# Living with Art

**Reproduced on the cover:**
Pierre-Auguste Renoir.
*Monet Painting in His Garden at Argenteuil,* detail.
1873. Oil on canvas, entire work (shown here) $19\frac{3}{4} \times 24\frac{1}{2}''$.
Wadsworth Atheneum, Hartford, Conn.

Cover design by Marlene Rothkin Vine

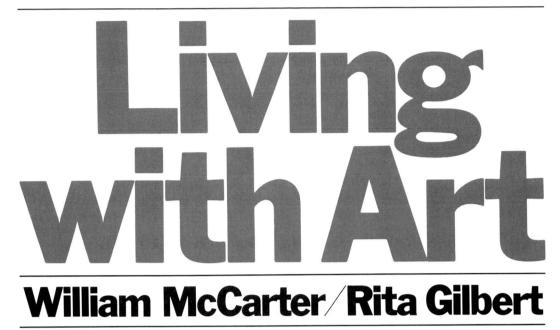

# Living with Art

## William McCarter/Rita Gilbert

*North Texas State University*

**Alfred A. Knopf**  **New York**

THIS IS A BORZOI BOOK
PUBLISHED BY ALFRED A. KNOPF, INC.

*Acquiring Editor*  Roth Wilkofsky
*Project Editor*  Dorchen Leidholdt
*Production Manager*  Della Mancuso
*Editorial Assistant*  Cindy Spiegel
*Designer*  Marlene Rothkin Vine

Line illustrations by Bill Evans, Denton, Texas; Vantage Art Studios, Massapequa, New York
Composition and camera work by York Graphic Services, Inc., York, Pennsylvania
Color separations by Chanticleer Company, Inc., New York/Switzerland
Printing and binding by W. A. Krueger Company, New Berlin, Wisconsin

**Library of Congress Cataloging in Publication Data**

McCarter, William, 1939–
  Living with art.

  Bibliography: p. 450.
  Includes index.
  1. Art appreciation.  I. Gilbert, Rita, 1942–
II. Title.
N7477.M35      1985      701'.1      85–15
ISBN 0-394-33589-9

Manufactured in the United States of America
First Edition
9 8 7 6 5 4 3 2 1

# Preface

*Living with Art* is a basic art text for college students and other interested readers. As such, it offers a broad introduction to the nature, vocabulary, media, and history of art, drawing on examples from many cultures.

The book is divided into five major parts. Part I serves as a general overview of the subject of art and its study. In the opening chapter are discussions about the importance of art in today's world; the basic impulse for art as exemplified in children's art and folk art; the phenomena of visual perception, including left brain and right brain dominance; the challenge of becoming an "intelligent" observer; and the role of the artist. Chapter 2 poses the question "What Is Art?" and gives readers a basis for answering it within their own frames of reference. The chapter considers "motel" or "sofa" art; the relationship art has to beauty and to the natural world; iconography; and standards for criticizing and evaluating art. Chapter 3 introduces several broad themes that run through the entire history of art and notes the various purposes that art has served and continues to serve.

Part II is a thorough analysis of the elements and principles of design in art, with detailed explanations and many illustrations. Part III covers the two-dimensional media, and devotes a full chapter to each of the major categories—drawing, painting, prints, photography, and graphic design. In Part IV the same comprehensive coverage is applied to three-dimensional media—sculpture, crafts, architecture, and environmental design. No comparable text, we believe, gives such an in-depth treatment of these important modes of expression. Techniques and materials are explained in relation to their expressive possibilities and, wherever appropriate, in relation to the visual elements and principles.

Part V is a brief, but comprehensive, chronological history of art from earliest times to the present. The final chapter in this part compares works of art from widely separated parts of the globe—Asia, Africa, South America, Europe, and North America—that were produced in approximately the same time period.

Illustrations are the "meat" of any art text; there can be no meaningful words without the pictures. *Living with Art* has six hundred illustrations. The book has been printed entirely on a four-color press, thus allowing for a large number of color reproductions placed alongside their textual references. Because our publisher believes (and we agree) that quality is at least as important as quantity, it was arranged for the color film separations to be made in Italy. Great care has been taken to ensure that the color reproductions are as nearly faithful to the original works of art as four colors of ink on paper can be.

Such a large number of illustrations permits flexibility. Readers will find works of art from many different cultures, works made by women and by men, works as old as civilization and others barely dry. Historical periods have been documented thoroughly. However, because we feel that students connect particularly well with the art of our own time, more than one hundred of the works shown in *Living with Art* date from the 1970s and 1980s. No work of art is discussed without being illustrated, and nearly every illustration falls on the page where it is discussed.

Students often are fascinated by the lives of artists they study. We are fascinated, too, and that interest prompted a unique feature in *Living with Art*. Spotted throughout are thirty-four brief biographies of artists, positioned near the text discussion of each artist's work. Set off from the text, the biographies include an image of the artist (usually a self-portrait, sometimes a photograph, occasionally a portrait by another artist), a brief life history, and a quote from the artist. The preparation of these biographies has been perhaps the most rewarding work on *Living with Art*. We have learned anew that artists are interesting people; we have speculated about which artists we would like to invite to dinner, which we would rather admire from afar. The individual personalities of the artists have resulted in a rich and complex heritage of art, and we in turn are enriched by learning who they are, who they were.

A number of additional resources have been provided in *Living with Art*. Extensive chronologies offer students both a geographical and a historical perspective. The chronologies are cross-cultural, listing periods and styles, important political and social events, and major artists. There is a bibliography with suggestions for further reading. A glossary of terms summarizes definitions given in the text. An Instructor's Manual is available, providing teaching strategies, sample tests, student projects, suggestions for further illustrations, and a list of teaching resources.

Living with art is something everyone does. In today's world we are surrounded, inevitably, by an amazing treasure house of art. To ignore that art, to let it pass before our eyes without our noticing, is like walking into the treasure house and turning off all the lights. By this book we have tried to turn on the lights.

## Acknowledgments

A book as complex as *Living with Art* does not really involve as many people as, say, the building of the pyramids, but at times it has seemed so. All the following have made important contributions.

First, we must thank the hundreds of museums, galleries, private collectors, and photographers who have provided the illustrations for *Living with Art*. They make a life filled with art possible—and joyful.

Numerous reviewers have helped to shape this text. They have corrected our mistakes, changed our emphases, and offered creative suggestions. Our special gratitude goes to the people who have stayed with us throughout the development of the manuscript and reviewed it several times, often calling us back, and back again, to the same problem until we got it right. They include: Michelle R. Banks, Tennessee Technological University; Betty Disney Durko, Cypress College; Robert N. Ewing, California State University, Fullerton; Paul Grootkerk, Mississippi State University; Sharon K. Hopson, University of Nebraska, Lincoln; John C. Riordan, State University of New York, College at Potsdam; and Claire Selkurt, Mankato State University.

We also received much constructive criticism and good advice from: George Arnott Civey, III, Eastern Kentucky University; Richard T. Doi, Central Washington University; Henry Drewal, Cleveland State University; Steve Eliot, Broward Community College; Neil Lafaye, University of South Carolina; Michael J. Smith, Southern Illinois University; Barbara von Barghahn, George Washington University; and Randy Wassell, Colorado State University.

Artist Joan Curtis served throughout as first-round critic and reviewer, and she also must be credited with suggesting a large number of the illustrations in the text. The lovely design and page-by-page layout in *Living with Art* are the work of Marlene Rothkin Vine, who has demonstrated once again that an art book can be made to look like a work of art.

The huge task of gathering six hundred illustrations was facilitated by B. H. Barcuse (assisted by J. H. Greene), who handled the thousands of pieces of correspondence associated with the illustrations, and we thank them for carrying through on this daunting work.

For the staff at Alfred A. Knopf we reserve a special gratitude. The degree of commitment and personal involvement shown by all is rare in today's publishing world, and we count ourselves fortunate. Dorchen Leidholdt brought an exceptionally sensitive knowledge of art—as well as skill and determination—to the job of project editor. Her contributions to the manuscript were invaluable. Production manager Della Mancuso proved that expertise and attention to detail can indeed control the enormous task of publishing an art book. Faced with one author who couldn't keep her fingers out of the production process, Della maintained a wonderful spirit of cooperation. Cindy Spiegel was a meticulous and conscientious editorial assistant. Laura Littwin managed much of the reviewing process and answered many cries of despair from the authors. All of them have our warm appreciation.

For our editor, Roth Wilkofsky, there can be no adequate thanks. This book is dedicated to him.

Two authors need two sets of personal acknowledgments.

**From William McCarter:** My first thanks must go to the thousands of students who have passed through my classes at North Texas State University. They shared excitement over their growing awareness of art and allowed me the privilege of being part of the process. The energy of this interaction naturally overflowed into *Living with Art*.

Similarly, I owe a debt of gratitude to the faculty and administration at NTSU. The university acted as a support system for my work, demonstrating an unusual collective ambition by urging that my classroom experience be extended into the printed word.

For a boy growing up in my section of North Carolina in the 1950s, the profession of artist or teacher of art was about as likely as the profession of astronaut. My mother, Nell McCarter, collaborated with a wonderful art teacher, Mrs. Eugenia Gerth, to provide me with the kind of training I so wanted. Today astronauts orbit the earth, and I am an artist and teacher of art. I must express here my profound gratitude to those two remarkable women.

Last is most important, and I save my best thanks for my wife, Mickey, and my son, Monte. They have proved that love takes many forms, including giving Dad enough space to get the book done.

**From Rita Gilbert:** Everybody seems to have had one teacher who was special, one who made a difference. Mine was Dr. Carol Krinsky at New York University. Her classes in art history created, for me, the fork in the road. She set me on the path that eventually resulted in this book. Dr. Krinsky also made substantial contributions to the architecture chapter in *Living with Art*.

Although they have been acknowledged elsewhere, Marlene Rothkin Vine and Joan Curtis must have my special thanks. Dear friends as well as colleagues, they have been integral to a creative collaboration stretching back more than fifteen years. I would not want to do anything important without them. They give me courage.

*November 1984*
*Denton, Texas*
*North Salem, New York*

W.McC.
R.G.

# Contents

*To Roth Wilkofsky*
*who gives honor*
*to the profession of editor*

*part one*

# INTRODUCTION

# 1

# Living with Art

It cannot be mere coincidence that most of the cultures we admire as having represented high points in the world's history also were great patrons of art. Among them we could include the Classical civilizations of Greece and Rome, the Gupta period in 5th- and 6th-century India, the Song dynasty in China, the Aztec Empire in Mexico, and the Renaissance in 15th-century Europe. Conversely, during periods that we have come to think of as low points—such as the Nazi regime in Germany—art has been systematically destroyed, controlled, and strangled. History tells us that art thrives in an atmosphere fostering the highest ideals and the greatest energy. Art grows alongside achievements in science, government, and commerce.

There are records to show how highly art was valued in some of these exemplary cultures. For instance, in 15th-century Italy, in the prosperous city-state of Florence, one family reigned supreme for three generations—the family of the Medici. The Medici were bankers and, although not of noble blood, ruled as virtual kings. They were also great patrons of art and supported Raphael, Michelangelo, Sandro Botticelli, and many other artists whose works appear in this book. Botticelli's *Birth of Venus* (**1**), one of the best-known paintings in the Western world, originally was created to hang in a villa belonging to the Medici. Lorenzo de' Medici had this to say about his vast expenditures for art: "Many deem that it would have been preferable to keep part of the funds in the treasury; I think that our patronage was the great splendor of our regime and, in my opinion, the money was well spent."[1]

Five centuries later we can only agree: the money was *very* well spent. Yet it is difficult for us to imagine such expenditure today. In a time when nations try to outdo one another in buying bombs and missiles and tanks, no government leader would empty the treasury to buy art. Lorenzo de' Medici brought into his palace a promising fifteen-year-old sculptor, a boy named Michelangelo. We cannot conceive of the President of the United States opening up a room in the White House for the Michelangelo of our era.

**1.** Sandro Botticelli. *Birth of Venus.*
c. 1480. Tempera on canvas, 6′7″ × 9′2″.
Uffizi, Florence.

Nevertheless, art patronage goes on. In place of government rulers, we have wealthy private individuals, foundations, and business corporations—all spending money to buy art and to support artists. Once a sculptor's masterpiece might have adorned the private sitting room of a king or dictator. Today it is more likely to rest in the lobby of a company's headquarters or in the street outside the building (**2**). If we can judge the achievements of a civilization by the amount of art it produced and by the quality and diversity of that art, then perhaps our own time will be looked back upon as one of history's high points.

Just as art patrons have changed, so too has the audience for art. The Medici bought paintings for themselves, their families, and their circle of friends. Not until hundreds of years later did the concept of the public museum emerge. (The Medici collections, in Florence's Uffizi Gallery, were opened to the general public in 1765.) Architecture, especially of churches and other public buildings, always has been available to everyone, but the public's access to paintings and sculpture has been limited until fairly recently.

There still are private art collections, to be sure, but most of the world's great art now resides in public museums, open to all. You needn't be rich or famous or aristocratic to walk into, say, the Metropolitan Museum of Art in New York and look at the Rembrandts. The same is true for museums throughout the United States and around the world (**3**).

Not all art, however, is lodged in museums. Actually, a growing number of art lovers feel that art, especially contemporary art, should *not* be lodged in museums, for it is therefore not sufficiently accessible to everyone. As reported by *The Christian Science Monitor* in 1983, many critics feel the museum setting is not the best environment in which to look at art.

**above: 2.** Arnaldo Pomodoro.
*Big Disc (Grande Disco).* 1965–68.
Polished bronze, diameter 11′10″.
Collection PepsiCo Inc., Purchase, N.Y.

**left: 3.** Honoré Daumier. *Connoisseurs.*
Watercolor, charcoal, and pen; $10\frac{1}{4} \times 7\frac{5}{8}$″.
Cleveland Museum of Art
(purchase, Dudley P. Allen Fund).

Let there be museums for the art of other times and places, and for the earlier art of our own period, but let us also make art more of an everyday activity, more of an everyday source of significance and pleasure. Let us remove today's art from the arid, sterilizing climate of the museums and bring it into our homes, streets, and offices, our working and recreational lives. Let us, in short, truly humanize it by making it a full and dynamic part of our lives rather than a cold and idealized by-product that bears as much relationship to humanity as a hard-boiled egg does to a chicken.[2]

When we begin to take a broader view of art, we realize that this desirable situation already exists. Art *is* all around us, if we but stop to notice it. You probably have a lot more art in your life than you realize. If you live in a city or town, artists have designed almost everything in your environment. The buildings in which you live and work, the furniture inside those buildings, the clothes you wear—all were designed by artists in specialized fields. Even this book you are reading was designed by a graphic artist, whose task was to make it visually appealing and easy to read.

Very likely the walls of your home are decorated with posters, prints, photographs, maybe original paintings, which you have hung to give personal meaning to your environment. Perhaps your school or office building has a large-scale sculpture out front, or a fabric hanging or mural inside. In the homes of friends you will see different kinds of art. One person may collect antique furniture, another Mexican pottery, yet another stamps or drawings or rare books.

The point is, all of us now *live* with art, every day of our lives. We can go through life like sleepwalkers, ignoring or taking for granted the art around us. Or we can enrich our lives by developing a more active appreciation of the art we live with. This book is about the appreciation of art, by which we mean a combination of understanding and enjoyment. It is possible to heighten our appreciation of art, to learn to see, to take an active interest in the visual world. When we do so, we are only following a basic *aesthetic* impulse—an urge to respond to that which we find beautiful.

**4.** Cave painting of horses.
c. 15,000–10,000 B.C. Lascaux, France.

**5.** Funerary urn, Chinese, from Kansu Province.
c. 2000–1500 B.C. Ceramic, height 12¼".
Nelson–Atkins Museum of Art, Kansas City (Nelson Fund).

## The Impulse for Art

Why did the Medici spend so much money for art, and why would IBM or AT&T or Union Carbide do so now? In fact, why is there art? Do we need it? Are such things as paintings and sculptures absolutely necessary to human existence?

The history of civilization suggests that we do need art, that it is basic to human expression. This seems to be equally true for those who make art, those who buy it, and those who simply admire it. The earliest people made art—whether they called it that or not—as evidenced by the cave paintings found in various parts of the world (**4**). And as primitive peoples advanced and learned to make objects for their daily use, they nearly always embellished them with artwork. A pot will hold water or cook food over the fire just as well if it is plain. Why decorate it (**5**)? A plain garment will keep the wearer warm. Why make it fancy? A shelter needs only to keep out the rain and wind. Why ornament it? Nevertheless, our long-ago ancestors did all these things. We must conclude that there is an inborn human urge to create and enjoy art.

There are two areas we might consider to see how this artistic impulse works. In neither case are the artists always aware that they are making "art." They are simply doing what seems to them perfectly natural, and it remains for others, outsiders, to declare that their efforts constitute art. The first of these areas is children's art, and the second is folk art.

### Children's Art

All of us begin to play with art as children, but in our teens most of us turn away from that kind of free expression in order to concentrate on learning the numerous rules of success in our complicated society. By looking at children's art we can get some idea of how an individual's power of expression grows. The book *Heidi's Horse*[3] follows the progress of one child, Heidi Scheuber, from age two to age nine.

**6.** Drawing at age 2.

**6–10.** Horse drawings by Heidi Scheuber, over a period of four years.
From *Heidi's Horse* by Sylvia Fein, published by Exelrod Press.

**7.** Drawing at age 4 years, 3 months.

At two Heidi began with random scribbling that expressed her joy in making marks (**6**). At three she made organized circular swirls, and at four separate shapes and shapes within shapes. At four years and three months human and animal figures appeared, made of circles and straight lines (**7**). A few months later Heidi produced a horse composed of the same elements (**8**). Heidi's progress reflects the normal pattern of human development, from formless marks to forms with meaning. This gradual expansion of form and meaning is the story of art, both for the individual artist and for the entire human race.

Heidi's drawings of horses when she was between five and nine years old show the burst of creative development we all go through at that age (**9,10**).

**8.** Drawing at age 4½.

**9.** Drawing at age 5.

**10.** Drawing at age 6.

This is my very best horse. And horse head

This urge, however, often is lost between age nine and the teens. The creative freedom of the younger child is overwhelmed by the desire, experienced by most older children, for realism and accuracy. Awareness of the world has expanded tremendously, and the set of marks that once seemed so satisfactory is suddenly inadequate. At this stage many children become so critical of their own efforts that they give up and never draw again. The ones who don't give up, who persevere and retain their ability to play freely with forms, become the people we call "artists."

We might speculate that there is something of the child in all artists—not in the sense of immaturity or lack of intellectual development, but in the ability to experiment, uncensored by conventional standards of good and bad. Pablo Picasso was an immensely sophisticated artist, and certainly he knew that what he made was called art—by himself and by the world. Yet throughout his life he retained this ability to play, even to joyfully "draw" in the air with a flashlight (**11**). Could it be that the artist lives in all of us until and unless something destroys it? Further evidence for this idea can be found in the expression of folk art.

**11.** Gjon Mili. *A Centaur Drawn with Light,* Pablo Picasso at the Madoura Pottery in Vallauris, France, 1949. Life Magazine © Time Inc.

## Folk Art

Folk art is a term applied to works made by individuals with no academic training in art and often with little or no formal education. Folk art exists outside the mainstream of Western art—that is, art that would be exhibited in the museums and galleries—yet it has a living current of its own. Some folk artists work within a longstanding tradition; skills are handed down from parent to child over many generations. Other such artists are true "originals," who begin to make art even though it might be considered a strange pursuit by their families and friends.

We tend to think of folk art as a country art, uncorrupted by slick urban values, but some folk art has been made in cities. There is folk painting and sculpture, even folk architecture. Much of this art, however, consists of objects for daily life, embellished to make them beautiful. In other words, everyday people take everyday objects and turn them into a special art form.

So much about folk art is appealing. Like the art of children, it often reveals a quite direct expression. Folk painters and sculptors have rarely been shown the works of Michelangelo or Rembrandt and made to believe that is the way art is "supposed" to look. They form images of what they see, colored by their feelings about what they see, and they are satisfied. They invent, they play with forms, they delight in colors and shapes, they decorate—free of the inhibition that comes from being told "That's not *real* art."

Another aspect of folk art, especially of functional items, is that it tends to be exceptionally well crafted. Pleasure is in the making, in the handling of materials, in taking the time to be sure the work is as perfect as it can be. No wonder "sophisticated" art lovers have begun to collect this work avidly.

What impulse causes folk artists to create? There seem to be a variety of motives. Vermont folk artist Stanley Marcile, who began drawing in his seventies, claims he did so because he had nothing else to do. He says, "I saw these pencils in the store, so I bought them and started drawing. I couldn't go hunting no more, so I just started inventing." Marcile's drawing of a house (**12**) shows an instinctive flair for composition, especially in the way the tree curves above the roof. Like most folk art, the drawing is decorative—full of patterns and lines and curls that please the eye as much as they must have pleased the hand in drawing them. This last might be considered a major (or *the* major) characteristic of folk art: it pleases the eye.

**12.** Stanley Marcile. *Untitled.* 1981. Ballpoint and felt pen on paper, 11 × 14". Courtesy the artist.

left: **13.** Simon Rodia.
Watts Towers, Los Angeles, detail.
c. 1921–54 (now partially destroyed).

right: **14.** Rya rug, from Finland. 1782. Wool.
National Museum, Helsinki.

Similar concerns must have motivated Simon Rodia, an immigrant tile-setter from Italy, who built, in the depressed area of Los Angeles known as Watts, a fantasy-land construction that has come to be called the Watts Towers. Working with bits of bottle glass, broken dishes, shells, pieces of mirrors, and other debris from the streets, Rodia patiently created a thing of beauty—a very personal expression of art, in monumental form—in his backyard. He labored over the towers for about thirty years, feeling that he thus paid a debt to the country that had given him a home and a living. But the Watts Towers are not just the obsession of an eccentric laborer. They are the product of a creative artist who has found a unique way to use his gift.

Whole cultures have established folk-art traditions because, for certain periods of time, they had little else to do. Before the advent of television or video games, before radio, before modern transportation made social contact easy, people were left to their own devices for long stretches of time. In rural areas, and particularly in cold climates, the winter months dragged on interminably. Shut inside their houses, people turned to making functional objects, and, since time was their greatest asset, they lavished attention on craftsmanship and decoration. In Scandinavia—where winters are among the coldest and darkest on earth—a tradition of weaving and rug-making sprang up, which continues to this day. A rug hand-knotted in Finland in 1782 (**14**) has a typical folk quality of allover decorative plant and animal forms. Characteris-

**15.** Ferris wheel toy, from Germany. Late 19th century. Tin. Bethnal Green Museum of Childhood, London.

**above: 16.** Angel Gabriel weathervane, from Massachusetts. 19th century. Copper. Index of American Design, Washington, D.C.

**below: 17.** Bridal chest, from Pennsylvania. 18th century. Painted pine and poplar. Metropolitan Museum of Art, New York (Rogers Fund, 1923).

tic, too, is the working into wool of the maker's initials and the date, for folk weavers take great pride in their accomplishments.

Time, therefore, seems to be an important element in the urge to make folk art, but it does not completely explain the phenomenon. The same people, faced with time on their hands, could equally have taken up gymnastics or dancing or indoor horticulture or games (and possibly they did all these as well). It seems evident that there is an inborn compulsion to make something wonderful, something that will last.

As suggested earlier, the inventiveness of folk art stems largely from a lack of knowledge or concern about how things "should" look, and this is true not only of drawings and paintings, but of handcraft objects as well. Toys serve as a good example. In our day most children's toys are turned out by the identical millions, geared to a child-consumer market that responds eagerly to television advertising. Before mass production, however, a toy was usually a one-of-a-kind item, its form determined only by the ingenuity of the maker. A tin ferris wheel made in Germany during the late 19th century (**15**) shows the lengths to which an interested and creative toy-maker might go in constructing a plaything to delight a child.

During the 18th and 19th centuries in the United States, the folk arts enjoyed an especially rich outpouring. All sorts of objects—furniture, toys, gateposts, trade signs, tableware, weathervanes (**16**)—were potential subjects for the folk artist's imagination. The great variety of styles can be explained partly by the ethnic diversity of the new nation. Settlers from Europe brought along their own folk traditions and transplanted these traditions in the new country. In Pennsylvania, for instance, the German settlers (sometimes known as Pennsylvania "Dutch") carried on the practice of painting furniture, especially bridal chests (**17**), in elaborate designs of flowers, plants, and figures.

To sum up, then, it seems that the conditions favorable for the development of a folk art are time, separation from the mainstream of art, and the desire to make something extraordinary out of the ordinary. Does this mean that, in our fast-paced world with global communication and mass production, the folk arts will die out? Apparently it does not. Thanks to the machine, leisure time is, if anything, more available than ever before. The mainstream of art, if known, can be disregarded; some contemporary folk artists know very well what is being shown in the galleries of New York, Chicago, and Los Angeles but don't care. Above all, the desire to make something wonderful appears to be basic and will not go away, no matter how our world changes. Indeed, our changing world has fostered the expansion of folk art into different realms. Perhaps there is a new "folk art," in tune with modern times.

## Modern "Folk Art"

If there is a contemporary folk art, we may seek it wherever people take something ordinary and make it extraordinary. Across the bay from San Francisco, in a spot bordered by the highway that daily carries commuters into the city, lie the depressingly named Emeryville mud flats. Prevailing winds and tides continually strew the mud flats with garbage—driftwood, old automobile parts, tin cans, junk of all sorts. But what might have been an ugly trash pile has turned into something quite different—a constantly changing folk-art gallery. Artists, nearly all anonymous, take the junk and turn it into sculptures of animals, human figures, fanciful creatures, abstract constructions—whatever the imagination can conjure from battered castoffs (**18**). Some of the sculp-

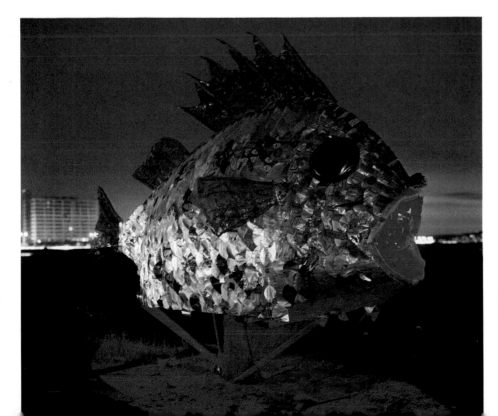

**18.** Anonymous. *Fish.*
Aluminum cans and mixed media.
Emeryville mud flats, California.

tures do not stand for long. When they fall, other artists come along and recycle the material into new works of art. Motorists driving by the mud flats are treated to an ongoing, vital art exhibition.

The mud-flat artists do not get any money for their efforts, nor do they get recognition as individual artists. So why do they do it? They do it for fun, for pleasure, for the sheer joy of creating something out of almost nothing. They are playing with art in the same way that Picasso might play with a flashlight. They make the extraordinary out of the ordinary. In a very real sense, they are today's folk artists.

As observers, we also can learn to play with art, but before we can play we must teach ourselves to *see* the art around us. It would be easy enough for a motorist passing the Emeryville mud flats to see nothing more than a junk pile. To see art, the motorist must rearrange his or her thinking to see junk-made-into-art. This way of seeing comes from training our visual perception.

## Perception

Our appreciation of art is directly tied to our individual *patterns of perception*— the specific ways in which we experience the world around us. In most cases art depends primarily on *visual* perception—the process by which our minds interpret the information that we collect with our eyes.

In visual perception our eyes take in information in the form of light patterns. Through a complex interaction that scientists do not entirely understand, the brain processes these visual images to give them meaning. The mechanics of perception work much the same way for everyone, yet in a given situation, we do not all see the same things. The human eye simply cannot take in all available visual information. Our world is too complex, and we are constantly bombarded with an incredible range of visual images. If the mind recorded all the visual detail that our eyes see at any given moment, it would "blow a fuse." To avoid overloading our mental circuits, the brain responds only to that visual information required to meet our needs at one moment.

Suppose you are driving along a busy street, assailed on all sides by demanding visual images (**19**). Your eyes "see" everything. But what does your brain register? If you are behind the wheel of the car, you will see the traffic signs and lights, because awareness of such details is necessary to survival. If

**19.** A view of the "Strip," Las Vegas, Nev.

**20.** E. G. Boring's
Object-Ambiguous Mother-in-Law.

you are very hungry, your attention may be attracted by fast food signs and restaurants. But if you are looking for a specific address—the home of a friend or the place where you have a business appointment—then you will focus on building numbers and block out nearly everything else. It is easier to cope with life and with our complex visual world if we simplify our perceptions and see according to our immediate needs.

At the same time, if we habitually allow ourselves to see *only* in terms of immediate needs, we miss many satisfying visual experiences. On a treacherous, icy day we may concentrate so hard on the problem of getting to class or to work that we do not see how beautiful the ice-covered tree branches are. Always busy, always preoccupied, we do not notice the striking design of a house or the beautiful cut of a garment. We walk past paintings and sculptures without ever really seeing these works of art. To enjoy fully the aesthetic experiences offered by our world, we must occasionally put aside immediate needs and really *look*. A quick glance is not enough.

Studies indicate that the brain is often more important than the eyes in determining what each of us sees as we move through the world. The brain's ability to control perception is obvious when we study ambiguous figures, such as the classic one reproduced here (**20**). When you first look at this drawing, you may see a young woman turning away from you so that only her cheek line, the tip of her nose, and her eyelashes are visible. Or you may see a toothless old woman with a large, warty nose, whose chin is buried in a dark collar. For you to be able to see both images, your brain must reorganize the lines in the drawing.

Even after you have been made aware of the two images, you must consciously work at going back and forth between them. You can feel your brain shifting as it organizes the visual information into first one image and then the other. But you *cannot* see both images at the same time. The important thing to remember as you shift your perception back and forth from the young woman to the old is that the visual image *always stays the same*. It is only your perception, as controlled by your brain, that changes.

This idea is vital to the appreciation of art. When you look at a painting, for example, at least three factors always are operating: the actual, physical substance of the painting, the artist's intention in making the painting, and your own perception of the painting. Each person who looks at that same painting will bring a different perception, so you can see how complex is the communication we call art. To get an idea of how this works, let us study one well-known painting.

# Vincent van Gogh

## *1853–1890*

The appeal of Van Gogh for today's art lovers is easy to understand. A painfully disturbed, tormented man who, in spite of his great anguish, managed to create extraordinary art. An intensely private, introspective man who wrote eloquently about art and about life. An erratic, impulsive man who had the self-discipline to construct an enormous body of work in a career that lasted only a decade.

Vincent van Gogh was born in the town of Groot-Zundert, in Holland, the son of a Dutch Protestant minister. His early life was spent in a variety of roles, including those of theological student and lay preacher among the miners of the region. Not until the age of twenty-seven did he begin to take a serious interest in art, and then he had but ten years to live. In 1886 he went to stay in Paris with his brother Theo, an art dealer who was always his closest emotional connection. In Paris Vincent became aware of the new art movements and incorporated aspects of them into his own style, especially by introducing light, brilliant colors into his palette.

Two years later Van Gogh left Paris for the southern provincial city of Arles. There he was joined briefly by the painter Paul Gauguin, with whom Van Gogh hoped to work very closely, creating perfect art in a pure atmosphere of self-expression. However, the two artists quarreled, and, apparently in the aftermath of one intense argument, Van Gogh cut off a portion of his ear and had it delivered to a prostitute living in a brothel. Soon after, Van Gogh realized that his instability had gotten out of hand, and he committed himself to an asylum, where—true

to form—he continued to work prolifically at his painting. Most of the work we admire so much was done in the last two years at Arles. Vincent (as he always signed himself) received much sympathetic encouragement during those years, both from his brother and from an unusually perceptive doctor and art connoisseur, Dr. Gachet, whom he painted several times. Nevertheless, his despair deepened, and in July of 1890 he shot himself to death.

Vincent's letters to his brother Theo represent a unique document in the history of art. They reveal a sensitive, intelligent artist pouring out his thoughts to one especially capable of understanding. In 1883, while still in Holland, he wrote to Theo: "In my opinion, I am often *rich as Croesus,* not in money, but (though it doesn't happen every day) rich, because I have found in my work something to which I can devote myself heart and soul, and which gives inspiration and significance to life. Of course my moods vary, but there is an average of serenity. I have a sure *faith* in art, a sure confidence that it is a powerful stream, which bears a man to harbour, though he himself must do his bit too; and at all events I think it such a great blessing, when a man has found his work, that I cannot count myself among the unfortunate. I mean, I may be in certain relatively great difficulties, and there may be gloomy days in my life, but I shouldn't want to be counted among the unfortunate nor would it be correct."[4]

Vincent van Gogh. *Self-Portrait.* 1890. Oil on canvas, $25\frac{1}{2} \times 21\frac{1}{2}''$. Jeu de Paume, Louvre, Paris.

left: **21.** Vincent van Gogh.
*The Starry Night* (detail).

below: **22.** Vincent van Gogh.
*The Starry Night.* 1889.
Oil on canvas, $29 \times 36\frac{1}{4}''$.
Museum of Modern Art, New York
(acquired through
the Lillie P. Bliss Bequest).

When you look at the image shown at top (**21**), you will see a layer of paint on canvas, the individual strokes of a brush. This is what you would see if you stood very close to the painting and focused on one area—globs of inert colored pigment attached to a canvas backing.

Now pull back farther and consider the whole painting (**22**). You see a brilliantly colored landscape with a tree, a village, a church, and a turbulent sky. This is Vincent van Gogh's masterpiece, called *The Starry Night*. If we limit ourselves to absolute scientific observation, no night sky ever looked like this. Stars do not race about in frenzied whirlpools. What was Van Gogh's perception of the scene that caused him to paint it this way? We know that he was a tormented, intense, and mystical man. Some of the torment, and a kind of ecstasy, are built into the painting.

And what is the viewer's perception? That depends, to a large extent, on the individual's perceptual habits and biases and on past experience. The cosmologist might think *The Starry Night* alludes magnificently to the formation of the universe. A Londoner who experienced the German blitz in World War II might see a bombing raid. Someone who has been in a fever or taken drugs might see a hallucinatory vision. A person with a certain visual disorder might think that is the way a sky always looks. And the individual who views nature in a meticulous, scientific way might think that Van Gogh was crazy.

The message Van Gogh (or any other artist) sends cannot be precisely the message you receive. Van Gogh brought to his work a whole set of experiences and emotions; no one else can duplicate them exactly. However, if you open yourself to looking at the art, to receiving whatever message it may have for you, then a communication exists. Communication, as we all know, is a two-way process. Two people cannot hold a conversation if one is doing all the talking and the other is sitting there dumbly. Van Gogh poured a lot of himself into *The Starry Night*. If you want to understand and enjoy—to appreciate—his art, then you also must bring something to the experience.

We have considered, then, two ways in which the brain influences our perception of art. It sorts out images and arranges them into patterns that are meaningful to us, and it stores memories, emotions, and associations—a frame of reference—through which we experience art made by someone else. There is yet a third way in which the brain controls our perception of art, and it is one whose complexities we are only beginning to understand.

## Left Brain, Right Brain

Scientists have known for many decades that the two halves of the human brain have some different functions, and that the left side of the brain controls verbal abilities. People who survive injuries to the left brain may lose their verbal skills, whereas those who suffer right-brain injuries do not. It was thought, therefore, that the left brain was somehow the more important half. But studies begun in the 1960s have demonstrated that the right side of the brain has equally complex and vital functions to perform in our perception and understanding of the world. The difference lies in the way the two sides of the brain process information.

Stated very briefly, the left brain is the custodian of words and logic, the right brain the keeper of images and analogies. The left brain gives names to things and describes them. It reasons sequentially, from one step to the next, and bases its conclusions on reason and facts. The right brain does not use words but relies on images. It is intuitive rather than logical, it lacks a sense of linear time, and it tends to seek relationships and associations between things. At any moment either one side or the other is dominant. For cognitive purposes, the two sides cannot operate simultaneously, although exceptional people can shift very rapidly.

You can test this idea yourself. While you are reading this book, following the words and their meanings, try to form an image in your mind of something familiar to you—a person, a room, or an object. You'll find it extremely difficult to do both at once; even if you think you are succeeding, you are probably making split-second shifts from one to the other. In order to create a mental image you must shut off the words and shift from one side of your brain to the other. To get back to the words, you must shift back again.

The right side of the brain is the dreamer, the imaginer, the taker of creative leaps. In the right side of the brain lives the artist. For art, by its nature, deals in images, not words. It is nonrational, not bound by time or logic, preoccupied with associations and metaphors. It is supposed that artists, without really knowing what they are doing, have learned to "turn on" the right brain when they want to work, although few can explain the process. And sometimes the right brain may turn itself on automatically (**23**).

If artists can switch to right-brain dominance to produce art, then it follows that observers may have a much-enhanced experience of art if they let their right brains take over, for a little while at least. How does one do this? As with many things, by practice. When you look at a work of art, try to avoid words, either spoken aloud or in your mind. Concentrate on what you are actually *seeing*, not what you think you should see or want to see. Focus on colors and patterns and shapes, but don't name them. Close your eyes and try to form a mental image of the work you have just been looking at, then open your eyes again. After a time you may find that your right brain takes charge automatically when you approach art. Of course, if you want to describe the art or share your perceptions with someone else or even analyze your own response, you'll need to shift back to the left brain. Ideally, both halves of the brain should participate in the experience.

All this is not to suggest that our appreciation of art should be purely intuitive. The small child who sees a painting for the first time may enjoy it at a certain level, but with nowhere near the richness of pleasure felt by someone who has dedicated a lifetime to studying art. Acknowledging the possibilities of your right brain is one step toward the greater appreciation of art, but that alone is not sufficient. You are still merely an observer. To achieve real satisfaction from the art you live with, you should go on to become an *intelligent* observer. Here the left brain goes back into business.

**cathy**®         **by Cathy Guisewite**

**23.** Cathy cartoon. October 3, 1984.
Copyright, 1984, Universal Press Syndicate.
Reprinted with permission. All rights reserved.

## The Intelligent Observer

There is a difference between being merely an observer and being an intelligent, *informed* observer. To understand this we might go back again to Van Gogh's painting, *The Starry Night*. Neither in this work nor in any other did the artist simply tune in to his right brain and let it run wild. Make no mistake, Van Gogh did not just toss onto canvas the outpourings of a psychotic personality. He studied, he worked, he learned from artists who had gone before, he planned his canvases carefully. The viewer owes him and every other artist a similar fund of education.

How, then, do observers of art proceed to educate themselves? Again, the more you put into it, the more you will get out of it. One can observe and enjoy art at many different levels. Some art is "easy." Record jacket design offers a good example. The graphic design is bright, colorful, and attractive.

**24.** Alma Woodsey Thomas.
*Light Blue Nursery.* 1968.
Acrylic on canvas, 4'2" × 4'.
National Museum of American Art,
Smithsonian Institution,
Washington, D.C.
(gift of Alma W. Thomas).

Its main purpose is to appeal superficially to the eye—and to encourage you to buy the record. Nearly anyone can admire the cleverness of the design without spending a lot of time studying it.

Other kinds of art are more "difficult" for the untrained observer. This could be said of the two paintings illustrated next (**24,25**). If you are not familiar with works of art in these particular styles, you may think that the first, a painting by Alma Thomas, is little different from a computer printout—perhaps in Arabic; and the second, a painting by Chuck Close, may strike you as resembling a photograph of an intense young woman. If you turn away from them quickly, the paintings may communicate nothing to you. On the other hand, if you have seen other works in these styles, if you have learned the process by which the two artists arrived at these kinds of expressions, then you may find some thread of communication.

In other words, there are two specific things that can enhance your appreciation of art: exposure and study. *Exposure* means simply looking at art, as much as possible, and really seeing it. You should be familiar with this process from your experience with music. The first time you hear a song or a symphony you may find it appealing. But when you have listened to the same piece of music over and over, you begin to greet it like an old friend. You hear patterns and rhythms and harmonies that you didn't notice before. Whereas the first exposure gave you sensory pleasure, repeated exposures bring emotional and perhaps intellectual pleasure. This, in turn, gives you greater appreciation of similar music by the same composer and by other composers.

Exposure alone, however, is not enough for understanding art. Art requires intellectual as well as sensory involvement. Your appreciation of art can

**above: 25.** Chuck Close. *Susan.* 1971.
Oil on canvas. Courtesy
Pace Gallery, New York.

**left: 26.** Figure of a man,
pre-Columbian Mexico. Ceramic.

be greatly improved by knowing how a work of art was made, why it was made, what went before and came after. This is where *study* comes in.

The understanding of process—the *how*—often contributes quite a lot to our appreciation of art. For example, you may look at a Mexican ceramic sculpture (**26**) and notice that it has very large feet. From this, you might conclude either that the tribe that made the sculpture had unnaturally large feet, or that they were trying to express the idea of being bound to the earth by

# Henri de Toulouse-Lautrec
## 1864–1901

Henri Marie Raymond de Toulouse-Lautrec Monfa was born at Albi, in the south of France, son of an aristocratic French family. From early childhood he showed talent for drawing and painting—a talent his family encouraged. The events that probably shaped the rest of his life and his career as an artist began at the age of thirteen, when he broke his left thigh in a fall. A year later he broke the other thigh. Although he recovered from the injuries, his legs never grew again. As an adult he stood just over 5 feet tall, with a fully developed body but shrunken legs, and he walked always with difficulty and pain.

By the age of seventeen Lautrec had begun serious art studies in Paris. He had also gotten his first taste of Montmartre—the rather seedy part of the city where writers, painters, and students congregated; where the brothels were located; and where soon would open the famed cabaret, the Moulin Rouge. At that time he wrote to his grandmother: "I am against my will leading a truly Bohemian life and am finding it difficult to accustom myself to this milieu." Later, that milieu would be the only one in which he seemed to belong.

The artist gradually began to achieve modest success with his paintings. He also began to accumulate a circle of friends—other artists, writers, intellectuals, performers—who were attracted by his great wit and unflagging high spirits. In 1889 the Moulin Rouge opened and quickly became the focus of this social life, as well as of Lautrec's art. Singers and dancers, prostitutes and poets, the highborn and the lowborn who came to the Moulin Rouge—Lautrec drew them all, with a style and originality that captured the essence of Paris nightlife.

After two years of popularity the Moulin Rouge fell upon hard times, and its owner decided to re-group. He hired new talent, planned a grand re-opening, and asked the all-but-resident artist to create a poster announcing the event. The poster Lautrec designed was unlike any Paris had ever seen—colorful, immediate, full of life, focusing on the image, not the printed words. Once again the Moulin Rouge was a sensation, and so were the artist and his poster.

In the years following his triumph as a graphic artist, Lautrec often had no regular home. He lived for periods of time at one or another of the brothels, among the prostitutes. Some of the women were his lovers, many were his friends, and all were potential subjects, whom he painted with sympathy and warmth. His dissipated life notwithstanding, he continued to work prolifically. Little by little, however, he began to drink more and work less, until the situation became so grave his family placed him in a sanitarium. A brief recovery was followed by yet more drinking, and at last the illness took over. In September of 1901, two months short of his thirty-seventh birthday, Lautrec died at his family's estate.

Lautrec's art is above all an art of people and life. He explained this himself after a brief visit to the countryside, meant to improve his health: "Only the human figure exists; landscape is, and should be, no more than an accessory; the painter exclusively of landscape is nothing but a boor. The sole function of landscape is to heighten the intelligibility of the character of the figure."[5]

Henri de Toulouse-Lautrec. *At the Moulin Rouge*, detail with artist's self-portrait. 1892–95. Oil on canvas, $4'\frac{1}{2}'' \times 4'7\frac{3}{8}''$ (entire work). Art Institute of Chicago (Helen Birch Bartlett Memorial Collection).

their agricultural life. The real answer is much simpler. This figure has large feet because otherwise it wouldn't stand up by itself. The statue was modeled from soft, heavy, weak clay. Given small feet, it would have toppled over in the making. Throughout this book you will find many such examples of the ways in which knowledge about process can heighten our perceptions of art.

An artist may create a specific work for any of a thousand reasons, and awareness of the *why* can also give the viewer greater understanding. We show here a late work by the American artist Charles Willson Peale (**27**). Peale was born in the colony of Maryland in 1741 and saw active service in the Revolutionary War. He is best known, perhaps, for his many portraits of George Washington, but they represent only a small portion of his achievement. Few other individuals typify so well the energy and ambition of a new nation.

Charles Willson Peale was passionately devoted to the pursuit of art (he named three of his sons Titian, Raphaelle, and Rembrandt) and its development in the new country. Beyond this, he was a talented inventor, a scientist, and an organizer of the first museum in the United States. *The Artist in His Museum*, painted when Peale was eighty-one, was done for a specific purpose. It is a kind of summing up of his lifetime achievements. He lifts the curtain on his museum and, with quiet pride, invites the viewer to share his pleasure. In the foreground are symbols of his various careers—his artist's palette, the tools of the taxidermist, the bones of a mastodon, which he excavated. Beyond the curtain, in the museum itself, are stuffed animals and many portraits by the artist and his sons. Peale might be saying, "Here are the fruits of my life, and they are good."

The historical place of a work or art—*what went before and came after*—can be most interesting. Artists borrow and learn from each other all the time. The

**27.** Charles Willson Peale.
*The Artist in His Museum*. 1822.
Oil on canvas, 8'7¾" × 6'7⅞".
Pennsylvania Academy of the Fine Arts, Philadelphia
(Joseph and Sarah Harrison Collection).

**above left: 28.** Henri de Toulouse-Lautrec.
*L'Estampe originale*, cover. 1893.
Color lithograph, $17\frac{3}{4} \times 23\frac{3}{4}''$.
Metropolitan Museum of Art, New York
(Rogers Fund, 1922).

**above right: 29.** Chobunsai Eishi.
*Komurasaki of Kadotama-ya*, from the series
*Greenhouse Beauties as the Six Poets.* c. 1795.
Woodcut, $15\frac{1}{4} \times 10\frac{1}{4}''$.
Art Institute of Chicago
(Clarence Buckingham Collection).

**left: 30.** David Hockney.
*Celia.* 1973. Lithograph, $42\frac{1}{2} \times 28\frac{1}{2}''$.
Courtesy André Emmerich Gallery,
New York.

myth of the lonely artist—starving in a garret, isolated from human contact, leaving behind a mass of brilliant work that no one had suspected—is mostly that, a myth. There have been a few such cases, but not many. On the whole, artists study each other's work carefully, adapt ideas to serve their own needs, and then bequeath those ideas to future generations of artists. The more you know about this living current of artistic energy, the more interesting will be any specific work of art.

The three pieces illustrated here (**28,29,30**) have two things in common: each is a picture of an elegant woman, and each is a *print*—a work designed for multiple reproduction (Chapter 8). But far more than that connects them to the artistic chain letter of seeing, adapting, and passing along.

The first print (**28**) is by the French artist Henri de Toulouse-Lautrec. Lautrec was an unexcelled master of the color lithographic poster for advertising. The illustration shown here is essentially a print about a print. It shows the entertainer Jane Avril, a close friend of the artist's, examining a freshly printed proof of a poster advertising her performance at the Moulin Rouge. In this lithograph Lautrec reveals his debt to Japanese art. In 1853 Commodore Matthew Perry, an American naval officer, had sailed with his fleet into Tokyo Bay and thereby "opened" Japan to the West, ending two centuries of that country's isolation. Soon afterward Japanese prints (**29**) began to flow into Europe, and artists studied them avidly. Lautrec took from them the ideas that were most useful for his own vision, especially the large flat areas of color and the elegant, flowing silhouette lines. If you compare *L'Estampe originale* with the Japanese print made a century earlier, you will see that both have a sharply drawn, curving outline around the rather flat figure.

And a century *after* Lautrec these influences—explored by him and by other artists of his time—have made their way into contemporary art. David Hockney's *Celia* (**30**), done in 1973, shows the same rather flat figure, the same elegant, curving silhouette line. Hockney has adapted the style for his own needs, but he has also tapped into the vibrant artistic current that inspired those earlier works.

As an observer, you will find that familiarity with this artistic current contributes quite a lot to your appreciation of art. Combined with the "how" and the "why" it will move you closer to being an intelligent observer. That is what this book is all about. It will give you a sample of the how, the why, and the when. With this knowledge you should have a much more active enjoyment of the art around you, the art you live with. And, in turn, you may find that you want to live much more actively with art.

There are great observers as well as great artists, each with their own special tendencies and interests. Whatever artists may say, their art is not done just for themselves. It is done for serious observers who, through education and experience, have made themselves sympathetic receivers of the messages of art. In the final analysis, it is for these observers that artists create.

## The Role of the Artist

What *about* these artists who create? So far in this chapter we have considered the role of the observer in living more actively with art, and we have posed the theory that there is an inborn urge to create and enjoy art. To end our introduction to the idea of living with art, we might focus briefly on those who do live actively with art every day of their lives—the artists themselves.

We should first consider who the artist is. Thanks to Hollywood movies and popular fiction, many people have a stereotype in mind. (The two artists whose biographies appear in this chapter were both subjects of sensationalized Hollywood films, thus contributing to the stereotype.) According to this idea, the artist is a free spirit, unbridled by any moral code; poorly dressed and not very well washed; high nearly all the time on drugs or drink or both; housed in a drafty but picturesque studio, surrounded by paint cans, nude models, and bohemian friends; apt to dash off at any moment to Majorca or the South Pacific to live primarily on peeled grapes, pausing every now and again to splash onto canvas the tortured outpourings of an Intense Inner Turmoil. The artist's death comes tragically early, usually by suicide or overindulgence in strong drink. Is this image romantic? Absolutely. Is it accurate? Almost never. The fact is that most great artists become great by channeling their personal vision into hard work and discipline.

This picture of the artist—a charming one, to be sure—really applies only to a few artists, influenced by Romantic ideals of the late 19th century.

Throughout history artists have filled many different kinds of social roles. In ancient Egypt, in Greece and Rome, most artists were slaves, carrying out in meticulous detail the artistic requirements of their masters. During the Middle Ages the artist moved into the realm of the craftsman, occupying a social level roughly equivalent to that of today's fine cabinetmaker. Only by the time of the Renaissance, the 15th century, were artists accepted in "good" society, and still their creations were under the rigorous control of wealthy patrons. Today's artists in most countries enjoy a social status like that of Renaissance artists—a special elite apart from class—but their freedom of expression is considerably greater than that of artists even a few generations ago.

The social role of artists has changed over time, but their function remains basically the same. Like their counterparts in earlier times, contemporary artists fulfill a practical function, designing virtually every structure and object in the environment. Today this practical role is carried out by artists with specialized, often technical, training—industrial and graphic designers, architects, craft artists, and fashion designers, among others. But what about the painters and sculptors, the photographers and cinematographers? What needs do they meet in our computer age? We can identify at least four basic functions for the artist—all of them age-old, all expanding in complexity.

First, artists *record*. They give us visual images that can be preserved for historical reference. This idea is so obvious that we take it for granted, forgetting how overwhelming our ignorance otherwise would be. Were it not for artists, we would have no idea what people from the past looked like! Nor could we form any visual image of historical places and events. Before the invention of the camera in the early 19th century, artists recorded images mainly through painting and sculpture. Today we rely more heavily on photography, cinema, and television to keep our history, but of course the people behind these media are also artists. Even with the prevalence of mechanical recording, there is in the 1980s a renewed interest in the painted portrait, and a great many well-known artists are thriving on portrait commissions.

Second, artists *give tangible form to the unknown*. In other words, they attempt to record what cannot be seen with the eyes or what has not yet occurred. This role has been important throughout the history of art, and it is no less vital today. Ancient artists had a somewhat different list of unknowns to contend with. They puzzled over and feared such things as tornadoes, floods,

**31.** *Calendar of the Sun.* Aztec, A.D. 1479. Stone, diameter 13′. National Museum of Anthropology, Mexico City.

**32.** University of Kansas students and residents of Lawrence, Kansas, holding a candlelight vigil after the telecast of *The Day After*. Copyright A. Tannenbaum-Sygma.

eclipses, and the wrath of spirits. The famous Aztec stone known as the *Calendar of the Sun* (**31**) is an elaborate representation of the Aztecs' many nature gods, who were thought to have close control over time and weather. At center is the sun-god—a concrete image of the unknown.

Even in an age when satellites predict the weather, there still are certain unknowns, and artists still are struggling to give them tangible form. One contemporary unknown is as terrifying to us as an eclipse of the sun must have been thousands of years ago. This fact was demonstrated on the evening of Sunday, November 20, 1983, when an estimated 100 million Americans watched a made-for-television movie called *The Day After* (**32**). In this film cinematographers—artists—tried to give tangible form to the biggest unknown in our world: What would a nuclear war be like? Much controversy surrounded the showing of the film. Critics complained that *The Day After* represented only one point of view, but of course this is inevitably true. Artists, being people, *can't not* have a point of view. But there is nothing to prevent other artists who hold opposing points of view from formulating equally creative images of the unknown. The viewer is free to choose the one he or she finds to have the greatest personal significance.

Third, artists *give tangible form to feelings*. Again, these are the artist's own feelings that are expressed in paint or marble or whatever the medium. But surely they are feelings shared by many people—love, hate, despair, fear, exhilaration, anger, admiration. When we respond to a work of art, when we pay attention to the emotions it evokes, we are communicating in a way with the artist and with other people who share these responses.

Fourth, artists *offer an innovative way of seeing*, a unique visual perspective. When we experience a work of art, we confront the artist's perspective, compare it to our own, and take note of both the similarities and the differences. We may find that just as Lautrec's appreciation of Japanese painting changed and enhanced his visual perception, our appreciation of the painting of Lautrec or Van Gogh or an inspired but still unrecognized folk artist contributes to our own way of seeing. This collaboration between artist and observer is also a kind of communication—one that enriches our perception of art.

Communication is the key word here, and it is a factor in each of the four functions that have just been described. Artists communicate what things look like, what things might look like, and how people feel and how they see. By learning to live with art we tap into this communication, so that we deepen our humanity and are less alone in the world.

# 2
# What Is Art?

Until about a hundred years ago almost no one would have thought to ask the question "What is art?" Everybody who considered art at all assumed they knew what it was. Only in the 20th century has the problem of definition arisen, and this is true for several reasons.

For one thing, people today are exposed to art from many different times and places—an available body of art far more varied than at any other period in history. If you walk into a large museum, you will see on display works of art from literally all over the world, and covering a time span of some 15,000 years. Magazines, newspapers, and television also bring us into contact with different types of art. Each work of art we see is the product of its own culture, with its own prevailing standards of taste. Each represents what the person who made the work—and those for whom it was made—considered to be art.

The citizen of ancient Athens might have said that art is a sculpture, perhaps depicting a goddess, modeled to look very much like a living woman, yet taller and more beautiful than life (**33**). The tribal member from the Baluba area in Africa might have said that art is a wood figurine, stylized and exaggerated in its features, that symbolizes the human figure (**34**). The aristocrat of 18th-century France might have said that art is a portrait of a queen (or king or duke) that is a good likeness of its subject but at the same time glorifies the subject and has a properly elegant setting (**35**). Each of these works met the standards of acceptable art for its audience, and yet we cannot apply the same standard to all three. We cannot even be sure that all the objects now housed in our art museums—the Baluba figurine, for example—were considered by their makers to be art in the sense that we mean it.

Before our age of easy worldwide communication, the art produced by any specific culture tended to be relatively homogeneous—much the same in style and expression. Of course, there always has been cross-fertilization of styles among cultures, and styles have changed over the years, but generally we can point to a pattern. We can say, "These are the general characteristics of

**above left: 33.** *Aphrodite of the Cnidians,*
Roman copy after an original of c. 330 B.C.
by Praxiteles. Marble, height 6'8".
Vatican Museums, Rome.

**above right: 34.** *Kneeling Woman Presenting a Bowl,*
from Luba, Zaïre. Wood, height 17⅛".
Royal Museum of Central Africa, Tervuren, Belgium.

**right: 35.** Elisabeth Vigée-Lebrun.
*Marie Antoinette.* 1778.
Oil on canvas, 36¾ × 30¼".
Private collection, New York.

4th-century B.C. Greek art" (or Italian Renaissance art or Song dynasty Chinese art), and then proceed to list them. Now, however, not only are we confronted with art from many different cultures, but the art of our own time defies such classification. Three works will demonstrate this (**36,37,38**). Each of these works was made by an artist in the United States, and all were made within three years of one another. But how difficult it would be to formulate a definition of art suitable for all three! So diverse are the styles of 20th-century art, even within the same decade, that we cannot assign them a uniform set of characteristics.

To further complicate the problem, we now have works of art created in media undreamed of a mere thirty or forty years ago. Electronic images of all kinds are made and accepted as art. Often there is no concrete "object," nothing you could hang on the wall or place on a pedestal. Some types of contemporary art are preserved only in the memory banks of computers, and some disappear forever within minutes or hours after they are created. Little wonder, then, that in our century, for the first time, we need to stand back and ask, "What exactly *is* art? How can we determine what is and what isn't?"

This book will not give the definitive answer to either question, about any particular work or about art in general. What it will do, however, is present some guidelines that will help individual viewers to make up their own minds. It will show what some people have considered to be art in different times and places, and what some people consider to be art now. With this information, the viewer should be able to make a better judgment about "What is art *for me?*"

In many parts of the United States today you will encounter the phenomenon known as "motel art." This will be a large inventory of original oil paintings, turned out by assembly-line methods, and sold on weekends at bargain prices in suburban motels—hence the name. You may also hear this work called "sofa art," because the most popular item is the 2-by-3-foot painting considered "correct" for hanging over a sofa. As a potential buyer you are encouraged to bring your wallpaper samples, your upholstery swatches, your paint chips when shopping. This will ensure that the painting you select "goes with" your decor. If you like the painting of the flowers but its colors clash with your sofa, chances are you can find the same flowers in a different range of hues. Your sofa is unusually small or large? No problem. That same bowl of flowers comes in various sizes, like shirts or shoes.

The people who paint these pictures do so on commission from an entrepreneur, who often tells them what to paint and which colors to use. When they gear up, they turn out thirty or forty paintings in a week. Of one such sale *The New York Times* reported: "Most of the paintings on display . . . were landscapes and seascapes with little detail. While each was an original, many were markedly similar, some virtually identical." The *Times* quoted one dealer as saying his artists "prefer doing landscapes, probably because if you make a mistake on a landscape, who can tell?" Moreover, "after a while [the artists] can do them in their sleep—with their eyes shut."[1]

Are these people making art? Certainly it is billed as art by the sellers, and many buyers would agree. A buyer might say, "I like it because it looks nice on my wall and makes me happy. *For me,* this is art." We cannot argue with this point of view. What is art for one person may not be art for somebody else, and that is the very problem we are addressing in this chapter.

Other critics might insist that the "motel artists" are not making art but are making *money*—and by a far safer system than printing up counterfeit bills in the basement. People on this side of the argument are disturbed by the concept of paintings that their makers can turn out "in their sleep."

The issues raised by motel art are those of motivation and satisfaction. What motivates the artist to make art? If money is the *primary* motive, can the result be art? If money is a *secondary* motive and the artist's expression comes first, is the product "more" art? Also, who is supposed to be satisfied by the art—the commissioner, the buyer, the artist, or all three? Again, there are no absolute answers to these questions. They raise issues for consideration and debate, and the answers each of us decides upon will help to clarify our own opinions about what is art.

We might compare the factory approach of motel art to a statement by the sculptor Reuben Nakian: "In art you have to shoot your grandmother. You can't compromise. I'll compromise in life. I'll clown, I'll get drunk. But not in art, which is a life-and-death matter. If it isn't 100 percent right, zing, I'll smash it."[2]

left: **37.** Ellsworth Kelly.
*Red White.* 1962.
Oil on canvas, 6'8⅛" × 7'6".
San Francisco Museum of Art.
(T. B. Walker
Foundation Fund Purchase).

right: **38.** Roy Lichtenstein.
*Girl with Hair Ribbon.* 1965.
Oil on canvas, 4' square.
Private collection, on loan to
National Gallery, Washington, D.C.

**39.** Michelangelo.
*Creation of Adam*, detail
of Sistine Chapel ceiling. 1511.
Fresco. Vatican, Rome.

When Nakian says "you have to shoot your grandmother," he means that the artist is searching for an ultimate truth, an ultimate perfection, an ultimate confrontation with the self and the art. Nothing short of this will do. By this definition, a work that is tossed off quickly to please someone else's specifications—the entrepreneur or the potential buyer—cannot possibly be considered art. Others will judge the merits of the work, but the first and most demanding judge is the artist.

This does not mean that art commissioned by someone else is necessarily inferior to art originated by the artist. As we saw in Chapter 1, artworks have always been commissioned, and throughout history there have been patrons with strong ideas about what they wanted. The ceiling of the Sistine Chapel in the Vatican—undoubtedly one of the best known works of art in the Western world—was painted by Michelangelo on commission from Pope Julius II (**39**). What's more, Michelangelo undertook the ceiling project with great reluctance. Despite these facts, the ceiling of the Sistine Chapel is not, to say the very least, in any way comparable to "sofa art." Michelangelo spent four years of arduous labor on the ceiling paintings, and many art historians consider it miraculous that he finished them in that time. Throughout his career the artist set for himself almost inhumanly high standards. (One of his sculpture commission contracts specified that he would carve the most beautiful statue ever made.) The original idea for the Sistine ceiling might have come from Julius, but the conception and execution were all Michelangelo's—at the height of his artistic powers. Figuratively speaking, Michelangelo "shot his grandmother," and in so doing produced one of the artistic masterpieces of all time. The artist satisfied his patron only after he had satisfied himself.

But what of the viewer? What does it take to satisfy the viewer and to convince him or her that a certain piece is art and is good art? Most people bring to art a set of aesthetic *values,* a collection of likes and dislikes that predispose their judgments about what art should be. Usually, these values are instilled during childhood. One person, fond of graphic detail, likes the painting that shows every blade of grass; another admires all paintings that have a lot of blue in them, because blue is a favorite color; and so on.

To study art on a more formal basis, however, you should try to suspend these value judgments for a little while. If you set aside preconceived ideas about art and open your awareness to other possibilities, you may find that your own area of "likes" has broadened considerably. At the very least you will have a sounder basis for your value system. As a first step toward a heightened appreciation of art, let us look at two of the most common preconceptions about art and see if they hold up.

# Art and Beauty

Many people take for granted that all art should be beautiful. They think of art as something to ornament one's home, like "sofa art." This line of thinking may cause trouble if you visit a museum exhibit, especially an exhibit of 20th-century art. You are almost certain to find a few things that you consider plain ugly. Why are they there?

We may as well face the question squarely, since it is basic to our whole attitude toward art. Why are there so many "ugly" works of art? There are several possible answers. We might reply that "beauty is in the eye of the beholder." In other words, beauty is subjective, and your personal taste leads you to reject things that might be beautiful to others. Both "beautiful" and "ugly" imply aesthetic value judgments.

Another possibility is that the ugly works of art are failures, which were hung because the museum director didn't look at them carefully or because the artist had a famous name. You might even imagine that you are the victim of a great plot designed to make a fool of you by showing you ugly things as if they were art (**40**). All these possibilities depend on the assumption that the artist's proper aim is the creation of beauty.

But there is another possibility. Perhaps the works are successes by artists who were sincerely aiming at something *other than* conventional, physical beauty. Would an artist intentionally make something ugly? And what, actually, do we mean by the words "ugly" and "beautiful"?

Over the centuries numerous writers have grappled with the concept of beauty and tried to understand it. One of the most entertaining was the 18th-century British statesman Edmund Burke, who wrote an essay called *The Sublime and the Beautiful*. In the essay Burke defined beauty as a positive and striking quality that produces pleasure by being small, smooth, gradually or gently varied, delicate, softly and variably colored. It is submissive and may arouse love. Beauty is not related to proportion, said Burke, nor to functional fitness, nor even to perfection. All these things are found apart from beauty.

The sublime, by contrast, is vast even to infinity, difficult, magnificent, dark, and rugged. According to Burke, it will "fill the mind with that sort of delightful horror, which is the most genuine effect and truest test of the sublime." A thing may be ugly and yet sublime if it is "united with such qualities as excite a strong terror." Burke made it clear that greatness lies on the side of the sublime, not of the beautiful.

**40.** From Charles Saxon, *One Man's Fancy* (New York: Dodd, Mead, 1977).

*"How do we know he isn't just trying to make damn fools of us?"*

# Pablo Picasso
## *1881–1973*

The life of Picasso defies summary in a one-page biography. Few artists have lived so long; none have produced such an immense volume of work in so diverse a range of styles and media; and only a rare few can match him in the richness and variety of personal history.

Pablo Ruiz y Picasso was born in the Spanish city of Málaga. He attended art schools in Barcelona and Madrid but became impatient with their rigid, academic approach and soon abandoned formal study. After two trips to Paris—where he saw the work of Van Gogh, Gauguin, and Lautrec—he settled permanently in that city in 1904 and never again lived outside France.

Although Picasso worked in many different styles throughout his life, much of his art is classifiable into the well-known "periods": the "Blue" period, when his paintings concentrated on images of poverty and emotional depression; the "Rose" period, whose paintings included depictions of harlequins and acrobats; the Cubist period, when he worked with the painter Georges Braque; and the "Neoclassical" period, in which the figures took on qualities resembling ancient Greek and Roman sculptures.

Success came early to Picasso. Except for brief periods when he was short of funds (usually because of some romantic entanglement), he lived well and comfortably, traveled widely, and enjoyed a large circle of friends. His work was always in demand, whether in painting, sculpture, prints (of which he made thousands), theatrical design, murals, or ceramics (he took up ceramic art in 1947 and decorated some two thousand pieces in a single year).

It would be impossible to discuss Picasso's life without reference to the women who shared it, because they are a constant presence in his art. Picasso married only twice, but he maintained long, occasionally overlapping, liaisons with several other women. His attachments included Fernande Olivier; Eva Gouel; Olga Koklova, his first wife and the mother of his son Paulo; Marie-Thérèse Walter, mother of his daughter Maïa; Dora Maar; Françoise Gilot, who bore him Claude and Paloma, then later wrote a scandalous memoir of her years with the artist; and finally Jacqueline Roque, whom he married in 1961, in his eightieth year. Their faces parade through his paintings.

Despite his international celebrity, Picasso gave almost no interviews. One of the few took place in 1935 and included this insight into the nature of art: "Everyone wants to understand art. Why not try to understand the song of a bird? Why does one love the night, flowers, everything around one, without trying to understand them? But in the case of a painting people have to understand. If only they would realize above all that an artist works of necessity, that he himself is only a trifling bit of the world, and that no more importance should be attached to him than to plenty of other things which please us in the world, though we can't explain them. People who try to explain pictures are usually barking up the wrong tree."[3]

Pablo Picasso. *Self-Portrait.* 1906.
Oil on canvas, $36\frac{1}{4} \times 28\frac{3}{4}''$
Philadelphia Museum of Art (A. E. Gallatin Collection).

This is quite a useful idea. Let's keep it in mind while we look at Ivan Albright's painting *Into the World Came a Soul Called Ida* (**41**). This work is not smooth, delicate, or soft, and it is not likely to arouse love. For most people, though, it would evoke delightful horror. What is the artist aiming at? We don't know, because Albright did not tell us. A common reaction is to say that the artist is showing us a person who is physically and mentally exhausted— even spiritually exhausted. According to this interpretation, Albright teaches us about spiritual decay by exaggerating the physical decay. Every bulge, every wrinkle, every wart stands for a nasty blow that life has dealt. Everything about the painting speaks of hopes destroyed. The articles on the table are delicate, dainty. Their owner is not. She looks into the hand mirror, but her gesture is one of pushing it away. The "delightful horror" Burke was talking about might be evoked in those who view *Ida* in this light.

*Ida* has elicited very different responses from people whose definitions of "beauty" differ from Burke's. One student, when she first saw the painting, exclaimed, "How beautiful!" When her classmates looked at her in astonishment, the student explained that *Ida* reminded her of her grandmother, who had taken her in as a young child, an orphan, and raised her with much love. To this viewer a woman like Ida, or a painting of such a woman, could never be anything but beautiful. Another student saw *Ida* as a "marvelous study in texture," which he could look at forever.

By Burke's definition, however, Albright's *Ida* is not beautiful, although it might be called sublime. But whether it repels or attracts, Ida is a moving and memorable work of art. A conventionally "beautiful" painting would not have such an impact.

We do not mean to imply that art should *not* be beautiful in the more conventional sense. Many artists aim at creating this kind of beauty. If that is their goal, then we measure their success according to how well they achieve it. The important point is that art can be many different things, and "beautiful" is only one of them.

**41.** Ivan Albright.
*Into the World Came a Soul Called Ida.* 1929–30.
Oil on canvas, 4'7" × 3'9".
Art Institute of Chicago
(gift of the artist).

**42.** Pablo Picasso.
*Olga Picasso in an Armchair.* 1917.
Oil on canvas, $4'3\frac{1}{4}'' \times 2'10\frac{5}{8}''$.
Musée Picasso, Paris.

It is odd that so many people expect all painting and sculpture to be "beautiful." They don't demand this quality in the other arts. Many of the great works of drama and literature are anything but pretty. Consider the tragedies of Shakespeare or the Greek epics or, for that matter, many current novels. They are powerful, shocking, disturbing, frightening—but not beautiful in the sense that a love sonnet is beautiful. The same could be said of much modern music. It is not beautiful, but a great many people respond to it.

The observer of art should be open to the widest possible range of experience. Art that momentarily pleases the eye offers only one level of experience. Art that touches the intellect and the emotions ultimately brings far greater satisfaction.

## Art and the "Real" World

Just as many people expect all art to be beautiful, many people expect all art to mimic the real world, to duplicate as closely as possible the appearance of nature. This is another preconception we might examine. If duplicating the natural world is the *only* thing art is supposed to do, why should artists bother? We already have the natural world, so why make another? No one expects this

**43.** Pablo Picasso.
*Dora Maar Sitting.* 1939.
Oil on canvas, $28\frac{5}{8} \times 23\frac{1}{2}''$.
Courtesy Perls Galleries,
New York.

kind of fidelity from any of the other arts. Few of us would enjoy listening to a symphony that precisely reproduced the sounds of a subway train, a pack of dogs barking, a jet flying overhead, or even bird songs. Similarly, the great works of literature are not real, they are made-up stories. There never was an Anna Karenina or Macbeth or Scarlett O'Hara. It has been said that in fictional literature you "have to tell a lie to tell the truth." In other words, a made-up story can touch basic truths more vividly than can a strict recitation of facts. In a sense, this is what artists are doing: looking for a basic truth that is more "real" than the everyday world we perceive with our eyes.

Have you ever heard someone say, "That guy's a terrible artist. He can't even draw!" There is a strong feeling among much of the public that a "good" artist should be able to draw well—to make pictures of horses or dogs or people that look like the real thing. To be sure, some modern artists cannot draw lifelike images. But far more of them can—and choose not to. Picasso is a prime example of this situation. By anyone's standard, he was one of the greatest draftsmen who ever lived (**42**). Nevertheless, through most of his long career he produced works that did not look anything like the "real" world (**43**).

Picasso himself addressed this problem. He said: "They speak of naturalism in opposition to modern painting. I would like to know if anyone has ever seen a natural work of art. Nature and art, being two different things, cannot be the same thing. Through art we express our conception of what nature is not."[4]

In looking at any work of art, we must always keep in mind that it *is* a work of art. A painting of a horse is not a horse, but daubs of pigment on a backing. A sculpture of a horse is not a horse, but a chunk of metal or wood or stone. The way these works should look is dictated by the artist's aesthetic sense, not by biological laws. Artists are looking for the "lie that tells the truth," for something "realer than real."

Only in Western culture has it been supposed that art should duplicate the natural world and, at that, only during certain periods of Western culture.

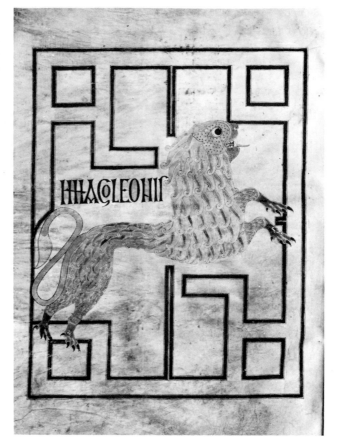

**44.** *Symbol of St. Mark,*
from *The Echternach Gospels.*
Anglo-Irish, c. 700.
Manuscript illumination.
Bibliothèque Nationale, Paris.

We owe this idea to the ancient Greeks and Romans. Plato put forth the notion in *The Republic*, written in Athens in the 4th century B.C. He believed that the aim of painters is to create imitations of objects they see before them, as a mirror reflects the appearance of its surroundings. Even the ancient Greeks, however, were capable of attempting something "realer than real." The Greek statue at the beginning of this chapter (**33**) looks like a human being, but probably not like any human being you know. Plato to the contrary, the Greek sculptor was more interested in the *ideal* than the real. The statue is a little taller than a person, a little more perfectly proportioned, a little more beautiful than nature usually manages to be.

We tend to think that this goal of imitating the natural world carried through from the Greeks to almost our own time, when 20th-century artists broke abruptly with tradition. However, this isn't really true. From the beginning of the Christian era in Europe until the 14th century, naturalism in art was not so highly valued. The manuscript drawing (**44**) makes a good example. This work, dated about 700, is called *The Symbol of St. Mark,* and it is a lion, but it is not the sort of lion you would see in a zoo. It is flat, stylized, and decorative. In its mock ferocity it conveys the *idea* of a lion, rather than the exact appearance of a lion. Much of medieval art is like this—decorative and abstracted, symbolic rather than naturalistic. Should we assume that medieval artists "forgot" how to draw, were not as good at it as their ancient counterparts? Definitely not. The artists of the Middle Ages simply did not care all that much about imitating the natural world. Their concerns were above all spiritual, so their eyes were on the heavens, not the earth.

In the Renaissance the idea of naturalism came back to life. This period began in Italy around 1400 and gradually spread to the rest of Europe. The word *renaissance* means "rebirth," and the rebirth in question was that of ancient culture—the culture of Classical Greece and Rome. In effect, the artistic

left: **45.** Sesshu. *Daruma.*
Japan, Ashikaga Period, 15th century.
Hanging scroll, ink on paper.
Yoshinari Collection, Tokyo.

above: **46.** Pablo Picasso. *Self-Portrait.* 1901.
Oil on canvas, $31\frac{1}{2} \times 23\frac{5}{8}''$.
Musée Picasso, Paris.

leaders of the Renaissance took a good look at ancient art and said, "This is the best that art has ever been."

During the Renaissance the imitation of nature in art became not a goal but a passion. Treatises were written. Artists made all kinds of mathematical studies to better simulate "reality." In some cases this resulted in great masterpieces, such as Michelangelo's (**39**). In others, it created works that are meticulously real—and also bland, lifeless, and boring (**141**).

Outside the European tradition, there was no progression away from naturalism and back again. The great artists of the Orient, of Africa, of pre-Columbian America had virtually no interest in reproducing the real world. Like so many artists today, they were seeking something "realer than real." In the 15th century the Japanese artist Sesshu painted a study of *Daruma,* the first Zen Buddhist patriarch (**45**). We may hope this is not what Daruma really looked like. The stark brushwork and the horribly staring eyes are meant to show Daruma's ardent devotion to the Buddha. (Legend tells that Daruma, while meditating on the Buddha one day, accidentally fell asleep. To punish himself, he cut off his eyelids, so that his eyes could never again close on the Buddha.)

We might compare Sesshu's painting to a self-portrait by Picasso, done in 1901 (**46**). There is an extraordinary resemblance—not in the features, but in the effect. We know that Picasso did not actually look just like this. He did have unusually piercing black eyes, and here he has emphasized that feature. He has also made his face gaunt and almost corpselike. Perhaps we are seeing the intensity of passion in a young man absorbed in his art, just as Daruma was absorbed in his adoration of the Buddha. Both paintings have given us a reality beyond mere illusion.

Before we leave this subject of art and the real world, it will be useful to discuss a few terms that will come up throughout the book. All have to do with the relationship between the artistic image and the appearance of objects in the natural world.

*Representational* or *naturalistic* images in art are those that look very much like images found in the natural world. The portrait of Marie Antoinette (**35**) falls in this category. You may also encounter the term *illusionistic*, which means images that are so natural they trick us into thinking they are real.

An extreme of illusionism is referred to as *trompe-l'oeil*, the French term for "fool the eye." The 19th-century American artist William Harnett specialized in still-life paintings that fool the eye so thoroughly as to cause the double- and triple-take. Viewers sometimes must restrain themselves from touching the canvas, so convincing is the illusion of three-dimensional objects in space. This *trompe-l'oeil* effect does not show up so well in reproduction, but we can get some idea of it in *Music and Good Luck* (**47**). Part of Harnett's visual deceit lies in his skillful painting of the objects in the composition. Far more important, however, is the meticulous rendering of textures and cast shadows. No matter how often we tell ourselves that this is absolutely flat paint on canvas, we still see the violin and other objects floating in front of the background.

*Trompe-l'oeil* illusionism has been out of fashion during most of this century, but recently there has been a revival of interest. In New York, artist Richard Haas has transformed several blank, depressing walls into fantasy cityscapes, like the one shown here (**48**). Both the lawyers' office and the bakery are inventions—stage flats with nothing behind them. Especially diverting is the bakery entrance, which appears to be recessed, with a "shadow" cast by the shop window.

We call a work of art *abstract* or *stylized* when the art has reference to the natural world but does not try to duplicate it exactly. In the illustration (**49**) the figure on the right is naturalistic. The figure on the left, a sculpture from the ancient culture of the Cyclades Islands, off Greece, is highly abstract. We

**49.** Comparison of abstract and naturalistic figures:

**left:** *Statuette of a Woman.* Cycladic, c. 3,000 B.C. Marble. Metropolitan Museum of Art, New York (gift of Christos G. Bastis, 1968).

**right:** Jean Antoine Houdon. *La Frileuse (Winter).* 1787. Bronze, height 4′9″. Metropolitan Museum of Art, New York (bequest of Kate Trubee Davison, 1962).

have no doubt that the Cycladic image is meant to portray the nude female figure, yet the form has been abstracted to an extreme. The face is a rough triangle, with another jutting triangle for the nose. The crossed arms are flat and geometric. Knees, pubic area, and the curve of the abdomen are suggested by simple incised lines. In a sense, the sculptor of this figure has given us the minimum visual information we need to identify the form. The sculpture thus becomes not any particular female figure, but the *essence* of the female figure.

*Nonrepresentational* art has no reference to the natural world of images. It does not show people or animals or mountains, but simply shapes and sometimes colors (**37**). This art bypasses known forms and touches directly upon our senses and emotions. It does not "represent" anything but itself. If, for instance, you were to see a painting that was entirely red, you might suppose it to be about fire or sunsets or a volcano. It might, however, be "about" *red*, and nothing else.

You may sometimes hear people use the terms *abstract* and *nonrepresentational* interchangeably. The distinction is convenient for talking about art, but not necessarily for understanding it.

Despite the apparent dissimilarities in these various kinds of art, they all share a common trait. They are expressions of the artists who made them.

## Art as Expression

Until now we have been talking about things that art can be but need not be. Now at last we come to something that art is always—the expression of the artist. By *expression* we mean an outward manifestation of the artist's emotions, thoughts, feelings, fears, dreams. We have got to the root of what Nakian meant when he talked about shooting his grandmother.

Expression means that the artist is always present in the work of art. No matter how straightforward a work may seem, the artist is always telling us more about her- or himself than about the subject of the art. This may be a difficult idea to grasp, at first. We can look at a beautiful painted landscape, for example, and think, "But that's just the way it *looks*. The artist isn't expressing anything." Is this really true?

To test the idea, we might compare two landscapes painted just four years apart—one by the American Thomas Cole, the other by the Englishman J. M. W. Turner (**50,51**). At first glance we are tempted to say that the Turner is expressive and the Cole is not. Turner's landscape is a fantasy of light and vapor and cloud and mist. We can scarcely identify any details. Cole's *Oxbow*, on the other hand, is a recognizable and very pretty scene on the Connecticut River. You could go there, find the right place, and it would look very much like the painting. The casual observer might say that Turner was inventing, but Cole was just recording nature.

The task of "just" recording nature, however, begins to seem rather formidable when we realize how many decisions Cole had to make in painting the scene. Why choose that particular spot? Why take the exact vantage point that he did? Why paint the scene by day instead of making a moonlit panorama? Why include a rainbow—wouldn't a violent storm have been more dramatic? The answer to all these questions is: That's what the artist wanted to express. That's what he felt about the painting. Cole is expressing himself in a naturalistic scene just as Turner is in his vapors and mist.

An artist's expression will be equally evident in a portrait, even though the portrait may "look like" the person depicted. The two paintings illustrated next (**52,53**) were done in the same year, and both are portraits of Vincent van

above: **52.** Paul Gauguin.
*Vincent van Gogh.* 1888.
Oil on canvas, $28\frac{3}{4} \times 35\frac{7}{8}''$.
National Museum Vincent van Gogh,
Amsterdam.

right: **53.** Vincent van Gogh.
*Self-Portrait.* 1888.
Oil on canvas, $24\frac{3}{8} \times 20\frac{1}{2}''$.
Fogg Art Museum, Harvard University,
Cambridge, Mass.
(bequest of Maurice Wertheim).

Gogh. The first is by Van Gogh's friend Paul Gauguin, and the second is a self-portrait. Without the titles and the background information, almost no one would identify these works as portraits of the same man at the same time. Each expresses what the artist felt about the subject—in one case, about the self.

Gauguin shows us a rather ordinary, heavy-set, middle-class man at work, delicately painting sunflowers. The subject is shifted far to the right in the composition and balanced against the sunflowers, which assume equal importance. It is as though Van Gogh and his sunflowers are two sides of the same coin. How different is Van Gogh's self-portrait! The artist strips away all background details and presents himself as a gaunt, brooding, almost monklike figure—totally introspective, totally isolated.

We may be tempted to ask ourselves, which of these two portraits is the more "real"? And the answer must be: both of them. Gauguin's portrait is the *real* Van Gogh as perceived by Gauguin, sifted through his friendship, memories, emotions, and indeed all of Gauguin's life experiences. Van Gogh's self-portrait is equally the real Van Gogh, as perceived by himself, sifted through the mental torment we know he endured, colored by the self-image he wanted to express to the world.

Two periods in the recent history of art have so intensely shown us the artist's expression that they have been labeled with the term. *Expressionism,* sometimes called *German Expressionism* because most of the leading artists worked in Germany, was a movement of the late 19th and early 20th centuries. Above all, this was an art that looked inward, to the soul and the psyche. Expressionist artists sought to explore their own emotions, their own passions and terrors. Among the most moving of these artists was Käthe Kollwitz, who worked chiefly in prints. Kollwitz drew images based on her own anguish to express her feelings about a world in which there could be war and brutal death. Throughout her difficult life she maintained a fascination for the self-portrait. The lithograph shown here (**54**) portrays an old woman beyond pain and despair, and reduced to an exhausted kind of acceptance. The artist is expressing her utter weariness in a stark, poignant image.

Another movement closely linked with the artist's expression came in the mid-20th century and was known as *Abstract Expressionism* (Chapter 17). Artists identified with this style also looked inward and sought a direct expression of their emotions. This expression, however, took the form of abstract—actually nonrepresentational—images: colors, shapes, lines.

**54.** Käthe Kollwitz. *Self-Portrait.* 1938.
Lithograph, $18\frac{3}{4} \times 11\frac{1}{4}''$.
National Gallery of Art, Washington, D.C.
(Rosenwald Collection).

# Jackson Pollock

## *1912–1956*

Jackson Pollock was born on a sheep ranch in Cody, Wyoming, the youngest son in a family of five boys. During his youth the family moved around a good deal and led a fairly unstable existence. By the age of fifteen Jackson had begun to show signs of the alcoholism that would plague him all his life.

In 1930 Pollock went to New York to study at the Art Students League. His principal teacher was Thomas Hart Benton, a realistic painter of regional Americana, best known for his murals. Later, Pollock would say he was glad to have had the experience with Benton, because he then had to struggle all the harder to make art so very different from that of his mentor.

Money was a critical problem throughout the early years in New York. By 1935 Pollock was employed on the Federal Art Project of the Works Progress Administration—a Depression-era program meant to provide employment for artists. He was required to turn out, every four to eight weeks, one painting suitable for installation in public buildings, for which he was paid a stipend of about $100 a month. Frequent alcoholic binges often interfered with this work, and in 1937 Pollock began psychotherapy in an attempt to overcome his addiction.

Pollock's work was first exhibited in 1942, as part of a group show that also included the work of painter Lee Krasner. Krasner and Pollock soon formed a close relationship, and they were married in 1945. Gradually, Pollock's work began to change, to be freer and more spontaneous, to contain fewer and fewer figural elements. During the late 1940s he began exhibiting works in his mature style.

Some critics praised Pollock as the greatest of all American artists, but the general public was very slow to accept his revolutionary art. *Time* magazine epito-mized the bewilderment of the popular press, dubbing him "Jack the Dripper." Nevertheless, there were some collectors willing to invest, so that finances became less pressing.

The years 1948 to 1952—Pollock's late thirties—were the artist's prime, when he was at the height of his creative powers. After that, he seemed less sure where to go with his art, and even the sympathetic critics were not so responsive to the work. Pollock began to paint less and drink more. On the night of August 11, 1956, Pollock—along with two young women friends—was driving his convertible near his home when he lost control of the car and rammed into a clump of trees. Pollock and one of the women were killed instantly. The artist was only forty-four years old.

Pollock drunk could be violent and brutish; Pollock sober was shy, introverted, and uncommunicative. Few ever succeeded in getting him to talk about his art, but there is one quote, reprinted many times, that gives voice to his truly remarkable vision: "On the floor I am more at ease. I feel nearer, more a part of the painting, since this way I can walk around it, work from the four sides and literally be *in* the painting. . . . When I am *in* my painting, I am not aware of what I'm doing. It is only after a sort of 'get acquainted' period that I see what I have been about. I have no fears about making changes, destroying the image, etc., because the painting has a life of its own. I try to let it come through. It is only when I lose contact with the painting that the result is a mess. Otherwise there is pure harmony, an easy give and take, and the painting comes out well."[5]

Jackson Pollock in his studio
at Easthampton, N.Y., 1950.

**55.** Jackson Pollock. *Convergence.* 1952. Oil on canvas, 7'11½" × 12'11". Albright-Knox Art Gallery, Buffalo, N.Y. (gift of Seymour H. Knox, 1956).

One of the best-known Abstract Expressionists was Jackson Pollock. In the late 1940s and early 1950s Pollock began showing works like *Convergence* (**55**). His style of painting was unusual, even revolutionary. Pollock set his huge canvases on the floor, stood above them (sometimes walked on them), and flung the paint from brushes, sticks, drippers, and even from the paint can itself. The result was an intricate web of lines and colors, with no beginning and no end. A viewer, once drawn into the painting, is led around and through it, with the eye moving continuously through a network of forms. What does the painting express? Movement, color, action, life, vitality—the spirit of the artist. As a matter of fact, many critics referred to this style as *action painting*. The artist's action in making the painting is communicated directly to the viewer. If you stand for a while in front of one of Pollock's paintings, you almost want to conduct it, as if it were an orchestra. The expression is open—available—to anyone who is willing to receive it.

An interesting point about Pollock's art is that its *form* and its *content* are hard to separate. Indeed, the two are almost identical. Form and content are important ideas for the study of art. An understanding of how they work together will bring us closer to answering the question "What is art?" These terms are also indispensable for communicating about art to other people.

## Form and Content

If a good idea were all it took to be a famous artist, we all would be famous. The world is full of people who are carrying around in their heads great ideas for novels, symphonies, and paintings. What is lacking is form. Unfortunately for the dreamers, form is essential to any work of art.

In simplest terms, *form* is the way a work of art looks; and *content* is what a work of art says. Form includes everything from the material the artist uses (oil paint, stone, paper, whatever), to the style in which the artist works, to the shapes and lines and colors in the art. It also includes how a work of art is put together—its *composition*.

Content refers to the message communicated by a work of art—what the artist expresses. Sometimes content begins with a story or an event or an image of something we recognize, which we could call the *subject matter*. For instance, in a painting called, say, *The Battle of Bull Run,* the subject matter would be a battle scene. The content would be a battle scene *and* what the artist wanted to communicate about that battle scene. (You can guess that the content would likely be very different if a Union sympathizer and a Confederate artist were painting the same scene.) Similarly, in a portrait, as in the two portraits of Van Gogh, the content begins with the subject and includes whatever the artist wishes to communicate about the subject.

In other types of art, however, the content may not be so clear. It could be anger or fear or loneliness or joy or, as in the Pollock, action and vitality. For an interesting study in form and content, we might look at Willem de Kooning's *Woman and Bicycle* (**56**), one of a series of "woman" paintings the artist did during the early 1950s. In form *Woman and Bicycle* is an oil painting, in a highly abstract style, consisting mainly of harsh, savage brush strokes.

**56.** Willem de Kooning.
*Woman and Bicycle.* 1952–53.
Oil on canvas, 6'4½" × 4'1".
Whitney Museum of American Art,
New York.

As to the painting's content, we have a clue in the title "woman," but that is only a starting point. De Kooning's women throughout this series are predatory monsters—all eyes and teeth and huge, engulfing breasts. The artist himself said that he always began with an image of a young, beautiful woman, only to see it transformed on canvas, as he worked, into a hideous nightmare creature. We have a sense of de Kooning struggling against the women in his paintings, struggling to carve them up and subdue them, while at the same time the painted women become more and more menacing, in danger of destroying the artist. The content of *Woman and Bicycle*, then, is not simply a woman, but de Kooning's conscious and unconscious feelings about women.

To fully understand content it is necessary to know something about the artist and especially about the culture in which the artwork was produced, because every work of art emerges from some particular cultural background. At the most basic level, it is important to know what is being depicted in a work of art (the subject matter) and why—its iconography.

## Iconography

Artists around the world always have assumed a certain knowledge on the part of their audiences. They have assumed their audiences would understand a work's *iconography*. Loosely, iconography is the "story" within a work of art. A viewer's comprehension of the iconography includes familiarity with the people, places, and events that are depicted, as well as any symbolism intended by the artist. Much of the history of art has some literary or historical or religious reference. Quite a lot of Western art is based on the Bible. Most of the time an artist's immediate circle of patrons and viewers will grasp the iconography at once. Problems arise, however, when we confront art from times and places other than our own.

Christians around the world are familiar with the story surrounding the birth of Christ. When a person with this background looks at Fra Filippo Lippi's *Nativity* (**57**), certain things are immediately apparent. There is the

**57.** Fra Filippo Lippi. *Nativity.* c. 1459. Tempera on wood, 4′2″ × 3′10″. Staatliche Museen, West Berlin.

# Albrecht Dürer
## *1471–1528*

**A**lbrecht Dürer is the first of the northern European artists who seems to us "modern" in his outlook. Unlike most of his colleagues, he had a strong sense of being an *artist,* not a craftsman, and he sought—and received—acceptance in the higher ranks of society. Moreover, Dürer appears to have understood his role in the history of art—sensed that his work would exert great influence on his contemporaries and on artists of the future. This awareness led him to date his works and sign them with the distinctive "AD" (visible in the left background of his self-portrait)—a fairly unusual practice at the time.

Born in the southern German city of Nuremberg, Dürer was the son of a goldsmith, to whom he was apprenticed as a boy. At the age of fifteen young Albrecht was sent to study in the workshop of Michael Wolgemut, then considered a leading painter in Nuremberg. He stayed with Wolgemut for four years, after which he began a four-year period of wandering through northern Europe. In 1494 Dürer's father called him back to Nuremberg to an arranged marriage. (The marriage seems not to have been a happy one and produced no children.) Soon afterward Dürer established himself as a master and opened his own studio.

Dürer made a great many paintings and drawings, but it is his output in prints (engravings, woodcuts, and etchings) that is truly extraordinary. Many people would argue that he was the greatest printmaker who ever lived. His genius derived partly from an ability to unite the best tendencies in northern and southern European art of the period, for Dürer was a well-traveled man. In 1494 he visited Italy, and he returned in 1505, staying two years in Venice, where he operated a studio. This second trip was a huge success, both artistically and socially. The artist received many commissions and enjoyed the high regard of the Venetian painters as well as of important patrons in the city. Upon his return to Germany Dürer took his place among the leading writers and intellectuals of Nuremberg, who seem to have valued him for his knowledge and wit, as well as for his art. In 1515 he was appointed court painter to the Holy Roman Emperor Maximilian I, a position he retained with the emperor's successor.

The last years of Dürer's life were devoted largely to work on his books and treatises, through which he hoped to teach a scientific approach to painting and drawing. As a Renaissance artist, he was fascinated by perfection and by an ideal of beauty. He wrote: "What beauty is, I know not, though it adheres to many things. When we wish to bring it into our work we find it very hard. We must gather it together from far and wide, and especially in the case of the human figure throughout all its limbs from before and behind. One may often search through two or three hundred men without finding amongst them more than one or two points of beauty which can be made use of. You, therefore, if you desire to compose a fine figure, must take the head from some, the chest, arm, leg, hand, and foot from others; and, likewise, search through all members of every kind. For from many beautiful things something good may be gathered, even as honey is gathered from many flowers."[6]

Albrecht Dürer. *Self-Portrait.* 1500.
Wood panel, $25\frac{5}{8} \times 18\frac{7}{8}''$. Alte Pinakothek, Munich.

child Jesus, watched over by his mother Mary (who wears a halo symbolic of her perfect sinlessness). To the left are Joseph, the child's foster father, and the young John the Baptist, identified by his staff. And at the top are God the Father and the Holy Ghost in the form of a dove, completing the Trinity. Someone with no knowledge of the Christian tradition, however, would probably see just a lovely mother-and-child scene and wonder who those other people are and why they are wearing such funny hats. We can try to imagine what an Inca in 15th-century Peru or a Samurai in 15th-century Japan (both contemporary with this painting) would see in Filippo Lippi's scene.

Even in the Western culture we have inherited the iconography can sometimes be unfamiliar. Albrecht Dürer, who worked in Germany during the late 15th and early 16th centuries, was a Christian. Much of his iconography is biblical, but it is overlaid with mystical northern European symbolism. In *The Fall of Man* (**58**) we see Adam and Eve about to be banished from the Garden of Eden after their sin of eating the forbidden fruit. Dürer has included symbols of the four humors, or temperaments, which were thought to rule the human body: the elk symbolizes gall; the ox, phlegm; the cat, choler; and the rabbit, blood. Each of these humors, in turn, was associated with a particular sin—avarice, gluttony, cruelty, and lechery—sins that the fallen Adam and Eve were now susceptible to. Dürer's iconography is incredibly rich, and we can only begin to explore it here. For the artist's learned contemporaries it was perfectly understandable; for us it is new territory.

**58.** Albrecht Dürer. *The Fall of Man.*
1504. Engraving, $9\frac{7}{8} \times 7\frac{5}{8}''$.
Metropolitan Museum of Art, New York
(Fletcher Fund, 1919).

**59.** *Sita in the Garden of Lanka with Ravana and His Demons.*
Guler School, India, c. 1720. Gold and color on paper, $22\frac{3}{4} \times 33\frac{1}{4}''$.
Cleveland Museum of Art (gift of George P. Bickford).

Now let us consider a work even farther outside the experience of most of us—a painting that portrays an episode from the *Ramáyana*, the classic epic poem of India (**59**). Probably composed in the 3rd century B.C., the *Ramáyana* is an integral part of daily life in India even today. Every character, every incident in the tale is as well known to the Indian public as the details of the Nativity are to practicing Christians.

Briefly, the *Ramáyana* tells the adventures of Rama—a prince who was the seventh incarnation of the god Vishnu—and his beautiful, faithful wife, Sita. Through a trick, the demon-king Ravana manages to abduct Sita and carry her off to his splendid palace at Lanka, which we see in the left half of this illustration. Ravana is so demonic, and so powerful, that he can assume any form he chooses—the worst one being a monster with ten heads and twenty arms. After kidnapping Sita, he gives her one year to renounce Rama and become his consort, and he exiles her to the forest in the keeping of demon-handmaidens. In this episode Ravana is paying Sita a visit to see if she has yet relented, but Sita remains steadfastly true to Rama.

Without this background information we find the painting lovely and exotic, but how much more interesting it becomes when we understand its iconography. Nowadays all of us are exposed to art from cultures other than our own, and it is well worth the effort to learn more about them.

We should also remember that our own culture could be equally mystifying to those outside it. What would Filippo Lippi or Dürer or the painter of the *Ramáyana* make of Audrey Flack's *Marilyn* (**60**)? The details of the tragic film star's life are well known to most Americans, and so we readily accept the symbols of glamor, of artifice, of lushness, and especially of time running out (the candle, watch, calendar, and egg timer). But to someone who has never heard of Marilyn Monroe, the painting would seem a meaningless jumble.

A knowledge of any work's iconography, therefore, can greatly enhance our appreciation, as can acquaintance with the culture that produced the art. We are ready now to sum up the method by which we can approach intelligent art criticism—to judge what is art and what is good art.

**60.** Audrey Flack. *Marilyn.* 1977.
Oil and acrylic on canvas, 8′ square.
University of Arizona Art Gallery, Tucson.

## Art Criticism

When you walk into a museum, or into someone's home where art is displayed, or down a street where there is sculpture or a new building, how do you approach this new visual experience? Is this particular object art? Is it good art? If a well-known critic says it is good, does that make it so? Not necessarily, for the critics have often been wrong. Far better to inform yourself fully and then make your own judgment. Here are some of the questions you might ask yourself when you encounter any new work of art:

1. Where does this work fit into the history of art? Does it remind me of any others I have seen, and in what way? Can I make any connection between this piece and others?
2. What do I know about the artist? Is there anything about his or her background that would influence my reaction to this work?
3. When and where was this work made? What else was going on in the world at the same time? What are the characteristics of the culture from which it emerges?
4. What is the form of this work? What is it made of, and how is it organized?
5. What is the content of this work? Is there a recognizable subject and, if so, how is that subject treated?

6. What feelings, memories, or associations does this work evoke in me? Does it make me feel happy, angry, sad, frightened, disgusted, uplifted, inspired? Can I imagine the artist felt the same way? Do I feel any sense of kinship with the artist?
7. How has the artist used his or her materials? Is the work well-crafted? Does the use of material enhance the content and the communication?

After a bit of practice this seven-step procedure—which sounds long in the telling—will become almost automatic. You will not have to think about it because the questions will arise, and be answered, whenever you give serious attention to a new work of art.

And so, to return to the title of this chapter: What is art? It is the "lie that tells the truth." Sometimes it is beautiful, but it may be ugly. It can look like things in the natural world, but frequently it does not. It is always the expression of the artist. It is always a product of the culture that produces it. It is the artist showing us something, telling us something, making us experience something. It is communication—if we but look, listen, think, and feel.

# 3
# Themes and Purposes of Art

There are several ways to approach the study of art. A popular one is to trace its history chronologically, from the earliest cave paintings of the Stone Age to the art of our own time. This method offers great advantages, because it places works of art in the context of the cultures from which they emerged and allows one to follow the development of art over the centuries. Part V of this book will present a brief chronological survey of art.

The chronological approach has one drawback, however, in that we may lose sight of the characteristics that works made by different cultures have in common. For instance, a sculpture produced today and one produced ten thousand years ago may seem very different, and a chronological approach emphasizes the differences by focusing on the cultural aspects that influenced each. But suppose the two sculptures are images honoring political leaders; then we would say they have the same *theme,* so we can make interesting comparisons between them. While it is useful to understand how and why works of art differ, it is also helpful to see how much they are alike, even when thousands of miles and years separate them.

In Chapter 2 we discussed content—the subject matter of a work of art and what the artist means to convey about that subject matter. Content can be considered as *theme* whenever similar material is treated by many artists at various times and places. A theme is therefore like a thread running through the entire history of art, and there are many such threads. No doubt every person setting out to name the important themes in art would produce a different list. We have chosen to consider these: magic and survival, religion, pride and politics, art as the mirror of everyday life, art and nature, imagination and fantasy.

The *purpose* of a work of art is what the artist hoped to achieve (or in some cases what the art patron hoped to achieve by commissioning it). Sometimes the two factors—theme and purpose—overlap, so it is difficult to tell them apart, but in other instances we can identify a separate purpose. For example, in a landscape painting the theme probably would be nature, and the purpose simply to depict some aspect of nature. But if the artist's goal in painting a landscape is to show the glory of God's creation, then the theme is still nature but we might consider the purpose one of religion. Let us therefore examine the six themes mentioned, with several examples of each, and see how they lend themselves to various purposes. We begin with what was probably the first preoccupation of artists and indeed of all people.

## Magic and Survival

Our illustration shows a little statuette that is nearly everybody's favorite way to begin the study of art (**61**). She is made of stone, was formed ten to thirty thousand years before the birth of Christ, and was found near a town in Austria. Her name: the *Venus of Willendorf.* At first her title of "Venus" may seem strange, given our usual image of the Goddess of Love. The name, of course, represents an application of modern-day standards to a world about which we know almost nothing. It seems clear, however, that the little figure was a fertility image, perhaps meant to be carried around as an *amulet,* or good-luck charm (the *Venus* is less than 5 inches tall). Only the features associated with childbearing have been stressed—the belly, breasts, and pubic area. Venus' face is obscured, her arms, crossed above the breasts, are barely defined, and her legs taper off to nothing. If we take this figure literally, she could not see or speak or walk or carry; what she could do was bear children and nurture them.

How difficult it is for us in this time to imagine what childbirth meant all those millennia ago. On the one hand it must have been a pressing necessity. Children were needed to help in the task of survival, and there may also have been an instinct to continue life through future generations. On the other hand, however, the process by which children are conceived and born was a mystery to these early peoples. The ovum and the sperm were unknown. Bringing forth a child must have seemed very much like the magician's trick of pulling a rabbit out of a hat. No wonder elements of magic became associated with childbirth. Many scholars assume that fertility figures like the *Venus of Willendorf,* which are extremely common in early art, were meant to play a cause-and-effect role. The sculptor would form an image of a woman with exaggerated reproductive features and this figure would *result* in a child (or children) being born. To primitive peoples this sequence must have made as much sense as any other.

Much primitive art seems to have been created for this purpose—to make sense out of the universe and to exert some control over the forces of nature. Today we have weather forecasters and meteorologists and seismologists and orbiting satellites and computers—but we are still not absolutely sure whether it will rain tomorrow. Early peoples had none of these, but they made the best out of what they had. Some of their arrangements startle us with their ingenuity.

On a plain in the south of England stand the enormous megaliths known as Stonehenge (**62**), much as they have stood for more than three thousand years. Stonehenge was built over a period of centuries, perhaps beginning as early as 2,000 B.C. It consists of four concentric rings of stones, the outermost ring being 100 feet in diameter. The basis of the structure is *post-and-lintel* construction (Chapter 13), in which two uprights are surmounted by a horizontal crosspiece, the *lintel.* One of the most fascinating aspects of Stonehenge is the puzzle of *how* it was built. The stones, some weighing 50 tons or more, were quarried many miles away and dragged to the site by whatever primitive means may have been available. Next came the staggering feat of raising the lintels into position, without benefit of the cranes and other modern devices we take for granted. There is no mortar holding up these immense rocks. The method used by Stone Age peoples to erect them has stood up ever since.

**above: 62.** Stonehenge. c. 2000–1500 B.C.
Height of stones 13′6″. Salisbury Plain, England.

**right: 63.** Double face mask, Baule tribe, Ivory Coast.
Wood with coloring, height 13¾″.
Metropolitan Museum of Art, New York
(Michael C. Rockefeller Memorial Collection).

Even more interesting is the problem of *why* Stonehenge was created. What purpose can have been so compelling as to stimulate this tremendous human effort? For centuries art historians debated the question. Then in 1964 a theory was advanced by astronomer Gerald S. Hawkins that appears to have solved the riddle of Stonehenge. By feeding complex measurements into a computer, Hawkins found that, at the moment of sunrise on the summer solstice (usually June 21), the sun shines through a key opening directly to an altar at the center. Similar computations showed that the position of the stones was organized to predict the winter solstice, the spring and autumnal equinoxes, and even eclipses of the sun and moon. In other words, Stonehenge apparently functioned as a giant calendar, codifying the mysterious changes of seasons and stars. Is Stonehenge a tool of magic, or the beginning of science, or a link between the two? Whichever the case, it provided the means by which its makers could plan for survival.

In many cultures throughout Africa, the Pacific, and elsewhere there has been a long tradition of making masks (**63**). These masks are usually ceremonial, magical, and related to such basic aspects of survival as birth, healing, puberty, marriage, fertility, success in the hunt, and death. (Death, seen as the transition to the afterlife, can be considered an aspect of survival.) A *shaman*—or healer-priest—may wear a mask as part of the healing ritual, thus combining the two elements of magic and survival.

Art whose theme is magic and survival has as its purpose the establishment of some sense of control. For nearly everyone, it seems, the most terrifying situation is that of being helpless, out of control, at the mercy of forces much bigger than we are. Worst of all, many psychologists contend, is the fear of *random* disasters. It is safer to believe that lightning strikes a particular spot because a spirit is angry than to know that lightning's path is arbitrary. At least a spirit can be placated, but randomness leaves us defenseless. Therefore, even if the control we take is imaginary—wearing a mask and beating a drum to quiet the lightning-god—we still are comforted.

Today's world is far more complex and calls for different kinds of control over powerful forces—the "magic" of the physicist, the neurosurgeon, the cosmologist, the mathematician. Even with all these specialists, there still are a great many areas of mystery in our world. Although we have learned much about the principles of birth and crop-raising and healing, we do not really know much about the nature of our universe. For most of us quasars and black holes do not seem any less magical than the idea that forming an image of a pregnant woman could produce a child. Perhaps that is why some contemporary artists have endowed their work with magical qualities not unlike those of the African shaman's art.

Among the artists who have carried this theme of magic into present-day and cosmic realms is the sculptor Alice Aycock. *Collected Ghost Stories from the Workhouse* (**64**) may remind you of an oil refinery or a factory set in the landscape. It does not seem out of keeping with the water tower at the right in this photograph, which is not part of the sculpture. *Collected Ghost Stories* is an attempt to make machinery do spiritual work. The ghosts from the title are contained in the eight round canisters in the right foreground. It is they who supply spiritual energy to power the two globes at top, which are models of the universe. According to the catalogue notes for this sculpture, Aycock requires the viewer to "ponder the magic of science." The sculpture "contains the power to conjure spirits and challenge the viewer's intellectual comprehension of material and psychic phenomena."[1] It would seem, therefore, that magic and survival are still potent issues in our world, and that artists are still striving to take control over what they cannot see.

Artists often use religion for much the same reason as magic: to explain that which cannot be seen or demonstrated. This brings us to our next important theme in art.

**64.** Alice Aycock. *Collected Ghost Stories from the Workhouse,*
from the series *How to Catch and Manufacture Ghosts.* 1980.
Installed on the campus of the University of South Florida, Tampa.

**65.** Ictinus and Callicrates. The Parthenon. 448–432 B.C. Acropolis, Athens.

## Art in the Service of Religion

Since earliest times art has served religion in two important ways. First, it has attempted to make specific and visible something that is, by its very nature, spiritual. Religious art provides images of Christ, Buddha, the whole galaxy of Greek and Roman gods, the saints and angels, and other figures. It portrays all the legends, stories, and events that make up the fabric of a faith. Artists depict—and help others to visualize—the Crucifixion of Christ or the cremation of the Buddha. Each of these depictions, of course, is the artist's own idea of what a particular being or situation looked like. But by giving the faithful an image to focus on, the artist makes religion more concrete, less abstract.

The second major task of artists has been to erect the sacred temples where believers join to profess their faith and to follow the observances it requires. A very large portion of the magnificent architecture we have was built in the service of religion. Naturally the architectural style of any religious structure reflects the culture in which it was built, but it is also dependent on the particular needs of a given religion. Three examples will help to show this.

On a high hill, or *acropolis*, overlooking the city of Athens stands the shell of what many consider the most splendid building ever conceived: the Parthenon (**65**). The Parthenon was erected in the 5th century B.C. as a temple to the goddess Athena, patroness of the city, and at one time its core held a colossal statue of the goddess. However, the religion associated with the Parthenon was not confined to worship of a deity. In ancient Greece, veneration of the gods was closely allied to the political and social ideals of a city-state that celebrated its own greatness. The statesman Pericles, under whose sponsorship the Parthenon was built, spoke of such matters in his famous Funeral Speech during the Peloponnesian War:

> Our love of what is beautiful does not lead to extravagance; our love of the things of the mind does not make us soft. We regard wealth as something to be properly used, rather than as something to boast about. . . . What I would prefer is that you should fix your eyes every day on the greatness of Athens as she really is, and should fall in love with her. When you realize her greatness, then reflect that what made her great was men with a spirit of adventure, men who knew their duty, men who were ashamed to fall below a certain standard.[2]

Rising proudly on its hill, visible from almost every corner of the city and for miles around, the Parthenon made it possible for all literally to "fix their eyes every day on the greatness of Athens." It functioned therefore as a symbol of the citizens' aspirations. Its structure as a religious shrine seems unusual for us in that it turns outward, toward the city, rather than in upon itself. Worshipers were not meant to gather inside the building; actually, only priests could enter the inner chamber, or *cella,* where the statue of Athena stood. Religious ceremonies on festal occasions focused on processions, which began down in the city, wound their way up the steep path on the west side of the Acropolis, and circled the Parthenon and other sacred buildings at the top.

Most of the Parthenon's architectural embellishment was intended for the appreciation of the worshipers outside. All four walls of the exterior were decorated with sculptures high up under the roof, and originally portions of the marble facade were painted a vivid blue and red. In Chapter 13 we shall consider details of the Parthenon's structure; here we concentrate on the theme of religion and on the Parthenon's purpose, which is both religious *and* political exaltation.

At about the same time the Parthenon was being constructed in Athens, but half a continent away, one of the world's great religions was developing and beginning to form its own architecture. Buddhism is predominantly a personal religion, and its observances depend less on communal worship than on individual contemplation. It places great emphasis on symbolism, much of it referring to episodes in the life of the Buddha. Both these aspects—the personal and the symbolic—are evident in one of Buddhism's finest early shrines, the Great Stupa at Sanchi, in India (**66**). Like the Parthenon, the Great Stupa turns more outward than inward, but its moundlike form is more sculptural, intended as a representation of the cosmos. At the very top is a three-part "umbrella," symbolizing the three major aspects of Buddhism—the Buddha, the Buddha's Law, and the Monastic Order.

Buddhist shrines—the word *stupa* means shrine—often housed relics of the Buddha, and worship rituals called for circumambulation ("walking around") of the stupa. Thus, on the outside of the Great Stupa we see a railed pathway, provided so that pilgrims could take the ritual clockwise walk following the Path of Life around the World Mountain. Elsewhere the stupa is embellished richly with carvings and sculpture evoking scenes from the Buddha's life. Every part of the stupa is geared to the pursuit of personal enlightenment and transcendence.

If the Buddhist temple is dedicated to private worship, then its extreme opposite can be found in the total encompassment of a community religious experience: the medieval Christian cathedral. And the supreme example of that ideal is the Cathedral of Notre Dame de Chartres, in France (**67**). Chartres Cathedral was built, rebuilt, and modified over a period of several hundred years, but the basic structure, which is in the Gothic style (Chapter 13), was established in the 13th century. A cathedral—as opposed to a church—is the bishop's domain and therefore always in a town or city. This one fact is crucial to understanding the nature of Chartres and the role it played in the people's lives.

Our illustration shows that the cathedral towers magnificently over the surrounding city, much as the Parthenon does over Athens, but here the resemblance ends. Whereas the Parthenon is above and apart from the city, accessible only by a steep path, Chartres Cathedral is very much a living presence *within* the city. In the Middle Ages houses and shops clustered right up to its walls, and one side of the cathedral formed an edge of the busy marketplace. The cathedral functioned as the hub of all activities, both sacred and secular, within the town.

Medieval France had one dominant religion, and that was the Christianity of Rome. One could assume that almost every resident of the town of Chartres professed exactly the same faith, and so the church was an integral part of everyday life. Its bells tolled the hours for waking, starting work, praying, and retiring for the evening rest. Its feast days were the official holidays. Chartres Cathedral and its counterparts served the populace not only as a setting for religious worship but as meeting hall, museum, concert stage, and social gathering place. Within its walls business deals were arranged, goods were sold, friends met, young couples courted. Where else but inside the cathedral could the townsfolk hear splendid music? Where else could they see magnificent art?

Three religious structures: the Parthenon, the Great Stupa, and Chartres Cathedral. Each was built in the service of religion but for each we can find another slightly different purpose. For the Parthenon the purpose is also *political*; for the Great Stupa there is the purely *private* observance of religion; and for Chartres the *social* role is almost as important as the religious.

These three structures demonstrate that religious art must always be understood in the context of the culture for which it was created. Moreover, that context changes as the culture develops. No religion is static. Every faith changes and grows, adapts to particular times and cultures, is influenced by individuals who practice it. The same is true of art that expresses aspects of that religion. We can see this by studying two interpretations of the Crucifixion, made by artists with very different views of the world.

The Crucifixion of Christ has been a frequent subject in Western religious art for many hundreds of years. In its essentials the story is simple. Jesus Christ, who was by birth a Jew, attracted a large following by preaching a new kind of faith and was believed by many to be the long-awaited Messiah. This disturbed the authorities, who were threatened by the prospect of having a powerful "king" of the Jews at large, and Christ was condemned to death. After a series of tortures and humiliations, he was nailed, by the feet and hands, to a cross and left to die—a customary method of execution in those times. His dying took three hours and was witnessed by his mother Mary, his beloved disciple St. John, and Mary Magdalene. Here is the way two artists responded to this scene of anguish.

Matthias Grünewald, a German artist of the early 16th century, painted the Crucifixion as the center of his great masterpiece, the *Isenheim Altarpiece* (**68**). Originally, the altarpiece reposed in the chapel of a hospital devoted to the treatment of illnesses afflicting the skin, including syphilis. This helps to explain the horrible appearance of Christ's body on the cross—pockmarked, bleeding from numberless wounds, tortured beyond endurance. Without question the patients in the hospital could identify with Christ's sufferings and increase their faith by being as one with him. The artist's purpose was undoubtedly in part to foster this identification.

**68.** Matthias Grünewald. *The Crucifixion,* center panel of the *Isenheim Altarpiece* (exterior). Completed 1515. Panel, 8'10" × 10'1". Musée d'Unterlinden, Colmar.

In Grünewald's version of the Crucifixion, the twists and lacerations of the body speak of unendurable pain, but the real anguish is conveyed by the feet and hands. Christ's fingers splay out, clutching at the air but helpless to relieve the pain. His feet bend inward in a futile attempt to alleviate the pressure of his hanging body. To the left of the Cross the Virgin Mary falls in a faint, supported by St. John, and Mary Magdalene weeps in an agony that mirrors Christ's own. To the right John the Baptist offers the only sign of hope. He points calmly at the dying Savior in a gesture that foreshadows Christ's Resurrection and eventual triumph. Grünewald's interpretation of this event is in keeping with a harsh northern tradition of art in which extremes of physical agony were commonplace. Much of northern European art from this period dwells on the more grisly aspects of faith—the martyrdom of saints and the inventive punishment of sinners.

Now let us consider a version of the same scene painted just about a hundred years later by an artist who was born in Crete, but who spent most of his professional life in Spain—the man known as El Greco (**69**). Can this possibly be the same execution scene? *This* Christ does not hang helplessly from the Cross but seems rather to float upward, lifting the Cross with him.

**69.** El Greco.
*Christ on the Cross with Landscape.*
c. 1610. Oil on canvas, 6'2" × 3'8".
Cleveland Museum of Art
(gift of Hanna Fund).

# El Greco
## *1541?–1614*

Not until the 20th century did El Greco become valued as one of the great artists of all time. Soon after his death he was all but forgotten, and nearly three centuries would elapse before serious attention was paid to his work. No doubt this is a major reason why so very little is known about his life.

The year 1541 is given tentatively as the date when Domenicos Theotocopoulos was born on the Greek island of Crete. It is believed that he began as a painter of small icons (religious images) of the sort then typical on that island. Sometime in the 1560s Theotocopoulos traveled to Venice, where he was taken as a pupil by the Renaissance master Titian, and in 1570 he moved on to Rome. There is a story that, while in Rome, Theotocopoulos—who had yet to prove himself as an artist—grandly offered to replace the *Last Judgment* fresco by Michelangelo and do a better job of it. If true, the story indicates both the artist's staunch faith in himself and a certain tactlessness in dealing with those who considered Michelangelo barely less than a god. (Many years later El Greco was quoted as saying: "Michelangelo was a good man, but he could not paint.")

Early in 1577, for reasons that are unclear, the artist left for Spain and settled in the city of Toledo, where he was to remain for the rest of his life. There he acquired the name by which he is always known: El Greco, the Greek. Possibly he had been attracted by news of the Spanish King Philip II's ambitious plans to restore his palace, which would mean many artistic commissions. However, El Greco's only commission from the king did not please its patron and was never hung in the intended spot. Thereafter, most of El Greco's commissions came from the clergy.

Not long after his arrival in Spain El Greco met a Spanish woman, Jerónima de las Cuevas, who became his lifelong companion, although they apparently never married. Almost nothing is known of Jerónima except for a lovely portrait, *Lady with a Fur*, that is assumed to be her image. In 1578 she bore El Greco's son, his only child, Jorge Manuel, who later became an artist and worked in his father's studio.

If ever an artist and a place were identified closely with one another, such was the case with El Greco and Toledo. Stronghold of Roman Catholicism, of the Spanish Inquisition and the Jesuit order, Toledo was a fervently religious city, which fit in excellently with El Greco's ardent spirituality. The artist's friends were the clergy and the intellectuals of the town, who formed an appreciative audience for his innovative treatment of religious themes. In the end, the painter who was not really a Spaniard at all is often called the greatest of all Spanish painters.

A contemporary who interviewed El Greco not long before the latter's death spoke of his extensive writings on art and philosophy. These, unfortunately, have been lost. But one comment reliably attributed to him is significant in view of his long centuries of obscurity before the world again discovered El Greco, and it is a comfort to struggling artists in our own time: "If once in a while popular taste is right, it is usually by accident and is not worth taking into account."

El Greco. *Portrait of a Man (Self-Portrait?)*. c. 1610. Oil on canvas, $20\frac{3}{4} \times 18\frac{3}{8}''$. Metropolitan Museum of Art, New York (purchase, Joseph Pulitzer Bequest, 1924).

His body twists, yes, but not so much in anguish as in a graceful transcendence over earthly concerns. No onlookers interrupt this otherworldly image of perfect goodness triumphing over pain and death.

In painting this Crucifixion, El Greco was responding to three impulses that set him apart from Grünewald. First of all, El Greco was a southern European artist, steeped in the traditions of Greece and Rome, aware of the Renaissance masterpieces of Michelangelo and Raphael, untouched by the harsh precedents of northern art. Second, El Greco was much an artist of the Counter-Reformation—the Roman Catholic struggle against the increasing strength of the new Protestant religions in northern Europe. El Greco reflects the Counter-Reformation mood with his supremely mystical vision of Christ on the Cross, poised in a landscape that is clearly not of this world. Catholic Spain turned its eyes upward, to the heavens rather than the earth, and forward, to eternal life rather than the earthly one. El Greco's pristine, elongated figure of Christ exactly satisfied this ideal. Finally, El Greco was himself a mystic, a visionary, a passionately religious man. His Crucifixion emerges from an intense and very personal faith, supported by his strong artistic background.

So we see that religious art is deeply affected by many forces: when it was made, where, why, by whom, and for what purpose. The same is true of art that deals in more earthly matters.

## Pride and Politics

It has been said that everything in life comes down to politics. All the worthy emotions—love, honor, patriotism, charity—have at their root a concern with politics, which means simply possessing the power to achieve one's desired goal. This is not the place to debate whether that theory holds true or not, but it is certainly clear that a great portion of the world's art has had political implications. The queen or pope or president who commissions an artist to make a particular work may have a true love of art, but that patron surely knows that a great masterpiece will enhance the patron's prestige and therefore increase his or her power.

Political art, and those who make it, can be divided between the "ins" and the "outs." The "ins" want to be even more in—to consolidate their power and enhance their prestige. The "outs," by and large, are unhappy with the existing political situation (whatever it may be) and hope to dislodge the "ins" and replace them. Art has traditionally served both ends, and we will look at a bit of each.

The structures that many consider to be the ultimate in kingly pride, the height of political power, were built four and a half millennia ago and have never been surpassed. At Giza in Egypt rise the three great pyramids, tombs of the Pharaohs Mycerinus, Chefren, and Cheops (**70**). Only an immensely

**70.** The Great Pyramids: Pyramid of Mycerinus (c. 2500 B.C.); Pyramid of Chefren (c. 2530 B.C.); Pyramid of Cheops (c. 2570 B.C.). Giza, Egypt.

prideful king would divert thousands of workers to the massive chore of erecting a burial mound on this scale. Cheops' pyramid, the largest of the three, is about 450 feet tall (roughly the height of a fifty-story building), covers more than 13 acres, and consists of some 2.3 million blocks of stone. Each of these blocks had to be quarried with hand tools, dragged to the site, and assembled without benefit of mortar.

Perhaps even more interesting than the difficulty of the task is the grandiosity of the kings who willed it. The pharaohs had a lofty purpose: they meant these pyramids to stand for all eternity, to strike a mark upon the landscape that could never be wiped away. The farthest extent of pride is to say, in effect, "*My* name will never be forgotten, *my* monument will endure through all the generations to come." And so far, despite the wars and political upheavals and natural disasters that the earth has witnessed, they were right.

Given what we know about the spread of the mighty Roman Empire in the few centuries surrounding the birth of Christ, it is not surprising that some of the most prideful and political art was created at that time. The Roman emperors, who eventually conquered most of the civilized world they knew of, understood the political value of celebrating themselves and their achievements. An example is the statue of Augustus, which is known as the *Augustus of Prima Porta* (**71**).

Augustus came to power in Rome in 31 B.C. by virtue of his military successes, and he reigned unchallenged for forty-five years—the first of the great Roman emperors. Under Augustus the Empire enjoyed peace, prosperity, administrative order, and a flowering of the arts. In those times the line separating admiration for the ruler and worship of a deity was a fine one;

**71.** *Augustus of Prima Porta.* c. 20 B.C.
Marble, height 6′8″.
Vatican Museums, Rome.

**72.** *Emperor Justinian and Courtiers.* c. 547. Mosaic. San Vitale, Ravenna.

emperors and heroes took on the attributes of gods. That Augustus deliberately sought to enhance this godlike image is clear, and recent scholarship provides fascinating clues about how this statue and others played a role in his "public relations" campaign.

Considerable evidence supports the theory that Augustus was in fact much less attractive than he appears here. In life he had unruly hair, a small chin, small eyes, big ears, a bony face, and thin lips. Scholars now believe that in about 27 B.C.—seven years before the presumed date of the Prima Porta figure—the emperor commissioned an idealized portrait head, which was to be used as a model for all later sculptures, regardless of the emperor's advancing age. The Prima Porta head was based on this model; it is not only beautiful and godlike but also resembles the idealized Greek style. What were Augustus' motives for promoting this idealized self-portrait? According to those who have studied the question, "the portrait was supposed to show that he had ideal human qualities and, at the same time, that he stood for a culture that combined the best traditions." Also, the Prima Porta style head "was part of a representational program which gave Romans hope for the future under Augustus, as a divinely inspired leader. He claimed to be acting as the agent of the gods on earth."[3] In other words, the emperor's purpose in commissioning this art was a political one—an attempt to consolidate his power and ensure its continuity.

Five centuries later Augustus' successor in the Eastern Empire, the Byzantine Emperor Justinian, was no less inclined to glorify himself by means of art. Justinian was a Christian emperor, and so he has made the subtle transition from identification with the old Greek and Roman gods to kinship with Christ. The illustration here (**72**) is a *mosaic*—a wall decoration (in this case) assembled from tiny pieces of colored glazed tile—in the Church of San Vitale, in Ravenna. Justinian stands at center in the composition, surrounded by twelve companions (symbolic of Christ's twelve Apostles). He alone has a halo of light around his head, suggesting that he is divine, not human. The arrangement of figures is meant to suggest a procession, yet there is little sense of movement as Justinian poses formally, accepting with solemn dignity the homage of his subjects.

For the ultimate in a political portrait, however, we must look several hundred years later, to a king who so wholeheartedly embraced his role as divine ruler that he dared to say "L'Etat, c'est moi" ("I am the state")—Louis XIV of France. Hyacinthe Rigaud's portrait (**73**) captures all the pageantry of a reign that was built on drama as carefully as any full-scale operatic performance might be.

Louis himself commented on the value of visible symbols: "Those who imagine that these are merely matters of ceremony are gravely mistaken. . . . The peoples over whom we reign, being unable to apprehend the basic reality of things, usually derive their opinions from what they can see with their eyes."[4] Louis ruled as the "Sun King" for an amazing seventy-two years, and during that time France experienced a period of political, social, and artistic achievement without parallel. At his death the nation was only seventy-five years away from revolution—a revolution that would bring down the monarchy—but while Louis sat on the throne he kept all eyes focused on himself as the personification of France in her glory.

To the modern viewer Louis' costume seems absurd, his pose more than a little affected, but his subjects must have found the picture inspiring. No detail that might have contributed to the king's grandeur has been spared, from the lavish ermine-lined robes, to the lush scarlet canopy of the backdrop, to the classical Greek column at left. Louis obviously realized that political power rests on an illusion. Art that fostered it could help to maintain the power.

So far in this section we have focused on the person who was the *subject* of political art, rather than the artist who made it—that is, the patron who was in control of whatever purpose was to be achieved, not the artist. Let us turn our attention now to the artist who chooses a specific political ideal and uses his or her talent to realize it. There can be no more interesting example than Jacques Louis David.

**73.** Hyacinthe Rigaud.
*Louis XIV.* 1701.
Oil on canvas, 9′1½″ × 6′2⅝″.
Louvre, Paris.

**74.** Jacques Louis David.
*The Death of Marat.* 1793.
Oil on canvas, 5′5″ × 4′2½″.
Musées Royaux des Beaux-Arts
de Belgique, Brussels.

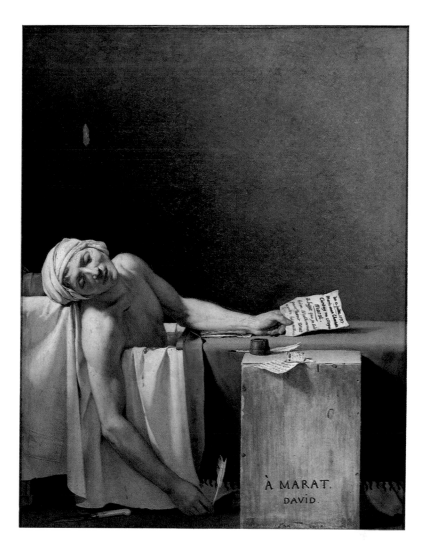

David was a painter of enormous skill who worked at a time of intense political turmoil. He epitomizes for the history of art the phrase "survival of the fittest." David's career began under the patronage of Louis XVI, descendant of the Sun King and last of the Bourbon monarchs before the revolution. When revolution came to France in 1789 the artist slipped, with apparent ease, into the revolutionary mode and became one of its leading propagandists. Then again, when the revolution faltered and Napoleon came to power as Emperor of France, there at the forefront of artistic service to the Empire was Jacques Louis David.

What many consider to be David's finest picture was made during the revolutionary period. Its subject is Jean-Paul Marat, one of the leaders of the Reign of Terror, who was responsible for the death-by-guillotine of hundreds of people. Because of a painful skin ailment Marat spent his days in the bathtub, which was fitted out with a writing desk so he could work, and there he received callers. A woman named Charlotte Corday, incensed by Marat's excesses with the guillotine, gained entry to his apartments and stabbed him to death. As a memorial to his friend, David painted *The Death of Marat* (**74**).

In lesser hands Marat's demise could have been laughable—a naked man murdered in his tub by an overexcited woman in visiting dress. But David has invested the scene with all the pathos and dignity of Christ being lowered into his tomb; Marat is shown, in effect, as a kind of secular Christ martyred for the revolution. All the forms are concentrated in the lower half of the composition, and light bathes the fallen leader in an unearthly glow, both of these

**75.** Pablo Picasso. *Guernica.* 1937.
Oil on canvas, $11'5\frac{1}{2}'' \times 25'5\frac{3}{4}''$. Prado, Madrid.

devices contributing to the sense of tragedy. It is probably safe to conclude that David's purpose in this work was to transform a man whom many considered Satan himself into a sainted hero.

David was demonstrably (though flexibly) on the side of the "ins." His artistic goals were compatible with the goals of those holding political power. Our next example, however, was created by an artist whose sympathies lay with those not in power, an artist who took up his brush with a sense of fury at the "ins" who caused devastation. From his fury came one of the great masterpieces of 20th-century art. The artist was Pablo Picasso, and the painting is called *Guernica* (**75**).

It is necessary to know the story behind *Guernica* to understand its power. In 1937 Europe was moving toward war, and a trial run, so to speak, occurred in Spain, where the forces of General Francisco Franco waged civil war against the established Republican government. Franco willingly accepted aid from Hitler, which allowed the Nazis to test their developing air power. On April 28, 1937, the Germans bombed the town of Guernica, the old Basque capital in northern Spain. There was no real military reason for the raid; simply, it was an experiment to see whether aerial bombing could wipe out a whole city. Being totally defenseless, Guernica was devastated and its civilian population massacred.

At the time Picasso, himself a Spaniard, was working in Paris and had been commissioned by the Republican government to paint a mural for the Spanish Pavilion of the World's Fair. For some time he had procrastinated about fulfilling the commission; then, within days after news of the bombing reached Paris, he started *Guernica* and completed it in little over a month. Despite the speedy execution, however, this was no unreasoning outburst of anger. Picasso controlled his rage, perhaps knowing that it could have better effect in a carefully planned canvas, and he made many preliminary drawings and sketches. The finished mural had a shocking effect on those who saw it; it remains today a chillingly dramatic protest against the brutality of war.

At first encounter with *Guernica* the viewer is overwhelmed by its size; it is more than 25 feet long and nearly 12 feet high. It dominates any space in which it is hung and seems to reach out and engulf the observer. Picasso used no colors; the whole painting is done in white and black and shades of gray, possibly to create a "newsprint" quality in reporting the event. Although the artist's symbolism is very personal (and he declined to explain it in detail), we cannot misunderstand the images of extreme pain and anguish throughout the canvas. At far left a shrieking mother holds her dead child and at far right another woman, in a burning house, screams in agony. The gaping mouths and clenched hands all speak of disbelief at such mindless cruelty.

Another victim is the dying horse to left of center, speared from above and just as stunned by the carnage as any of the human sufferers. Various writers have interpreted the bull at upper left in different ways. Picasso drew much of his imagery from the bullfight, an ingrained part of his Spanish heritage. Perhaps the bull symbolizes the brutal victory of the Nazis; perhaps it, like the horse, is also a victim of carnage. There is even more confusion about the symbols of the lamp and the light bulb at top center. These may be indications that light is being cast on the horrors of war, or they may be signals of hope. Picasso did not tell us, so we are free to make our own associations.

With *Guernica* Picasso functioned as an artist of the "outs"—a voice crying against those who had power to do something of which he disapproved vehemently. Much political art of the 20th century has this purpose. Perhaps art throughout history has spoken against injustice, but until our era (and in our relatively free society) the "ins" were able to suppress their critics. In the United States one group, black Americans, has a long history of being "out"— out of power, out of work, out of schools, out of the material pleasures of society. No wonder, then, that oppression of blacks should have found a political expression in art.

Jacob Lawrence, who is himself black, took up this theme in the early 1940s with an ambitious sixty-panel series called *The Migration of the Negro*. We illustrate here the best-known panel from that series, *One of the Largest Race Riots Occurred in East St. Louis* (**76**). As a work of social protest, Lawrence's painting can be compared, in concept if not in style, to Picasso's *Guernica*. Rather than depicting realistically the bloody violence of a race riot, Lawrence has transformed the action into a stylized ballet of flat, abstract shapes. Interpreted this way, the conflict takes on universal implications, revealing not just a vicious clash of individuals, but the underlying hatreds of "us" against "them" that mark a pattern throughout human history. Lawrence's composition is a masterful geometric arrangement, all forms leading to the clenched fist holding a knife—the one form silhouetted above the horizon line.

**76.** Jacob Lawrence. *One of the Largest Race Riots Occurred in East St. Louis,* Panel 52 from *The Migration of the Negro*. 1940–41. Tempera on composition board, 12 × 18″. Museum of Modern Art, New York (gift of Mrs. David M. Levy).

right: **77.** Robert Rauschenberg. *Retroactive I.*
1964. Silkscreen,
Wadsworth Atheneum, Hartford, Conn.
(gift of Susan Morse Hilles
by Deed of Gift, 1964).

**above: 78.** Limbourg Brothers.
*February* page, from *Les Très Riches Heures
du Duc de Berry*.
1416. Illumination, $8\frac{7}{8} \times 5\frac{3}{8}''$.
Musée Condé, Chantilly.

**right: 79.** Jan van Eyck.
*Giovanni Arnolfini and His Wife*.
1434. Oil on wood, $33 \times 22\frac{1}{2}''$.
National Gallery, London
(reproduced by courtesy of the Trustees).

Our final example in this brief survey of political art does not really fit either of the two categories—the "ins" or the "outs." Robert Rauschenberg's *Retroactive I* (**77**) does contain political images, notably a silkscreened version of a photograph of President John F. Kennedy, but the purpose is neither to damn nor to praise Kennedy. Rauschenberg as an artist stands outside politics, viewing it objectively as one of the phenomena that touch his life, assembling images that are meaningful to him, and presenting them without comment.

In *Retroactive I* Rauschenberg concentrates on the media—many of them, including painting—as a potent visual and symbolic force upon our lives. John Kennedy's picture (probably the best-known photo of him) is the focus of the composition, and the gesturing right hand is repeated at left. Also included is an image closely associated with the Kennedy years and the sixties in general—an astronaut in space. The patch at lower right is part of a photograph Rauschenberg found in *Life* magazine. *Collage*—assemblage of fragments or separate works into a single composition—suits Rauschenberg's style. By these means he can select from among the millions of images that bombard us daily and make connections that express his personal view of the world.

We might say that Rauschenberg's art is political in theme but *not* political in purpose. The artist's aim is not to achieve any political goal. Rather, he selects from the phenomena of everyday life—some of which are political—and shows them to us in new ways. In a sense, this is just a more complicated version of what artists have done for centuries.

## Art as the Mirror of Everyday Life

When children start to draw and paint, they deal in the images they know best: mother and father, sisters and brothers, the teacher, the house, the dog. Many artists never lose this preoccupation with everyday things, and so we have a rich heritage of art depicting those concerns that are closest to the artist's personal world.

Art that depicts the little moments of everyday life and its surroundings is known as *genre*. Often, its purpose is a simple one—to record, to please the eye, to make us smile. A series of charming genre paintings occurs in an early French manuscript, one page of which is reproduced here (**78**). During the Middle Ages wealthy patrons customarily would commission artists to *illuminate,* or hand-illustrate, books, particularly prayer books. In the early 15th century a close relationship existed between the Duc de Berry, brother of the French king, and three artist brothers, the Limbourgs. The Limbourgs painted for the duke what has become one of the most famous illuminated books in the history of art, *Les Tres Riches Heures* ("the very rich book of hours"). It contains a calendar, with each month's painting showing a typical seasonal activity of either the peasantry or the aristocracy.

The *February* page, shown here, focuses on a small peasant hut with its occupants clustered around the fire, their garments pulled back to get maximum benefit from the warmth. (Underwear as we know it had not yet been invented, and so this forthright image has occasionally been censored.) With a touch of poetic license, the artists have removed the front of the hut so that we may look inside. Outside the hut we see what may be the earliest snow-covered landscape ever painted. Sheep cluster in their enclosure, a peasant comes rushing across the barnyard pulling his cloak about his face to keep in the warm breath. From there the movement progresses diagonally up the slope to a man chopping firewood, another urging a donkey uphill, and finally the church at the top. Such was the everyday life of the lower classes in medieval France, and the Limbourgs have left us a capsule picture of it.

Some twenty years later another northern European artist, Jan van Eyck, painted a picture that is quite literally the "mirror" of life, this time of bourgeois life. *Giovanni Arnolfini and His Wife* (**79**) is believed by many experts to have a specific purpose; it apparently served as a marriage document, made to

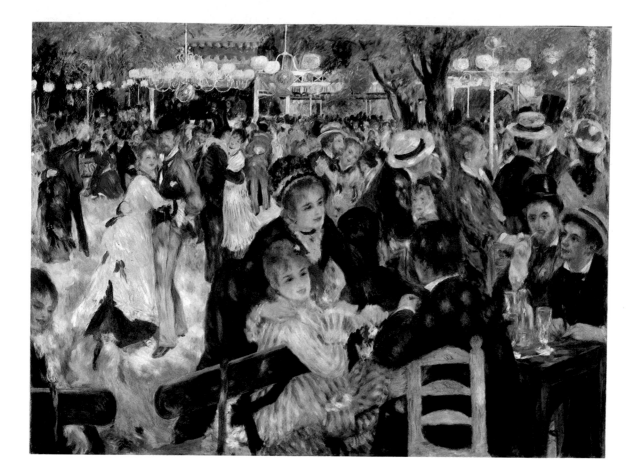

above: 80: Pierre-Auguste Renoir.
*Le Moulin de la Galette.* 1876.
Oil on canvas, 4′3½″ × 5′9″.
Louvre, Paris.

below: 81. Paula Modersohn-Becker.
*Mother and Child.* 1906.
Oil on canvas, 2′10½″ × 4′1″.
Ludwig-Roselius Collection, Bremen.

record and legitimize the nuptials between the merchant Arnolfini and his bride Giovanna Cenami. At center in the painting is a mirror reflecting the artist, who has come to bear witness to the ceremony, adding his signature "Jan van Eyck was here, 1434." To reinforce the solemn nature of the occasion, the artist has included many symbols, such as the little dog at the couple's feet—an emblem of fidelity. Arnolfini has removed his shoes to indicate that he is standing on sacred ground—the ground on which are pledged the holy vows of matrimony. Many symbols relate to the potential fruitfulness of marriage, from the actual fruits on the windowsill to the marriage bed in the

**82.** George Segal.
*Next Departure*. 1979.
Bronze, metal, plaster, wood,
paper, and vinyl; 7 × 6 × 8'.
Installation 1982
at Port Authority of N.Y. and N.J.
Bus Terminal, New York.
Courtesy Sidney Janis Gallery,
New York.

background. In fact, some observers have concluded that the new wife is already pregnant, but her gesture and rounded form are probably due more to the fashions of the day than to anticipating the wedding ceremony.

As the mirror of everyday life has recorded important occasions, so it has been used to capture life's little moments, the fleeting experiences that last for an instant and then are gone. This type of subject was a particular favorite with the Impressionist painters of the late 19th century, whose goal was to record that which is transitory—an impression. In Pierre-Auguste Renoir's *Le Moulin de la Galette* (**80**) young couples meet at the outdoor café, they dance, they fall in love. The viewer has a quick impression of the most delightful of all ways to spend a summer day. As observers, we seem to have glanced briefly at the scene and absorbed its essence, rather than its details. We can almost hear the bright music (a waltz tune unquestionably), feel the warm breezes, sense the atmosphere of innocent flirtation and fun.

Another of life's little moments, this time a very private one, is recorded by Paula Modersohn-Becker in her *Mother and Child* (**81**). What might have been simply a woman nursing her baby has been given a universal quality by Modersohn-Becker, so that the image seems to be *all* mothers nursing all babies since time began. The mother's body, heavy and solid as the earth itself, curves protectively around the child, who in turn curves into the mother's belly. Both figures are anonymous; the baby's face is obscured, and the woman's barely articulated. This, however, is a far cry from the faceless fertility of the *Venus of Willendorf* (**61**). Modersohn-Becker's image speaks not of mindless childbearing but of the unbreakable attachment, the love, between mother and child—the most basic aspect of everyday life that allows it to continue.

Everyday life in the late 20th century may take on a different kind of timeless quality, as evidenced by the sculptures of George Segal (**82**). In 1982 Segal set up three of his life-size figures in New York City's Port Authority bus terminal, ostensibly waiting in line to buy a ticket. The figures are naturalistic, having been cast from living models (Chapter 11 and **361**), but they are made of unpainted white plaster. And they wait. Patiently, eternally, they wait in line, much as the modern-day individual has to wait for the bureaucratic realities of life to sort themselves out. Commuters moving through the bus terminal were much taken by Segal's waiting people. Some good-humored passersby fell casually in line behind them, prepared to stand immobile as long as they did, entranced by this image of themselves. Segal, himself a commuter, managed to capture what is for the urban person, unfortunately, a faithful mirror of everyday life.

## Art and Nature

If art is the mirror of everyday life, it is also the mirror of everyday surroundings. Drive out into the country on a splendid autumn day, and along the road you are likely to see cars parked, easels set up, amateur painters trying to distill, on canvas or watercolor paper, the glories of the natural landscape. Throughout history professional artists, too, have responded to this impulse and have turned their eyes to nature as an engrossing subject for art. What they have seen depends on many things, including the cultures in which they worked and their own artistic visions.

A hanging scroll attributed to Li Cheng shows how a Chinese painter of the 10th century might interpret nature according to the magnificent landscape style that flourished in that period (**83**). Li Cheng's painting, characteris-

**83.** Li Cheng (?).
*A Solitary Temple
amid Clearing Peaks.* 919–967.
Hanging scroll,
ink and slight color on silk;
3'8" × 1'10".
Nelson–Atkins Museum of Art,
Kansas City (Nelson Fund).

tic of the Northern Song dynasty "monumental" style, emphasizes naturalism in details of the landscape. It was considered important for the viewer to be able to "walk through" the painting visually and to imagine him- or herself actually walking through the terrain. One is led into the landscape at the bottom, then the eye moves upward gradually, much as the traveler would cross the bridge, walk up from the buildings at the base of the hill, climb to the temple, and then progress farther to the towering peak in the background. Especially typical of Li Cheng's style is the gnarled quality of the trees, each of which is seen as an individual entity. As viewers we stand apart from the landscape and see it in the distance, yet it is accessible if we choose to enter.

How different is our experience of John Constable's landscapes, such as *The White Horse* (84). Constable was perhaps the greatest of the English 19th-century landscape artists, and, like Li Cheng, he was concerned with absolute naturalism, a sense of what—for that artist—the landscape *really* looked like. In Constable's paintings, however, the viewer does not stand outside but seems almost to be surrounded by the natural scene, inside it without taking a step. To stand before one of these huge canvases is to be transported to another world, a peaceful corner of the rural English countryside. Constable was meticulous about recording details of foliage and other features, but his main fascination lay in transitory effects of light and changing patterns in the sky. The sunlight dapples through the leaves, reflects off the water, and picks out the white horse that gives the painting its name. Clouds scuttling across the sky seem actually to be in motion; we know that a second earlier or later the effect would be different. Whereas a Chinese landscape seems frozen in peace for eternity, Constable's visions capture a moment that will never come again.

**84.** John Constable. *The White Horse.* 1819.
Oil on canvas, 4′3⅝″ × 6′2⅛″.
Frick Collection, New York (copyright).

# Paul Cézanne
## 1839–1906

Paul Cézanne remains one of the most enigmatic figures in modern art history, even though the details of his life are well known. A word often used to describe his personality is "difficult." Clearly, he was a man of intelligence and great sensitivity, yet he could be rude to strangers and boorish with his friends. Although he was acquainted with most of the leading artists then working in Paris, he spent the greater part of his life in isolation in the southern French town of Aix-en-Provence, where he was born.

Cézanne's banker father tried to steer his son into his own profession or the law, but the young man showed so little talent and inclination for either that eventually the father gave up and permitted him to undertake art studies. Cézanne's first attempts at exhibiting his work met with disastrous results; the critics' reactions ranged from ridicule to outrage. Nevertheless, he persevered, struggling on alone to achieve the form in art that was his vision. Cézanne's paintings are difficult to date, because he worked on many canvases at once and often labored over the same painting for several years. So demanding was he with live models that few sitters were willing to pose for him. One who did pose, the art dealer Ambroise Vollard, reported that he was forced to endure 115 sittings, some lasting three hours or more.

In 1869, while visiting Paris, Cézanne met a young woman, Marie-Hortense Fiquet, and she became his mistress. Some three years later their son Paul was born. Cézanne went to extraordinary lengths to conceal this liaison from his domineering father, for fear his allowance would be cut.

For most of Cézanne's life only the very discerning—and they were few—recognized the genius of his art. After his initial disappointments, the artist stopped exhibiting in Paris for twenty years. Then in 1895 Ambroise Vollard decided to mount a show—Cézanne's first one-man exhibition—and asked the artist to send all available work. Cézanne bundled up 150 canvases (not on stretchers) and shipped them off to Paris from Aix. The show took Paris completely by surprise and was an immediate sensation. From that time until his death the artist gradually acquired the recognition he deserved; ironically again, his personality had so deteriorated that the acclaim seems to have given him little pleasure.

While alternately mocked and ignored by critics and the general public, Cézanne never lost faith in himself and his art. In 1874 he wrote this to his mother: "I am beginning to find myself stronger than any of those around me. . . . I must go on working, but not in order to attain a finished perfection, which is so much sought after by imbeciles. And this quality which is commonly so much admired is nothing but the accomplishment of a craftsman, and makes any work produced in that way inartistic and vulgar. I must not try to finish anything except for the pleasure of making it truer and wiser. And you may be sure that there will come a time when I shall come into my own, and that I have admirers who are much more fervent, more steadfast than those who are attracted only by an empty outward appearance."[5]

Paul Cézanne. *Self-Portrait with a Beret.* c. 1906. Oil on canvas, 25¼ × 21″. Museum of Fine Arts, Boston (Charles H. Bayley Picture and Painting Fund and partial gift of Elizabeth Paine Metcalf).

Yet another approach to the theme of nature can be found in Paul Cézanne's many versions of Mont Sainte-Victoire (**85**), a mountain near his home in Provence. We may be amazed to see that less than a hundred years and only the breadth of the English Channel separate Cézanne's landscape from Constable's. During this time the Impressionist painters—who sought to interpret nature in visual effects of light and color (Chapter 17)—had come and gone. Cézanne often is referred to as a *Post-Impressionist*, meaning that he adapted and built upon the theories of the Impressionists. Through the later years of his life Mont Sainte-Victoire obsessed him, but his interest was less in recording nature than in searching for a solidity and unity of form. To Cézanne, geometry served as the basis for all forms, including those in the landscape. He sought to discover the forms of geometric solids—the cone, the sphere, the cylinder—in nature and record them in his paintings.

Naturalism is not important to this expression. Cézanne's purpose was to explore the landscape as a vehicle for the study of forms in space, much as a grouping of objects would in a still life study. He has reduced this vista of Mont Sainte-Victoire to a pattern of color patches, with individual brush strokes defining planes and surfaces. Details generally are obscured, because this is not a landscape inhabited by people. One does not walk through it or repose within it; one stands back and considers it objectively as a perfect realization of form.

**85.** Paul Cézanne.
*Mont Sainte-Victoire.* 1902–04.
Oil on canvas, $27\frac{1}{2} \times 35\frac{1}{4}''$.
Philadelphia Museum of Art
(George W. Elkins Collection).

Finally, we turn to an artist who, rather than viewing nature from a distance, zooms in on it as tightly as possible. The paintings of Georgia O'Keeffe, such as *The White Calico Flower* (**86**), are extreme close-ups, almost to the point of abstraction. O'Keeffe examines every nuance of the form minutely, as though a whole universe were unfolding within the flower. Much has been made of the apparent sexual symbolism in these paintings, and, although the artist denies it, there is an elemental quality in the flower's lush opening.

So far we have considered artists who look primarily to the outside for their inspiration. Our final thematic category focuses on artists who turn inward, to their own brains and psyches, for the genesis of their art.

## Imagination and Fantasy

The purposes of imaginative art are as complex and as individual as imagination itself. An artist may look inward and paint what he or she sees in an attempt to understand this inner life, to purge it of its terrors, or simply because the products of the imagination seem more interesting than the realities of every day. We may be tempted to think of imaginative art as a purely 20th-century phenomenon, a product of the Freudian era or even of the "me generation." Looking closely at one's dreams and fantasies—and then recording them as art—does indeed seem to be a peculiarly modern preoccupation. Nevertheless, we can trace imaginative art back at least to the 16th century, where it flourished in the hands of the extraordinary Netherlandish artist Hieronymus Bosch.

When we first encounter *The Garden of Earthly Delights* (**87**), we might think we have wandered into a fun house of a particularly macabre kind. Bosch's large *triptych* (a three-section panel, of which we show only the middle portion) is like a peep into Hell—but this is an X-rated earthly Hell. Hundreds of nude human figures cavort in a fantasy landscape peopled also by giant plants, animals no biologist ever classified, and strange creatures that are part human, part vegetation. Humans ride upon, emerge from, are devoured by,

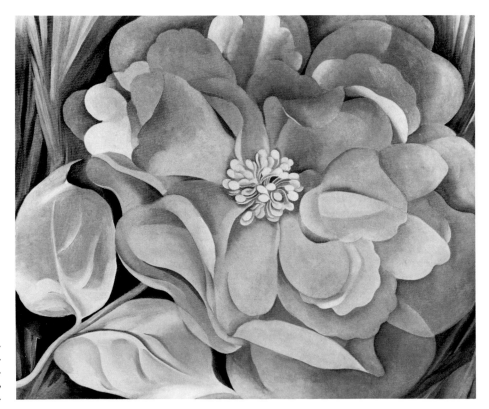

**86.** Georgia O'Keeffe. *The White Calico Flower*. 1931. Oil on canvas, 30 × 36″. Whitney Museum of American Art, New York (purchase).

**87.** Hieronymus Bosch. *The Garden of Earthly Delights,* center section. c. 1505–10. Panel, 7'2⅝" × 6'4¾". Prado, Madrid.

or become part of the plant and animal forms. It is as though Bosch has let his imagination and perhaps his dream imagery go wherever it might. Bosch drew upon many sources for his creations, including folklore, literature, astrology, and religious writings, but only his own inventiveness could have constructed a fantasyland like this one.

Artists who deal in the realm of the imagination are often quite interesting as personalities. This was true of Bosch, and it was true also of an English artist/poet who worked during the late 18th and early 19th centuries. William Blake was, by the standards of his time and most others, a thoroughgoing eccentric. He was foremost a poet and will be remembered by generations of college literature students for the lines "Tyger, tyger, burning bright/In the forests of the night." Much of Blake's production as an artist involved the illustration of books, not only of his own volumes of poetry but also of the Bible, Shakespeare, and Dante. In these he expressed a kind of personal theology, which he claimed had been revealed to him in visions of God, Christ, various angels, and certain notable personages from history.

Typical is his *Satan Watching the Caresses of Adam and Eve* (**88**), an illustration for John Milton's epic poem, *Paradise Lost*. The scene depicted does not appear in the Scripture, nor in Milton's poetic version of the fall from grace of Adam and Eve. According to standard Christian doctrine, Adam and Eve were innocent and free of carnal desire before eating the forbidden fruit. William Blake, however, had other ideas, and he followed his own theological and sexual interpretation in this work. Years later, in discussing the illustration, he insisted: "I saw Milton in imagination, and he told me to beware of being misled by his *Paradise Lost*. In particular he wished me to shew the falsehood of his doctrine that the pleasure of sex arose from the Fall. The Fall could not produce any pleasure."[6]

**above: 88.** William Blake.
*Satan Watching the Caresses of Adam and Eve*,
illustration for *Paradise Lost*. 1808.
Pen and watercolor on paper, $19\frac{7}{8} \times 15''$.
Museum of Fine Arts, Boston
(gift by Subscription, 1890).

**left: 89.** Salvador Dali.
*The Temptation of St. Anthony*.
1947. Oil on canvas, $35\frac{1}{4} \times 47''$.
Musées Royaux des Beaux-Arts
de Belgique, Brussels.

Blake's picture, therefore, shows the first couple, still not having touched the apple, still in the Garden of Eden, engaged in a decidedly erotic pursuit. They are enveloped in a lush circle of fantasy foliage, and their bodies are muscular and full-fleshed in the manner of Dürer or Michelangelo, both of whose works were known to the artist. Floating above the pair is the figure of Satan—part angel (it must be remembered that Satan was the fallen angel Lucifer) and part serpent. Soon afterward, Satan, in the guise of a serpent, will tempt Eve to eat the apple, resulting in banishment from the Garden of Eden. Blake's Satan looks down upon the lovers with something rather like jealousy, which gives new meaning to the story of the temptation. The artist's imagery comes not from the Bible, not from Milton, but from his own imagination.

Imaginative treatment of a religious subject also appears in the work of the 20th-century Spanish artist Salvador Dali. In *The Temptation of St. Anthony* (**89**) Dali addresses a subject that had been popular throughout the Middle Ages and early Renaissance. The story concerns efforts by the holy man, St. Anthony, to fend off temptations of the flesh that tormented him in his thoughts and dreams. Earlier representations showed the saint being assailed by all manner of hellish demons and often being lured by a lustful woman or women. Dali has perhaps come closer to the truth by reinterpreting the temptation as a dream/nightmare landscape.

Dali's art, often identified as *Surrealism* (Chapter 17), is predominantly an art of the unconscious. The artist explored his own dreams, studied case histories of psychotic individuals, and even toyed with waking hallucinations, which he claimed he could summon on command. In *The Temptation* St. Anthony appears as a gaunt figure, besieged yet strong, holding off a nightmare parade of fantastic creatures stalking across an endless plain on giant insect-legs. Dali's demons are not actual monsters from Hell, but the demons of the mind.

Another 20th-century artist who explored the mysteries of the mind was the Russian-born painter Marc Chagall. In his most famous work, *I and the Village* (**90**), Chagall interweaves many diverse memory images from his childhood to evoke a warm and happy picture of village life. At right we see a green-faced young man, at left a transparent cow through which is visible a milkmaid tending another cow. A farmer carrying a scythe strides toward an

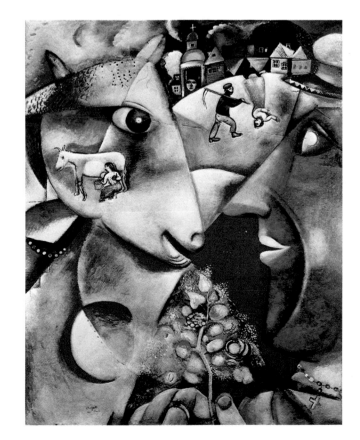

**90.** Marc Chagall.
*I and the Village.* 1911.
Oil on canvas, 6'3½" × 4'11½".
Museum of Modern Art, New York
(Mrs. Simon Guggenheim Fund).

**91.** Joan Curtis. *Border Crossing (Lament).* 1982. Acrylic and mixed media relief with colored pencil drawing, $17\frac{1}{2} \times 19\frac{1}{2}''$. Courtesy the artist.

upside-down peasant woman against a background of colorful Russian provincial architecture. All conventions of realistic color, size, and placement have been abandoned in favor of an inner reality—the reality of the mind. Chagall chooses and arranges his elements according to their importance for him, his private associations, and the structural needs of the painting as he conceives it.

The work of contemporary artist Joan Curtis represents not a deliberate dip into the unconscious, but instead a willing surrender to its magic. *Border Crossing (Lament)* (**91**) combines a delicate colored-pencil drawing in the center with a rough outer "frame" modeled into sculptural thickness. The focus is a wolflike animal figure standing on a similar horizontal figure and reaching out to emblematic objects—a comb, a spoon and bowl, a key, and others—floating in a mysterious space. Animal imagery has been an important theme in Curtis' art for some twenty years; it is an obsession that seems to have chosen her rather than the other way around. The artist, who sketches constantly, has found "certain images cropping up again and again" in her sketchbook, and she has made the conscious decision to let these unconscious forces enter her art. The symbolism in *Border Crossing (Lament)* is not something about which one can intellectualize and make neat lists of "what this means," as one can about a painting by Van Eyck (**79**). This symbolism is far more personal, more *felt* than understood, perhaps not entirely clear to the artist herself. Fantasy art comes from the subconscious; the viewer to whom it speaks most eloquently will experience it through the subconscious, not through the methodical left side of the brain.

These, then, are some of the recurring themes in art and a few of the purposes various types of art have served. In the chapters that follow we shall consider works of art from other points of view; but it will be useful to keep in mind that each of them, while it is analyzed for its medium or its place in history, also is part of a basic theme—one of those discussed here or possibly another that you can identify.

*part two*

# THE VOCABULARY OF ART

# 4
# The Visual Elements

If somebody asked you what you see in our first illustration (**92**), you probably would say something like "a picture of a little boy on a donkey." You know it isn't a real little boy or a real donkey, but a representation in paint on canvas. This is a painting by Pablo Picasso of his own small son Paulo.

Now look closer and observe how the painting is constructed. You will see that Picasso has used *lines* to draw around the boy's head and figure, to show the hairs on the donkey's body, to suggest blades of grass in the background. He has created the *shapes* of a boy and a donkey and differentiated them from the open *space* of the sky and earth. The animal's body has a rough *texture*, similar to the texture of the grass but contrasted with the smoother texture of the boy's outfit. The painting is full of *light*, which illuminates this daytime scene. Picasso has used a range of *colors*—white for the boy's costume, gray-black for the donkey, rust for the donkey's blanket, blue for the sky, and so on.

These six things that Picasso used to construct his picture—line, shape, texture, light, color, and space—are the ingredients an artist has available in making any work of art. They are called the *visual elements*. (As we shall see, some works of art also depend on time and motion, so these two are sometimes added to the list.) No matter what kind of art, no matter where or when it was made, the character of these elements, and how they are organized, determine what the work of art will be like.

In this chapter we shall look closely at the visual elements—what they are, how they are used, and how they affect a work of art. Chapter 5 deals with organization of these elements according to the principles of design.

## Line

By conventional definition, a line is the path left by a moving point. You put down your pencil on a sheet of paper and *move* its point across the paper to make a line. We can also think of line as an extended mark. Line is so basic to art that it is difficult to conceive of any work of art *not* having lines.

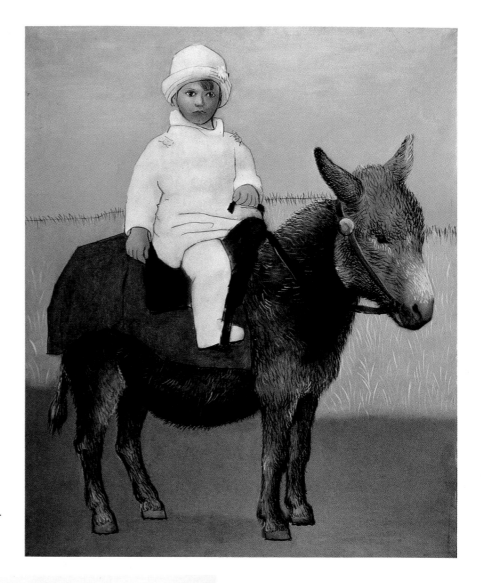

right: **92.** Pablo Picasso.
*Paulo on a Donkey.* 1923.
Oil on canvas, 39¾ × 31⅞".
Collection Bernard Picasso, Paris.

below: **93.** Ellsworth Kelly. *Apples.* 1949.
Pencil, 17⅛ × 22⅛".
Museum of Modern Art, New York
(gift of John S. Newberry).

When you sit down to write a letter or an examination paper or a note to yourself, you are making lines, whether you think of it that way or not. The letters of the alphabet are lines, and they are also symbols of sounds. Artists, too, use lines as symbols. In Picasso's painting of Paulo, the oval line around Paulo's face is a symbol. People don't actually have lines around their faces; people's faces are composed of flesh and bone. At the point where flesh meets space, our eyes see an imaginary line, so Picasso has drawn that line in his painting to symbolize "face." This task of symbolically outlining form is only one of the many functions line performs in a work of art.

## Functions of Line

**Outline and Form**    In Ellsworth Kelly's drawing *Apples* (**93**) a thin, elegant line describes the shape of the fruit. This is called an *outline drawing*. There is no shading, no interior detail, and no background. By this amazingly economical line Kelly convinces us that we see a group of rounded apples resting on an invisible surface. As in Picasso's painting, the line creates a boundary. It marks the point where the apples stop and the surrounding area begins. This function of line as outline is extremely important to art.

Whereas Kelly uses line to create the illusion of three-dimensional form, Alexander Calder, in *The Hostess* (**94**), uses line to create a form that is actually three-dimensional. This witty little sculpture consists of a few pieces of wire welded and twisted together—the wire drawing lines in space. Somehow, Calder makes these few thin lines suggest a very proper society matron ready to entertain guests. Details drawn in line are the key to this sculpture—the curls of the hair, the long nose, the lorgnette poised in one hand, the high heels. We imagine this figure walking along in jerky little steps. Line alone, when used by a master like Calder, has the power to convey a whole character.

**Movement and Emphasis**    Line often implies movement, and this is another of its functions. Every line goes somewhere, and the viewer's eye naturally follows it. Frank Stella's *Itata* (**95**) uses lines to reinforce the unusual shape of the canvas and to enhance the sense of movement. The lines draw our eyes across, down, and across; and because we expect lines to be continuous, we tend to follow the lines even beyond the composition to an imaginary space outside.

**right: 94.** Alexander Calder. *The Hostess.* 1928.
Wire, height 11½″.
Museum of Modern Art, New York
(gift of Edward M. M. Warburg).

**below: 95.** Frank Stella. *Itata.* 1964.
Metallic powder and polymer emulsion
on canvas, 6′5″ × 10′2″.
Courtesy Leo Castelli Gallery, New York.

**96.** Paul Cézanne. *The Great Bathers.* 1898–1905.
Oil on canvas, 6′11″ × 8′2″.
Philadelphia Museum of Art (purchase: the W. P. Wilstach Collection).

Line also plays a role in creating emphasis in a work of art. In Paul Cézanne's painting *The Great Bathers* (**96**), diagonal lines of trees bend inward to form a triangle in the center of the canvas. The figures all lean in such a way as to echo the diagonal line. By means of this triangle Cézanne focuses attention on the main figures at the bottom center of the composition. His diagonal lines create a frame-within-a-frame, so we concentrate on forms within or making up the triangle.

**Pattern and Texture**    Yet another function of line in art is the creation of pattern and texture. We saw the latter in Picasso's painting (**92**), where closely spaced short lines suggest the texture of animal hair and grass. Saul Steinberg has used

**97.** Saul Steinberg. *Hen.*
1945. Pen, brush,
and India ink;
14½ × 23⅛″.
Museum of Modern Art,
New York (purchase).

90

line to great effect in creating the ornate texture of chicken feathers in his ink drawing *Hen* (**97**). Repeated, interwoven squiggly lines suggest a fabulous plumage that any bird would be proud of. The face and feet of the hen seem almost an afterthought to this wonderful, rich display of texture.

Pattern is usually considered to be any repetitive, decorative design, such as that of dress fabric or wallpaper. Very often line is the means by which pattern is created. An unusual adaptation of this idea can be found in the tattooed face of a Maori tribesman in New Zealand (**98**). These patterns are especially interesting because of the way in which they follow the lines of the face. Swirling linear circles decorate the nostrils, the beard line, and the temples. Lines curving outward on the cheeks mimic the "smile lines" that may occur naturally in the face, and "rays" in the forehead suggest fierce frown lines. The use of line to create pattern is especially common in the crafts and in graphic design.

**Modeling and Shading**    One very important function of line, especially in drawing and printmaking, is the creation of shaded effects and/or the illusion of three-dimensionality on a flat surface. An artist who wishes to suggest roundness often will *model* by means of closely spaced short lines (**99**). *Hatching* is an area of parallel lines, and *cross-hatching* is the same thing but with intersecting parallel lines. Both types of marks are obvious in Albrecht Dürer's superb *Head of a Child* (**100**). Dürer uses hatching for the hair, the left cheek, and most of the neck. But where he wants to show the swell of the nose and the right cheek, he builds up a varying cross-hatch that follows the planes of the face. If you could erase the cross-hatched marks, the child's face would seem flat. *Stippling* results when the lines are reduced to dots and spaced closer together or farther apart to create modeling. Because of the nature of certain printmaking tools, stippling is particularly important for that medium.

**98.** Maori man with tattooed face.

**above: 99.** Line techniques to create modeling: hatching, cross-hatching, and stippling.

**right: 100.** Albrecht Dürer. *Head of a Child.* Pen and ink with white ink. Louvre, Paris.

## Types of Lines

The preceding sections have dealt primarily with actual lines—visible marks made in pencil or paint or some other medium. In studying art, however, we often have to take into account other types of lines (**101**). Actual lines are the most familiar, so we begin with them.

**Actual Lines**    Actual lines are obvious in Robert Motherwell's *Procession, with Oil* (**102**); in fact, they are the dominant element in the composition. Bold, thick, black lines are arranged in such a way that they resemble Oriental calligraphy—the art of "beautiful writing." The sheer size of the painting (it is more than 5 by 7 feet) gives the lines tremendous force. This work is totally nonobjective, or free of any visual reference to the natural world. Its interest lies in the interplay between black lines and space, the dynamic shapes created between the lines, and—above all—the energy implicit in the powerful lines. We imagine Motherwell drawing the lines with a sweeping arc of the whole arm, not a careful motion of the wrist.

**Implied Lines**    When a person stops on a street corner and gazes upward, other passersby will also stop and look up, following the "line" of sight. When someone points a finger, we automatically follow the direction of the point. Artists often exploit this natural response by using implied lines in their work. In Raphael's painting called *The Madonna of the Meadows* (**103**), implied lines of sight between the Virgin and the two children help to pull the composition together and direct the eyes of the viewer to the most important figure in the painting—the child Jesus (**104**). The Madonna casts her eyes downward toward John the Baptist, who, in turn, gazes upward at the baby Jesus, establishing a triangular flow. As observers, we unconsciously follow these lines of sight around and through the painting, just as we would glance upward if we saw someone in the street staring up. Implied lines here give both unity and a subtle sense of movement to the painting.

**Lines Formed by Edges**    If you press the palms of your two hands flat together in a praying gesture, you will see that a "line" seems to form where they meet. There is no line, in reality, but the point where the edge of one form meets the edge of another form creates the impression of a line. This can happen in two-dimensional art as well, wherever one shape or color area

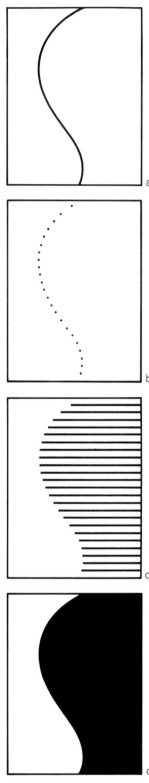

**above: 101.** Actual line (**a**), implied lines (**b, c**), and line created by edge (**d**).

**right: 102.** Robert Motherwell. *Procession, with Oil.* 1981. Oil and acrylic on canvas, 5′6″ × 7′6″. Courtesy M. Knoedler & Co., Inc., New York.

**left: 103.** Raphael. *The Madonna of the Meadows.*
1505. Oil on Panel, 44½ × 34¼".
Kunsthistorisches Museum, Vienna.

**above: 104.** Line analysis of Raphael's
Madonna of the Meadows.

meets another shape or color area. The line created by edge is evident in our
next illustration—a sculpture by Claes Oldenburg in the Dallas Museum of
Art (**105**). *Stake Hitch,* with its giant "rope" stretched from floor to ceiling, is
actually a three-dimensional form, but in contrast to the light-colored background we perceive a wavy, scalloped line on either side of the rope. The
edges of buildings, of sculptures, of any shapes isolated against a plain background fool the eye into seeing lines where none exist.

Let's return again to Picasso's painting of Paulo (**92**). The line of the
child's chin and cheeks would have been an edge line in real life, the sense of
a line formed by the juncture of face and background. Picasso turned an
imaginary line into an actual line for the painting.

**105.** Claes Oldenberg.
*Stake Hitch.* 1984.
Painted epoxied aluminum,
urethane foam, polyester resin,
and fiberglass; height 39'.
Dallas Museum of Art
(commissioned to honor
John Dabney Murchison, Sr.,
for his arts and civic leadership
and presented by his family).

# Raphael
## *1483–1520*

According to the 16th-century biographer Giorgio Vasari, we find in Raphael "an artist as talented as he was gracious," possessed of unbounded "grace, industry, looks, modesty, and excellence of character." Whereas both Michelangelo and Leonardo da Vinci emerge as rather moody, solitary figures, their younger colleague seems to have been the sort of person who charms everybody and to whom success comes as naturally as breathing.

Born in the town of Urbino, Raffaello Sanzio received his first art training from his father, then later became an assistant to the early Renaissance master Pietro Perugino. At twenty-one Raphael struck out on his own, but he continued to study avidly the work of other artists—including Leonardo and Michelangelo, both of whom influenced him greatly. (Vasari claims that Raphael was secretly let into the locked Sistine Chapel when Michelangelo had temporarily stopped work on the ceiling frescoes so that he could get an advance look at the figures.)

Raphael established his reputation early and throughout his career never lacked for patrons. A major preoccupation was the madonna and child group, of which he made numerous versions. In 1508 Pope Julius II called Raphael to Rome, where the artist began the decoration in fresco of four rooms in the Vatican. Among these frescoes was the famous *School of Athens* (**225**).

By his early thirties Raphael had become a busy person indeed, testing his artistic skills in many areas. Increasingly, the work of carrying out his commissions was delegated to assistants. He had been named chief architect of Saint Peter's Basilica in the Vatican and was also director of excavations for ancient Greek and Roman art in and around the city of Rome. On commission from Pope Leo, Julius' successor, Raphael designed ten huge tapestries for the Sistine Chapel and perhaps executed the cartoons (drawings to guide the weavers) himself, although this point is in dispute.

Raphael's private life seems to have been as full and satisfying as his artistic career. At home in any social situation, sought-after as a friend, he played as energetically as he worked. He never married—possibly because he hoped to be made a cardinal of the Church—but he lived for many years with the same woman. The biographer Vasari refers to "secret love affairs" and comments that the artist "pursued his pleasures with no sense of moderation." If we are to believe Vasari, Raphael's death at the tragically premature age of thirty-seven came as the aftermath of such lack in moderation, which brought on a "violent fever" made fatal by unwise medical attention.

Among Raphael's great talents was the ability to please his patrons while at the same time fulfilling his own ideals of art. In about 1514 he wrote this to a noble client: "I should consider myself a great master if [a drawing of Galatea] had half the merits you mention in your letter. However, I perceive in your words the love that you bear me; . . . I am making use of a certain idea which comes into my mind. Whether it is possessed of any artistic excellence I do not know. But I do strive to attain it."[1]

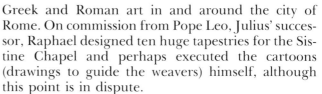

Raphael. *School of Athens,*
detail with presumed self-portrait. 1510–11.
Fresco. Stanza della Segnatura, Vatican, Rome.

## Characteristics of Lines

When someone mentions the word "house," everyone who hears forms a different mental image. Listeners might picture anything from a small cabin in the woods to Buckingham Palace, depending on their frame of reference. So it is with line. Line is such a broad term that it can encompass everything from Motherwell's huge black strokes to the delicate pencil marks of Kelly's *Apples*. The characteristics of any given line have much to do with how that line performs in a work of art. Two important characteristics are direction and linear quality.

**Direction**    Most of us have instinctive reactions to the direction of line, which are related to our experience of gravity. Flat, horizontal lines seem placid, like the horizon line or a body in repose. Vertical lines, like those of an upright body or a skyscraper jutting up from the ground, may have an assertive quality; they defy gravity in their upward thrust. But the most dynamic lines are the diagonals, which almost always imply action. Think of a runner hurtling down the track or a skier down the slope. The body leans forward, so that only the forward motion keeps it from toppling over. Diagonal lines in art have the same effect. We sense motion because the lines are unstable; we half expect them to topple over. (One exception is the diagonal line that makes up part of a triangle or pyramid, as in Cézanne's painting [**96**]; such lines are very stable because the triangle form is closed and solid.) To see how linear direction works, let us compare two paintings that both show a boat in the water.

In Thomas Eakins' *The Biglen Brothers Racing* (**106**) nearly all the lines are horizontals. The two boats, the shoreline, the ripples on the river, the treetops, even the clouds scuttling across the sky are horizontal. Only the diagonal lines of the oars and the rowers' arms and bodies suggest that this is a race. Why should a race be so placid? Eakins has captured the essence of sculling, races involving flat, long-oared boats powered by one or two rowers. Usually done on calm bodies of water, sculling has an odd, streamlined quality in the way the boats knife through the still water. The only apparent motion is in the bodies of the rowers, whose brisk, automaton movements in tandem make them seem, from a distance, like little mechanical toys. Eakins, therefore, has given his painting an overall serenity, broken only by the diagonals of the men.

**106.** Thomas Eakins.
*The Biglen Brothers Racing.* 1873.
Oil on canvas, $24\frac{1}{8} \times 36\frac{1}{8}''$.
National Gallery of Art,
Washington, D.C. (gift of Mr. & Mrs.
Cornelius Vanderbilt Whitney, 1953).

# Eugène Delacroix
## *1798–1863*

Art lovers may be secretly pleased to discover that certain artists look just the way one expects them to. Such is the case with the portrait above. If we wanted an image of a 19th-century aristocrat, a suave and polished man-about-Paris, the preeminent painter of the Romantic movement in art—surely that image would look like Delacroix.

Born in a suburb of Paris, Ferdinand Victor Eugène Delacroix claimed descent from an upper-class family, although his true parentage is in doubt. One theory maintains he was the natural son of the controversial statesman Talleyrand, which would help to explain the artist's securing of considerable government patronage even while his art was still extremely unpopular. In any event, he was never without funds to enjoy the rather dashing "upper bohemian" life style that placed him in the company of the leading French writers, musicians, and intellectuals of the day.

Delacroix had little formal education as an artist, but he was much influenced by the work of his older colleague Théodore Géricault, as well as by the masters he admired most—Michelangelo ("God! What a man!") and especially Rubens. Delacroix first exhibited at the annual Paris Salon in 1822, when he was only twenty-four; his real arrival on the public scene, however, came two years later, when he exhibited a work so innovative in its treatment of colors that it caused a scandal and attracted few defenders. Intense colors, applied with great originality, remained a hallmark of his art throughout his career.

A major turning point in Delacroix's art came in 1832, when the artist made a trip to Morocco. So overwhelmed was he by the colors, the exotic people and scenes, the exciting discovery of a life entirely alien to him, that his art was affected permanently. Not only did he often treat "Oriental" or exotic subjects, but his approach to traditional themes became more intense and colorful.

As leader of the Romantic school of painting, Delacroix found himself thrust into bitter rivalry with Jean Auguste Dominique Ingres, the great master of the cooler, more subdued classical style. Older by nearly twenty years, the methodical Ingres seems to have considered his younger rival little short of a barbarian for his vibrant colors and energetic brushwork. Undismayed by the attacks, Delacroix continued to work and to prosper, leaving counterattack to his followers. The Delacroix-Ingres feud, kept at high pitch by the supporters of the two artists, enlivened the Parisian art scene for a quarter century.

Delacroix was as prolific a writer as he was a painter, and the voluminous journal he left is among the most articulate in the history of art. He expressed himself on almost every subject imaginable, including (perhaps as a none-too-subtle slap at Ingres) the idea of perfection in art: "I have told myself a hundred times that painting—that is to say, the material thing called painting—was no more than the pretext, the bridge between the mind of the painter and that of the spectator. Cold exactitude is not art; ingenious artifice, when it *pleases* or when it *expresses*, is art itself. The so-called conscientiousness of the majority of painters is only perfection applied to the *art of boring.* . . . It would be interesting to write a treatise on all the falsehoods which can add up to truth."[2]

Eugène Delacroix. *Self-Portrait.* 1860.
Oil on canvas, 26 × 21¼″. Uffizi, Florence.

A diagram will help to show the great differences in linear direction, and thus in emotional effect, between Eakins' work and our next illustration (**107**). Serenity was the last thing Théodore Géricault wanted for his painting *The Raft of the Medusa* (**108**). Géricault's work is based on an actual event—the wreck of the French government ship *Medusa* off North Africa in 1816. Only a few of those on board survived, some by clinging to a raft. The artist has chosen to depict the dramatic moment when those on the raft sighted a rescue ship. Virtually all the lines in the composition—the men straining forward, the arc of the sail, the bodies of the dead and dying in the foreground—are diagonal. Their thrust reinforces that of the raft plunging toward safety. And all these exciting diagonals build toward the climax of the one vertical—the man signaling to the rescue ship. The artist's use of line direction may be overt or subtle, but we can rarely fail to respond to it.

**Linear Quality** As with direction, the artist's use of linear quality does much to influence the overall impact of the work, including the viewer's emotional response. Lines can be any length, thick or thin or tapered, straight or curved or angular. For example, we might compare the linear quality—and the emotional content that corresponds to the particular quality—in three works reproduced here.

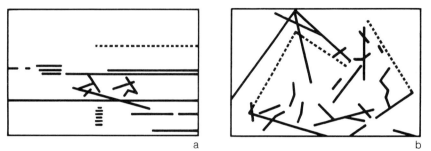

a                                                                    b

**above: 107.** Line analyses of Eakins' *The Biglen Brothers Racing* (**a**) and Géricault's *The Raft of the Medusa* (**b**).

**below: 108.** Théodore Géricault. *The Raft of the Medusa.* 1818–19. Oil on canvas, 16'1⅜" × 23'9". Louvre, Paris.

**109.** Vincent van Gogh. *Cypresses with Two Women*, detail. 1889. Reed pen and ink, chalk, and touches of oil; $12\frac{5}{8} \times 9\frac{1}{2}''$. Rijksmuseum Kröller-Müller, Otterlo, The Netherlands.

A drawing by Vincent van Gogh, *Cypresses with Two Women* (**109**), consists almost entirely of short, wavy, flame-like lines—a style characteristic of Van Gogh's later drawings. The cypress trees seem to be in undulating motion, their leaves perhaps shivering in the wind, and this movement is differentiated from the more stable foreground foliage defined in curling lines.

Henri Matisse's lithograph has a very different subject—the curve of a woman's back (**110**). The artist has employed a long, elegant, gently curving line to convey the sensual, ripe quality of the form. So delicate is the line that in places it disappears altogether, leaving a space—and an implied line to connect the two sections.

How different is the linear quality and emotional content of the lines in Eugène Delacroix's drawing (**111**). The lines in *Study for the Death of Sardanapalus* swoop and swirl with tremendous energy. Just by looking at these turbulent lines we know that Delacroix made them swiftly, not with studied deliberation. The emotional tumult all but leaps out of the boundaries of the paper, carrying the viewer along with it.

This brief discussion of linear quality ends our discussion of line. We turn next to a second vital element in art—shape, and its three-dimensional counterpart, mass. However, it must be remembered here and throughout the chapter that all the elements are interdependent and affect each other continually. The quality of a line, for example, will influence the quality of a shape it produces.

## Shape and Mass

A *shape* is a two-dimensional area having identifiable boundaries. Shapes are created by lines, by color areas, by being set off against space, or some combination of these. If the artist draws a circle and colors it blue inside the line, the result is a round blue shape. Even if there is no line, if there is just a roundish daub of blue paint, we still perceive a circular blue shape set off from the surrounding space because of the edges of blue.

In everyday conversation we also use the term shape to refer to three-dimensional forms, such as the shape of a car or a house or a person. More formal art analysis, however, usually prefers the word *mass* for objects that have depth. A blue tennis ball is a spherical blue mass whose boundaries we perceive as distinct from the surrounding space. In a slightly different though related sense, mass refers specifically to bulk, density, and weight. We might speak of the mass of a heavy paperweight or the mass of a natural rock formation, for example. Another term often used in connection with mass is *volume*. Generally speaking, mass and volume mean much the same thing, but volume can also refer to a void, an empty but enclosed space, whereas mass always refers to solid form. From the outside we notice the mass of a large building, such as the Guggenheim Museum (**426**), but inside we can talk about the volume enclosed and created by the structure (**134**).

**right: 110.** Henri Matisse.
*Study: A Woman's Back.* 1914. Lithograph.
Metropolitan Museum of Art, New York
(Rogers Fund, 1921).

**below: 111.** Eugène Delacroix.
*Study for the Death of Sardanapalus.*
1827–28. Pen, watercolor, and pencil;
$10\frac{1}{4} \times 12\frac{1}{2}''$.
Cabinet des Dessins, Louvre, Paris.

Shape on a two-dimensional surface may give the *illusion* of mass. In Picasso's painting (**92**) we see the flat shape of a boy on a donkey, drawn so as to create the illusion of roundness. A real boy on a real donkey—or a sculpture of them—would be an actual mass.

It is customary to distinguish two broad categories in both shapes and masses: organic and geometric. Geometric shapes, based on the mechanically drawn line, include the square, the rectangle, the circle, and the triangle. Organic shapes are based on the forms in nature, which are usually rounded, irregular, and curving. Many works of art combine these two categories, but often one or the other will predominate.

One artist who devoted a career to exploring the potential of geometric shape was the Dutch painter Piet Mondrian (**112**). Mondrian's *Composition with Red, Yellow, and Blue* is typical of his mature work and represents the artist's search for what he called a "pure reality." Mondrian felt that certain things are universal, common to all people—the rectangle, the vertical and horizontal, the primary colors red, yellow, and blue, plus black and white. By these means he hoped to cut through cultural and emotional differences among people and make a visual statement that would be meaningful to all. Mondrian's canvases, apparently so simple, rest on the hair's-breadth balance of line, shape, and color. Shift one line, alter the dimensions of one rectangle, change one area of color, and the entire composition falls apart—that is the kind of dynamic equilibrium Mondrian achieved with geometric shapes.

Organic shapes prevail in Joan Miró's *Carnival of Harlequin* (**113**). This fantasy landscape is aswarm with odd little creatures—animals and fish and insects and perhaps a snake or two—as well as nameless organic forms that participate in Miró's madcap carnival. Much of Miró's imagery suggests a very cheerful sexuality, as though the whole space of the world were occupied with light-hearted erotic play and reproduction. To achieve this effect the artist

**112.** Piet Mondrian.
*Composition with Red, Yellow, and Blue.*
1928. Oil on canvas, 4'¾" × 2'7½".
Courtesy Sidney Janis Gallery,
New York.

employed nearly all organic shapes, except for the mysterious square, circle, and triangle at upper right.

Before we complete our discussion of two-dimensional shape, we should touch upon one more aspect of it, and that is the concept of positive/negative shape, sometimes called *figure-ground relationship*. A painting or other work of two-dimensional art usually has one or more shapes meant to be perceived as positive. In a representational work, they are the shapes of the subject; in a nonrepresentational work, they are the shapes that seem active or dominant. For instance, in Picasso's painting of Paulo, the little boy and the donkey are positive shapes, or figure. Everything else is negative shape, or background. If you compare this to a work by M. C. Escher (**114**), you will find it hard to decide which are the positive shapes and which are the negative ones. Focus

**above: 113.** Joan Miró.
*Carnival of Harlequin.* 1924–25.
Oil on canvas, $26 \times 36\frac{5}{8}''$.
Albright-Knox Art Gallery, Buffalo, N.Y.
(Room of Contemporary Art Fund, 1976).

**left: 114.** M. C. Escher.
*Study of Regular Division of the Plane
with Horsemen.* 1946.
India ink and watercolor.
Escher Foundation, Gemeentemuseum, The Hague.

**115.** Sculpture at Centre Street, New York.

your eyes on the dark figures, and the light ones become ground; focus on the light ones, and the opposite is true. Escher meant this drawing to be a clever visual puzzle, but it makes an important point about art in general. Looking back at Motherwell's painting (**102**), maybe the white in this painting really is "figure" and the black lines are negative, or "ground." We don't usually think in these terms until an artist gives us figure and ground that can exchange "roles," as Escher has done. What Escher's drawing emphasizes is that both positive and negative shapes are dynamic elements in art.

Three-dimensional mass also can be considered either geometric or organic. The sculpture illustrated here (**115**) consists of a series of shallow, hollowed-out cubes (a geometric mass) arranged in a broken spiral. Although the plain shape of the cube can seem static, even boring, this work is full of movement. No single cube stands flat on its side; all are caught in a precarious teetering pose and dependent on their neighbors for stability. The sculpture seems particularly effective in contrast to the traditional equestrian statue in the background—an organic mass.

Perhaps no elements are more important to the visual impact of a work of art than shape and mass. When describing a work it is usually the shapes we talk about first. The next two elements, however, are also crucial, for they dramatically influence our response to art.

## Light and Color

Light and color are intimately connected elements. Color is a function of light and therefore directly dependent on its presence. Apart from the purely sensory pleasure we derive from it, color helps to define shape and mass. For example, we notice the *green* hills largely because they are set off against *blue* sky. In a nonobjective painting color may be the only means by which we identify shapes and spaces. Color is also used by artists to convey emotion.

In this section we take up the subjects of light and color insofar as they affect our perception of art. Both involve complex sciences, but only a little of the science is necessary to understand how light and color operate.

### Light

**Natural Light**     In architecture and in sculptures meant to be exhibited outdoors we are particularly aware of the influence of natural light. The architect of an old cast-iron building in New York, photographed by Evelyn Hofer (**116**), probably realized how important would be the play of light and shadow on its ornate facade. The photographer has seen this too and has captured a moment when patterns of light are especially dramatic. One could say that this photograph is "about" light, as light interacts with three-dimensional mass.

Dazzling natural light admitted by a glass roof is virtually the most important element in the great hall of Vancouver's new courthouse (**117**). Reacting against the usual image of a courthouse as stuffy and claustrophobic, architect Arthur Erickson has "turned the traditional courthouse inside-out." Shadow patterns over the course of a day make a fascinating, ever-changing mosaic on the floors and throughout the interior. Erickson has welcomed light as an important part of his design, but any artist whose work will be exposed to natural light must take it into account.

**The Illusion of Light**     Artists working in two-dimensional art—painting or drawing or prints, for instance—often wish to create the impression of light illuminating their subjects. This apparent light may be daylight evenly illuminating a scene or dappling the leaves in a landscape or the light cast by a lamp, candle, or fire. In some cases the supposed light source is included in the image, as when a

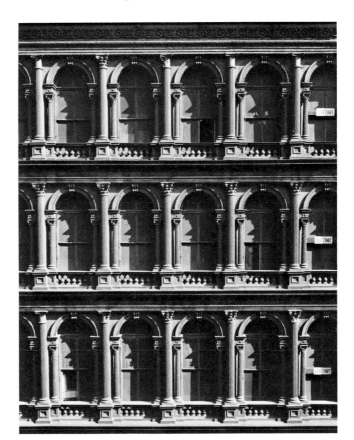

**right: 116.** Evelyn Hofer.
*Cast-Iron Building,*
*Broadway and Broome Streets, New York.*
1965. Photograph.
Courtesy the photographer.

**below: 117.** Arthur Erickson.
Great Hall, Courthouse, Vancouver, B.C.

**left: 118.** Thomas Eakins. *The Concert Singer*. 1892. Oil on canvas, 6'3⅛" × 4'6¼".
Philadelphia Museum of Art (given by Mrs. Thomas Eakins and Miss Mary A. Williams).

**right: 119.** *The Concert Singer,* reproduced in black and white, to show gray values.

painter depicts figures clustered around a lamp. At other times the light source is assumed to be outside the frame of the picture, but we see its effects clearly. A subject bathed in light from a definite angle, with the resultant shadows, may seem more lifelike and three-dimensional. (When light is general and comes from no specific source, figures tend to be flattened.)

We can see how light enhances the sense of depth in Thomas Eakins' painting *The Concert Singer* (**118**). This work shows the singer Weda Cook in a solo perform- ance. The strong light coming from below and to her left is apparently from a footlight on the concert stage. Eakins obviously was intrigued with the effects of light on form. The lower part of the gown is the most brilliantly illuminated, while more than half the face remains in shadow. Light picks out folds in the dress, hollows in the singer's throat, the musculature of the arms—all of these details contributing to the roundness of the figure.

**Value and Contrast**   The term *value* means relative lightness or darkness, whether in color or in black and white. Values are perhaps easier to see in black and white than in color; we are accustomed to their effects in black-and-white television, photography, and reproductions, such as the ones in this book. When *The Concert Singer* is reproduced in black and white (**119**), the very pale pink on the near side of the dress is seen as a very light gray, the singer's illuminated arm and cheek slightly darker grays, and so on, to the very dark grays that represent the shadows behind the singer and on her right side. Color values are translated into values of gray. In black and white, then, lacking the color cues we have in most situations, we rely to a large extent on contrasts of grays to help us distinguish one form from another.

For purposes of analysis, value is usually considered in terms of a value scale (**120**), ranging from white (the lightest) to black (the darkest), with several gradations in between. (The same value scale can be applied to colors, as we shall see.) Works of art in which light values predominate are called high-key, those in which dark values predominate low-key.

Value contrasts—contrasts of light and dark—may be used in a painting or drawing to create the effects of light and shadow in the natural world. This technique is called *chiaroscuro*, which literally means "light / dark." In Georges Seurat's drawing *Child in White* (**121**) there is no explicit light source within the painting, yet light seems to be coming from above. The child's hat and dress are rendered in very light values, as though light-struck, but her face is bathed in shadow, a dark value. Seurat has created this impression of light and shade entirely by varying the values in the drawing. By this method also he models the figure into apparent three-dimensionality.

Seurat's drawing is in black and white. The effects of value, light, and contrast become even more complex when we add the ingredient of color.

**120.** Value scale in gray.

| white | high light | light | low light | medium | high dark | dark | low dark | black |

**121.** Georges Seurat.
*Child in White.* 1884.
Conté crayon and chalk, $12 \times 9\frac{1}{4}''$.
Solomon R. Guggenheim Museum, New York.

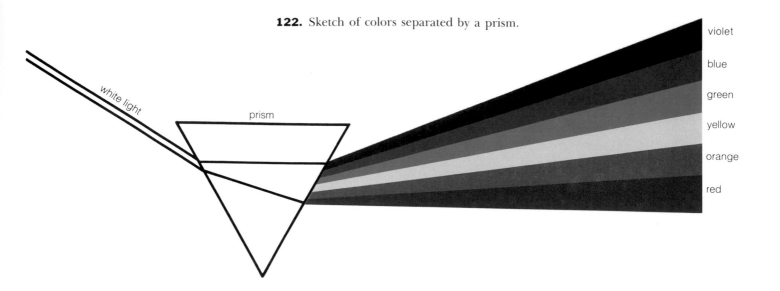

**122.** Sketch of colors separated by a prism.

white light

prism

violet
blue
green
yellow
orange
red

## Color

It is probably safe to say that none of the visual elements give us so much pleasure as color. You will understand this if you have ever been restricted to watching a black-and-white television and then suddenly have access to a color set. With the color in front of you, you will watch almost anything, even the commercials, for sheer visual delight. Or, imagine that you have been living or working in a drab, colorless room, and then, overnight, the room is painted in bright colors. Not only will you probably work more energetically, but your spirits may rise.

Various studies have demonstrated that color affects a wide range of psychological and physiological responses. Restaurants often are decorated in red, which is believed to increase appetite and therefore food consumption. A common treatment for premature babies born with potentially fatal jaundice is to bathe them in blue light, which, for reasons not fully understood, eliminates the need to transfuse their blood. Blue surroundings also will significantly lower a person's blood pressure, pulse, and respiration rate. In one experiment subjects were asked to identify, by taste, ordinary mashed potatoes colored bright green. Because of the disorienting color cues, they could not say what they were eating. And in one California detention center violent children are routinely placed in an 8-by-4-foot cell painted bubble-gum pink. The children relax, become calmer, and often fall asleep within ten minutes. This color has been dubbed "passive pink." The mechanism involved in all these color responses is still unclear, but there can be no doubt that color "works" on the human brain and body in powerful ways.

In this book you will find about one hundred fifty works of art reproduced in full color. This color does not exactly duplicate the colors you would see if you stood in front of the actual works, because mechanical reproduction on paper is never wholly accurate. But you will no doubt look at these color reproductions first—before the black-and-white pictures—and will look at them more often. Color always draws the eye.

At the beginning of this section we said that color is a function of light. Without light there can be no color. The principles of color theory explain why this is so.

**Color Theory**    Much of our present-day color theory can be traced back to experiments made by Sir Isaac Newton, who is better known for his work with the laws of gravity. In 1666 Newton passed a ray of sunlight through a prism, yellow

yellow-orange    yellow-green

orange    green

red-orange    blue-green

red    blue

red-violet    blue-violet

violet

**123.** Color wheel.

a transparent glass form with nonparallel sides. He observed that the ray of sunlight broke up or *refracted* into different colors, which were arranged in the order of the colors of the rainbow (**122**). By setting up a second prism Newton found he could recombine the rainbow colors into white light, like the original sunlight. These experiments proved that colors are components of light.

In fact, all colors are dependent on light, and no object possesses color intrinsically. You may own a red shirt and a blue pen and a purple chair, but these items have no color in and of themselves. What we perceive as color is reflected light rays. When light strikes the red shirt, for example, the shirt absorbs all the color rays *except* the red ones, which are reflected, so your eye perceives red. The purple chair reflects the purple rays and absorbs all the others, and so on. Both the physiological activity of the human eye and the science of electromagnetic wavelengths take part in this process.

If we take the colors separated out by Newton's prism—red, orange, yellow, green, blue, and violet—add the transitional color red-violet (which does not exist in the rainbow), and arrange these colors in a circle, we have a *color wheel* (**123**). Different theorists have constructed different color wheels, but the one shown here is fairly standard.

*Primary colors*—red, yellow, and blue—are labeled with the numeral *1* on the color wheel. They are called primary because (theoretically at least) they cannot be made by any mixture of other colors.

*Secondary colors*—orange, green, and violet—are labeled with the numeral *2*. Each is made by combining two primary colors. For most of us this information is not new. Even in kindergarten children working with poster paints learn to make green by mixing yellow and blue.

white | high light | light | low light | medium | high dark | dark | low dark | black

**124.** Color chart, showing value and intensity.

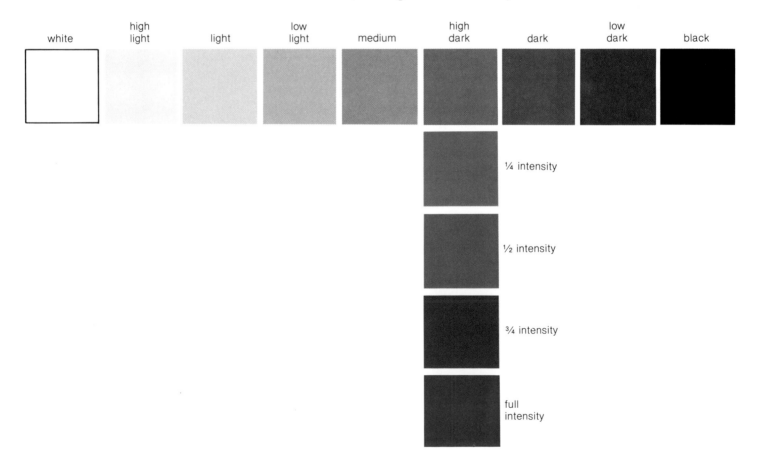

white | high light | light | low light | medium | high dark | dark | low dark | black

¼ intensity

½ intensity

¾ intensity

full intensity

*Tertiary colors*, labeled number *3*, are the product of a primary color and an adjacent secondary color; for instance, mixing yellow with green yields yellow-green.

*Complementary colors* are those directly opposite one another on the color wheel. They are assumed to be as different from one another as possible. The relationship between complementary colors, as we shall see, is extremely important in such areas as the optical and emotional effects of color.

**Color Properties**     Any color has three properties: hue, value, and intensity.

*Hue* is the name of the color—green or red or violet-blue. In any serious discussion of color it is important to avoid the poetic color names promoted by the fashion industry, such as "fuchsia" or "topaz." The hues listed on the color wheel and the designations on the color chart (**124**) are meant to be standard, so that people can agree on their meanings.

*Value,* again, refers to relative lightness or darkness. Most colors are recognizable in a full range of values; for instance, we identify as "red" everything from palest pink to darkest maroon. In addition, all hues have what is known as a *normal value*—the value at which we expect to find that hue. We think of yellow as a "light" color and violet as a "dark" color, for example, even though each has a full range of values. The various hues of the color wheel can be organized in relation to the values of gray on the color chart (**124**).

A color lighter than the hue's normal value is known as a *tint*; therefore, pink is a tint of red. A color darker than the hue's normal value is called a *shade*; maroon is a shade of red. (This terminology is specific to color theory and differs from everyday usage of the word "shade" to mean any variation of a color, as in "My coat is a lovely shade of blue.")

*Intensity*—also called *chroma* or *saturation*—refers to the relative purity of a color. The difference between intensity and value can be a bit difficult to understand until you see how it works on the color chart (**124**). Colors may be pure, or saturated, as they appear on the color wheel, or they may be grayed and softened to some degree. The purest colors are said to have high intensity, those grayer to have lower intensity. To lower the intensity of a color when mixing paints or dyes, the artist may add a combination of black and white (gray) or may add a little of the color's complement.

**Light and Pigment**     Colors behave differently depending on whether the artist is working with light or with pigment. In light, as we said, white light is the sum of all colors. In other words, if you combine all colors, you will get white. This is not true for pigment—artists' colors or dyes. If you mix all these colors together, you will get a *neutral*—either black or an almost colorless brownish-gray.

Artists who work in light—including video artists, photographers, and filmmakers—need to master a complex technology of light/color dynamics. For instance, the image shown here (**125**) was made in a machine known as a

**125.** Composite image created in a quantizer, photographed from the screen.

**126.** Arshile Gorky.
*One Year the Milkweed.* 1944.
Oil on canvas, 37 × 47".
National Gallery of Art,
Washington, D.C.
(Ailsa Mellon Bruce Fund, 1979).

color *quantizer,* which combines television imagery with sophisticated color technology. The operator begins by focusing a black-and-white camera on a subject, such as a person, and thus breaking up that subject into values of gray. Next, by manipulating dials on the quantizer, the operator can substitute colors for each of the values in the subject. The operator might decide, say, that all the high-dark values in the image (see value scale, **120**), should be replaced with a golden orange.

Often the colors in this type of imagery are *arbitrary*—unrelated to colors in the natural world. In effect, the artist is working with an "electronic palette," which allows him or her to choose from an infinite range of colors and combinations with just the twist of a dial. The colors can be tried, adjusted, rejected, retrieved, and recombined indefinitely. This is where video art gets its expressive and individual power; the machine does not control the artist, but rather the artist controls the machine. As we see in this illustration, the quantizer can also merge two or more images and vary their sizes—perhaps to attach a bird's wings to a full-grown human male.

Artists using real light usually select their colors mechanically, at a distance, by pushing buttons or choosing filters or adjusting dials. Their work requires a sophisticated knowledge of color science. By contrast, artists who work in pigments—watercolors or oil paints or similar media—usually blend their colors by trial and error, using their own hands. In both cases, familiarity with the color wheel and the color properties can help, as can understanding of the color harmonies.

**Color Harmonies**   A color harmony, sometimes called a *color scheme,* is the selective use of two or more colors in a single composition. We tend to think of this especially in relation to interior design; you may say, for instance, "The

**127.** Demonstration of the effects of afterimage in colors. Stare at the dot in the center of the flag for at least 30 seconds. Then, quickly turn your eyes to a white paper or a white wall. The flag should appear in its usual colors.

color scheme in my kitchen is blue and green with touches of brown." But color harmonies also apply to the pictorial arts, although they may be more difficult to spot because of differences in value and intensity.

Usually, an artist's choice of colors is intuitive, so that it is only after a work of art has been completed that observers can identify the color harmony involved. These harmonies do, however, help us to understand why certain combinations of colors produce certain visual effects. There are several categories of color harmonies.

*Monochromatic* harmonies are composed of variations on the same hue, often with differences of value and intensity. A painting all in reds, pinks, and maroons would be considered to have a monochromatic harmony. It is important, however, to understand this term in context. Sometimes, especially in reference to drawings, the word "monochromatic" is used to mean works entirely in one color, as well as works in black and white.

*Complementary* harmonies involve colors directly opposite one another on the color wheel. Arshile Gorky's painting *One Year the Milkweed* (**126**) illustrates such a harmony, being composed primarily of different reds and greens.

*Analogous* harmonies combine colors adjacent to one another on the color wheel, such as green, blue-green, and blue. And *triad* harmonies use three colors equidistant on the color wheel, such as blue, yellow, and red-orange. In addition, there are several more complicated color harmonies that are significant mainly to color theorists. For our purposes here it is enough to know that such harmonies exist and that they may sometimes help us to understand why particular colors work together.

**Optical Effects of Color**    Certain uses and combinations of colors can "play tricks" on our eyes, or, more accurately, on the way we perceive colors registered by our eyes. For one thing, there is the phenomenon known as *simultaneous contrast*. If you place two complementary colors next to each other, both of them will seem more brilliant: red seems redder, green greener, and so forth. Food merchandisers understand this well. Strawberries are nearly always packaged in green, the complement of red, and the meat counter in a grocery store often will have some touch of green. Both the fruit and the meat therefore seem redder and more appetizing. Similarly, the home decorator might create an instant "still life" by piling fresh oranges into a blue bowl on the table; the two colors spark against each other and dazzle the eye.

Another phenomenon associated with complementary colors is *afterimage*. If you stare fixedly at the color areas in the illustration (**127**) for half a minute or so, and then turn your eyes quickly to a white page or white wall, you will see a faint afterimage of the color patches in their complementary colors.

Some colors seem to "advance," others to "recede." Interior designers know that if you place a bright red chair in a room it will seem larger and farther forward than the same chair upholstered in beige or pale blue. Thus, color can dramatically influence our perceptions of space and size. In general, colors that create the illusion of large size and advancing are those with warmer hues (red, orange, yellow), high intensity, and dark value; small size and receding are suggested by colors with cooler hues (blue, green), low intensity, and light value.

Colors can be mixed in light or pigment, but they can also be mixed by the eyes. When small patches of different colors are placed close together, the eye may blend them to produce a new color. This is known as *optical color mixture*, and it is an important feature in the painting of Georges Seurat. Seurat's style of painting, known as *pointillism*, depends on the painstaking arrangement of many, many tiny dots of color very close together. From a distance of a few inches a Seurat painting looks like a meaningless jumble of color dots (**128**). But as the viewer moves back, the dots merge to form soft, subtly gradated colors (**129**). Although Seurat's work is the epitome of optical color mixture, many artists use the effect in less extreme forms.

**Emotional Qualities of Color**    Endless books have been written in an attempt to explain the emotional effects of color. Why does a bull chase something red? Why does a person wearing a red shirt or dress immediately attract our attention? Why are red, white, and silver status colors for an automobile, whereas orange is not? Whatever the reasons, one group of experts—packaging designers—have been aggressive in exploiting these qualities. If you scan the shelves of the supermarket, you will discover that few packages are entirely free of red, because red seems to attract attention better than any other color. (One exception is foods promoted as being "natural," whose packages will usually feature beige and brown.)

In our language we have given specific emotional symbolism to the different color names. Green is associated with envy; blue, with sadness; red, with anger; yellow, with cowardice; and so on. Beyond this, we think of colors as having different "temperatures," as suggested earlier. Red and orange are thought of as being "warm" colors, perhaps because of their association with fire, sunsets, and the like. Conversely, blue and green are considered "cool."

An artist choosing colors for a particular work will expect those colors to have some emotional impact on the viewer, an impact that supports the intent in that work of art. We can see this by comparing two paintings with very

above: **128.** Georges Seurat. *Une Baignade*, detail.

right: **129.** Georges Seurat. *Une Baignade.* 1883–84. Oil on canvas, 6'7" × 9'10½". National Gallery, London (reproduced by courtesy of the Trustees).

different emotional qualities. Both paintings show figures floating in a swirling space, but here the resemblance stops.

Jean-Honoré Fragonard's *Bathers* (**130**) is a masterpiece of the mid-18th-century style known as Rococo (Chapter 16). Fragonard's work celebrates an ideal of frivolous, light-hearted love, frolicking play, and gentle sensuality. No serious concerns intrude in this artist's world. His people might have moved straight into adulthood from the nursery and simply incorporated the pleasures of the flesh into their play. Nearly all the colors in the painting are soft pastels, with special emphasis on abundant pink bodies. The mood is supposed to be light and charming, and Fragonard's colors foster this.

How different is *Incident at the Cafè Tintoretto* (**131**) by the contemporary Italian artist Sandro Chia. Often identified as one of the *neo-Expressionists*

**above: 130.**
Jean-Honoré Fragonard.
*Bathers*. c. 1765.
Oil on canvas, $25\frac{1}{4} \times 31\frac{1}{2}''$.
Louvre, Paris.

**right: 131.** Sandro Chia.
*Incident at the Cafè Tintoretto*.
1984. Oil on canvas,
$8'5'' \times 11'2''$.
Courtesy the artist.

*113*

(Chapter 17), Chia paints simple everyday events and yet gives them cosmic importance. The "incident" depicted here might be an ordinary fight in a café, but it has all the drama of a scene from Dante's *Inferno.* Part of the reason for its impact is the dense, seething composition, but another part is the color. Chia's color absolutely *shrieks* at us, compelling attention with its vividness and "clash." Our emotional response to this work cannot help but be poles apart from our response to the Fragonard.

These two examples should be enough to demonstrate how potent a force color can be in a work of art, just as it is in life. Our next element is also a major factor in the experience of everyday life, and artists have learned to explore its power in art.

## Texture

Texture refers to surface quality—a perception of smooth or rough, flat or bumpy, fine or coarse. Our world would be bland and uninteresting without contrasts of texture. Most of us, when we encounter a dog or cat, are moved to pet the animal, partly because the animal likes it, but also because we enjoy the feel of the fur's texture against our hands. In planning our clothes we instinctively take texture into account. We might put on a thick, nubby sweater over a smooth cotton shirt and enjoy the contrast. We look for this textural interest in all facets of our environment. Few people can resist running their hands over a smooth chunk of marble or a glossy length of silk. This is the outstanding feature of texture: it makes us want to touch it.

### Actual Texture

All the textures referred to above are *actual* or *tactile;* we experience them through the sense of touch. The rougher the texture, the greater is the difference in surface elevation. If we cannot touch these surfaces, as it is forbidden to touch most sculptures in museums, we understand their actual textures by remembering similar objects we *have* touched.

Actual texture in art is usually associated with sculpture, architecture, and the crafts. But many paintings also have actual texture. When an artist lays on the paint in thick layers (a technique known as *impasto*), with some areas thicker than others, the painting may have actual surface texture (**230**). Sometimes, too, an artist may attach three-dimensional objects to a canvas, giving it actual surface texture. More often, of course, the textures we see in a painting are visual ones.

**132.** Jean Dubuffet. *Paysage avec un personnage.* 1980. Black ink on paper with collage, 13¾ × 10″. Courtesy Pace Gallery, New York.

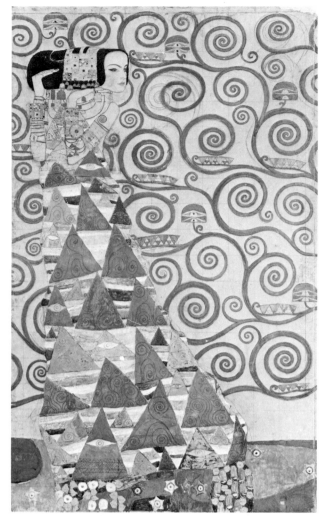

**133.** Gustav Klimt. *Expectation*. c. 1905–09. Mixed media with silver and gold leaf on paper, 6'4" × 3'9⅜". Osterreichisches Museum für Angewandte Kunst, Vienna.

## Visual Texture

Jean Dubuffet's *Paysage avec un personnage* (**132**) illustrates the concept of visual texture. If you could touch the paper, you would find it to be primarily flat. Nevertheless, the eye perceives a texture because of the irregular scribbled lines and the contrasts of light and dark. This work reminds of objects that in fact do have texture, so we apply remembered perceptions of tactile texture to the visual form.

We saw another type of visual texture in Steinberg's *Hen* (**97**). In this drawing Steinberg used ink lines to evoke a tactile texture from the natural world—the feathers of a hen. Throughout history artists have attempted to simulate, on the flat surface of a canvas, natural textures—textures of fur and hair and fabric, for example, or textures of fruits and vegetables in a still life.

A visual texture, therefore, may be aimed at creating an illusion, or it may exist simply for its own sake, to provide visual interest. Either way, the texture helps to enliven a work of art.

## Pattern

As was mentioned in the section dealing with line, pattern is any repetitive motif. There is often a relationship between pattern and certain kinds of texture; when a visual texture is highly repetitive and evenly spaced over an area, we are more likely to call it pattern. A good example is the drawing by Gustav Klimt (**133**). Klimt's subject in this work, a common one for him, is a woman in a long, flowing dress. But the dress has been fragmented into a series of irregular triangles. Only this pattern separates the figure from its background, which consists of spiraling plantlike tendrils. The figure, then, becomes a point of departure for the overall decorative patterns.

Klimt's drawing is full of movement and energy, thanks to the background spirals, which seem to spin like whirlpools. It is meant to be decorative, not naturalistic. You may observe that there is no impression of roundness in this figure, no distinction of foreground and background, no sense of looking through the "window" of the picture area into a real world. Klimt meant his picture to be "flat," but other artists have had very different goals. This brings us to consideration of the most complex visual element—space.

## Space

The word "space," especially in our technological world, sometimes conveys the idea of nothingness. We think of outer space as a huge void, hostile to human life except when protected by complex support systems. A person who is "spaced out" is blank, unfocused, not really "there." But the space in and around a work of art is not a void, and it is very much there. It is a dynamic visual element that interacts with the lines and shapes and colors and textures of a work of art to give them definition. Consider space in this way: How could there be a line if there were not the spaces on either side of it to mark its edges? How could there be a shape without the space around it to set it off?

In this section we will look at the different types of space an artist deals with and how these spaces affect the other elements.

### Three-Dimensional Space

Sculpture, architecture, and all forms with mass exist in three-dimensional space—that is, the actual space in which our bodies also stand. These works of art take their character from the individual ways in which they carve out sections of space within and around them.

Architecture, in particular, can be thought of as a means of carving space. Without the walls and the roof of a building, the space would be limitless; with them, the space has boundaries and therefore has volume. For instance, in a very simple house, say a shoebox-shaped house, the walls and roof create a "cube" of space that could be measured in terms of its volume. If the house is subdivided into rooms, then several smaller cubes of space have been created. The interior of the Solomon R. Guggenheim Museum in New York, designed by Frank Lloyd Wright (**134**), provides a more complex example. Inside the building Wright constructed a huge, bubble-like space enlivened by curved forms cutting in and out, and culminating in the skylight dome overhead. Of course, we could also talk about this structure in terms of its *mass* alone and consider the interior space to be merely passive. But really the space and the mass are equal partners. Neither could exist without the other. What is especially fascinating is the way in which Wright *shaped* this interior space.

Space is also a vital element of sculpture, and this is even true of prehistoric sculptures such as the ancient burial chamber at Pentre-Ifan (**135**). This form is exciting because of the spaces between the stones and especially the open space under the balanced capstone. If you try to visualize how the form would look if all the spaces were closed up by solid rock, you will begin to understand the active role of space in three-dimensional art.

## Two-Dimensional Space

Two-dimensional space refers to the space in a painting, drawing, print, or other type of flat art. As the name implies, this kind of space has only height and width, no depth. There are two major considerations in dealing with this space. The first is the way in which shapes, lines, and other elements are arranged vertically or horizontally within the space. The second is the possibility of visual depth, or the *illusion* of three-dimensional space on a two-dimensional surface.

**Spatial Organization**    Working on a picture surface that is flat and has no depth, the artist has to decide where to place forms in that flat space—high or low, left or right, centered or off to one side. Each time the artist makes a mark of any kind, the space is divided into segments that were not there before.

In Jean Arp's collage *Arrangement According to the Laws of Chance* (**136**) the square forms have been organized more or less evenly throughout the space.

**136.** Jean Arp.
*Arrangement According to the Laws of Chance.* 1916–17. Torn and pasted papers, 19⅛ × 13⅝".
Museum of Modern Art, New York (purchase).

The spaces between squares are similar, as are the top and bottom spaces. Now let us compare the spatial organization in Edgar Degas's *Dancers Practicing at the Barre* (**137**). The two major forms are crowded into the upper-right quadrant of the painting, leaving the rest of the canvas as open space. Why would Degas design such an unusual division of space? Partly because he was influenced by Japanese art, in which asymmetrical balance is common (**253**). Also partly because he was fascinated by the unexpected angle of vision, such as a viewer might catch by peeping in a window or over a balcony. Even with the eccentric placement of the dancers at upper right, the space below and to the left does not seem "dead." Quite the opposite—the daring composition and sharp diagonal bring the whole space to life.

**Illusion of Depth**     In some works of art the artist will try to create on a flat surface the illusion of deep, three-dimensional space, as one might see in a natural landscape. This space appears to go backward in depth "behind" the front surface of the painting, which is referred to as the *picture plane*. When artists establish illusionary depth, they create the impression that some forms in the composition are farther away than others, and that some forms are in front of or behind others in space.

At different times in history and in different cultures there have been several methods used to create the illusion of depth on a two-dimensional surface. One of the simplest of these is *overlapping*. If one form overlaps another, that form appears to be in front of the other one. We see this effect in the mosaic of *The Good Shepherd Separating the Sheep from the Goats* (**138**). The composition is essentially flat with virtually no suggestion of background depth. Still, because the animals are placed in front of the angels and Christ's hand overlaps the angel at our left, we perceive the animals and the Christ figure to be farther forward in space. This picture could be read as having two very shallow planes—one at the picture plane, where Christ and the animals stand, one slightly farther back.

Another device to show spatial depth is *position,* which is especially common in Persian and Indian art. In a Persian painting illustrating the verses of the great 14th-century poet Hafiz, *Dervishes Dancing* (**139**), all the figures are

**137.** Edgar Degas.
*Dancers Practicing at the Barre.* 1877.
Oil, freely mixed with turpentine,
on canvas; $29\frac{3}{4} \times 32''$.
Metropolitan Museum of Art, New York
(H. O. Havemeyer Collection,
bequest of Mrs. H. O. Havemeyer, 1929).

roughly the same size, and the landscape background is more decorative than lifelike. But the figures placed *higher* in the composition are assumed to be farther back in space than those toward the bottom. The audience for whom this painting was made understood the convention perfectly, though it seems unusual to Western eyes. In addition to the placement of the forms, the artist has used some overlapping to foster the sense of spatial depth.

During the 15th century in Italy artists perfected the science of *linear perspective*—the most "realistic" method of portraying in two dimensions the visual depth of the natural world. Although linear perspective can be extremely complex and mathematical, it is based on the application of two sim-

**above: 138.**
*The Good Shepherd Separating the Sheep from the Goats.*
c. 520. Mosaic.
Sant' Apollinare Nuovo, Ravenna.

**right: 139.**
School of Bihzad.
*Dervishes Dancing,*
leaf from the *Diwan.* c. 1490.
Color on paper.
Metropolitan Museum of Art,
New York (Rogers Fund, 1917).

horizon

vanishing
point

one point
linear perspective

one point
linear perspective

square in linear perspective

square in isometric perspective

two point
linear perspective

isometric perspective

**140.** Sketch of linear
and isometric perspective.

ple, observable phenomena: First, forms that are far away from the viewer seem smaller than those that are close up. Second, parallel lines receding into the distance seem to converge, until they meet at a point on the horizon line where they disappear. This point is known as the *vanishing point*. You can visualize this second idea if you remember gazing down a straight highway. As the highway recedes farther from you, the two edges seem to come closer together, until they disappear at the horizon line (**140**). All linear perspective is a translation into drawing principles of these two ideas.

Renaissance artists took up linear perspective with as much delight as a child takes up a new toy. For the first time in the history of civilization (as far as they knew) they could depict absolutely naturalistic scenes, and this was an important goal at the time. Several paintings were done as academic exercises to test the new science of perspective, including *View of an Ideal City* (**141**). In this work the ground lines, the facades of the buildings, the roof lines, and the protruding architectural elements recede in a perfectly contrived scheme toward a vanishing point somewhere behind the circular building. Also, the buildings get smaller and smaller as they go back into space.

Linear perspective may seem "correct" to our eyes because of our experience with photographs; many photographs, especially of architecture, look much like a drawing in careful linear perspective (**142**). Nevertheless, it is not the ultimate key to perfect art, as some Renaissance artists thought. This per-

**top: 141.** Piero della Francesca and Luciano Laurana. *View of an Ideal City.* c. 1460. Tempera on panel, 1'11⅝" × 6'6¾". Galleria Nazionale della Marche, Palazzo Ducale, Urbino.

**left: 142.** Berenice Abbott. *Exchange Place.* Photograph. Courtesy the artist.

spective works only if the viewer stands motionless and fixes his or her eyes (or, even better, one eye with the other closed) on a particular spot. For this reason the results of academically perfect linear perspective may seem static and lifeless—much like the *Ideal City*, which reminds us less of a living metropolis and more of a ghost town abandoned after some catastrophe. Expanding the perspective to include two or more vanishing points (**140**), a more complex form of perspective, helps to give a more vital image, but the results may still be rather rigid. Linear perspective is only one of many tools artists can use when they wish to portray three-dimensional space.

In Eastern art linear perspective has played much less of a role. Instead, artists often have relied on a system of *isometric perspective,* in which distant forms *are* made smaller, but parallel lines do not converge. The Shinto shrines depicted in the *Kumano Mandala* (**143**) might be considered the Japanese equivalent of a Renaissance "ideal city." As usual in isometric perspective (**140**), lines that would be perpendicular to the picture plane are drawn as sharp diagonals. Whereas linear perspective turns the square into a trapezoid, isometric perspective turns the square into a parallelogram. Architects and industrial draftsmen often use this type of perspective for their drawings, because it allows them to indicate accurate measurements.

In conjunction with linear or isometric perspective, the artist may employ the device of *atmospheric perspective.* This means that forms meant to be perceived as far in the distance are blurred, indistinct, and misty—much as the eye perceives distant forms in nature. You can see something of this effect in the *Kumano Mandala* and in many landscape paintings reproduced throughout this book.

**left: 143.** *Kumano Mandala*, Japan. Kamakura Period, c. A.D. 1300. Color on silk, 4'4¾" × 2'3⅜". Cleveland Museum of Art (purchase, John L. Severance Fund).

**above: 144.** Andrea Mantegna. *Dead Christ.* After 1466. Tempera on canvas, 26¾ × 31⅞". Brera Gallery, Milan.

When linear perspective is applied to human or animal forms or to objects receding into depth, the result is called *foreshortening*. Literally, the body, or part of it, is "shortened" from its normal vertical height to better convey the appearance of figures that are perpendicular to the picture plane. A classic example of foreshortening is Andrea Mantegna's *Dead Christ* (**144**). If you could lift this figure out of the painting and stand it upright, its proportions would seem very strange indeed. The legs are far too short for the body, and the entire figure would be absurdly short compared to its breadth. Mantegna's composition, however, seems entirely believable given the unusual angle of vision. And his choice of this angle makes the body of the dead Christ all the more poignant and vulnerable.

The aim of all perspective systems, including the device of foreshortening, is to create the impression of realism. Yet once the artist has the *ability* to convey the idea of depth on a flat surface, the question remains, how much sense of depth does he or she want in any given work? Most Renaissance artists would have answered this question by saying "the more the better," the more depth in a painting, the better the artist has succeeded. Later artists, however, have had many different goals, and illusion of depth is only one of them.

The space in Romare Bearden's *Miss Bertha & Mr. Seth* (**145**) is almost entirely flat. The figures stand flush at the picture plane, and the backdrop pushes up very close behind them. Moreover, the figures themselves have no full-bodied roundness; they are more like paper dolls or the large cardboard cutouts one might see in a shop window. Only in the extreme right-hand side of the composition has Bearden given us a suggestion of depth. We see a hint

**145.** Romare Bearden.
*Miss Bertha & Mr. Seth.* Collage.
Private collection, New Jersey.

# Suzanne Valadon
## *1867–1938*

In 1867, in a small town in central France, was born an illegitimate child named Marie-Clémentine Valade. When Marie was three years old her mother brought her to Paris, where they lived in extreme poverty, subsisting on vegetables discarded as garbage at the market. Little Marie worked as a laundress and, later, joined a circus as animal rider and trapeze artist. At the age of eighteen she, in turn, gave birth to an illegitimate child, who would become the painter Maurice Utrillo. During her childhood she taught herself to draw—first with cinders given to her by a coal-hauler, then with whatever drawing materials she could find. After an accident at the circus, she became an artist's model, posing for Degas, Renoir, and the young painter Henri de Toulouse-Lautrec. The latter formed a friendship, perhaps a romance, with Marie, and is said to have given her a new name—Suzanne Valadon.

Although she never had a formal lesson, Valadon received much encouragement from her artist-patrons, whose work she was able to study at close range. She began to paint, and then to make prints. By the time she was twenty-eight she had had her work exhibited by an important dealer and had sold many drawings and etchings. Some compared her painting to that of Paul Gauguin, whom she much admired, yet always she retained an originality and reliance on her own instincts, especially in her use of the bold, definitive outline.

In 1894 Valadon took up with a rich banker, Paul Mousis, and spent the next fourteen years living as his wife—they never married legally—in a large house in the Paris suburbs. Despite the slightly scandalous nature of their unwed relationship and the presence of Valadon's illegitimate (and alcoholic) son, this proved to be the *least* bohemian period in her colorful life. Valadon continued to work and to exhibit, and she taught Maurice to paint, apparently in the hope that it would help him to overcome his alcoholism. But in 1908 Valadon herself slipped back into what most people considered a bohemian life style. She fell in love with a young painter, André Utter, a friend of Maurice's twenty-one years her junior, and went to live with him. On one occasion the three—Valadon, Utter, and Utrillo—held a joint exhibition in Paris, but the public was more interested in the trio's sins than in their art.

Toward the end of her life Valadon achieved some measure of fame and considerable financial security. Until her last year she continued to paint and to show, in both solo and joint exhibitions. Indeed, death came, in the form of a stroke, while she was at her easel working on a new painting. The mourners at her funeral included virtually the whole Paris art community, among them Picasso.

Certainly the details of Valadon's life are interesting, and they mark her as a genuine individual. In her life, as in her art, she followed her own path, copying no one, offering no explanation. She seldom spoke, and never wrote, about her art, but one comment that was recorded seems to sum up her faith in her own vision: "I don't understand the experts, neither their explanations, nor their comparisons. When they speak of technique, balance and values they simply make me dizzy. Only two things exist for me and all others who paint: good pictures and bad pictures, that's all."[3]

---

Suzanne Valadon. *Self-Portrait.* 1927.
Oil on wood, $24\frac{1}{2} \times 19\frac{3}{4}''$. Courtesy Paul Petrides, Paris.

**146.** Suzanne Valadon. *Reclining Nude.*
Oil on canvas, $23\frac{5}{8} \times 31\frac{11}{16}''$. Metropolitan Museum of Art,
New York (Robert Lehman Collection, 1975).

of a deep landscape, but this serves to make the space of the entire work even more complicated. Bearden knows how to draw deep space, but in this case he chooses not to. He stands his figures flat at the front of the canvas, thereby giving them an importance and a dignity they might not have had were they worked into a conventional landscape.

The French artist Suzanne Valadon also knew how to draw deep space, but for her *Reclining Nude* (**146**) she has chosen to keep the space of the painting quite shallow. The figure is posed rather awkwardly on a too-small sofa, with legs crossed and one arm clutched across the breast in a self-protective gesture. This model presents herself for our inspection, but at the same time she pulls away and keeps to herself. Valadon has outlined the figure in a strong black line and concentrated especially on the powerful volumes of thigh and belly and upper arm. But the most fascinating aspect of this painting is its claustrophobic space. We as viewers seem to be very close to the model, who is hemmed in on three sides by the sofa. The tight space creates a tension, a psychological confrontation, between the viewer and the model. She is naked but private; the viewer is perhaps embarrassed and sympathetic, surely intrigued.

So we see that pictorial depth, or the lack thereof, is a powerful tool that an artist can use for whatever effect is desired. Once the skill is acquired, the possibilities are endless. Yet no matter how skilled the artist, it is not possible to make a painted scene look exactly like a real scene for one simple reason: Our world does not stand still. At every moment there is the sense of passing time, the sense of movement. Some works of art, however, do deal in the realms of time and motion. We turn finally to a consideration of these two factors.

**147.** Le Corbusier. Notre-Dame-du-Haut, Ronchamp, exterior.     **148.** Le Corbusier. Notre-Dame-du-Haut, Ronchamp, interior.

## Time and Motion

The ancient Egyptians undoubtedly would have been puzzled to find time and motion included in a discussion of art. In Egyptian culture, and in many others, art was supposed to be time*less*, motion*less* for all eternity. Our own world, however, is considerably more dynamic. Most of us, especially in the industrialized nations, are obsessed with time, and motion is a fact of everyday life. Both time and motion have come to be recognized as important elements in art.

### *Elapsed Time*

In the three-dimensional arts, especially sculpture and architecture, time is always a factor in the observer's reaction. When you walk through a building or walk around a sculpture, your viewpoint changes with every split second that elapses. Usually, you *cannot* experience every aspect of the structure from one vantage point or at one moment. You must expend time to accumulate all the different points of view and assemble them into an understanding of the whole. The architects of the great cathedrals knew this, and so did the architect of one of the great modern churches.

Set high in the Vosges Mountains of eastern France, near Switzerland, is the Chapel of Notre-Dame-du-Haut (Our Lady on High), designed by the contemporary architect known as Le Corbusier. The little church sits atop a pinnacle, overlooking the town of Ronchamp (**147**). There is only one access road, so the visitor's viewpoint while approaching the church is controlled at every turn. Having reached the summit, the visitor finds no obvious entrance to the church on the facing side, and so must walk all around to enter. The exterior of Notre-Dame-du-Haut is endlessly unpredictable. Each new viewpoint, each moment of elapsed time, brings a different perspective.

The inside of the chapel (**148**) is equally unusual. Irregular openings cut into the thick walls admit light according to a constantly changing pattern—a pattern affected by time during the day. No one vantage point will reveal

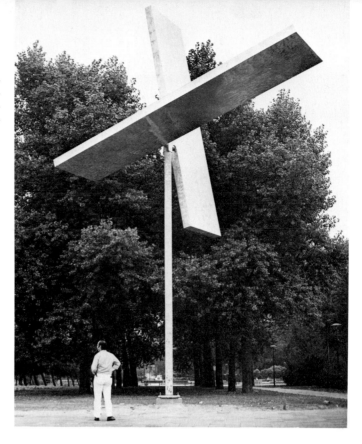

**149.** George Rickey.
*Two Rectangles Vertical Gyratory.* 1969.
Stainless steel, height 45'.
Collection City of Rotterdam.

everything about the chapel. The visitor must walk around, move from spot to spot, draw closer and then pull away to get a full sense of the building's architecture. Notre-Dame-du-Haut is as much a masterpiece of time as it is of mass and space and light.

## Actual Motion

When time is a factor in art, it is often assumed that the viewer is in motion. In some cases, however, the work of art is also in motion. One sculptor whose special preoccupation has been forms in motion is George Rickey. In any Rickey sculpture the shape of the object is less important than the movements that may be produced by that shape. *Two Rectangles Vertical Gyratory* (**149**) floats above the streets of Rotterdam, its two rectangular slabs set in constant, nonrepetitive motion by the wind. The balance of these slabs makes them receptive to any passing breeze, but no one can predict exactly what configuration they will take at any moment. Their polished surfaces reflect light from above, the street scene from below, in an ever-changing pattern.

## Illusion of Motion

Just as artists have long attempted to create the illusion of deep space on a flat surface, so have they often tried to create the illusion of motion where there is none, and, as with spatial depth, the artist has a choice. Some works of art are planned to be rather static and motionless and a sense of movement would actually be harmful to the artist's intent. Picasso's *Paulo* (**92**) and Valadon's *Reclining Nude* (**146**) both fit this category. In other cases a sense of movement contributes much to the success of the work. Géricault's *The Raft of the Medusa* (**108**) seems dynamic because the artist has created an illusion of the raft plunging through the water, an illusion of motion. We could find many other examples of this situation. Indeed, in Gustav Klimt's drawing (**133**) the illusion of motion—caused by the repetitive pattern of spirals that seem to spin—becomes one of the most important elements in the composition.

below: 151. Andy Warhol.
*Superman,* from the series *Myths.* 1981.
Silkscreen, 38″ square.
Courtesy Ronald Feldman Fine Arts, New York.

above: 150. Bridget Riley. *Current.* 1964.
Synthetic polymer paint
on composition board, 4′10⅜″ square.
Museum of Modern Art, New York
(Philip Johnson Fund).

The same is true for the two works illustrated here. Bridget Riley's *Current* (**150**), an example of the style known as *Op Art,* has as its theme the illusion of motion caused by optical effects, a direct response by the retina of the eye to lines and colors arranged in certain ways. The lines in this painting are just that—precisely drawn lines on flat canvas—but as we stare at them they begin to swim before our eyes, and the painting actually seems to be in motion. Some viewers have experienced vertigo or even nausea after spending time in front of an Op canvas, so powerful is the effect on one's central nervous system.

Andy Warhol's screenprint *Superman* (**151**) shows another device by which motion can be suggested. The ghost image to the right of Superman's full-color form creates the impression of him streaking through the sky so fast that he registers as a blur. Here Warhol is capitalizing on our familiarity with motion photography (Chapter 9) to present an image of believable motion.

Line, shape and mass, light, color, texture, space, time and motion—these are the raw materials, the visual elements, of a work of art. Some people are troubled by this approach to works of art, taking them apart and putting them back together again like jigsaw puzzles. And how can we justify discussion of the art elements in the face of utterly down-to-earth and commonsensical remarks like Suzanne Valadon's declaration that such analyses made her "dizzy"?

Whether she cared to talk about it or not, Valadon understood the art elements. She had absorbed them into her eye and her hand and her soul as an artist. For the rest of us, a discussion of the elements gives systematic and intellectual order to our aesthetic appreciation of art. With a knowledge of the elements, we begin to understand *why* we love one work of art, why we do not much like another. And then we—along with Valadon—can make intelligent judgments about "good pictures and bad pictures, that's all."

# 5
# Principles
# of Design
# in Art

When an artist sets about making any work, he or she is faced with infinite choices. How big or small? What kinds of lines and where should the lines go? What kinds of shapes? How much space between the shapes? How many colors and how much of each one? What amounts of light and dark values? Somehow, all the elements discussed in Chapter 4—line, shape, light, color, texture, space, and possibly time and motion—must be organized in such a way as to satisfy the artist's expressive intent. In two-dimensional art this organization is often called *composition,* but the more inclusive term, applicable to all kinds of art, is *design.* The task of making all the decisions involved in designing a work of art would be paralyzing were it not for certain guidelines that, once understood, become almost instinctive. These guidelines are usually known as the *principles of design.*

All of us have some built-in sense of what looks right or wrong, what "works" or doesn't. Some—including most artists—have a stronger sense of what "works" than others. If two families each decorate a living room, and one room is attractive, welcoming, and pulled-together while the other seems drab and uninviting, we might say that the first family has better "taste." Taste is a common term that, in this context, describes how some people make visual selections. What we really mean by "good taste," oftentimes, is that some people have a good grasp of the principles of design and how to use them.

The principles of design are a natural part of perception. Most of us are not conscious of them in everyday life, but artists usually are very aware of them, because they have trained themselves to be aware. These principles codify, or explain systematically, our sense of "rightness" and help to show why certain designs work better than others. For the artist they offer guidelines for making the most effective choices; for the observer an understanding of the principles of design gives greater insight into works of art.

It must be stressed that the principles of design are not rules or laws. If they were, nearly every great artist would have been guilty of breaking them at one time or another. They are, as we said, guidelines that apply in most situations. There are circumstances, however, in which an artist may choose deliberately to violate or ignore these guidelines to achieve a particular effect.

The principles of design most often identified are unity and variety, balance, emphasis and focal point, proportion and scale, and rhythm. This chapter illustrates some forty works of art that show these principles very clearly. But *any* work of art, regardless of its form or the culture in which it was made, could be discussed in terms of the principles of design, for they are an integral part of all art.

**above: 152.** Ben Jones.
*Black Face and Arm Unit.* 1970.
Mixed media, lifesize.
Courtesy the artist.

**right: 153.** Stuart Davis.
*Ready to Wear.* 1955.
Oil on canvas, 4′8¼″ × 3′6″.
Art Institute of Chicago
(Sigmund W. Kunstadler
Gift and Goodman Fund).

# Unity and Variety

Unity is a sense of oneness, of things belonging together and making up a coherent whole. Variety is difference, which provides interest. We discuss them together because the two generally coexist in a work of art. A solid wall painted white has unity for sure, but it is not likely to hold your interest for long. Take that same blank wall and ask fifty people each to make a mark on it and you will get plenty of variety, but there probably will be no unity whatever. In fact, there will be so *much* variety that no one can form a meaningful visual impression. Unity and variety exist on a spectrum, with total blandness at one end, total disorder at the other. For most works of art the artist strives to find just the right point on that spectrum—the point at which there is sufficient visual unity enlivened by sufficient variety.

Ben Jones' *Black Face and Arm Unit* (**152**) illustrates the way unity and variety work together. This wall-mounted sculpture consists of several units of a painted masklike face above a decorated arm. We get the impression of a whole personality from each of the units; each face-and-arm pair stands for an entire human being. There is unity in the basic forms—face above arm—and in the spacing of the forms. Yet the artist has provided great variety in facial expressions, decorative motifs, even the direction in which the arms are bent.

How does an artist achieve unity? One way is by holding one or two elements constant and varying the others. Jones, in his sculpture, kept the elements of shape and space constant and varied the lines, colors, and visual textures. Similarly, in Stuart Davis' *Ready to Wear* (**153**) shape is the unifying element. Nearly all the shapes in Davis' painting are roughly geometric, and most are variations on the rectangle or oval. Yet we see great variety in color, size, placement, angle, and overlapping of the shapes. The composition is unified and at the same time excitingly diverse.

Henri Matisse used color to unify *The Red Studio* (**154**). Walls and floor are saturated with a vivid scarlet, and some of the furniture is drawn as though transparent to let the red show through. By this method Matisse pulls together

**154.** Henri Matisse.
*The Red Studio.* 1911.
Oil on canvas, 5'11¼" × 7'2¼".
Museum of Modern Art, New York
(Mrs. Simon Guggenheim Fund).

# Jean Baptiste
# Siméon Chardin
*1699–1779*

**C**hardin's career provides a refreshing antidote to the myth of the passionate, tormented artist. His life was unremarkable, and so were the subjects he chose to paint. His personality, insofar as it has been recorded, seems little different from that of any other hard-working bourgeois of the period. Actually, the most interesting fact about this artist is that he managed to make an extraordinary art out of the very ordinary. Chardin's attitude was businesslike, his paintings luminous, elegant, and almost magical in their perfect composition.

Jean Baptiste Siméon Chardin was born in Paris, the eldest son of a cabinetmaker. He pursued a conventional art-training program, and his first recorded work was an enormous signboard intended to advertise the skills of a surgeon who was a friend of his father's. In 1728 he presented several works to the French Academy, which chose two paintings and elected him a member. Thereafter, his progress as an artist was steady, if unspectacular.

In an age when the fashionable artists were painting frothy visions of aristocratic life and play, Chardin took an entirely different road. His two areas of concentration were the still life and the genre painting—the scene of everyday life—and he stands now as the acknowledged master of both. Eventually his works became so popular that Chardin was kept busy painting copies of them for sale, and engravings after his paintings (done by other artists) were much in demand.

Chardin's personal life was as measured and undramatic as his artistic career, although it did contain its share of tragedy. The artist's first wife, Marguerite Saintard, bore him a son and a daughter, but she died only four years after their marriage, at the age of twenty-six. Nearly a decade later Chardin married again, and this union produced a daughter. Through all the ups and downs of his life, he continued to work methodically. The results, however, were anything but boring, for Chardin created a brilliant expression in areas he carved out for himself.

Too busy all his life to do much but work at his art, Chardin did not leave much of a verbal record. His few recorded thoughts on art may have been adapted from others, but they ring true to him: "The eye must be taught to look at nature; and how many have never seen and will never see it! It is the agony of our lives. . . . Talent does not declare itself in an instant. It is not at the first attempt that one has the honesty to admit one's inabilities. How many attempts, now happy, now unhappy! . . . He who has not felt the difficulties of his art does nothing that counts."[1]

---

Jean Baptiste Siméon Chardin. *Self-Portrait.* 1775. Pastel, 18⅛ × 15″. Louvre, Paris.

the variety of what might be any artist's home-studio—paintings displayed and stacked against the wall, a clock and bureau, drawing and eating utensils. Although the spatial organization may at first glance seem random, we get a strong sense of unity due largely to the color.

Unity is especially important in architecture, because one is working on such a grand scale. Think how unsettling it would be to see a large building in which the parts didn't seem to belong together. Not only the major forms but also the decorative design should contribute to the overall effect intended by the architect. In Moscow, which we often consider to be a stronghold of stern, bureaucratic drabness, stands one of the most delightfully ornate churches in the world, the Cathedral of St. Basil (155). Many domes—some of them called "onion" domes because of their bulbous shape—crown this magnificent structure. The amazing richness of detail makes us think more of a fairy-tale castle than a Christian church. Points and arches, triangles and half-circles and zig-zags, round and square and octagonal shapes—everything the creative imagination can dream up has been lavished on this design. The major factor in pulling it all together is a unifying texture. Although the shapes are riotously varied, their surface texture, which catches the light and casts shadows, creates a harmonious pattern.

The classic exercise in achieving unity-with-variety is the still-life painting. To make a still life, the artist brings together a number of diverse objects having different colors, shapes, sizes, and textures, and arranges them into a pleasing composition. The usual goal is to make these forms belong together, to harmonize with and yet play against one another. Chardin's glorious *Kitchen Still Life* (156) consists of homely objects one might expect to find in an 18th-century kitchen—earthenware jugs, a casserole, a deep cooking pot, a bit of raw meat, some fish, two eggs. Shape is a unifying element here, as most of the forms are round or curves, including the table edge. But beyond this, Chardin has made the curves echo one another, in a gentle, rhythmic motion. For the viewer there is little "stillness" in this still life. Our eyes move up and around and down, following the rounded shapes. Each object is treated as though it were perfect, the most beautiful form in the world, yet all are drawn together in a harmoniously balanced composition.

**155.** Cathedral of St. Basil, Moscow.

**156.** Jean Baptiste Siméon Chardin. *Kitchen Still Life*. c. 1730–35. Oil on canvas, $12\frac{1}{2} \times 15\frac{1}{4}''$. Ashmolean Museum, Oxford.

**157.** Don Eddy.
*Hosiery, Handbags,
and Shoes.*
Acrylic on canvas.
Soarland-Museum,
Soarbrücken,
West Germany.

In a sense Don Eddy's painting *Hosiery, Handbags, and Shoes* (**157**) might be considered a still life, but of a vastly different kind. Eddy works in the *Photorealist* style—a style marked by such precision of detail that the result looks like a photograph. Here he portrays a display of colorful, gaudy shoes and the reflections on the plate glass of the window. Unity comes from the repetition of similar forms in the shop display. Variety is provided by the fragmented reflections of a street scene, which overlay the still life of shoes.

Building unity by keeping one or more elements constant is probably the most common method, but there are others. Another way to achieve unity in a

**158.** Joseph Cornell. *The Hotel Eden.* 1945.
Assemblage with music box, $15\frac{1}{8} \times 15\frac{5}{8} \times 4\frac{3}{4}''$.
National Gallery of Canada, Ottawa.

composition is by *enclosure*. Joseph Cornell devoted most of his career to making box-like structures that enclosed many dissimilar but related objects (**158**). Contained within the boxes, these objects build their own private worlds, apart from the larger world. Cornell collected things, odds and ends, wherever he went. His studio held crates of stuff filed according to a personal system. There were even crates labeled "flotsam" and "jetsam." When making his box sculptures, Cornell would select and arrange these objects to create a *conceptual* unity—a unity of ideas—that was meaningful to him, based on his dreams, nostalgia, and fantasies. This is not sufficient to provide a *visual* unity, and so the boxed enclosure and the smaller boxes within it take care of the latter.

All the works we have looked at so far strike a balance between unity and variety, and this is most often the artist's goal. Sometimes, however, an artist will aim at extreme unity or extreme variety. Andy Warhol's *200 Campbell Soup Cans* (**159**) is an example of the first. No one would question that this composition has unity. What little variety Warhol gives us comes in the different soup names, and this is a subtle variety to say the least. Warhol, like many "Pop" artists of the 1960s, is commenting on the packaged uniformity of our society. He might be saying that we have sacrificed variety for efficiency, in manufacture and in life, so that this is our world—row upon row of sameness.

When a composition is as unified as the *200 Campbell Soup Cans*, there is likely to be a side effect in the automatic achievement of compositional balance. In most works of art, however, balance is more subtle and somewhat more difficult to create.

## Balance

How can a ballet dancer stand, poised on the toes of one foot, with arm and chest thrust out in one direction, extended leg thrust out in the other direction? The answer, of course, is balance. The dancer has instinctively calculated

**159.** Andy Warhol. *200 Campbell Soup Cans.* 1962. Casein on canvas, 6' × 8'4⅛". Courtesy Leo Costelli Gallery, New York.

# Henri Matisse
## *1869–1954*

**H**ow ironic it is that Matisse, of all people, should have provoked a critic to call him a "wild beast," for, while his art may indeed have seemed a bit wild at first, the artist himself could scarcely have been less so. Cautious, reserved, cheerful, a hard worker, a dedicated family man, frugal, painstaking—these are the qualities that describe Matisse. His longtime friend and rival Picasso captured more of the headlines, but the steadfast Matisse created art no less innovative and enduring.

Matisse's father intended him to be a lawyer, but a bout of appendicitis at the age of twenty-one changed his life—and changed the course of all modern art. Henri's mother bought him a box of paints as a diversion, and, for once, Matisse reacted strongly. Much later he said of this experience, "It was as if I had been called. Henceforth I did not lead my life. It led me."[2]

Matisse enrolled at the Ecole des Beaux-Arts in Paris and studied with the painter Gustave Moreau, a brilliant teacher who is said to have told his young pupil, "You were born to simplify painting." After a period of experimentation in various styles, Matisse burst on the Parisian art scene at the Salonne d'Automne (autumn salon) in 1905, when he exhibited, along with several younger colleagues, works of such pure, intense, and arbitrary color that a critic labeled the artists *fauves*—wild beasts. In these early years Matisse did not fare much better with the general public. However, he had the good fortune to attract the attention of certain wealthy Americans who have achieved fame as inspired collectors, including the Stein family (Gertrude and her brothers) and the eccentric Cone sisters of Baltimore.

Considering the period in which he lived, encompassing two world wars, Matisse kept himself remarkably outside the fray. His art did not touch upon politics or social issues. Throughout his life, his favorite subjects remained the human body (usually a beautiful female body) and the pleasant domestic interior. The joys of home life, of family, of cherished objects dominate his expression. In 1898 Matisse married Amélie Parayre, with whom he maintained a contented relationship for many years. Mme. Matisse was lovely, a willing model, charming and lively, and devoted to her husband's career. Their three children all chose art-related lives, Pierre becoming a prominent art dealer in New York.

We think of Matisse as a painter, but he worked in many fields—sculpture, book illustration, architectural design (of a small, jewel-like chapel near his home), and finally in *decoupage*. By the early 1930s Matisse had begun to use cut-up paper as a means of planning his canvases, and a decade later the cut paper had become an end in itself. When he was very old and could no longer stand at his easel, Matisse sat in his wheelchair or in his bed, cutting and arranging segments of pre-painted paper into compositions, some of mural size.

Perhaps it was at the end that he came nearest to his goal: "What I dream of is an art of balance, of purity and serenity, devoid of troubling or depressing subject matter, an art which might be for every mental worker, be he businessman or writer, like an appeasing influence, like a mental soother, something like a good armchair in which to rest from physical fatigue."[3]

Henri Matisse, photographed by Robert Capa.

**160.** Rudolph Nureyev, as Apollo.

his bodily weight so it is dispersed and balanced perfectly around the supporting leg (**160**).

If our bodies were not balanced in standing and walking and running, we would topple over. We have an innate desire for balance and stability. Maybe this is why we seek balance in a work of art, why we feel threatened by instability when it is absent. *Actual weight*, physical weight in pounds, is important in some types of art, such as sculpture and architecture. All art, however, must deal with the concept of *visual weight*. Visual weight refers to the apparent "heaviness" or "lightness" of forms arranged in a composition. When two sides of a flat composition have the same visual weight, the composition is in balance. Let us see how this works by considering the three types of balance—symmetrical, asymmetrical, and radial.

## Symmetrical Balance

Symmetrical balance, sometimes called *formal balance,* means that the two halves of a composition—on either side of an imaginary vertical line running down the middle—form a mirror image of one another. Since the two sides are identical or nearly so, they must have the same visual weight, and therefore they are balanced. The Matisse collage (**161**) is symmetrically balanced; if you were to fold this image down the middle and match the two sides, they would fit almost exactly. Except for color variations, the forms on one side of the center axis are the mirror image of those on the other side.

**161.** Henri Matisse.
*Large Composition with Masks.* 1953.
Collage, paper on canvas,
$11'7\frac{1}{4}'' \times 32'8\frac{1}{2}''$.
National Gallery of Art,
Washington, D.C.
(Ailsa Mellon Bruce Fund, 1973).

**162.** Joseph H. Davis.
*Portrait of James and Sarah Tuttle*. 1836.
Watercolor on paper, 9½ × 14½".
New York Historical Society,
New York.

**163.** Paul Gauguin.
*Day of the God (Mahana no Atua)*.
1894. Oil on canvas, 27⅜ × 35⅝".
Art Institute of Chicago
(Helen Birch-Bartlett
Memorial Collection).

Much the same is true of the folk painting by Joseph H. Davis (**162**). James and Sarah Tuttle, the subjects, have been arranged carefully, in the similar poses, on either side of a table, with the painting centered over the table and the cat centered beneath. Even the rug under their feet has a symmetrically balanced pattern.

Lest you think that symmetrical balance is confined to folk art and abstract designs, let us look at a famous painting by Paul Gauguin, *Day of the God* (**163**). Here the balance is not quite so rigid, but it is nonetheless predominantly symmetrical. The "god" is centered at the top of the composition, with the main figure directly below flanked by two curled-up reclining bodies. In the background paired figures stand at either side of the god. These major forms establish the symmetry and therefore the essential balance.

When you stand with your feet flat on the floor and your arms at your sides, you are in symmetrical balance. But if you thrust an arm out in one direction and a leg out in the other, or take a pose like that of the dancer (**160**), your balance is asymmetrical (*not* symmetrical). Of the two, asymmetrical balance is often considered to be the more interesting and dynamic.

## Asymmetrical Balance

An asymmetrical composition has two sides that do not match. If it seems to be balanced, that is because the visual weights in the two halves are very similar. What looks "heavy" and what looks "light"? Unfortunately, there are no mathematical formulas to follow. The drawing (**164**) illustrates some very general precepts about asymmetrical or *informal balance*:

**1.** A large form is visually heavier than a smaller form.
**2.** A form that is dark in value is visually heavier than a light form of the same size.
**3.** A textured form is visually heavier than a smooth form of the same size.
**4.** A form placed close to the central axis may be visually heavier than a similar form placed near the outer edge of the composition.
**5.** Two or more small forms can balance a larger one.
**6.** A smaller dark form can balance a larger light one.

These are only a few of the possibilities. Keeping them in mind, you may still wonder, but how does an artist actually go about balancing a composition? The answer is unsatisfactory but true: The composition is balanced when it looks balanced. An understanding of visual weights can help the artist achieve balance or see what is wrong when the balance doesn't work, but it is certainly no exact science.

**164.** Sketch showing some of the different factors in visual balance.

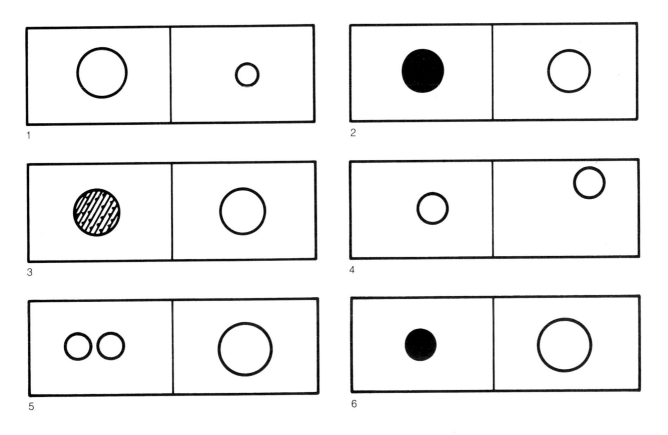

left: 165. Paul Klee. *Costumed Puppets.* 1922.
Ink on paper, mounted on board, $9\frac{1}{2} \times 6\frac{3}{4}''$.
Solomon R. Guggenheim Museum, New York.

below: 166. Photographic postcard, early 1900s.
Gotham Book Mart Collection.

A fairly straightforward example of small forms balancing a large one (#5 in the drawing) can be found in Paul Klee's *Costumed Puppets* (165). The single large form to right of the center axis is offset by two smaller forms at the left. Because Klee was a brilliant draftsman and designer, the balance does not seem static. The lower small figure curves in toward center, and Klee's endlessly inventive pen line animates the entire composition.

A photographic postcard from the early 1900s (166) has much more complicated balance, involving placement, size, value, and several other variables. The man sitting just to right of the center axis provides most of the visual weight in the right side of the composition. Not only is he the largest form and placed close to the center axis, but he is a human being. People attract our attention, thereby gaining a lot of visual weight. To balance this weight on the right, the photographer has made the crescent moon (a large form and light value) curve upward on the left side and also placed the flag on the left. The hat perched on the tip of the crescent is crucial; it finishes the perfect balance. Our eyes are drawn to it immediately because, after all, it's rather silly to have a hat on the point of a moon. If you put your finger over the hat, you'll find that the balance is upset and the composition tilts to the right.

An equestrian sculpture from Africa also reveals an elegant asymmetrical balance (167). The upraised horse's head and longer front legs balance the shape of the rider, who is mounted very far to the rear. Obviously, the Mali sculptor who made this figurine knew that horses do not have much longer front legs, that people do not have arms twice the length of their legs, and that

**167.** *Equestrian Figure,*
Prim-African, Dogon tribe, Mali.
Wood, height 27⅛".
Metropolitan Museum of Art, New York
(Michael C. Rockefeller Memorial Collection,
Bequest of Nelson A. Rockefeller, 1979).

riders do not sit just over the horse's tail. These features have been adjusted and stylized to create a sculptural balance.

At first glance we might think that Dürer's *Reclining Female Nude* (**168**) is out of balance. Nearly the whole figure, and most of its bulk, lies in the right half of the composition. But the subtitle, *Proportion Study,* gives us a clue to Dürer's intent. He was undoubtedly studying not only the proportions of the human body but also the placement of a figure within the picture space. The figure gazes to the left, and we, as observers, follow her gaze. Thus we find a center of interest in the left side of the drawing when nothing is there! In our minds we fill in the blank of whatever the woman is looking at. This is not imbalance but a daring balance created by conceptual rather than visual cues.

Balance in architecture has special importance because of the size of the object. Any flaws in balance will be greatly enlarged and evident to all pass-ersby. Moreover, unlike a painting or sculpture or print, architecture often changes over the years, especially the architecture of houses. A wing may be

**168.** Albrecht Dürer.
*Reclining Female Nude
(Proportion Study).* 1501.
Pen and brush on green paper,
6¾ × 8⅝". Albertina, Vienna.

added, a garage tacked on, a porch removed. With any such changes the balance of the whole structure must somehow be maintained.

Like any other work of art, a building can be balanced symmetrically or asymmetrically. The two houses illustrated here show these different approaches. An 18th-century Philadelphia mansion in the style known as "Georgian" (**169**) is absolutely symmetrical. The entrance opens precisely in the middle of the facade, and windows, chimneys, and all other architectural details are paired on the two sides. Symmetrical balance is thought to give a building stateliness and quiet grandeur. For this reason it has been, and sometimes still is, used for official government buildings. Even a small house seems dignified when its balance is symmetrical.

By contrast, a vacation house in California (**170**) was designed with dramatic, exciting asymmetry. Part of the reason for this was functional. The house is set on a very steep slope; any symmetrical design probably would

**right: 169.** Mt. Pleasant, Philadelphia. c. 1761.

**below: 170.** Michael Moyers. Vacation house near Dunsmuir, California.

have seemed *un*balanced against the slant of the hill, so the architect has considered the landscape as a factor in the design. In this photograph the mass of the facade juts out to the left, and this thrust is counterbalanced by that of the stairway/deck to the right. Asymmetrically balanced structures may seem less formal and more dynamic than symmetrically balanced ones.

We said at the beginning of this discussion that an artist may choose deliberately to violate the principles of design. Occasionally, asymmetrical balance may be carried to such an extreme that the composition appears unbalanced. We find this often in the work of Chinese and Japanese painters. Nonomura Sotatsu's *Zen Priest Choka* (**171**) shows the priest perched in a tree that barely makes it into the composition. In Oriental art as much importance may be placed on what is *not* there as on what is there. The empty space to the right and below may be visually empty, but it is animated by the daring unbalanced design. In looking at this work we feel a tension, a lack of resolution or closure. Imbalance might be compared to someone's starting a story "Once upon a time. . . . ," but never getting to ". . . and they lived happily ever after." We are left feeling keyed up, still waiting for something else to happen.

Another painting (**172**), this one by a Western artist, is balanced (asymmetrically and perfectly) from left to right, but it seems unbalanced vertically. Nearly all the forms appear in the top half of the composition. This is the reverse of what we expect. We are used to gravity, to heavy things being down. In most works of art of all kinds you will find the greatest weight—visual or actual—toward the bottom, so that the composition is firmly rooted in the

**left: 171.** Nonomura Sotatsu.
*Zen Priest Choka.*
Late 16th–early 17th century.
Hanging scroll,
ink on paper, $37\frac{3}{4} \times 15\frac{1}{4}''$.
Cleveland Museum of Art
(purchase, Norman O. Stone and
Ella A. Stone Memorial Fund).

**right: 172.** Ilia Chashnik.
*Floating Suprematist Forms.* 1922.
Watercolor, $29 \times 20\frac{7}{8}''$.
Courtesy Leonard Hutton Galleries,
New York.

**left: 173.** *Baptism of Christ and Procession of Twelve Apostles.* Dome mosaic, Arian Baptistry, Ravenna. c. 520.

**above: 174.** Grant Wood. *Parson Weems' Fable.* 1939. Oil on canvas, $3'2\frac{3}{8}'' \times 4'2\frac{1}{8}''$. Amon Carter Museum, Fort Worth.

ground. Ilia Chashnik's watercolor catches us, quite literally, off balance. We get a sense of the rectangular shapes falling continuously. The forms never actually fall, of course, but against all reason we feel that they are doing so. By using imbalance artists are able to make us see movement where none exists.

## Radial Balance

There is a third possibility for balance, which is more common in architecture and the crafts than in the pictorial arts. Radial balance means that elements in the composition radiate outward from a central point. The most frequent expression of this is the architectural dome (**173**). The dome of the Baptistry in Ravenna, Italy, has the scene of Christ's baptism in the center with the twelve Apostles arranged in a radial pattern around the outside. Radial balance works especially well with a circular format, and it nearly always focuses attention on the central point.

## Emphasis and Focal Point

Emphasis means that the viewer's attention will be centered more on certain parts of a composition than on others. A focal point is a specific spot to which one's attention is directed. Our everyday perception is structured around focal points. Walking down a crowded street, we naturally pick out from the throng the person who is dressed bizarrely; the one person who is exceptionally tall; the person who is waving to attract attention. Not all works of art have a focal point—Warhol's *Soup Cans* does not—but the vast majority do have areas of greater emphasis and one or more focal points. Without them, the composition might seem bland and repetitive, more like a patterned wallpaper or a dress fabric than a work of art.

There are several methods by which an artist can create a focal point or center of emphasis in a work of art. One is by directional lines, as in Grant Wood's painting *Parson Weems' Fable* (**174**). The fable in question is the story of young George Washington chopping down the cherry tree. Although the boy George is one of the smaller elements in the picture, we have no doubt that he is the center of interest. Both Parson Weems and George's father point their fingers at him, so naturally we follow the direction of the fingers. Also, the curve of the drapery at right and the opposing curve of the half-chopped tree frame little George between them. Just in case we still miss the point, the artist has placed George almost precisely in the middle of the composition and given him a white shirt—the only white in the painting. (Although this has nothing to do with emphasis, we might notice for fun that Wood has painted George's head like that of a full-grown man, the Father of his Country, and put that venerable head atop a boy caught red-handed.)

Another device for creating emphasis is the manipulation of light. We see this in Artemisia Gentileschi's painting of *Judith and Maidservant with the Head of Holofernes* (**175**). In this work light is used much as it would be in the theater, to spotlight attention. Gentileschi took her subject from the biblical story of Judith. According to the Scripture, Judith, a pious and beautiful Israelite widow, volunteered to rescue her people from the invading armies of the Assyrian general Holofernes. Judith charmed the general, accepted his invitation to a banquet, waited patiently until he drank himself into a stupor, then calmly beheaded him, wrapped up his head in a sack, and escaped. In the painting the light, apparently coming from a single candle, focuses attention on Judith's upraised hand and on the other arm holding the sword. The gory deed is done, and Judith signals for silence and caution, so she can flee with Holofernes' head.

**175.** Artemisia Gentileschi.
*Judith and Maidservant
with the Head of Holofernes.*
Oil on canvas, 6'$\frac{1}{2}$" × 4'7$\frac{3}{4}$".
Detroit Institute of Arts
(gift of Mr. Leslie H. Green).

# Francisco de Goya
## *1746–1828*

**W**riters on Goya have long been fascinated by the close friendship between him and the Duchess of Alba, the powerful aristocrat whom many considered the most beautiful woman of her time in Spain. It is a measure of this artist's complexity and uniqueness that the haughty Duchess should form a special bond with one who emerged from quite humble origins, whose temperament was often morose and reclusive, and whose imagery could be shockingly gruesome.

Francisco José de Goya y Lucientes was born in a village in the bleak northeast section of Spain. While a young man Goya may have supported himself partially as a bullfighter, but this is one of many unverifiable stories about his intriguing life. By the age of twenty he was in Madrid.

Goya's earliest commissions were for church murals and tapestry cartoons. In 1783 he was launched in one of the two artistic arenas for which he is best known—portraitist to the nobility. Within a few years he was active at the royal court, and in 1799 he was appointed court painter to Charles IV, King of Spain. Some of Goya's portraits, including two of the Duchess of Alba, are exquisitely lovely; others have a darker side to them. According to some critics, Goya's pictures of the royal family, while appearing to flatter, were actually subtle revelations of the subjects' greed, stupidity, and corruption.

Goya's other major field of expression was prints, of which he was an unexcelled master. Two major series, each having about eighty images, constitute the bulk of his work: *Los Caprichos*, in which the many follies of human nature are satirized; and *The Disasters of War*, an often brutally explicit catalogue of the cruelties prevalent in wartime.

Goya achieved both fame and financial success relatively early. While his career prospered, however, his personal life was repeatedly marked by tragedy. His marriage to Josefa Bayeu seems to have been more of a convenience than a passion. She bore him many children—perhaps as many as twenty—but only one survived to maturity. In 1792 the artist was struck by a severe illness that left him almost totally deaf. Another near-fatal illness in 1819 increased his isolation and pessimism; Goya bought a home outside Madrid, known as La Quinta del Sordo ("The House of the Deaf Man"), to which he retired and painted a series of works known as the "Black Paintings," for their dark tonality and aura of despair. After all, the artist's relationship with the Duchess of Alba, whatever it might have been (some maintain that they were lovers), seems to have been one of the few bright periods in his life.

Goya's education was sketchy, and as an adult he read and wrote with some difficulty. An announcement for *Los Caprichos* probably was written with the help of a friend, but it captures Goya's attitude toward his art: "Painting, like poetry, selects in the universe whatever she deems most appropriate to her ends. She assembles in a single fantastic personage circumstances and features which nature distributes among many individuals. From this combination, ingeniously composed, results that happy imitation by virtue of which the artist earns the title of inventor and not of servile copyist."[4]

Francisco de Goya. *Self-Portrait.* 1815.
Oil on canvas, $18\frac{1}{8} \times 15\frac{3}{4}''$.
Prado, Madrid.

Both directional lines and light create the focal point in Francisco de Goya's *Executions of the Third of May, 1808* (**176**). The event Goya depicted was the invasion of Spain by Napoleon's armies and their savage execution of Spanish resisters. Our interest is centered on one heroic but doomed Spaniard, his arms raised in a pose of crucifixion. This tragic figure is bathed in light, while most of the rest of the painting remains in shadow. Moreover, the faceless figures of the soldiers point their rifles at him, and even the stance of their bodies focuses our attention on the victim. Goya's sympathies clearly lay with the killed, not the killers. He therefore chose to emphasize the poignant bravery of one man, to deemphasize the mechanical slaughter by the others.

Emphasis by placement is evident in Grandma Moses' painting, *Hoosick Falls, N.Y., in Winter* (**177**). In this tranquil town landscape Grandma Moses

**above: 176.** Francisco de Goya.
*Executions of the Third of May, 1808.* 1814–15.
Oil on canvas, 8'9" × 13'4". Prado, Madrid.

**left: 177.** Anna Mary Robertson
("Grandma") Moses.
*Hoosick Falls, N.Y., in Winter.* 1944.
Oil, 19¾ × 23¾".
Phillips Collection, Washington, D.C.

has chosen to emphasize the locomotive of the train steaming across the picture. To accomplish this, she has placed the locomotive just on the bridge crossing the river, with the pale blue of the water acting as a contrasting background. The horseshoe curve of the river also helps to direct our attention to the train.

A variation on emphasis by placement is emphasis by isolation. Kliban's Fourth of July parade of cats (**178**) has row upon row of cats in scout kerchiefs marching before a line of spectators, indicated only by their feet. One cat (the Catmaster?) is isolated from the others against a white background, and this leader immediately becomes the focal point of the cartoon.

Emphasis by contrast works much the same way. In Roy De Forest's painting *Let Sleeping Dogs Lie* (**179**) the three spotted white dogs, especially the large one at lower right, provide focal points, because they stand out boldly from the highly colorful background. The dogs are practically the only areas of white in an otherwise riotously colored canvas.

Finally, we should mention emphasis by content. Regardless of other focal devices employed by an artist, certain visual images, when included in a composition, will draw the viewer's attention. Blood and gore attract attention; anything shocking or surprising will act as a focal point. In a figural work the face is nearly always the major focal point, because we are used to looking at people's faces rather than their elbows or hips. And in general, as mentioned earlier, the human figure will tend to draw the viewer's eye.

**left: 178.** B. Kliban.
"July" page from the 1982 Cat Calendar.
Copyright © B. Kliban.

**below: 179.** Roy De Forest.
*Let Sleeping Dogs Lie.* 1979.
Polymer on canvas, 6 × 7′.
Courtesy Fuller Goldeen Gallery, San Francisco.

above: **180.** René Magritte. *La Folie des grandeurs.*
1948. Oil on canvas, $39\frac{1}{8} \times 32\frac{1}{8}''$.
Hirshhorn Museum and Sculpture Garden,
Smithsonian Institution, Washington, D.C.

right: **181.** Morris Hirshfield. *Boy with Dog.*
1945. Oil on canvas, $32 \times 23''$.
Courtesy Sidney Janis Gallery, New York.

## Proportion and Scale

Proportion and scale both have to do with size. Sometimes the two words are
used interchangeably, but there is a difference. *Scale* means size in relation to
some constant or "normal" size. For example, a model airplane is small scale in
relation to a real airplane, or to the usual size for an airplane. *Proportion*, on
the other hand, refers to size relationships between parts of a whole, or between two or more people or objects perceived as a unit. When we see a
skyscraper next to a two- or three-story apartment house, we always notice,
because the two seem out of proportion to one another. René Magritte played
with this idea in *La Folie des grandeurs* (**180**). The three sections of the nude
torso are in different proportions, so they do not fit together at all.
Magritte, of course, used this jarring disproportion on purpose to create an
intriguing image.

There are many reasons an artist may choose to violate normal proportions in a work of art. In Morris Hirshfield's *Boy with Dog* (**181**), for instance,
the disproportion was undoubtedly made to serve decorative purposes.
Hirshfield, known as a folk or "naive" painter, relished decorative pattern.
Here the boy's dog, even if it is a toy poodle (though it looks a bit like a
miniature horse) is much too small in relation to the boy. And the boy's arms,
hands, and feet are far too small for his body. Yet there is a pleasing sense of
flow in the figures of the boy and dog—a flow that echoes the rhythm of the
wave-like background. The boy's tiny right arm curves downward in an arc, is

met by the opposing arc of the leash, and then again by the arc of the dog's body. From head to shoulder to tail we can draw a lovely, undulating S-curve—all of which is mirrored in the background. Similar curving lines move from the boy's hair down through the shirt and coat tails to the legs, and terminate gracefully in the boy's minute feet. If the proportions had been accurate, this decorative effect could never have been achieved.

Disparate proportions can also indicate status—of a religious or political figure, for instance. According to this system, sometimes known as *hierarchical* proportioning, the more important a figure is, the larger will be its size relative to others in the composition. In the watercolor of the *Tathagata Buddha* (**182**), the figure of the Buddha is much larger than the surrounding personages because the Buddha is the most important element in the composition. This work is meant to be symbolic and reverential, not naturalistic, so the disproportion seems fitting.

Since the time of the ancient Greeks people have been seeking the "ideal" proportions in art. Much classical Greek figure sculpture was based on a *canon*, or set of rules, of ideal proportions in which the figure's head was to be one-eighth of the total height, the width of the chest one-quarter of the total height, and so on (**183**). (These proportions would remain the same regardless of the figure's scale.) Similarly, in Greek architecture, vase-making, and presumably painting, proportions derived from what is known as the *golden section*, or *golden mean*. Stated algebraically, the golden mean says that a:b = b:(a + b). Suppose that *a* is the width of a temple and *b* is its length. The ratio

**left: 182.** *A Tathagata Buddha*, from Tibet. 13th–14th century.
Opaque watercolors on cloth, $36\frac{1}{4} \times 26\frac{7}{8}''$. Los Angeles County Museum of Art
(Nasli and Alice Heeramaneck Collection, Museum Associates Purchase).

**right: 183.** *Poseidon* or *Zeus*. c. 460–450 B.C.
Bronze, height 6'10". National Museum, Athens.

of width to length should be the same as the ratio of length to width-plus-length. The drawing (184) shows a rectangle and a segmented line based on these proportions. Undeniably, the visual result is satisfying and appealing.

Proportion and scale must be considered together because they nearly always operate simultaneously. A painting that is, say, 10 feet by 15 feet is certainly large scale; it is larger than most of the paintings we have seen. We must also take into account, however, where the painting is to be hung. If it is hung in a small house, it will be out of proportion to its surroundings. But if it is hung in a huge auditorium, the proportions may be just right.

Scale and proportion can work side by side *within* a work of art. The figures in Nicholas Africano's *Whiskey per tutti!* (185) and the figures in Pieter Bruegel's *Wedding Dance* (186) are all small scale. If you were standing in front

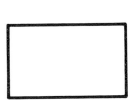

**184.** Sketch of proportions in the Golden Section.

**above: 185.** Nicholas Africano. *Whiskey per tutti!* 1980–81. Oil, acrylic, and Magna on enamel on Masonite; 4 × 7'. Courtesy Holly Solomon Gallery, New York.

**right: 186.** Pieter Bruegel the Elder. *Wedding Dance.* c. 1566. Oil on panel, 3'11" × 5'2". Detroit Institute of Arts (City of Detroit Purchase).

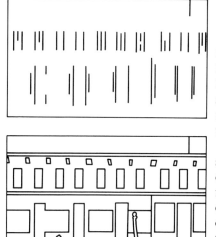

of the actual paintings, the figures would be just a few inches tall. The proportions in the two paintings, however, are quite different. Africano's little people are set in a huge, almost empty canvas, so they seem tiny and lost. They are out of proportion to the field they inhabit. Bruegel's painting has many figures, arranged to fill the composition, so its proportions seem perfectly normal. The reason for this discrepancy lies in the different intents of the two artists. Bruegel was drawing a naturalistic festive scene. Africano is aiming at a grand theatrical image, a vision of tiny people lost on an enormous opera stage. Manipulations of scale and proportion serve both these goals.

## Rhythm

People who are totally deaf can learn to dance. No one is quite sure how they keep time when they cannot hear the sounds, but they do. Apparently, they have some perception of rhythm that is independent of aural cues. All of us are accustomed to rhythm in music, in dance, in poetry (where it is called meter), and in many other aspects of life. Intuitively, we seek this rhythm in the visual arts.

Visual rhythm depends upon the repetition of accented elements, usually shapes. In Edward Hopper's *Early Sunday Morning* (**187**) we find several different rhythms moving horizontally across the canvas (**188**). At top there is the rhythm of the eaves under the roof, and below that the strong rhythmic pulse of the second-story windows alternating with plain wall. At bottom the rhythm of the repeated storefronts counters the two patterns above. Although this is a very repetitive rhythm, we do not find it boring, because there is enough variation of color and light to create interest. The two focal points of fire hydrant and barber pole interrupt the rhythm so it is not stagnant.

The rhythm in Piet Mondrian's *Composition in Blue B* (**189**) is sharp and staccato. Rectangles of color, many of them overlapping, intersperse with smaller black rectangles that act as weaker beats in the pulse. There is so much energetic movement in this composition that it could almost be set to music.

Rhythm is crucial to Van Gogh's *Starry Night* (**190**)—a swirling, swooping rhythm made up of both the pattern of lighted forms and their frenzied circular motion. An important function of rhythm in art is that it keeps the viewer's eye moving through the composition. Nowhere is this more evident than in *The Starry Night*. Our eyes follow the tumbling shapes up, around, down, and back again in a constant motion. Even the vertical tree form at left participates in this, as it carries the eye upward to start the roller-coaster ride all over again.

**opposite: 187.** Edward Hopper. *Early Sunday Morning.* 1930. Oil on canvas, 2′11″ × 5′. Whitney Museum of American Art, New York.

**opposite below: 188.** Sketch of the visual rhythms in *Early Sunday Morning.*

**right: 189.** Piet Mondrian. *Composition in Blue B.* 1917. Oil on canvas, 24 × 19″. Kröller-Müller Museum, Otterlo, The Netherlands.

**below: 190.** Vincent van Gogh. *The Starry Night.* 1889. Oil on canvas, 29 × 36¼″. Museum of Modern Art, New York (acquired through the Lillie P. Bliss Bequest).

**191.** Johnson/Burgee.
Fort Worth Water Garden, Texas.

**192.** Pablo Picasso.
*Girl Before a Mirror.* 1932.
Oil on canvas, 5′3¾″ × 4′3¼″.
Museum of Modern Art, New York
(gift of Mrs. Simon Guggenheim).

As in music, there are different kinds of rhythm in the visual arts. One is simple repetition of regular beats. Another is alternating rhythm—stronger beats alternating with weaker ones, as in Mondrian's painting. A third is progression. Progression means that the visual beats gradually increase (or decrease) according to a definite pattern. We see this in Philip Johnson's *Water Garden* fountain in Fort Worth (**191**). While some of the slab forms are repetitive, others gradually increase in size and/or height to create a sense of progressive rhythm. The water, of course, adds its own rhythm to play against that of the constructed forms.

## Elements and Principles: A Summary

In this chapter and the preceding one we have focused one by one on the elements of art and principles of design, isolating each for individual scrutiny. Every member of the ensemble, so to speak, was brought before the curtain and allowed to take a separate bow. Now, to finish this section, we should put the actors back together, reunite the company into a performing unit. By analyzing one work of art in some detail, we can begin to see how the elements and principles influence one another. It should become clear that we cannot easily talk about one element or principle without involving several of the others. The painting for analysis is Pablo Picasso's *Girl Before a Mirror* (**192**).

In *Girl Before a Mirror* a young woman (at left) contemplates her nude image in a mirror (at right) just at the time when she is entering womanhood and becoming aware of her future sexual and childbearing capabilities. The reproductive organs are therefore prominent in the image. This is a very brief summary of the painting's content. Now let us consider its visual design.

Unity is achieved in several ways, including the predominance of curved lines (**193a**). There are very few straight lines (horizontals and diagonals) but these provide linear variety (**193b**). Unity of shape is particularly important to this work; the circle motif—be it face, breast, womb, or buttock—recurs in a rhythmic pattern (**193c**). The concept of unity with variety becomes clear when we see how straight lines and curved shapes are integrated (**193d**).

Colors are brilliantly varied, but they fall generally in the same range of values and intensities, thus contributing unity. A skeleton of dark, almost black values in both shape and line provides the structure on which the whole picture is "hung" (**193e**).

The balance of *Girl Before a Mirror* is not perfectly symmetrical, but it is generally so (**193e**). Picasso has even provided a vertical line exactly in the center of the composition to divide the two halves. Subtle differences between the girl's body and the mirror reflection enliven the symmetry. There is almost

**193.** Linear analyses of Picasso's *Girl Before a Mirror*.

**193.** Linear analyses of Picasso's *Girl Before a Mirror*.

a pendulum effect as our eyes shift back and forth rhythmically between one side and the other—a pendulum effect enhanced by the curve of the arm.

There are several areas of emphasis in *Girl Before a Mirror*, most of which can be found in the shapes painted with the lightest values (**193f**). Also, the two faces—the white luminous face of the girl and the darker and more menacing one of the reflection—are emphasized by their colors, their placement, and simply by the fact that they *are* faces. Secondary areas of emphasis are the reproductive organs below, shown in a kind of X-ray vision, which gain emphasis by their bright white and by the repetition of the round form. Even with these areas of emphasis, however, it should be borne in mind that the background of this painting is almost as important as the figures. There is no "dead" space, no area of rest for the eyes; every inch of the canvas is important to the artist's expression.

In scale the *Girl Before a Mirror* is rather large, but not unusually so. The proportions are more interesting. Picasso has filled almost the entire space of the composition with the two figures; they jam the picture space from top to bottom and left to right. Also interesting are the proportions of shapes to one another. Small circles and ovals play off against larger and larger circles, to the oval of the mirror image.

Finally, we have alluded before to the rhythms in this work—the rhythm of echoing curved lines, of repeated circular forms, of the pendulum swing from side to side (**193g**). Besides the pendulum swing, there is a figure-8 rhythm that swoops us through the two figures. By introducing these rhythms Picasso has made what might have been a static image—a girl facing a mirror in a flat space—assume qualities of almost dancelike grace.

Picasso had no program when he painted *Girl Before a Mirror*. He did not stand before his easel with a checklist and make sure that all the visual elements had been accounted for in the proper amounts of unity, variety, balance, scale, proportion, and rhythm. He *knew* what he was doing but perhaps could not have articulated it. Being able to articulate these elements and principles does, however, help the viewer to better understand works of art, and to penetrate, a little, the genius of those who make them.

*part three*

# TWO-DIMENSIONAL MEDIA

# 6
# Drawing

Everybody draws. There can scarcely be a person above the age of two who has never made a drawing. Many people take photographs, some paint, a few make sculpture, and a very few may even design a building. But everybody draws. You see a patch of wet sand at the beach, a dusty tabletop, or a blank note pad while you are sitting in class or at a business meeting—and your natural impulse is to draw something, even if it is only a stick figure.

Children begin to draw long before they begin to write, sometimes before they can talk intelligibly, and their drawings give us fascinating insight into the child's perspective on the world (**194**). In drawing far more than in speech, children reveal their fantasies and their fears. Whatever the content, nearly all children draw, which shows how truly universal is this method of expression.

Two qualities often associated with drawing are familiarity and intimacy. Drawing is familiar in that it uses the materials we are all accustomed to—the pencil, the pen, the stick of chalk. There are no mysterious or exotic ingredients. You can pick up a pencil and draw somebody's likeness on paper and so can a great draftsman like Ingres (**198**). Your drawing almost certainly will not look as good as his, but it is the same kind of expression.

Drawing seems intimate because it is frequently—although not always—the artist's private note-taking. Many drawings are not intended for exhibition and therefore are not shown publicly during the artist's lifetime. They may be preliminary sketches for some other work of art or just the artist's refined doodling. We think of such drawings as direct expression—from brain to hand—without the intervening censor of desired public approval. In looking at a sketch by Michelangelo (**195**), for example, we can speculate about what he was actually thinking as he drew those lines.

The drawing illustrated here is a notebook page showing studies for the ceiling paintings of the Sistine Chapel (**39**). When we look at the finished paintings, they seem so perfect that we cannot imagine the forms being any other way. It is almost as though the composition sprang fully realized from

**194.** Bay Baxter, age 6½.
*This Is Bay When She Is Grown Up.*
1979. Colored pencils.

Michelangelo's brush. But, of course, it did not. The artist tried and rejected forms repeatedly, as this drawing demonstrates. Here he is testing various poses for the arm of God in the act of creating Adam, one of the best-known painted forms in Western art. Through the drawing Michelangelo becomes more human to us, as we watch him experimenting, correcting, playing with new shapes. Drawings give a clue to the often agonizing path of genius.

Other factors may contribute to drawing's sense of intimacy. Most drawings are relatively small (compared to paintings), and many are executed quickly. Drawings are often made in great quantities; some artists do hun-

**195.** Michelangelo.
*Arm Studies for the Lord,
and Studies for Angels
in the Creation of Adam,*
preparatory drawings
for Sistine Chapel ceiling. 1511.
Red chalk over black chalk,
8⅜ × 11″.
Teylersmuseum, Haarlem.

dreds of drawings for every "finished" work. There are exceptions to this generalization—drawings that are large and/or are executed with painstaking attention to detail, including several examples in this chapter (**198**, **200**, **203**). But part of the charm of drawing as a medium must surely be the fact that, even when a work *is* intended for exhibition and is finished carefully, it still retains an air of intimacy.

We usually associate drawings with paper, but paper as we know it did not appear in Europe and the Western world until the 12th century. Before that, we must assume, people drew images on any available surface, and most of these drawings have been lost. The oldest artworks we know of are the cave drawings found in southern France and in Spain (**4**). The artists who made these drawings worked directly on the stone walls of caves, and one of the great mysteries about the images is why their makers chose such inaccessible spots, deep underground. Many later cultures had a strong tradition of pottery making, including the ancient Greeks (**450**) and the Mochica of pre-Columbian Peru (**196**). The images drawn on ceramic vessels tell us much about the drawing styles of these early peoples.

According to legend, the Chinese invented paper in A.D. 105. Despite this, they continued to draw on silk, their special material. Other cultures worked on papyrus (a paper-like material made from pressed plant stems) or on parchment (treated animal skins). It was the Moslems who spread the knowledge of paper-making from the Orient to the West. The drawing of a camel (**197**), from a manuscript dated about 1299, shows a typical flat, decorative design, with stylized foliage filling and overlapping the background. The square, or picture frame, was a new idea to these artists and had not yet become an absolute boundary, so the design has been allowed to burst exuberantly outside its limits.

Nowadays, the artist who wants to make a drawing has a dizzying array of surfaces and materials to choose from. Some materials are ancient, while others depend on space-age technology. In this chapter we shall look first at the range of materials used for drawing and the effects each can produce. Then we will consider the unique linear characteristics of drawing. Finally, we will explore the various purposes for which a drawing can be made.

**left: 196.** Stirrup vessel, from Chicama Valley, Peru. Mochica, A.D. 500–700. Ceramic, height $10\frac{5}{8}''$. Metropolitan Museum of Art, New York (gift of Nathan Cummings, 1964).

**right: 197.** *Camel,* miniature in a manuscript, from Persia. 1297–1299. Pierpont Morgan Library, New York.

# Materials for Drawing

Some artists draw almost exclusively in one favorite material, whereas others experiment widely and are eager to try each new medium that comes along. It would be difficult to say how much a choice of material influences the resultant work. Of course, the potential for expression comes from within the artist, not from any substance, but it is nevertheless true that different materials tend to produce particular effects. By "playing" with many tools and papers the artist may be inspired to create new types of imagery.

All drawing media (and, for that matter, all painting media) are based on *pigment*—coloring material in a neutral or some version of a hue that has been ground and mixed with a substance that enables it to adhere to the drawing surface. Drawing materials generally are divided into two categories—dry media and liquid media. The dry media tend to be abrasive. They "scratch" across a paper or other surface, depositing particles wherever they come in contact with the surface. Liquid media, in contrast, have particles of pigment suspended in fluid, so they flow onto the surface much more freely.

## Dry Media

**Pencil**   The graphite pencil, sometimes called a "lead" pencil, probably has made more drawings than any other medium. Pencils are cheap, readily available, and easy to work with. Mistakes can be erased. If the drawing turns out badly, it can be thrown away at no great expense.

In spite of the pencil's humble status, however, some of the most sensitive, elegant drawings we know have been done with graphite pencil. The acknowledged master of this technique was Jean Auguste Dominique Ingres. In the work shown here (**198**) Ingres used the sharp point of a pencil to draw an exquisite portrait of a woman and her daughter. The figures are idealized—cool, pale, reserved, and aristocratic—and the delicate pencil line is perfectly suited for rendering this ideal.

Pencil can also be a warm medium, especially the colored pencils that some artists favor. David Hockney's portrait of *Marinka Nude* (**199**) exemplifies this quality; it is wonderfully vibrant. The artist has reserved his strongest colors for the model's hair and eyes, making her head the focal point. Marinka is naked and thus, we might think, exposed; but she holds her body primly, and her expression is very private. In Hockney's interpretation, the body, the chair, and the background all serve to focus attention on that compelling face.

**Metalpoint**   Metalpoint, the ancestor of the graphite pencil, is an old technique that was especially popular during the Renaissance. Few artists use it now, because it is not very forgiving of mistakes or indecision. Once put down, the lines cannot easily be changed or erased. The drawing material is a thin wire of metal, often of pure silver (in which case the medium is called *silverpoint*), mounted in some kind of holding device, such as a wooden shaft or a modern mechanical pencil. The drawing surface must be specially coated with white poster paint or a similar ground—historically, the coating was bone dust and glue—and the lines produced by the metalpoint are thin and of uniform width.

Metalpoint drawings are characterized by a fine elegance, a finished perfection. Because of the thin, uniform lines it is somewhat difficult to model rounded forms, so artists often highlighted their drawings in white to enhance the illusion of depth, as in Perugino's magnificent *Man in Armor* (**200**). This drawing undoubtedly was meant to be a finished work, not a preliminary sketch. It is as carefully planned as any painting, in its subtle effect of gray line against lovely blue ground.

**Charcoal**   Charcoal's effects are almost the exact opposite of those offered by metalpoint. Where metalpoint produces a thin, delicate line, charcoal's line is dark, sometimes very soft, occasionally harsh. Charcoal is actually burned sticks of

wood—the best quality being special vine wood heated in a kiln until only carbon remains. Charcoal lines can be thin or thick, pale to velvety black. If charcoal is used on a paper with a "tooth," or heavy grain, the results are textured. Honoré Daumier used charcoal to create the drawing called *Fright* (**201**). The undulating charcoal line and repeated form make the figure seem actually to be trembling in fear. No delicate medium could so easily have produced this chilling image.

**Chalk and Crayon**   A wide range of chalks and crayons are available to the artist, and nearly all of them offer color effects. The main difference between them is the *binder*—the substance that holds particles of pigment together. Chalks have nonfat binders, whereas crayons have a fatty or greasy binder, so there is considerable variation in the way these materials react to contact with paper. (If you imagine blackboard chalk and ordinary children's crayons, this difference should be clear.)

**left: 201.** Honoré Daumier. *Fright.*
Charcoal over pencil, $8\frac{1}{4} \times 9\frac{3}{8}''$.
Art Institute of Chicago
(gift of Robert Allerton).

**below: 202.** Georges Seurat.
*Seated Boy with Straw Hat,*
study for *Une Baignade.* 1882.
Conté crayon, $9\frac{1}{2} \times 12\frac{1}{4}''$.
Yale University Art Gallery, New Haven, Conn.
(Everett V. Meeks Fund).

**203.** Dante Gabriel Rossetti. *Jane Burden.*
1858. Crayon, 17 × 13″.
National Gallery of Ireland, Dublin.

The greasier crayons adhere well to paper, but they are difficult to blend with one another for subtle tones and gradations. However, the newer oil-based crayons can be finger-blended almost as easily as oil paints blend. They offer more brilliant colors than children's crayons. Chalks, being drier and more crumbly, blend well and can be overlaid (two or more colors on top of one another) to produce shaded effects.

Crayon can mean anything from the wax crayons used by children through the lithographic crayon meant for drawing on stone in printmaking (Chapter 8). But the commonest drawing material is *conté crayon*—a fine-textured stick medium with an oil binder.

The artist who comes to mind most readily in discussing conté crayon drawings is Georges Seurat. In Chapter 4 we looked at Seurat's painting technique, called *pointillism,* in which tiny dots of color are massed together to build form (**128, 129**). Seurat also did many drawings. By working in conté on rough-textured paper he could approximate the effect of color dots in paint. *Seated Boy with Straw Hat* (**202**) is a preliminary study for Seurat's large painting *Une Baignade* (**129**). Unlike Michelangelo's rough sketches for the arm of God, however, this drawing, along with many of Seurat's studies, is a fully realized work of art. The figure is shown in soft silhouette, blending into the even softer background. It was Seurat's practice to work out his figures very completely as separate units in drawing, and then to transfer them to the painted canvas.

A harder crayon and smoother paper resulted in the much more detailed modeling in Dante Gabriel Rossetti's portrait of *Jane Burden* (**203**). Rossetti was one of a group of mid-19th-century artists known collectively as the "pre-Raphaelites." One characteristic of their art is concentration on a specific ideal of female beauty— thick, flowing hair, enormous eyes, and a pursed rosebud mouth. Jane Burden was the perfect embodiment of this type. In the drawing Rossetti has taken advantage of the precision afforded by the hard crayon, which can produce either a

**204.** Rembrandt.
*A Thatched Cottage by a Tree.* c. 1652.
Reed pen and bistre, $6\frac{7}{8} \times 10\frac{1}{2}''$.
By permission of the Trustees
of the Chatsworth Settlement.

sharp line or a shadowy gray one. He has left the figure and gown pale and only slightly defined, to focus on the model's haunting pre-Raphaelite face.

One other medium that should be mentioned along with the chalks and crayons is pastel. Because it is very soft and offers a full range of colors, pastel is a borderline medium, producing effects somewhere between painting and drawing. It lends itself especially well to the kind of blending of hues that creates gradated tones. The drawing by Edgar Degas (**210**) was done in pastel.

**205.** Vincent van Gogh.
*A Peasant of the Camargue.* 1888.
Quill and reed pen and ink
over soft graphite, $19\frac{1}{2} \times 15''$.
Fogg Art Museum,
Harvard University, Cambridge, Mass.
(Grenville L. Winthrop Bequest).

166

**206.** Alexander Calder.
*The Circus.* 1932.
Pen and ink, $20\frac{1}{4} \times 29\frac{1}{4}''$.
Courtesy Perls Galleries, New York.

## Liquid Media

**Pen and Ink**     Ink flowing onto paper gives a smooth, uninterrupted line. As with other relatively permanent media, such as silverpoint, there is little possibility for correction once the lines have been inscribed. A major variable in the ink drawing, however, is the relative thickness or thinness of lines, which depends on the pen point used. The lines can be all one width, ranging from fine to heavy, or they can vary. A single line may change, perhaps starting as a fine thread, broadening into thickness, and then tapering down again to a slender mark. Such thick-and-thin lines are often referred to as *calligraphic* or *gestural*.

As crayon makes us think of Seurat, pen and ink makes us think of Rembrandt—one of the greatest draftsmen who ever lived. Rembrandt made thousands of drawings during his long career, and he drew almost everything imaginable. But it is his landscapes that perhaps more than any other theme reveal Rembrandt's personal "handwriting." In *A Thatched Cottage by a Tree* (**204**) the curling penwork in the trees and foreground foliage, drawn with a reed pen, is typical of his rapid, sketchy style. The stiff reed point yields a rather bold line with much visual character. We know that trees have leaves, not swirling shapes, and yet ever since Rembrandt this curving line seems to us the very essence of "tree." The drawing may seem sketchy and quick, but the artist has given us a strong sense of forms in space.

Another artist who achieved a distinctive style in pen and ink—quite a different style—was Van Gogh. In *A Peasant of the Camargue* (**205**) the pen marks are short, choppy, and massed together to produce texture. Van Gogh combined a reed pen with the more flexible quill to obtain quite varied lines—fine and thready in the face, heavy in the shirt and around the hat, and stubby in the background. All the splendid modeling in the face is accomplished by patterning of these thick and thin lines. The background texture of dots and tiny strokes makes the figure stand out plainly. Van Gogh made this drawing as a study for a painting, so the different types of pen marks and textures take the place of contrasting colors in the later work.

Still another use of the pen line can be seen in Alexander Calder's circus drawings of the 1930s (**206**). These drawings are related to Calder's thin wire sculptures from that period (**94**), and they are just as economical in form, just as uniform in line as the three-dimensional wires. The artist gives us only the barest outlines of the figures, the minimum needed to show shape and position. This

# Käthe Kollwitz
## *1867–1945*

In a time when the word "artist" usually meant a painter or a sculptor, Kollwitz did the bulk of her work in prints and drawings. In a time when vivid, sometimes startling color was preoccupying the art world, Kollwitz concentrated on black and white. And, in a time when nearly all artists were men, Kollwitz was—triumphantly—a woman, a woman whose life and art focused on the special concerns of women. This combination of oddities might have doomed a lesser artist to obscurity, but not one of Kollwitz' great gifts and powerful personality.

Käthe Schmidt was born in Königsberg (then in Prussia, now part of the U.S.S.R.), the second child in an intellectually active middle-class family. Her parents were remarkably enlightened in encouraging all their children to take an active part in political and social causes, and to develop their talents—in Käthe's case a talent for drawing. Käthe received the best art training then available for a woman, in Berlin and Munich. In 1891, after a seven-year engagement, she married Karl Kollwitz, a physician who seems to have been equally supportive of his wife's career. The couple established themselves in Berlin, where they kept a doctor's office and artist's studio for fifty years.

During her student days Kollwitz had gradually focused on line and had come to realize that draftsmanship was her genius. Her conventional artistic training must have intensified the shock when she "suddenly saw that I was not a painter at all."[1] She concentrated thereafter on drawings and prints—etchings and woodcuts early on, lithographs when her eyesight grew weaker.

Five major themes dominate Kollwitz' art: herself, in a great many self-portraits and images for which she served as model; the ties between mothers and their children; the hardships of the working classes, usually interpreted through women's plight; the unspeakable cruelties of war; and death as a force unto itself. As a socialist Kollwitz identified passionately with the sufferings of working people; as a mother she identified with the struggle of women to keep their children safe.

Kollwitz bore two sons—Hans in 1892 and Peter in 1896. The first of many tragedies that marked her later life came in 1914, with the death of Peter in World War I. She lived long enough to see her beloved grandson, also named Peter, killed in World War II. During the almost thirty years separating those losses, she continued to work prolifically, but her obsession with death never left her.

Few artists have so touchingly described their attempts to achieve a certain goal, and their continual frustration at falling short. In Kollwitz' case, the artistic goals were generally realized, but the emotional and political goals—never: "While I drew, and wept along with the terrified children I was drawing, I really felt the burden I am bearing. I felt that I have no right to withdraw from the responsibility of being an advocate. It is my duty to voice the sufferings of men, the never-ending sufferings heaped mountain-high. This is my task, but it is not an easy one to fulfill. Work is supposed to relieve you. . . . Did I feel relieved when I made the prints on war and knew that the war would go on raging? Certainly not."[2]

Käthe Kollwitz. *Small Self-Portrait, Facing Left.* 1922. Lithograph, $13\frac{5}{8} \times 9\frac{7}{8}''$. National Gallery of Art, Washington, D. C. (Rosenwald Collection).

type of drawing is a kind of visual shorthand, energetic and playful. Calder suggests the huge space of the Big Top by his placement of curving parallel lines. The figures are transparent, as they would be when done in wire, but we have no doubt about their arrangement in space. Only a skilled draftsman can give us so much sense of place with so little.

**Brush and Ink**     The brush has long been the favorite drawing tool of Oriental artists. Because in the East the brush is commonly used for writing, its handling seems as natural there as using a pencil does to Westerners. When the brush is manipulated in the Oriental way, it is the ideal tool (better than a pen) for producing the calligraphic line—thin at the beginning, broadening along its length, and then tapering again to very thin. We see this effect in a marvelous drawing by Wu Zongyuan, *The Procession of the Five Heavenly Rulers* (**207**). No other medium but fluid ink could have yielded these graceful, swirling lines, which give the drawing so much energy.

When ink is diluted with water and applied with a brush, the result is called a *wash* drawing. Käthe Kollwitz used touches of wash and thick, aggressive lines of pure black for the powerful image of a *Fettered Man* (**208**). Kollwitz made a great many drawings, and nearly all of them are in charcoal, a much softer medium. For this figure of extreme anguish she chose the far bolder black ink.

**above: 207.** Wu Zongyuan (attributed by Zhao Mengfu). *The Procession of the Five Heavenly Rulers*, detail. First half of 11th century. Ink on silk. Collection C. C. Wang and family, New York.

**left: 208.** Käthe Kollwitz. *Fettered Man.* 1927. Pen and wash, $17\frac{1}{2} \times 14\frac{1}{2}''$. Private collection, New York.

*Materials for Drawing*     **169**

Kollwitz' drawing shows plainly the interaction between drawing medium and imagery. In this case we might suspect that the artist had an image in mind and selected the medium that would best fit that image. Other times the reverse may occur: an artist experiments with a particular medium and thus is inspired with an image idea.

Artists today have a broad spectrum of drawing media to work with, and they do not limit themselves to the traditional materials we have just described. In this electronic age drawings are made by computer, by video technology, by all kinds of sophisticated equipment (209). But whether the image is made by pencil or by computer terminal, the quality of line remains a vital aspect of drawing. We turn, therefore, to a brief discussion of the different kinds of lines and their effects.

170

# Line Quality in Drawing

Chapter 4 discussed line quality in some detail (pp. 97–98); here we might focus, with just a few examples, on the drawing as a work of art, and how line quality affects it. Our first two examples (**210**, **211**) show the same subject, a nude or partially nude woman arranging her hair, in almost identical poses. Yet how different are the effects of the two drawings. The first, a pastel by Degas, is softly modeled, almost painterly in its subtle shadings that mold the fully rounded form. Modeled lines are usually drawn in very soft dry media, often with the side of a pencil or a piece of chalk. We might not even call these blurred outlines "lines," so gently do they define the contours of the human body. The second drawing, by the great Japanese artist Katsushika Hokusai, is sketched in a few quick calligraphic lines. In spite of this, the second figure seems as full-bodied and round as the first. One deft stroke down the center of the back, combined with the curve of breast and belly, and Hokusai has made us believe in the three-dimensional form.

The soft modeled line and the calligraphic line are but two possibilities for drawing. Another is the contour line. A contour line describes only the outlines of a subject, with no shading and often very few inside details. The line is usually continuous and of unvarying width. We see a good example in Matisse's still life (**212**). Especially fine is the handling of the pears and peaches in the foreground. With the simplest of possible outlines Matisse presents these fruits unmistakably.

So we have seen three of the possibilities in line quality: the soft, modeled line; the thick-and-thin calligraphic line; and the uniform contour line. Although it is not in quite the same category as the other types of lines, we cannot leave out the purely decorative line. Picasso, whose play instinct never left him in his ninety-odd years, delighted in making lines for the sheer joy of pattern and decoration. In *Head of a Man* (**213**) it is difficult to separate the lines defining facial features from those drawn for their own sake. For in-

**left: 212.** Henri Matisse.
*Nature Morte, Fruits et Potiche.* 1941.
Pen and ink, $20\frac{3}{4} \times 16\frac{3}{4}''$.
Musée National d'Art Moderne,
Centre Georges Pompidou, Paris.

**right: 213.** Pablo Picasso.
*Head of a Man in Profile.* 1967.
Ink on paper, $25\frac{5}{8} \times 19\frac{3}{4}''$.
Collection Sandra Rotman, Toronto.

**214.** Elisha Gray.
Drawing for a proposed telephone.
1876. Courtesy Regional
Economic History Research Center,
Wilmington, Del.

*Feb 11- 1876*
*apparatus for talking through a telegraph wire —*

*Line*

stance, which curly lines are hair or beard and which are just curly lines? Many of Picasso's drawings seem like complicated doodles, like the work of someone who says, "Let's start this line and see where it might go."

Simple doodling is one of the many purposes of drawing. Practically everyone does it. When you doodle, your goal may be nothing more than to pass the time or to fill up white space on a page. Like the rest of us, great artists often doodle, but, as we have seen, they also make drawings with specific artistic goals in mind. In the following section we will consider some of these purposes.

## Purposes of Drawing

### Preliminary Study

Many of the drawings reproduced in this chapter—including those by Michelangelo, Seurat, and Van Gogh—were done as preliminary studies for paintings. Before committing time and material to a finished painting, the artist will often sketch and experiment until the form seems exactly right. Artists working in all fields do the same thing. Sculptors, architects, interior designers, printmakers, ceramists, landscape architects, and industrial designers—all make preliminary drawings. Probably you have done this yourself at some time or other. Suppose you decide to build a stereo cabinet or to rearrange the furniture in your room. You may do a few quick sketches to make sure your design is workable.

We need not be concerned with whether the design whose sketch is reproduced here (**214**) would have been workable. Dated February 11, 1876, this drawing, made by an inventor named Elisha Gray, shows a rudimentary type of telephone. Even without considering the scientific principles involved, we find the drawing itself delightful. It is simple and straightforward, like the invention it describes. Unfortunately, Gray's version of the machine never came into use. His patent application arrived at the U.S. Patent Office on February 14, 1876, but only a few hours earlier the office had received a similar application from another inventor, a man named Alexander Graham Bell. A century later we still have Bell's telephones, but we can enjoy the charm of Gray's drawing.

The next drawing (**215**), by the sculptor Henry Moore, is a general exploration of the volumes and masses of the nude female figure—the subject of many of Moore's works. It does not, however, look very much like Moore's finished sculptures (**216**). The drawing is naturalistic, while the sculpture is much more abstract. We can learn a good deal about the process of abstraction

right: 215. Henry Moore.
*Reclining Nude.* 1931.
Brush and wash in sepia,
$9\frac{15}{16} \times 18\frac{1}{4}''$.
Victoria and Albert Museum,
London.

below: 216. Henry Moore.
*Reclining Figure.* 1935.
Elmwood, $19 \times 35 \times 15''$.
Albright-Knox Art Gallery,
Buffalo, N.Y.
(Room of
Contemporary Art Fund).

by comparing the two. As mentioned in Chapter 2, abstraction is always based on forms from the natural world. Clearly Moore understands the forms of the human body thoroughly. Once he has mastered them—by studying the volumes and weights and interplay of parts—he can show them to us in a new way, as in the sculpture.

Architects use drawing throughout the process of designing a building. At the beginning they may make very rough sketches, which they gradually refine as the idea takes shape. They may also make detailed sketches of certain parts of the building. Finally they make a finished drawing for presentation to the client, to sell the idea. Most architects get by with basic drafting skills, but a few have delighted in drawing for its own sake. One such architect was Frank Lloyd Wright. Wright liked to work in colored pencils, and he nearly always sketched in much of the landscape surrounding the proposed building, in keeping with his belief that a structure should be integral with its environ-

# Henry Moore
## b. 1898

**O**n the occasion of Henry Moore's eightieth birthday, art critic John Russell wrote that "it is a great thing to be before the public uninterruptedly for the best part of half a century and still stand up, erect and uncontaminated, as a completely honorable human being."[3] Few people would argue with Russell's assessment. If fate smiles on certain individuals, Moore is surely one of them, but one cannot begrudge this "completely honorable" man having enjoyed rich talents as a draftsman and sculptor, international fame, a warm and loving family, respect from his friends, and a long, productive life.

Born in a small mining town in the north of England, Moore was the seventh child of a miner and his wife. Quite early he settled upon the career of sculptor as his goal. ("When I was 11, I was in Sunday school and I heard a story about Michelangelo. I can't remember the story, but what I retained was that Michelangelo was esteemed the greatest sculptor who ever lived. That unremarkable bit of information moved me, then and there, to decide to become a sculptor myself."[4]) After a brief stint in the army during World War I, Moore entered art school in the city of Leeds and first encountered modern art in a private collection there. Later he moved on to London's Royal College of Art.

Henry Moore was no overnight sensation; the type of sculpture he made was too new, too innovative for the public at large to accept. During the 1920s and 1930s Moore patiently laid the groundwork for what would become a world-class career. He worked steadily, exhibited often, taught first at the Royal College and later the Chelsea School of Art. In 1929 he married Irina Radetzky, a painting student, to whom he has remained happily wed all his life. (Their daughter Mary was born in 1946.)

The year 1940 marked something of a turning point for Moore. England was at war, and he became an official war artist. His drawings of Londoners huddled in shelters to escape the Nazi bombing raids have become famous, both because of their unique circumstances and because the artist's sensitive rendering turned the act of hiding underground into a heroic gesture. The English people never forgot that it was Moore who showed them so poignantly in their "finest hour." After the war he was recognized as one of England's foremost artists, and his stature thereafter increased steadily.

Whether in stone or wood or metal, Moore's sculptures have continued to focus on three great themes: the family group (or mother and child), the reclining female figure, the form within a form. These sculptures are in the collections—and often adorn the outsides—of the world's great museums. And always this prolific artist has drawn, both for study and for drawing's own sake.

Reflecting on a lifetime devoted to art, Moore seems to have retained the joy and excitement that motivated a little boy who learned about Michelangelo: "Art is not practical, and shouldn't be practical. Art is not to earn a living. It's to make the difference between us and animals, like cows. I mean a cow doesn't stop and look at a field and say, isn't it a beautiful green. Painting and sculpture . . . are there to make life more interesting, more wonderful than it would be without them."[5]

Photograph of Henry Moore, 1980.

ment. His project drawing for a hunting lodge at Lake Tahoe (**217**) is almost as lyrical as a Chinese landscape painting. Wright has sketched this tree-house-among-trees as though the house had simply grown there, just like any other natural element. Typical touches are the bird in the upper left and the woman with a parasol faintly visible at the far right. For this master builder, at least, drawing was not only a means to an end but an end in itself.

What was true of Wright is true for many artists. A drawing that is preliminary to something else is not necessarily trivial or hasty. For any artist who enjoys the act of drawing, each drawing is potentially a perfect work of art.

## Illustration

Another purpose for drawing is illustration, and this field is enormous. Illustrations are made for books, for magazines, for newspapers, for advertising, for fashion displays. Before the advent of the camera, drawn illustrations were the only kind available. Illustrators today still make drawings to record events where the camera is not permitted, such as at many courtroom trials.

One of the most famous illustrators of all time was the 19th-century English artist Aubrey Beardsley. Beardsley was a fascinating character who achieved international recognition by the age of twenty, was enormously productive, and died of tuberculosis at twenty-six. His style is distinctive, bringing together elements of the erotic and the grotesque with the curving decorative patterns of plant and flower forms. The style has influenced many later illustrators but has never quite been imitated. Beardsley's illustrations for books and magazines (**218**) have strong contrasting areas of black and white. The drawing is broad and exaggerated—in this example almost a caricature. Like any great illustrator, Beardsley went beyond the story he was illustrating to create a whole new world from his own imagination. Once you get to know Beardsley's style, you cannot fail to recognize it. For an illustrator, the style, the personal view of the world, is all important.

There are two major areas in which drawn illustration has never given way to the camera but is still used extensively—fashion illustration and the

**left: 217.** Frank Lloyd Wright.
Project drawing for Hunting Lodge,
Tahoe Summer Colony,
Lake Tahoe, Calif. 1923.
Pencil and colored pencils
on tracing paper, $21\frac{7}{8} \times 15\frac{1}{8}''$.
Copyright ©
The Frank Lloyd Wright
Foundation, 1957.

**right: 218.** Aubrey Beardsley.
Cover design for *The Forty Thieves*.
Pen and black ink,
brush and black chalk; $9\frac{7}{16} \times 7\frac{13}{16}''$.
Fogg Art Museum, Harvard University,
Cambridge, Mass.
(Grenville L. Winthrop Bequest).

illustration of children's books. Both fields have enjoyed unwavering popularity, and their styles have kept pace with other types of art.

The fashion drawing (**219**) may not give you an exact picture of what, for example, a particular hat looks like, but it captures a certain tone, an impression that the woman who might buy such a hat would like to achieve. Fashion merchandising is, after all, based on fostering an illusion—an illusion that the buyer will look as good as the model—and drawings help to preserve that illusion.

Illustration for children's books has been greatly influenced by the innovative work of Maurice Sendak. Sendak's drawings are not the gentle, benign images that several previous generations had thought appropriate for children. Sendak draws monsters, monsters who dwell somewhere between the naughty and the truly wicked. In his book *Where the Wild Things Are* (**220**) the artist gives concrete form to the dreadful creatures that inhabit children's fantasies. Some critics have attacked the drawings as being too frightening for children. Others suggest that the drawings have psychological value, in that Sendak's stories allow children to confront their monsters and conquer them.

**above: 219.** Harvey Boyd. Fashion drawing for *The New York Times Magazine,* April 15, 1979.

**top: 220.** Maurice Sendak. Drawing from *Where the Wild Things Are.* 1963. Courtesy Harper & Row Publishers, Inc., New York.

**right: 221.** "Does it strike anyone else as weird that none of the great painters have ever been men?" Drawing by Lorenz; © 1980, The New Yorker Magazine, Inc.

*"Does it strike anyone else as weird that none of the great painters have ever been men?"*

From the audience, however, there has never been any argument. Children love the drawings, scary though they be.

There is one more type of drawing associated with illustration—the cartoon. Cartooning is a terrifically demanding art. Most cartoons have specific narrative content, which may be amusing, dramatic, satirical, political, or a combination of these. The artist has to convey this content in one drawing, or, in the case of a comic strip, in a few economical drawings. If the cartoon has a caption, it too must be economical. Perhaps more than any other art, the cartoon must live up to the old saying, "One picture is worth a thousand words." By the clever marriage of a few words and an image, the cartoonist may clarify a very complex idea (**221**).

## Expression

All drawings are made for the expression of the artist, regardless of any other purpose they might serve, and self-expression was a key motivation for most of the drawings we have seen in this chapter. Artists record on paper what they see, in the unique way they see it. Drawing is just one way in which the imagination takes concrete form.

Contemporary artists have expanded the potential for expression in drawing, as in every other artistic medium. For example, the work by Larry Rivers (**222**), which most people would call a painting, actually contains a great many areas that qualify as drawing, including the sketch of a painting by Rembrandt at center right. To make this intricate, combination work of art, Rivers obviously dipped into his own sketchbook, choosing drawings that pleased him and that had some meaning for his overall concept. Above all, this work shows us that the line between drawing and painting—at least for some artists—has all but disappeared.

With the work of Jonathan Borofsky we have come full circle from the cave drawings of earliest history. Borofsky draws directly on the walls of a room, and his images are those remembered and recorded from dreams (**223**). Many historians speculate that the cave artists as well were recording dreams, and their surfaces too were the walls around them. In bypassing conventional surfaces, such as paper, Borofsky shows us that drawing today need accept no limits, no restrictive sizes or shapes. Drawing is so much a natural impulse that it can be around us and among us in the most natural way.

**left: 222.** Larry Rivers.
*Golden Oldies 60's.* 1977–78.
Acrylic and mixed media on canvas,
8'10" × 12'.
Collection Jeffrey H. Loria, New York.

**right: 223.** Jonathan Borofsky.
Installation on four walls, floor,
and ceiling, Venice Biennale, 1980.
Mixed media, wall height 20'.
Courtesy Paula Cooper, Inc., New York.

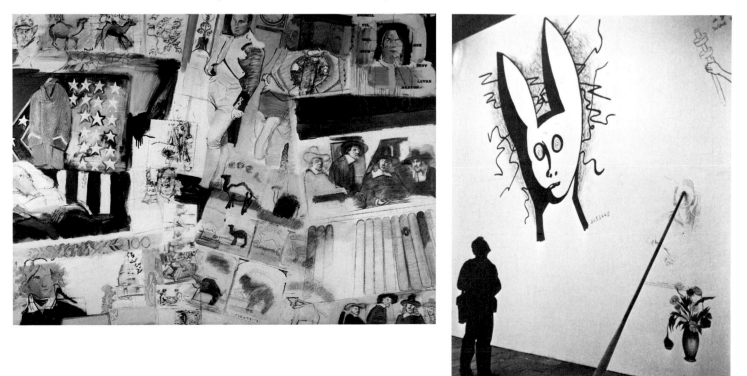

# 7
# Painting

Painting is the queen of the arts. Ask ten people to form a quick mental image of "art," and nine of them are likely to visualize a painting on a wall. There are several reasons for the prominence of painting. For one thing, paintings usually are full of color, and—as was noted in Chapter 4—color is a potent visual stimulus. For another, paintings often are framed, some quite elaborately, so that one has the impression of a very precious object set off from the rest of the world for our visual excitement. Even without a frame a painting may seem a thing apart—a focus of energy and life, a universe unto itself. Whatever the painting shows, it establishes its own visual scope, sets its own rules.

If we consider some of the earliest cave images, especially the more elaborate and colorful ones, to be paintings, then the art has been practiced for at least twelve thousand years. During that long history the styles of painting have changed considerably, as have the media in which paintings are done— the physical substances the painter uses. In the latter case it might be more accurate to say broadened, rather than changed, for few media have been completely abandoned while many new options have been added to the painter's repertoire.

To begin this discussion of painting, we should define certain terms crucial to the understanding of how, physically, such a work of art is put together. As with drawing media (Chapter 6), the color element in paint is the *pigment*, which consists of natural or synthetic color particles. Pigments usually come in the form of a powder, which by itself cannot be spread or made to adhere to the painting surface.

The *medium* or *binder* is the substance in which the pigment is suspended. ("Suspension" here means that the particles are mixed with a liquid or semi-liquid material without dissolving or changing chemically.) Linseed oil—as in oil paint—is possibly the best-known medium, but there are many others. A successful medium allows the painter to spread the colors on a surface as desired and, when it dries, adheres securely to the surface. The name of the medium of a particular work is often used to describe the work: an oil painting, a watercolor painting, and so on.

The *solvent* or *vehicle* enables the artist to thin the paint so as to control its flow and also to clean the brushes. A solvent is selected according to whether the paint is *aqueous* (water-solvent) or *nonaqueous* (dissolved by other than water). Most of us are familiar with the distinction used for house paints—water-base or oil-base. For water-base paints you can wash the brushes with tap water, but for oil-base paints you need turpentine. Much the same distinction applies to artists' paints.

Finally, there is the painting *support*, which is the canvas, paper, wood panel, wall, or other surface on which the artist works. The painter may first apply a preliminary coating known as a *ground* or *primer* to make the support more receptive to the paint and/or to create certain effects.

In this chapter we shall first discuss the painting media—the mechanics and expressive possibilities of each. Then we will look at how different artists have adapted the various media to meet their own expressive needs.

## Painting Media

As suggested earlier, practically every painting medium ever invented is still in use somewhere, by somebody. Artists interested in history or chemistry love to experiment with obscure techniques that went out of fashion centuries ago. Most of the painting media that have fallen out of favor have been abandoned because they were cumbersome or because they were replaced by similar media that had certain advantages—lower cost, clearer colors, easier preparation, better adherence to the support, quicker drying time, slower drying time—whatever artists might wish.

It is impossible to tell which painting medium is the oldest, but we know that ancient peoples mixed their pigments with such things as fat and honey. Apparently, the first widespread and well-perfected technique came into use in the Classical period, the few hundred years surrounding the birth of Christ. This was encaustic painting.

### Encaustic

For encaustic, the pigment particles are suspended in hot beeswax, which must be kept at the proper temperature for spreading on a support (often a wood panel). Encaustic is an extremely demanding medium, and few contemporary artists want to cope with its difficulties. However, the wax gives a clear, luminous quality that almost no other medium can rival. The early Christians in Eygpt, the Copts, were especially proficient at encaustic painting, and their works retain a splendid brilliance even two thousand years later (**224**).

### Fresco

To make a fresco the artist paints in water-suspended pigment on a surface of freshly spread plaster. As the plaster dries, the colors are absorbed into it, so that the two substances—paint and plaster—fuse. The painting will survive in good condition as long as the plaster remains intact.

Fresco is above all a wall-painting technique, and it has been used for large-scale murals since ancient times. Probably no other painting medium requires such careful planning, such meticulous attention to the chemical properties of the medium, and such hard physical labor. The plaster can be painted only when it has the proper degree of dampness; therefore, the artist must plan each day's work and spread plaster only in the area that can be painted in one session. (Michelangelo could cover about 1 square yard of wall or ceiling in a day.)

**224.** *Young Woman with a Gold Pectoral.* Egypto-Roman (Coptic), c. A.D. 100. Encaustic. Louvre, Paris.

There is nothing tentative about fresco. Whereas in some media the artist can experiment, try out forms, and then paint over them to make corrections, every touch of the brush in fresco is a commitment. The only way an artist can correct mistakes or change the forms is to let the plaster dry, chip it away, and start all over again. Usually, the artist begins with a preliminary drawing called a *cartoon*. This may be a scaled-down or full-size version of the finished painting. If the cartoon is full size, the artist may cut it up into pieces, each the size of a day's work. Next the artist outlines major forms by placing the drawing on the surface and poking through its lines with a sharp tool to leave a row of pinholes in the plaster.

There have been three great eras of fresco painting in the history of art: the Classical period in the Aegean and Rome, the Renaissance in 15th- and 16th-century Italy, and the early 20th century in Mexico. Only a few of the Classical frescoes have survived (**456**); as buildings become ruins, so do their frescoed walls. But among the works we consider the greatest in all of Western art are the magnificent frescoes of the Italian Renaissance.

While Michelangelo was at work on the frescoes of the Sistine Chapel ceiling (**39,478**), Pope Julius II brought in an artist named Raphael to decorate the walls of several rooms in the Vatican Palace. Raphael's fresco for the end wall of the Stanza della Segnatura, a room that may have been the Pope's library, is considered by many to be the summation of Renaissance art. It is called *The School of Athens* (**225**) and depicts the Greek philosophers Plato and Aristotle, centered in the composition and framed by the arch, along with their followers and students. The "school" in question means the two schools

of philosophy represented by the two Classical thinkers—Plato's the more
abstract and metaphysical, Aristotle's the more earthly and physical.

Everything about Raphael's composition celebrates the Renaissance ideals
of perfection, beauty, natural representation, and noble principles. The towering architectural setting provides an arena for quiet intellectual debate, and
it is drawn in masterful linear perspective (Chapter 4, p. 120; the vanishing
point is between the heads of the two philosophers). The figures, perhaps
influenced by Michelangelo's figures on the Sistine ceiling, are idealized—
more perfect than life, full-bodied and dynamic. *The School of Athens* perfectly
reflects Raphael's vision of one Golden Age—the Renaissance—and establishes its kinship with the Golden Age of Greece two thousand years earlier.

The era that spawned the great fresco artists of Mexico, while scarcely
"golden," was a fertile and turbulent one. The Mexican Revolution began in
1911 and continued for twenty years. It launched a period of great economic
and social upheaval, overlapping with the social upheaval of Depression in the
United States. A number of Mexican artists, trained in Mexico but influenced
by European art of the time, sought to revive fresco painting, and in this they
were supported by the Mexican government.

Diego Rivera's enormous frescoed murals in many public buildings in
Mexico and the United States typify this style. *Detroit Industry* (226), an ambitious four-wall panorama at the Detroit Institute of Arts, illustrates the grand
scale and monumental quality that often characterize mural painting. Conceived as a tribute to the city and the worker, Rivera's mural has a complex
iconography. The detail shown here portrays the manufacture of the 1932

Ford V-8 automobile. Every step of the job, every event in the worker's day is represented, from the punching of the time clock through steel processing, molding, welding, drilling—even the lunch break. The mural treatment bestows a grandeur on the everyday operations of the assembly line. In fact, the frescoed mural probably served Rivera's expressive needs better than any other medium could have done.

## Egg Tempera

Anyone who has washed breakfast dishes knows about the adhesive strength and quick drying of egg yolk. A painting medium based on egg yolk, called tempera, was preferred by artists throughout the medieval period, until the introduction of oil paint. Tempera's yellow color is too weak to distort a pigment color, and, strangely enough, tempera works tend to yellow less with age than do those in oil. Paintings done in tempera hundreds of years ago retain their brilliant glow and clear colors. The one disadvantage is that tempera is not as flexible as oil or the synthetics, not nearly as convenient in the application. Oils or acrylics can be laid on in large strokes, small strokes, thick or thin. But in tempera forms must be built up slowly, with small, individual brush strokes. For those few contemporary artists who care to take the trouble, the rewards are gratifying.

Among 20th-century artists one painter in particular has made tempera his own medium—Andrew Wyeth. Wyeth's painting *The Virgin* (**227**) shows

**227.** Andrew Wyeth. *The Virgin.* 1969. Tempera on canvas, 46 × 36″. Brandywine River Museum, Chadds Ford, Pa. Copyright © 1973 by the Tri-County Conservancy of the Brandywine, Inc.

this luminous technique at its best. The artist himself has spoken about the difficulties and the joys of creating form in the method of egg tempera:

> I think it's some of the purest tempera painting I ever did in that torso, because it almost becomes an abstraction of the truth. There are parts of the picture that are almost watercolor. But I thought this is the flash in the picture. This is the sparkle. I think you run from that waxen quality of the lower part of the figure going up all of a sudden to the sunlight on the upper body. I had to paint like mad to get it. But, fortunately, I had the whole figure painted in and could work quite directly on the head and hair. I refined it, of course, later on, but to get it there had to be some pretty excited strokes when that sun came out.[1]

## Oil

A popular legend says that oil painting was invented early in the 15th century by the great Netherlandish artist Jan van Eyck, who experimented with it for this portrait (**228**). However, Van Eyck probably learned the technique from another artist and merely perfected it himself. From that time and for about five hundred years the word "painting" was virtually synonymous with "oil painting." Only in the 1950s, with the introduction of acrylics, was the supremacy of oil challenged, and even then many artists clung to their oil paints.

The outstanding characteristic of oil paint is that it dries very slowly. This creates both advantages and disadvantages for the artist. On the plus side, it means that colors can be blended very subtly, layers of paint can be applied on top of other layers with little danger of separating or cracking, and the artist can rework sections of the painting almost indefinitely. This same asset becomes a liability when the artist is pressed for time—perhaps when an exhibition has been scheduled. Oil paint dries so *very* slowly that it may be weeks or months before the paint has truly "set."

Another great advantage of oil is that it can be worked in an almost infinite range of consistencies, from very thick to very thin. The German Expressionist painter Oskar Kokoschka often used thick oil paints straight from the

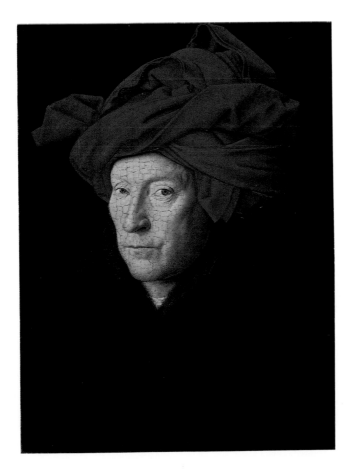

**228.** Jan van Eyck.
*Man in a Red Turban
(Self-Portrait?).* 1433.
Oil on panel, $10\frac{1}{4} \times 7\frac{1}{2}''$.
National Gallery, London
(reproduced by courtesy of the Trustees).

left: **229.** Oskar Kokoschka.
*Self-Portrait.* 1917.
Oil on canvas, $31\frac{1}{8} \times 24\frac{3}{4}''$.
Von der Heydt Museum, Wuppertal, West Germany.

right: **230.** Detail of Oskar Kokoschka's
*Self-Portrait,* **229.**

tube, occasionally squeezing them directly on the canvas without a brush (**229**). He could then mold and shape the thick paint with a palette knife (a spatula-shaped tool) to create actual three-dimensional depth on the canvas (**230**). Any thick application of paint is referred to as *impasto*, and Kokoschka's is an extreme version of this. The ability to use paint in this way was important for Kokoschka's expression, because the sinewy coils of paint in the *Self-Portrait* trace the artist's passionate exploration of his inner self. A smoother medium could not so define his anguished personality.

Oil paint can with equal ease be diluted and applied in very thin layers called *glazes*. By painting glaze upon glaze the artist can achieve a sense of depth, a subtle coloration, and a luminous quality that are very different from the effect of impasto application. This was the technique of many European artists during the 16th and 17th centuries. We find a masterful example in Jan Vermeer's *Woman Holding a Balance* (**231**). The warm, rich glow of this work comes from the application of many glazes and is intensified by Vermeer's method of placing tiny light dots of opaque paint as highlights. Like many artists of his time, Vermeer was much concerned with naturalism, and the thin application of oil paint in layers lends itself to lifelike portrayal.

Another generation of artists, many years later, also concerned themselves with naturalism, but the techniques and the visual results were quite different. This group, who worked in France during the late 19th century, were known as the Impressionists. We can see the basic characteristics of their style and method of working with oil paint in Claude Monet's *Sunflowers* (**232**).

The Impressionists attempted to paint what the eye actually sees, rather than what the brain interprets from visual cues. For example, if you look at a house in the distance and you know intellectually that the house is painted a uniform color of yellow, you might "see" all one shade of yellow, because your brain tells you that is correct. In purely visual terms, however, your eyes register many variations of yellow, depending on how light strikes the house and the shadows it creates. This is what the Impressionists were after—the true visual impression, not the version filtered through the knowing brain.

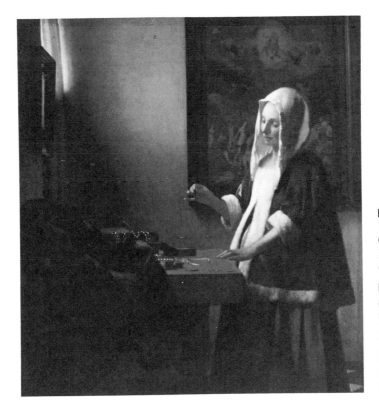

**left: 231.** Jan Vermeer.
*Woman Holding a Balance.* c. 1664.
Oil on canvas, $16\frac{3}{4} \times 15''$.
National Gallery of Art, Washington, D.C.
(Widener Collection, 1942).

**below left: 232.** Claude Monet.
*Sunflowers.* 1881.
Oil on canvas, $39\frac{3}{4} \times 32''$.
Metropolitan Museum of Art, New York
(H. O. Havemeyer Collection,
bequest of Mrs. H. O. Havemeyer, 1929).

**below right: 233.** Detail of
Claude Monet's *Sunflowers,* **232.**

The Impressionists strove to capture what the eye actually sees by applying oil paint using many individual brush strokes of varying colors, with no blending. Viewed up close, an Impressionist painting seems a meaningless jumble of color daubs (**233**). When you move farther away, however, your eyes "mix" the colors to produce a recognizable subject with shimmering effects of light. This is yet another example of the kind of effects that oil can produce.

# Rembrandt
## *1606–1669*

**O**f the few artists classified as "greatest of the great," Rembrandt is the most accessible to us. Through more than one hundred self-portraits, we follow his path from the brashness of youth to the high good spirits and prosperity of middle life to the melancholy loneliness of old age. Rembrandt's penetrating self-portraits represent a search for the self, but to the viewer they are a revelation of the self.

Born in the Dutch city of Leiden, Rembrandt Harmensz van Rijn was the son of a miller. At fourteen he began art lessons in Leiden and later studied with a master in Amsterdam. By the age of twenty-two he had pupils of his own. About 1631 he settled permanently in Amsterdam, having by then attracted considerable fame as a portrait painter. Thus began for Rembrandt a decade of professional success and personal happiness—a high point that would never come again.

In 1634 Rembrandt married Saskia van Uijlenburgh, an heiress of good family, thus improving his own social status. The pair must have been rather a dashing couple-about-Amsterdam. The artist's portraits were in demand, his style was fashionable, and he had money enough to indulge himself in material possessions, especially to collect art. One blight on this happy period was the arrival of four children, none of whom survived. But in 1641 Rembrandt's beloved son Titus was born.

Rembrandt's range as an artist was enormous. He was master not only of painting but of drawing and of the demanding technique of etching for prints. (It is said that Rembrandt went out sketching with an etcher's needle, as other artists might carry a pencil.) Besides the many portraits, the artist dis-played unparalleled genius in other themes, including landscape and religious scenes.

In 1642 Rembrandt's fortunes again changed, this time, irrevocably, for the worse. Saskia died not long after giving birth to Titus. The artist's financial affairs were in great disarray, no doubt partly because of his self-indulgence in buying art and precious objects. Although he continued to work and to earn money, Rembrandt showed little talent for money management. Ultimately he was forced into bankruptcy and had to sell not only his art collection but even Saskia's burial plot. About 1649 Hendrickje Stoffels came to live with Rembrandt, and she is thought of as his second wife, although they did not marry legally. She joined forces with Titus to form an art dealership in an attempt to protect the artist from his creditors. Capping the long series of tragedies that marked Rembrandt's later life, Hendrickje died in 1663 and Titus in 1668, a year before his father.

Rembrandt's legacy is almost totally a visual one. He does not seem to have written much. Ironically, one of the few recorded comments comes in a letter to a patron, begging for payment—payment for paintings that are now considered priceless and hang in one of the world's great museums. "I pray you my kind lord that my warrant might now be prepared at once so that I may now at last receive my well-earned 1244 guilders and I shall always seek to recompense your lordship for this with reverential service and proof of friendship."[2]

Rembrandt. *Self-Portrait*, detail. 1652.
Oil on canvas, $44\frac{1}{2} \times 31\frac{7}{8}''$ (entire work).
Kunsthistorisches Museum, Vienna.

**234.** Rembrandt. *Sortie of Captain Banning Cocq's Company of the Civic Guard (The Night Watch).* 1642. Oil on canvas, 12'2" × 14'7". Rijksmuseum, Amsterdam.

Before we leave the topic of oil paints, we might mention one more interesting fact about the medium. Oil paintings very often are coated with a top layer of varnish to protect the painted forms underneath. Although many types of paintings and drawings are framed behind glass, oils seldom are. The varnish therefore serves roughly the same purpose as glass would in preserving the artwork. Sometimes the varnish does more to distort than it does to protect. This was the case with one of Rembrandt's most famous paintings.

*Sortie of Captain Banning Cocq's Company of the Civic Guard* (**234**) shows a kind of private elite militia guard going out on an exercise. In the center is Captain Cocq, giving orders to his lieutenant, and grouped around are members of the company who seem especially pleased to be dressed up and playing at war games. For many years Rembrandt's painting was known as *The Night Watch,* and it still is informally called by this name. The reason has nothing to do with the artist's intent. A heavy layer of varnish applied on top of the oil paint, combined with smoke from a nearby fireplace, had gradually darkened the painting's surface until it seemed indeed to portray a nighttime scene. No one alive remembered it any differently.

During World War II Rembrandt's masterpiece was put away for safekeeping. Before it was returned to exhibition after the war, the varnish was removed and the surface thoroughly cleaned. What emerged was a painting very different from the one art lovers had become accustomed to. *The Night Watch* is shot through with light and is, in fact, a daytime scene. Details that had long been obscured were once again visible, as Rembrandt painted them.

**235.** Maurice Prendergast. *Sunlight on the Piazzetta, Venice.* c. 1888–89. Watercolor over graphite. Museum of Fine Arts, Boston (gift of Mr. and Mrs. William T. Aldrich).

## Watercolor

Watercolor is thought of as an intimate art, usually small in scale and executed with great freedom and spontaneity. Watercolor straddles the border between painting and drawing.

The pigments for watercolor are suspended in gum arabic (a gummy plant substance), thinned with water, and painted with a flowing motion onto paper of good quality. Generally, the watercolor is translucent, so that much of the white paper shows through. Watercolors are meant to be done quickly, according to the inspiration of the moment. Mistakes cannot easily be corrected, and too much overworking spoils the spontaneity of the medium.

Maurice Prendergast's painting *Sunlight on the Piazzetta, Venice* (**235**) illustrates the watercolor technique at its most vibrant. Prendergast, an American artist who worked at the turn of the 20th century, was much influenced by the French Impressionists. His style is filled with light and color—the quick blink-of-an-eye impression of life in motion. Watercolor captures the immediacy of the moment, the gaiety and fleeting charm of a sunlit outdoor scene.

Watercolor has been an important part of traditional Chinese painting, where it is often combined with ink or ink washes (sweeps of diluted ink). The Chinese skill with the brush lends itself especially well to a rapid, assured execution. Qiu Ying's hanging scroll, *A Lady in a Pavilion Overlooking a Lake* (**236**), exemplifies the watercolor refined to miniature proportions. The artist's brushwork, so precise in detailing the architecture of the pavilion, changes subtly to create a sense of lushness in the foreground trees and then changes again to suggest the mountains in the distance. Watercolor is often thought to be exclusively a broad technique, with flowing washes and large color areas, but Qiu Ying uses it with the most delicate precision.

## Gouache

When opaque (nontranslucent) white is added to watercolors, the result is known as gouache. The white may be either mixed with the paints or coated on the support before the watercolors are applied. Because gouache is exceptionally quick-drying, it is well suited for sketches and preliminary drawings, but this also means that brush strokes do not blend well. The artist must adapt to this characteristic by placing colors and forms side by side, rather than overlapping them or blending them into one another. Wassily Kandinsky has exploited this quality splendidly in *Russian Beauty in a Landscape* (**237**). Individual daubs of flat, opaque paint are laid down like the tiles in a mosaic to create a shimmering, exotic image. There is something almost magical about this gorgeous figure set against a fairy-tale landscape.

## Distemper

Distemper, commonly known as poster paint, is a medium based on water-soluble glue into which pigments are mixed. Like gouache, it dries very quickly, so that the blending of brush strokes or the glazing of colors is almost impossible. We often think of distemper as the best painting medium for children because it is inexpensive, covers mistakes solidly, and cleans up easily. But it is also a respectable medium for adult artists who are willing to adjust to its difficulties. The French artist Edouard Vuillard, who began his career paint-

**left: 236.** Qiu Ying.
*A Lady in a Pavilion
Overlooking a Lake.*
China, Ming Dynasty, c. 1552–60.
Hanging scroll, ink and color
on paper; height 35⅛".
Museum of Fine Arts, Boston
(Chinese and Japanese Special Fund).

**right: 237.** Wassily Kandinsky.
*Russian Beauty in a Landscape.*
1904. Gouache. Städtische Galerie
im Lenbachhaus, Munich.

left: 238. Edouard Vuillard.
*The First Steps.* 1902.
Distemper, $19\frac{1}{2} \times 13\frac{3}{4}''$.
Private Collection, Dallas,
courtesy Acquavella Galleries, Inc.,
New York.

right: 239. Rufino Tamayo.
*El Hombre (The Man).* 1953.
Vinyl with pigment on Masonite
(mural), $18' \times 10'6''$.
Dallas Museum of Art
(commissioned by the
Dallas Art Association
through Nieman-Marcus
Exposition Fund).

ing stage flats for the theater, developed an affinity for this fast-drying medium and later adapted it to his large paintings, such as *The First Steps* (238). The color transitions, which with less expert handling might have seemed abrupt, are softened by Vuillard's use of closely related, subtle pastel colors.

## Synthetic Media

The enormous developments made in chemistry during the early 20th century had an impact in artists' studios. All painting media available up to that time had certain limitations. Oil, the most widely used, had the disadvantage of excessively slow drying time. The new synthetic media offered the promise of more control—control of fluidity, color fidelity, drying time, and durability. It should be noted, however, that there is still no *one* perfect medium for all types of expression and for all artists. The introduction of synthetic media, especially the acrylics, has simply expanded the range of possibilities.

By the 1930s the chemical industry had learned to make strong, weatherproof paint based on plastic resins, as well as new fade-proof colors for use in industry. The first painter known to have adapted these paints to art was the Mexican artist David Alfaro Siqueiros. In Los Angeles in 1932 Siqueiros organized his students into an industrial crew to paint outdoor murals with plastic resin paints, using slide projectors to transfer designs to the walls and spray guns to apply the paint. The murals, like those of Rivera, were meant to convey a social message. But the most revolutionary part of Siqueiros' work was the way the murals were made. The acrylic paints many artists use today are a development of these early synthetic resins, with similar characteristics of quick drying and resistance to weather and fading.

Siqueiros' countryman, Rufino Tamayo, adopted another synthetic medium, a vinyl emulsion (or polyvinyl acetate) for large-scale murals such as *El*

*Hombre* (**239**). Whether applied thick or thin, vinyl emulsion offered a high degree of permanence suitable for withstanding the wear and tear to which publicly available murals may be subjected.

The most popular synthetic paints are the water-base acrylics, which were introduced in the 1950s. Acrylics offer quick drying time (though not as unmanageably quick as that of the earlier synthetic resins), pure and intense colors, and great flexibility in methods of application. While many artists still paint with conventional brushes, others have adapted the acrylic medium to pouring, throwing, or dripping. Thinned down, acrylics can be shot through an airbrush—a tool that sprays a controlled mist of paint—as in the work of Chuck Close and Audrey Flack (**25,60**). It has been suggested that the "hard-edge" painting of the 1960s (**241**) could not have developed without acrylic paints, because they permit the artist to block off areas with masking tape to achieve an absolutely straight line. The masking tape could not be put down on top of slower-drying oils or most other media. Acrylics also can be applied to many kinds of supports (not just primed canvas), and they combine well with certain other techniques, such as silkscreen (Chapter 8).

New media and methods can enlarge an artist's scope, can make possible new types of expression, but they do not dictate form. It is up to the artist to apply the specific qualities of any given medium to his or her thematic and formal needs. Throughout history artists have used the same medium to achieve very different artistic goals.

## Medium and Expression

The next three paintings (**240,241,242**) all were done with acrylics, yet they have little else in common. The first, a "stained" work by Helen Frankenthaler (**240**), shows how acrylic behaves when it is thinned to the consistency of a dye and applied to raw canvas, which partially absorbs the color. In

**240.** Helen Frankenthaler. *Enigma.* 1975.
Acrylic on canvas, 10′ × 5′10″.
Courtesy André Emmerich Gallery, New York.

below: 241. Kenneth Noland.
*Bridge.* 1964.
Acrylic on canvas, 7′5″ × 8′2″.
Collection Mrs. Harry Davidson, Toronto.

right: 242. Ronald Markman.
*Fish Dinner.* 1981.
Acrylic on wood, 4′ × 3′2″.
Courtesy Terry Dintenfass Gallery, New York.

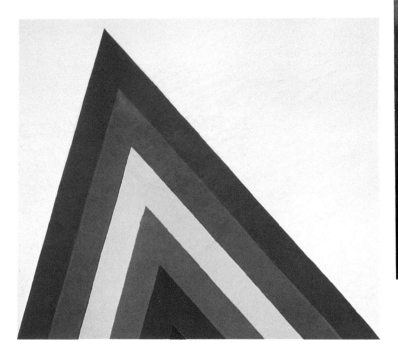

Frankenthaler's work there is little actual surface texture and practically no illusion of pictorial depth. The forms are organic, creating a color landscape of their own within the rectangle of the painting, but they make no specific reference to the natural landscape. Free-flowing washes of color spread and overlap on the canvas in what appears to be an immediate, spontaneous burst of imagery. Like Jackson Pollock (**55,523**), Frankenthaler often places her canvases flat on the floor, the better to control the flow of paint.

Almost the exact opposite of Frankenthaler's style is the razor-sharp geometry of the "hard-edge" painters, such as Kenneth Noland (**241**). Noland and other painters of the 1960s and 1970s sought to refine painting to its most basic elements—pure color and pure shape. The colors are flat and unvaried, the forms are geometric, and lines are drawn literally with a straightedge. Just as Frankenthaler exploited the acrylic medium for its flowing qualities, Noland found in acrylic the perfect material for precision.

As painting in the past few years has moved away from the more abstract and nonrepresentational styles of the last three decades and back toward greater use of figures and representation, acrylics have followed suit. Ronald Markman's work, such as *Fish Dinner* (**242**), is a good example of the trend toward patterned, decorative painting and explicit subject matter. Acrylics lend themselves well to the intricate pattern and vivid color of this expression.

The same divergence of styles that we find in acrylics can be found in other media. Both John Marin and Winslow Homer were noted for their watercolors; in fact, Marin worked primarily in this medium. If you compare their paintings, however, you will see that the two artists used the watercolor technique in very different ways. Marin's cityscapes, such as *From the Bridge,*

*New York City* (**243**), capture the essence and the spirit of the metropolis, rather than its actual appearance. Full of vigor and color and exciting diagonals, they make us feel the city's pulse, its movement. The brushwork is loose and free, with form only barely sketched in. Marin's style exploits the fluidity of watercolor to the fullest extent.

Homer's watercolor style, while retaining the freedom and spontaneity of the medium, is far more contained. In *For To Be a Farmer's Boy* (**244**) the forms are defined by small color patches—in contrast to Marin's long sweeps of liquid color. Homer was certainly capable of dramatic diagonals, but here there is a predominance of serene horizontal lines, broken only by the vertical of the boy's figure. Homer's more controlled handling of watercolor in this work shows us the pleasures of a peaceful summer afternoon on the farm.

And what of oil? Still considered by many to be the only "true" painting medium, oil has for nearly five centuries met the requirements of artists from every possible school. Three portraits will illustrate oil's amazing range.

**right: 243.** John Marin.
*From the Bridge, New York City.* 1933.
Watercolor, $21\frac{7}{8} \times 26\frac{3}{4}''$.
Wadsworth Atheneum, Hartford.

**below: 244.**
Winslow Homer.
*For To Be a Farmer's Boy.* 1887.
Watercolor, $14 \times 20''$.
Art Institute of Chicago
(gift from Mrs. George T. Langhorne
in Memory of Edward Carson Waller).

# Alice Neel
## *1900–1984*

When an acquaintance once remarked that Alice Neel painted "like a man," the artist retorted, "No, I don't paint like a man; but I don't paint like they expect a woman to paint." As a matter of fact, this extraordinary woman spent a long lifetime doing the unexpected, with cheerful disregard for the prevailing mores and fashions.

Alice Neel was born in Merion Square, Pennsylvania, the daughter of a proper middle-class family that she described as "anti-bohemian." She studied at what was then the Philadelphia School of Design for Women—"a school where rich girls went before they got married"—and received a thorough, if conventional, grounding in art.

Her personal life, too, was conventional up to that point, but soon it changed drastically. Neel referred to the men who played important roles in her life by stereotype, rather than by name. Upon leaving art school she married "the Cuban." The couple moved to Havana, where Neel continued to paint and had her first exhibition in 1926. The Cuban marriage eventually broke up, after which Neel returned to New York and worked on the W.P.A. project—the government-sponsored Depression program to help support artists. Along the way she took up with "the sailor," with whom she lived until he cut up and burned all her work. ("You know how men are, they get jealous, they're possessive.") With "the Harvard man" she maintained a friendship for several decades, but she claimed he was most useful during the thirties, because, when everyone was very poor, he took her to expensive places to eat. There was also "the Puerto Rican singer."

From the beginning Neel was a portraitist, although she preferred to call herself a "people painter," feeling that portraitists are looked down on. This assessment actually proved correct through most of her career. Just at the point when Neel should have been in her artistic prime—the 1940s and 1950s—abstraction had completely taken over the art world. The painter of figures was out of fashion and remained so for at least twenty years. Not until 1974, at the age of seventy-four, did Neel have her first important show—at the Whitney Museum in New York. The show included some fifteen pictures that had not previously been "off the shelf." Alice Neel waited a long time to hear an important critic name her as the best portrait painter of the 20th century, and then she herself did not contradict that statement. The pictures, however, have transcended portrait status in the sense of recording someone's looks. They are major paintings that just happen to have people as their subjects.

Quite obviously, Alice Neel was an original, an exceptionally self-directed artist and human being. Neither her personal life nor her career was modeled after any example, nor did she follow anything but her own inclinations: "When they asked me if I had influences I said I never copy anybody. I never did, because I feel that the most important thing about art and in art—and I tell students this—is to find your own road."[3]

Alice Neel. *Nude Self-Portrait.* 1980.
Oil on canvas, 4'6" × 3'4".
Courtesy Robert Miller Gallery, Inc., New York.

John Singleton Copley's portrait of *Mrs. Thomas Boylston* (**245**) might be considered the "hard-edge" painting of its day. Forms are perfectly and clearly defined; there is a definite break between hand and skirt, face and cap, figure and background. Copley has given meticulous attention to such details as the veins in the hands and the lines of the face. His treatment of the shimmering folds of satin in the dress is a virtuoso performance in handling the oil medium. Copley's brush strokes are tiny and almost indistinguishable except at very close range.

By contrast, Frans Hals' portrait of *Willem Croes* (**246**) is much more in the style called "painterly." Edges are blurred and indistinct, brush strokes are clearly visible and overlap, and there is more of a sense of surface texture. We can see this especially in the treatment of the hands in the two paintings. Copley's is precise, but Hals manages to capture the impression of full-fleshed solidity with far broader strokes. Each artist had a vision, and each found a realization of that vision in oil paint.

**left: 245.** John Singleton Copley.
*Portrait of Mrs. Thomas Boylston.* 1766.
Oil on canvas, 4'1½" × 3'4¼".
Harvard University Portrait Collection,
Cambridge, Mass.
(bequest of Ward Nicholas Boylston
to Harvard University, 1828).

**right: 246.** Frans Hals.
*Willem Croes.* c. 1660.
Oil on canvas, 18½ × 13⅜".
Alte Pinakothek, Munich.

**247.** Alice Neel. *Nancy.* 1981.
Oil on canvas, 5′ × 3′4″.
Courtesy Robert Miller Gallery, Inc.,
New York.

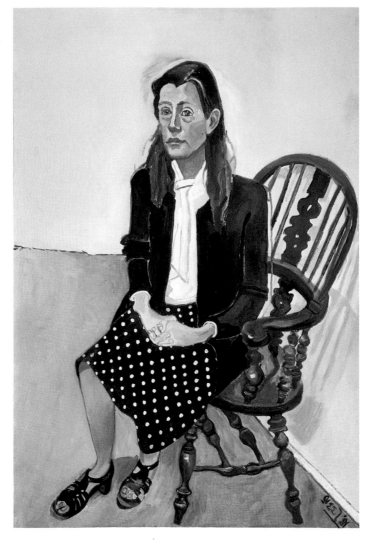

To prove that oil can hold its own in the late 20th century, we need only look at Alice Neel's picture of *Nancy* (**247**). As is typical of a Neel portrait, this image gives a portrait of the whole body, not just the face. The clasped hands, the pushed-up sleeves, the pose perching tentatively on the outside of the chair, even the feet in their too-large sandals—all contribute to our insight into the sitter's character. If we did not know this painting's medium, we might be tempted to think it was acrylic, especially seeing it in reproduction. The rather flat color areas and defining lines seem too "modern" somehow for oil paint. But that is just the point, that oil has the flexibility to be a great many things. In this thoroughly contemporary painting, oil seems every bit as modern as any substance invented by chemistry.

This brief survey should have demonstrated that the various painting media and the artists who use them yield endless possibilities. It would be difficult to say which comes first—the artist's imagery or the material. Did the first cave artist have the impulse to paint something and search about for a material with which to do it? Or did the cave artist find some pigmented material and then speculate about what would happen if the substance were applied to a wall? The answer is not important, but the two aspects—idea and medium— feed upon each other. No visual image could be realized without the medium in which to make it concrete. And no medium would be of any consequence without the artist's idea—and the artist's compelling urge to paint.

# 8
# **Prints**

If you have ever received a handmade greeting card for Christmas, for a birthday, or as an invitation to a party, then you will appreciate the difference between an art print and a mass-produced reproduction. Commercial greeting cards are cranked out by the thousands, even millions, by the major card manufacturers. But many people like to make their own cards with their own original designs. Usually they will *print* the cards by some type of stamping process. The design is carved out on a printing block made of wood, linoleum, or even the cut side of a potato, leaving some areas raised as in a rubber stamp. Then the printing block is coated with ink and pressed carefully onto paper to make the card.

An image made this way is special. For one thing, the design is unique—a personal expression of the individual who conceived it. Also, each card will be slightly different from all the others because of variations in pressure, placement on the paper, and steadiness of the hand. There is a human touch, which we find missing from commercial products. For each separate image, *one* person made it, judged its quality, and was satisfied. All these factors apply equally to art prints.

Prints differ from most other works of art in two important respects. First, they are made by an indirect process. The artist does not draw or paint directly on the work of art, but instead creates the surface that *makes* the work of art. (In some cases the artist may add special touches to each print, but this is not the most common practice.) Second, the printing process results in many nearly identical images, which is the reason it is called an art of *multiples*. Each image—called an impression—is considered an original work of art. This latter point is crucial to an understanding of art prints, so we need to discuss it more fully.

Before the 1950s there were no strict guidelines for what could genuinely be labeled an "original" print. In the past twenty to thirty years, however, certain criteria have been established, and the value of recent prints has much to do with their adherence to these criteria. The guidelines were set up in an attempt to avoid abuses that had crept into the print market, such as inferior, shoddy, or inauthentic works being passed off as fine art.

Printmaking procedures now are rigidly controlled. The artist works on a plate or stone or some other surface to make the image. Then the image is printed on paper, by hand or by a hand-operated machine, either by the artist or by someone under the artist's immediate supervision. Each print is examined to make sure it meets the artist's standards, and any faulty impressions are destroyed. Usually the artist and printer decide in advance how many impressions will be made—ten, fifty, a hundred or more—and this number is referred to as the *edition*. The size of the edition may be determined by the material used for printing. Hard metal can print many perfect impressions, but a softer material, such as linoleum, will begin to wear down, resulting in a blurred image. Once the planned number of prints has been made, the plate or block is *canceled* (by scratching cross marks on it) or destroyed, so that no more prints can be struck. Finally, the artist signs each print individually and numbers each one. For example, if you buy a print marked 10/100, you will know you have the tenth print made in an edition of one hundred. Prints made earlier in the edition are sometimes considered more valuable.

The type of print we are talking about must be distinguished from posters and other reproductions made by mechanical or photographic processes, such as the illustrations in this book. You can buy a color reproduction of a Rembrandt or Picasso painting, or a poster featuring a rock star or film personality, but these are not prints in the sense that we are discussing in this chapter, not original works of art. The artist who made the image has no supervision over the printing process, may not even know about it, and did not sign the finished product. The quality of the reproduction is nowhere near as meticulously controlled as that of a print. Such reproductions are useful for study purposes and they often give pleasure, but they have little artistic or monetary value.

Today's art print, above all, is designed to *be* a print. It is not a copy of a work done in some other medium, although it may be adapted from an image in another medium. Some artists, for instance, will take a theme they have used in painting and explore its possibilities in prints. But in this case the artist adjusts the image to fit the physical qualities and expressive potential of the particular print medium chosen.

Like drawings, prints are a great boon to the art lover and the collector. At a time when original paintings by well-known artists are beyond the means of any but the very rich, prints by equally well-known artists—sometimes the same ones—often can be purchased for just a few hundred dollars. (The most fashionable artists command several thousand dollars for each print, but this price range is limited to a small group.) Young collectors starting out, and even large corporations with huge resources, have eagerly taken to buying prints. They may be a sound financial investment, but far more important is the fact that they give aesthetic pleasure and the joy of owning original art.

There are four basic methods for making a print (**248**)—relief, intaglio, lithography, and screenprinting. In this chapter we shall look at each in turn and then consider a few advanced and combined techniques.

## Relief

The term relief describes any printing method in which the image to be printed is *raised* from a background (**248**). Think of a rubber stamp. When you look at the stamp itself, you may see the words "First Class" or "Special Delivery" standing out from the background in reverse. You press the stamp to an ink pad, then to paper, and the words print right side out—a mirror image of the stamp. All relief processes work according to this general principle. The most common of the relief methods is the woodcut.

relief

intaglio

lithography

screenprinting

**248.** The four basic print methods: relief, intaglio, lithography, and screenprinting.

**249.** Anonymous master, Bohemia. *Rest on the Flight into Egypt.* c. 1410. Hand-colored woodcut. Albertina, Vienna.

## Woodcut

To make a woodcut the artist first draws the desired image on a block of wood. Then all the areas that are not meant to print—the background areas—are cut and gouged out of the wood so that the image stands out in relief. When the block is inked, only the raised areas take the ink. Finally, the block is pressed onto paper, or else paper is placed on the block and rubbed to transfer the ink and make the print.

Woodcut is the oldest of the printmaking methods, having been developed in the Western world as soon as paper became available, about 1400. In fact, even before papermaking techniques were introduced in Europe, wood blocks were used to stamp designs on textiles. It was a simple transition from cloth to paper, and so the new art form advanced rapidly.

Early woodcut prints were used for both religious and secular purposes. Until the 15th century only the very rich could afford to own religious pictures, which had to be drawn by hand. Prints put such images into the reach of anyone who wanted them. An early example is *Rest on the Flight into Egypt* (**249**), made about 1410 by an unknown artist in Bohemia.

This charming woodcut depicts a scene in the life of the infant Christ, when the Virgin Mary and Joseph, with their child, have fled Jerusalem to escape the terrors of King Herod. Here they have stopped by the wayside to rest from their journey. Mary nurses the child Jesus, while Joseph stoops over the fire to prepare a hasty meal. Despite the halos and Mary's crown, these figures seem very down-to-earth, like ordinary people one might meet on a trip. The artist's style is graceful, especially in the drapery of the Virgin's gown, in Joseph's beard, and in the flames of the cooking fire. An angel perched over the rather small figure of Joseph balances the composition.

Besides teaching the common people about religious tradition, woodcut served another basic need—for amusement. Early playing cards were made by

250. "Steward" and "barber," playing cards of a courtly pack with illustrations of trades, from south Germany or Austria. 1453–57. Hand-colored woodcut, each 5⅜ × 3⅞". Kunsthistorisches Museum, Vienna.

wood blocks, and our illustration (250) shows part of the earliest surviving woodcut "deck" of cards. An anonymous master from South Germany or Austria made these cards about the middle of the 15th century. They depict the various trades—barber, baker, metalsmith—which must have made their users feel right at home while playing games of chance. The little figures, going about their work, are cheerful and charming. And, while the drawing style is fairly simple, the bodies and clothing of the tradesmen seem animated, and their faces suggest individual personality.

251. Albrecht Dürer.
*Rhinoceros.* 1515.
Woodcut, 8⅜ × 11⅝".
Metropolitan Museum of Art,
New York
(gift of Junius S. Morgan, 1919).

The woodcut print reached a high point in Germany and northern Europe during the 15th and 16th centuries, with the work of such masters as Albrecht Dürer. Dürer's *Rhinoceros* (**251**) represents an attempt by a highly imaginative artist to depict a beast he had never seen, but knew only from description. The artist must surely have amused himself very much in creating such wonderful decorative detail, and his results amuse us equally today. (Dürer also worked in other print media, and we shall look at one of his engravings later in this chapter.)

By the 17th century prints began appearing in the Orient, where Japanese artists, in particular, experimented with the new medium. In the mid-18th century Japanese printmakers perfected the technique of full-color woodcut printing, using several blocks. This method required careful planning in the design and cutting of the wood blocks.

For color printing the artist must cut one block for each color that is to appear in the print. On the "red" block, for instance, only the areas that are to print in red are raised; on the "blue" block only the blue areas are raised; and so forth. Then the blocks are printed one color at a time on each sheet of paper in the edition. The impressions made by the various color blocks must be lined up very carefully, one on top of the other, so there are no unintended gaps or overlapping in the finished print. This process is known as *registration*.

The two names most often associated with masterful Japanese woodcut prints are Hiroshige and Hokusai. Ando Hiroshige was renowned for his landscapes, such as *Rain Shower on Ohashi Bridge* (**252**). As in many of Hiroshige's prints, the work is composed primarily of diagonals—the bridge

**252.** Ando Hiroshige.
*Rain Shower on Ohashi Bridge.*
19th century. Color woodcut, $13\frac{7}{8} \times 9\frac{1}{8}''$.
Cleveland Museum of Art
(gift from J. H. Wade).

# Katsushika Hokusai
## *1760–1849*

One of the most delightfully eccentric figures in the history of art is the Japanese painter and woodcut designer who has come to be known as Hokusai. During his eighty-nine years Hokusai lived in at least ninety different houses and used some fifty names. The name that stuck for posterity—Hokusai—means "Star of the Northern Constellation."

Hokusai was born in the city of Edo (now Tokyo), the son of a metal engraver. At the age of eighteen he was sent as an apprentice to the print designer Katsukawa Shunsho. So impressed was the master with his pupil's work that he allowed the young man to adopt part of his own name, and for several years Hokusai called himself "Shunro." Later the two quarreled, and Hokusai changed his name.

Even in his early years Hokusai always worked very quickly, producing huge quantities of drawings. As he finished a drawing, he would toss it on the floor, until there were papers scattered all over the studio, making cleaning impossible. When the house got too filthy and disorderly, he would simply move to another, followed by his long-suffering wife.

Hokusai's first book of sketches was published in 1800 and showed various scenes in and around Edo. That same year the artist produced a novel, which he sent off to a publisher accompanied by the self-portrait here. (Hokusai's head is shaved in the manner of Japanese artists and writers of that time.) Both books achieved popular success, but, characteristically, Hokusai never bothered to open the packets of money sent by his publisher. If a creditor stopped by, he would hand over a packet or two without counting it. Throughout his life he remained indifferent to money and despite his accomplishments was usually at the brink of starvation.

As Hokusai's fame spread he was often invited to give public drawing demonstrations. Legends of his virtuosity abound. On one occasion, the story goes, he stood before the assembled crowd outside a temple and drew an immense image of the Buddha, using a brush as big as a broom. Another time he drew birds in flight on a single grain of rice. Hokusai's sense of humor, never far below the surface, came bubbling out when he was asked to perform for the Shogun (the military governor). As onlookers gathered at the palace, Hokusai spread a large piece of paper on the floor, painted blue watercolor waves across it, then took a live rooster, dipped its feet in red paint, and allowed it to run across the painting. Bowing respectfully, he announced to the Shogun that this was a picture of red maple leaves floating down the river.[1]

Though well aware of his own skill, Hokusai often amused himself by pretending modesty. In the preface to one of his books he wrote: "From the age of six I had a mania for drawing. At seventy-three I had learned a little . . . in consequence when I am eighty I shall have made still more progress, and when I am a hundred and ten, everything I do . . . will be alive." But the artist did not make it quite that far. As he lay on his deathbed, he cried out: "If Heaven would grant me ten more years!" And then: "If Heaven would grant me *five* more years, I would become a real painter."[2] His grave is marked by a slab on which is carved the last of his many names: Gwakio Rojin—Old Man Mad About Drawing.

---

Katsushika Hokusai. *Self-Portrait,*
from *The Tactics of General Oven.* 1800.
Woodcut. Art Institute of Chicago.

**253.** Katsushika Hokusai.
*View of Fuji from Seven-Ri Beach.* 1823–29.
Color woodcut, $10\frac{1}{8} \times 15''$.
Metropolitan Museum of Art, New York (Rogers Fund, 1914).

slanting from lower left to middle right, the rain slashing down at a different angle, the riverbank cutting across at yet another diagonal. The figures crossing the bridge, typically, are small and are depicted not as individuals but as people responding to, and buffeted by, the weather. In a Hiroshige landscape nature is grand and people are small. The long parallel lines of the rain give this print a wonderful rich texture.

Katsushika Hokusai also made many landscapes during his prolific career. Best known are his numerous views of Mt. Fuji—the cone-shaped volcano that is the highest mountain in Japan and also is considered a sacred spot to the Japanese. Hokusai drew Fuji in all seasons, in all weathers, and from many vantage points. *View of Fuji from Seven-Ri Beach* (**253**) presents a vista that seems not entirely of this world. The white cone of the mountain hovers tranquilly in a realm of puffy green foliage and spreading clouds of vivid blue.

As was mentioned in Chapter 1, Japanese woodcut prints were imported to Europe in great quantities during the latter part of the 19th century. Many artists were influenced by aspects of their style, including the emphasis on diagonals, the subtle use of asymmetrical balance (note that Fuji is thrust far to right in the composition and balanced by the calligraphy at upper left), and the areas of flat, unshaded color in many prints. This special view of the world has been absorbed into the mainstream of contemporary art, so that it no longer seems "Japanese" but is part of a universal visual expression.

The German Expressionist artists of the early 20th century found in woodcut a medium uniquely compatible with their style. A splendid example

above left: 254. Emil Nolde.
*The Prophet.* 1912.
Woodcut, $12\frac{5}{8} \times 8\frac{5}{8}''$.
National Gallery of Art,
Washington, D.C.
(Rosenwald Collection).

above right: 255. Carol Summers.
*Road to Ketchikan.* 1976.
Color woodcut, 37″ square.
Courtesy Associated American Artists,
New York.

below: 256. Susan Rothenberg. *Pinks.*
Hand-wiped woodcut, $20 \times 27\frac{3}{4}''$.
Courtesy Multiples, Inc., New York.

is Emil Nolde's *The Prophet* (254). Expressionism's imagery is stark, somewhat primitive, and occasionally shocking. Woodcut readily lends itself to this style by allowing harsh contrasts of black and white as well as broad—even crude—drawing and cutting. Expressionism is just what its name implies—expressive, and also brooding, emotional, uncompromising. Of all the print methods, woodcut offers the greatest possibilities for realization of that expression.

A number of contemporary printmakers work in woodcut. Carol Summers' prints (255) seem at first to be totally nonobjective. In looking at them we respond to the broad areas of lush color, the graceful forms. But as the title *Road to Ketchikan* suggests, there is a reference to the natural world. The intense blue bands may be part of the road, and the triangular red form could be a mountain. Viewed in this way, the composition takes on a spatial depth. Many of Summers' prints offer this type of visual puzzle. At first we see flat color patches, but after a while we begin to perceive a landscape—a very abstract landscape to be sure, but a landscape nevertheless.

At the beginning of this chapter we said that some artists work directly on the prints, so that each one is different. Susan Rothenberg's *Pinks* (**256**) is an extreme version of this approach. Each print in the edition of twenty has a hand print on the left and a crude face on the right superimposed over a hand outline, with the fingers becoming hair and perhaps ears. Rather than using an inking roller, the artist has hand-wiped each print individually over the ink, so the intensity of the color varies. Rothenberg has confined herself to three colors—black, pink, and white—but the use of these colors varies from impression to impression. She has also allowed the grain of the wood block to take part in the image, using rough wood with ridges and knots. From Rothenberg's example we can see that the oldest printmaking technique still has much potential to be explored.

## Linocut

A linoleum cut, or linocut, is very similar to a woodcut. The major difference is that the material is much softer than wood, which makes it both easier to carve and less durable in printing multiple impressions, resulting in smaller editions. Linoleum has no grain, so it is possible to make cuts in any direction with equal ease. Some artists dismiss linoleum as being suitable only for schoolchildren (or for greeting cards), but Picasso never let such preconceived ideas interfere with his creativeness. His color linocut depicting a *Seated Woman (after Cranach)* (**257**) is, as the title implies, an interpretation of a painting by the 16th-century German artist Lucas Cranach, but a more abstract

**257.** Pablo Picasso.
*Seated Woman (after Cranach)* 1958.
Color linocut, $25\frac{5}{8} \times 21\frac{1}{8}''$.
Museum of Modern Art,
New York (gift of
Mr. and Mrs. Daniel Saidenberg).

treatment than Cranach could ever have imagined. The splendid colors result from printing with several linoleum blocks, just as is done with color wood blocks. The richly detailed textures in the hair, arm bands, and jewelry may have been made easier to achieve by the relatively soft linoleum.

## Wood Engraving

Wood engraving differs in several respects from woodcut. For one thing, it is done on the end grain of the wood. If you imagine a board, say a 2-by-4, the long, smooth plank sides would be used for woodcut, but the grainy cut end would be used for wood engraving. The end grain can be cut in any direction, without chipping or splintering, unlike the plank sides.

A distinctive characteristic of wood engraving is that it is a "white-line" technique. The tool used for cutting makes fine, narrow grooves in the wood, and these grooves, which do not take the ink, result in a white line when the inked wood block is pressed to paper. Woodcut, by contrast, usually has larger, broader, more irregular uninked white areas because of the coarser tools that gouge out background areas.

During the 19th century wood engraving was used widely for printing books and journals. The cut end of the wood could easily be prepared to be "type high"—the same height (7/8 inch) as the wooden alphabet letters that printers worked with at the time. Therefore, both images and text could conveniently be printed together. Photography was a young art, and methods for reproducing photographs had not been perfected. Most illustrations still were made in the form of prints. In the United States this art of illustration was dominated by Winslow Homer, who worked for several periodicals during the latter half of the 1800s. Homer depicted events of the Civil War, important political figures, and scenes of everyday life.

One of Homer's best-known prints was *The Robin's Note* (**258**). We can see the white-line effect clearly in the woman's dress, the column, and the background foliage. This is a simple enough scene—a young woman lying in a hammock—but Homer has composed it brilliantly. The strict vertical of the pillar, the diagonal of the porch floor, the arc of the hammock, the spill of the dress over the side, and the rich texture of the background—all these add up to a striking, almost classical composition. The robin of the title is isolated in the sky, centered in the V of the hammock. Wood engraving's capacity for fine detail was especially suited to Homer's style.

# Intaglio

The second major category of printmaking techniques is intaglio, which includes several related methods. Intaglio is exactly the reverse of relief, in that the areas meant to print are *below* the surface of the printing plate (**248**). The artist uses a sharp tool or acid to make depressions—lines or grooves—in a metal plate (**259**). When the plate is inked, the ink sinks into the depressions. Then the surface of the plate is wiped clean. When dampened paper is brought into contact with the plate under pressure, the paper is pushed into the inked depressions to pick up the image.

There are five basic types of intaglio printing: engraving, drypoint, mezzotint, etching, and aquatint.

## Engraving

The oldest of the intaglio techniques, engraving developed from the medieval practice of incising (cutting) linear designs in armor and other metal surfaces. The armorer's art had achieved a high level of expertise, and it was just a short step to realizing that the engraved lines could be filled with ink and the design transferred to paper.

below: 260. Albrecht Dürer.
*St. Jerome in His Study.* 1514.
Engraving, 9¾ × 7½". British Museum, London.

above: 258. Winslow Homer.
*The Robin's Note.* 1870.
Wood engraving, 8⅞ × 9".
New York Public Library, Prints Division
(Astor, Lenox and Tilden Foundation).

below: 259. Plate-making methods
for intaglio printing:
engraving, drypoint, mezzotint,
etching, aquatint.

engraving

drypoint

mezzotint          etching          aquatint

   The basic tool of engraving is the *burin*, a sharp, V-shaped instrument used to cut lines into the metal plate (**259**). Shallow cuts produce a light, thin line, while deeper gouges in the metal result in a thicker and darker line. Engraving is closely related to drawing in pen or sharp pencil in both technique and the visual effect of the work. Looking at a reproduction it is hard to tell an engraving from a fine pen or pencil drawing. As in these drawing media, modeling and shading usually are achieved by hatching, cross-hatching, or stippling (**99**).

   One of the first great masters of engraving, perhaps the greatest ever, was Albrecht Dürer. In *St. Jerome in His Study* (**260**) we seem to stand on the threshold of a quiet room, where Jerome is at work—perhaps on his major project,

**261.** William Hogarth.
*The Marriage Contract,*
from *Marriage à la Mode.*
1745. Engraving.
New York Public Library,
Prints Division.

the translation of the Bible into Latin. Light streams in through the window of the study, which is drawn in careful perspective. According to legend, St. Jerome once removed a thorn from a lion's paw, and so he is often depicted with a lion at his feet. Here the dozing, friendly lion and a dog add to the overall impression of serenity and quiet work. The scene is rich with detail, for Dürer has exploited the possibilities of the engraving technique with remarkable skill.

In Dürer's time one great benefit of engraving was the dissemination of artistic ideas and innovations. Because prints were circulated throughout Europe, noted artists were able to study each other's work and learn from one another with far greater ease than ever before. Previously, an artist's masterworks were known only to those who lived in the city where a given work was kept or who traveled to that city. Journeys to Italy from the northern countries

**262.** Reuben Nakian.
*Myths and Legends.*
Drypoint, $19\frac{3}{4} \times 25\frac{5}{8}''$.
Courtesy HMK Fine Arts, Inc., New York.

were common; those from south to north less so. Engraved copies enabled artists to examine the work of their distant colleagues without leaving home, and soon influences among artists occurred more rapidly. Art styles of the various regions gradually became less distinctly different.

Around the 18th century engraved copies of well-known paintings became sought-after items for middle-class people. The change came about largely through the efforts of the English artist William Hogarth. Hogarth is best known for three large series of paintings—*The Rake's Progress, The Harlot's Progress,* and *Marriage à la Mode.* Each series was a "picture story" with a moral, and each portrayed the progress of an individual (or in the last case, a couple) from innocent beginnings through increasing sin to complete ruin. Being short of funds, Hogarth hit on the idea of making engraved copies of the paintings, copyrighting the engravings, and selling them cheaply in great quantities. This plan worked splendidly. (It also formed the basis for English copyright law in regard to art.)

The first scene in *Marriage à la Mode* (**261**) sets the stage for eventual disaster. A poverty-stricken nobleman is marrying off his son to the daughter of a rich but middle-class merchant. The two fathers settle the details of the marriage contract as they would any business deal. Meanwhile, the engaged couple, at right, ignore each other. Hogarth is not subtle in pointing out that this is not a love match. In fact, the future bride is already responding to the attentions of Counsellor Silvertongue, the lawyer, who will soon become her lover. Later scenes in the series portray infidelities by both partners, great excess of all kinds, a duel, and ultimately the death of the husband.

Hogarth's satire may seem a bit heavy-handed to us today, but his eye for the telling detail—such as the groom's father having a bandaged foot as a result of gout, a disease supposedly caused by excesses of food and drink—must have greatly amused his public. Engraving was the ideal technique for Hogarth, for its precision enabled him to capture a wealth of detail. Not surprisingly, Hogarth's satirical prints were extremely popular with members of the working class.

## Drypoint

Drypoint is similar to engraving, except that the cutting instrument used is a drypoint needle. The artist draws on the plate, usually a copper plate, almost as freely as one can draw on paper with a pencil. As the needle scratches across the plate, it raises a *burr,* or thin ridge of metal (**259**). This burr holds the ink, making a line that is softer and less sharply detailed than an engraved line. If engraving is like fine pen drawing, sharp and distinct, then drypoint is more like drawing in soft pencil or crayon, with slightly blurred edges. This soft, sketchy quality is obvious in the figures of Reuben Nakian's drypoint *Myths and Legends* (**262**).

## Mezzotint

Mezzotint is a reverse process, in which the artist works from dark to light. To prepare a mezzotint plate, the artist first roughens the entire plate with a sharp tool called a *rocker.* If the plate were inked and printed after this stage, it would print a sheet of paper entirely black, because each roughened spot would catch and hold the ink. Lighter tones can be created only by smoothing or rubbing out these rough spots so as not to trap the ink. To do this, the artist goes over the image portions of the plate with a burnisher (a smoothing tool) and/or a scraper to wear down the roughened burrs (**259**). Where the burrs are partially removed, the plate will print intermediate values. Highlights—very light values—print in areas where the burrs are smoothed away.

The major advantage of mezzotint is that it is capable of subtle gradations from dark to light. Whereas engraving and drypoint are predominantly line techniques, mezzotint is based on values. We see this effect in Peter Pelham's portrait of *Cotton Mather* (**263**), one of the earliest prints made in the American colonies. So finely modeled is this portrait of the great Puritan leader that, in reproduction, we might almost mistake it for an oil painting. The face, in particular, is wonderfully naturalistic because of the skillful use of values. This naturalism would be hard to achieve in an engraving or in one of the relief processes.

## Etching

Etching is done with acids, which "eat" lines and depressions into a metal plate much as sharp tools cut those depressions in the other methods. To make an etching the artist first coats the entire printing plate with an acid-resistant substance called a *ground*, made from beeswax, asphalt, and other materials. Next, the artist draws on the coated plate with an etching needle. The needle removes the ground, exposing the bare metal in areas meant to print (**259**). Then the entire plate is dipped in acid. Only the portions of the plate exposed by the needle are eaten into by the acid, leaving the rest of the plate intact. Finally, the ground is removed, and the plate is inked and printed as usual. Etched lines are not as sharp and precise as those made by the engraver's burin, because the biting action of the acid is slightly irregular.

Rembrandt, who was a prolific printmaker, made hundreds of etchings. Unfortunately, many of his plates were not canceled or destroyed. Long after his death, and long after the plates had worn down badly, people greedy to produce yet more "Rembrandts" struck impressions from the plates. These later impressions lack detail and give us little idea of what the artist intended. Our reproduction of *Arnold Tholinx* (**264**), one of Rembrandt's magnificent portraits, is an excellent early impression. In this work the artist brought to bear all his genius as an etcher, accomplishing the fully rounded modeling

**left: 263.** Peter Pelham. *Cotton Mather.* 1727. Mezzotint, 11 × 15". Courtesy Kennedy Galleries, Inc., New York.

**right: 264.** Rembrandt. *Arnold Tholinx.* c. 1656. Etching, drypoint, and engraving; 7$\frac{13}{16}$ × 5$\frac{7}{8}$". Louvre, Paris (Cabinet Rothschild).

entirely with hatching and cross-hatching (**99**). The face is serious, the man almost severe, possibly impatient with having his portrait done. Rembrandt's triumph is in conveying not just the physical image but the psychological depth as well. Perhaps no one else could give us so sensitive an insight into character in this demanding medium.

Another master of the etching technique was the Spanish artist Francisco de Goya. Goya made several ambitious series of prints, and he worked in all the various print media, sometimes, as here, in more than one technique for a single print. The soft, occasionally irregular line of etching gives it a rather "dark," brooding quality, suited to Goya's political and social satire. *Hasta la muerte (Until Death,* **265**) is from one of his major series, called *Los Caprichos,* meaning caprices, whims, eccentricities, freakishness. We see an old, grotesque woman primping absurdly for her seventy-fifth birthday party, reflected even more horribly by her mirror. The look of satisfaction on her face suggests that *she* does not see the ugliness that we and the mocking onlookers see. Goya is poking none-too-gentle fun at her vanity, her girlish costume, her attempt at gilding a very faded lily. The message of this print, as of many of *Los Caprichos,* might be: "We do not see ourselves as others see us."

If etching can produce the dark, gruesome qualities that Goya was looking for, it is also capable of quite delicate effects, as in the work of contemporary printmaker Donald Saff. *Our Lady of Sarcasm* (**266**) presents an airy female figure apparently floating in a garden of pale flowers. There are many ambiguities in this etching. Is the woman reclining, or is she drifting gently from right to left? Why are the beautifully drawn flowers at left canceled out by the harsh black scribbling at right? Why is the woman's expression so melancholy, why is her form barely suggested, and what is the round ball halfway down her figure? Above all, what is the meaning in the title *Our Lady of Sarcasm*? These mysteries draw us back again and again to study the print. We may understand imperfectly and yet be hypnotized by the fragile image.

**left: 265.** Francisco de Goya.
*Hasta la Muerte,*
from *Los Caprichos.*
Etching and aquatint, first edition.
Meadows Museum,
Southern Methodist University, Dallas.

**right: 266.** Donald Saff.
*Our Lady of Sarcasm.* 1978.
Etching with hand coloring, 24 × 19″.
Courtesy Getler/Pall Gallery, New York.

## Aquatint

A variation on the etching process, aquatint is a way of achieving flat areas of tone—gray values or intermediate values of color. To understand why this is desirable, we need only look back at the portrait of *Arnold Tholinx* (**264**). In that etching Rembrandt created the *illusion* of tone and shading by means of lines, hatched and cross-hatched. But aquatint allows the intaglio printmaker to produce real, not simulated tone.

To prepare the plate, the artist first dusts it with particles of resin. Several methods are available to control where and how thickly the resin is distributed on the plate. Then the plate is heated, so the resin sticks to it. When the plate is dipped in acid, the acid bites everywhere there is no resin, all around the particles (**259**). For instance, if the particles are thinly dusted and far apart, the acid will be able to bite into larger areas of the plate, but if the particles are close together the acid will have limited space to penetrate. Different tones, from light to dark, can be produced depending on the density of the particles, the length of time the plate is held in the acid, or the strength of the acid bath.

Because aquatint does not print lines but only areas of tone it is nearly always combined with one or more of the other intaglio techniques—drypoint, etching, or engraving. The 19th-century American artist Mary Cassatt, who was much influenced by the flat areas of color in Japanese woodcuts, adopted aquatint for a great many of her prints. *In the Omnibus* (**267**) has broad areas of soft tone in the women's dresses, the baby's bunting, and part of the background. But the faces and other details have been precisely rendered in drypoint and etching. The overall effect, in its softness and subtle shading, resembles a pastel drawing.

By combining techniques the intaglio artist can get almost any result he or she wishes. Because the artist can achieve effects ranging from the most precisely drawn lines to the most subtle areas of tone, the possibilities for imagery are much greater than in the relief methods. We turn now, however, to a branch of printmaking that is even more flexible in its effects.

**267.** Mary Cassatt. *In the Omnibus.* 1891. Color aquatint with drypoint and soft-ground, $14\frac{15}{16} \times 10\frac{1}{2}''$. Cleveland Museum of Art (bequest of Charles T. Brooks).

# Lithography

All the printmaking techniques except one have origins going far back into history, having developed from other art forms, such as decoration of armor, printing on fabrics, and so on. That one exception is lithography. Lithography was invented in a particular place at a particular time by a particular individual—a man named Alois Senefelder.

Senefelder was a young German actor and playwright living in Munich during the 1790s. Frustrated by the expense of publishing his plays, he began experimenting with the etching process as a cheap method of reproducing them. He was too poor to invest much money in copper plates, so he tried working on the smooth Bavarian limestones that lined the streets of Munich, which he excavated from the street and brought to his studio. One day, when he was experimenting with ingredients for drawing on the stone, his laundress appeared unexpectedly, and Senefelder hastily wrote out his laundry list on the stone, using his new combination of materials—wax, soap, and lampblack. Later, he decided to try immersing the stone in acid. To his delight he found that the words of the laundry list appeared in slight relief on the stone. This event paved the way for his development of the lithographic process. While the relief aspect eventually ceased to play a role, the groundwork for lithography had been laid.

Lithography is a *planographic* process, which means that the printing surface is flat—not raised as in relief, or depressed as in intaglio (**248**). It depends, instead, upon the principle that oil and water do not mix. To make a lithographic print the artist first draws the image on the stone with a greasy material—usually a grease-based lithographic crayon composed of such materials as wax, soap, and shellac. (Senefelder's Bavarian limestone is still in use as a surface, but zinc plates are also common.) Then the whole stone is treated with a light acid bath to fix the image and is soaked in water. Water is absorbed by the stone only in the areas *not* coated with grease. When the stone is inked, the greasy ink sticks to the greasy image areas and is repelled by the water-soaked background areas. Although the printing surface, stone or plate, is flat, only the image areas print on paper. (This book was printed by a mechanical version of lithography, known as *offset lithography.*)

Within a few years after Senefelder's discovery, many artists familiar with the relief and intaglio methods had taken up lithography. One of the first was the French artist Honoré Daumier. Some of Daumier's prints involve harsh political criticism, but *The Hot Bath* (**268**) is in a lighter vein. Daumier has comically depicted a man lowering himself into the bath, oh-so-gingerly. The

**268.** Honoré Daumier.
*The Hot Bath.* 1839.
Lithograph, $8\frac{1}{2} \times 10\frac{7}{8}''$.
Minneapolis Institute of Arts
(gift of Mrs. C. C. Bovey, 1924).

pained expression on the man's face tells us the bath is very hot indeed. While his outer clothing is scattered about, the man is wearing a shirt, since bathing naked was not at all common in those times. We can see that Daumier has mastered the lithographic technique, then barely forty years old. There is a full range of textures, from the patterned background at both sides to the white cloud of steam in the center, echoing the curve of the bather's body.

The potential of lithography was recognized almost immediately. By this method artists could create a wide range of effects, both linear and tonal, with relative ease and consequently low cost. The general public thus could be supplied with inexpensive, high-quality prints suitable for framing. Many companies on both sides of the Atlantic went into the business of making lithographs, but in the United States one firm so dominated the market that its name became almost automatically associated with the word "lithograph." That firm was Currier & Ives.

Nathaniel Currier established his lithographic company in New York City in 1834, and in 1857 James Merritt Ives joined him as a partner. During the nearly seventy years the firm was in business it produced an estimated seven thousand lithographs on a wide variety of subjects. There was something for every taste—Civil War battles, landscapes, religious themes, famous disasters (especially fires, which allowed for lurid red effects in the sky), great trains and ships, scenes from the American West, sports (from prize fighting to fishing), and many other categories.

Currier & Ives devised an ingenious system for manufacturing the prints. They employed a great many artists to do the original drawings, after which the image was transferred to stone by professional lithographers. Although color printing, which required several stones, was feasible, Currier & Ives rarely used this expensive method. Instead, after the prints had been run off in black and white, each one was individually hand-colored in assembly-line fashion by platoons of young women sitting at long tables—one color per person. The colorists were supposed to follow color keys supplied by the artist, but quite often—perhaps to break the tedium of the job—they would select colors according to the whim of the moment. A catalogue from 1860 lists prices ranging from 8¢ to $3.75 for each print. Today a good Currier & Ives lithograph might be sold for many thousands of dollars.

One of the most talented and certainly the busiest of Currier & Ives' artists was Flora Bond (Fanny) Palmer. During her career with the firm Palmer made an astonishing number of prints, on all the various subjects. Her detailed drawing style, plus an instinct for what the public would like, put her work greatly in demand. *American Express Train* (**269**) shows a favorite subject, drawn with her usual attention to detail and set in a picture-perfect landscape where every leaf is a work of art.

Most of the Currier & Ives artists were anonymous. It was the firm name that mattered, not the names of individual artists. Even Fanny Palmer signed few of her lithographs; later experts have identified her prints by analyzing the drawing style. By the end of the century, however, a number of well-known artists, especially in Europe, had taken up the new process. The Frenchman Henri de Toulouse-Lautrec has become closely identified with the lithograph because of one of those rare perfect convergences: He had the right artistic style for the right medium at the right time.

As we saw in Chapter 1, Lautrec practically invented the color lithographic poster, with the designs he made to advertise the Moulin Rouge nightclub and its performers. *La Goulue at the Moulin Rouge* (**270**) is a superior example. One of the featured dancers at the Moulin Rouge, La Goulue (the Glutton) is shown doing the can-can before an audience rendered in silhouette. Lautrec understood well that a poster must, above all, catch the eye. Its message is simple: Come to the Moulin Rouge, where you will have a good time. The influence of Japanese prints is obvious in the flattened forms, the broad color areas, and the sharply up-tilted perspective, which is visible espe-

AMERICAN EXPRESS TRAIN.

cially in the floorboards. Despite the apparent foreground (the master of ceremonies in silhouette), middle ground, and background, we get little sense of
spatial depth. The composition is meant to be flat and decorative. Lithography provided Lautrec with the means to achieve, with relative ease, both the
definite outline and the flat areas of tone. In all, the effect is frivolous, bohemian, and just a trifle sinister—like the Moulin Rouge itself.

above: 269. Flora Bond Palmer,
for Currier & Ives.
*American Express Train.* 1864. Lithograph.
Museum of the City of New York
(Harry T. Peters Collection).

left: 270. Henri de Toulouse-Lautrec.
*La Goulue at the Moulin Rouge.* 1891.
Color lithograph, 5'5" × 3'10".
Philadelphia Museum of Art
(gift of Mr. and Mrs. R. Sturgis Ingersoll).

# Edvard Munch
## *1863–1944*

The picture reproduced above, *Self-Portrait Between Clock and Bed,* was completed by Edvard Munch two years before his death. Munch chose to portray himself in light of the short time left to him (symbolized by the clock), beside the bed on which he would die. It is not surprising that a man in his eightieth year was anticipating death, but for Munch it was nothing new. Death obsessed him throughout his life and was an ongoing presence in his art.

Born in a small town in Norway, Munch was raised in Christiania, as Oslo was then called. When he was five his mother died, and nine years later his beloved older sister died of tuberculosis. These events haunted the artist and no doubt contributed much to his extreme anguish and anxiety. At seventeen he began art studies in Christiania, becoming involved as well in the rather morbid, sexually permissive bohemian life of the city. In 1885 Munch paid the first of many visits to Paris. There he saw, and was influenced by, the work of the Impressionists and Post-Impressionists, especially that of Paul Gauguin. Although Munch borrowed aspects of painting techniques, his themes remained very personal ones—death and dying, generalized anxiety, the despair of loneliness and abandonment, the passions between men and women, the sexual force of Woman as a source of terror.

Munch's first one-man show, in Berlin in 1892, was a disaster. His powerful subject matter and (to onlookers) harsh painting style caused an uproar, and the show was closed within a week. Nevertheless, the artist decided to take a studio in Berlin, where he remained for several years. The sixteen years following the Berlin exhibition, spent mainly in Germany and Paris, were Munch's most fertile period. It was then that he developed his interest in prints—woodcuts, lithographs, etchings—of which he eventually made more than seven hundred. Prints allowed him to explore, in many variations, the subjects that absorbed him. Often a subject he had tried in painting became starker, more disturbing, more intensely colored in subsequent print versions.

By 1908 Munch had become internationally famous, but his personal life was far from tranquil. Alcoholic, worn out with hard work, overstimulated by the bohemian clique in Berlin, tormented by at least one miserable love affair—Munch suffered a nervous breakdown and checked himself into a sanitarium in Copenhagen. There he underwent electric shock therapy to counteract effects on his brain of "persistent battering from an obsessive idea."[3]

If there is such a thing as a "Norwegian temperament"—brooding, melancholy, dark as the long nights of northern winter—Munch had it. Certainly it is difficult to visualize imagery like his coming from a French or Italian artist. After the breakdown, however, Munch's torments eased, and the output from his later years lacks the power of the Berlin/Paris period. It is as though the therapy that healed him took away all the passion, and the passion was necessary to his art. Perhaps he understood this. As he himself said, "I shouldn't like to be without suffering. How much of my art I owe to suffering!"[4]

Edvard Munch. *Self-Portrait between Clock and Bed.* c. 1940. Oil on canvas, $5'7\frac{3}{8}'' \times 3'11\frac{5}{8}''$. Oslo Kommunes Kunstsamlinger.

Lithography also was well adapted to the stark, intense, brooding imagery of the Norwegian artist Edvard Munch (**271**). Munch's lithograph *Sin* is done almost entirely in red, symbolic of the title, and we find it shocking to see such an intense color used so freely. Because the green eyes are the only contrast, they rivet our attention. The eyes seem at once to be looking inward and gazing at some dreadful horror. This image associates women's sexuality with evil and shame—a theme that obsessed Munch throughout his life. Women's hair, especially in quantity as here, was seen by Munch as both an allurement and a potential danger for men. This effect of voluptuous hair—gorgeous yet menacing—was enhanced by the free-drawing capabilities of the lithographic crayon on stone.

A number of contemporary artists who are best known as painters have taken up lithography as a means of broadening their range of expression. Among them is Jim Dine. In recent years Dine has used lithography and other printmaking media to explore the expressive possibilities of a series of motifs, or repeated images. For some time his motif was a disembodied bathrobe, representative of himself. Then he turned to the motif of the heart shape (**272**). Dine uses the heart as a pure shape, interesting in itself and adaptable to many variations, yet its association with love gives added symbolic meaning.

Lithography has been a favorite technique of contemporary artists, because it offers so much freedom in drawing and design. The technical limits of the medium are few. Our final branch of printmaking, however, gives even greater freedom in one particular respect—the use of color.

**left: 271.** Edvard Munch. *Sin.* 1901. Color lithograph, $27\frac{3}{8} \times 15\frac{1}{2}''$. Rijksmuseum, Amsterdam.

**272.** Jim Dine. *The Earth.* 1983. Lithograph, $46\frac{1}{4} \times 32''$. Courtesy Pace Gallery, New York.

# Screenprinting

To understand the basic principle of screenprinting, you need only picture the lettering stencils used by schoolchildren. The stencil is a piece of heavy cardboard from which the forms of the alphabet letters have been cut out. To trace the letters onto paper, you simply place the stencil over the paper and fill in the holes with pencil or ink.

**above left: 273.** Andy Warhol.
*George Gershwin,*
from *Ten Portraits of Jews
of the Twentieth Century.*
1980. Silkscreen, 40 × 32″.
Courtesy Ronald Feldman
Fine Arts Inc., New York.

**above right: 274.**
Robert Rauschenberg.
*Arcanum IV.* 1981.
Silkscreen with silk collage
and watercolor, $22\frac{1}{2} \times 15\frac{3}{4}$″.
Courtesy Styria Studio, Inc.,
New York.

**right: 275.** Alan Shields.
*Color Radar Smile A.* 1980.
Multicolored handmade paper
with etching, aquatint, and relief;
25″ square. Courtesy
Tyler Graphics, Inc., Bedford, N.Y.

Today's art screenprinting works much the same way. The screen is a fine mesh of silk or synthetic fiber mounted in a frame, rather like a window screen. (Silk is the traditional material, so the process is often called *silkscreen* or *serigraphy*—"silk writing.") Working from drawings, the printmaker blocks *(stops out)* areas in the screen that are *not* meant to print by plugging up the holes, usually with some kind of glue, so that no ink can pass through. Then the screen is placed over paper, and the ink is forced through the mesh with a tool called a *squeegee*. Only the areas not stopped out allow the ink to pass through and print on paper (**248**).

To make a color screenprint, the artist prepares one screen for each color. On the "blue" screen, for example, all areas not meant to print in blue are stopped out, and so on for each of the other colors. The preparation of multiple color screens is relatively easy and inexpensive. For this reason it is not unusual to see serigraphs printed in ten, twenty, or more colors. This color flexibility would be very difficult to achieve in any of the other methods. (Imagine preparing twenty-five Bavarian limestones, each weighing many pounds, for a single color lithograph!)

Andy Warhol's portrait of *George Gershwin* (**273**) exploits another capability of screenprinting—its potential for flat areas of color. A broad area of unshaded color can be achieved simply by not stopping out the screen in that area. In Warhol's print the composer's face, in profile, is divided into four quadrants, each in a different electric color, with the linear detail kept to a minimum. Take away the startling color, and this print would be just a rather straightforward sketch of Gershwin. By treating an ordinary likeness in such an unexpected way Warhol jolts the viewer into a new awareness of how colors and forms influence one another.

One of the most appealing qualities of screenprinting for the contemporary artist is its ability to be used in combination with other techniques. Such combining has become a favorite practice for Robert Rauschenberg. Rauschenberg's *Arcanum IV* (**274**) is part silkscreen, along with silk collage (layers of silk are applied to the backing) and watercolor. The surface of the print is richly textured with many different images, screened on both paper and silk, overlapping and sometimes seen through a film of translucent silk. The imagery itself is complex—bits of machinery, bombs, spaceships, a race horse, flowers, parts of Old Master paintings—all suggesting a riddle or puzzle to be solved, as the title *Arcanum* ("a mystery") implies. Rauschenberg's combination of techniques adds to the mystery, while the silkscreening pulls the composition together.

Much of Rauschenberg's work, and that of other contemporary artists, depends on technology developed only in the last decade or two. So enormous have been the technical innovations in recent years that no artist need feel confined by the limits of any one medium. In fact, it is not uncommon for the two aspects—imagery and process—to feed upon one another. The idea for an image stimulates new advances in technology, which in turn suggests new possibilities for imagery, and back and forth indefinitely. To see how this works, let us consider a few advanced and combined techniques.

## Advanced and Combined Techniques

Alan Shields' *Color Radar Smile A* (**275**), made by at least four different printmaking techniques, is so exciting that, according to a writer for *Art News*, it makes "a person want to drop everything and join in the fun of making objects like these." Shields begins with handmade paper—a multicolored paper that has been molded and shaped with openings to allow light to pass through. Printing on the front is by etching and aquatint, on the reverse by relief, so the print should be free-hanging and seen from both sides. The image does actually remind us of a radar screen (as in the title), with its blips and dashes, but it is also a bit like a computer punch card gone wild with color.

# Robert Rauschenberg

*b. 1925*

**B**orn in Port Arthur, Texas, Milton Rauschenberg—who later became known as Bob and then Robert—had no exposure to art as such until he was seventeen. His original intention to become a pharmacist faded when he was expelled from the University of Texas within six months, for failure (he claims) to dissect a frog. After three years in the Navy during World War II, Rauschenberg spent a year at the Kansas City Art Institute, then traveled to Paris for further study. At the Academie Julian in Paris he met the artist Susan Weil, whom he later married.

Upon his return to the United States in 1948, Rauschenberg enrolled in the now-famous art program headed by the painter Josef Albers at Black Mountain College in North Carolina. Many of his long-term attachments and interests developed during this period, including his close working relationship with the avant-garde choreographer Merce Cunningham. In 1950 Rauschenberg moved to New York, where he supported himself partly by doing window displays for the fashionable Fifth Avenue stores Bonwit Teller and Tiffany's.

Rauschenberg's work began to attract critical attention soon after his first one-man exhibition at the Betty Parsons Gallery in New York. The artist reports that, between the time Parsons selected the works to be exhibited and the opening of the show, he had completely reworked everything, and that "Betty was surprised." More surprises were soon to come from this unpredictable artist.

The range of Rauschenberg's work makes him difficult to categorize. In addition to the paintings, prints, and combination pieces, he has done extensive set and costume design for dances by Cunningham and others, as well as graphic design for magazines and books. "Happenings" and performance art played a role in his work from the very beginning. In 1952, at Black Mountain College, he participated in *Theater Piece #1,* by the composer John Cage, which included improvised dance, recitations, piano music, the playing of old records, and projected slides of Rauschenberg's paintings. Even the works usually classified as paintings are anything but conventional. One has an actual stuffed bird attached to the front of the canvas. Another consists of a bed, with a quilt on it, hung upright on the wall and splashed with paint. Works that might be called sculptures are primarily assemblage; for example, *Sor Aqua* of 1973 is composed of a bathtub (with water) above which a large, irregular chunk of metal seems to be flying, attached by rope to a glass bottle in the tub.

We get from Rauschenberg a sense of boundaries being dissolved—boundaries between media, between art and nonart, between art and life. He has said: "I don't think any artist sets out to make art. You love art, you live art, you are art, you do art, but you are just doing something, you are doing what no one can stop you from doing, and so it doesn't have to be art, and that is your life. But you also can't make life, and so there is something in between there, because you flirt with the idea that it is art."[5]

Robert Rauschenberg, photographed by Hans Namuth.

As printmaking techniques have advanced, so have methods of making paper. It may be difficult to think of paper as being "made." For most of us, paper comes in tablets or sheets or rolls, and we don't give much thought to how it got that way. But paper is composed of vegetable fibers, pounded into a pulp and then pressed into sheets. There is no reason why it cannot be pressed into other forms—forms that are quite different from the pages of this text or the blue books in which you write your examinations.

One artist who has explored the realm of pressed paper is Louise Nevelson. Nevelson's molded paper works, such as *Night Star* (**276**), are formed around handmade rubber molds. They may remind you of prints made in sand or of Egyptian rock carvings. Like other prints, these cast-paper images can be duplicated for an edition, because the mold is reusable. The image is not in lines and colors but is an actual three-dimensional impression.

Once prints start expanding into the third dimension, there is no stopping them. Contemporary printmakers are masters of the "why not try . . . ?" Take an artist whose imagination and sense of humor are manic, who understands the lithographic process, who appreciates pop-up books and paper dolls—and you get *Gertrude* (**277**). Red Grooms made *Gertrude*—who is the famous writer and art collector Gertrude Stein—from two lithographic prints, cut, folded, and mounted in three dimensions within an acrylic box. She (we cannot think of the work as "it") is a multiple, but she might just as well have fit into the sculpture chapter of this text. There she sits, pudgy in her flowered blouse in her pudgy flowered chair—an example of where prints might go if artists don't take themselves too seriously.

If you had any doubt at the beginning of this chapter that printmaking is a lively art, chances are you have changed your mind by now. In some ways it is an art ideally suited to our life style. The painter, the sculptor, the architect—all these make *one* work of art at a time, that will reside in one place. People who want to see the original must journey to do so. But the print made in an edition of three hundred will reside in three hundred different places and be enjoyed by thousands of people. Truly, the print allows nearly anyone to corner a small piece of the world of art.

left: **276.** Louise Nevelson.
*Night Star.* 1981.
Cast paper, $32\frac{3}{8} \times 36''$.
Courtesy Pace Gallery, New York.

right: **277.** Red Grooms.
*Gertrude.* 1975.
Six-color lithograph, cut out, mounted, and boxed in Plexiglas; $19\frac{1}{4} \times 22 \times 10\frac{1}{2}''$.
Courtesy Brooke Alexander, Inc., New York.

# 9 Photography

Photography is the art form that best demonstrates a basic truth: Artistry resides not in the hands but in the head. People who cannot draw well sometimes think that painters have some unusual skill in their hands, just as a singer may have an exceptional voice. But while some art forms do demand manual skill, the difference between a merely competent mechanical performance and a great work of art lies not in the artist's hands but in the brain—in the artistic inspiration that tells the hands what to do.

It is this confusion between mechanical skill and inspiration that has caused some people to question photography as an art form. After all, painters and sculptors *create* forms; photographers only *find and record* forms. Nevertheless, just as the painter's brain tells the hands what marks to make on canvas, so the photographer's brain interprets what is seen by the eyes and tells the camera what to do. Whereas the average person walks through the world seeing trees and buildings and people, the creative photographer walks through the world seeing compositions—possible photographs. We might almost say that the photographer has an invisible frame somewhere behind the eyes—a frame that is constantly composing pictures.

In composing a picture the photographer makes many decisions. We might analyze one well-known photograph to see how this works (**278**). The American photographer Russell Lee took the picture in Missouri during the Great Depression. Writing for the Museum of Modern Art, John Szarkowski said this about it:

> The simplicity of photography lies in the fact that it is very easy to make a picture. The staggering complexity of it lies in the fact that a thousand other pictures of the same subject would have been equally easy. Should the picture be made from farther away, or closer? Perhaps only the top of the dresser with the oil lamps and the boy's reflection in the mirror would be better; one step to the left might show the curve of the boy's cheek, but his head now touches the oil lamp, and the tape on the broken mirror falls on the reflection of his face. The feet are

**278.** Russell Lee. *Son of a Sharecropper Combing Hair in Bedroom of Shack, Missouri.*
1938. Gelatin-silver print from original negative in the Library of Congress,
$7\frac{3}{8} \times 9\frac{1}{2}''$. Museum of Modern Art, New York.

necessary. Would a vertical be better? Are the hats and the romantic landscapes on the wall, and the slop pail, part of the picture? How large is the boy and how small the room? What is the proper relationship between them? An infinite number of possibilities present themselves simultaneously, to be instinctively resolved, well or badly, in a moment, while the situation itself continues to change.

No one can now know what other pictures might have been made here, but the one that Russell Lee made is perfect.[1]

Szarkowski's analysis of the Russell Lee photograph makes us question the popular idea that photography simply "tells the truth," or that the "camera can't lie." Lee's photograph of a sharecropper's little boy is obviously the "truth" of what took place at that particular time in a shack in Missouri. But suppose, for example, Lee had zeroed in on the child, screening out nearly everything else; we would have had a charming photo of a little boy combing his hair. Or suppose the child had not appeared in the picture; the image would have shown disorder and poverty, but not the poignancy of poverty reflected in a child. Each situation, therefore, contains many truths, and the truth of a particular picture is whatever the creative photographer selects for us to see, selects to become part of the final image.

## The Camera and Its Beginnings

History books usually report that photography was invented in 1837 by the Frenchman Louis Jacques Mandé Daguerre. However, others besides Daguerre had been working on the principles of photography, and the idea of forming images by means of light had been known since the 16th century. Painters of the Renaissance, including Leonardo da Vinci, experimented with methods of recording objects and people by focusing light upon them in controlled ways. Daguerre's contribution was in finding a method to make those images permanent.

Despite the amazing sophistication of modern photographic equipment, the underlying principle of the camera is simple. A camera is a light-tight box (**279**) with an opening at one end to admit light, a lens to focus and refract the light, and a light-sensitive surface to receive the light-image and hold it. In today's cameras the light-sensitive surface is the film, but early experimenters used various materials. Daguerre recorded his first photographic image on a copper plate and christened this method the *daguerreotype*. Other pioneers worked with light-sensitive paper (the *calotype*), glass (the *ambrotype*), and dark metal (the *tintype*).

Daguerre's invention caused great excitement throughout Europe and the United States. Entrepreneurs and the general public alike were quick to see the potential of photography, especially for portraits. It is hard to realize now, but until photography came along only the rich could afford to have their likenesses made, by sitting for a portrait painter. Within three years after Daguerre made his first plate, a "daguerreotype gallery for portraits" had opened in New York, and such galleries soon proliferated. To our eyes the portraits seem stiff and posed, which they were. Subjects had to remain motionless, without blinking, for between half a minute and a full minute. (If this doesn't seem long to you, try doing it.) What's more, the idea of sitting for an "official" portrait was very new to most of these subjects. The sitters look awkward, and the results are often amusing—and charming (**280**).

The desire to record what people look like remains an important function of photography, for professionals and amateurs alike. Nearly everyone has a drawerful of photographs and slides, recording significant events from birth (some have been photographed *during* birth) through childhood, adolescence, romance, marriage, parenthood, and old age. Despite the popularity of amateur photography, the professional still plays a role in recording what people look like. Portraits comprise one of the major categories in photography.

**279.** The basic parts of a camera.

## Subject Matter in Photography

### Portraits

The professional portrait, at its best, goes beyond merely recording the subject's physical attributes. Like any other photograph, it tells one "truth"—a selected version of all the possible things one could record about the subject. And, like any other portrait—an oil painting, for example—it may serve as a revelation of the subject's character. Certain photographers have demonstrated a particular genius for portrait photography.

In the middle of the 1800s one man, by virtue of creative talent, enterprise, and sheer hard work, dominated the field of photography in the United States. That man was Mathew Brady. Brady opened a daguerreotype studio in New York in 1844, at the age of twenty-one. Later there was a studio in Washington and more studios in New York. From these bases he set out to photograph all the illustrious people of the time, and he very nearly succeeded. He employed many assistant photographers, called "operators," including Timothy O'Sullivan, whose work we shall see later in the chapter (**288**, **289**). In many cases it is impossible to tell which pictures Brady himself took, because his name appears on all of them.

The photograph shown here, however, almost certainly came from Brady's own camera. In 1860, when Abraham Lincoln was running for election to the Presidency, he arrived in New York to make a speech at Cooper Union, an important college. During his visit he presented himself at Brady's studio, where this sensitive portrait was made (**281**). Brady shows us a young Lincoln, clean-shaven, not yet torn by the heartache of war, fresh out of the back country of Illinois. His suit is obviously new, bought for the occasion, with the shirt cuff hanging down awkwardly from the jacket sleeve. Lincoln's facial

**above: 280.** Anonymous photographer, Great Britain. *An Elderly Veteran of Waterloo Posed with His Wife.* c. 1885. Hand-colored ambrotype, $4\frac{3}{4} \times 3\frac{1}{2}''$. Rubel Collection, courtesy Thackrey and Robertson, San Francisco.

**right: 281.** Mathew Brady. *Cooper Union Lincoln Portrait.* 1860. Photograph. Library of Congress, Washington, D.C.

expression is stern and dignified, but we also sense a bit of apprehension—perhaps caused by the leap into national politics, perhaps caused by the novel experience of having his portrait done.

Lincoln's Cooper Union speech was a success. Brady's photograph was in great demand, and thousands of copies were sold. After the election, Lincoln reportedly said, "Brady and the Cooper Union speech made me President."

Another famous portraitist of the 19th century—and an equally fascinating personality—was Frances Benjamin Johnston, who, without benefit of multiple assistants, was almost as prolific as Brady. Like Brady, she photographed an extraordinary range of subjects. Johnston was a niece of Mrs. Grover Cleveland, so she had access to the White House and, by extension, to many illustrious people, and she photographed them all. One of her most

**above left:**
**282.** Frances Benjamin Johnston.
*Self-Portrait.* 1895. Photograph.
Library of Congress, Washington, D.C.

**above right:**
**283.** Berenice Abbott. *James Joyce.*
1928. Gelatin-silver print,
$13\frac{3}{8} \times 10\frac{3}{8}''$.
Museum of Modern Art, New York
(Stephen R. Currier Memorial Fund).

**right: 284.** Edward Steichen.
*Carl Sandburg.* 1936.
Montage, gelatin-silver print;
$13\frac{11}{16} \times 16\frac{7}{8}''$.
Museum of Modern Art, New York
(gift of the photographer).

memorable works, however, is her portrait of herself (**282**). As we can see, Johnston was a strong personality who flouted convention. This seems to have helped rather than hindered her career. She has chosen to portray herself with a beer stein in one hand and a cigarette in the other—both virtually unheard of for a woman in 1895. Most shocking of all, though her costume is in line with the demure fashions of the day, her pose is decidedly "unladylike." She leaves us with the impression of a woman who lives and works exactly as she wishes, does it well, and answers to no one.

As we have said, the true photographic portrait is not just an accurate likeness but an interpretation of character. This is particularly clear in Berenice Abbott's portrait of James Joyce, made in Paris in 1928 (**283**). Joyce poses in an elegant costume, with a fine beaver hat and cane, but everything about him speaks of exhaustion and near-despair. His body seems shrunken within the suit, his hands too weary to hold themselves up. Abbott has lighted the scene so that her camera picks up every detail, even to the unspeakably sad expression in the writer's eyes.

Another writer, the poet Carl Sandburg, inspired photographer Edward Steichen to create a multiple image (**284**). It is as though Sandburg was so alive, so animated, so full of wisdom and charm that one likeness alone would not do to convey his character. Moreover, the repetition of Sandburg's head creates a visual rhythm that suggests the cadence of his poetry. Steichen's trademark was the dramatic use of light, especially of light-and-dark contrasts, and nowhere did he put it to better effect than in this portrait. Only the head is lighted, sometimes only the face. It is easy to imagine how much *less* striking this photograph would have been if the whole figure had been included.

Steichen's picture of Carl Sandburg gives us the impression of movement, of the poet carrying on a lively discourse. This idea of capturing motion has been another preoccupation of photographers from the beginning.

## Motion

Throughout history artists have tried to create the illusion of motion in a still image. Painters have drawn galloping horses, running people, action of all kinds—never being sure that their depictions of the movement were "correct" and lifelike. To draw a running horse with absolute realism, for instance, the artist would have to freeze the horse in one moment of the run, but because the motion is too quick for the eye to follow, the artist had no assurance a running horse ever does take a particular pose. In 1878 a man named Eadweard Muybridge addressed this problem, and the story behind his solution is a classic in the history of photography.

Leland Stanford, a former governor of California, had bet a friend twenty-five thousand dollars that a horse at full gallop sometimes has all four feet off the ground. Since observation by the naked eye could not settle the bet one way or the other, Stanford hired Muybridge, known as a photographer of landscapes, to photograph one of the governor's racehorses. Muybridge devised an ingenious method to take the pictures. He set up twelve cameras, each connected to a black thread stretched across the racecourse. As Stanford's mare ran down the track, she snapped the threads that triggered the cameras' shutters—and proved conclusively that a running horse does gather all four feet off the ground at certain times. Stanford won the bet, and Muybridge went on to more ambitious studies of motion.

In 1887 Muybridge published *Animal Locomotion*, his most important project. Somehow, he persuaded a great many of his friends to take off their clothes and move about doing specific physical activities—in this case, inexplicably, kicking a pith helmet—while he photographed them (**285**). There were

**285.** Eadweard Muybridge. *Woman Kicking*, Plate 367 from *Animal Locomotion*. 1887. Collotype, $7\frac{1}{2} \times 20\frac{1}{4}''$. Museum of Modern Art, New York (gift of the Philadelphia Commercial Museum).

781 plates in the series—many of nude people, some of clothed people, some of animals—all in motion. For the first time ever the world could see what positions living creatures really assume when they move.

A hundred years after Muybridge's pioneering work, the capturing of motion by the camera has become commonplace. Developments in mechanical equipment have expanded the possibilities to include such things as the motion picture and stop-action photography, which today we take for granted. Even so, we cannot help but admire a photograph like Michael C. Hayman's picture of football players in action (**286**). Had Hayman snapped the shutter a split second earlier or later, the picture would have been routine. In another instant, we know, there would have been just a pileup of bodies. But Hayman has captured the player from Michigan (in the white jersey) in flight with the ball, as opposing players from Ohio State try to tackle him. This picture could not have been made without today's sophisticated equipment, nor without the sure instincts of the photographer.

Both Muybridge's and Hayman's photographs show *arrested* motion—action frozen at a critical moment. Other pictures, however, attempt to capture in a still image the experience of continuing motion. Gerry Cranham's photograph of *Sprinters* (**287**) falls into this second category. Cranham, who

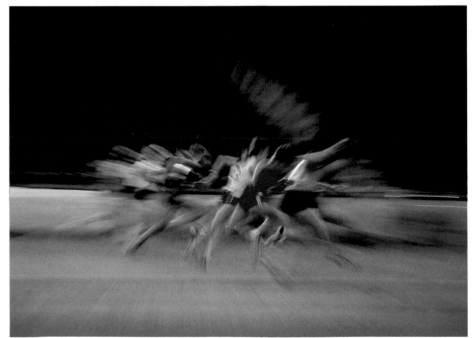

left: **286.** Michael C. Hayman. Photograph of college football players. 1974.

below: **287.** Gerry Cranham. *Sprinters*. Photograph.

specializes in sports photography, here deliberately blurs details in order to enhance the sense of great speed. The image of runners straining forward has become a kaleidoscope of bright colors that is full of energy. The photographer today has an extremely wide range of choices in the subject of motion.

## Landscape

From the first, landscape has been a popular subject for photographers, whether it was the natural beauty of the countryside or the constructed landscape of the city. Some early photographers, like Timothy O'Sullivan, went to great extremes to capture nature's forms. The photo here (**288**) shows a member of O'Sullivan's team perched dangerously on a rocky overhang to make one of the photographer's many studies of the American West. Hauling what was then very cumbersome photographic equipment through mountains and desert presented a real challenge, but the results were well worth the effort.

In 1867 O'Sullivan signed on as official photographer to an expedition commissioned by the federal government to explore the territories of Nevada and Colorado. One of his most dramatic photos from this trip (**289**) shows the mule-drawn ambulance O'Sullivan had hired to carry water for his traveling

**left: 288.** Timothy O'Sullivan.
*Photographing the West.* c. 1870.
Wet-plate photograph.
Library of Congress, Washington, D.C.

**below: 289.** Timothy O'Sullivan.
*Sand Springs, Nevada.* 1867.
Photograph.
Library of Congress, Washington, D.C.

darkroom. Tiny and stark against the vast shifting dunes, the vehicle looks like a dignified toy. We imagine that the footprints and grooves left by the wheels were the first marks ever made in this spot by anything but the wind.

The acknowledged master of 20th-century landscape photography was Ansel Adams. Our illustration (**290**) shows one of his most famous pictures, *Moon and Half Dome*. Although the scene that Adams chose to photograph is undeniably dramatic, that alone does not account for the artistry of this picture. Adams had "set up" the shot by choosing a precise vantage point; by *framing* the photo precisely (that is, including just the portion of landscape he wanted and no more); and by waiting until the moon, light, and shadows seemed just right. The composition is perfectly balanced, with the dark foreground rock at left and the dark shadow at right framing the lighted expanse of the rock known as Half Dome. The brilliant moon at top not only completes the balance of the picture but is its major focal point. Light is used to define and shape the natural forms, to create contrast, to define textures and details; indeed, light structures the entire photograph. Adams demonstrates that the successful landscape photo, far from being a happy accident of nature, is a demanding art.

## Genre

In the visual arts, as we have seen, the theme of genre focuses on everyday life. Usually people are included, but the intention is not to make a portrait of individuals. Instead, a genre photograph captures one of life's "little moments," as in André Kertész' *Couple in the Park* (**291**). The young couple, strolling through a park in Budapest, have paused for a moment to kiss. Who they are is not important; what matters is the sweetness of life and of young love. We see both tenderness and sensuality in this picture, heightened by the dark background and the light falling on the woman's face. Is she pulling away slightly? Perhaps, but her hands are clasped firmly behind her lover's back.

Our next photographer's pictures, while not strictly genre, expand that theme. The work of Diane Arbus concentrated on people who are unusual, apart from the norm—some would say "freaks." Arbus photographed a sword swallower, aging nudists, and people with physical abnormalities of all kinds.

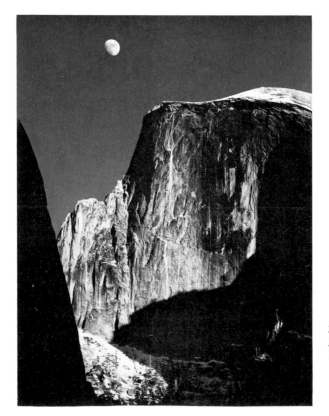

**290.** Ansel Adams.
*Moon and Half Dome.* 1966. Photograph.
Estate of the photographer.

291. André Kertész.
*Couple in the Park.* 1915.
Photograph. © André Kertész.

Her goal was to look directly, unflinchingly, at that which others turn away from. Often, her pictures reveal jarring incongruities. *The King and Queen of a Senior Citizens Dance* (**292**) shows a couple decked out in absurdly elaborate robes and crowns, which seem all the more absurd against their banal street clothing. Presumably, this is meant to be a festive occasion, but the "king" and "queen" have such mournful expressions that we doubt any pleasure in their monarchy. Their postures are weary, and the woman in particular looks as though she has just plopped herself down in exhaustion. Arbus might be showing us that any attempt to impose gaiety or celebration on this couple will be futile.

292. Diane Arbus.
*The King and Queen
of a Senior Citizens Dance,
New York City.* 1970.
Gelatin-silver print, 15 × 11¾".
Copyright © The Estate
of Diane Arbus, 1970.
Museum of Modern Art, New York
(Mrs. Armand P. Bartos Fund).

**293.** Skeet McAuley. *Roller Coaster,*
from the *Barriers* series.
Color coupler photograph.
Courtesy the photographer.

## Abstraction

As has been noted before, abstraction is a process by which natural forms are
simplified and reduced to their most characteristic aspects. We might think the
camera, which tells only the "truth," cannot do this, but indeed it can. Abstraction in photography can result from viewpoint, angle, distance (including
close-up), special lenses, darkroom techniques, or any combination of these.

Viewpoint is the factor in Skeet McAuley's *Roller Coaster* (**293**), part of a
series the photographer has made on barriers of different kinds. Here we can
identify the rising and falling tracks of the amusement park ride, but because
of the camera's viewpoint, and the screening out of other identifying details,
these tracks tend to be abstracted into curving, intersecting lines. Also, and
again because of the absence of extraneous details, we lose our sense of this
structure's scale, which further contributes to the abstraction of form.

Many of Edward Weston's photographs are extreme close-ups of familiar
objects, such as the *Artichoke, Halved,* shown here (**294**). Without the title, you
might not be able to identify the picture's subject matter. By moving in close
and picking up the exquisite detail of the vegetable, Weston gives it a majestic
quality. All sense of scale is destroyed; this could just as easily be a huge
underground cavern or a mysterious growth in a tropical rain forest—or a
modern abstract painting. In creating this abstraction Weston challenges our
preconceived notion of what an artichoke looks like. He may also encourage
us to look beyond the overly familiar appearance of other common objects and
consider their possibilities for abstraction of line, form, and texture.

A special lens known as a wide-angle lens produced the dream-like abstraction of Bill Brandt's *Nude on a Pebbled Beach* (**295**). Under some circumstances the wide-angle lens distorts what it records, stretching out shapes horizontally. Here the photographer has manipulated it in such a way that the
nude figure takes on a monumental quality, not unlike Henry Moore's sculptural abstractions of the human form (**216**). Only the most essential features
give us clues to the identity of this subject—the flow of hair, the swell of the
hips, and the line between the buttocks. The last is most important. If the left
quarter of the picture is covered up, the form could be almost anything.

below: **294.** Edward Weston.
*Artichoke, Halved.* 1930. Photograph.
© 1981 Arizona Board of Regents,
Center for Creative Photography.

right: **295.** Bill Brandt.
*Nude on a Pebbled Beach,*
*East Sussex Coast.* 1953. Photograph.

From a straightforward portrait to a naked monolith on a beach, the subject matter of photography includes everything in this world and—since the advent of space travel and sophisticated telescopes—more than a few things that are out of our world. The choice of imagery is limited only by the limits of the photographer's imagination. In some cases, however, the choice of subject matter may be influenced by the photographer's circumstances. Like drawings, photographs often are made for specific applications. The following section explores some of the purposes of photography.

## Purposes of Photography

Many photographs are made for specific commercial applications, such as publication in books, magazines, and newspapers, and their purpose is primarily illustrative or documentary. Other pictures have no external incentive beyond the photographer's urge for self-expression. The dividing line between these two categories is not a rigid one. The photographer on assignment from a magazine may make an image that survives for its artistic qualities long after that issue of the magazine has been forgotten. And, of course, art photographs often are reprinted in books and magazines. Nevertheless, our appreciation of photographs can be enhanced by considering the primary purpose for which each was taken, because this strongly affects the photographer's expression.

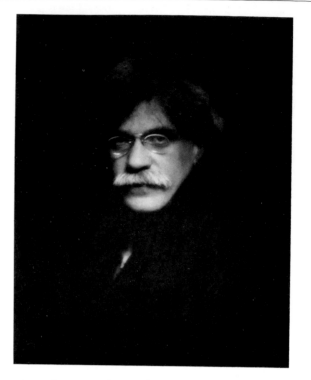

# Alfred Stieglitz
## *1864–1946*

The person most responsible for introducing modern art to the United States was not a painter or sculptor, but a photographer. Alfred Stieglitz was born in Hoboken, New Jersey, the eldest child of German parents. His youth was spent in travel between Europe and the United States, and he studied at both the City College of New York and the University of Berlin. In 1883, at the age of nineteen, Stieglitz bought his first camera in Berlin; thereafter his life's work seems never to have been in question.

Stieglitz settled more or less-permanently in New York in 1890, although he continued to travel widely. The first of his major efforts to promote photography as an art form came in 1896, when he was instrumental in founding the Camera Club of New York. The following year he became editor of its quarterly publication, *Camera Notes*. But the group most closely associated with his name was "Photo-Secession," founded in 1902. A loosely structured national organization of photographers, Photo-Secession was devoted to promoting exhibitions of photographers, later of contemporary painters and sculptors as well. Stieglitz served as editor of its quarterly, *Camera Work*, which maintained extremely high standards for photographs published and reproduction quality.

Along with the photographer Edward Steichen, Stieglitz in 1905 opened the Little Galleries of the Photo-Secession at 291 Fifth Avenue in New York, usually called "291." There the American public had its first opportunity to see the works of Picasso, Matisse, Cézanne, and other avant-garde European artists, as well as the most innovative of the Americans.

As a photographer, Stieglitz dedicated his talents to demonstrating that the medium was accessible to anyone, even those with unsophisticated equipment and little training. He often worked with the simplest cameras, had his photographs printed commercially, and delighted in shooting under difficult conditions—in rain, fog, and darkness. His pictures were exhibited widely and were collected by major museums during his lifetime.

Among the artists showing at 291 was the painter Georgia O'Keeffe. In 1918 Stieglitz left his first wife and moved in with O'Keeffe, whom he married after his divorce became final. His portraits of O'Keeffe, including many close-up studies of her hands, are among his most sensitive and striking images. Although Stieglitz and O'Keeffe were frequently apart, often at different parts of the globe (their chronology for the next twenty years or so reads like a travelogue), they remained married until his death at the age of eighty-two.

Stieglitz wrote extensively about his work, but perhaps the most characteristic statement can be found in his catalogue notes for an exhibit of his photographs in 1921: "My teachers have been life—work—continuous experiment. Incidentally a great deal of hard thinking. Any one can build on this experience with means available to all. . . . I was born in Hoboken. I am an American. Photography is my passion. The search for Truth my obsession."[2]

Alfred Stieglitz. *Self-Portrait.* c. 1894. Photograph.

left: **296.** Alfred Stieglitz.
*The Steerage.* 1907. Photograph.
Art Institute of Chicago
(Alfred Stieglitz Collection).

right: **297.** Harry Callahan.
*Eleanor, Port Huron.* 1954.
Photograph, $6\frac{5}{8} \times 6\frac{1}{2}''$.
Courtesy Zabriskie Gallery, New York.

## The "Art" Photograph

By art photograph, we mean a picture that is specifically intended for exhibition as art. Such photos are appreciated for their formal qualities and for their expressiveness, rather than for any illustrative value. Almost since the beginnings of the medium photographers have explored the purely expressive potential of the camera. But what we think of as today's art photography owes a great deal to the influence of one man in particular, both because of his own work and because of his efforts to promote photography as an art form. That man was Alfred Stieglitz, and his most famous picture is *The Steerage* (**296**).

The story of how *The Steerage* was made illustrates our point about photographers moving through the world with an invisible frame behind their eyes. In 1907 Stieglitz was aboard ship on his way to Europe, traveling first class. One day as he was walking the deck, he happened to look down into the steerage section—that portion of the ship where the poorest passengers, paying the lowest fares, were herded together like cattle. Before him he saw a perfectly composed photograph—the smokestack leaning to the left at one end, the iron stairway leaning to the right at the other, the chained drawbridge cutting across, even to such details as the round straw hat on the man looking down and the grouping of women and children below. Stieglitz knew he had only one unexposed plate left (the equivalent of one exposure at the end of a roll of film). He raced to his cabin to get his camera. When he returned, the scene was exactly the same; no one had moved. That one plate became *The Steerage*.

By the 1950s photography had definitely come into its own as an art medium, and among those recognized as master photographers was Harry Callahan. Over the years Callahan has made many pictures of his wife, Eleanor, but they are in no sense portraits. Some are quite abstract, and many, like *Eleanor, Port Huron* (**297**), show her distant and small in a large, tranquil landscape. Callahan's photographs are very personal, a direct expression of his inner emotions. Their trademark is the use of strong contrasts between light and dark values, as here. If you squint your eyes, the brilliant white form of

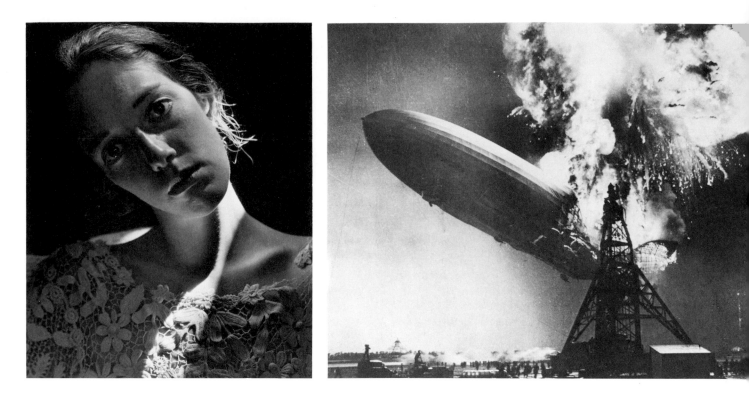

the woman's body almost seems to be floating in the lush dark background foliage. This image conveys utter serenity. Perhaps it speaks of Callahan's love for his wife, better than any portrait could do, in a grander way—as part of his love for life and nature.

Most of Judy Dater's photographs also include people, but like Harry Callahan's they are not, strictly speaking, portraits. Her subjects have often been urban California women, strangers to her before the photographing session, chosen because something in their faces connected with Dater's artistic vision. Rather than seeking the essence of the subject, Dater's pictures focus on one dimension of the subject's personality. For instance, the photograph of *Gwen* (**298**) shows a face of almost unbearable sorrow and loneliness. This does not mean, necessarily, that Gwen herself is sorrowful and lonely. Instead, she has chosen this role to play for the camera, and Dater has encouraged her. The picture is brilliantly composed. Gwen's side-tilted head almost fills the upper-half of the frame, and her face is kept in deep shadow. Both the extreme angle of the head and the dramatic lighting foster the impression that this is not a face at all but a theatrical mask—the mask of tragedy. Especially important is the streak of light cutting down the neck, which almost severs the head from the body.

## Photojournalism and Editorial Photography

Until the 19th century the only pictures that ever appeared in newspapers and magazines were made from drawings or from prints, usually engravings (**258**). Then photography came along, opening the potential for actual documentation of events. Mathew Brady, whose portrait of Lincoln we saw earlier (**281**), was among the first to exploit the potential of photographs for journalism. When North and South went to war in 1860, Brady and his team also went to war, carrying their equipment in peculiar horse-drawn wagons that the soldiers dubbed "Whatsits." Because his photos still required a fairly long exposure time at sittings, Brady could not photograph actual battles (which obviously would not stand still for the camera), but he recorded scenes of camp life, important generals and their aides, and especially the poignant aftermath of battle. The American Civil War, therefore, was the first major war photographed for posterity.

Because no method had yet been perfected to reproduce the photographs accurately and clearly, early photographs like Brady's were first translated into drawings and then into woodcuts for reproduction. Then, about 1900, the first process for photomechanical reproduction—high-speed printing of photographs along with type—came into being.

Today nearly every event that might remotely be considered newsworthy is covered by photojournalists, from the carnage of war to the escape of a pet snake in a residential neighborhood. News photographers must depend to a certain extent on luck. Their best pictures result when they are in the right place at the right time, when some extraordinary event occurs. Nevertheless, it is the photographer's skill that turns a record of an event into a great picture.

On May 6, 1937, the enormous German airship *Hindenburg* was scheduled to land at Lakehurst, New Jersey. Even though it was the dirigible's seventh trans-Atlantic crossing, the arrival was still considered remarkable enough that a crowd gathered, and twenty-two photographers from the New York and Philadelphia papers had been sent to cover the landing. The photographers were set up to compose shots for feature stories. Just as the giant silver balloon was about to be secured to the ground, it exploded and burst into flames. Of the ninety-two people on board, thirty-six were killed. Every one of the photographers, despite the tremendous heat and danger, managed to snap a few pictures before dashing to cover. Sam Shere's photo, with the crane silhouetted in front of the inferno, is one of the more memorable (**299**).

The burning of the *Hindenburg* was the first disaster to be thoroughly documented in photographs. During the decade of the thirties, however, another disaster—not a sudden one, but a long and painful one—was covered in depth by the most creative photographers of the time. The Great Depression, which began in 1929 and lasted until the onset of World War II, caused hardships for photographers as well as for the population as a whole. To ease the first problem and document the second, the Farm Security Administration (FSA) of the U.S. Department of Agriculture subsidized photographers and sent them out to record conditions across the nation. One of these was Russell Lee, whose picture of a sharecropper's son we saw at the beginning of this chapter (**278**). Another was Dorothea Lange.

Lange devoted her attention to the migrants who had been uprooted from their farms by combined effects of the Depression and drought. *Heading West, Tulare Lake, California* (**300**) shows a mother and her two children, dirty

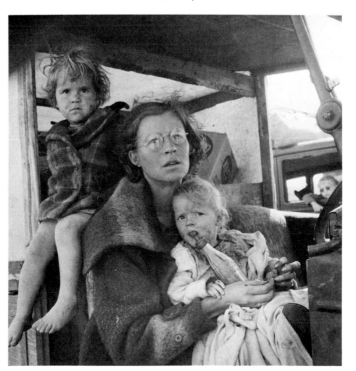

**300.** Dorothea Lange.
*Heading West, Tulare Lake, California.* 1939. Photograph.
Library of Congress, Washington, D.C.

and disheveled, in a battered truck. Despair is written on all three faces, as the eyes stare off at some distant point that may offer no relief from misery. Lange's masterful composition gives an importance, a universal quality, to the tragedy of one family. The picture's basic structure is a triangle, with the boy's head at the apex, one side running down through his leg, the other diagonal through the mother's head and the younger child, and the base resting on the bottom of the photo. (Compare Raphael's *Madonna*, **103**.) FSA photos like this one were offered free to newspapers and magazines across the United States. After the government project ended, Lange published her Depression photographs in a book, *An American Exodus: A Record of Human Erosion*.

Dorothea Lange's travels for the FSA took her to nearly every part of the country. In one summer alone she logged 17,000 miles in her car. Photojournalism is hard work. It may also be dangerous, as when the *Hindenburg* exploded. But the most difficult and dangerous job is that of war photographer.

W. Eugene Smith, who was on assignment for *Life* magazine for many years, worked as a combat photographer during World War II. Smith is a man with deep compassion for human suffering and a commitment to using photography to help alleviate that suffering. The picture shown here (**301**) was taken in Saipan in 1944, during the closing months of the Pacific campaign. A soldier in battle dress holds a naked infant from the local population. The

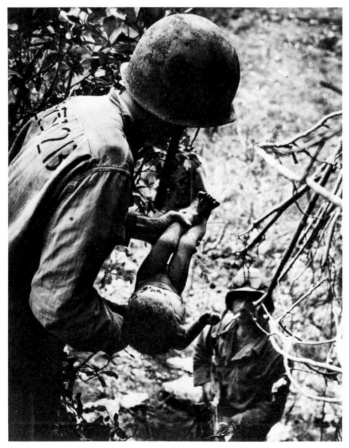

**above: 301.** W. Eugene Smith.
*Saipan.* 1944. Photograph.
© 1944 W. Eugene Smith/Black Star.

**right: 302.** Irving Penn.
*Woman in Black Dress.* 1950.
Gelatin-silver print, 16¼ × 11″.
Museum of Modern Art,
New York (gift of the photographer).

**303.** David Attie.
*Child Stuttering.* 1981. Photograph.
Courtesy the photographer.

picture raises many questions: What is the baby doing there? Where is its mother? Is it dead or alive? Did the soldier just stumble upon the child in the underbrush? The contrast between the burly soldier and the tiny, helpless child tells us *this* is the reality of war.

The photojournalist, as we said, needs a certain amount of luck. He or she must wait for the picture to happen in order to cover a story. There is another branch of journalistic photography, however, that *makes* pictures happen. This is editorial photography. Editorial photographers may deal in fashion, in food, in architecture, or many other areas. Their goal is to make the subject attractive and appealing, or possibly to interpret an idea photographically. Their pictures are "set up" very deliberately to achieve this purpose.

Fashion photography, like fashion illustration (**219**), usually aims at creating an illusion—the illusion of an impossible, idealized beauty that the viewer will feel compelled to emulate. No one has mastered this art of illusion better than Irving Penn. Penn's *Woman in Black Dress* (**302**) is almost an abstraction. The model, impossibly tall and thin, does not seem to resemble any living creature. We cannot imagine her walking or moving. If you cover up the head, you would be hard-pressed to identify the rest as a human body. Penn has posed the figure exactly in the center of the composition, and he has balanced one outstretched arm against the froufrou at the back of the dress. What matters here is not depiction of reality but a glimpse of unearthly elegance.

The job of the editorial photographer often is to interpret visually the ideas in a story or article. Special effects made possible by today's technology bring another dimension to this role. Photographer David Attie has used such effects for an article about childhood stuttering in *Smithsonian* magazine (**303**). By superimposing rows of colored blips across the photo, Attie ingeniously suggests the efforts of the boy to bring out a word or sound. The photographer has created a word-picture of stuttering.

Attie's picture, with its superimposed colored blips, can serve as an introduction to the final section in this chapter. So far, most of the photographs we have seen are essentially "straight." None employ complicated darkroom techniques or other special effects. The camera clicks, and the photograph is finished. With Attie's image we see a certain amount of manipulation, but for other photographers the click of the shutter is only the beginning of a process that will create an image very different from the one actually recorded on film.

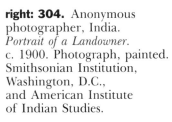

**right: 304.** Anonymous
photographer, India.
*Portrait of a Landowner.*
c. 1900. Photograph, painted.
Smithsonian Institution,
Washington, D.C.,
and American Institute
of Indian Studies.

**below: 305.** David Hockney.
*Celia, Los Angeles.* 1982.
Polaroid assemblage,
$14\frac{1}{2} \times 26\frac{1}{2}''$.
Copyright David Hockney, 1982,
courtesy André Emmerich Gallery,
New York.

## Special Effects and Techniques

The idea of using the photographic image only as a starting point is not a new
one. We have already explored the problem of photography as truth-teller
and asked, *which* truth? To this we must add another question: *whose* truth?

Photography reached India in the 1840s and was eagerly adopted by the
populace. The Indian approach to the medium was very different from that in
the West, however. Europeans, steeped in Renaissance concepts of depth and
perspective, greeted photography as an ever more "real" depiction of the natural world. The Indians, by contrast, had a tradition of miniature painting in

which the illusion of deep space was irrelevant. Paintings were flat, all in one plane, and highly decorative. So when they took up photography, the Indians proceeded to paint over the camera image until it looked "correct" to *them*.

Our illustration shows a splendid example (**304**). This portrait of a landowner, taken about 1900, has been meticulously painted all over. While the subject's face and hands retain a suggestion of roundness from the photograph, the rest of his body is flat, thanks to the painting. The chair seems to float in space, while the meeting of patterned rug and wall is just a vertical division of the picture plane, not an indication that the rug is perpendicular to the picture plane. (Possibly the rug was a plain floor in the photograph; it has been painted with no perspective at all, as though it were parallel to the picture plane.) The background wall—which in the photo must have showed another room opening to the left and a vista out the window at right—now seems more like a painted backdrop for the theater.

There is a lesson to be learned from this approach to photography. Our understanding of how things "are" and how things "should be" has much to do with cultural conditioning. The Indians' cultural heritage predisposed them to the belief that a flat, decorative image is the ideal expression of art; Western cultural heritage predisposes us to believe that the illusion of depth on a flat surface is superior. Actually, neither is right or better. Through understanding and exposure, we can learn to appreciate aesthetic values different from our own. This applies to all aspects of art and culture, not just to photography.

A century later and half a world away, the English artist David Hockney has also taken a fresh approach to perspective, with a different technique. Hockney's *Celia, Los Angeles* (**305**) is an assemblage of thirty-two Polaroid shots, each focusing on one part of the subject. Taken all together, the thirty-two images give a recognizable picture of the woman Celia. However, because each shot has a different perspective and scale, the effect is jarring and disorienting. Celia has been fragmented; the fragments add up to a whole, but it is a disturbing whole.

Jerry Uelsmann is another photographer who likes to combine images for special effect—not side by side but one on top of another. *Apocalypse II* (**306**) was printed from three negatives—two for the ghost-like white tree and a third for the silhouetted children on the beach. Cleverly, the photographer left: **307.** David Vine. *The Old Man of the World.* 1984. Solarized print. Courtesy the photographer.

right: **308.** Charles Swedlund. *Red Chair.* 1977. Dye-transfer photograph. Courtesy the photographer.

has made it seem that the figures are staring at the tree as though it were some mysterious cosmic force. You may be reminded of contemporary horror movies in which children possess demonic powers.

The Surrealist artist Man Ray experimented with several unusual photographic techniques in the 1920s and 1930s. One of them was *solarization,* a process by which an exposed negative is briefly reexposed to light during development. This causes chemical changes in the photographic emulsion—the light-sensitive coating on film. Contemporary photographer David Vine used solarization in *The Old Man of the World* (**307**). This image combines the visual effects we would expect to see in a photographic negative *and* a positive print. Most of the left side of the photo, except the hat, is "negative." The rest is "positive." Together, these effects give the old man's portrait an eerie quality but also an imposing dignity.

*In-camera color separation* is a technique that has been developed extensively by Charles Swedlund. Although fairly complicated, it basically involves "separating" the colors in an image by means of filters, photographing each individually, and then recombining them to make the print, much as one would print several colors together for a woodcut or silkscreen (page 201). The brilliant tones and soft focus in *Red Chair* (**308**) result from this method.

Interesting photographic images are possible even when the camera is bypassed altogether. Another of Man Ray's preoccupations was the photogram, which he called a *rayograph.* In this technique objects are placed directly on photographic paper and exposed briefly to light. The resulting print is developed and processed in the usual way. Philip Molten's *Bonegram #1* (**309**) is a contemporary version of this method. An exercise in form and design, the *Bonegram* sets white, shadowless bones against an inky black background. The highlights on the bones make them shine like polished silver. There is a strange contradiction in this image. The bones are primitive shapes, like magic artifacts in a shaman's kit, yet the design is entirely modern.

Finally, some artists have explored the potential of machine-mounted photographic equipment meant for copying documents, such as Xerox. You know that if you put your hand on the copying surface of a Xerox machine and push the button, you will get a "print" of your hand. But when you control the exposure time and set up the shot more deliberately, the machine becomes a creative tool, like a hand-held camera. Joan Lyons used a Xerox machine to make her *Self-Portrait* (**310**), which she then transferred to a lithographic plate for printing.

**309.** Philip L. Molten.
*Bonegram #1.* Photogram.
Courtesy the photographer.

We might very well ask, what will photography do next? It is now possible to photograph the vastness of the universe through telescopes and the most minute forms of life through electron microscopes. Just as quickly as scientists have developed new techniques for their studies, creative artists have adapted those techniques for aesthetic purposes. In a mere century and a half photography has come farther and faster than any of the media that have been with us for thousands of years.

It is important to remember, though, that the impulse for a photograph comes from the photographer, not from the technology. Any camera, from the simplest to the most sophisticated, is just so much hardware until it is brought to life by the eye, the mind, and the heart of a creative photographer.

**310.** Joan Lyons.
*Untitled, Self-Portrait.* 1974.
Xerox transfer-lithograph, 19 × 26".
Courtesy Visual Studies Workshop Gallery,
Rochester, N.Y.

# 10
# Graphic Design

All art has to do with communication, but this is uniquely true of graphic design. Graphic design has as its goal the communication of some *specific* message to a group of people, and the success of a design is measured by how well that message is conveyed. The message may be "This is a good product to buy" or "This is an important, respected company" or "This way to the elevators (or rest rooms or newsstand)" or any of countless others. If it can be demonstrated that the public received the intended message—because the product sold well or the company's stock went up or the traveler found the right services—then the design has worked.

Not all graphic design has to do with selling, but much of it does, and so for a long time it was known as "commercial art." The term "graphic design" is more inclusive and describes more accurately what artists in this field really do. They create a visual image by some combination of words and/or pictures to communicate a message quickly and effectively. Graphic artists design books and packages and advertisements. They devise the trademarks and symbols (logos) that construct a special corporate identity for firms doing business around the world. They invent symbols that have the same meaning to people who speak different languages. They provide the colorful images that introduce television programs and movies. Graphic designers even are responsible for the visual appeal of video games.

Printed words play a role in many graphic designs, but graphic designers rely heavily on recognizable visual images. Their art rarely involves subtle, complicated symbolism, as is often true of painting. The image presented must have an immediate *shared* impact on a large number of people in order for the communication process to work. Seldom are these designs meant to be savored, studied, and enjoyed at leisure—although they can be. The effect is supposed to be immediate and lasting.

A prime example of a design with a quick, lasting effect is the corporate logo, the symbol intended to represent a certain company. Logos have two major criteria for success: They must register instantly on the observer, and

**311.** Pepsi-Cola logo in Russian. Courtesy PepsiCo., Inc., owners of the trademark.

244

they must stick in the observer's mind so that every time the logo appears the observer will be reminded of that company. For instance, the Pepsi logo (311,312), with its distinctive colors and circle-around-a-wave, is recognized everywhere, even when the product name is in Russian or Chinese.

Because of our constant exposure to images like the Pepsi logo, graphic design seems very much a phenomenon of the 20th century, but in fact it has existed almost since the beginning of civilized life. Street signs and shop signs were used in ancient Rome. We might speculate that graphic design was invented when a hunter first managed to kill two bison in a single day and, unable to consume both before they spoiled, drew a crude sketch of a slain bison outside the cave to attract potential buyers. Of course, this is supposition, but we do know that graphic design gradually took hold through the centuries until it became a central part of urban life.

Three factors are ultimately responsible for the growing influence of graphic design: the invention of the printing press in the 15th century; the Industrial Revolution in the 18th century; and the revolution in travel and communication in the 20th century.

Anyone can paint one sign, or two or three. The printing press, however, made it possible to reproduce a graphic image many hundreds or thousands of times. This gave designers the *ability* to communicate with a broad public. The *need* for such communication was largely a result of the Industrial Revolution, which began in Europe in the latter part of the 18th century. Before that time, most products were grown or made locally to serve a local population. The person who wanted, say, a new pair of shoes could walk down the road to the village cobbler, or perhaps wait for the monthly fair at which cobblers from the neighboring towns might appear, but the choices were fairly limited. With the advent of machines huge quantities of goods were produced in centralized factories for wide distribution, and competition between producers became intense. It was necessary, therefore, to inform the buying public about the availability of certain goods and their relative merits. Graphic design in the form of advertising filled that need.

The history of graphic design for travelers is interesting, too. No doubt Robin Hood could have benefited from a sign pointing the way to Nottingham, and the pilgrims Chaucer wrote about looked for road signs to Canterbury. One of the more intriguing of travelers' communication systems is the one traditionally practiced by hobos in the United States. "Hobo signs" are simple, graphic images, usually scratched in chalk on a fence or post or sidewalk (313). The casual passerby would not notice them, but for those intrepid souls who ride the freight trains, sleep under bridges, and catch a meal wherever they can—the signs have meaning. Some are *pictographic*, or visually suggestive of what they mean ("good place to catch a train"), while others are purely arbitrary and convey meaning from hobo to hobo because they have been learned. The message conveyed by "hobo signs" is one of comradeship: "This is the experience I had at this place, and I want you to profit by it."

**below: 312.** Pepsi-Cola logo in Chinese. Courtesy PepsiCo., Inc., owners of the trademark.

**bottom: 313.** Hobo signs, United States.

| | | |
|---|---|---|
| DOCTOR HERE, WON'T CHARGE | COWARDS, will give, to get rid of you | GOOD PLACE to CATCH a TRAIN |
| JUDGE LIVES HERE | MAN with a GUN LIVES HERE | AUTHORITIES HERE ARE ALERT |
| IF YOU ARE SICK, they'll care for you | FREE TELEPHONE | RELIGIOUS TALK gets FREE MEAL |
| HOLD YOUR TONGUE | KIND LADY LIVES HERE | JAIL |

**left: 314.** Graphics from the
1984 Summer Olympic Games, Los Angeles.
Courtesy Los Angeles Olympic Organizing Committee.

In the last few decades international travel has increased dramatically. People journey to foreign countries, without knowing the local language, and expect to get around comfortably and safely. Such travel has opened up a whole new realm for the graphic designer. Nowhere is the need to communicate without words more evident than at the Olympic Games, which draw athletes from scores of countries into one location. Somehow all the athletes must be housed, must find the places where they are supposed to be at various times, and must obtain the services they need. Preparing signs written in all the languages represented would be tedious and cumbersome. So each time the games are held, graphic images are designed to mark basic areas and functions. The images are designed anew each time, but always they are simple, straightforward, and free of cultural biases (**314**). Even without captions you should have little difficulty identifying the sports they portray.

So in international travel as well as international commerce the need for graphic design has burgeoned. Fortunately, the *ability* to communicate graphically has also increased, thanks to new mechanical and electronic processes. Together, need and ability have yielded an unprecedented outpouring of graphic design. With this background, let us look first at the tools used by the graphic designer and then at some of the many categories of graphic design.

## The Tools of the Graphic Designer

Regardless of the kind of graphic design or the method of reproduction, the graphic designer works with three tools: *type* (printed letters), *photography,* and drawn *illustration.* Every design has at least one of these resources and usually has two or more in combination. We must also take into account the variable of color, because color is often responsible for much of a design's impact. And motion—whether in television or in computer graphics—can dramatically influence the way these three elements operate.

Type design has come a long way since the invention of movable type about 1450. Contemporary graphic designers have a bewildering array of typefaces and styles to choose from, in an infinite range of sizes. This book, for instance, is printed in a typeface known as *New Baskerville,* which is popular for books because it is easy to read, legible in fairly small sizes, and not tiring to the eyes after sustained reading. Some of the headings, including the one just above that says "The Tools of the Graphic Designer," are printed in a face called *Franklin Gothic.*

With so many typefaces and sizes to choose from, the designer can select one that best fits the character of the design and the tone of the message to be communicated. Moreover, type design itself has changed radically. In earlier times the letters of type were painstakingly carved out of wood or cast in metal. Today, type is "set"—or created and placed in position—by computer and photographic methods, so it is relatively easy to design an original typeface for a specific purpose. The designer can make a "word picture" that symbolizes the idea of the graphic design. Inventive use of typography is one trademark of New York designer Ellen Shapiro, whose logos for The O'Neill Theater Center and Home Box Office cable television network are very different but both distinctive (**315**).

Typography and color together have made *Life* magazine's logo instantly recognizable. Gilbert Lesser, promotion director of *Life,* has used the logo so extensively that, according to the design magazine *Graphis,* he has "provided a powerful lesson in the use of colour. He has monopolized a red-and-white format (corresponding to the magazine's logo) so well that . . . red-and-white has come to symbolize *Life*." Thus in totally unexpected contexts the magazine name still evokes an immediate response (**316,317**).

One of the major decisions for any graphic designer is whether to use photography or drawn illustration. In either case the options are limitless, so the choice becomes one of finding the image that will best present the idea for a particular audience. Fashions in graphic imagery change. What might have been suitable for a public of half a century ago now seems quaint and naive. We can demonstrate this point by showing two covers for piano sheet music, one from 1926 and the other from 1983. The 1926 cover, for a song called "I'd Climb the Highest Mountain If I Knew I'd Find You" (**318**), is charming and romantic, with the woman's head floating ethereally above a mountain that looks surprisingly like the Japanese Mt. Fuji (**253**).

**above: 315.** Type designs by Ellen Shapiro for *The O'Neill Theater Center* and *Home Box Office*.

**left: 316.** "Paint the town red," New Year's, promotional mailing by LIFE Magazine. Designer: Gilbert Lesser; copy chief: Richard B. Lawrence. Courtesy LIFE Magazine.

**above: 317.** "LIFE wishes you the reddest, hottest, firiest of Valentine's Days," Valentine's Day promotional mailing by LIFE Magazine. Designer: Gilbert Lesser; copy chief: Howard R. Klein. Courtesy LIFE Magazine.

**right: 318.** Sheet music cover for Irving Berlin's "I'd Climb the Highest Mountain If I Knew I'd Find You." 1926. Collection Rita Gilbert.

By contrast, there is little of a conventional romantic mood in a sheet music cover for Culture Club's "It's a Miracle," dating from 1983 (**319**). Here the designer has used a photograph, with three photographic inserts, to convey a brooding, emotional, perhaps "miraculous" quality, quite devoid of the sentimentality we find in the previous music cover. In part, the difference between these two compositions is created by time—the distance of nearly sixty years—but another part has to do with the choice between drawing and photograph. Photos are always more "real," more direct.

These three tools—type, photography, and illustration—lend themselves to literally infinite combinations. The following brief survey of graphic design categories should give some idea of the scope and variety in this field. We begin with the most pervasive design category of modern times.

## Advertising

Imagine that you have bet someone that you could get through an entire day without being exposed to a single advertisement. How would you go about winning the bet? You couldn't watch television or listen to the radio, of course, or read any magazines or newspapers. You'd have to be careful about the food you ate; so many packages and cans have advertising on them, for themselves or for some other product. You couldn't go to work or to class: too many billboards on the street, advertising posters on the bus, people handing out flyers on street corners. Should you settle down with a good book? Many books carry advertising for other books, either on the back cover or bound inside. A day at the beach? No, there's a skywriting airplane flying overhead and somebody's radio turned up loud. Perhaps a walk in the woods. But will it rain? You decide to call the weather service on the telephone. You've lost the bet! The weather report now includes commercial messages.

**below: 319.** Sheet music cover for Culture Club's "It's a Miracle." Copyright © 1983 Virgin Music (Publishers) Ltd./ Warner Bros. Music Ltd. (Columbia Pictures publications)

**right: 320.** "Looking Good Mona," generic image promotion for WHAS-TV, Louisville, Ky. Designer: Teresa Heintzman.

**321.** "Moving billboard" truck advertising for Levi's. Courtesy Levi Strauss & Co.

More than any other time in history we are bombarded from every side with advertising. So many products are made, so many consumers are there to buy them, so many millions of dollars are at stake in bringing the two together. Many times the success of a product has more to do with the advertising campaign than with the product's intrinsic worth. This is especially true when products are alike. How different, really, are household cleaners? All have more or less the same ingredients, and all will get the sink clean. The manufacturer's job, therefore, is to fix the product name in the consumer's mind and have that consumer *perceive* a difference. For this the manufacturer relies on advertising.

The question then arises, what makes a successful advertisement? Why do some ads work better than others? Countless books have been written on this subject, and the answer sometimes involves complex psychological responses. Certain key factors can be identified, however, as contributing to an advertisement's effectiveness.

First of all, the ad must be noticed. Getting the viewer's attention is the advertising designer's first task, especially given the huge number of commercial messages constantly assailing us. One very popular technique for getting attention is consumer identification, as in ads for expensive items. While flipping through a magazine or newspaper, you see a picture of an elegant person or group and think to yourself, "I want to be just like that." After a barrage of such ads, you associate the product name with that desirable image.

A related approach is to take the expected, the familiar, and do something unexpected with it. Practically everyone knows the *Mona Lisa,* but few have ever imagined her in any of the guises shown in an advertisement for television station WHAS (**320**). This device is bound to attract attention, then generate a few chuckles, then possibly cause the observer to think, "How witty and creative those people must be"—which is no doubt the impression WHAS wanted to achieve.

Yet another method of attracting attention is by sheer size. Levi Strauss & Company tapped an unexpected resource when it decided to turn its three hundred trailer trucks into "moving billboards," with huge 6-by-8-foot decal advertisements on the sides (**321**). In the language of the market researchers who participated in this ad campaign, each truck-billboard would garner seventy "consumer impressions" for every mile the truck was driven. Consumer impressions, naturally, translate into consumer purchases—or so it is hoped. An expected bonus from this campaign is that fewer trucks will be hijacked and fewer truckloads of jeans—a very popular item for pirating—will be lost.

Most advertisements, regardless of what they are selling, are planned to appeal to the self-interest of the people at whom they are directed. The viewer is supposed to think, "This would be good for *me*." Advertising designers have known this for at least a hundred years. An ad for Arbuckles' coffee, dating from the 1880s (**322**), suggests that home-roasting of coffee beans in those days was both a common practice and a "burning issue." The little dialogue in the ad is straightforward. It presents the problem in such a way that consumers can perceive a need, and then it offers a solution in comforting terms: "You will have no trouble." Since everybody wants to have "no trouble," the ad was probably quite successful.

Today's advertisements occasionally take the opposite view, by pointing out the harmful consequences of *not* buying what the ad has to sell—in this case an education (**323**). "Drop out of school and take it easy for the rest of your life," combined with a picture of a derelict sleeping on a park bench, is an ingenious approach, because it lets the viewer do some of the selling work. It would have been easier, but much less effective, to caption this picture "Drop out of school and you will become a bum." Instead, the reader must think

**left: 322.** Chromolithograph poster, advertisement for Arbuckles' Coffee. 1880s. New York Historical Society (Bella C. Landauer Collection).

**below: 323.** "Drop Out of School," advertisement for Cincinnati Public Schools. 1981. Bill Sontag, art director; Bill Sontag and Don McMillar, designers; Don Kortekamp, writer; Mark Alexander and M. Caporale, photographers; SIVE Associates, agency.

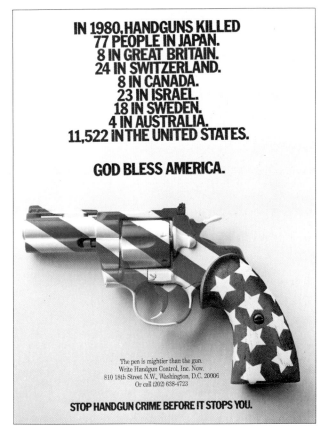

IN 1980, HANDGUNS KILLED
77 PEOPLE IN JAPAN.
8 IN GREAT BRITAIN.
24 IN SWITZERLAND.
8 IN CANADA.
23 IN ISRAEL.
18 IN SWEDEN.
4 IN AUSTRALIA.
11,522 IN THE UNITED STATES.

**GOD BLESS AMERICA.**

The pen is mightier than the gun.
Write Handgun Control, Inc. Now.
810 18th Street N.W., Washington, D.C. 20006
Or call (202) 638-4723

**STOP HANDGUN CRIME BEFORE IT STOPS YOU.**

through the message to connect "taking it easy" with being a bum, so the message is more likely to sink in and stick. The humor helps the ad avoid a tone of preachiness.

An ad placed by Handgun Control, Inc. (**324**) combines several elements to achieve a powerful impact. It attracts attention by means of its simple, symmetrical layout plus the startling image of a gun decorated in the Stars and Stripes. Having gotten the viewer's attention, the ad slowly piles up evidence about the number of handgun deaths in various countries, culminating in the shocking U.S. figure at the bottom. And finally it appeals to the self-interest of the reader: "Stop handgun crime before it stops you." The reader who thinks, "*I* could get hurt" is likely to be more highly motivated than one who thinks, "Some other people might be hurt." Regardless of one's point of view about gun control, there can be no question that this is an effective advertisement.

## Print Media: Books, Magazines, and Posters

Book designers, of all graphic artists, often have the most difficulty making people understand what they do. In this book, for example, the designer selected the two typefaces; chose the appropriate sizes of type for text, headings, captions, and so forth; and decided how much space to allow for margins and between various elements. She also devised a way to set the artists' biographies off from the main text and planned how illustrations could be integrated with the written material. Many, many decisions go into making a book appear to be a coherent whole.

Cover design is easier to fathom. Usually, a book's cover will have an image—photograph or illustration—and the book's title and author's name printed in a suitable typeface. Cover design has two related purposes: to make the book attractive and appealing, and to encourage a potential reader to pick it up. The old adage says, "You can't judge a book by its cover," but to some

GAVE HUBBY A WHIPPING.
BECAUSE HE INTERFERED WITH HER AN ACTRESS REPRIMANDS HIM, AT DENVER, COL.

extent you can. Certainly the reader browsing in a library or bookstore will often be drawn by a cover, then moved to explore the book further.

Most cover designs attempt to interpret the book's content. We find a good example in the cover for Judith Rossner's *August* (**325**), a novel about psychoanalysis focusing on the month when analysts traditionally go on vacation. The graphic designer's interpretation captures this idea with clever simplicity: an empty analyst's couch, a shaft of sunlight, a picture of a sailboat on the ocean.

The design of magazine covers, while drawing on the same elements as book cover design (type, photography, illustration), differs in certain respects. For one thing, magazine covers are more influential in a reader's decision to purchase. You may be motivated to buy a particular book for any of several reasons—it's on the best-seller list, you heard about it from a friend, you are familiar with the author's work, and so on. But buying a magazine is more often a spur-of-the-moment decision. You are dashing for the train, waiting to check out at the supermarket, faced with a boring evening when your friends are away and there's nothing on television. You scan the magazine racks looking for diversion. Chances are, the magazine whose cover attracts you will be the one you choose.

Another difference between magazine and book cover design has to do with longevity. Books often are kept, in homes and libraries, for many years. Magazines tend to be read quickly and then thrown away. (There are exceptions; in 1982 a Connecticut couple narrowly escaped disaster when several years' worth of stored *National Geographic* issues crashed through the floor of their attic to the bedroom below, landing on the bed to which they would soon have retired. For the most part, though, magazines are soon discarded.) Because of their short life span, magazines can have covers that are contemporary, following up-to-the-minute fashions and current events.

The history of magazine cover design is fascinating. We may think that today's magazines are often sensational in their attempts to capture the consumer dollar. But a glimpse back into the last century shows that, even in one of the most straitlaced periods of our history, magazines used scandalous subject matter on the cover to attract readers (**326**).

When a drawn illustration is to be used for a cover, the choice of an illustrator is up to the designer of the cover or the magazine's art director—the person in charge of the visual aspects of the whole magazine. Occasionally a particular illustrator is used over and over, has a distinctive style, and therefore becomes closely associated with that magazine. There could be no better example of such a partnership than the one that existed between Norman Rockwell and the *Saturday Evening Post*.

In 1916 a very young Norman Rockwell, just twenty-two years old, presented himself at the Philadelphia offices of the *Saturday Evening Post*, a popular weekly magazine. He carried two paintings meant as potential *Post* covers and a sketch for a third. The *Post*'s art director was impressed and immediately bought the young artist's illustrations, requesting more. Rockwell's first *Post* cover appeared in May of that year, and his covers continued to appear regularly until 1963, when the artist branched out to other magazines. His last *Post* cover was a portrait of President John F. Kennedy, used as a memorial on the December 14 issue—three weeks after the President's death. During those forty-seven years Rockwell averaged about six covers each year—an amazing feat when one considers that each of the illustrations was a fully developed painting, often including many characters. Every Rockwell cover was greeted with delight by *Post* readers and guaranteed an increase in sales.

Rockwell's task was not an easy one; working in the magazine's format imposed many restrictions (**327**). Obviously, the image had to fit within a certain vertical framework—the shape of the magazine cover. Space had to be

# Norman Rockwell

## *1894–1978*

**N**orman Rockwell, chronicler of small-town America, was born in New York and raised in a section of that city known as the Bronx. By the age of fourteen, already determined on a career as an artist, he assumed responsibility for his own education—selecting the art schools he would attend (which eventually included the Art Students League) and finding odd jobs to support himself. One such job was as an extra, often a spear carrier, at the Metropolitan Opera, where he became rather a pet of the legendary tenor Enrico Caruso.

At eighteen Rockwell began to get his first professional commissions, most of them for illustrations in boys' magazines and children's books. Then in 1916 came the first *Saturday Evening Post* cover. After his early triumph at the *Post*, Rockwell never again lacked for assignments. His career blossomed, and he remained busy trying to keep up with the demand for his work until the onset of his last illness at the age of eighty-four.

Rockwell's great success was based on the simplest of formulas: He drew ordinary people in ordinary situations doing the sorts of things all the *Post*'s readers were accustomed to doing. He drew them with a gentle humor that poked fun at the situations while never poking fun at the people. The magazine's readers could laugh at themselves, at the odd and funny plights they got themselves into, because they sensed the artist was one of *them*, subject to the same foibles as anybody else.

After leaving New York, Rockwell first lived in a suburb of the city, then for many years in Vermont. Ultimately he settled in Stockbridge, Massachusetts, the town with which he is most closely associated. His models for *Post* covers and other illustrations were the townspeople—the mayor, the barber, the village clerk, the children of the neighborhood. In the early years Rockwell painted them from life, but later he developed a system of photographing the scenes and models, then painting from the photographs. Not all Rockwell's subjects were Stockbridge villagers, however. Routinely he was called upon to paint the famous and the mighty—Presidents and presidential candidates, from Eisenhower onward; heads of state; sports heroes and astronauts; and many entertainment figures, including Bob Hope, Frank Sinatra, John Wayne, and even Lassie.

Rockwell married three times—the latter two marriages were apparently very happy ones—and had three sons. Apart from the sudden death of his second wife, little trouble marred a peaceful, productive life. Although the major art critics always were harsh in their assessment of Rockwell's work, he enjoyed enormous popularity with the general public. In 1969 Rockwell had his first one-man show of paintings in New York; the local critics savaged the show, but nearly every painting sold at the preview, before the exhibit opened officially.

Actually, the problem of criticism arose only when people tried to evaluate the artist as a *painter*; few ever questioned his gifts as an illustrator. Rockwell himself commented once on this distinction: "Some people have been kind enough to call me a fine artist. I've always called myself an illustrator. I'm not sure what the difference is. All I know is that whatever type of work I do, I try to give it my very best. Art has been my life."[1]

Norman Rockwell. *Triple Self-Portrait,* cover for *Saturday Evening Post,* February 13, 1960. Reprinted from *The Saturday Evening Post* © 1960 The Curtis Publishing Company.

allowed at the top for the magazine's title and the date. Sometimes "teaser" blurbs for articles were superimposed over the artwork; Rockwell once mildly complained that the blurbs always seemed to fall just over the spot where he had drawn his most interesting detail. Nevertheless, Rockwell's association with the *Saturday Evening Post* proved to be a long and happy one for all concerned. As with many enduring works of art, Norman Rockwell's illustrations offered the right style in the right medium at the right time.

Some of today's magazine covers might dismay an artist of Rockwell's generation, but they are as reflective of our own time as Rockwell's were of his era. *New York* magazine recently published an issue devoted to the "wounded city" and tackled the problem of "What's Happened to Our Life Here?" Appropriately enough, the cover illustration resembles the all-pervasive graffiti that decorate (?) that city's subways and many buildings (**328**). In analyzing the "wounds" of New York, the magazine presents a wounded cover—a mess. This is a far cry from Rockwell's charming, small-town scenes, but so is contemporary urban life.

From the magazine cover to the poster is not a large step; in fact, some exceptional magazine covers have been transformed into posters and found their way onto college dormitory and apartment walls around the country. Posters are by no means new, but only since the 1960s have they been such an ever-present factor in our lives. Nowadays, it is the rare individual who has never hung up a poster from a museum exhibition, a travel poster, a poster featuring a film or music star, even an advertising poster, if it is particularly attractive. Museum posters are among the most popular, because they usually have interesting images and high-quality printing. Exhibition posters often feature a work of art from the show, but in our example (**329**) the Kentucky Arts Commission took a different approach. New paintings are interpreted as "fresh paint," all in intense color that makes a viewer eager to see the exhibition that inspired such a splash of hues.

Most graphic artists greatly enjoy the challenge of designing a poster, but there is one design assignment that nearly every graphic artist covets: the design "package"—or, in other words, total design.

**left: 328.**
Cover for *New York* magazine, 1982.

**right: 329.**
Poster for an exhibition
of the Kentucky Arts Commission.
Julius Friedman and Nathan Felde,
art directors and designers;
Warren Lynch, photographer;
Implement Limited, design firm.

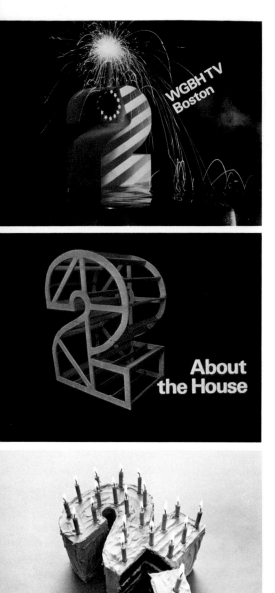

# Total Design

Total design gives the graphic artist an opportunity to create a unified design program that runs through many different applications. The goal may be to build a certain "image" for a business firm, or simply to present an ongoing reminder to the public. For instance, if a museum is having a special exhibit, the designer may use the same motif on a poster, the catalogue cover, advertisements, ticket stubs, and perhaps a banner on the front of the museum. Total design works on the principle, familiar from music and some works of art, of theme and variations. An idea is held constant but subject to many variations depending upon need.

Television station WGBH in Boston took as its motif the numeral 2—its channel number. By playing with variations on the 2, the station hoped to project a visual personality that was "eclectic, unorthodox, witty, heterogeneous, and otherwise unpredictable." Madcap versions of the 2 included promotion slides of various kinds (330,331), and even a giant 2-mobile (332), an astonishing vehicle set on top of a '68 Volkswagen and used in a fund-raising drive. When a campaign of this sort is carried through long enough, and

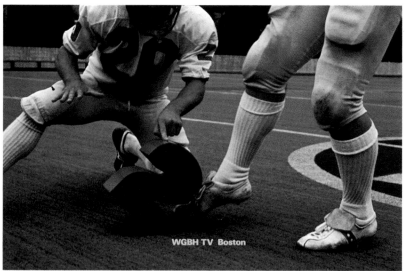

**330.** Station promotional slides for Channel 2, WGBH-TV, Boston.

**above: 331.** Station promotional slide for Channel 2, WGBH-TV, Boston.

**right: 332.** 2-Mobile, WGBH-TV, Boston.

creatively enough, the public begins to look forward eagerly to new incarnations of the theme. In other words, people think, "What will they do next?" No better response could be prompted by total design.

Being a television station, WGBH naturally set some of its 2's in motion. This brings us to our final category for this chapter—one that has utterly revolutionized the field of graphic design.

## Graphics in Motion: Television and Computers

Television commercials have been with us since the 1950s, but only in the last decade or so has the medium begun to be explored for its full potential. Some commercials are irritating (especially after much repetition); some are neutral and can be ignored; but some are more entertaining than the programs they interrupt. The designer of commercials has great resources available—motion photography, animation, computer-generated graphics, spoken or printed words, music, and of course color. A commercial can be considered successful if it is appealing *and* sells the product.

A typical commercial lasts for about thirty seconds. During that brief time it must do essentially the same things a printed advertisement does—attract attention and appeal somehow to the self-interest of the viewer. A "groundbreaking" commercial for Diet Pepsi (**333**) handles these problems in an exceptionally creative way. Bold, brilliantly colored shots of a model alternately sipping the cola and displaying a slim, attractive body are flashed against the sung theme "Now you see it, now you don't." (The viewer is left to make the connection between seeing "it"—the can of soda—and no unpleasant consequences on the model's waistline.) All the frames of film are very tightly cropped, so that usually the model's head is not visible (**334**). Attention is assured, and the message ("buy Diet Pepsi") manages to be both straightforward and subtle.

Many commercials, especially those involving dramatization, follow what communication theorists refer to as "Monroe's Motivated Sequence," named after Purdue speech professor Alan Monroe. A five-step sequence, this method is based on the psychology of persuasion. In a typical situation, the commercial works like this:

1. *Attention.* A customer walks into a coffee shop calling a big hello to the waitress; sits down at counter.
2. *Need.* Clumsy customer knocks over a glass and spills liquid on the counter.

**3.** *Satisfaction.* Waitress mops up the spill with wonderfully absorbent paper towel.

**4.** *Visualization.* Waitress demonstrates how strong this paper towel is.

**5.** *Action.* Voice-over announcer urges the viewer to buy this particular brand of paper towel.

If you analyze current commercials, you will discover that quite a few familiar ones follow this pattern.

Certain commercials are so attractive, so witty, or so immediately relevant to our life styles that they are absorbed into the popular culture. We find ourselves humming the tunes of commercial jingles or repeating phrases identified with commercials ("Where's the beef?"). Very occasionally the star of a commercial becomes a popular cult hero. Perhaps the best example of this phenomenon is Morris, the 9-Lives Cat (**335**). Morris is finicky. Morris is a grouch. Morris is decidedly "laid back." For all these reasons, and some we

**335.** Morris in "Clambake," commercial for 9-Lives cat food. "Morris the 9-Lives Cat" is a registered trademark of Star-Kist Foods, Inc. © Star-Kist Foods, Inc., 1982.

above: **336.** "Peace on Earth"
greeting card, 1981.
Reprinted by permission
of Information International,
Inc., Copyright 1981.
All rights reserved.

right: **337.** Television
computer graphics.

can't quite pinpoint, Morris has attracted a tremendous following. A secretary
is required to handle his fan mail, especially since his life story, *Morris: An
Intimate Biography*, was published in 1965. When he appeared on the Mike
Douglas Show, Morris received a standing ovation. Truly this is commercial
magnetism raised to a high level.

The computer has done more to influence graphic design than anything
since the invention of the printing press. Each of the three tools available to
the designer—type, photography, and illustration—can be manipulated in
special ways when the computer's help is enlisted.

Computer-designed typography is now commonplace. Unique typefaces
can be created, stored, rearranged, and redesigned with a speed and flexibility
unheard of until just a few years ago. The computer influences the character
of mechanically produced alphabets as surely as the quill and ink influenced
the design of letters centuries ago. A design for a Christmas card celebrating
"Peace on Earth" (**336**) was generated entirely by computer; its suggestion of
three-dimensionality is created by shading and by the perspective of the interior lines.

Photography is an equally fertile area for the computer's ingenuity. Photographs can be bent, twisted, segmented, and otherwise distorted by means of
the computer in ways that make their creative potential infinite. As one example, we might consider the photograph of a night cityscape (**337**), into which
the animated image of a Pegasus—a flying horse—has been introduced so
that the horse seems about ready to circle the buildings.

The major contribution of the computer to graphic design is in the field of animation—the creation of illusory movement through a series of drawn illustrations, as in cartoons. Walt Disney Productions perfected the technique, known as the "cel" method, that was in use for many years. This consists of a series of drawings, each slightly different from the last, all done laboriously by hand. Even a short cartoon required thousands of such drawings, whereas a feature-length motion picture like *Snow White* demanded the services of armies of illustrators.

The computer changed all this virtually overnight. Now, animation can be accomplished directly on the computer terminal display, using light rather than paint. The artist can draw an original picture and then program the computer to "draw" the changing images that simulate action. Images and colors can be varied at will, live action can be combined with animation—the possibilities are literally endless. It seems appropriate that the landmark movie *TRON* (**338**) was produced by Walt Disney Productions, because this was the first major motion picture to combine live action with computer animation.

*TRON* represents the ultimate application of technology that had been common on television for some years. Computer animation is responsible for the colorful graphics that appear in advertising and that often introduce television programs, especially news and sports shows (**339**). Logos streak across the screen, explode in many-hued sunbursts, evolve into other words or images, pulsate to rock music. Much the same technique is being used for wonderfully creative movie title sequences.

The computer has also changed the way graphic artists in *all* media work. Even if the end result is to be a printed design—an advertisement or magazine cover, for example—some graphic designers have replaced their sketch pads with computer terminals. Designing, testing of ideas and forms and color, is done on the screen with as much flexibility as could be obtained from the pencil or pen, but with much greater speed. The design can then be transmitted almost instantly anywhere it needs to go—to the client, the art director, or the home office.

One hesitates to say too much about computer graphics, because the field is evolving so rapidly. In the short time that elapses between the writing of this book and its publication, tremendous expansion of computer graphics will undoubtedly take place. Without question we are in the middle of another revolution in graphic design. It will be fascinating to watch its development.

*part four*

# THREE-DIMENSIONAL MEDIA

# 11
# Sculpture

The study of sculpture confronts us with the third dimension, with the concept of *depth*. This seems like an easy and obvious point, but there is more to it than you might imagine. In everyday life we are faced constantly with situations in which our brains have to make adjustments for depth. Just walking down the street requires the brain to make a thousand calculations. How far away is that building? If you misjudge the distance, you may bump into it. How high is the curb? Unless you estimate correctly, you may trip and fall. The mass media require us to make a similar set of adjustments. We see images of people on the movie screen or television set. Even though these are, in reality, flat images, we perceive the people as being full-bodied and three-dimensional.

To appreciate fully how complex is our perception of depth we might consider what happens when that perception is absent. M. von Senden's book, *Space and Sight*, describes experiments with people who were blind from birth and then gained their sight through surgical techniques. The results of these experiments are fascinating. Von Senden concluded that, after regaining their sight, most patients were unable to see depth or distance. Accustomed always to making judgments about depth by touch, they could not convert their knowledge to an understanding of visual cues. One patient confused depth with roundness; for her, three-dimensionality always meant the globe form of a ball or an orange, for instance. Another patient, when shown photographs and paintings, wanted to know "Why do they put those dark marks all over them?" She was told the dark marks were shadows, and that without them everything would look flat. The patient replied, "Well, that's how things do look. Everything looks flat with dark patches." Once patients learned to recognize faces and other familiar things in photographs, they were startled to discover that the *photographs* were flat and did not have the same bumps and textures they were used to sensing by touch.

Distance presented similar problems. Until their operations the patients' entire concept of distance had been limited by what they could reach with their hands. One man said that everything he could not touch with his hand was "to the side." The researchers gradually understood that, as far as this man was concerned, objects across the room, in the next room, or on the other side of town were all the same distance away. Many of the newly sighted people had difficulty grasping the idea that their sight could travel farther than their hands. Some thought at first that seeing involved bringing an object into *contact* with the eyes.

One of the newly sighted people worked out a method to practice his visual apprehension of distance. He would take off one of his boots, throw it some distance away, then estimate how far it was from him and how many steps it would take to reach it. If he failed to reach it, he'd take another step or two and try again until he could touch the boot. In effect, this adult man was trying painstakingly to learn depth perceptions that sighted people have assumed since babyhood—and to *un*learn the different perceptions he had mastered while blind.

Those of us sighted from birth have learned to make enormously complicated judgments about depth, size, and distance. But as we approach sculpture, we ought to place ourselves in the position of the formerly blind man with his boot. We should train our eyes to see in new ways and to be aware of seeing. We should train our minds to understand the dynamics of three-dimensional form. Heightened awareness of the third dimension is crucial to our appreciation of sculpture. Sculptures are like our selves, full-bodied and substantial. Usually they look different when viewed from different angles. The experience of looking at a flat painting on a wall is quite unlike the experience of walking up to a freestanding sculpture, circling it, observing it from various viewpoints, and then integrating many visual perceptions into an understanding of the sculpture as a whole.

This chapter will explore a wide range of three-dimensional forms, from many times and places. Sculpture has one of the longest histories of any art medium, and yet it is especially vital and exciting today. A major reason for this vitality in contemporary sculpture is its use of materials and techniques that were unheard of just a century ago. We will look first at the sculptor's methods, how materials are handled, and how sculptures are designed.

## Methods of Sculpture

There are four basic methods for making a sculpture: modeling, casting, carving, and assembling. Modeling and assembling are considered *additive* processes. The sculptor begins with a simple framework or core or nothing at all and *adds* material until the sculpture is finished. Carving is a *subtractive* process in which one starts with a mass of material larger than the planned sculpture and *subtracts*, or takes away, material until only the desired form remains. Casting really doesn't belong in either category. It involves a mold of some kind, into which liquid or semiliquid material is poured and allowed to harden. Often casting is used to make several identical sculptures.

Let us consider each of these methods in more detail.

### *Modeling*

Modeling is familiar to most of us from childhood. As children we experimented with Silly Putty or clay to construct lopsided figures of people and animals. For sculpture, the most common modeling material is clay, an earth substance found in most parts of the world. Wet clay is wonderfully pliable; few can resist the temptation to squeeze and shape it. As long as clay remains wet, the sculptor can do almost anything with it—add on more and more clay to build up the form, gouge away sections, pinch it outward, scratch into it with a sharp tool, smooth it with the hands. But when a clay form has dried and been *fired*—heated to a high temperature in a kiln (Chapter 12, p. 288)—

it becomes hard. Fired clay, sometimes called by the Italian name *terra cotta*, is surprisingly durable. Much of the ancient art that has survived was formed from this material.

A female figure made in Cyprus more than three thousand years ago (**340**) is typical of the fertility images found in most early cultures. The artist who created this little statue had learned to exploit many of the possibilities of clay. After the overall form had been shaped by the fingers, delicate lines defining the form were incised with a sharp tool. The arms and "earrings" were shaped of separate pieces of clay and then added to the main piece.

Throughout their history the Chinese have been masters of ceramic sculpture—sculpture made from clay—but not until recently has the enormous scope of their production been fully appreciated. In 1974 well diggers near the central Chinese city of Xi-an accidentally uncovered part of the tomb complex of the first Emperor of China, Shi Huang Di. Buried since 210 B.C., guarding the tomb in military formation, were a whole army of life-size clay soldiers, horses, and attendants—at least seven thousand of them (**341**). The warriors' faces and bodies are modeled with amazing naturalism, and each variety of provincial headdress is rendered in specific detail. The horses stand waiting to be harnessed and ridden off into battle. More recent digs have unearthed a similar array of scribes, or clerks, suggesting that the entire court, represented in clay, may have gone into the emperor's tomb. We can only speculate how many sculptors labored to build this immense ceramic population, especially in view of the high quality maintained in the figures.

Clay served the Chinese tomb builders well, because of its permanence and potential for naturalism. But later artists have prized clay for other qualities. Sculptors often use clay modeling in the same way that painters traditionally have used drawing, to test ideas before committing themselves to a finished sculpture. As long as the clay is kept damp, it can be worked and reworked almost indefinitely. Even the terminology is the same; we call a clay test piece a "sketch."

**340.** Female figure holding a fluttering bird (fertility image?), from Cyprus. c. 1500–1200 B.C. Terra cotta, height 8⅜". Metropolitan Museum of Art, New York (Cesnola Collection; purchased by subscription, 1874–1876).

**341.** *Cavalryman and Saddle Horse from Earthenware Army of First Emperor of Qin.* c. 210 B.C. Terra cotta, height of man 5'10½". Cultural Relics Bureau, Beijing, and Metropolitan Museum of Art, New York.

Our illustration (**342**) shows a clay study for Eustache de St. Pierre, one of the figures in Rodin's *Burghers of Calais* (**357**), a life-size bronze piece. We can learn much about the sculptor's creative process by comparing the little terra cotta sketch—only about a foot tall—to the large finished work. Most obvious is the fact that the clay model is nude, while the figures in the *Burghers* are clothed. Undoubtedly Rodin wanted to explore the way this man would hold his body, to capture every line of muscle and bone, to study the movement of legs, arms, and shoulders, the curve of the back—before draping the figure in garments. In our photograph of the completed *Burghers* (**357**) Eustache de St. Pierre appears just to right of center, facing us. Rodin has changed the pose from that of his terra cotta study. In the modeled clay figure the arms are held out from the body, almost as though in supplication. But the bronze Eustache—more inward-looking, more self-contained—holds his arms closer to his sides. Only after many such sketches, in clay and plaster, did Rodin settle upon the final composition for his work. We are fortunate in having the clay study, not only because it helps us to understand the creative process, but also for its own sake. Despite this figure's small size, the clay modeling is wonderfully lifelike and expressive.

Rodin also made studies in plaster, and this too has traditionally been a common material for preliminary models. But in contemporary sculpture plaster has come into its own as a medium for finished work. Modern sculptors seem to like the flat, white impersonality of plaster, as well as its ready acceptance of bright color. Manuel Neri's *Red Legs* (**343**), modeled in plaster over a steel frame or *armature,* seems almost cheerful in its vivid colors and jaunty pose. But this gaiety is in direct contradiction to the flat blue face. A face without features is depersonalized and frightening. We cannot tell where the figure is looking or what it is thinking, and it cannot speak to us. There is only that blank, staring oval of blue.

In some ways modeling is the most direct of the sculpture methods. The workable material responds to every touch, light or heavy, of the sculptor's fingers, so that the maker and the made become almost one.

# Casting

In contrast to modeling, casting seems like a very *indirect* method of creating a sculpture. Sometimes the sculptor never touches the final piece at all. Metal, and specifically bronze, is the material we think of most readily in relation to casting. Bronze can be superheated until it flows, will pour freely into the tiniest crevices and forms, and then hardens to extreme durability. Even for a thin little projection, like a finger, there is no fear of it breaking off. Other materials also can be cast, including many plastics and clay.

The simplest type of casting is *solid* casting—that is, solid as opposed to hollow. You make a solid cast every time you make an ice cube. You pour liquid material (water) into a mold (the ice cube tray), cause it to harden (by freezing), and then remove the cast (the ice cube). Novelty ice cube trays can make cast-ice "sculptures" in the shape of hearts or flowers or any number of other shapes. Some plastics are cast by a very similar method. Liquid plastic is poured into a mold and allowed to set, after which the mold is removed.

There are three problems with solid casting. First, it uses quite a lot of material, and this can be expensive, especially with metal. Second, solid-cast objects tend to be very heavy unless they are made of lightweight plastic. Third, many materials, including metal and clay, develop cracks if cast solid. For all these reasons various methods have been developed to make *hollow* casts—that is, casts with an inner core of air.

Metal usually is cast by the *lost-wax* method, sometimes known by the French name, *cire-perdue*. This is an extremely complex process. The following description and the illustration (**344**) outline its basic principles.

1. The sculptor works in clay or plaster to create a full-size model of the intended sculpture (**344a**). For the sculptor this may end the creative part; very likely specialized technicians will take over afterward to complete the casting.
2. A coating of synthetic rubber is applied to the clay or plaster model, thus making an outside mold of the sculpture's contours that is accurate in every detail (**344b**).
3. The synthetic rubber mold is removed from the outside of the model. It is now a *negative* or exterior mold of the sculpture (**344c**). Wax is coated on the inside of the synthetic rubber mold to a depth of about 1/8 inch. This wax layer is the exact shape and thickness that is wanted for the final metal sculpture.
4. The space inside the wax walls of the sculpture is filled with a mixture of wet plaster, which is then allowed to dry (**344d**). This plaster core is held in place by a series of metal pins. Then the synthetic rubber mold is removed from the outside of the wax layer. A network of wax rods is constructed all over the outside of the wax model. (Later, when the wax is melted away and the metal poured in, these wax rods will serve as channels for the flow of material.)

**344d**
cutaway view of wax figure
showing walls and plaster core

**344.** Sketch of the major steps in lost-wax casting.

**344a**
clay or plaster original

**344b**
synthetic rubber mold creating negative impression of original

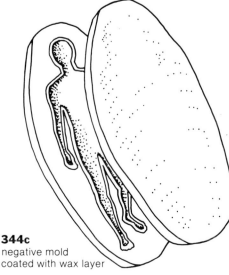

**344c**
negative mold coated with wax layer

**5.** The wax model, complete with rods and plaster core, is coated with a layer of plaster, and the whole assembly is placed in a kiln (**344e**). The heat of the kiln melts away the wax—hence the term *"lost" wax*—leaving an empty space between the inner core and outer layer of plaster that is exactly the shape and thickness of the desired sculpture. (The metal pins maintain the gap between these two sections of plaster, now that the wax is no longer there to hold them apart.) Molten metal is poured into the space that once held the wax, filling every crevice and filling all the rod-like channels. Metal, therefore, has replaced the wax, which is why casting is often known as a *replacement* method. Depending on the size of the sculpture, it may take several days for the metal to cool and set.

**6.** The new metal sculpture is taken from the kiln, and both inner core and outer layer of plaster are removed. Then the rods, now also metal, are cut from the sculpture (**344f**), rough spots are filed away, and the sculpture is cleaned and polished.

A common application for lost-wax casting has been the large equestrian (rider on horseback) statues we see in parks and plazas. The ancient Romans were masters of the equestrian portrait, and it remained popular for depicting military heroes well into this century. Almost no material except bronze would be strong enough, for the horse and its rider, life-size or larger, must be balanced on slender legs in an animated pose. An outstanding example is the statue of *Colleoni* (**345**) by the 15th-century Italian sculptor Andrea del Verrocchio. The sculptor has shaped the tense muscles and alert poses of both figures with such skill that the horse, although cast in rigid bronze, seems about to leap off its pedestal and gallop away.

Besides providing the necessary strength to make thin forms and projections, cast metal offers the sculptor two other great advantages. First, because the mold is generally reusable, one can make several identical casts of the work. Each is considered an original sculpture, just as each impression of a

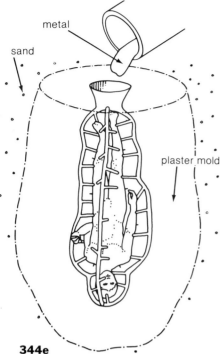

**344e**
pouring molten metal into the mold to replace the "lost" wax

**344f**
completed figure as metal rods are being removed

**345.** Andrea del Verrocchio. *Equestrian Monument of Colleoni.* c. 1483–88. Bronze, height c. 13′. Campo SS. Giovanni e Paolo, Venice.

above: **346.** Alberto Giacometti. (left to right) *Diego au Manteau; Diego au Chandail; Buste de Diego.* All 1954. Painted bronze, height of tallest figure 22⅜". Collection Raymond D. and Patsy R. Nasher, Dallas.

right: **347.** Detail of Tlingit totem pole, Ketchikan, Alaska. 1901.

graphic print is considered an original work of art (Chapter 8). Second, casting makes permanent the most fleeting gesture of the sculptor's hands. The sculptor can work freely, spontaneously, in some soft material like clay or wax, and then translate that free expression into a more durable material. Such is the case with Alberto Giacometti's three heads (**346**). In these figures we can see the roughness of the modeling and every mark of the sculptor's fingers and tools. In spite of their hard bronze material, the heads seem remarkably alive.

## Carving

Carving is more aggressive than modeling, more direct than casting. In this process the sculptor begins with a block of material and cuts, chips, and gouges away until the form of the sculpture emerges. Wood and stone are the principal materials for carving, and both tend to resist the sculptor's tools. When approaching the block to be carved, the sculptor must carefully study the grain of the material—its fibrous or crystalline structure—so as to work *with* that material. Any attempt to violate the grain would probably result in a failed sculpture.

Wood carving reached an especially high level of expertise among the Indians of the Pacific Northwest. The totem pole, unique to this area, served as a historical record of the tribe or clan for which it was made. Totem poles usually were carved out of a single huge trunk of cedar, and no two poles are alike (**347**). Stylized forms of birds, fish, animals, and humans tested the ingenuity of the carver. Areas of shallow cutting alternate with sharp indentations and projections to create a dramatic, striking design.

Stone carving has known no greater genius than Michelangelo, who—despite his massive production in painting and ventures into architecture—always considered himself a stone sculptor above all. Michelangelo believed that the sculptor's task is simply to free the subject from its imprisoning block of stone. So perfectly did he visualize the figure inside a block of marble that he announced one had only to cut away those parts of the stone that *weren't* the figure. Few other sculptors would be quite so confident, for stone carving holds tremendous risks. One false move and the sculpture is ruined. The sculptor cannot put back a piece mistakenly cut away.

**left: 348.** Michelangelo. *Boboli Captive*.
c. 1530–34. Marble, height 7'6½".
Academia, Florence.

**below: 349.** Henry Moore. *Reclining Interior: Oval*.
1963–69. Red travertine marble, height 39½".
Courtesy Marlborough Gallery, New York.

We can get an idea of Michelangelo's approach to sculpture by considering a work he left unfinished, the so-called *Boboli Captive* (**348**). This tortured figure appears to be struggling to tear itself free from the stone. Clearly visible are the marks of the toothed steel chisel, which was used to rough out the broader outlines of the figure. Had Michelangelo finished the piece, he would have smoothed the tool marks away. But one reason later generations are so fascinated by the *Captive* is that we can still see the rough marks made by Michelangelo's hand.

Given the fact that stone carving was the ultimate achievement of ancient Greek and Renaissance sculptors, it may seem old-fashioned to our eyes. But many contemporary sculptors work in stone, including one of the great masters of the 20th century, Henry Moore. Moore's *Reclining Interior* (**349**) is so organic, so much a part of the earth that it might have been carved by nature. No other material but stone is so solid and yet so alive, so cold and yet so inviting to the touch, so resistant yet so satisfying. It is no wonder that sculptors return to it over and over again.

## Assembling

Assembling is a process by which individual pieces or segments or objects are brought together to form a sculpture. Some writers make a distinction between *assembling*, in which parts of the sculpture, often "found" objects, are

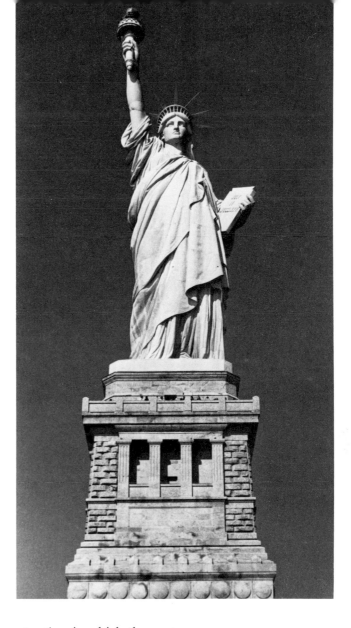

**350.** Frédéric-Auguste Bartholdi.
*Liberty Enlightening the World
(Statue of Liberty)*. 1874–75.
Copper and iron, height of figure 151'.
Liberty Island, New York City.

simply placed on or near each other, and *constructing,* in which the parts are actually joined together through welding, nailing, or a similar procedure. We have chosen to use the term *assemblage* for both types of work, because often the line separating one from the other is a fine one. A given sculpture might, for example, consist partly of wooden boards nailed together (construction) and partly of found objects placed on top of the wood structure (assembling). Use of a single term avoids such complication.

Assemblage was the method employed to make the sculpture that, for people in the United States, is better known than any other. We are so used to thinking of it as a "statue," a symbol, that we forget it is a sculpture. It is the Statue of Liberty (**350**). Formally named *Liberty Enlightening the World,* the statue was conceived by the French sculptor Frédéric Auguste Bartholdi and was presented to the United States by the people of France on the one hundredth anniversary of American independence. Bartholdi's grand scheme required unusual means. From top to toe the figure is 151 feet high, or about the size of a seventeen-story building. Liberty's index finger is 8 feet long.

No conventional sculpture method could have produced this immense piece. Its sheer size made ordinary casting impractical. Instead, the statue was divided up into manageable segments, and an outside mold was made for each segment. Individual sheets of copper were hammered into the molds, and then the entire sculpture was riveted together under the sculptor's supervision. On the outside the joints are practically invisible, but inside the statue

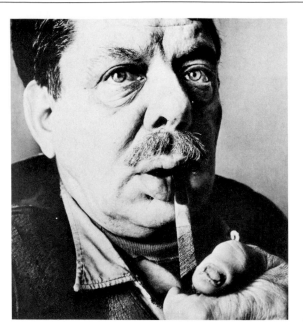

# David Smith
## *1906–1965*

David Smith holds a special interest for students of art history because, more than most artists of past or present, he was extremely articulate about his work and wrote widely about the business of making art. The man himself was something of a paradox. Physically strong and burly, he personified what we would now call a "macho" life style, having worked as a logger, an oilman, and a welder; as a sculptor his expression depended on the physical skills of the blacksmith. But from the noisy atmosphere of the machine shop Smith produced sculptures of shimmering pure form, and this same macho hero was also a lover of classical music, a lifelong poet, a gourmet cook, and a sensitive father to two daughters.

Smith was born in Decatur, Indiana, where he remained for the first twenty years of his life. By 1926 he was in New York, studying painting at the Art Students League. He took a variety of jobs to support himself, including one that proved crucial for his later work—that of metal welder in an automobile factory. In 1927 he married the artist Dorothy Dehner; two years later the couple bought the now-famous farm in Bolton Landing overlooking Lake George, New York, where Smith worked until his death and where he eventually displayed quantities of his large sculptures outdoors.

About 1933 Smith turned from painting and collage to sculpture. Influenced by the iron sculptures of Picasso, he focused on metal and began using his welding skills to assemble the forms. Finding a suitable place to work became a problem. As he told it: "One Sunday afternoon we were walking on a navy pier [in Brooklyn]. Down below on the ferry terminal was a long rambly junky looking shack called Terminal Iron Works. Wife said, 'David that's where you ought to be for your work.' Next morning I walked in and was met by a big Irishman named Blackburn. 'I'm an artist. I have a welding outfit. I'd like to work here.' 'Hell! yes—move in.' I learned a lot from those guys."[1]

From that point Smith worked almost exclusively in metal, soon focusing on steel. He had his first exhibition in New York in 1937, after which his reputation as a sculptor grew steadily. Whether in New York or Bolton Landing, he worked prolifically, and he also played with gusto, enjoying a wide range of friendships with many of the most successful artists of the period. After the breakup of his first marriage, Smith married Jean Freas in 1953, and his daughters Rebecca and Candida were born in the following two years. The artist's life ended prematurely when, driving near the farm, he failed to negotiate a turn in the road, crashed his truck, and was killed.

The sculpture of David Smith is represented in nearly every major collection of modern art, but the works housed indoors in museums may strike the viewer as out of place, almost uncomfortable. Smith always preferred his pieces to be displayed outdoors. He wrote: "I like outdoor sculpture and the most practical thing for outdoor sculpture is stainless steel, and I make them and I polish them in such a way that on a dull day, they take on the dull blue, or the color of the sky in the late afternoon sun, the glow, golden like the rays, the colors of nature. . . . They are colored by the sky and the surroundings, the green or blue of water. Some are down by the water and some are by the mountains. They reflect the colors. They are designed for outdoors."[2]

Photograph of David Smith by Irving Penn.

left: **351.** David Smith. *Cubi XVII.* 1963.
Stainless steel, height 9'.
Dallas Museum of Fine Arts
(Eugen and Margaret McDermott Fund).

above: **352.** Deborah Butterfield.
*Horse #4.* 1978. Mixed media, 31 × 30".
Courtesy Fuller Goldeen Gallery,
San Francisco.

one can see how Liberty was put together. Upon her arrival from France, Liberty was widely heralded as "the most expensive statue in the world." Correcting for inflation, she may still be.

The 20th-century American sculptor David Smith came to assemblage in an unusual way. While trying to establish himself as an artist, Smith worked as a welder. Later, when he began to concentrate on sculpture, he readily adapted his welding skills to a different purpose. His mature works broke new ground in both materials and forms (**351**). Sculptures like *Cubi XVII* are of steel, which eventually became Smith's favorite material. Steel had long been used for the framework of cars, of refrigerators, of locomotives, but Smith explored its aesthetic potential. He polished the surfaces so they would shine in the sunlight when exhibited outdoors. The form of these works is also daring—cube piled upon cube in a seemingly precarious structure. Steel, with its great strength, makes possible the dynamic balance of *Cubi XVII*, and assemblage makes possible the soaring composition.

The sculptures of Deborah Butterfield also are assembled, but in comparison to Smith's, her forms are deliberately crude. A favorite subject of Butterfield's is the horse (**352**). Her horses, built on metal armatures, are put together from sticks, twigs, chicken wire, pipes, and sometimes mud. The finished works remind us of primitive art and of children's art (Chapter 1, **6–10**) in their concentration on the basic segments—head, neck, horizontal body, four legs, and tail. The horse is a motif that runs through the entire history of art in most cultures. By reducing the horse to its essential forms, Butterfield reminds us of how universal this motif is.

# Louise Nevelson

*b. 1899*

As a sculptor and as a person, Louise Nevelson has long projected the image of royalty. Many of her large works have names suggesting royal subjects—kings, queens, palaces—and the artist has made it her personal trademark to dress with an exotic flamboyance suitable for an eastern princess. This preoccupation seems related to her expressed conviction that one can make one's life be anything one chooses. She says that royalty is "dressing beautifully and having comfort and great houses and great art. Who wouldn't want it? Who wants to live in a hut?"[3]

Born Louise Berliawsky in Kiev, Russia, Nevelson emigrated with her family to Rockland, Maine, in 1905. She claims she was drawn to art as a child because the schoolhouse in Maine was always cold, and the art room was the only warm place. When she was just twenty-one she married Charles Nevelson. Decades later she would say the marriage was the only thing in her life she would have done differently, because she was not equipped for it. Nevelson's son Mike was born in 1922, but only a few years later the marriage collapsed, and the artist has remained single ever since.

Nevelson attended the Art Students League in New York for three years, then traveled to Europe where she studied briefly with the painter Hans Hoffmann. Her first one-woman show came in 1941 at an important New York gallery. Despite favorable critical notice, many years passed before the public showed any interest in her work and it became financially sustaining. The artist feels this was because the components of her sculptures have little material value. From her earliest years in New York (where she still lives) she formed the habit of picking up castoff wooden objects in the street—bits of furniture, old tools, sections of architectural elements, and the like. Her most characteristic sculptures are complex assemblages of these "found" objects in shallow, boxlike grids, many of which are wall- or room-size. The assemblages are each spray-painted a uniform color—occasionally white or gold, but most often black, an "aristocratic" color.

In the late 1960s and 1970s Nevelson experimented with new materials—aluminum and steel—and made several large outdoor sculptures that echo the feeling of her box assemblages. She also accepted an unusual commission for the complete interior design of a Christian church (Nevelson is Jewish) in New York, including architectural details, sculptural decoration, even the priest's vestments.

Louise Nevelson has always been an extremely prolific worker. All through the years of struggle she continued to produce. She maintains that she had a preconceived blueprint for her life and that, by and large, she has fulfilled it. "I remember my mother telling me, 'You know, art is a very difficult life, and why do you want to choose that? You won't live as well as you could otherwise.' And I said, 'It's not how I live, it is how I finish my life.' And I did it."[4]

---

Photograph of Louise Nevelson.

One great advantage of assemblage, as suggested earlier, is that it allows a sculptor to introduce "found" objects—objects made by others, by hand or by machine—and to combine them, making a connection never made before. Louise Nevelson has done this throughout most of her career. Her sculptures, like *Mrs. N's Palace* (**353**), consist of odds and ends, mostly pieces of wood, that she has accumulated in her studio over many years. Assembled in box-like forms, painted a uniform color (often black), they create a rich, intricate, serene world of their own.

## Sculpture and the Third Dimension

Most of the sculptures we have looked at so far are *in the round*, or freestanding and completely finished on all sides, like the human body. Nevelson's box sculpture, however, is usually described as a *relief*, which means it is supposed to be placed against a wall and viewed from the front only. Relief sculptures have three-dimensional depth, but they do not occupy space as independently as do sculptures in the round. Often they are used to decorate architecture or functional objects.

If you have a nickel in your pocket, take it out and look at it. On the face you'll see a profile of Thomas Jefferson and on the back an image of his home, Monticello. Both images are in *low relief*, sometimes called by the French name, *bas-relief*. The subjects project very slightly from their background. Many kinds of flat surfaces serve as fields for low-relief sculpture—coins,

**left: 354.**
*Tutankhamun and His Queen*,
relief on the back
of the Golden Throne
found in the tomb
of King Tutankhamun. c. 1325 B.C.
Sheet gold, silver,
colored glass, and carnelian.
Cairo Museum.

**355.** Lorenzo Ghiberti.
*The Story of Jacob and Esau*,
detail from *The Gates of Paradise*. c. 1435.
Gilt bronze, 31¼″ square.
Baptistry, Florence.

tombstones, walls, decorative plates, book covers. The illustration here (**354**) shows the back of a throne found in the tomb of the Egyptian king, Tutankhamun. A low relief applied to pure sheet gold depicts the young King "Tut" and his queen in graceful poses. The flowing clothes of the two monarchs are of silver, and their headdresses and jeweled collars are inset with colored glass and gemstones.

When a sculpture projects more boldly from the background, we call it *high relief* (or *haut-relief*). To qualify for this category, the sculptured elements should project by at least half their depth, and parts of the figures may be in the round, unattached to the background.

Both low and high relief are evident in *The Story of Jacob and Esau* (**355**), one panel of Lorenzo Ghiberti's famous bronze doors for the Baptistry of Florence Cathedral (**470**). The arched openings, the figures at upper right, and some of the background figures are in low relief. But nearly all the foreground figures are in very high relief—still attached to the background, but

# Errata

## LIVING WITH ART
### by William McCarter and Rita Gilbert

Ten of the 600 illustrations in *Living with Art* were positioned incorrectly. All ten illustrations are positioned correctly below and will be positioned correctly and reproduced in color in the second printing of the book.

Alfred A. Knopf     New York

**1.** Sandro Botticelli. *Birth of Venus.* c. 1480. Tempera on canvas, 6'7" × 9'2". Uffizi, Florence. Scala/Art Resource.
**page 4**

**31.** *Calendar of the Sun.* Aztec, A.D. 1479. Stone, diameter 13′. National Museum of Anthropology, Mexico City. Lee Boltin Picture Library.

page 26

**240.** Helen Frankenthaler. *Enigma.* 1975. Acrylic on canvas, 10′ × 5′10″. Courtesy André Emmerich Gallery, New York.

page 191

below: **241.** Kenneth Noland. *Bridge.* 1964. Acrylic on canvas, 7′5″ × 8′2″. Collection Mrs. Harry Davidson, Toronto. Courtesy André Emmerich Gallery. New York.

page 192

above: 456. Wall painting, from the Villa of the Mysteries, Pompeii. c. 50 B.C. Fresco. Scala/Art Resource.
page 353

458. *Empress Theodora and Retinue.* c. 547. Mosaic. San Vitale, Ravenna. Scala/Art Resource.
page 355

right:
461. *St. Matthew the Evangelist,* from *The Gospel Book of Archbishop Ebbo.* Before 823.
Illumination, 10¼ × 7⅞". Bibliothèque de la Ville, Epernay.
page 356

468. Giotto. *The Lamentation.* 1305–06. Fresco, 7'7" × 7'9". Arena Chapel, Padua. Scala/Art Resource.

**page 361**

**left:**
Leonardo da Vinci. *Self-Portrait.* c. 1512. Chalk on paper, 13 × 8¼". Biblioteca Reale, Turin. Scala/Art Resource.

**page 370**

**right:**
Gianlorenzo Bernini. *Self-Portrait.* c. 1625. Oil on canvas. Galleria Borghese, Rome. Scala/Art Resource.

**page 382**

**356.** Timothy Woodman. *Odysseus and the Sirens*. 1980. Painted aluminum, 5'1" × 5'7" × 1'3". Courtesy Zabriskie Gallery, New York.

fully round and almost freestanding. Ghiberti used these gradations in relief to create a sense of deep space, which is heightened by the receding perspective of the arches. The impression of depth is enhanced even more by the figures that overlap the frame at left and right, in such a way that they actually seem to advance into our space.

We may be tempted to think of figural relief sculpture as "primitive"— something artists of earlier centuries did before they developed the skill necessary to make fully round sculptures. This isn't true at all. The Egyptians and certainly the sculptors of the Renaissance, like Ghiberti, were quite capable of undertaking freestanding works. Moreover, in our own time sculptures still are made to decorate the walls of buildings, and a few contemporary artists have experimented with relief sculpture for its own sake.

Works by Timothy Woodman, such as *Odysseus and the Sirens* (**356**), are modern versions of high-relief sculpture. In Woodman's sculptures little people, usually about 10 inches tall, go cheerfully about their business, whatever that might be. In this piece the artist has interpreted a classic theme—the Greek hero Odysseus and his men being tempted by siren-mermaids. As seen by Woodman, the sailors look like members of a college crew out for a practice on the river, waving their oars to members of the women's swim team on the shore. The oars and most of the figures project from the surface like characters in a pop-up book.

Although we have already looked at several examples of sculpture in the round, it will be useful here to consider one work primarily from the standpoint of its complex interaction with space. Sculpture in the round exists wholly in our world. We can walk around it and see it from every angle. This is a terrific challenge to the sculptor's compositional ability, since every viewpoint must be under control. Even when there is a definite front and back, as there usually is in figurative sculpture, all viewpoints should be interesting. And the fact that the work looks different from every angle makes the observer's experience much richer.

**357.** Auguste Rodin. *The Burghers of Calais.* 1886. Bronze, 6'10½" × 7'11" × 6'6". Hirshhorn Museum and Sculpture Garden, Smithsonian Institution, Washington, D.C.

An excellent example of sculpture in the round is Rodin's *Burghers of Calais* (**357**), whose preliminary study we examined earlier in this chapter (**342**). Rodin made this sculpture for public display in the city of Calais, and it depicts an episode in the town's medieval history. Six men have offered to give their lives to ransom their city from the English, who hold it captive. Each of them faces certain death, but they confront their sacrifice in different ways. One is angry, one sorrowful, one merely resigned, and so on—but each is unique, facing a personal tragedy amid shared crisis. We can read the men's emotions from their various postures, facial expressions, and gestures. The six hostages march in an irregular circle, some determinedly erect, others drooping in despair. And the viewer must also walk in a circle, because there is no angle from which all the faces are visible. Rodin's message is complex, and so he has expressed it in the complex form of sculpture in the round.

## The Human Figure in Sculpture

We humans tend to be egocentric. We are interested in ourselves, in anything that touches upon our immediate concerns. Artists throughout history have expressed this egocentrism with the self-portrait. So it should come as no surprise that the human figure has always been a basic subject of sculpture. What could be more interesting than oneself—or a figure shaped like oneself? We respond psychologically to the sculpture of a human form much as we would to a real human being. What is that person like? Why does he or she look that way? What is that person thinking?

When children see a figurative sculpture, they often arrange their bodies into the same pose as that of the sculpture. As adults we may be tempted to do the same thing, but we have learned to be more inhibited in public. We may be surprised to discover that we have the same impulse to let our bodies mimic the shape of *abstract* sculptures, but this is not really so strange. There is considerable similarity in the way naturalistic and abstract (or nonobjective) sculptures are designed. By studying the figure in sculpture, we can learn much about the way nonfigurative sculptures are designed—how the sculptor handles weights, balances, stresses, and the composition in general. Some nonobjective sculptors go back occasionally to study the human figure, in order to test their understanding of forms in space.

In ancient sculptures there were two major categories of poses for the human figure—the *frontal* and the *contrapposto.* The frontal pose is rigid and immobile. We find it where great formality is desired, as in Egyptian tomb sculptures. Just as the Egyptians built their pyramids for all eternity, so they meant their kings and queens to be posed in eternal serenity. The sculpture of *Mycerinus and His Queen* (**358**) offers a good example. Both figures stand proudly erect, facing straight ahead. Although each has the left foot planted slightly forward, there is no real suggestion of walking. The shoulders and hips are level, the arms frozen at solemn attention.

Contrapposto means "counterpoise" or "counterbalance." In contrast to the frontal pose contrapposto, introduced by the ancient Greeks, is natural, curving, and relaxed. Whereas the frontal pose suggests immobility, the contrapposto always implies action. We have the impression that the sculptor has caught the figure in the middle of a movement, and that one second earlier or later the pose would have been different. You can see this effect in *Hermes with the Infant Dionysus* (**359**), which is probably an original by the famous Greek sculptor Praxiteles. Hermes' weight is on his right foot, so that his right hip is

left: **358.** *Mycerinus and His Queen,* from Giza, Egypt. 2599–2571 B.C. Slate, height 4'6½". Museum of Fine Arts, Boston (Harvard–Boston Expedition).

right: **359.** Praxiteles(?). *Hermes with the Infant Dionysus.* c. 330 B.C. Marble, height 7'1". Museum, Olympia.

raised and his left leg bent and relaxed. To counterbalance this, Hermes' left shoulder is raised, and the whole figure stands in a gentle S-curve. This elegant curve was Praxiteles' trademark and has been copied ever since. We find exaggerated versions of it today in the poses of such "living statues" as fashion models and professional body builders, who use contrapposto to show off to best advantage accomplishments in fabric or muscle tissue.

In Eastern art as well we find both the frontal and the contrapposto poses. The Buddha, who exists in eternity like the monarchs of Egypt, is routinely shown in a frontal pose (**547**). But less exalted beings may be modeled in animated motion. Our illustration (**360**) shows Krishna, one of the most charming personages in Indian mythology. The Krishna legend is full of tales about his boyish pranks and escapades. Here he is "the butter thief," stealing butter from his cowherd foster parents. The child Krishna dances impishly as he runs away with the butter. All his weight is balanced on one leg, with the other bent and his arms held out in counterbalance. We expect him to dance right off the pedestal in delight at his trick.

Contemporary sculptors are less committed to specific categories of poses, yet they are no less interested in the human figure as a subject. One modern sculptor who has concentrated on the figure almost exclusively is George Segal. Segal works in plaster, and his figures are cast from living models. The "sculpting" is done by selecting, dressing, and posing his subject. After that, technology largely takes over. The artist pastes plaster-saturated cloth squares over the model to form a perfectly defined shell of the body. After the plaster

**left: 360.**
*Krishna as the Butter Thief,*
from Tanjore, India.
13th century. Bronze, height 19″.
Nelson-Atkins Museum of Art,
Kansas City (Nelson Fund).

**below: 361.** George Segal.
*Blue Girl on Park Bench.* 1980.
Painted plaster and aluminum, lifesize.
Collection Melvin and Harriet Golder,
Melrose Park, Pa.

**362.** Duane Hanson. *Self-Portrait with Model.* 1979. Painted polyester and mixed media, lifesize. Courtesy O.K. Harris Gallery, New York.

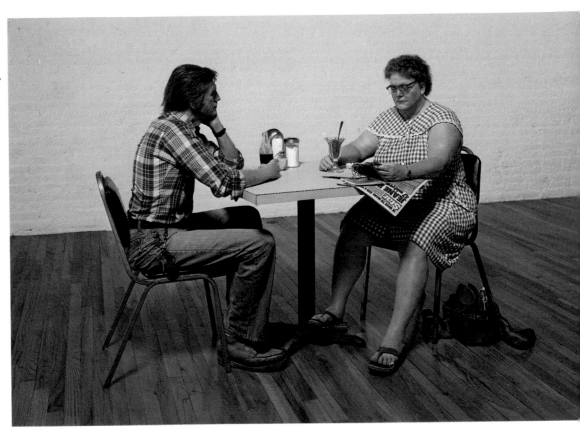

has hardened, the shell is removed in sections. Later, Segal reassembles the sections and uses this shell as a mold in which to make a plaster cast. Earlier works were left in the pure chalky white of the plaster, but of late Segal has begun to paint some of his people in vivid colors, as evidenced by *Blue Girl on Park Bench* (**361**).

Segal likes to place his figures in a setting of objects from the real world, such as the actual park bench supporting the *Blue Girl* (or the real-life bus terminal, **82**). His expressionless people suggest isolation, boredom, and mental stagnation in a packaged society. The *Blue Girl* might be waiting for a bus, but one has the feeling that if the bus doesn't come, she will go on waiting impassively for all time. These figures are antiheroic. Just as heroic figures show us that we might aspire to be, Segal's show us what we might fear to become.

When you look at the next illustration (**362**), Duane Hanson's *Self-Portrait with Model*, you may think you are seeing a photograph of two people sitting at a table. But in fact this is a photograph of a sculpture, and the two figures are made of polyester and fiberglass. Like Segal's plaster people, Hanson's figures are cast from life, but they are painted to be as naturalistic as possible and have been dressed in real clothes and hair and positioned at a real table. If you see an exhibition of Hanson's work, you may have to keep reminding yourself that the real people are the ones who move, the sculptures are the ones who don't.

Hanson makes us look at people, really look at them, the way they are in everyday situations—in the supermarket, at the lunch counter, on the beach. His figures may be "types," but they are the types that make up the bulk of our society. Normally we wouldn't pay much attention to such people. By making something fake, Hanson confronts us with what is real. He deals in middle-aged, middle-class, middle-Americans who cope with life as it comes along from day to day. Perhaps this is one reason why much contemporary figurative sculpture is so approachable. It is not up on a pedestal, far away, to be admired. It is us.

**363.** Red Grooms.
*Ruckus Rodeo.* 1976.
Mixed media, including
sculpture wire, celastic, acrylic,
canvas, and burlap.
Fort Worth Art Museum
(purchased with funds from the
National Endowment for the Arts
and the Benjamin J. Tillar
Memorial Trust, 1976).

**364.** Judy Pfaff.
*Kabuki (Formula Atlantic).* 1980.
Mixed media. Installation
February 12 to May 3, 1981,
at the Hirshhorn Museum
and Sculpture Garden,
Washington, D.C.
Courtesy Holly Solomon Gallery,
New York.

## Sculpture and the Environment

The term "environmental sculpture" may cause some confusion, because it is used in at least three different ways. First, it can refer to sculptures that are large enough for viewers to enter and move about in, sculptures that create their own environments. Second, it can mean large sculptures designed for display in the outdoor environment, such as a sculpture commissioned for a city square. And third, it can be sculptures that are actually a part of the natural environment, such as the presidents' heads carved out of the natural rock of Mt. Rushmore. We will look at one or two examples of each type.

Red Grooms' *Ruckus Rodeo* (**363**) is a giant walk-in cartoon of a rodeo show. Occupying 1,237 square feet of gallery space, it depicts the riotous action of major rodeo events—Brahma bull riding, bareback bronco busting, steer wrestling, rodeo queens, and clowns—all in a colorful, madcap, environment. Full-size figures occupy this outlandish landscape, but these are not the

left: 365. Claes Oldenburg.
*Clothespin*. 1976. Cor-Ten steel, height 45'.
Centre Square, Philadelphia.

above: 366. Robert Smithson. *Spiral Jetty*. 1970.
Rock, salt crystals, earth, algae; coil length 1500'.
Great Salt Lake, Utah.

meticulously lifelike figures of a Duane Hanson. Grooms' fun-house people
are built of any material at hand—wire, cloth, wood, plastic, metal. And they
are painted, but not with the naturalistic skin tones favored by Hanson.
Grooms paints his figures the way a clown puts on makeup—the broader, the
more exaggerated, the more colorful, the better. *Ruckus Rodeo* demonstrates
Grooms' desire for active audience participation in large-scale works of art.
Viewers are allowed to walk among the structures and interact with the zany
creatures who dwell there. To enter this environment is to suspend judgments
about reality and let the wit and magic and color take over.

Also full of vivid colors, Judy Pfaff's environmental sculptures are not
figurative but instead are abstract and poetic. Walking into a work like *Kabuki*
(**364**) is not unlike carrying around with you the vague memory of a dream
whose details you can't quite recall. Everything in Pfaff's environment comes
into play—the walls, ceiling, floor, and objects placed or suspended in the
composition. Viewers who venture in are surrounded by a self-contained
world of colors and shapes. Because the work is entirely nonrepresentational,
it is even truer than usual that each viewer experiences the environment differently. Pfaff controls the visual stimuli, but she cannot control the associations we bring to her work.

Claes Oldenburg's *Clothespin* (**365**) is a giant representation in steel of
exactly what the title says—an everyday clothespin. It is meant to be exhibited
outdoors, seen against the cityscape, and the very size of the sculpture makes
this virtually necessary. By taking an ordinary object, blowing it up to huge
size, and setting it in a public place, Oldenburg makes the form heroic. In
effect the artist is saying, "Look at this form, look at it in the new way I have
shown it to you." In the laundry room a clothespin is boring and mundane. In
a city square, 45 feet tall, it is both amusing and awesome. The simplicity of
the form makes a striking contrast to the ornate building behind it.

Environmental sculpture on a grand scale occurs when an artist sets out to
sculpt the earth itself. Robert Smithson's *Spiral Jetty* (**366**) is such a construction, and it has become one of the classics of modern sculpture. The *Spiral Jetty*
is a 1,500-foot-long ramp of earth and rock, bulldozed into position in a se-

cluded part of the Great Salt Lake in Utah. When the *Jetty* was constructed in 1970, the United States was actively involved in space exploration, and for the first time we could see photographs of what our planet looks like from "the outside." We became aware that Earth is always in a state of change, with forms continually building up and breaking down. Smithson's work exemplifies this process on an enormous scale; although intended as a permanent structure, the *Spiral Jetty* is no longer visible, because the lake has risen to cover it. The long curl of the spiral also reminds us of old legends about the Great Salt Lake being connected by an underground canal to the Pacific Ocean. According to these legends, the flow of water back and forth created huge whirlpools in the lake, similar to the form of the spiral. Above all, the spiral is a timeless symbol. Spirals have been a recurring motif in the arts since earliest ages. Smithson took the bold step of carving a giant spiral into the very land we inhabit.

A similarly ambitious work, Christo's *Running Fence* (**367**), never was intended to be anything but temporary. Constructed of 20-foot-high nylon panels set on steel posts, the *Running Fence* meandered over the hills and fields of northern California for 24 miles, starting at the Pacific Ocean and moving inland. It was built by a team of volunteers, stood for two weeks, and then, as planned, was demolished. All that remain of it are photographs, films, and preliminary drawings.

Christo's work is an example of *conceptual art*, which we shall explore in more detail in Chapter 17 (pp. 429–433). More important than the physical structure itself is the concept underlying it—in this case the experience of conceiving, planning, building, recording, and destroying a monumental work. This artist's sculptures make a mark upon the landscape; they confront nature on a giant scale. The impulse is similar to, though grander than, that of drawing one's initials in wet concrete or painting them on a rock. And yet, after all, one cannot leave a 24-mile fence across California. Christo deliberately chose to create a structure that had to come down, that had demolition built into its concept, in order to focus attention on the process.

## Motion, Light, and Time

The world we live in is preoccupied with action—change and movement and energy—so it is only natural that some of our sculpture would reflect this. *Kinetic sculpture* is a broad term generally used to describe works that incorporate motion as part of their artistic expression. The mobiles of Alexander Calder (**368**), for instance, are light and fluid, balanced so that the slightest current of air will set them moving. In a sense they are *about* motion, which is

**367.** Christo. *Running Fence.* 1972–76. Nylon fabric and steel poles, 18′ × 24½ miles. Installed in Sonoma and Marin Counties, California, for two weeks, fall 1976.

**368.** Alexander Calder.
*Untitled.* 1976.
Painted aluminum
and tempered steel,
29'10½" × c. 76'.
National Gallery of Art,
Washington, D.C. (gift of the
Collectors Committee).

to say their subject is constant change and a never-ending formation of new relationships in space. Implicit in these mobiles is the element of time. We said of Rodin's *Burghers* (**357**) that you have to move around the sculpture to appreciate it fully. You can also move around a Calder mobile, but *it* is moving too, so the experience of elapsed time, of changing forms and spaces, is even more complex.

Weightless as they seem to be, Calder's mobiles still have substance. If you could touch one, you would feel thin, rigid pieces of metal. Other sculptors have created works based on an element with no substance at all—light. The light sculptures of James Turrell are designed to "make light inhabit space so it feels materially present," according to the artist. In *Afrum* (**369**), for instance, we see what appears to be a solid cube hovering in the air. Closer inspection, however, leads us to discover that the cube consists entirely of light. Turrell's work is based on illusion, and that illusion is very persuasive—so much so, in fact, that a 1980 exhibition of his work at the Whitney Museum of American Art resulted in two lawsuits. In both cases visitors to the exhibition leaned against what seemed to be a wall but was only a light-illusion, lost their balance, and fell to the floor.

**369.** James Turrell.
*Afrum.* 1967. Xenon light.
Installation 1976 at the
Stedelijk Museum, Amsterdam.
Collection Dr. Giuseppe Panza di Blumo,
Varese, Italy.

*Motion, Light, and Time* 285

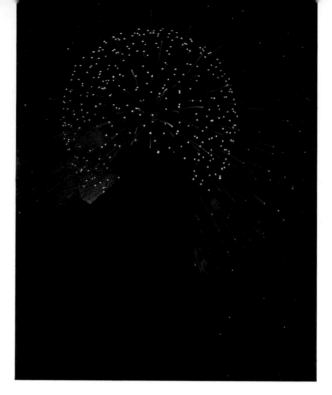

**370.** Fireworks display over the Brooklyn Bridge, New York, at its centennial celebration, May 24, 1983. Courtesy New York Convention and Visitors Bureau.

To the person whose idea of sculpture is the stone carvings of Michelangelo, this conception of light as sculpture may be strange, even shocking. But somehow it seems appropriate that our electronic world should produce sculptures this transitory and just this susceptible to a modern phenomenon—the power failure.

If we take light, expand it in space, add motion, throw in a loud noise, and include the element of time, we have . . . fireworks. Fireworks have been with us for quite a while, but only recently have we begun to think of them as sculptures in the sky (**370**). Are they really sculptures? Perhaps, by some definitions. They have form, they exist in three dimensions, they are a human creation for the purpose of aesthetic expression. The only thing unusual is that they exist for just a few seconds and then fade, never to be duplicated exactly.

One thing is clear: we cannot evaluate sculptures according to how long they last. Classical civilizations made sculptures to survive for all eternity, but they will not. Wood sculptures may burn, stone sculptures are eaten away by acid rain and industrial pollution. In times of war metal sculptures have sometimes been melted down to be turned into bullets. What remains, what cannot be taken away, is the sculptor's expression and the experience of the viewer—even if it lasts only for a moment.

# 12
# Crafts

The works of art considered in this chapter have certain things in common with one another, but they also share traits with other media, such as sculpture. Most of them have roots in the traditional trades of the Middle Ages—potter, blacksmith, woodworker, and so forth. It is from this background that the word *craft* derives, referring to expert work done by hand. We still describe as "well-crafted" anything finely made, including a chair, an automobile, a house, even sometimes a painting or sculpture. The specific connotation of craft, however, is an object made by hand, not by machine, and that is true of all the works shown in this chapter.

A common assumption people make about the crafts is that objects are made for some functional use, such as eating, drinking, wearing, or sitting. For this reason they have often been called the "functional arts" or the "applied arts"—that is, applied to everyday necessities. And, to be sure, many of the objects we will look at have that very reason for being. A beautifully hand-made dinner plate or wine goblet is a craft object, meant to be used for eating or drinking. However, it has never been true that all works considered crafts are purely utilitarian, and it is much less true today than in the past.

Our first three illustrations (**371**, **372**, **373**) show objects made of clay, made by hand. We would probably call the first one (**371**) a pot or a cup. It was made specifically for holding tea and was deliberately made simple and rough, according to the requirements of the Japanese tea ceremony. The second piece (**372**) might be called a sculpture; it is not different in concept from many of the works in Chapter 11, several of which are also made of clay. But how do we classify the third example (**373**)? This is a "stirrup vessel" made by the Mochica Indians of ancient Peru, dating from about A.D. 200–500. Although it was made to hold liquids and actually has a pouring spout (the name "stirrup" comes from the arc-shaped spout), the piece is so masterfully sculpted that its form takes precedence over any practical use. Most people would be more inclined to put it on display as an art object than to store it in a kitchen cupboard. Would we then call it a "sculptural pot"?

right: 371. Choniu. Tea bowl,
from Japan. c. 1760.
Raku ware, height 3½".
Metropolitan Museum of Art,
New York (Mansfield Collection,
gift of Howard Mansfield, 1936).

below: 372. Viola Frey.
*Lady in Red Dress.* 1983.
Ceramic, height 7'7½".
Collection Nancy and Bernard Kattler,
Los Angeles.

The problem is that we can draw no definite line between the functional object and the art object, between the piece meant to be used and the one meant only to be admired. Furthermore, the object intended for use will still be admired for its beauty of form and the unique expression of its maker. Many craft artists move freely back and forth from the functional to the sculptural. For example, it is not uncommon for the ceramist who worked all day yesterday making a set of coffee mugs to spend today building a large ceramic sculpture. This kind of versatility is true for the glass blower, the weaver, the metalsmith, and the woodworker as well.

What may distinguish the crafts from the other arts is their emphasis on particular materials. The traditional materials of the crafts are clay, glass, fiber, metal, and wood. While a sculptor might be equally proficient in several different materials, most craft artists concentrate on one material only and have learned to realize its potential for many different kinds of expression. Each of these materials has its own capabilities and limitations, and each lends itself to certain kinds of structural and decorative design. In this chapter, then, we shall consider each of these materials in turn.

## Clay

The craft of *ceramics* involves making objects from clay, a naturally occurring earth substance. When dry, clay has a powdery consistency; mixed with water it becomes *plastic*—that is, moldable and cohesive. In this form it can be modeled, pinched, rolled, or shaped between the hands. Once a clay form has been built and permitted to dry, it will hold its shape, but it is very fragile. To ensure permanence the form must be *fired* in a kiln, at temperatures ranging between about 1,200 and 2,700 degrees Fahrenheit, or higher. Firing changes the chemical composition of the clay so that it can never again be made plastic. A fired ceramic object, especially one fired at a high temperature, is quite durable. It can be shattered by a hard blow, but the pieces will not disintegrate. A sizable portion of the ancient art that has survived is ceramic, because—unlike wood or fiber—fired clay is highly resistant to the elements. Most large museums have very old ceramic treasures that have been patiently reassembled from the fragments discovered at archaeological sites.

Nearly every culture we know of has practiced the craft of ceramics, and civilizations in the Middle East understood the basic techniques by as early as 5,000 B.C. The first ceramic ware was undoubtedly made by *pinching*—simple molding and squeezing of a lump of clay between the fingers. This method is adequate for making a small figurine or a miniature bowl, but it would be inefficient to impossible for larger items.

A major requirement for most ceramic objects is that they be hollow, that they have thin walls around a hollow core. There are two reasons for this. First, many ceramic wares are meant to contain things—foods or liquids, for instance. Second, a solid clay piece is difficult to fire and may very well explode in the kiln. To meet this need for hollowness, ceramists over the ages have developed specialized forming techniques.

One such technique is called *slab construction*. The ceramist rolls out the clay into a sheet, very much as a baker would roll out a pie crust, and then allows the sheet to dry slightly. The sheet, or slab, can then be handled in many ways. It can be cut into pieces for assembly into a box form, curled into a cylinder, draped over a mold to make a bowl, or shaped into free-form sculptural configurations. Slab building is usually the method of choice for forming rectilinear objects.

Slab construction was used to create the little horse shown here (**374**). This charming figure is an example of *haniwa*—clay figures placed around Japanese burial mounds between the 3rd and the 6th centuries. *Haniwa* were made to represent many subjects—horses, warriors, birds, and elegant costumed ladies. Usually there was little attempt at naturalism; the subjects were rendered in simple, tubular forms—the word *haniwa* means "circle of clay." This figure intentionally looks more like a toy horse than a real one. The slab construction lends itself readily to the creation of these basic sculptural forms.

*Coiling* is another technique for making a thin, hollow form. The ceramist rolls out ropelike strands of clay, then coils them upon one another and joins them together. A vessel made from coils attached one atop the other will have a ridged surface, but the coils can be smoothed completely, to produce a uniform, flat wall. The Indian tribes of the southwestern United States (who never developed the potter's wheel common in most other parts of the world) made extraordinarily large, finely shaped pots by coiling. In this century their

**left: 373.** Stirrup vessel in the shape of a kneeling warrior. Mochica culture, Peru, A.D. 200–500. Earthenware, height 9⅛".
Metropolitan Museum of Art, New York
(gift of Nathan Cummings, 1963).

**right: 374.** *Haniwa: Horse*, from Japan. A.D. 3rd–6th century. Terra cotta, height 23½".
Cleveland Museum of Art
(gift of Mrs. R. Henry Norweb).

# María Martínez
## *1881(?)–1980*

It is a long way in miles and in time between the tiny pueblo of San Ildefonso in New Mexico and the White House in Washington, D.C. But the extraordinary ceramic artist María Martínez made that journey, and many others, in a long lifetime devoted to the craft of pottery-making. María—as she signed herself and is known professionally—began her career as a folk potter and ended it as a first-ranked potter of international reputation.

A Pueblo Indian, María most likely was born in 1881, but there are no records. As a child she learned to make pottery, using the coil method, by watching her aunt and other women of the community. Part of her youth was spent at St. Catherine's Indian School in Santa Fe, where she became friends with Julián Martínez. The couple married in 1904.

Although the husband worked at other jobs, the two Martínezes early formed a partnership for making pottery—she doing the building, he the decorating. Between 1907 and 1910 he was employed as a laborer on an archaeological site near the pueblo, under the direction of Dr. Edgar L. Hewett. The amazing career of María Martínez was launched in a simple way: Dr. Hewett gave her a broken piece of pottery from the site and asked her to reconstruct a whole pot in that style using traditional Indian black-ware techniques.

About 1919 the Martínezes developed the special black-on-black pottery that was to make them and the pueblo of San Ildefonso famous. The shiny black ware—created from red clay by a process of smothering the dung-fueled bonfire used for firing—was decorated with matte-black designs. This black-on-black ware was commercially quite successful.

María Martínez and her husband became wealthy by the standards of the pueblo and, as was customary, shared that wealth with the entire community.

María bore four sons who survived. Eventually they and their wives and children and grandchildren became partners in her enterprise. One shadow on her domestic life was her husband's serious alcoholism, which began early in their marriage and contributed to his death in 1943. After he was gone, María's daughter-in-law Santana took over much of the decorating of pots, to be followed by María's son Poponi Da.

As María's fame spread, she traveled widely, giving demonstrations at many world's fairs. Among the awards she received were an honorary doctorate from the University of Colorado and the American Ceramic Society's highest honor for a lifetime of devotion to clay. Her visit to Washington during the 1930s was a highlight. President Franklin D. Roosevelt was not at home, but Mrs. Eleanor Roosevelt was, and she reportedly told María, "You are one of the important ones. We have a piece of your pottery here in the White House, and we treasure it and show it to visitors from overseas."

Undoubtedly, María's greatest achievement was in reviving and popularizing the traditions of fine pottery-making among the Pueblo Indians. Not long before her death, according to her great-granddaughter, she said: "When I am gone, essentially other people have my pots. But to you I leave my greatest achievement, which is the ability to do it."[1]

---

Photograph of María Martínez.

craft has been revived by a few supremely talented individuals, including the famous Indian potter María Martínez (**375**).

By far the fastest method of creating a hollow, rounded form is by means of the *potter's wheel* (**376**). Egyptian potters were using the wheel by about 4,000 B.C. Despite some modern improvements and the addition of electricity, the basic principle of wheel construction remains the same as it was in ancient times. The wheel is a flat disk mounted on a vertical shaft, which can be made to turn rapidly either by electricity or by foot power. The ceramist centers a mound of clay on the wheel and, as the wheel turns, uses the hands to shape, "open," and lift the clay form—a procedure known as *throwing*. Throwing on the wheel always produces a rounded or cylindrical form, although the thrown pieces can later be reshaped, cut apart, or otherwise altered. Two or more thrown forms can also be joined together.

The most suitable technique, therefore, is one choice the ceramist needs to make in planning a particular work; another choice is the type of clay to be used. Clays differ in their composition, and this in turn affects the character of pieces made from them. Usually a clay is categorized by its firing temperature— the optimum temperature needed to permanently change the clay's chemical composition and make it hard. *Earthenware* clays, generally red or brown, fire at the lowest temperatures. Fired earthenware objects are often called *terra cotta* ("baked earth"). They tend to be coarse and porous and will not hold liquids unless coated with a glaze (see below). *Stoneware* clays, which fire at medium temperatures, are generally brown or grayish. Much commercial dinnerware is made of stoneware, and these clays have been extremely popular among artist-potters.

The aristocrats of clays are the pure white *porcelains*, which fire at the highest temperatures. Porcelain is the material of the finest dinnerware and in the past was used for the most elegant of commercial vases and figurines. Until recently, individual artist-potters seldom worked in porcelain because the high firing temperatures are difficult to achieve with noncommercial

**left: 375.** María Martínez. Black-on-black jar.

**right: 376.** Elmer Taylor, North Texas State University, throwing on the potter's wheel.

**377.** *Hippopotamus,* from the tomb
of Senbi at Meir, Egypt.
XII Dynasty, 2000–1788 B.C.
Egyptian faience, height 4⅜".
Metropolitan Museum of Art, New York
(gift of Edward S. Harkness, 1917).

equipment and because porcelain clays are less plastic and thus more difficult to handle than earthenware or stoneware. In the last few years, however, additives have been developed for porcelain clays that decrease the problems, so there has been renewed interest in porcelain among craft artists. (A term often used—and misused—by commercial ceramics manufacturers is *china,* which refers to a ware not unlike porcelain but firing at a lower temperature. China clays have little plasticity, and they are rarely used by the craft artist.)

While clays themselves may have interesting colors and textures, much of the potential for decoration in ceramics comes from the glaze. A *glaze* is a

**378.** *The Calydonian Boar,*
decorated plate
from Urbino, Italy. c. 1542.
Majolica ware, diameter 10¾".
Victoria & Albert Museum, London.

**379.** Elena Karina.
*Botticelli.* 1979.
Porcelain, height 13″.
Collection Mr. and Mrs. Alvin Ferst, Jr.

glass-like material usually applied to the surface of a ceramic piece and then fired on so as to fuse the glaze with the clay body. Nearly always this is a second firing, which follows the preliminary one to harden the clay. There is virtually no limit to the different effects that can be produced by combining glazes or by the various methods of applying them. While there are clear glazes, most glazes have color, and this is a major reason for their application. A secondary purpose of the glaze is to make an object watertight and nonabsorbent—especially important for cooking and eating vessels and for the more porous low-fired clays.

One of the earliest glazes, in use by 3,000 B.C., is known as *Egyptian paste.* Unlike most glazes, this material is mixed into the clay rather than applied on top of it. When the piece is fired (in a single firing) a glassy coating, often turquoise in color, forms on the surface. We see this in the Metropolitan Museum's famous hippopotamus figure, affectionately known to museum-goers as "William" (**377**).

Conventional glazes can be applied in many ways—by pouring, dipping, or spraying, for example. When properly compounded, glazes can also be painted onto a surface with all the precision and potential for color effects available to an artist using oil paints on canvas. The best examples of this technique appear in the decorated plates from Renaissance Italy and Spain, known as *majolica* ware (**378**). Elaborate painted scenes, some of them quite naturalistic, were achieved through the use of multicolored glazes. In this type of expression the form of the ceramic piece is much less important than its decoration. The plate becomes just another surface on which to paint.

In contemporary ceramics we are more likely to find a balance of form and decoration—a blend so perfect that one could not exist without the other. This is apparent in the work of Elena Karina (**379**). Karina's forms may remind us of seashells, but if so, they are the most delicate, intricate, and complex seashells ever made. Shaped by hand from porcelain, Karina's vessels shimmer with a variable opalescent glaze that seems like a natural extension of the form.

Today's ceramic artists have many advantages over those of the past. Improvements in technology have encouraged a new willingness to experiment with form and design. Above all, size is no longer a limitation. Whereas most ceramists up to the last decade focused on the individual piece, the one perfect object, now it is common for ceramic artists to assemble components separately formed and fired into a larger structure or an environment. Viola Frey's

**380.** Betty Woodman. *Cloistered Arbor Room.* 1981. Handmade earthenware tiles with glaze, height of columns 5'. Installation at Bennington College, Vermont. Courtesy Hadler/Rodriguez Galleries, New York and Houston.

**381.** Peter Bramhall blowing glass with a blowpipe.

**382.** *Portland Vase.* A.D. 3rd century. Cameo-cut glass. British Museum, London.

*Lady in Red Dress* (**372**), which is more than 7 feet tall, was made this way, as was Betty Woodman's *Cloistered Arbor Room* (**380**). The columns that make up this "room" are composed of individual glazed tiles, assembled and attached to the wall. What intrigues us about the *Arbor Room* is its unexpected use of the material. We expect to see tiles on a wall, but not arranged into column-like forms; and we may expect to see flat columns on a wall, but usually they are of wood or stone. Arranged in an orderly progression, the ceramic columns have a monumental, dignified quality. Woodman's work pushes ceramic art into a new dimension, one that defines space rather than just ornamenting it.

# Glass

If clay is one of the most versatile of the craft materials, glass is perhaps the most fascinating. Few people, when presented with a beautiful glass form, can resist holding it up to the light, watching how light changes its appearance from different angles.

While there are thousands of formulas for glass, its principal ingredient is usually silica, or sand. The addition of other materials can affect color, melting point, strength, and so on. When heated, glass becomes molten, and in that state it can be shaped by several different methods. Unlike clay, glass never changes chemically as it moves from a soft, workable state to a hard, rigid one. As glass cools it hardens, but it can then be reheated and rendered molten again for further working.

Glass as a material holds many risks, both during the creative process and afterward. The shaping of a glass object demands split-second timing—quick decisions and quick handwork—while the glass remains hot. What's more, a finished glass piece is the most fragile of all craft wares. One quick blow can shatter it irreparably. There is something almost heroic about an artist who would spend days, weeks, even months making an object that is so vulnerable.

Glassmaking is nearly as old a craft as ceramics, but it was not until the Roman era, shortly before the birth of Christ, that the first great period of glassmaking as an art began. The Roman era saw the invention of the blow-pipe—an instrument that has changed very little in two thousand years (**381**). To blow glass, the artist dips up a portion of molten glass at the end of the pipe and then blows through the pipe to produce a bubble. The bubble can be shaped or cut by various methods while it is still hot. Besides blowing, other ways of forming glass include molding, pressing, and rolling.

The Roman historian Pliny the Elder wrote of large "statues" made from glass, but almost nothing is known about them. It is assumed that they were chiseled out of solid glass blocks and then polished. Although we can only speculate about such pieces, many examples of glassware from the Roman period have survived, including what is perhaps the most famous glass object in the world—the *Portland Vase* (**382**). The incredible virtuosity displayed in this vessel testifies to long experience in glassmaking. The vase was made in three stages. First the basic form of dark blue glass was blown, and then a layer of semi-opaque white glass was added to the outside. Next the vase was given over to a cameo cutter—a carver of low-relief figural designs—who patiently chipped away the white glass to create a relief design of many gradations. In some areas the dark blue shows faintly through the white to give a shaded effect. Later glass artists have tried to duplicate the remarkable cameo quality of the *Portland Vase* and have failed.

About a thousand years later, another great era of glassmaking took place in Italy. This time it centered on the city of Venice. By the year 1291 there were so many glass factories in Venice, with so many furnaces burning day and night, that the entire city seemed in danger of going up in flames. As a result, the Senate demanded that all the glass factories be removed to the island of Murano, where many remain to this day.

Venetian glassmakers excelled in decorative design and perfected many elaborate techniques. Among their specialties were enameling ("painting" with colored glass), etching with acids, gilding, trailing on thin ribbons of molten glass in preplanned designs, and combinations of these. Ornate examples of Venetian glass like this elaborately decorated goblet (**383**) were highly sought throughout Europe. Because their glasswares were such valuable trading items, Venetian glassmakers were forbidden to leave Murano, and the techniques were closely guarded secrets. Nevertheless, several of the artisans escaped, and their knowledge spread across Europe and to North America.

Contemporary glass artists, like their counterparts in ceramics, strive for a balance of form and decoration. In glass—in the hands of a sensitive artist—

**383.** Goblet, from Venice. Early 16th century. Cristallo with enameled and gilt decoration, height 9¼". Corning Museum of Glass, Corning Glass Center, Corning, N.Y.

**above left: 384.** Peter Bramhall.
*Water Series Interior.*
Blown glass, diameter 16″.
Collection Mr. & Mrs.
Lawrence Rockefeller.

**above right: 385.** Dale Chihuly.
*Macchia Seaforms.* 1983. Blown glass
with applied threading
and glass "jimmies," width c. 25″.
Courtesy Charles Cowles Gallery,
New York.

**below: 386.** *Tiger,* from China.
Middle Zhou period,
c. 900–600 B.C.
Bronze, length 29⅝″.
Freer Gallery of Art,
Smithsonian Institution,
Washington, D.C.

this balance may develop as the piece is conceived. Peter Bramhall's *Water Series Interior* (**384**), a hand-blown glass piece more than a foot in diameter, exemplifies this exquisite partnership of shape and expressive design. The title suggests a flow of underwater reeds and grasses in constant, gentle motion, yet these forms are merely implied, not deliberately drawn. They emerge from the fluid nature of the glass and create their own universe inside the perfect bubble.

Dale Chihuly's designs are more exuberant, more deliberately sculptural (**385**). Their decoration seems to evolve from the form itself, rather than being applied to an existing structure. Chihuly's blown-glass works are very thin and translucent; they have a fluid quality reminiscent of shapes in the natural world, without referring specifically to any particular natural form.

In spite of the fact that glassmaking is an ancient art, its popularity as an expressive craft medium faded after the Venetian era. Not until the 1960s did craft artists rediscover glass, so that all the traditional techniques had to be relearned—and then applied to contemporary styles. Nevertheless, glass artists have made tremendous strides in catching up with the other craft media.

# Metal

From the most fragile craft material we turn to the most indestructible. Metals rust and corrode under some circumstances, but they do not shatter, chip, or rot away. Indeed, sometimes the action of the elements has a beneficial effect on metals, giving them a surface color, or *patina*, that is more attractive than their original appearance.

Ever since humans learned to work metals, they have made splendid art, as well as functional tools, from this versatile family of materials. Given all the sophisticated technology we have available today, we might think that metalwork would simply get better and better. Yet for sheet beauty of form and decoration, few artists have matched the skill of bronze craftsmen in China during the Shang and Zhou dynasties three thousand years ago.

Ornate bronze vessels were made in China as early as the 16th century B.C. The piece illustrated here (**386**) is later, dating from the Middle Zhou dynasty (c. 900–600 B.C.). It is interesting to note that this work predates by hundreds of years the art of Classical Greece, which many Westerners consider to have been the beginning of all civilized art. Chapter 11 (p. 267) explained the process of lost-wax casting. The Shang and Zhou bronzes also were cast, but by a far more demanding method. Archaeologists now speculate that the Chinese metalworkers were able to build a two-piece "sandwich" mold without benefit of the wax layer to hold the two sections apart—an inexplicable and astonishing feat for that time or any other. The tiger shown here is thought to have been made as a base support for some large structure, perhaps a throne. Like most works from this period, it is covered with stylized geometric designs in relief.

One distinctive aspect of metal is that it is equally at home in the mundane and the sublime—the bridge that spans a river or the precious ring on a finger; the plow that turns up the earth or the crown on a princess' head. Whatever the application, the basic composition of the material is the same, and the methods of working it are similar.

Casting is but one of several methods for working metal. Another ancient technique is *forging*—the art of the blacksmith. Forging involves heating a chunk of metal over a fire until it is red-hot, then beating and shaping it with hammers. This is how horseshoes traditionally were made, and it is also the method of making wrought iron.

A hundred years ago there was a blacksmith in every town. This was necessary to serve the needs of a populace that could travel only when its animals were properly shod. The more inventive of these blacksmiths also answered the enormous demand for decorative metal objects—doorways, grilles, balconies, hinges, door knockers, and many others. Today such commissions are rare, partly because the public taste for ornamental metal has declined, partly because most such objects are mass-produced. However, when it was decided to restore the Senate Chamber of the state capitol building in Albany, New York, the planners found themselves a modern counterpart of yesterday's creative blacksmith.

Albert Paley, a noted metalsmith who teaches at the State University of New York, was commissioned to execute new doors for the Senate chamber, first designed in the 1870s. Paley's gates (**387**), forged and fabricated from steel, brass, and bronze, are modern in their streamlined, linear design, yet they harmonize extremely well with the century-old structure. His design is so elegant and classic as to seem timeless.

Forging is the method of hammering heated metal, but some metals can also be hammered cold. This is the technique of many fine silversmiths. The artisan begins with a thin sheet of metal and, working from the back, strikes it repeatedly with small hammers, a technique known as *repoussé*. In some cases the metal sheet is placed on top of a mold and hammered so as to conform to the shape of the mold. Silver, in particular, is a soft enough metal to endure this kind of constant pounding, yield to it, but seldom break or develop holes. The vase illustrated (**388**) is a wonderful example of this technique. It was made by Tiffany and Company for the World's Columbian Exposition in 1893, and no effort was spared to make it as elaborate—and as uniquely American—as possible. Hammered into relief are flowers and plants from every region of the United States. Both the overall shape of the vase and the handles at the top were inspired by pottery forms from the ancient tribes that inhabited the Americas before the arrival of Columbus.

**below: 387.** Albert Paley. *Portal Gates.* 1980. Mild steel, brass, and bronze; height 13′6″. Commissioned for the Senate Chambers, Capitol Building, Albany, N.Y. Courtesy Fendrick Gallery, Washington, D.C.

**right: 388.** Tiffany and Company. *Magnolia Vase,* made for World's Columbian Exposition, 1893. Silver, gold, and enamel; height 31″. Metropolitan Museum of Art, New York (gift of Mrs. Winthrop Atwell, 1899).

**below right: 389.** Merry Renk. *Arizona Conference.* 1980. Necklace of silver, carved coral, sawed from sheet, cast, soldered, and hammered; 11 × 7″. Courtesy the artist.

One of the oldest uses of metal as an expressive medium is for jewelry. This has been true since prehistoric times. Early cultures believed that wearing special stones or special metals could ward off disease and evil spirits—a practice continued today in the wearing of copper bracelets for therapeutic purposes. Apart from its supposed magical powers, metal has great symbolic value. People wear jewelry to symbolize wealth and status. They also wear jewelry to symbolize belonging—to a person (a wedding ring), to an institution (a school ring), to a group (a club or fraternity or religious ring).

Among contemporary metal artists jewelry has been a major preoccupation—not the jewelry of the perfect one-carat diamond in a traditional setting, but far more creative forms. Any of the various metalworking techniques can be used for jewelry, and sometimes two or more are combined in the same piece. For instance, Merry Renk's necklace *Arizona Conference* (**389**) was created by a combination of sawing, casting, soldering, carving, and hammering. The design represents an interesting trend among some contemporary jewelry makers, in that its symbolism is meaningful to the artist, not the buyer. Usually we expect symbolism in jewelry to reflect the wearer's life, as does a charm bracelet, but *Arizona Conference* recalls an event in the life of the artist. We might liken this trend to the work of painters and sculptures who explore their own realms of symbolism, but whose works are eagerly collected by those for whom the symbolism may not have direct personal meaning.

Heikki Seppä's metalwork, like the piece shown here (**390**), is generally free-form, an abstraction in metal meant to evoke but not duplicate flower or plant forms. Its curving shape beautifully exploits metal's primary qualities—its shine, its smoothness, its fluidity. The individual who would choose to buy and display such a piece is responding to the metalworker's interpretation of form. Contemporary metalwork, thus, is an expression of both the artist's personal approach to the material and the collector's aesthetic taste.

# Wood

There are two reasons for the extreme popularity of wood as a craft material throughout the entire history of art. One is that it is relatively easy to work. The simplest tools will shape it, and there is no need for extreme heat, as with clay, glass, or metal. The second reason is that wood is so widely available. In most inhabited areas of the globe wood is abundant and relatively easy to obtain.

These two qualities would make wood the ideal material were it not for certain drawbacks. Because of its organic nature, wood is not very durable. Cold and heat distort it, water rots it, and insects can eat it away. More than one collector has tried to import a gorgeous wood carving from Africa, only to find it contained an active colony of insects that left nothing but a crumbling shell. We must assume that only a tiny fraction of the wood artifacts made over the centuries have survived. Perhaps that is why the few very old wood pieces we have seem all the more marvelous.

A particularly rich trove of carved-wood objects was found at Oseberg in southern Norway, in a buried Viking ship dating from the early 9th century. The Oseberg ship, itself made of wood and decorated with a wonderfully carved prow, is believed to have been a luxury vessel intended for cruising the coastline and rivers. Among its contents was a splendid animal head (**391**) that adorned the top of a post—the sort of post probably carried in religious processions. In style the head represents an artistic tradition, the so-called *animal style*, common in northwestern Europe from about the 5th to the 10th century. The main feature of this style is a delicate, interlacing of lines, seen here on the neck of the animal. Obviously, enormous skill was required to plan and execute this intricate design in wood.

Wood carving, especially of figures, reached a high point in the United States during the 19th century. Certain types of figures flourished: cigar-store

**392.** Carousel figure.
19th century. Wood, length 5′2″.
Smithsonian Institution, Washington, D.C.
(Van Alstyne Collection).

Indians and other images that adorned the fronts of shops; magnificent fig-
ureheads, usually of women with long, flowing hair, that crowned the prows
of sailing ships; and marvelously ornate carrousel animals. Generations raised
on look-alike merry-go-round horses can scarcely comprehend the ingenuity
of carrousel figures carved a century ago. Not only horses, but lions and gi-
raffes and elephants and camels—all were meticulously hand-carved and im-
aginatively painted (**392**). The thrill of the ride was far less important than the
exotic experience of sitting atop one of these fanciful sculptures in wood.

Carving is only one of several methods for working with wood. It is a
subtractive process (pieces of wood are cut away), but there are also additive
processes for wood, such as nailing and gluing pieces together. One of the
more interesting of these is the old technique of *inlay,* in which small pieces of
wood, often with different grains and colors, are glued together to make a
pattern. When this method is used to decorate a wall or the face of a piece of
furniture, it is often called *marquetry.* A splendid example of this art comes
from the Ducal Palace at Gubbio, in Italy (**393**). Small pieces of different
woods have been cleverly combined to give a *trompe-l'oeil* (fool-the-eye) effect
of three-dimensional space, even though the wall is absolutely flat. The open
cabinet doors, the benches below them, even the shadows are all illusions! This
type of visual deceit was much prized in earlier centuries, and it still astonishes
us as we move closer to see that, yes, it really *is* a flat surface of wood.

**393.** Francesco di Giorgio of Siena.
Room from the Ducal Palace,
Gubbio, Italy. Late 15th century.
Trompe-l'oeil inlay of walnut, oak,
beech, rosewood, and fruitwoods;
height of room 8′10″.
Metropolitan Museum of Art,
New York (Rogers Fund, 1939).

For most of us, of course, wood is usually associated with furniture, which is generally constructed by a process of nailing and/or gluing. Contemporary wood artists have interpreted the basic furniture designs in wholly new ways to enhance the special qualities of wood. A walnut rocking chair by Peter Korn (**394**) reminds us of classic designs from the past, yet it is strikingly modern in its elegant shape and line.

When furniture craft and wood carving merge, we may get a zany result like the bedstead illustrated here (**395**). Klindt Houlberg's *Phantasy Plenishing* looks like a normal, well-crafted bed frame—up to about a foot from the floor. Above that the artist's imagination runs wild. One bedpost is a nude female figure, another a fantasy tree with a bird perched on top, and so on. Houlberg's work makes us realize how rich our environment could be if more everyday objects were treated with this kind of delightful expressiveness.

## Fiber

The design possibilities for works of fiber are enormous. By fiber we mean a narrow strand of vegetable or animal material (cotton, linen, wool, silk) or the modern-day synthetic equivalents. Like wood, fiber is widely available and quite perishable, but the construction methods used for fiber are unique to this pliable medium.

For centuries the most common method of working with fiber has been *weaving*. Weaving involves placing two sets of parallel fibers at right angles to one another and interlacing one set through the other in an up-and-down movement, generally on a loom or frame. One set of fibers is held taut; this is called the *warp*. The other set, known as the *weft* or *woof*, is interwoven through the warp to make a fabric. Nearly all fabrics, including those used for our clothing, are made by some variation of this process.

A complex loom is a little like a computer. Much of the designing of fabric takes place when the loom is "programmed." The weaver decides in advance how the warp yarns are to be arranged on the loom and also decides on the

**left: 394.** Peter Korn. Rocking chair. 1981. Walnut with upholstered seat. Courtesy the artist.

**right: 395.** Klindt Houlberg. *Phantasy Plenishing.* 1980. Wood, height 7'. Courtesy the artist.

pattern of interlacing for the weft yarns. After the planning stage, the weaving often progresses more or less automatically. Amazingly intricate fabrics can be created on the loom, and some of the most magnificent are the brocades of the traditional Japanese kimono (396). Perhaps no wearing apparel ever has been so richly decorated, so sumptuous to the touch, as the court dress of Japan.

*Tapestry* is a special type of weaving in which the weft yarns are manipulated freely to form a pattern or design on the front of the fabric. Often the weft yarns are of several colors, and the weaver can use the different colored yarn almost as flexibly as a painter uses pigment on a canvas. The weavers of ancient Peru specialized in tapestry weaves with geometric forms or marvelous stylized animal figures (397). The shirt illustrated here seems even more remarkable when we consider that it was woven on the simplest, most primitive of looms.

**left: 396.** Noh robe, with autumn flowers, from Japan. Edo Period, 18th century. Kara-ori brocade, length 5′3½″. Art Institute of Chicago (gift of Miss Nathalie Gookin).

**below: 397.** Shirt, Ica, south coast of Peru. 13th–15th century. Tapestry of wool and cotton, height 23½″. Metropolitan Museum of Art, New York (Michael C. Rockefeller Memorial Collection, bequest of Nelson A. Rockefeller, 1979).

**below: 398.** *Norman Fleet Sailing to England,* detail of the *Bayeux Tapestry.* c. 1073–88. Wool embroidery on linen; height 20″, overall length 231′. Town Hall, Bayeux, reproduced with special authorization of the City of Bayeux.

**399.** Lynda Benglis. *Patang*. 1980. Satin appliqué on canvas, 15 × 90'. Atlanta Airport Commission, Courtesy Paula Cooper Gallery, New York.

One of the most famous examples of fiber art in the Western world once hung in the Cathedral of Bayeux and now is preserved in the Town Hall of that French city. This is the *Bayeux Tapestry* (**398**)—misnamed, because it is actually a work of embroidery. (In the past, large-scale fabrics, especially those hung in buildings, often were loosely called "tapestries," regardless of the construction method.) *Embroidery* is a technique in which colored yarns are sewn to an existing woven background; frequently the sewing takes the form of decorative motifs or images, as here. The *Bayeux Tapestry* is like a long picture book—20 inches high and 231 feet long—telling the story of the conquest of England by William of Normandy in 1066. The scene illustrated, one of seventy-two separate episodes reading from left to right, shows the Norman boats setting sail to wage war on Saxon England. The fabric's pictorial design is simple and flat. The two smaller boats, meant to be seen as farther away than the three large ones, do not contribute to any sense of spatial depth; instead, they seem to be floating in the air. Despite the charming naïveté of these images, however, scholars have learned more about the events surrounding the Norman Conquest from the *Bayeux Tapestry* than they have from any of the literature of the time.

Centuries later and light-years away in expression, Lynda Benglis' *Patang* (**399**) shares one of the functions of the *Bayeux Tapestry*—to cover the bare walls of a public building. It is a work in *appliqué,* or pieces of fabric stitched onto a fabric backing, and hangs above a check-in counter at Atlanta's new airport. Benglis' work makes an interesting contrast with the *Bayeux Tapestry*. Where the latter originally hung, high up on the walls in a dim cathedral, it is unlikely that viewers could see much of its detail, and this was apparently of little concern to its makers. *Patang*, on the other hand, was designed for maximum impact at a distance in a large, open space. Planned for this location, it presents large, bold, abstract designs in brilliant colors.

Benglis' work represents a revival of the use of fabric to decorate large expanses of wall. Ten years ago the architects of this building probably would have left the wall plain. Fifty years ago they might have commissioned a painter to do a mural. Today, increasingly, architects and interior designers seek the work of the fiber artist. Why is this so, why has fashion turned in this direction? We cannot say for sure, but it is certainly true that fiber brings a warmth, a softness, a flexibility to the often-forbidding steel and concrete of our world.

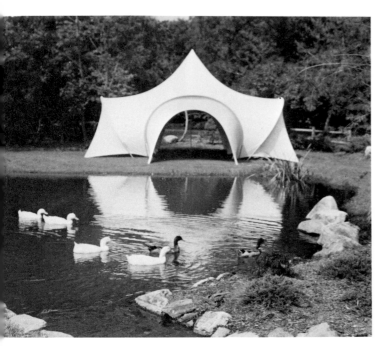

above: **400.** Ina Kozel.
*The Seven Sisters.* Hand-painted fabric.
Installed in the Ashford-Green Building, Atlanta.
Courtesy Paula Cooper Gallery, Atlanta.

left: **401.** Bill Moss.
*Optimum 350.* 1978.
Tent of cotton duck
and aluminum, 12 × 24 × 24'.
Courtesy Moss Tent Works, Inc., Camden, Maine.

While fiberworks can be stretched taut or laid flat against the wall or even sculpted into three-dimensionality, we usually associate fabric with pliability. Clothing flows around our bodies as we move, sails puff out and fill with the wind, flags flutter. This association of fabric with movement is inherent in Ina Kozel's *Seven Sisters* (**400**). Installed in the atrium of Atlanta's Ashford-Green Building, *Seven Sisters* is an assemblage of hand-painted "kites" that swoop and pivot constantly as they are propelled by air currents. Within this six-story glass enclosure has been contained a gentle reminder of all graceful things that fly.

From the fabric *in* architecture to the fabric *as* architecture is but a short step. Tents are almost as old as human civilization, yet certain innovative designers have adapted them to fit the styles and needs of contemporary life. The Moss *Optimum 350* tent (**401**) is an elegant, sculptural interpretation of fiber art as dwelling. It curves gracefully to carve and define the space both outside and in. This illustration leads us naturally to architecture—the subject of the next chapter.

The illustrations in this chapter cover five different families of materials and four thousand years of human history. They are very different, yet they have certain things in common. Each of them represents a perfect use of the material from which it was made. Each has been formed with the highest possible standards of craftsmanship. Above all, each shows the striving for aesthetic satisfaction that is part of humanity.

# *13*
# **Architecture**

Architecture satisfies a basic, universal human need for a roof over one's head. More than walls, more than a chair to sit down on or a soft bed upon which to lie, a roof is the classic symbol of protection and security. We've all heard the expression "I have a roof over my head," but it would be unusual to hear someone say, "I'm all right because I have walls around me." Of course, in purely practical terms a roof does keep out the worst of the elements, snow and rain, and in warm climates a roof may be sufficient to keep people dry and comfortable. In Mexico City the much-admired National Museum of Anthropology (**402**) was built around a large open courtyard, covered only by a massive roof supported atop a central column. The climate is mild, but there is much rain in the winter; a roof protects museum-goers as they move from gallery to gallery.

The roof, therefore, seems to be symbolic of the nature of architecture. There are, however, structures that have no roofs, and, except for rare and striking examples like the Mexico City museum, most buildings also have walls to enclose and protect from the sides. As was discussed in Chapter 4 (p. 116), the walls and roof of a building shape space and define it. We can discuss architecture equally in terms of the spaces and volumes created within a structure and in terms of the forms that create those spaces.

More than any of the other arts, architecture demands structural stability. Every one of us daily moves in and out of buildings—schools, houses, offices, stores, churches, bus stations, banks, and movie theaters—and we take for granted, usually without thinking about it, that they will not collapse on top of us. That they do not is a tribute to their engineering; if a building is physically stable, this means it adheres faithfully to the principles of the particular *structural system* or systems on which its architecture is based.

## **Structural Systems in Architecture**

Any building is a defiance of gravity. Since earliest times architects have tackled the challenge of erecting a roof over empty space, setting walls upright,

Courtyard, National Museum
of Anthropology, Mexico City.

**below: 403.**
Mission St. Francis of Assisi,
Ranchos de Taos, New Mexico. 1722.

and having the whole stand secure. Their solutions have depended upon the materials they had available, for, as we shall see, certain materials are better suited than others for a particular structural system. There are two basic families of structural systems: the *shell* system and the *skeleton-and-skin* system.

In the shell system one building material provides both structural support and sheathing (outside covering). Buildings made of brick or stone or adobe fall into this category (**403**). The structural material comprises the walls and roof, marks the boundary between inside and outside, and is visible as the exterior surface.

The skeleton-and-skin system might be compared to the human body, which has a rigid bony skeleton to support its basic frame and a more fragile skin for sheathing. We find this method of construction in modern skyscrapers, with their steel frames (skeletons) supporting the structure and a sheathing (skin) of glass or some other light material.

Skeleton-and-skin construction is largely a product of the Industrial Revolution; nearly always the skeleton is made of steel, which could not be manufactured in practical quantities until the mid-19th century. Most architecture before that time was of the shell type, and today the development of strong cast materials, including many plastics, has brought renewed interest in this type of construction.

Two factors that must be considered in any structural system are *weight* and *tensile strength*. Walls must support the weight of the roof, and lower stories must support the weight of upper stories. In other words, all the weight of the building must somehow be carried safely to the ground. You can get a sense of this if you imagine your own body as a structural member. Suppose you are lying flat on your back, your body held rigid. You are going to be lifted high in the air, to become a "roof." First you are lifted by four people: one supports you under the shoulders, one under the buttocks, one holds your arms extended above your head, another holds your feet. Your weight is therefore channeled down through four vertical people to the ground, and so you can hold yourself horizontally with some ease. Next you are lifted by two people, one holding your shoulders, another your feet. A lot of your weight is concentrated in the center of your body, which is unsupported, so eventually you sag in the middle and fall to the floor. Then you are lifted by one person, who holds you at the center of your back. The weight at both ends of your body has nowhere to go, nothing to carry it to the ground, and you sag at both ends.

Tensile strength is the ability of a material to span horizontal distances with minimum support from underneath. Returning to the analogy of the body, imagine you are not made of flesh and blood but of strong plastic or metal. Regardless of how you are held up in the air, you can stay rigid and horizontal, because you have great tensile strength.

If you keep these images in mind, you may find it easier to understand the various structural systems we shall consider below. They are introduced here in roughly the chronological order in which they were developed. As was mentioned earlier, all will be of the shell type until we reach the 19th century.

## Load-Bearing Construction

Another term for load-bearing construction is "stacking and piling." This is the simplest method of making a building, and it is suitable for brick, stone, adobe, ice blocks, and certain modern materials. Essentially, the builder constructs the walls by piling layer upon layer, starting thick at the bottom, getting thinner as the structure rises, and usually tapering inward near the highest point. The whole may then be topped by a lightweight roof, perhaps of thatch or wood. This construction is stable because its greatest weight is concentrated at the bottom and weight diminishes gradually as the walls grow higher.

Load-bearing structures tend to have few and small openings (if any) in the walls, because the method does not readily allow for support of material above a void, such as a window opening. This was the system used to construct the Ranchos de Taos church in New Mexico (403,404), a piled-up mass of sun-dried mud—adobe. Although the Taos church is hollow, meant to contain worshipers inside, many load-bearing structures are solid all the way through, or perhaps have only small open chambers within them. Indeed, some of the ancient pyramids of the Americas are more accurately referred to as "mound temples," because all ceremonies were conducted outside atop the pyramids and there are no interior spaces. We find such a structure in the colossal Pyramid of the Sun at Teotihuacán, near Mexico City, part of a giant temple complex built in the 6th or 7th century A.D. (405).

above: **404.** Mission St. Francis of Assisi, interior.

below: **405.** Pyramid of the Sun, Teotihuacán, Mexico. c. 510–660.

post–and–lintel

## Post-and-Lintel

We encountered post-and-lintel construction earlier, in the discussion of Stonehenge (62). After stacking and piling, it is the most elementary structural method, based on two uprights (the posts) supporting a horizontal crosspiece (the lintel, or beam). This configuration can be continued indefinitely, so that there may be one very long horizontal supported at critical points along the way by vertical posts to carry its weight to the ground. The most common materials for post-and-lintel construction are stone and wood. Since neither has great tensile strength, these materials will yield and cave in when forced to span long distances, so the architect must provide supporting posts at close intervals.

Post-and-lintel construction has been, for at least four thousand years, a favorite method of architects for raising a roof and providing for open space underneath. Tracing its history back to the first culture we know well, we find post-and-lintel used widely by the ancient Egyptians. At Luxor on the east bank of the Nile in Egypt stand the ruins of the mighty temple of Amen-Mut-Khonsu (406), planned by the pharaoh Amenhotep III in the 14th century B.C. The heavy lintels of the colonnade are supported solidly by tall, massive columns, almost too massive for the job they had to do. Perhaps the builder deliberately made the columns heavier than necessary in order to create an imposing effect.

Possibly the best-known and most impressive post-and-lintel building of all time is the Parthenon in Athens (407). We have already studied the Parthenon as a religious and political structure (Chapter 3, pp. 59–60); here we will focus on its construction. Had the Parthenon been simply an academic exercise in placing horizontal members atop vertical supports—a kind of Classical

Age prefabrication—it never would have been so admired for its architectural purity. What sets it apart are the many subtle refinements in its structure.

To begin with, the Parthenon has a particularly satisfying proportion of width to length to height—many would say a "perfect" proportion. Legend claims there are no straight lines in the Parthenon, but this is probably a romantic exaggeration. Many of the lines we expect to be straight, however, are not. What the builders did was adjust the physical lines of the temple so they would appear to be straight visually. For example, tall columns that are absolutely straight may appear to bend inward at the center, so the columns on the Parthenon have been given a slight bulge, known as *entasis*, to compensate for the visual effect. Also, a long horizontal, such as the Parthenon's porch steps, may appear to sag in the middle; to correct for this optical illusion, the level has been adjusted very slightly, rising about $2\frac{1}{2}$ inches to form an arc higher at the center. A large building rising perpendicular to the ground may loom over the visitor and seem to be leaning forward; to avoid this impression, the architects of the Parthenon tilted the whole facade back very slightly. Corner columns, seen against the sky, would have seemed thinner than inside columns, which have the building as a backdrop; therefore, the outside columns were made slightly heavier than all the others. These are only a few of the structural refinements that resulted in a beautiful temple.

Because the Parthenon looks so visually perfect, these optical corrections are not noticeable to the casual viewer. Precise measurements have revealed the secrets of the Parthenon's majesty. The point is, post-and-lintel construction, which at first appears to be so rudimentary, can embody the most sublime forms ever conceived by an architect's mind.

People often assume the Parthenon is a ruin simply because it is old, but this is far from true. Not only is post-and-lintel construction highly stable, but the builders who took such trouble about visual details were equally careful about structural soundness. In fact, were it not for an unfortunate incident in the 17th century, the Parthenon would stand today much as it did twenty-four hundred years ago. In 1687 the Turks, who then controlled Athens and were at war with the Venetians, used the Parthenon as an ammunition dump. The Venetians laid seige to the city, a bullet fell on the Acropolis igniting the ammunition, and the Parthenon blew up. No structural system yet devised can withstand the tragic consequences of conflict between nations.

The post-and-lintel system, then, offers potential for both structural soundness and grandeur. When applied to wood or stone, however, it leaves one problem unsolved, and that is the spanning of relatively large open spaces. The first attempt at solving this problem was the invention of the arch.

## Round Arch and Vault

Although the round arch was used by the ancient peoples of Mesopotamia several centuries before the birth of Christ (**449**), it was most fully developed by the Romans, who perfected the form in the 2nd century B.C. To get a sense of how the arch works, we might go back to the analogy of the body. Imagine that, instead of lying flat on your back, you are bent over forward into a curve, and again you will be lifted into the air. One person will support your hands, another your feet. As long as your body follows the proper arc—that is, your two supporters stand the correct distance apart—you can maintain the pose for some time. If they stand too close together, you start to topple first one way and then the other; if they move too far apart, you have insufficient support in the middle and plunge to the floor. An arch incorporates more complex forces of *tension* (pulling apart) and *compression* (pushing together), but the general idea is the same.

The arch has many virtues. In addition to being an attractive form, it enables the architect to open up fairly large spaces in a wall without risking the building's structural soundness. These spaces admit light, reduce the weight

keystone

round arch

barrel vault

round arches in the
Romanesque style

of the walls, and decrease the amount of material needed. As utilized by the Romans, the arch is a perfect semicircle, although it may seem elongated if it rests on columns. It is constructed from wedge-shaped pieces of stone that meet at an angle always perpendicular to the curve of the arch. Because of tensions and compressions inherent in the form, the arch is stable only when it is complete, when the topmost stone, the *keystone,* has been set in place. For this reason an arch under construction must be supported from below, usually by a wooden framework.

Over the centuries arches have been made of just about any building material imaginable, but there seems to be a natural affinity between this form and brick or stone. The Romans clearly understood this, and so did 20th-century architect Louis Kahn (**427**), who said:

> In consultation with nature you will discover the order of water, the order of wind, the order of light, the order of certain materials. If you think of brick and you're consulting the orders, you consider the nature of brick, you say to brick: "What do you want, brick?" Brick says to you: "I like an arch." If you say to brick: "Arches are expensive, and I can use a concrete lintel over an opening, what do you think of that, brick?" Brick says: "I like an arch."[1]

Among the most elegant and enduring of Roman structures based on the arch is the Pont du Gard at Nîmes, France (**408**), built in A.D. 15 when the Empire was nearing its farthest expansion through Europe. At this time industry, commerce, and agriculture were at their peak. Roman engineering was applied to an ambitious system of public-works projects, not just in Italy but in the outlying areas as well. The Pont du Gard functioned as an aqueduct, a structure meant to transport water, and its lower level served as a footbridge across the river. That it stands today virtually intact, after nearly two thousand years, testifies to the Romans' brilliant engineering skills. Visually, the Pont du Gard exemplifies the best qualities of arch construction. Solid and heavy, obviously durable, it is nevertheless shot through with open spaces that make it seem light and its load-bearing capabilities effortless.

When the arch is extended in depth—when it is, in reality, many arches placed flush one behind the other—the result is called a *barrel vault* or *tunnel vault.* This vault construction makes it possible to create large interior spaces. The Romans made great use of the barrel vault, but for its finest expression we look many hundreds of years later, to the cathedrals of the Middle Ages.

The church called La Madeleine (**409**), in the French town of Vézelay, is an example of the style prevalent throughout western Europe from about 1050 to 1200—a style known as *Romanesque.* Romanesque builders adopted the old Roman forms of round arch and barrel vault so as to add height to their churches. Until this period most churches had wooden roofs, which not only posed a threat of fire but also limited the height to which architects could aspire. With the barrel vault, they could achieve the soaring, majestic space we

**408.** Pont du Gard, Nîmes, France. Early 1st century A.D. Length 902′.

see in the *nave* (the long central area) of La Madeleine. Round arches set on half columns punctuate the ceiling at regular intervals, leading one's eye forward to the altar.

On the side aisles of La Madeleine (not visible in the photograph) the builders employed a series of *groin vaults*. A groin vault results when two vaults are crossed at right angles to each other, thus directing the weights and stresses down into the four corners. By dividing up a space into square segments known as *bays*, each of which contains one groin vault, the architects could cover a long span safely and economically. The arrangement of bays also creates a satisfying rhythmic pattern down the length of the structure.

## Pointed Arch and Vault

While the round arch and vault of the Romanesque era solved many problems and made many things possible, they nevertheless had certain drawbacks. For one thing, a round arch, to be stable, must be a semicircle; therefore, the height of the arch is limited by its width. Two other difficulties were weight and darkness. Barrel vaults are both literally and visually heavy, calling for huge masses of stone to maintain their structural stability. Also, the builders who constructed them dared not make light-admitting openings in or around them, for fear the arches and vaults would collapse, and so the interiors of Romanesque buildings tend to be dark. The *Gothic* period in Europe, which followed the Romanesque, solved these problems with the pointed arch.

The pointed arch, while seemingly not very different from the round one, offers many advantages. Because the sides arc up to a point, weight is channeled down to the ground at a steeper angle, and therefore the arch can be taller. The vault constructed from such an arch also can be much taller than a barrel vault. Architects of the Gothic period found they did not need heavy masses of material throughout the curve of the vault, as long as the major points of intersection were reinforced. These reinforcements, called *ribs*, are visible in the nave ceiling of Chartres Cathedral (**410**; see also **67,432**). The lighter vault also enabled builders to introduce stained-glass windows in the

**left: 409.** Nave, church of La Madeleine, Vézelay, France. 1120–40.

**right: 410.** Nave and choir, Chartres Cathedral. c. 1194–1260.

groin vault

pointed arch

**411.** Giovanni Paolo Panini. *Interior of the Pantheon.* c. 1740. Oil on canvas, 4′2½″ × 3′3″. National Gallery of Art, Washington, D.C. (Samuel H. Kress Collection, 1939).

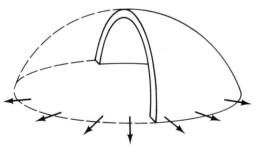

dome

stone walls, and so the Gothic church generally is much brighter inside than its Romanesque predecessor.

Gothic architecture was the first major step toward the skeleton-and-skin construction mentioned at the beginning of this chapter, although the method would not truly be realized until the 19th century. In the Gothic cathedral most of the weight rested on heavy stones in the walls, columns, and ribs, so that there could be large areas of "skin," such as thin masonry inserts and windows of stained glass.

## The Dome

A dome is an architectural structure generally in the shape of a hemisphere, or half globe. One customary definition of the dome is an arch rotated 360 degrees on its axis, and this is really more accurate, because, for example, the dome based on a pointed arch will be pointed at the top, not perfectly hemispherical. The stresses in a dome are much like those of an arch, except that they are spread in a circle around the dome's perimeter. Unless the dome is *buttressed*—supported from the outside—from all sides, there is a tendency for it to "explode"—for the stones to pop outward in all directions.

Like so many other architectural structures, the dome was perfected under the incomparable engineering genius of the Romans, and one of the finest domed buildings ever erected dates from the early 2nd century. It is called the Pantheon, which means a temple dedicated to "all the gods"—or, at least, all the gods who were venerated in ancient Rome. We reproduce here an 18th-century painting of the interior (**411**) because the circular building is so vast that it is impossible to find a camera angle to convey adequately its shape and scale.

As seen from the inside, the Pantheon has a perfect hemispherical dome soaring 142 feet above the floor, resting upon a cylinder almost exactly the same in diameter—140 feet. At the very top of the dome is an opening 29 feet in diameter called an *oculus,* or eye, thought to be symbolic of the "eye of heaven." This opening provides the sole (and plentiful) illumination for the building. In its conception, then, the Pantheon is amazingly simple—equal in height and width, symmetrical in its structure, round form set upon round form. Yet because of its scale and its classic proportions, the effect is overwhelming. The fact that the Romans, in ancient times, could enclose such a huge space without interior supports today seems extraordinary.

When an architect wishes to set a round dome atop a square building, as is very often the case, the structural problems become more complex. Some transitional device is required between the circle (at the dome's base) and the square (of the building's top), preferably one that bolsters the dome. An elegant solution can be found in Hagia Sophia (The Church of the Holy Wisdom) in Istanbul (**412**). Hagia Sophia was built as a Christian church during the 6th century, when Istanbul, then called Constantinople, was the capital of the great Byzantine Empire (p. 354). When the Turks conquered the city in the 15th century, Hagia Sophia became an Islamic mosque, and it is now preserved as a museum. In sheer size and perfection of form it was the architectural triumph of its time and has seldom been matched since then.

The dome of Hagia Sophia rises 183 feet above the floor, with its weight carried to the ground by heavy stone *piers*—in this case, squared columns—at the four corners of the immense nave. Around the base of the dome is a closely spaced row of arched windows, which make the heavy dome seem to "float" upward. Each of the four sides of the building consists of a monumental round arch, and between the arches and the dome are curved triangular sections known as *pendentives*. It is the function of the pendentives to make a smooth transition between rectangle and dome.

Because domes have so much been a feature of public buildings, both religious and political, we may think of them as the capstones of "official" architecture. St. Peter's Basilica in Rome (**479**), the U. S. Capitol in Washington (**422**) and its many offshoots in the state capitals, the great cathedrals of London—all are monumental structures topped by imposing domes. One of the loveliest of all domed buildings, however, originally was constructed for a private purpose, and despite its size it has a more intimate quality. This is the famous Taj Mahal in Agra, India.

The Taj Mahal (**413**) was built in the mid-17th century by the Moslem emperor of India, Shah Jahan, as a tomb for his beloved wife, Arjummand Banu, who died at the age of thirty-nine after having borne fourteen children. Although the Taj is nearly as large as Hagia Sophia and possessed of a dome

plan of the Pantheon

pendentive

dome with pendentives

**413.** Taj Mahal, Agra, India. 1632–53. White marble.

313

rising some 30 feet higher, it seems comparatively fragile and weightless. Nearly all its exterior lines reach upward, from the graceful pointed arches, to the translucent pointed dome, to the four slender towers—minarets—poised at the outside corners. The Taj Mahal, constructed entirely of pure white marble, appears almost as a shimmering mirage, which has come to rest for a moment beside the peaceful reflecting pool but may float away at any time.

## Cast-Iron Construction

With the perfection of the post-and-lintel, the arch, and the dome, construction in stone and brick had gone just about as far as it could go. Not until the introduction of a new building material did the next major breakthrough in structural systems take place. Iron had been known for thousands of years and had been used for tools and objects of all kinds, but only in the 19th century did architects realize that its great strength offered promise for structural support. This principle was demonstrated brilliantly in a project that few contemporary observers took seriously.

In 1851 the city of London was planning a Great Exhibition, under the sponsorship of Prince Albert, husband of Queen Victoria. The challenge was to house under one roof the "Works of Industry of All Nations," and the commission for erecting a suitable structure fell to Joseph Paxton, a designer of greenhouses. Paxton raised in Hyde Park a wondrous building framed in cast iron and sheathed in glass—probably the first modern skeleton-and-skin construction ever designed (**414**). The Crystal Palace, as Paxton's creation came to be known, covered more than 17 acres and reached to a height of 108 feet. Because of an ingenious system of prefabrication, the whole was erected in just sixteen weeks.

Visitors to the exhibition considered the Crystal Palace a curiosity—a marvelous one, to be sure, but still an oddity outside the realm of architecture.

They could not have foreseen that Paxton's design, solid iron framework clothed in a glass skin, would pave the way for 20th-century architecture. In fact, Paxton had taken a giant step in demonstrating that as long as a building's skeleton held firm its skin could be light and non-load-bearing. Several intermediary steps would be required before this principle could be translated into today's architecture.

Another bold experiment in iron construction came a few decades later just across the English Channel, in France, and involved a plan that many considered to be foolhardy, if not downright insane. Gustave Eiffel, a French engineer, proposed to build in the center of Paris a skeleton iron tower nearly a thousand feet tall, to act as a centerpiece for the Paris World's Fair of 1889. Nothing of the sort had ever been suggested, much less built. In spite of loud protests, the Eiffel Tower (**415**) was constructed, at a cost of about a million dollars—an unheard-of sum for those times. It rises on four arched columns, which curve inward until they meet in a single tower thrusting up boldly above the cityscape of Paris. The tower's importance for the future of architecture rests on the fact that it *was* a skeleton that proudly showed itself without benefit of any cosmetic embellishment. No marble, no glass, no tiles, no skin of any kind—just the clean lines drawn in an industrial-age product. Two concepts emerged from this daring construction. First, metal in and of itself can make beautiful architecture. Second, metal can provide a solid framework for a very large structure, self-sustaining and permanent. Today the Eiffel Tower is the ultimate symbol of Paris, and no tourist would pass up a visit. From folly to landmark in less than a century—such is the course of innovative architecture.

It is unclear how much direct influence the Crystal Palace and the Eiffel Tower had on the development of what we now call "modern" buildings. Change was in the air. The movement toward bigger, taller, more innovative seemed to spring up independently in many places, on both sides of the Atlantic. An economical method of steel production had been developed in 1855, and by the latter part of the century its potential for architecture was beginning to be realized. The time was ripe for architects to exploit this new material, which, no doubt, the Romans would have envied.

**415.** Alexandre Gustave Eiffel.
Eiffel Tower, Paris. 1889.
Iron, height 934'.

left: **416.** Louis Sullivan.
Wainwright Building, Saint Louis.
1890–91.

right: **417.** Gordon Bunshaft
of Skidmore, Owings, and Merrill.
Lever House, New York. 1952.

steel–frame construction

## Steel-Frame Construction

Although multistory buildings have been with us since the Roman Empire, the development of the skyscraper, as we know it, required two late-19th-century innovations—the elevator and steel-frame construction. Steel-frame construction is a true skeleton-and-skin arrangement. Rather than piling floor upon floor, with each of the lower stories supporting those above it, the builders first erect a steel "cage" that is capable of sustaining the entire weight of the building, and then apply a skin of some other material.

What many consider to be the first genuinely modern building was designed by Louis Sullivan and built between 1890 and 1891 in St. Louis. Known as the Wainwright Building (**416**), it employed a steel framework sheathed in masonry. Other architects had experimented with steel support but had carefully covered their structures in heavy stone so as to reflect traditional architectural forms and make the construction seem reliably sturdy. Centuries of precedent had prepared the public to expect bigness to go hand-in-hand with heaviness. Sullivan broke new ground by making his sheathing light, letting the skin of his building echo, even celebrate, the steel framing underneath. Regular bays of windows on the seven office floors are separated by strong vertical lines, and the four corners of the building are emphasized by vertical piers. The Wainwright Building's message is subtle but definite: the nation had stopped growing outward and started growing *up*.

Sullivan's design looks forward to the 20th century, but it nevertheless clings to certain architectural details rooted in classical history, most notably the heavy *cornice*—the projecting roof ornament—that terminates upward movement at the top of the building. In a very few decades even these backward glances into the architectural past would become rare.

Toward the middle of the 20th century skyscrapers began to take over the downtown areas of major cities, and city planners had to grapple with unprecedented problems. How high is too high? How much air space should a building consume? What provision, if any, should be made to prevent tall buildings from completely blocking out the sunlight from the streets below? In New

**418.** Verrazano-Narrows Bridge, New York. 1964. Ammann and Whitney, consulting engineers; John B. Peterkin, Aymar Embury II, and Edward D. Stone, consulting architects.

York and certain other cities ordinances were passed that resulted in a number of look-alike and architecturally undistinguished buildings. The laws required that, if a building filled the ground space of a city block right up to the sidewalk, it could rise for only a certain number of feet or stories before being "stepped back," or narrowed; then it could rise for only a specified number of additional feet before being stepped back again. The resultant structures came to be known as "wedding-cake" buildings. A few architects, however, found more creative ways of meeting the air space requirement; those working in the style known as *International* (in fact, European) designed some of the most admired American skyscrapers, such as Lever House.

Lever House in New York (**417**), designed by the architectural firm of Skidmore, Owings, and Merrill and built in 1952, was heralded as a breath of fresh air in the smog of look-alike structures. Its sleek understated form was widely copied but never equaled. Lever House might be compared to two shimmering glass dominoes, one resting horizontally on freestanding supports, the other balanced upright and off-center on the first. At a time when most architects of office buildings strove to fill every square inch of air space to which they were entitled—both vertically and horizontally—the elegant Lever House drew back and raised its slender rectangle aloof from its neighbors, surrounded by free space. Even its base does not rest on the ground but rides on thin supports to allow for open plazas and passageways beneath the building. Practically no other system of construction except steel frame could have made possible this graceful form.

## Suspension

Also made feasible by steel, suspension is the structural method we associate primarily with bridges, although it has been employed for some buildings as well. The concept of suspension was developed for bridges late in the 19th century. In essence, the weight of the structure is suspended from steel cables supported on vertical pylons driven into the ground. A long bridge, such as the Verrazano-Narrows Bridge in New York (**418**), may have only two sets of

trusses

pylons planted in the riverbed, but the steel cables suspended under tension from their towers are strong enough to support a span between them more than four-fifths of a mile long. Suspension structures are among the most graceful in architecture, involving as they do long sweeping curves and the slender lines of the cables. A bridge in particular, suspended over water, may seem almost weightless when viewed from a distance, and there is a sense of flexibility—both visual and physical, because the roadbed may rise and fall several feet depending on winds and passing traffic.

## Truss Construction

By contrast, the truss is one of the most rigid structural systems in architecture. It is based on the triangle, and it derives its stability from the fact that the triangle, unlike other geometric shapes, cannot be bent out of shape without changing the length of one of its legs. The truss, therefore, can be used to span horizontal distances much in the way post-and-lintel is employed, but with far less support from underneath.

Although truss construction has been known since the Middle Ages, its principles have been fully developed only in the 20th century. It is most often associated with wood, since the triangular arrangement gives that inexpensive material greater strength than it otherwise would have, but there are also trusses in iron and steel. In the Federal Correctional Institution at Bastrop, Texas (419), thick wood trusses are part of a design that constitutes a startling departure from our usual image of prison architecture. The trusses support the roof and are angled so that their long sides provide a surface on which to rest solar energy collectors. Beyond this, the repeated trusses set up a rhythmic pattern that unifies the entire complex of the buildings.

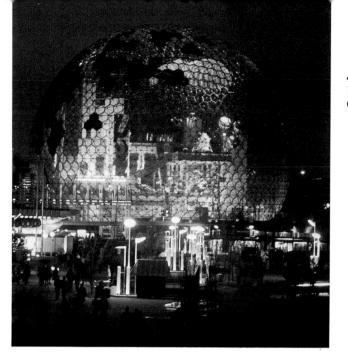

**421.** R. Buckminster Fuller.
U.S. Pavilion, Expo 67, Montreal.
Geodesic dome, diameter 250′.

## Reinforced Concrete Construction

Concrete is an old material that was known and used by the Romans. A mixture of cement, gravel, and water, concrete can be poured, will assume the shape of any mold, and then will set to hardness. Its major problem is that it tends to be brittle and has low tensile strength. This problem is often observed in the thin concrete slabs used for sidewalks and patios, which may crack and split apart as a result of weight and weather. Late in the 19th century, however, a method was developed for reinforcing concrete forms by imbedding iron rods inside the concrete before it hardened. The iron contributes tensile strength, the concrete shape and surface. In the 20th century reinforced concrete, also known as *ferroconcrete*, has been used in a wide variety of structures, often in those with free-form, organic shapes. While it may seem at first to be a skeleton-and-skin construction, ferroconcrete actually works more like a shell, because the iron rods and concrete are bonded permanently and can form structures that are self-sustaining, even when very thin.

A special kind of ferroconcrete construction—precast reinforced sections—was used to create the soaring shell-like forms of the famous Sydney Opera House in Australia (**420**). The Opera House, which is really an all-around entertainment complex, is almost as famous for its construction difficulties as it is for its extraordinary design. So daring was its concept that the necessary technology virtually had to be invented as the project went along. Planned as a symbol of the great port city in whose harbor it stands, the Opera House gives the impression of a wonderful clipper ship at full sail. Three sets of pointed shells, oriented in different directions, turn the building into a giant sculpture in which walls and roof are one. Reinforced concrete is the sort of material that allows the builder to experiment and try new techniques, that allows the architect to dream impossible dreams.

reinforced concrete

## Geodesic Domes

Of all the structural systems, probably the only one that can be attributed to a single individual is the geodesic dome, which was developed by the American architectural engineer R. Buckminster Fuller. Fuller's dome (**421**) is essentially a bubble, formed by a network of metal rods arranged in triangles and further organized into tetrahedrons. (A tetrahedron is a three-dimensional geometric figure having four faces.) This basic metal framework can be sheathed in any of several lightweight materials, including wood, glass, plastic, even paper.

geodesic dome

# R. Buckminster Fuller

## 1895–1983

The term "eccentric genius" might have been coined for the 20th-century architect/engineer/inventor/philosopher R. Buckminster Fuller, known to his friends as "Bucky." Whether history will characterize him as more of an eccentric or more of a genius remains to be seen.

Born in a suburb of Boston, Fuller was the black sheep of a distinguished New England family. He attended Harvard University for a short time, but, as he explained afterward, "I cut classes and went out quite deliberately to get into trouble, and so naturally I got kicked out." There followed a variety of odd jobs and a stint in the Navy. After he married Anne Hewlett in 1917, Fuller went into partnership with his father-in-law, an architect, in a building-block company. The year 1922 marked a crisis in his life. The business did not prosper, and the Fullers' daughter Alexandra died on her fourth birthday. Fuller sank into a terrible depression—working all day and drinking all night. At the lowest ebb he seriously considered suicide. Then in 1927, for some reason, he reached a critical turning point. One night, he later recalled, he found himself saying, "You do not have the right to eliminate yourself. You do not belong to you. You belong to the universe." From that moment he dedicated his life to discovering "the principles operative in the universe and [turning] them over to my fellow men."

The theory Fuller eventually formulated was both simple and extraordinarily grandiose: any problem in the world can be solved by design and technology. He believed wholeheartedly that "there is absolutely nothing that cannot be done." Fuller liked to talk about our planet as "Spaceship Earth" and felt that it should be designed as efficiently as any space vehicle; one of his twenty-five books is entitled *Operating Manual for Spaceship Earth*.

The first practical application of Fuller's theories was the Dymaxion House, patented in 1927. This experimental dwelling had glass walls, rooms hung from a central mast, and such energy-efficient devices as an automatic vacuum-cleaning system. Next came the Dymaxion automobile, a three-wheeled vehicle capable of speeds up to 120 m.p.h. Neither invention achieved any popular success, but in 1947 Fuller patented the design for which he is most famous—the geodesic dome. Based on a system of triangles arranged into four-planed figures, or tetrahedrons, the geodesic dome could enclose a huge amount of space without interior support and allow for total climatic control. Thousands of Fuller's domes have been built around the world. One of his most ambitious projects, however—the complete enclosure of midtown Manhattan in a dome three miles across—was (understandably) considered impractical.

Fuller remained active until about a month before his death, at the age of eighty-seven. He traveled widely, lecturing about his theories, and particularly enjoyed speaking to college audiences, among whom he attracted something of a cult following. Education was one of his many interests, for, as he explained: "Every child is born a genius. It is my conviction, from having watched a great many babies grow up, that all of humanity is born a genius and then becomes de-geniused very rapidly by unfavorable circumstances and by the frustration of all their extraordinary built-in capabilities."[2]

Photograph of R. Buckminster Fuller.

The geodesic dome offers a combination of advantages never before available in architecture. Although very light in weight in relation to size, it is amazingly strong, because its structure rests on a mathematically sophisticated use of the triangle. It requires no interior support, and so all the space encompassed by the dome can be used with total freedom. The geodesic dome can be built in any size. In theory, at least, a structurally sound geodesic dome 2 miles across could be built, although nothing of this scope has ever been attempted. Perhaps most important for modern building techniques, Fuller's dome is based on a modular system of construction. Individual segments—modules—can be prefabricated to allow for extremely quick assembly of even a large dome. And finally, because of the flexibility in choice of sheathing materials, there are virtually endless options for climate and light control.

Fuller patented the geodesic dome in 1947, but it was not until twenty years later, when his design served as the U. S. Pavilion at Montreal's World's Fair, that the public's attention was awakened to its possibilities. The dome at Expo 67, shown here, amazed the architectural world and fairgoers alike. It was 250 feet in diameter (about the size of a football field rounded off) and, being sheathed in translucent material, lighted up the sky at night like a giant spaceship set down on earth.

After Expo 67 some predicted that before long all houses and public buildings would be geodesic domes. This dream has faded considerably, but Fuller's dome has proved exceptionally well-suited for government and scientific operations in arctic climates. To build a habitable structure in the freezing wastes of Antarctica, for example, one needs a lightweight material that can be shipped and assembled easily, great strength to withstand below freezing temperatures and high winds, and control of the interior environment. The geodesic dome meets all these requirements.

In this brief survey of the major structural systems we have seen that the form of architecture and its method of construction are largely determined by the materials available. Wood readily lends itself to post-and-lintel construction or the truss; stone works for post-and-lintel also, as well as for the arch and dome; metal allows for steel-frame construction, suspension, or reinforced concrete; and so on. But there is another factor—often a more important one—that affects the shape of architecture, and that is the purpose a building will serve. For the rest of this chapter we will look at some of the possibilities.

# Purposes of Architecture

Most architecture throughout the ages fits into one of five major categories: government buildings, other public buildings, commercial buildings, religious buildings, and residences. In other words, nearly all buildings have been designed to serve one of five basic purposes. In this section we will consider the five categories and show three examples of each. The examples are not meant to cover the entire range of possibilities for any given architectural purpose. Rather, they have been chosen because they provide interesting comparisons with one another, and because they reveal how architects have attempted to serve these purposes at different times, in different places.

## Government Buildings

The function of government is ruling, managing, controlling, protecting the people it governs. In order to do so it must establish and maintain its legitimacy. A government that was not taken seriously by those it governs would have difficulty sustaining itself. For this reason most governments throughout history have taken pains to create outward symbols of their legitimacy, and some of the most powerful of those symbols have been in the form of official architecture. Anyone who has visited the United States Capitol building in

Washington will understand this (**422**). Its architecture states emphatically: *Here* is something of stability and order; *here* is a foundation on which a nation stands.

The original Capitol building was begun in 1793, a mere four years after the new government of the United States had been established, and George Washington himself laid the cornerstone. After many embellishments, repairs (following a severe fire in the War of 1812), and additions, it assumed in 1865 the form it has now. It is easy to look back and understand why the framers of this newly independent nation would want an impressive building. Just broken free from England, just victorious in war, just come from formulating an innovative method of government—the founders celebrated their achievements in marble and stone and classical architecture. Their choice was a structure that combines the best of Greek and Roman architecture.

Even today, accustomed as we are to enormous sports arenas and the like, we find the Capitol awe-inspiring. To enter one climbs a steep flight of marble stairs and passes through a formal Greek-style porch, continually aware of the immense building flanking out in both directions. Above the whole is the dome, 268 feet high, circled with columns and arches, crowned by a monumental statue representing freedom. Inside the building, under the dome, those with a taste for history may feel brushed by the ghosts of Washington, Adams, Jefferson, Madison—the nation's past standing by to oversee the nation's present. The best of government buildings, like the U. S. Capitol, represent the legitimacy and continuity of the government; at the same time they reach back to the past and forward to the future. The purpose of a government building, therefore, is not just to house the machinery of government but to symbolize the solidity of government.

At roughly the same time that the U. S. Capitol was completed, the former mother country, across the Atlantic, also was building a structure to serve its legislative body. The Houses of Parliament in London (**423**), finished in 1860, aimed at quite a different architectural ideal. Washington's Capitol looked backward to Greece and Rome for legitimacy, but the Houses of Parliament sought another precedent on which to base England's national pride— the Gothic period of the Middle Ages. The Gothic style, as exemplified by Chartres Cathedral (**410,432**), had prevailed throughout western Europe starting in the 13th century, but each nation, including England, claimed it as its own. For England, Gothic represented a Golden Age. In contrast to the stately, dignified U.S. Capitol, the Houses of Parliament, with its three Gothic-Revival towers of different heights and shapes, seems to be all lightness and vertical thrust—more like a castle than a sober government building.

Government buildings today project many different kinds of images; they interpret in varied ways the purpose of housing the machinery of state. One of the more interesting of recent structures is the City Hall in Dallas, designed by I. M. Pei (424). Its sharp diagonal overhang of glass serves a functional purpose—to keep out the relentless sun of a Texas summer. Beyond this, however, the dramatic overhang may suggest either the protective roof of government or the looming presence of Government with a capital G, depending on your point of view. Government buildings nearly always evoke powerful associations of some kind.

## Non-Governmental Public Buildings: Three Museums

Aside from state and municipal buildings, there are many other structures to which the public has frequent access—theaters, opera houses, libraries, post offices, schools, and museums. Art museums, in particular, make an interesting study in architectural design, because they are works of art that display other works of art. How they go about fulfilling this purpose tells us much about the nature of architecture.

**424.** I.M. Pei. City Hall, Dallas.

left: **425.** Charles Perrault. Louvre, east facade, Paris. 1667–70.

below: **426.** Frank Lloyd Wright.
Solomon R. Guggenheim Museum, New York. 1957–59.

One of the largest museums in the world, and probably the most famous, is the Louvre in Paris (**425**). It houses the *Mona Lisa* (**476**)—the best-known painting in the western world—and literally millions of other priceless works of art. The Louvre, however, was not originally designed to be a public museum. Built on the site of a 13th-century castle, the Louvre was erected as a royal palace in the 16th century, and it did not assume its present role as a museum until some two hundred years later, following the French Revolution. As a consequence, it does not always provide the ideal setting in which to view art. The long, classically decorated building, intended for the display of kingly power, has sapped the energy of many an art-loving tourist. Inside, the lighting and display surfaces are less than perfect, and the architecture is too grand to seem welcoming.

**427.** Louis Kahn. Kimbell Art Museum, Fort Worth. 1966–72.

In company with the British Museum in London and the Metropolitan Museum of Art in New York, the Louvre exists as a kind of stately shrine to art—a huge, imposing, somewhat intimidating monument filled with treasures beyond compare. The art-lover approaches it with awe and reverence. One finds it virtually impossible to walk through its doors without being overcome by the feeling, "I am in THE LOUVRE!" So authoritative is its presence that any object contained within its walls takes on the automatic stamp of "greatness." This is due largely to the nature of the architecture; a building so utterly sure of itself could not accept anything but the most sublime of art.

Quite different standards may prevail when someone sets out to design a building specifically for the display of art. Such was the case with the Solomon R. Guggenheim Museum in New York (**134,426**). The commission fell to master architect Frank Lloyd Wright, who created a museum unlike any before or since. Wright's architecture in general is distinguished by its coherence of interior and exterior; and nowhere is this more apparent than in the Guggenheim Museum. The outside consists of a series of curves arranged into a cylinder, and this structure is duplicated inside the museum. There is a long, curving ramp that spirals from the top of the building to the ground level, so that one must take an elevator to the top and walk down the entire ramp.

When the Guggenheim Museum opened, it attracted much controversy. Some people said that Wright had pulled off a great joke on painters and sculptors, whom he did not much admire. It is true that Wright's building carefully *controls* the circumstances under which one may view art. The viewer cannot get very far away from any work of art, because of the width of the ramp, and the ramp keeps one always slightly off-balance, going uphill or downhill. Also, the form of the museum itself is so intriguing that it competes with anything that is put inside it. But after some twenty-five years, most of the shouting has died down, and the Guggenheim has settled peaceably into the art community. It has a dynamic of its own, a tension of push and pull, that acts with, not against, the art it contains.

In the late 1960s architect Louis Kahn, whose comments on the arch we encountered earlier in this chapter, designed a museum for the city of Fort Worth, Texas—the Kimbell Art Museum (**427**). In planning the new museum, Kahn had one major goal: to allow the works of art to be viewed in natural light. This is unusual in contemporary museums; most rely entirely on artificial light, because sunlight can seriously damage paintings. However, Kahn devised an ingenious method for admitting light through skylights and filtering it in such a way that it would reflect off the ceilings, rather than beaming directly on the works of art. He felt that natural light, which is ever-changing, gives a life to paintings that is absent in the controlled, laboratory-like atmosphere of an artificially lighted museum. In all, Kahn's design for the Kimbell embodies a wonderful respect for the works of art it would house. The purpose of museum architecture—to make art available to the public—is excellently served.

## Commercial Architecture: Three Skyscrapers

The architecture of commerce, like that of government, often has strong symbolic value. Its primary purpose is to house offices, but a secondary one may be to make a statement about the firm that owns the building. When a company decides to erect a new office building, its leaders give serious thought to the image that will be projected by that building and lodged in the minds of the public. Unlike the government structure, however, the office building rarely seeks a model in traditional architecture, but rather attempts to convey the impression of dynamic modernism—of a company forging ahead to the future. The skyscraper, the office building of the 20th-century, has therefore tended to be a creature of fashion, taking its design from the trend of the times. Three examples will illustrate this.

**428.** William Van Alen. Chrysler Building, New York. 1930.

The Chrysler Building in New York, indisputably the gem of early skyscrapers, was completed in 1929 and was the first office building to rise above 1000 feet. Its slender, elegantly pointed spire (**428**) changed the skyline of New York dramatically and still remains distinctive, in spite of later, taller buildings around it. We might list three elements that contributed to this splendid building: the great success of the automobile industry, which enabled Walter Percy Chrysler to erect a monument to his name; the relative cheapness of fine building materials and labor; and the prevalence of the style known as Art Deco.

Art Deco, then at the height of fashion, was marked by geometric patterns and a rich display of surface decoration. (The term "deco" came from the Exposition des Arts Décoratifs, held in Paris in 1925, where the style first appeared as a significant force.) Art Deco was definitely a product of the machine age, for its favorite materials were chrome and steel and glass and aluminum—modern materials that glitter and sparkle, preferably in elaborate combinations to dazzle the eye. Its symbolism, indeed, is razzle-dazzle, and it celebrates the speed of the automobile and the airplane, people on the move. The top of the Chrysler Building is layered in an overlapping sunburst pattern pierced with triangular windows—a streamlined, geometric sculpture cutting through the sky. All throughout the building, inside and out, attention was lavished on decorative detail for even the most functional elements, such as the elevator cabs. When Art Deco passed out of fashion, much of the elaborate decoration of the Chrysler Building fell into disrepair, but it has recently been restored to its former splendor.

The patterned forms of Art Deco gave way in the 1940s to the pared-down, austere design aesthetic of the International Style. In a sense the roots of the International Style might be traced back to Louis Sullivan (**416**), who insisted that "form follows function." In other words, the form of a building or any other object should be expressive of what it is supposed to do, not overlaid with arbitrary decoration. This theme was taken up by two European architects, Le Corbusier and Ludwig Mies van der Rohe, and translated into a style that dominated American architecture through the 1970s. Mies van der Rohe added another catch phrase to the history of art when he made his often-quoted statement: "Less is more." By this he meant that architects (and other designers) must strip their forms to the barest essentials, the parts necessary to the work's function, and by so doing they would achieve a more honest, satisfying design.

As mentioned earlier, the International Style was introduced to the United States by such buildings as Lever House (**417**). Diagonally across the street from Lever House is a building many consider to be the quintessence of that style. The Seagram Building (**429**), designed by Mies van der Rohe and Philip Johnson, is almost the direct opposite of the Chrysler Building in its design aesthetic. A stark vertical slab resting on stilts, the Seagram Building rises abruptly from the base and terminates abruptly at the top, with no attempt at accent or decoration. Its form is the extended cube, and much of its visual appeal comes from the combination of bronze-colored steel and amber glass sheathing.

For more than twenty years after the Seagram Building was completed, through the 1970s, the International Style held sway as the most luxurious and sophisticated style for skyscraper architecture. Across the United States towers of steel and glass vied with each other for height and simplicity of design. By about 1980 it became clear that some change was due, that the pendulum would swing back again and bring a return to decoration. Even so, the architectural world was startled when AT&T (American Telephone and Telegraph) unveiled its model for a new corporate headquarters in New York.

The AT&T building (**430**), finished early in 1984, was designed by Philip Johnson, co-architect of the Seagram Building and long one of the leaders of the International Style. But this new structure was about as far from the Inter-

**left: 429.** Ludwig Mies van der Rohe and Philip Johnson. Seagram Building, New York. 1958.

**below: 430.** Philip Johnson for Johnson/Burgee. AT&T Corporate Headquarters Building (model), New York. 1984.

national Style as one could go. It has two quite distinctive architectural features: at the base a series of towering arches several stories high; at the top a classical broken pediment (a triangular form interrupted at the peak) of the sort found on furniture of the 18th century. In 1983, as the building was nearing completion, a reviewer for *The Wall Street Journal* recalled the jolt of its announcement:

> When Philip Johnson and John Burgee first made public their design for American Telephone & Telegraph Company's new corporate headquarters on Madison Avenue, critics responded with alarm, calling the proposed building any number of unkind names, including a grandfather's clock, a Renaissance Revival pay phone and a Chippendale highboy. When built, they warned, it would be a postmodern joke at the city's expense.[3]

However, the article in which this comment appeared is entitled "Learning to Love Ma Bell's New Building," and it points out that, "after all the fuss," most critics have reversed their earlier opinions. One irony about the AT&T building, though, is that its summit, which one might expect to make a dramatic change in the city's skyline, is barely visible in the forest of tall structures around it.

## Religious Architecture

We have already looked at several examples of religious architecture in this book, especially in Chapter 3. Here we will concentrate on the symbolic meaning of the architecture, the image of religion that is meant to be conveyed by the structure. Three very different Christian churches will give some idea of the possibilities.

Many of the colonists who settled in North America in the 17th century, in the area that would become the United States, sought religious freedom. Those who established themselves in New England brought with them a Protestant religion that was free of material trappings, even austere. Early churches in the northern colonies (**431**) consciously avoided any superficial embellishment—no statuary, no stained-glass windows, no arches or domes or columns, just a bare and simple meeting place where people could worship their God. The architecture expresses a religious ethic that hoped to strip itself of all worldliness.

The colonists' simple taste in religious architecture was a reaction to the heavily ornate churches of Europe. In Chapter 3 we considered the religious and social role of Chartres Cathedral in France (**432**; see also **67,410**). It may be interesting to compare this stately medieval church to a counterpart that could not have existed in any century but our own. The Garden Grove Community Church, usually known as the Crystal Cathedral (**433,434**), sits in the middle of a busy commercial section of suburban Orange County, California, surrounded by fast-food restaurants and shopping centers. Designed by Philip Johnson and completed in 1980, the Crystal Cathedral is the product of an immense "television ministry" organized by its leader, the Reverend Robert H. Schuller, whose sermons reach millions of people each week. Just as Chartres Cathedral served as the hub of its community, the Crystal Cathedral is the hub of a vast electronic community made possible by mass communication.

Chartres Cathedral, as we have seen, is a massive edifice of stone, built in the Gothic style. Inside it creates a world of its own, separate from the workaday world outside, dedicated to the worship of God in an other-worldly setting. By contrast, the Crystal Cathedral is all glass, and it was planned deliberately to allow those outside to have a clear view of the interior, and those inside to have unobstructed sight of the traffic and activity around the church. In fact, worshipers are encouraged to remain in their cars, if they choose, and participate in the service from the vast parking lot. The Crystal Cathedral is a church of the freeway world.

Many other comparisons—or contrasts—suggest themselves. Chartres Cathedral was a symbol of the enormous power held by the medieval Christian church, but the Crystal Cathedral symbolizes another great power—that of mass communication. All of the latter's cost, estimated at between $16 million and $18 million, was donated by the members of a fervent television audience. At Chartres much of the architecture and especially the sculpture and stained-glass windows were designed to create an atmosphere of mystical faith; also,

**left: 431.** Rocky Hill Meeting House, Amesbury, Mass. 1785.

**right: 432.** Chartres Cathedral, west facade, France. 12th–16th century.

this visual imagery helped to instruct a populace, most of whom could not read, in the history of their religion. The Crystal Cathedral has very different goals. Its architecture was planned, as we noted, to allow for a minimal barrier between inside and outside, and it was specifically designed to work well with television lights and cameras.

And what of the sense of community? The community of Chartres and that of the Crystal Cathedral are very different. We know that Chartres was built by the tradesmen of the town, the guilds of stonemasons and glaziers and carvers who would someday worship within its walls—or whose children, or children's children, would do so. But most of the people who contributed to the Crystal Cathedral will never actually see it, except on their television screens. Their community is an electronic one, not a physical one. In our time the coming together for worship may no longer mean groups of people wending their way up the hill to the church, but rather millions of people simultaneously pushing a button in their own homes. In the Crystal Cathedral, religious architecture has met the challenge of a new world by creating vital new forms.

## Domestic Architecture: Three Houses

Ever since humans came down from the trees or out of their caves, most of the architecture built has been in the form of houses. It would be impossible in a book of this scope to cover all the styles of domestic architecture that have prevailed in various parts of the world. So again we will focus on a trio—three houses that reflect very different points of view about what it means to dwell within a building, what kind of roof one should have over one's head.

Some of the most interesting domestic architecture can be found in cities or regions that grew up very quickly, for one reason or another. This is true of Washington, D.C.—a "planned" city that was deliberately selected to be the nation's capital (438). It is true of Rotterdam, in the Netherlands, which was heavily damaged in World War II but rebuilt valiantly afterwards. And it is true of San Francisco.

In 1847 San Francisco, then known as Yerba Buena, had a population of about 800 people. A year later gold was discovered at Sutter's Mill, and the famous gold rush was on, drawing thousands of potential millionaires to the area. By 1850, when San Francisco was incorporated as a city and California was admitted to the Union as a state, the population had increased to more than 10,000. A tremendous building boom started, meeting the needs not only of gold prospectors but of more respectable citizens with pioneering spirit, and San Francisco grew up in the blink of an eye, or so it seemed.

**433.** Philip Johnson.
Garden Grove Community Church (Crystal Cathedral).
Garden Grove, Calif. 1980.
*left:* exterior;
*right:* interior.

# Frank Lloyd Wright

## 1867–1959

Many critics consider Frank Lloyd Wright to have been the greatest American architect of his time; certainly few would dispute the claim that he was the greatest designer of residential architecture. To see a Wright-designed building from the first decade of this century is to be shocked by how remarkably contemporary it seems.

Wright had very little formal education. He attended high school in Madison, Wisconsin, but apparently did not graduate. Later, he completed the equivalent of about one year's course work in civil engineering at the University of Wisconsin, while holding down a job as a draftsman. In 1887 he moved to Chicago and eventually found work in the architectural firm headed by Louis Sullivan, the great designer of early office buildings. Before long Wright had assumed responsibility for fulfilling most of the residential commissions that came into the company, and in 1893 he opened a firm of his own.

During the next two decades Wright refined the principles of the "Prairie houses" that are his trademark. Most are in the Middle West, and they echo that flat expanse of the Great Plains—predominantly horizontal, stretching out over considerable ground area but usually in one story. All expressed Wright's special interest in textures and materials; he liked whenever possible to build with materials native to the immediate surroundings, so that the houses blend with their environments. Interiors were designed on an open plan, with rooms flowing into one another (an unusual practice for the time), and the inside and outside of the house were also well integrated. These ingredients added up to what Wright referred to as "organic" architecture.

For most of his long life Wright's personal situation was far from tranquil. His parents seem to have had a bitterly unhappy marriage, and they divorced in 1885, when Wright was seventeen—an extraordinary event for that era. Wright himself had a troubled marital history. His first marriage ended when he eloped to Europe with Mamah Brothwick, the wife of a former client, leaving his own wife and six children behind. Five years later, back in Wisconsin, Brothwick was brutally murdered by a deranged servant while Wright was out of the house. This tragedy sent the architect off on a period of wandering through faraway parts of the world. A final marriage in the late 1920s lasted out his lifetime and appears to have given him his first real happiness.

Although he is best known for his domestic architecture, Wright also designed many large-scale commercial and public buildings, including the Solomon R. Guggenheim Museum in New York. His innovative design for the Imperial Hotel in Tokyo, planned to be stable in an area plagued by earthquakes, proved successful when the hotel survived without damage a devastating quake just a year after it was completed.

Wright was the author of several books on his theories of architecture, and always he focused on the organic nature of his work and on his own individuality. "Beautiful buildings are more than scientific. They are true organisms, spiritually conceived, works of art, using the best technology by inspiration rather than the idiosyncrasies of mere taste or any averaging by the committee mind."[4]

Photograph of Frank Lloyd Wright.

**434.** Victorian Gothic house, San Francisco. Late 19th century.

During this period Queen Victoria sat on the throne of England, and the style known as "Victorian" or "high Gothic revival" dominated much of San Francisco's new architecture. Victorian architecture is not simple. A late-19th-century house in San Francisco (which survived the disastrous earthquake and fire of 1906) will demonstrate this (**434**). Every surface that might conceivably be decorated has been decorated. There are turrets and towers and columns and arches and gables and moldings and scrollwork. There are squares and triangles and cones and pyramids and cylinders. We might suspect that the person who designed this building threw open the whole architect's bag of possibilities and said, "Let's use one of everything." This is decidedly a city house, and a house planned to advertise the success of its owners. Mies van der Rohe may have thought that "less is more," but the prosperous citizens of Victorian San Francisco obviously felt that more is better.

A mere half-century later a kind of architecture was being built in the United States that almost seems to have emerged from a totally different culture, thousands of years and miles away. The architect was Frank Lloyd Wright, who designed the Guggenheim Museum (**134,426**). Wright's theory of domestic architecture was characterized by two related principles: first, a house should blend with its environment; second, the interior and exterior of a house should be visually and physically integrated.

The Kaufmann House in Bear Run, Pennsylvania, usually known as "Fallingwater," is considered to be Wright's masterpiece (**435**). Sited beside a waterfall, it was designed to take best advantage of the surrounding landscape.

**435.** Frank Lloyd Wright. "Fallingwater" (Kaufmann House), Bear Run, Pa. 1936–37.

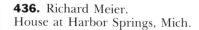
**436.** Richard Meier.
House at Harbor Springs, Mich.

Much of the house is built of stone, quarried from the immediate area, so that it seems to grow up from the site, rather than being set down upon it. One departure from this use of natural materials comes in the three terraces of reinforced concrete, two of them cantilevered over the waterfall. A *cantilever* is a horizontal form supported at only one end, jutting out into space at the other. Reinforced concrete, with its high tensile strength, makes such a construction possible, and Wright was among the first to exploit the cantilever for domestic architecture. Although not strictly "natural," the concrete cantilevers emphasize the waterfall and make it seem a natural extension of the house. Wright's architecture, then, blends with the natural surroundings and at the same time makes use of them.

Our third example is a house that shuns any superficial decoration and that proclaims its separateness from the landscape (**436**). Designed by Richard Meier, the house, on a steep hill overlooking Lake Michigan, is uncompromisingly a product of the technological age, with its shimmering white color and sharply angled geometry. No one would imagine that this building "grew" from the landscape. It contrasts sharply with its surroundings and thereby makes a statement: 20th-century humans made this building and 20th-century humans live in it. The architect might be suggesting that we have advanced far beyond the time when a roof meant simply the top of the cave or thatches gathered and woven together—or even rocks quarried in the neighborhood. Our century has made awesome technological advances, and we might as well acknowledge them in the homes we inhabit.

It is probably safe to say that architecture touches us more directly than any of the other arts. As we move through our everyday lives, we are influenced continually by the structures we enter, leave, or pass by. A huge, forbidding structure makes us feel uncomfortable; a warm and welcoming one makes us feel secure. Moreover, when we seek to learn about other cultures—far away or long ago—it is often their architecture that we study most closely. The people who built the Parthenon, the Taj Mahal, the Sydney Opera House, the Pyramid of the Sun—yes, even the Victorian house in San Francisco—were telling us much about their way of life and the values they considered to be important. A society's choice of materials, structural systems, and styles of architecture make a fundamental statement. Architecture tells us who we are. It shows us the face we want to present to the world.

# 14

# Environmental Design

When Buckminster Fuller proposed to build a 3-mile-wide geodesic dome over the whole midtown area of Manhattan Island, he probably knew that his idea would never be put into practice. Fuller was a visionary, and visionary plans usually falter before the realities of everyday life. In the abstract, however, the dome concept had its attractions. Think of it: The business district of New York City no longer would be plagued by the stifling heat of August or the cold and slush of January. Snow removal—a huge expense in the city's budget—would become a thing of the past. Individual buildings would not need to be heated or cooled; the entire atmosphere under the dome would be climatically ideal year-round. Air pollution, too, would become obsolete. No more would prevailing winds carry the smoke from factories to the west of the city into its heart, and whatever exhaust fumes were produced inside the dome could be vacuumed away efficiently. Hence, there would no doubt be a sharp decrease in respiratory ailments, along with a reduction in medical costs and therefore medical insurance premiums. Flying insects, such as flies and mosquitoes, could be all but eliminated, as could New York's perennial pigeon problem. There would be no more gloomy Mondays. Workers returning from their weekends would be greeted by a light (artificially lighted, if necessary), cheerful environment. Perhaps depressions would lift, psychological problems diminish, crime rates plummet . . . . One could go on listing the possibilities.

In proposing to "dome" Manhattan, Fuller was responding to an impulse that has tempted many artists—the urge to design an entire environment, to improve the quality of life through total design. *Environmental design* can be defined as large-scale planning to improve the aesthetic quality of the surroundings in which we live and make them more habitable. This type of design may involve architects, urban planners, landscape designers, and even psychologists and sociologists. While modern technology has greatly expanded the potential scope of the environmental designer, the concept of environmental design has actually been around for thousands of years.

# Environmental Design in History

The planned city may seem as new as today, but we have only to look back to the ancient city of Babylon to realize how long has been the human quest for order in the environment. Babylon was a city of Mesopotamia (the ruins are in modern Iraq, near Baghdad), and it was built over a period of many years—from the 18th to the 6th century B.C. Its history includes several famous rulers, from Hammurabi (who wrote an exemplary legal code) to Nebuchadnezzar (under whose reign was built the Ishtar Gate, **449**).

According to the old writings, Babylon was constructed as a square, bisected by the Euphrates River. Its perimeter was about 60 miles. Walls 300 feet high and 75 feet thick surrounded the city, and outside the walls was a large water-filled moat. The Greek historian Herodotus wrote that Babylon "surpasses in splendor any city of the known world." It had broad, even streets, crossing each other at right angles, and a covered bridge over the river. In one sector of the city were the legendary Hanging Gardens of Babylon, one of the Seven Wonders of the Ancient World; in another was the tower that probably inspired the biblical story about the Tower of Babel. All told, the planners of Babylon seem to have thought of everything important that touched upon their way of life: the security of the city, convenience of movement, and a pleasant visual aspect.

Like the Babylonians the ancient Greeks and Romans—master designers—favored the *grid* system for city planning. Streets crossed at right angles, with broader avenues allocated for the passage of many chariots. The Romans also pioneered in a surprisingly modern approach to high-density living in downtown areas—apartment houses of four and five stories. But after the Roman Empire and through the Middle Ages, environmental design as such was apparently not considered a priority. Cities grew up as they would, following the contours of the landscape and of well-traveled paths, with major access routes leading to the churches and markets. Not until the Renaissance did total design again excite the interest of artists.

Several artists of the Renaissance, including Michelangelo and Leonardo da Vinci, turned their attention to the concept of "ideal" cities and large urban spaces. One Renaissance architect, Antonio Filarete of Florence, actually planned such a city in detail, naming it Sforzinda after his patron, the duke Francesco Sforza. Sforzinda was to have broad, straight streets, large public spaces, and housing and work areas for every level of society. Filarete's plan was never realized, but during the 15th and 16th centuries a number of European cities, most notably Rome, were substantially rebuilt in an effort to eliminate the crowded, dirty, and disorganized conditions that had developed in cities during the Middle Ages.

In the 17th century the quest for large, well-planned urban spaces gathered momentum. One such example, designed by the Italian architect and sculptor Gianlorenzo Bernini, was the plaza in front of St. Peter's Basilica at the Vatican in Rome. St. Peter's—the heart of the Roman Catholic Church—had been under construction since 1450, on the site once occupied by a 4th-century church. This site is the presumed burial place of the Apostle Peter, the first Pope. In the mid-16th century Michelangelo designed the dome and the main section of the church containing the altar (**479**). The remainder of the basilica and the facade were completed in the first quarter of the 17th century by the architect Carlo Maderno. There remained the problem of creating a suitable plaza in front of the church, and this problem was addressed immediately after the election of Pope Alexander VII in 1655. As the story goes, before the sun set on the first day of his papacy, Alexander sent for Bernini.

Bernini's challenge was to design an enclosed area capable of holding the enormous crowds that converge on St. Peter's to receive the pope's blessing on ceremonial occasions, particularly on Easter Sunday. His solution was a structure consisting mainly of a double set of roofed colonnades (rows of columns) creating a wedge-shaped space in front of the church and then bulging into an enormous oval that encompasses the plaza (**437**). Thus enclosed, the space can hold as many as two million people. The colonnades are symbolic of the "arms of the church" reaching out to embrace the faithful. Atop them are scores of monumental marble statues of the saints carved by Bernini's assistants following his designs.

Besides providing a suitable and awe-inspiring setting for the pope's appearances, Bernini had another architectural goal in mind. He felt that Maderno's facade was too wide and too low, that its proportions were incorrect. Since he could not adjust the proportions physically, he did so visually. The colonnades, like pincers, visually "squeeze" the facade to make it seem taller and narrower. In all, Bernini's design was a brilliant conclusion to what had been a somewhat disjointed architectural scheme, for it pulled together into one cohesive unit all the diverse elements in the papal enclave. In its giant scale the plaza of St. Peter's has not been equaled before or since.

Beginning in the late 18th century and continuing through the 19th, two extremely ambitious city-planning projects were underway. Both involved great capital cities, and both took place in the aftermath of political revolution. Moreover, both were based on a combination of the grid plan, with streets at right angles to one another, and the *radial* plan, which has streets radiating outward on the diagonal from central points like the spokes in a wheel. The two cities in question were Washington, D.C., and Paris.

The construction of Washington was an adventure, and one at first plagued by tremendous difficulties. In its conception it reflected the ideals of the newly independent United States. Just as the founders of the young country set out to construct a totally new model of government, so too they set out to build, from the ground up, a grand and glorious capital city on an unoccupied spot—a spot, in fact, consisting principally of swampland. George Washington chose the site, and his selection had to do more with political considerations than with physical ones. The area of the city was then roughly equidistant from the northernmost states and the southernmost states. In terms of climate, however, the first President's choice was not a happy one; a swamp is a swamp. Letters written by the early government leaders are filled with complaints about the city's oppressive heat in summer, the mosquitoes, the generally unhealthful atmosphere. Not until the advent of modern air conditioning did Washington become a truly comfortable place to be.

To design the city, the President called in Pierre Charles L'Enfant, a young French engineer who had volunteered his services in the American Revolution. L'Enfant's plan is surprisingly ambitious and innovative, considering that he worked in a time when most cities had rather narrow and often

**437.** Gianlorenzo Bernini. Plaza and colonnades, St. Peter's Basilica. 1656–63. Vatican, Rome.

winding streets. At the very center of the then-city limits stands the Capitol building (**422**). From the Capitol, running along a north-northwest axis, is the main thoroughfare, Pennsylvania Avenue, which is 160 feet wide and leads directly to the White House. The Capitol also serves as the eastern anchor of The Mall (**438**), a parklike area lined with museums and government buildings. The Mall has three main focal points, arranged precisely in an east-west row: the Capitol at the east, the Washington Monument in the center, and the Lincoln Memorial at the west end of The Mall, on the banks of the Potomac River. (Not all of these buildings existed in L'Enfant's plan. Lincoln had not yet been born when the plans were drawn up.) The President and the Congress can look at each other from their windows, and now the Congress can look down the Mall for inspiration from Washington and Lincoln.

L'Enfant's design provided for several elements deemed desirable for an important capital city—broad, ceremonial avenues, imposing vistas, open public areas, major buildings as focal points. All these are possible when one is building from "scratch" and has a master plan. It is far more difficult to impose such an order on an existing city, one that has grown up haphazardly over the centuries. To a large extent, the city of Paris accomplished this.

The transformation of Paris from a medieval town to a city of many monuments, imposing public buildings, and majestic avenues took place over several centuries. Nearly always the construction was undertaken to satisfy grandiose, ego-enhancing ambitions of a monarch. The last Bourbon kings of France, in the 17th and 18th centuries, made a number of major contributions in and around Paris, including Louis XIV's gigantic conception for the Versailles Palace and gardens (**493**). During the French Revolution beginning in 1789 the mood ran more to tearing down than to building up. The main square of Paris, the Place de la Concorde, became the headquarters of the guillotine, the device invented as a "humane" method of severing heads. In the Place during the Revolution more than 2,500 people were executed, among them the king and queen.

A mere fifteen years after the Revolution began, Napoleon came to power in France, styled himself Emperor, and set out to create a regime equal in glory to the Empire of ancient Rome. To this end he ordered built numerous monuments, streets, plazas, gardens, and bridges. His projects included first one and then a second huge triumphal arch, modeled on Roman designs.

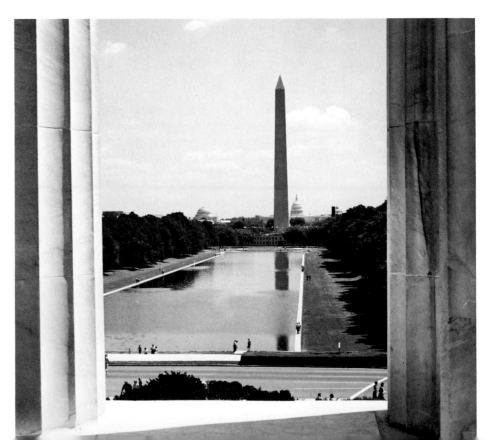

**438.** The Mall, Washington, D.C., viewed from the steps of the Lincoln Memorial, with the reflecting pool, the Washington Monument, and the Capitol dome in the distance.

The Arc de Triomphe at the Place de l'Etoile is the grander of the two (**439**),
placed in the center of a circle that interrupts Paris' main avenue, the Champs-
Elysées. Later, during the third quarter of the 19th century and under the rule
of Napoleon III, the first emperor's nephew, yet more grand-scale city planning was undertaken. Large sections of the city were flattened to allow for the
construction of diagonal avenues radiating outward from important monuments. At the Place de l'Etoile, as shown in the illustration, *six* major thorough-
fares intersect, to create a focal point for the arch and a traffic problem of
staggering proportions.

Both Washington and Paris demonstrate that when it comes to environmental design the grand and the efficient do not always coexist. Washington,
too, has traffic problems. To anyone not intimately familiar with the city, the
business of getting around by car can be formidable. Generously proportioned
boulevards tend to stop abruptly—at one of those majestic focal points!—and
though they pick up on the other side of the monument, one has no clear idea
how to *get* to the other side. Neither city, in fact, was conceived with the
automobile in mind.

The automobile is but one of many developments that have changed the
character of environmental design. Others include the challenge of cities
housing millions of people, the blight of urban slums, air pollution, the concentration of office buildings, mass transportation and communication, limited natural resources, and the desire for open space on a crowded planet.
Environmental designers of the 20th century have far more complex problems to solve than their predecessors ever dreamed of.

## Environmental Design in the 20th Century

To compare the environmental designs of our own age with those of previous
ones, we might look at a 20th-century architect's scheme for the same city in
which Louis XIV and Napoleon erected their tributes to kingly power. The
architect who in 1925 planned a drastic renovation of Paris was Charles Edouard Jeanneret, known as Le Corbusier, designer of Notre-Dame-du-Haut at
Ronchamps (**147,148**).

Le Corbusier, in his way, could be just as grandiose as a king or an emperor. What he proposed for Paris was no less than to level a large area in the

center of the city—600 acres—and start all over again. His design for a new Paris (**440**) would have concentrated the central Parisian population into sixteen tall, glass-sheathed skyscrapers, with open spaces around them. The old public spaces would be abolished; for example, Le Corbusier wrote that his dream was "to see the Place de la Concorde empty once more, silent and lonely." In this vision of the ideal city, the automobile would rule. Motorized traffic would be given a priority, and pedestrian traffic would cease to exist.

Not being a king, Le Corbusier had neither the power nor the funds to put his idea into practice, and subsequent generations have expressed gratitude that that is so. The trouble with Le Corbusier's plan—and Fuller's dome plan for Manhattan—is that it ignores how people *do* live and *want* to live, and reflects instead one artist's idea of how people *should* live. And people, by and large, resist doing what they "should" do. A population such as that of Paris, accustomed to small, individual houses and used to living an energetic life in the streets and squares, would take up arms before being stacked into vertical towers of glass. The more far-sighted contemporary environmental designers strive to understand the fabric of people's lives and make their plans an enhancement, not a restructuring, of modern civilization.

Today's environmental design is as varied as the populations it attempts to serve. At its best it looks at the city, the suburbs, and the country, examines the character of each, and attempts to improve that character without distorting it. In the suburbs this type of design has sometimes taken the form of "planned" or "ideal" communities, with specified amounts of space allocated to housing, recreation, schools, shops, and transportation. But as creative as environmental planning has been in the suburbs, it has been especially innovative in contemporary cities, because the problems of the cities are many.

One problem often addressed by urban planners is the rejuvenation of decaying sections of the city, especially waterfront areas. So many of the old cities in the United States were founded initially as major ports, but with the decline of the shipping trade the waterfront sections fell into disrepair. Designers have confronted this question: What do you do with a seaport that is no longer a seaport? In New York and Baltimore, in Boston and San Francisco, the answer has been to turn a waterfront area into a community center.

Boston's harbor renewal is a good example (**441**). Decrepit buildings in a once-seedy part of town have been renovated to house restaurants, shops, and artists' studios. Charming pedestrian walkways make the area a pleasant place by day or night. A sector that good Bostonians once skirted and tourists avoided has become a focus of the city's social life and a tourist attraction.

One important aspect of the Boston harbor renewal, as in other port cities, has been maintaining the character of the old sections, yet making them

**440.** Le Corbusier. Drawing of the "Voisin" Plan for Paris. 1925. Fondation Le Corbusier, Paris.

**441.** Boston waterfront district, with Faneuil Hall at right.

suitable for modern living. At Boston's harbor stands historic Faneuil Hall, originally constructed in 1742, then rebuilt in 1763 after a fire. The structure was used extensively as a meeting place for patriots during the Revolutionary period, and now it is open as a museum. Preserving Faneuil Hall, and making its surroundings hospitable, has been a part of the overall waterfront renewal project. In the best of such programs, then, the old is maintained and the new is added in such a way as to blend gracefully.

Port cities are not the only ones with decaying older sections. Many cities in the interior of the country have seen their downtown areas become shabby and deserted as a result of a post-World War II trend—the flight from the cities to the suburbs. The burgeoning of huge shopping malls in the suburbs has caused many downtown stores to close for lack of customers. Then, as stores and restaurants have moved out of the inner city, downtown areas have become unpleasant places to be, especially at night, and so increasing numbers of residents have also fled to the suburbs. Many large cities have found that, in the heart of town, a formerly bustling district has become desolate, run-down, and dangerous.

Dayton, Ohio, is one of a number of cities that has taken active steps to remedy this problem. In downtown Dayton are many fine old buildings, constructed between 1902 and 1904, that once housed such facilities as a farmer's market and government offices. These buildings now form the center of Arcade Square (**442**). This project, undertaken in the late 1970s, involved a part-

**442.** Lorenz & Williams, Inc. Rotunda, Arcade Square, Dayton, Ohio.

**443.** Atrium, Citicorp Building, New York.

nership between the City of Dayton and a private corporation backed by individual and business funds. The result is an exciting mix of the old and the new. While the basic architectural character of the buildings has been retained, the interiors have been substantially remodeled to allow for retail stores, restaurants, and apartments. So far, the outcome has been promising, largely because of the civic leaders' quest for excellence. As *Progressive Architecture* commented, "Not every city, of course, has officials with the sensitivity and/or the wisdom to hire talented design people and listen to them. It is much to the credit of both this city and this developer that, for the most part, they listened."[1]

Renewal is one solution to keeping the city alive and thriving, but innovative new construction is another. In New York the Citicorp atrium (**443**) represents a particularly creative use of urban space, for it gives city workers a planned and streamlined version of exactly the sort of space they are used to occupying. The Citicorp tower is an office building in midtown Manhattan. On its ground and below-ground levels is a three-tiered area that merges with the outdoors and that includes many restaurants, shops, bookstalls, sitting areas, "green spots" of plantings, and walkways. Here New Yorkers can stroll through to take a shortcut, meet their friends, get a meal or a snack, browse in the shops, or simply "hang out." The realities of city life—the way people do live, not how someone believes they should live—are given a splendid setting.

If we try to envision the environmental design of the future, we will be in precisely the position of Pierre L'Enfant, who laid out the city of Washington without knowing about the automobile. We don't know what lies ahead. We don't know what factors will influence human life fifty or a hundred years hence. Yes, certain things probably can be taken for granted. Population will increase, and there will be a greater need for housing. Industrial pollution must be eliminated or counteracted. But how will the dominance of the computer affect life and the environment? How will space travel influence future generations? Must we plan now for the colonization of the Moon and of distant planets? Should the L'Enfant of our day set out to plan a capital city in the "swampland" of our galaxy? Environmental design is among the most dynamic and most perplexing of all the arts, because the environment keeps changing before our very eyes.

*part five*

# ARTS
# IN TIME

# 15

# The Ancient World to the Middle Ages

A major factor in the understanding and appreciation of art is knowledge of its time frame—when a work of art was made and under what circumstances. For this reason the final part of this book has been devoted to a brief chronological survey, tracing the major movements in art from earliest times to the present. The four chapters here, together with the time lines beginning on page 447, should help in placing *all* the works of art discussed throughout the text in their historical context. At the same time, the artworks illustrated in this section can be considered primarily for their themes, their design components, and their media.

Some of the earliest surviving works of art have already been presented in this book—the cave paintings of southern Europe (**4**) and the figurines made by very early peoples (**61**). For the most part these are isolated examples, deriving from cultures that were essentially nomadic, oriented toward hunting to meet their needs for food. Not until we come to two cultures, both in the Middle East, do we find a coherent, reasonably intact artistic production about which we know a great deal. These are the ancient cultures of Egypt and Mesopotamia—the ancestors of Western art and civilization.

The Egyptians and Mesopotamians built their societies around mighty rivers, which enabled them to develop agriculture and therefore establish permanent settlements. This permanence, in turn, led to the development of architecture, the standardization of religions and rituals, and the creation of a social climate in which art could flourish. Our brief survey of art history, therefore, begins in the regions of these mighty rivers—the Nile in Egypt, the Tigris and Euphrates in Mesopotamia.

## Egypt

The principal message of Egyptian art is continuity—a seamless span of time reaching back infinitely into history and forward into the future. The Sphinx

**444.** *The Great Sphinx.*
c. 2530 B.C. Stone, height 65'.
Giza, Egypt.

(**444**), the symbol of this most important characteristic of Egyptian art, is the essence of stability, order, and endurance. Built about 2530 B.C. and towering to a height of 65 feet, it faces into the rising sun, seeming to cast its immobile gaze down the centuries for all eternity. The Sphinx has the body of a reclining lion and the head of a man, thought to be the Pharaoh Chefren, whose pyramid tomb is nearby. Egyptian kings ruled absolutely and enjoyed a semi-divine status, taking their authority from the sun-god, Ra, from whom they

**left: 445.**
*Palette of King Narmer,*
from Hierakonpolis.
c. 3100 B.C. Slate, height 25".
Egyptian Museum, Cairo.

**right: 446.**
*Queen Nefertiti.* c. 1365 B.C.
Limestone, height 20".
State Museums, West Berlin.

were assumed to be descended. Power and continuity both are embodied in this splendid monument.

An even earlier relic from Egyptian culture, the so-called *Palette of King Narmer* (**445**), illustrates many characteristics of Egyptian art. The Greek philosopher Plato wrote that Egyptian art did not change for ten thousand years; while this may be something of an exaggeration, there were many features that remained stable over long periods of time. The palette (so named because it is thought to have been a slab for mixing cosmetics) commemorates a victory by the forces of Upper Egypt, led by Narmer, over those of Lower Egypt, resulting in a unified kingdom. Narmer is the largest figure and is positioned near the center of the palette to indicate his high status. He holds a fallen enemy by the hair and is about to deliver the death blow. In the lowest sector of the tablet are two more defeated enemies. At upper right is a falcon representing Horus, the god of Upper Egypt. In its organization of images the palette is strikingly logical and balanced. The central section has Narmer's figure just to left of the middle, with his upraised arm and the form of a servant filling the space, while the falcon and the victim complete the right-hand side of the composition.

Narmer's pose is peculiar to Egyptian art and one of its most distinctive features. In depicting an important personage, the Egyptian artist strove to show each part of the body to best advantage. Thus, Narmer's lower body is seen in profile, his torso full front, his head in profile, but his eye front again. This same pose recurs throughout most two-dimensional art in Egypt. It is believed that the priests, who had much control over the art, established this figure style and decreed that it be maintained, for the sake of continuity. Obviously, it is not a posture that suggests much motion, apart from a ritualized gesture like that of Narmer's upraised arm. But action was not important to Egyptian art, no more in the smaller objects than in the large monuments; order and stability were its primary goals.

One brief period in the history of Egyptian culture stands apart from the rest and therefore has fascinated scholars and art-lovers alike. This was the reign of the pharaoh Amenhotep IV, who came to power in 1372 B.C. For a civilization that prized continuity above all else, Amenhotep was a genuine revolutionary. He changed his name (to Akhenaten), moved his capital, attempted to establish monotheism (belief in one god) among a people who worshiped many gods, and fostered a new, more relaxed style in art. Nowhere is this last more apparent than in the famous portrait bust of his queen, Nefertiti (**446**). While enchanted by Nefertiti's beauty, the modern viewer is perhaps even more taken by how contemporary she seems, how she appears to bridge the gap of more than three thousand years to our own world. Despite the regal headdress and elongated neck, Nefertiti might be a model in this month's fashion magazine. When the opportunity presented itself, the Egyptian sculptor was quite capable of great humanity and warmth, of letting a subject's real characteristics transcend convention.

## Mesopotamia

At the same time that ancient Egypt was flourishing, another great civilization had established itself to the east, in Mesopotamia, roughly in the area of modern-day Syria and Iraq. The two cultures had contact with one another but maintained their separate identities, and their styles in art were quite different. Mesopotamia occupies a large, flat area made fertile by its two rivers but offering few natural defenses from invasion (unlike Egypt, which is protected on two sides by the sea, elsewhere by the desert). Successive waves of people conquered the region of Mesopotamia—the most important being the Sumerians, the Assyrians, and the Babylonians. Judging by the surviving art, each culture centered around the temple as a place of worship and a focus of daily life.

The unique character of Sumerian art is exemplified by a group of marble statues from the Abu Temple at Tell Asmar, approximately contemporary with the Sphinx (**447**). The tallest figure is Abu, the god of vegetation, and just to the right is a mother goddess, while the rest of the statues represent priests and worshipers. No real attempt has been made to carve these figures naturalistically; the bodies are extremely stylized and some of the figures seem rather like decorated cylinders. Each has the hands clasped in the ritual Sumerian gesture of worship. The male figures show the heavily textured beards characteristic of this art, and the lips are curved upward as though to smile—a convention that means the persons depicted are alive, not dead, though not necessarily happy. The most extraordinary and riveting feature of each statue is, of course, the eyes, which are enormous, especially in the two gods. Outlined in black and inset with colored stones and shells, the eyes apparently served as the medium of communication between the worshipers and their gods. They give to these sculptures an exotic appearance very different from that of most Western art from ancient times.

**left: 447.** Group of votive statuettes, from the Square Temple of the god Abu, Tell Asmar, İraq. c. 2900–2600 B.C. Marble, height of tallest figure 30″. Iraq Museum, Baghdad, and Oriental Institute, University of Chicago.

**below: 448.** Outer Portal of the Citadel, Palace of Sargon II, Dur Sharrukin, Iraq. c. 721–705 B.C.

**449.** Ishtar Gate (restored), from Babylon. c. 575 B.C. Enameled sun-dried brick, height 48′9″. Near Eastern Museum, State Museums, East Berlin.

Mesopotamia's history over the centuries is a turbulent one marked by almost continual warfare and conquest. A major goal of architecture, therefore, was the erection of mighty citadels to ensure the safety of temples and palaces. Such a citadel was that of the Assyrian ruler Sargon II, built at Dur Sharrukin in the 7th century B.C. One of its gates (**448**) shows the monumental stone slabs that protected the entrance, which have been carved into guardian demons meant to impress—and intimidate—any visitor to the citadel.

The Babylonians, who followed the Assyrians, surely must be ranked among the great architects of the ancient world, although far less of their production remains than does that of Greece and Rome. We get some idea of their skill from the Ishtar Gate (reconstructed in a German museum), which was built in the 6th century B.C. under the great king Nebuchadnezzar (**449**). Made of thousands of glazed mud bricks, the gate has two massive towers flanking a central arch—the latter proving that, although the Romans developed the arch extensively (**457**), the Babylonians had discovered its uses earlier. On ceremonial occasions Nebuchadnezzar would sit under the arch in majesty to receive his subjects. The walls of the gate are decorated with processions of glazed ceramic animals, probably meant as spirit-guardians.

Both Mesopotamia and Egypt had access to the Mediterranean Sea, the "highway" of the ancient world. By the 11th century B.C. another civilization was developing on the north shore of the Mediterranean. The culture we identify as ancient Greece survived at its height for only a few hundred years, but for many people its art remains a standard against which all other art is measured.

## Greece

No doubt a major reason we so admire the ancient Greeks is that they seem to have excelled at everything. Their political ideals serve as a model for contemporary democracy. Their poetry and drama and philosophy survive as living classics, familiar to every serious scholar. Their architecture and sculpture have influenced most later periods in the history of Western art and continue to do so. We have seen examples in earlier chapters (**33**, **65**, **183**, **359**, **407**).

It is assumed the Greeks' genius shone equally in painting, but we know very little about this because most painted works have been lost. We would know even less were it not for the large number of painted clay vases that were produced between the 8th and 5th centuries B.C. In Chapter 11 we noted that terra cotta (baked clay) is an extremely durable material; it can shatter but will not disintegrate, and so the pieces can be reassembled. For this reason a large quantity of Greek art has survived to our day.

Few cultures can match the Greeks in the elaborate painting of vases, which represent a major part of their artistic output. These terra cotta vessels served as grave monuments, storage urns for wine or oil, drinking cups, and so forth. Our illustration (450) shows a *kylix* (a drinking cup) representing *Eos and Memnon.* The painting is done in the *red-figure style,* which developed late in the 6th century B.C. A background of black was created from glaze, leaving the figures in the natural red color of the clay. Sometimes details were added with white highlights. Given what sounds like a rather primitive technique, the painting is remarkably fine. Eos, the goddess of dawn, holds the body of her dead son, Memnon, who has been killed by the hero Achilles. There is a suggestion of depth in the overlapping of Memnon's body in front of Eos, as well as in the crossed legs; the dangling arms of the body visually balance Eos' outspread wings. The finely-drawn textures of gown, hair, and wings reveal the great skill of the vase painter's brush. As a mark of the esteem in which vase-painters were held, and the pride they took in their work, this kylix is signed by the painter, Douris.

Despite the Greeks' prolific output of painted vases, most people, at the mention of Greek art, think of sculpture. Between the 6th and 2nd centuries B.C. the Greeks gradually developed a type of sculpture that many succeeding generations have considered the ultimate expression of that medium. Its highest achievement was in the human figure. Although many figures, especially in later decades, were female, the most typical Greek statue is male, a nude athlete superbly proportioned to indicate an ideal of physical perfection.

The Greeks' approach to sculpture was a radical departure from artistic precedents in other parts of the Mediterranean world. Egyptian sculptures generally were attached to a background; Greek figures are freestanding, in the round. Egyptian figures usually were clothed; the Greeks introduced total nudity in the male figure and in later centuries moved toward increasing nudity in female statues (33). Most of the Egyptian sculptures we know are of pharaohs, their queens, their children, and other members of the court. The Greeks seem to have been far more interested in physical beauty than in high status. To be sure, some of their finest sculptures represent gods, but they are gods in human form—magnificent human form. And many are depictions of anonymous athletes, to whom scholars have given the name *kouros,* meaning "youth" or "boy."

**450.** Douris. *Eos and Memnon,* interior of an Attic red-figure kylix. c. 490–480 B.C. Terra cotta, diameter 10½". Louvre, Paris.

left: **451.**
*Kroisos (Kouros from Anavysos).*
c. 525 B.C. Marble, height 6'4".
National Museum, Athens.

right: **452.**
*Doryphorus (Spear Bearer).*
Roman copy after a Greek original
of c. 450–440 B.C.
by Polyclitus. Marble, height 6'6".
National Museum, Naples.

The reasons for this new approach to sculpture are clear from Greek philosophy and literature. Whereas the Egyptians emphasized continuity of the state, the Greeks sought perfection of the state *through* perfection of the individual. The ideal human body symbolized an ideal divine soul, dedicated to the highest principles. If perfection could be chiseled into marble, then perhaps the sought-after perfection in human affairs could be attained.

Two male figures, made perhaps seventy-five years apart, will show the enormous progress of Greek sculptors in striving toward an ideal of naturalism and physical perfection. The first is a *kouros* of about 525 B.C. (**451**), dating from the *Archaic* period. This sculpture is ambitious in depicting the figure in the round, but, compared with later works, it is a fairly crude attempt at freeing the nude body from its original block of stone. We can almost envision the cube of marble the sculptor began with from the square appearance of the form. The left foot is set slightly forward to suggest motion, but we do not really believe in that motion because the hips and shoulders are level and the arms held rigidly at the sides. If you try to assume this pose, you will find it almost impossible, for when you take a step forward with one foot, the opposing hip and shoulder go up, and your arms move in counterbalance. There is no indication of this in the statue. Even so, the sculptor made a serious effort at depicting the musculature of the body in a naturalistic way, especially in the knees and pelvic area, but the chest and arms are not well defined. On the *kouros'* face is an expression that has been dubbed the "archaic smile"—a rather forced grimace that was apparently meant to convey animation.

Now we might compare the *Spear Bearer* by the great sculptor Polyclitus (**452**), carved less than a century later, in the *Classical* period. (Like so many Greek statues, the original of the *Spear Bearer* has been lost and is known to us only through later, and probably inferior, Roman copies.) Here we find the

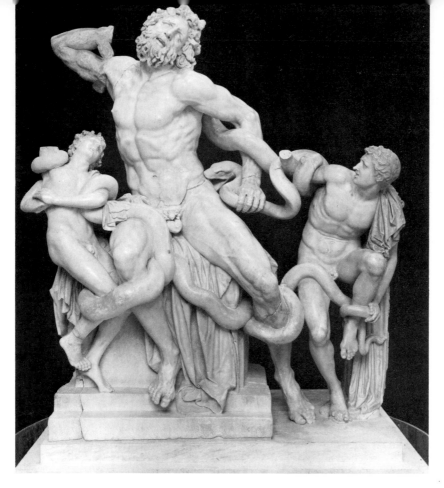

**453.** Agesander, Athenodorus, and Polydorus of Rhodes. *Laocoön Group.* Late 2nd century B.C. Marble, height 8'. Vatican Museums, Rome.

*contrapposto* of a figure in motion (p. 279). With the weight on the right foot, the left knee is bent, the left hip and shoulder rise, the arms reach outward from the body, and the whole form stands in a relaxed S-curve suggestive of movement. The musculature of a well-developed body has been carefully observed and recorded. Gone is the archaic smile, to be replaced by a natural, pensive expression. We must consider this sculpture in terms of what the Greeks had set out to do. They intended to show a perfectly formed body, at the peak of its youthful strength, rendered in as lifelike a manner as possible. At this they succeeded admirably.

The last phase of Greek art, occurring roughly in the 3rd and 2nd centuries B.C., is known as *Hellenistic*—a term that refers to the spread of Greek culture eastward to Mesopotamia and Egypt. Hellenistic sculpture tends to be more dramatic and emotional than that of the Classical 5th century; it has more of a tendency to push out into space and is more dynamic. One of the best-known examples of this style is the *Laocoön Group* (**453**), dated to the late 2nd century B.C.

Laocoön was a priest of the sun-god, Apollo, and his story involves one of the most famous events in Greek mythology. In the last year of the war between the Greeks and the Trojans, the Greeks devised a fabulous ruse to overrun the city of Troy. They built a giant wooden horse, concealed inside it a large number of Greek soldiers, and wheeled it up to the gates of Troy, claiming it was an offering for the goddess Athena. While the people of Troy were trying to decide whether to admit the horse, their priest, Laocoön, suspected a trick and urged the Trojans to keep the gates locked. (Here is the source of the well-known warning about "Greeks bearing gifts.") This angered the sea-god, Poseidon, who held bitter feelings toward Troy, and he sent two dreadful serpents to strangle Laocoön and his sons. The sculpture depicts the priest and his children in their death throes, entwined by the deadly snakes.

Compared to statues from the Classical period, such as the *Spear Bearer*, the *Laocoön Group* seems almost theatrical. Its subject matter, filled with drama and tension, would have been unthinkable three centuries earlier. The Classical sculptor wanted to convey an outward serenity, and thus showed the hero in perfection but not in action, outside of time, not throwing the spear but merely holding it. Hellenistic sculptors were far more interested than their predecessors in how their subjects reacted to events. Laocoön's reaction is a violent, anguished one, and the outlines of the sculpture reflect this. The three figures writhe in agony, thrusting their bodies outward in different directions, pushing into space. Unlike the dignified reserve of earlier figures, this sculpture projects a complicated and intense movement.

According to legend, the Trojans disregarded Laocoön's warning and brought the Trojan horse into their city. That night the Greek soldiers slipped out of the horse, pillaged Troy, and destroyed it. Only a few of the Trojans escaped, including Aeneas, who sailed away and, after many adventures, landed at the mouth of the Tiber River and founded the city of Rome. Whether or not one chooses to believe the old myths, it is nevertheless true that the history of art and civilization now shifts westward, to the great empire that conquered Greece and virtually all of the Mediterranean world.

## Rome

To understand the art of Rome we need to backtrack slightly to a people who inhabited the Italian peninsula from about the 7th century B.C. or earlier—the Etruscans. When the Roman Empire was established and its art began to flower, it drew on not only the traditions of the conquered Greeks but also styles of art nurtured on home soil.

The afterlife is the focus of a large part of Etruscan art—tombs and *sarcophagi* (burial coffins) and funerary vases. From the example illustrated here (**454**) and many others, we can deduce that the Etruscans held a more serene view of death than most cultures before and after. A couple, presumably husband and wife, recline comfortably on the lid of their sarcophagus, their demeanor suggesting that not only their spirits but their bodies are enjoying the hereafter. Their expressions are those of people at a pleasant dinner party, engaged in animated conversation with other guests, whom we cannot see. Part of the appeal of Etruscan sculpture is its material. While contemporary Greek artists to the east were working in marble, the Etruscans preferred terra cotta, which seems warmer than marble and can be modeled into a softer, more fluid form.

**454.** Sarcophagus, from Cerveteri. c. 520 B.C. Terra cotta, length 6'7". Museo Nazionale di Villa Giulia, Rome.

**455.** *Double Portrait of Gratidia M.L. Chrite and M. Gratidius Libanus.* Last quarter of 1st century B.C. White marble with traces of color, height 23¾". Vatican Museums, Rome.

Possibly it was the warmth and humanity of these Etruscan images that inspired a special category of Roman sculpture—one that differentiated Roman art from Greek. There can be no doubt that the Romans greatly admired the work of their conquered subjects. They made numerous copies of Greek sculptures (including our example of the *Spear Bearer*) and imitated the Greek style for much of their "official" sculpture, such as emperor figures. Sculptures of this sort are interesting historically and some are distinguished, but they pale by comparison to the Greek precedents. Where the Romans truly excelled was in a type of sculpture to which the Greeks had paid little attention—the portrait bust of an ordinary citizen.

One such example (**455**) is a portrait of a Roman husband and wife who are fully realized as individuals. Obviously, we cannot know what these people actually looked like, but it is safe to assume the sculptor made a good likeness, with a minimum of idealizing. The husband is old, the creases in his face well-defined, his expression patient; we might read from his image a long experience in the trials of the world and gentle resignation to those trials. His wife seems stronger, less marked by pain, and her supportive clasp of the husband's hand is touching. Scholars have read into this pose the highly esteemed Roman virtues of *fides* (faith or fidelity) and *concordia* (harmony). Whereas the Greek sculptures, and many of the Roman ones (**71**), seem to exist in a world apart, these portrait busts are wonderfully accessible. They allow us to identify with people who have been dead for two thousand years.

Were it not for a tragedy that occurred in A.D. 79, we would know little more about Roman painting than we do about the Greek, so fragile and vulnerable to the elements is this medium. But in that year Mt. Vesuvius, an active volcano, erupted and buried the town of Pompeii, about a hundred miles south of Rome, along with the neighboring town of Herculaneum. The resulting lava and ashes spread a blanket over the region, and this blanket acted as a kind of time capsule. Pompeii lay undisturbed, immune to further ravages of nature, for more than sixteen centuries. Then in 1748 excavations were undertaken, and their findings were made public by the famous German archaeologist Joachim Winckelmann. Within the precincts of Pompeii the diggers found marvelous frescoes that were exceptionally well-preserved. Pompeii was not an important city, so we cannot assume that the most talented artists of the period worked there. In fact, there is some evidence to suggest that the fresco painters were not Roman at all, but immigrant Greeks. Nevertheless, these wall paintings do give some indication of the styles of art practiced within the Empire at the time.

One fresco, from a house known as the Villa of the Mysteries (**456**), shows a scene believed to represent secret cult rituals associated with the wine-god, Dionysus. The figures stand as though on a ledge, in shallow but convincing space, interacting only slightly with one another. Although the artist has segmented the mural into panels separated by black bands, the figures overlap these panels so freely that there is no strong sense of individual episodes or compartments. Rather, the artist has established two rhythms—one of the figures and another of the dividing bands—both contributing to a strong design unity.

For all their production in painting and sculpture, the Romans are best known for their architecture and engineering. Earlier sections of this book have discussed the Pont du Gard (**408**) and the Pantheon (**411**). But the most familiar monument—indeed, for many travelers the very symbol of Rome—is the Roman Colosseum (**457**).

The Colosseum was planned under the Emperor Vespasian and dedicated in A.D. 80 as an amphitheater for gladiatorial games and public entertainments. A large oval covering 6 acres, the Colosseum, when in use, could accommodate some 50,000 spectators—about the same number as most major league baseball stadiums today. Few of the games played inside, however,

**above: 456.** Wall painting, from the Villa of the Mysteries, Pompeii. c. 50 B.C. Fresco.

**below: 457.** Colosseum, Rome. A.D. 72–80. Concrete (originally faced with marble); height 160′, diameters 620′ and 513′.

were as tame as baseball. Gladiators vied with one another and with wild animals in extraordinarily bloody and gruesome contests, made possible because an extensive system of sewers under the Colosseum could drain away the gore. On special occasions the whole structure could be filled with water for quite realistic naval battles.

While the Colosseum served as headquarters for some rather bloodthirsty activity, its architectural achievement represented the highest ideals of the Romans. Even in its ruined state this structure displays the genius of the Romans as builders. The Colosseum rises on three tiers of arches, each of the levels distinguished from the next by a different style of column between the arches. Around the base are eighty arched openings for entry and exit; it is said that the entire building could be emptied in a matter of minutes. Above all, the structure is logical and coherent. Roman architects tell us in visual detail exactly how the building is organized—which parts are separate from other parts, where to enter, where to go, and so on. The exterior view gives us a clear sense of the inside, the walkways, the scheme as a whole. Today the Colosseum seems romantic; tourists dream of exploring it by moonlight. In its prime, with the sides intact and sheathed in marble, it must have been the crown of the Empire.

Rome persisted as the capital of the civilized Western world until A.D. 330, when the Emperor Constantine moved his government to Byzantium, which he renamed Constantinople (today Istanbul, in Turkey). This change ushered in a new phase in the history of art.

# Byzantium

Byzantine art differs from its Greek and Roman precursors in two distinct ways. First, it is an art based on Christianity. Constantine was converted to the Christian faith, and, with a few exceptions, his successors followed that religion. No longer was art diffused into the portrayal of many gods and ideals. One God, one faith, one tradition—these became the standards of Byzantine art. Second, Byzantine art has an Eastern flavor in both style and materials. It seems more closely related to Russian models than to Western European ones. The Byzantine style, even for figurative art, is essentially flat, with an emphasis on elaborate decoration rather than naturalistic depiction. And, whereas the Greek or Roman artist might prefer to work in paint or marble, the Byzantine artist concentrated on the art of *mosaic*—small stones or pieces of tile arranged in a pattern.

We see an excellent example of this mosaic art in the portrait panel of the 6th-century Emperor Justinian (**72**) and its companion piece, a mosaic depicting Justinian's queen, Theodora (**458**). The *Theodora* mosaic is especially splendid in its rich, vibrant colors and elaborate decorative details. Many scholars feel it was intended to reinforce the royal status of—perhaps even give religious status to—Justinian's queen, who was of low birth and had been an actress before her marriage. The quiet dignity of the figures and elaboration in details seems even more remarkable when we realize this image was put together from tiny pieces, like a giant picture puzzle.

The flatness of Byzantine art is well illustrated by this mosaic. Theodora is supposed to be in procession, with her retinue trailing behind her, but we get little sense of this. Even though the artist has used some overlapping, especially in the figures at right, all the figures appear to be in the same plane, and that plane is identical with the ornately-decorated background. Compared to Greek and Roman figures, such as those on painted vases and Pompeiian frescoes, Theodora stands before us as a paper doll. She is, however, one of the loveliest, most sumptuous paper dolls ever.

Both Justinian's and Theodora's mosaics are housed in a building that represents one of the high points of Byzantine art—the church of San Vitale (**459**), built in the early 6th century about the same time that the great cathe-

458. *Empress Theodora and Retinue.* c. 547. Mosaic. San Vitale, Ravenna.

dral of Hagia Sophia was constructed in Istanbul (412). At this point Eastern styles of art and architecture had spread westward; San Vitale is in the Italian city of Ravenna. Its ground plan (460) reveals its somewhat unusual arrangement of spaces—unusual, that is, for a church in Western Europe. Most Early Christian churches were simple rectangles; later, churches in the West adopted the cross plan, consisting of a long main section intersected by a shorter section at right angles to the first. In either of these plans one enters through a door at one end, and straight ahead at the other end is the altar. The axis, or main line of sight, is from door to altar, horizontally through the church. San Vitale, with its Eastern character, is not like that. It is a central-plan church, built in the form of an octagon, and so the focus of attention is in the center of the building, immediately under the dome. The major axis, therefore, is vertical, from floor to dome (or earth to Heaven), with the altar off to one side. The central plan remained a feature of Eastern churches long after the cross plan had become firmly established in the West.

**left: 459.** Exterior of apse, San Vitale, Ravenna. c. 527–547.

**above: 460.** Plan of San Vitale, Ravenna.

right: **461.** *St. Matthew the Evangelist,*
from *The Gospel Book of Archbishop Ebbo.*
Before 823. Illumination, $10\frac{1}{4} \times 7\frac{7}{8}''$.
Bibliothèque de la Ville, Epernay.

below: **462.** Salisbury Cathedral. 1220–70.

**463.** Plan of Salisbury Cathedral.

# The Middle Ages in Europe

Medieval European art is also a Christian art. It would be nearly impossible to understand Western art, from the time of Constantine's historic move of his capital in 330 until well into the 17th century, without taking into account the Roman Catholic faith. Of course, secular art was produced throughout this period, but a major portion of the art was done in the service of the Church or based on religious themes. This is not to say that one must *be* a Christian to appreciate the art. Art is art, and religion is religion. Some of the greatest artists drew freely upon all the sources available to them, including religion, classical myths, historical events, literature, and drama. It is natural, though, that artists would turn to the subjects most familiar to them, and for which they found a ready audience and patronage. During the Middle Ages and beyond, this meant the Christian church.

Christianity centers on the Bible, a collection of sacred writings put down over many centuries and collected into one book (the word "bible" comes from the Greek and Latin words for "book") probably in the 8th century. For the teaching and practice of faith, it was essential to possess a Bible, and in this era, long before the invention of the printing press, manuscripts had to be copied laboriously by hand. Most of the work was done by monks, who toiled in special writing centers known as *scriptoria*. Gradually, the practice evolved of decorating, or *illuminating*, the prose manuscripts with drawings and paintings. Illuminated Bibles appeared in Western Europe as early as the 8th century, and the custom prevailed well into the 15th century. These volumes preserved not only the literary and theological traditions of the Bible and other writings, but also an artistic heritage. Painting in the sense that we know it—that is to say, a large, freestanding painted work, such as an easel painting—did not really emerge in Western Europe until the late 13th century, and even fresco painting was not widespread. So we rely on these exquisite miniatures—called *illuminations*—to follow the development of painting during the period.

`Many illuminated books concentrated on the gospels of the New Testament, written by the four Evangelists, Matthew, Mark, Luke, and John. An illumination from the 9th-century *Gospel Book of Archbishop Ebbo* (**461**) shows St. Matthew hard at work transcribing his Gospel. Everything about him suggests a frenzy of creative inspiration, from the agitated drapery of his clothing to the intense concentration on his face. Even his feet and toes seem tensed by the effort of his project. Each of the Evangelists has a traditional symbol, and Matthew's is a winged man, which appears in the upper right corner of the painting. For the most part the monks who made these splendid illuminations were anonymous. We might suspect, however, that the artist of the St. Matthew painting suffered greatly over his arduous task, and felt a certain empathy with Matthew struggling to get his Gospel written down.

The Middle Ages was the period when most of the great cathedrals of Europe were built. As discussed in Chapter 13 (pp. 310–312), the architectural style favored from about 1050 to 1200 was the Romanesque, based on round arches and vaults. After 1200 and into the 15th century the Gothic style prevailed, with its pointed arches and vaults and its emphasis on large stained-glass windows. The term "Gothic" was actually used by later writers of the Renaissance, who considered this architecture vulgar and used the word to mean "barbarian." Gothic-style architecture originated in France (**410,432**) and eventually spread to most of Western Europe.

Salisbury Cathedral in England, built in the 13th century, is a splendid example of the developed Gothic style (**462**). Its graceful spire, the tallest in England, rises to 404 feet—or nearly the height of a modern fifty-story apartment building. On the outside, the pointed arch is visible everywhere, and this theme is carried through inside the church. The ground plan (**463**) makes an interesting comparison to that of San Vitale (**460**). Salisbury is a very long church with a true cross plan and the spire located over the exact center. As

**464.** *The Gero Crucifix.* c. 975–1000. Wood, height 6'2". Cathedral, Cologne.

with most other great churches of the period, Salisbury Cathedral is heavily ornamented with sculpture.

In the sculpture of the Middle Ages, the theme again was usually a sacred one. A life-size work from the 10th century, the *Gero Crucifix* (**464**) shows the enormous skill a medieval carver could attain, as well as the willingness to portray Christ in relatively naturalistic, not symbolic, fashion. Here Christ is shown, not as a deity, but as a suffering flesh-and-blood human. There is great pathos in this figure, especially in the face, which combines the agony of pain with resignation to the fate of violent death. Christ's body pulls downward, its flesh and muscles straining against the hands nailed to the cross. The sculptor of this figure clearly wished to elicit a direct, emotional response from the viewer and identification with Christ's torment and death.

In contrast to the *Gero Crucifix*, a small wooden pietà from the 14th century (**465**) distorts natural appearances for a different effect. Harsh and angular, the *Röttgen Pietà* portrays in ghastly detail the results of Christ's final suffering and the anguish of his mother. If the crucifix was meant to elicit from the viewer a sigh of compassion, the pietà would be more likely to call forth a shriek or a moan. Although less than a foot tall, this little sculpture captures in shocking precision the physical results of crucifixion. Christ's body is shrunken virtually down to the bone, drained of its lifeblood, which pours out from the five wounds in hands, feet, and side. For both compositional and expressive reasons, the sculptor has adjusted proportions in the figures. The Virgin's head is too large for her body, but this is necessary to convey properly the grief on her face, which is a major focal point. Christ's body, on the other hand, is proportionately too small in relation to that of his mother. If it had been carved in correct scale, the effect might have been strange—head and legs jutting out too far in both directions—and the sculpture would lose its compact form and powerful message.

Not all religious sculpture of the Middle Ages has this emotional quality. In the work of Claus Sluter, a Dutch artist who worked in France and who was interested in Greek and Roman sculpture, we find a cool majesty that anticipated the Renaissance. Sluter's most ambitious sculpture was the so-called *Moses Well* (**466**), a six-sided stone pedestal featuring life-size portraits of six

Old Testament prophets, carved in very high relief. The view illustrated here shows Moses on the right, Isaiah on the left. Perhaps the word "portraits" seems unusual, since no one really knows what the patriarchs looked like. But Sluter has taken pains to depict them as individual personalities, vibrant and animated, so that we feel he has captured the character of each. The prophets do not stand rigidly, bonded to their background, but instead reach out to interact with one another and with the viewer. The figures are monumental, seeming especially massive because they are encased in a heavy swirl of drapery. This last point is the key to why the *Moses Well* appears in this chapter rather than the next one. Sluter's work serves as a bridge between the art of the Middle Ages and the art of the Renaissance. In true Renaissance style the sculptor has carved lifelike, mobile figures; yet so profuse is the mountain of drapery that we have little sense of the body underneath. It remained for the next generation of artists to strip away the garments and study the entire human form.

Our two final artists in this chapter could easily be placed in the one that follows, as masters of the Renaissance. Some scholars would insist upon their being accorded this honor for having begun, through their own creative genius, the tremendous artistic outpouring that marked the Renaissance period. Others consider them to represent the last gasp of the Middle Ages. The point is that, like Claus Sluter, both artists were transitional, both were influential in making the leap between two quite different styles of art. We place them here mainly because their major sources of inspiration were the vestiges of Byzantine art to the East and the medieval Gothic tradition to the North. Succeeding generations of artists would look instead to Greece and Rome.

**left: 465.** *Röttgen Pietà*. c. 1370. Painted wood, height 10½". Rheinisches Landesmuseum, Bonn.

**right: 466.** Claus Sluter. *Moses Well*. 1395–1406. Stone, height of figures c. 6'. Chartreuse de Champmol, Dijon.

Duccio was an artist of Siena, in Italy. His masterpiece was the *Maestà Altar*, a multisection panel meant to be displayed on the altar of a church, of which we illustrate the part showing *Christ Entering Jerusalem* (**467**). What is most interesting about this painting is Duccio's attempt to create believable space in a large outdoor scene—a concern that would absorb painters of the next century. Christ's entry into the city, celebrated now on Palm Sunday, was thought of as a triumphal procession, and Duccio has labored to convey the sense of movement and parade. A strong diagonal thrust beginning at the left with Christ and his disciples cuts across the picture to the middle right, then shifts abruptly to carry our attention to the upper left corner of the painting—a church tower that is Christ's presumed goal. The architecture plays an important role in defining space and directing movement. This was Duccio's novel, almost unprecedented, contribution to the art of the period, the use of architecture to enclose and demarcate space rather than to act as a simple backdrop.

Duccio's contemporary, a Florentine artist named Giotto, made an even more remarkable break with art traditions of the Middle Ages. Most of Giotto's best work was in fresco (Chapter 7), and the most notable examples are in a small church in Padua, called the Arena Chapel. *The Lamentation* (**468**), a work depicting Mary, St. John, and others mourning over the dead Christ, illustrates Giotto's highly original use of space in painting. The scene has been composed as though it were on a stage and we the viewers are an audience participating in the drama. In other words, space going back from the picture

**467.** Duccio.
*Christ Entering Jerusalem,*
detail of *Maestà Altar.*
1308–11. Panel, 40 × 21″.
Cathedral Museum, Siena.

**468.** Giotto.
*The Lamentation*. 1305–06.
Fresco, 7'7" × 7'9".
Arena Chapel, Padua.

plane seems to be continuous with space in front of the picture plane, the space in which we stand. Accustomed as we are now to this "window" effect in painting, it is difficult to imagine how revolutionary it was to medieval eyes, used to predominantly flat, decorative space in painting (**44,461**). Moreover, Giotto seems to have developed this concept of space largely on his own, with little artistic precedent. The figures in *The Lamentation* are round and full-bodied, clustered low in the composition to enhance the effect of an event taking place just out of our reach.

Giotto's grouping of the figures is unusual and daring, with Christ's body half-hidden by a figure with its back turned. This arrangement seems casual and almost random, until we notice the slope of the hill directing attention to Christ's and the Virgin's heads, which are the focal point. Yet another innovation—perhaps Giotto's most important one—was his interest in depicting the psychological and emotional reactions of his subjects. The characters in *The Lamentation* interact in a natural, human way that gives this and the artist's other religious scenes a special warmth.

Neither Duccio nor Giotto had an especially long career. Each did his most significant work in the first decade of the 14th century. Yet in that short time the course of Western art history changed dramatically. Both artists had sought a new direction for painting—a more naturalistic, more human, more engaging representation of the physical world—and both had taken giant steps in that direction. Their experiments paved the way for a flowering of all the arts that would come in the next century and would give us some of the greatest artists of all time—the Renaissance.

# *16*

# Renaissance to Revolution

This chapter encompasses about four hundred years in the history of Western art—from the beginning of the 15th century to near the end of the 18th. The title "Renaissance to Revolution" is appropriate, because the period begins with the emergence of the Renaissance in Italy and concludes with three different revolutions—the French, the American, and the Industrial—all of which occurred at roughly the same time. One could argue, however, that the title "Revolution to Revolution" would have done just as well, for in a very real sense the Renaissance was a revolution in the world of art. Nearly everything about art changed, and changed quickly—the types of art being made, the way works of art looked, the materials used, the role of the artist, the identities and influence of patrons, and the artistic precedents that served as inspiration.

Before discussing the components of this "revolution" that was the Renaissance, we might address the question of why it occurred, especially why it occurred at the time and place it did. Italy in the 15th century offered a perfect combination of circumstances. For one thing, the conditions for artistic patronage were unusually favorable. Italy had developed powerful city-states engaged in extensive trade and banking. The members of the merchant class, at the head of this commerce, had a great deal of money to spend, were well-educated, and were highly motivated for reasons of prestige and temperament to invest in art. Also, the Christian church was centered in Italy, and it provided another important source of patronage.

Besides the abundance of customers for art, there was ready inspiration for art. During this period a growing interest in the past led to the excavation of Classical Greek and Roman ruins, which revealed architecture and sculpture that had not been seen for centuries. Many of the leading artists of the Renaissance studied these works and took them as models.

Finally, we might be tempted to say that the Renaissance began in Italy in the 15th century because Michelangelo, Leonardo, Raphael, and others were there. But perhaps another age with the same social and historical advantages would have spawned artists of equal genius. We cannot know for sure, but the problem is intriguing. Let us now sum up the changes that took place in art; we will refer to them again as they are illustrated in specific examples. Some have already been mentioned in previous chapters.

The types of art made during the Renaissance included all those that had been popular during the Middle Ages—sculpture, architecture, tapestry, and so forth—but there was a much greater emphasis on painting. Throughout the medieval period, painting, except for miniatures and some frescos, had languished. In the Renaissance it came back to life, with an energy perhaps never before seen. The Renaissance has been called "the age of painting"; this may be an overstatement in view of the splendid sculpture and architecture it produced, but the phrase is certainly true when we compare the Renaissance to the several centuries preceding it.

For the first time since the Classical periods of Greece and Rome the quest for "realism"—the faithful representation of the natural world—dominated art. Painters and sculptors dissected corpses to better understand the mysteries of human anatomy. Elaborate studies of perspective were undertaken (p. 121) to create the illusion of accurate three-dimensional space. It was during the Renaissance that the notion of art as mirror of the physical world became established, a notion that persists in some people's minds even today.

Since painting was newly popular, artists took great interest in its physical properties, and the materials of that medium changed radically. Oil paint, which was introduced in northern Europe (perhaps by Jan Van Eyck, **228**), soon eclipsed the more cumbersome tempera (Chapter 7, p. 182). New techniques of fresco painting were perfected. On the whole, there was a great deal of experimentation with materials, some of it rewarding, some of it disastrous. Leonardo da Vinci, whose curiosity about the world seems to have been boundless, was most prone to try new techniques, and some of his best-known works have deteriorated badly. Nevertheless, the experimentation led to some extraordinary developments.

The changing role of the artist is a fascinating aspect of the Renaissance. Up until that time the vast majority of Western artists had been anonymous. In isolated cases we have a name; we know, for example, that Praxiteles was the great genius of Greek sculpture, and we know what his work looked like (**359**). Beyond that, we have little information about the man himself. Even this much is an advantage over our knowledge of most artists in the 13th and 14th centuries. The medieval artist, in general, was considered a skilled craftsman, little more. A talented wood- or stone-carver might be given the same respect that today is accorded to a first-rate carpenter—valuable, indispensable when needed, forgotten when the job is finished. Of course, there were exceptions, and a few names have come down to us, but not many. It is for this reason that none of the artists' biographies in this book predate the 15th century.

Starting with the great masters of the Renaissance we suddenly have rather complete portraits of the artists—who they were, how they lived and worked, what they thought about art and life in general. For the first time artists were considered a breed apart, comprising a class of their own that transcended the social class determined by birth—not nobility, not bourgeoisie, not clergy, but a separate and elite category of people respected not because of who they were, but because of what they could *do*. They lived in the courts of the nobles and popes, they moved freely in good society, their company was sought after, their services in demand. That role has remained essentially unchanged into the 20th century—except that few patrons today keep an artist in residence.

As mentioned earlier, the character of art patronage reflected the changing times. Before the Renaissance only two groups of people could afford to be art patrons—the nobility and the clergy. Both continued to be active sponsors of art, but they were joined in the 15th century by a new merchant class, very rich, socially ambitious, fully able to support extravagant spending on art. These were the forerunners of today's corporate patrons of the arts. The climate could not have been more fertile for a flowering of art: the best artists were available, and virtually unlimited funds existed to support them.

One more element is needed to complete our picture of the Renaissance artist—the changing sources of inspiration. The Renaissance individual was very much aware of being part of a Golden Age, an age of reason and enlightenment and achievement. Only twice, to anyone's knowledge, had such a situation existed before. Renaissance artists cast their eyes backward to those they considered their natural teachers—the great masters of Greece and Rome. To their everlasting credit these later artists were not satisfied merely to imitate, but forged a new style of art that at least equaled the standards of the Classical world. With this preamble, then, let us look at the artists of the Renaissance.

## The Renaissance in Italy

In 1401 the city of Florence announced an artistic competition, the winner of which would be awarded the commission for making sculptured bronze doors to decorate the Baptistry of the Cathedral. At least six artists were invited to submit trial pieces. The subject was to be the sacrifice of Isaac, from the biblical story in which God tested the faith of Abraham by requiring him to slay his son, Isaac. (At the last moment the Lord, convinced of Abraham's obedience, spared the boy.) Among those submitting designs to the competition was a twenty-three-year-old goldsmith, Lorenzo Ghiberti. Ghiberti's trial panel (**469**) shows a strong sense of composition; its action is compact, with a subtle curving rhythm from lower right to upper left, and the figures of Abraham and Isaac at middle right are emphasized to create a focal point. Isaac's nude body reveals Ghiberti's admiration for ancient statues and is a true Renaissance figure. Ghiberti won the prize and spent much of the next two decades working on the doors.

Shortly after the doors were installed, Ghiberti was asked to make another set, this time for the east side of the Baptistry, and this time without any need to prove himself in competition. The east doors were more than twenty-five years in the making, and finally were installed in 1452. So marvelous were their design and craftsmanship that Michelangelo termed them the "Gates of Paradise," and so they have been called ever since (**470**).

Between the time of the first competition and the completion of the "Gates of Paradise"—half a century—Ghiberti's style had matured considerably. We saw one panel of the later doors in Chapter 11 (**355**). The artist had made extensive studies of perspective, allowing him to create the illusion of spatial depth on the shallow bronze doors. And he is in full control of three-dimensional volumes; some of the figures on the east doors are virtually in the round. The composition is simplified, less cluttered, easier to understand. In the span of time from the trial panel to the "Gates of Paradise," Ghiberti made the transition from the first tentative gropings of the Renaissance to a more assured style that foreshadowed the sculptures of Michelangelo's generation.

While Ghiberti was working on the first set of bronze doors for the Baptistry, he was assisted by, among others, the young sculptor Donatello. Donatello was born in Florence in about 1386 and was apprenticed to Ghiberti by the age of seventeen. During his long career he worked in many different styles and in all the sculptural media then available—wood, stone, and metal. An early work, the statue of *St. Mark* in Florence (**471**), depends on Donatello's familiarity with two sources of inspiration—ancient Greek and Roman sculptures and the Scriptures. The figure is as naturalistic as any of the Greek statues, yet there is a stamp of individual personality in both face and body that may have come from Donatello's reading of Mark's Gospel.

*St. Mark* shows many of the characteristics that came to typify Donatello's work and helps to explain why some writers consider Donatello to be the

**469.** Lorenzo Ghiberti.
*Sacrifice of Isaac.* 1401.
Gilt bronze, $21 \times 17\frac{1}{2}''$.
National Museum, Florence.

**left: 470.** Lorenzo Ghiberti.
"Gates of Paradise,"
east doors of the Baptistry, Florence.
1425–52. Gilt bronze, height 18′6″.

**above: 471.** Donatello. *St. Mark.*
1411–13. Marble, height 7′9″.
Or San Michele, Florence.

founder of modern sculpture. This statue is enclosed within a niche but is by no means dependent on the architectural framework for support. For the first time in centuries we see a sculpture that is totally self-sustaining—fully rounded and capable of standing on its own. Moreover, Donatello's figure is remarkably lifelike. St. Mark seems caught in the act of movement, and his body underneath the garments seems real, substantial, made of flesh and bone. If you compare this statue to the figures on Sluter's *Moses Well* (**466**), carved a mere decade earlier, you will appreciate Donatello's originality. Sluter's prophets are wrapped in massive drapery that has a life of its own, independent of the body. But St. Mark's clothing responds to the form underneath. Where the left knee bends outward, the robe falls back; where the right arm is pressed to the body, the sleeve wrinkles. We know that if St. Mark moved, the garments would move with him.

At the same time that Donatello was exploring the potential for naturalism and animation in sculpture, the first painters of the Renaissance were grappling with the problems of conveying these qualities on a flat surface. Among the first of those who could indisputably be called a Renaissance artist was the young genius known as Masaccio, whose name has been variously translated as "wicked Tom" and "slovenly Tom." Masaccio lived for only twenty-seven years, and there are just four works that can be attributed to him definitely. Nevertheless, his contribution to the development of Early Renaissance art was immense.

Masaccio's best-known painting is *The Tribute Money* (**472**), a fresco in the Brancacci Chapel in Florence. The story related in this fresco is taken from the Gospel of St. Matthew and concerns an event in the life of Christ. Christ's disciples, especially Peter, had questioned whether it was proper to pay taxes to the Roman government, considering that Christ was the Messiah and above such authority. But Christ pointed out the difference between earthly and spiritual obligations and counseled that the taxes be paid, saying "Render therefore unto Caesar the things which are Caesar's; and unto God the things that are God's" (Matthew 22:21). He urged Peter to go and catch a fish, which would have a coin in its mouth and to pay that coin to the tax collector.

To portray this fairly complicated story Masaccio has employed a device known as *continuous narrative*. Three different parts in the sequence of events are shown in the same painting. In the center, Christ is conferring with his disciples and instructing Peter to pay the tax. At left, Peter goes fishing and finds the coin; at right, he turns the coin over to the Roman tax collector. Such a running narrative might have seemed awkward were it not for Masaccio's compositional powers. The most important scene is the conference among Christ and his twelve Apostles, just off center in the composition. Here the figures are drawn together in dramatic tension by their grouping and their gestures. The fishing segment is least important to Masaccio; he thrusts it far to the left in his composition. For the paying of the tribute money, the climax of the event, Masaccio has separated the two key figures—Peter and the tax collector—by an architectural background, with St. Peter framed in an arch.

All of Masaccio's figures are well-constructed, standing in relaxed *contrapposto* poses (p. 279). This effect is especially apparent in the legs of the tax collector in his two appearances. Like Donatello's *St. Mark*, the figures have real, living bodies under their garments, bodies that seem to have the muscle and bone to move. A comparison of this work with Duccio's *Christ Entering Jerusalem* (**467**), painted just a little over a century earlier, will show that great strides had been made in using linear perspective to depict architecture in three-dimensional space. Also, Masaccio's shading and treatment of drapery give convincing roundness to the bodies. The figures have a dignity and gravity that mark them as true products of the Renaissance.

Masaccio's art had a profound influence on another Florentine painter, who came into prominence about a generation later—Piero della Francesca. In Piero's fresco, *The Resurrection* (**473**), we can see the artist's debt to Masaccio in the sure handling of linear perspective and the wonderful roundness of the bodies. Piero, however, was a skilled mathematician, and that is one of the things that sets his composition apart from the work of the earlier master. This picture is constructed as a triangle, with Christ's head at the apex. The triangle moves down to the two lower corners of the painting and cuts across the bottom, pulling the figures of Christ and the sleeping soldiers into one coherent group. There is a pronounced vertical axis from Christ's face straight

**opposite: 472.** Masaccio.
*The Tribute Money.* c. 1427.
Fresco, 8'2⅜" × 19'8¼".
Brancacci Chapel,
Sta. Maria del Carmine, Florence.

**right: 473.** Piero della Francesca.
*Resurrection.* c. 1460.
Fresco, 9'6" × 8'4".
Gallery, Palazzo del Commune,
Borgo San Sepolcro, Italy.

**474.** Sandro Botticelli.
*Primavera.* c. 1478.
Tempera on panel, 6′8″ × 10′3¾″.
Uffizi, Florence.

down to the bottom of the painting. In spite of this structure, the picture does not seem rigid. The poses of the soldiers, as they lie sprawled in sleep, are by no means stiff. Also, Piero has introduced elements of asymmetrical balance to offset the predominantly symmetrical balance of the triangle. Christ's upraised arm with the banner juts out to one side of the central axis while his bent left knee pushes out to the other side. At their best, Renaissance painters imposed an order, often a geometrical order, on their compositions, but they did not let that order overwhelm the expressiveness of their art.

Yet another Florentine painter, a quarter-century younger than Piero, was Sandro Botticelli. Botticelli was rather more sophisticated and worldly than most of his artist-contemporaries. While he painted many religious subjects, his earlier works took their subjects from Greek and Roman culture and the classical myths. Also, he had a special fascination with detail and with the depiction of women as graceful, exquisite beings, so weightless they often seem about to float out of the paintings. Early in his career Botticelli had the great fortune to enjoy the patronage of the Medici, the ruling merchant family of Florence. At the beginning of this text, in Chapter 1, we pointed out that the famous *Birth of Venus* (**1**) was painted for a villa belonging to the Medici. Apparently, two large works were commissioned from Botticelli for that same villa, and the second was *Primavera* (**474**).

*Primavera* is the Italian word for "spring," and Botticelli's painting has a lusty, earthy, playful quality the artist clearly associated with that season. At center is Venus, the goddess of love, identified by the little figure of Eros (Cupid), who often accompanies Venus, hovering around her. To the left dance the three Graces—goddesses of joy, charm, and beauty—in flowing gowns that are virtually transparent, and at far left is the messenger-god Mercury. At right the wind-god, Zephyr, pursues a nymph who, at his touch, is transformed into Flora, goddess of flowers and springtime. Although Venus occupies the center of the painting, its main focal point surely is Flora—the very personification of spring and one of the loveliest images to emerge from the Renaissance. The mood of the painting is charming and undeniably erotic—a perfect evocation in classical terms of what today we might call "spring fever."

As we can see in *Primavera,* Botticelli has mastered the technique of painting round, full-fleshed bodies. However, he is not nearly as interested as later artists would be in depicting deep, three-dimensional space. The space in *Primavera* is actually quite shallow, with the trees serving as a backdrop, almost a stage set. And the figures, though somewhat overlapped, stretch out in a row from side to side. These characteristics mark Botticelli as an artist of the Early Renaissance. Painters of the next generation would strive to set their figures naturally in a deeper landscape.

We come now to a period known as the *High Renaissance*—a brief but glorious time in the history of art. In barely twenty-five years, from shortly before 1500 to about 1525, many of the most celebrated works of Western art were produced. Many artists participated in this brilliant creative endeavor, but the two giants among them were unquestionably Leonardo da Vinci and Michelangelo.

The term "Renaissance man" is applied to someone who is very well informed about, or very good at doing, many different, often quite unrelated, things. It originated in the fact that several of the leading figures of the Renaissance were artistic jacks-of-all-trades. Michelangelo was painter, sculptor, poet, and architect—incomparably gifted at all. Leonardo was painter, inventor, sculptor, architect, engineer, scientist, musician, and all-around intellectual. In our age of specialization these accomplishments seem staggering, but during the heady years of the Renaissance nothing was considered impossible.

Leonardo is the artist who most thoroughly embodies the term "Renaissance man"; many people consider him to have been the greatest genius who ever lived. Leonardo was possessed of a brilliant and inquiring mind that accepted no limits. Throughout his long life he remained absorbed by the problem of how things work, and how they might work. A typical example of his investigations is the well-known *Study of Human Proportions* (**475**), in which

**475.** Leonardo da Vinci.
*Study of Human Proportions
According to Vitruvius.*
c. 1485–90.
Pen and ink, 13½ × 9¾".
Academy, Venice.

# Leonardo da Vinci
## *1452–1519*

No clues are offered by the scant knowledge about Leonardo's origins to explain what spawned perhaps the most complex imagination of all time. Leonardo was the illegitimate son of a peasant woman known only as Caterina and a fairly well-to-do notary, Piero da Vinci. He was raised in his father's house at Vinci and, when he was about fifteen, apprenticed to the Florentine artist Andrea del Verrocchio, in whose workshop he remained for about ten years.

In 1482 Leonardo left Florence for Milan, where he became official artist to Lodovico Sforza, duke of that city. There the artist undertook many projects, foremost among them his famous painting of the *Last Supper,* for which he used an experimental mural technique that caused the painting to deteriorate badly soon after its completion. Leonardo remained with Sforza until the latter's fall from power in 1499, after which he returned to Florence.

Sketches and written records indicate that Leonardo worked as a sculptor, but no examples remain. Only about a dozen paintings can be definitely attributed to him, and several of these are unfinished. There are, however, hundreds of drawings, and the thousands of pages from his detailed notebook testify to the man's extraordinary genius. If Leonardo completed relatively few artistic works, this can only be ascribed to the enormous breadth of his interests, which caused him repeatedly to turn from one subject to another. He was a skilled architect and engineer, engrossed in the problems of city planning, sanitary disposal, military engineering, and even the design of weapons. He made sketches for a crude submarine, a helicopter, and an airplane—with characteristic thoroughness also designing a parachute in case the airplane should fail. He made innovative studies in astronomy, anatomy, botany, geology, optics, and above all mathematics. His contemporaries reported his great talent as a musician—he played and improvised on the lute—as well as his love of inventive practical jokes.

In 1507 Leonardo was appointed court painter to the King of France, Louis XII, who happened to be in Milan at the time. Nine years later the aging artist was named court painter to Louis's successor, Francis I. Francis seems to have revered him for his towering reputation as an artist and his crisp intellect, but to have expected little artistic production from the old man. The king provided comfortable lodgings in the city of Amboise, where Leonardo died.

Solitary all his life, Leonardo did not marry, and he formed very few close attachments. His obsession seems to have been with getting it all down, recording the fertile outpourings of his brain and hand. In his *Treatise on Painting,* assembled from his notebook pages and published after his death, he advised painters to follow his method: "You should often amuse yourself when you take a walk for recreation, in watching and taking note of the attitudes and actions of men as they talk and dispute, or laugh or come to blows with one another . . . noting these down with rapid strokes, in a little pocket-book which you ought always to carry with you . . . for there is such an infinite number of forms and actions of things that the memory is incapable of preserving them."[1]

Leonardo da Vinci. *Self-Portrait.* c. 1512. Chalk on paper, 13 × 8¼". Biblioteca Reale, Turin.

**476.** Leonardo da Vinci. *Mona Lisa.* c. 1503–05. Oil on panel, $30\frac{1}{4} \times 21''$. Louvre, Paris.

the artist sought to establish ideal proportions for the human body by relating it to the square and the circle. Above and below the figure is Leonardo's eccentric mirror writing, which he used throughout his notes and journals.

Despite his vast accomplishments, Leonardo often had difficulty completing specific projects; many of his most ambitious works were left unfinished, including his best-known painting, the *Mona Lisa* (**176**). The *Mona Lisa* has been the object of special fascination ever since it was painted. Songs, poems, and treatises have been written about the sitter's smile, and her image often turns up in remarkably unexpected contexts (**320,521**). Just what is so magical about this painting is hard to define. Certainly the "mysterious" smile on the woman's face contributes to the *Mona Lisa*'s special aura, but it alone is not sufficient to explain the painting's fascination. For this work Leonardo was in masterful control of a newly developed technique known as *sfumato* (deriving from the Italian for "smoke"), which involves painting in thin glazes to achieve a hazy, cloudy atmosphere and a sense of three-dimensional form. Behind the model is a fantasy landscape, vague and undefined, another element of the painting's mystery. Some of the intrigue of the *Mona Lisa* must lie in its contradictions. It presents to us a Florentine matron, not at first glance beautiful, posed almost rigidly in the exact center of the painting, showing little of her emotions. Yet further acquaintance with the subject reveals beauty so unique as to ignore conventional ideas of beauty, a pose that is not rigid but serene, and a personality which, though elusive, draws us to her.

During the years when Leonardo was painting the *Mona Lisa,* Michelangelo, a quarter-century younger, also was in Florence, at work on one of the projects for which he is best known. That two such extraordinary figures could live and work in close proximity, surrounded by numerous others of scarcely lower stature, demonstrates how remarkable a time the High Renaissance was.

# Michelangelo

## 1475–1564

He is beyond legend. His name means "archangel Michael," and to his contemporaries and those who came after, his stature is scarcely less than that of a heavenly being. He began serious work as an artist at the age of thirteen and did not stop until death claimed him seventy-six years later. His equal may never be seen again, for only a particular time and place could have bred the genius of Michelangelo.

Michelangelo Buonarroti was born in the Tuscan town of Caprese. According to his devoted biographer and friend, Giorgio Vasari, the young Michelangelo often was scolded and beaten by his father for spending too much time drawing. Eventually, however, seeing his son's talent, the father relented and apprenticed him to the painter Domenico Ghirlandaio. At the age of fourteen Michelangelo was welcomed into the household of the wealthy banker Lorenzo de' Medici, who operated a private sculpture academy for promising young students. There he remained until Lorenzo's death, after which Michelangelo, just seventeen years old, struck out permanently on his own.

He traveled to Venice and Bologna, then finally to Rome, where he attracted the first of what would become a long list of patrons among the clergy. A *Pietà* (Virgin mourning the dead Christ) made in 1500 and now in the Vatican established his reputation as a sculptor. From that time until his death he never lacked for highly placed patrons. He served—and survived—six popes, and in between accepted commissions from two emperors, a king, and numerous members of the nobility. All his life he struggled to keep a balance between the work he wanted to do and the work demanded of him by his benefactors.

His relationships with these powerful figures were marked continually by squabbles about payment, insults given and forgiven, flight from the scene of a particular commission followed by penitent return to continue the work.

Michelangelo served these masters, at various times, as painter and architect, but he always considered himself above all to be a sculptor. Much of his time was spent supervising the quarrying of superior stones for sculptural projects. His greatest genius lay in depictions of the human figure, whether in marble or in paint. Vasari writes that "this extraordinary man chose always to refuse to paint anything save the human body in its most beautifully proportioned and perfect forms." To this end he made extensive anatomical studies and dissected corpses to better understand the inner workings of the body.

Michelangelo never married, though he formed a number of passionate attachments during his life. These inspired the artist, always a sensitive and gifted poet, to write numerous sonnets. One of his most poignant verses, however, was not addressed to a loved one but to his friend Vasari, a few years before his death:

> The course of my long life has reached at last
> In fragile bark o'er a tempestuous sea,
> The common harbor, where must rendered be
> Account of all the actions of the past. . . .

> Painting and sculpture satisfy no more
> The soul now turning to the Love Divine,
> That oped, to embrace us, on the cross its arms.[2]

Anonymous artist. *Portrait of Michelangelo*. 16th century. Staatliche Museen Preussischer Kulturbesitz, Berlin.

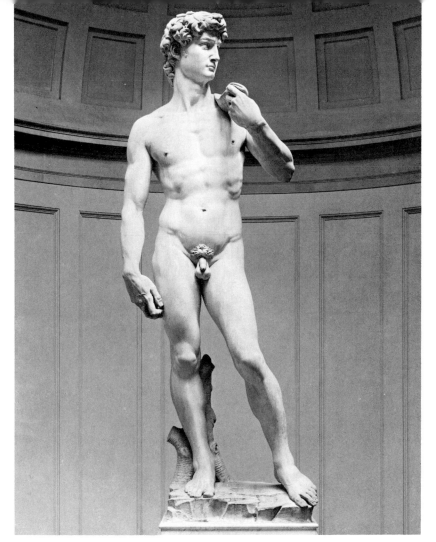

**477.** Michelangelo. *David.* 1501–04. Marble, height 18′. Academy, Florence.

By the age of twenty-five Michelangelo had established his reputation as a sculptor. A year later he received the commission for, and began work on, a colossal image of the biblical hero David (**477**), the young Hebrew shepherd who killed the giant Goliath with a single stone from his slingshot. The *David* statue reveals Michelangelo's debt to Classical sculptures; we might compare it to the Roman copy of the Greek *Spear Bearer* (**452**). *David* is not, however, a simple restatement of Greek art. The Greeks knew how bodies looked on the outside. Michelangelo knew how they looked on the inside, how they worked, because he had studied human anatomy and had dissected corpses. He translated this knowledge into a figure that seems made of muscle and flesh and bone, though all in marble.

There are other characteristics that make *David* a Renaissance sculpture, not a copy of a Greek one. For one thing, it has a tension and energy that is missing from Greek art. Some writers have suggested that the statue is a self-portrait—not so much that it duplicates Michelangelo's features, but that it expresses the creative tension of its maker. The hands especially are taut and strong, held at the ready for action. Another Renaissance quality is the expression on David's face. Classical Greek statues generally bore an expression of beatific calm, showing the subject to be above earthly concerns. But David is young and vibrant—and angry, angry at the forces of evil represented by the giant Goliath. Michelangelo equated perfect beauty with perfect truth and honor; he seems to have found these qualities in the story of David and to have embodied them in his statue of the young conqueror.

Four years after the completion of *David*, Michelangelo was in Rome, working on sculptures for the tomb of Pope Julius II (to be completed in the

**478.** Michelangelo. Ceiling, Sistine Chapel. 1508–12. Fresco, 44 × 128′. Vatican, Rome.

Pope's lifetime). Julius interrupted this project and persuaded, some would say coerced, his young artist to undertake another commission, the decoration in fresco of the ceiling in the Sistine Chapel at the Vatican (**478**). Such was the power of the Papacy and of patronage in those times that even an artist of Michelangelo's stature could be readily controlled, and Michelangelo writhed under this system.

Chapter 7 explained some of the difficulties of the fresco technique. Paint must be applied to the fresh plaster just when it has the proper degree of dampness; only a small area can be covered at a time; and the painting must be done directly, with no allowance for correction of mistakes. Add to these problems the fact that Michelangelo had to cover an area 44 by 128 feet (700 square yards), working on a scaffolding 68 feet above the floor, lying always on his back in a cramped position with paint and plaster dripping into his face, and you can appreciate how arduous was this task that he undertook.

Even more overwhelming than the physical difficulties was the challenge of making a coherent composition in such a huge area. Because the artist was Michelangelo, the composition is not merely coherent but is one of the great masterpieces of all time. Michelangelo organized the ceiling into a painted architectural framework of squares, rectangles, and triangles. These segments depict Old Testament stories of the creation of the world, the creation of Adam (**39**) and of Eve, the Fall of Man, and other biblical events. The figures have the same anatomical fullness and muscular energy as Michelangelo's sculptures; indeed, many of them have the cool, "stone-like" appearance of painted sculptures.

**479.** Michelangelo. St. Peter's, apse and dome. 1546–64. Vatican, Rome.

Just as Pope Julius II had urged Michelangelo to work as a painter, one of Julius' successors, Pope Paul III, encouraged the sculptor to work as an architect. In 1546 Paul named Michelangelo the official architect of the new St. Peter's—the basilica (or ceremonial cathedral) that is the "headquarters" of the Roman church (**479**). By the time he began work on this project he was an old man, well into his seventies and physically tired, but his creative vigor was undiminished. Michelangelo designed a majestic cross-shaped structure that now comprises the *apse* of St. Peter's (the section containing the altar) and topped it with a towering dome, which he did not live to see completed. (The building was substantially enlarged over the next hundred years; Bernini's colonnade, which we saw in Chapter 14 [**437**], was added in the 17th century.) Even at his advanced age Michelangelo did not relax his lifelong perfectionism. He studied the engineering problems of the huge building, and he mastered them. Today Michelangelo's dome stands as the symbol around the world for the Roman Catholic Church.

Although Michelangelo could be pressed into service as an architect, other 16th-century artists specialized in this field. Foremost among them was Andrea Palladio, architect of the Villa Rotonda (**480**), near Vicenza—the architect's birthplace. The Villa Rotonda, strange as it may seem to modern tastes, was planned as a country house for its owners. Like most of his contemporaries, Palladio looked to ancient Greece and Rome for inspiration, and he

**480.** Andrea Palladio. Villa Rotonda, Vicenza. Begun 1550.

apparently believed that the Roman nobility lived in houses of this sort. The villa is absolutely symmetrical all around. Its basic structure is a square, with identical Greek-style porches on each of the four sides, not unlike the entrances to Greek temples (**407**). At the very center is a round salon (the word "rotonda" refers to a round room) reaching up through the building and capped with a low dome. Palladio's architecture epitomizes the "classic" style that would send out echoes for centuries to come. Across the United States, even in small towns, you can see banks and government buildings that resemble the Villa Rotonda.

Besides Leonardo and Michelangelo, three other painters, each just a few years younger than Michelangelo, made far-reaching contributions to the art of the High Italian Renaissance. They are Giorgione, Raphael, and Titian.

The iconography of Giorgione's painting, *The Tempest* (**481**), is unknown. Even the artist's contemporaries seem not to have known what story he was depicting or to have been able to identify the nude woman nursing a child at right and the soldier (or shepherd) at left. Most likely Giorgione was making reference to some event in Greek or Latin poetry, or perhaps he was trying to evoke a classical mood. But regardless of the meaning of its subject, *The Tempest* makes an important contribution to Renaissance art in the way it is composed. Artists of earlier generations, even up to Botticelli (**474**), would compose a scene by concentrating on the figures and painting the landscape as a kind of backdrop. Giorgione, however, has started by constructing a landscape and then placing his figures in it naturally. This approach paved the way for the great landscape paintings of the centuries to follow. In *The Tempest*, as the title implies, the subject is really the approaching storm, which closes in dramatically over the city while the two foreground figures are still bathed in sunlight. Giorgione's principal interest seems to have been the contrast of bucolic foreground against the city rendered in careful perspective, with the two

above: **481.** Giorgione. *The Tempest*. c. 1505. Oil on canvas, 32¼ × 28¾″. Academy, Venice.

right: **482.** Raphael. *Pope Leo X with Two Cardinals.* c. 1518. Oil on wood, 5′⅝″ × 3′8⅞″. Uffizi, Florence.

drawn together by the violent effects of nature. The storm and the lush vegetation create a world in which nature dominates, not people, and the painting evokes a powerful, compelling mood of apprehension and anticipation.

Raphael also was capable of placing figures in a believable setting, as we saw in his brilliant fresco *The School of Athens* (**225**). But for the painting illustrated here, *Pope Leo X with Two Cardinals* (**482**), the artist has deemphasized the architectural setting and moved in close to create a true and perceptive portrait. As Julius II had been Michelangelo's great patron, Leo X was Raphael's. Leo was the son of Lorenzo de' Medici (Chapter 1, pp. 3–4), and the cardinals on either side of him are his nephews. Raphael has not flattered the Pope. The pontiff we see is seriously overweight and has a puffy face and rather coarse features. Despite its unflinching realism, the portrait conveys Leo's majesty and power, emanating not just from the office but from the man.

Even before Raphael painted the portrait of Leo X, the artist Titian, Raphael's contemporary, had declined to become the Pope's official artist. Possibly Titian hoped that a career of greater scope awaited him. If so he was not disappointed, for Titian eventually achieved an international reputation, numbering among his many royal patrons King Philip II of Spain, King Francis I of France, and, above all, the Holy Roman Emperor, Charles V.

The term "Roman" requires some explanation. In the mid-16th century the Holy Roman Empire comprised an area of Europe reaching from the borders of France at the west to Poland and Hungary in the east—roughly the size of modern-day Germany, Austria, and parts of northern Italy. Its ruler, Charles V, was not Roman at all but Austrian, and he reigned as the most powerful monarch in the West. Such was the patron that Titian secured.

After a time the Emperor refused to be painted by anyone *but* Titian. In *Charles V at Mühlberg* (**483**) the artist has created the image of a great hero—majestic yet honorable, stalwart yet kind, the defender of the Christian faith

**483.** Titian.
*Charles V at Mühlberg.* 1548.
Oil on canvas,
10'10¾" × 9'1⅞".
Prado, Madrid.

on the field of battle. We know that Charles was quite short in stature, and so the artist has cleverly bowed the horse's head, to make its rider more imposing. Unlike Raphael, Titian did not limit himself to a strict duplication of his subject's features; he probably improved a bit on nature in drawing the Emperor's face. Also, he made sure to pose Charles in splendid royal armor, on a prancing horse, isolated against a vivid sky—all of these factors designed to enhance the ruler's power.

By the time of Titian and his contemporaries, the style that can be identified as Renaissance had begun to spread outward from the Italian peninsula. When Renaissance ideals penetrated the North—Germany, Switzerland, northern France, and the Netherlands—they swept away the last vestiges of the Middle Ages.

## The Renaissance in the North

The first half of the 16th century was a time of tremendous spiritual, intellectual, and artistic upheaval in northern Europe. The Protestant Reformation was in full swing, bringing with it the establishment of new Christian denominations—Anglican, Lutheran, and Calvinist—which would split away large numbers of people from the Church of Rome. Literary and philosophical explorations emphasized the Greek and Roman classics, and gave rise to the movement known as *Humanism*. And Renaissance styles in art, which had appeared in Italy a century earlier, now sprang up in the North. All this activity can be traced in part to the new ease of communication. The printing press, developed in the mid-15th century, made possible a dramatic increase in the spread of books and artistic images. Travel throughout Europe became far more common, not just for trade, but for pleasure and study. Many Northern artists made pilgrimages to Rome and Florence to examine the work of their Italian contemporaries.

We have already seen several works by two of the greatest Northern masters, Jan van Eyck (**79**, **228**) and Albrecht Dürer (**58**, **100**, **168**, **251**, **260**). Here we turn to Hans Holbein the Younger, a German artist who was among the first of the true cosmopolitans—well-educated, well-traveled, at home in many cities. Holbein was born in Augsburg, in southern Germany, but lived for many years in Switzerland. After traveling extensively in France, Italy, and the Netherlands, he eventually settled in London, where he became court painter to King Henry VIII. It is largely through Holbein that we have a visual record of that most intriguing of monarchs (**484**). The painting shows two characteristics of the style that made Holbein one of the greatest portraitists ever. On the one hand, every aspect of the subject's appearance is rendered in careful detail, from the hairs in his beard to the textures of skin, clothing, and fur. On the other, the artist has penetrated surface appearance to give us an imposing character study. He has posed the monarch full front, so that he dominates and fills the picture space, the very image of arrogant kingship at the height of its powers. Henry confronts and overwhelms the viewer—much as he must have confronted the papacy, his own ministers in England, and, for that matter, all six of his wives.

Pieter Bruegel the Elder, an artist who worked in Antwerp and Brussels, also was well-educated and well-traveled, but his work took an opposite path from that of Holbein. Whereas Holbein concentrated on extravagant portraits of the nobility, Bruegel is best known for his animated genre scenes of the peasantry at work and play. *Peasant Wedding* (**485**) depicts the celebration, held in a barn, after the nuptials of a young couple. Just to right of center a hanging cloth, on which is suspended something like a crown, isolates the bride, who sits looking rather pleased with herself—presumably because she has made a good match. There is disagreement about which figure is the groom; some art historians identify him as the man in dark clothing leaning backward just at the center of the composition.

left: **484.** Hans Holbein the Younger.
*Henry VIII.* 1540. Panel, $32\frac{1}{2} \times 29''$.
National Gallery, Rome.

below: **485.** Pieter Bruegel the Elder.
*Peasant Wedding.* c. 1565.
Oil on panel, $3'8\frac{7}{8}'' \times 5'4''$.
Kunsthistorisches Museum, Vienna.

Bruegel employed an interesting compositional device for this painting. The table, slanting diagonally from lower right to upper left, pulls together a large number of people in conviviality but without confusion. His special genius, however, lies in painting these people as *types*—as "cheerful peasants"— yet also as individuals. If you examine each character, you begin to speculate about emotions, thoughts, reactions. The bagpiper at center left: Surely he wishes he could stop playing and eat some of the delicious food going by. The pair at far right: Are they discussing the details of the marriage contract and assessing the match? The couple immediately to the bride's left, variously identified as her parents or the groom's: They don't look especially happy. In fact, they look downright grim. Have they made a poor bargain, or are they pessimistic about the outcome of this marriage? All in all, the *Peasant Wedding* is a marvelous study in personality and in visual organization.

Once the Northern Renaissance caught up with its Italian predecessor, the North never again lagged behind. Starting with the 17th century, although there continued to be special regional styles, art developments throughout western Europe moved forward at the same pace.

## 17th-Century Europe: Post-Renaissance and Baroque Styles

The Protestant Reformation in northern Europe was extremely successful and drew large numbers of people away from the Roman Catholic Church. Deeply wounded, the church centered at Rome regrouped itself and struck back. The Catholic Counter Reformation, begun in the second half of the 16th century and continuing into the 17th, aimed at preserving the strength it still had in the southern countries, and perhaps recovering some lost ground in the North. Spain and Italy were the two major centers of the Counter Reformation, and some artists we shall look at were deeply involved in its activities.

Our first two artists in particular are associated with the Counter Reformation and can serve as a transition from the 16th century to the 17th. They are difficult to categorize, because their styles, while very different from those of the High Renaissance, do not fit either with the Baroque style we shall consider presently. Some writers have labeled their work *Mannerist*—a term that implies a dramatic use of space and light and a tendency toward elongated figures.

The first of the two artists was the Italian master Tintoretto, born in Venice. His *Last Supper* (**486**) makes an interesting comparison with Bruegel's

*Peasant Wedding.* Like Bruegel, Tintoretto has organized a large group of people by means of a table set in a sharply diagonal composition. The mood of the two paintings, however, could hardly be more different. Bruegel's atmosphere is one of light-hearted—even slightly vulgar—celebration. But Tintoretto's picture portrays a religious subject, and he has given it an intensely dramatic and mystical treatment.

The scene of the *Last Supper* takes place a few days before Christ's death and depicts the moment when Christ breaks bread and gives it to his disciples to eat—the basis for the sacrament of Holy Communion. Christ's head is brilliantly lighted, and clouds of angels waft toward him, making it clear that a supernatural event is taking place in this ordinary setting. The serving attendants, who are tied to earthly concerns, go about their business, oblivious to the spiritual drama, but Christ's disciples are very much caught up in the great mystery. Small halos of light form around all their heads to indicate their holiness—except for the head of Judas, who would soon betray Christ, and who sits alone on the opposite side of the table.

The artist most closely associated with the Catholic Counter Reformation was Domenicos Theotocopoulos, known as El Greco. We saw his *Crucifixion* in Chapter 3 (**69**). Another work from the same period, *The Vision of St. John* (**487**), depicts a scene from the biblical Book of Revelation, when all those martyred for their religion rise up and demand vengeance, and all of them are given white robes. El Greco's figures are extremely elongated; they reach upward in nervous movement like licks of flame. St. John, author of the Book of Revelation, is pictured on the left, transported in visionary rapture, the effect of which El Greco conveys by the turbulent movement of John's robe. Actually, the important point about this painting is that it *is* a vision, and is not meant to be realistic or earthly in any way. El Greco was striving to create an image that transcends this world, that provides a key to the spiritual world.

Tintoretto's and El Greco's works have some elements in common, especially in their emphasis on the spiritual, but we cannot link them with each other or with the products of other artists as constituting a particular style, as we could with the Renaissance. The last half of the 16th century and beginning of the 17th was a period of much experimentation in art, but no single coherent trend. Not until about the second decade of the 17th century can we again identify a definite style and give it a label. That label is *Baroque.*

**opposite: 486.** Tintoretto.
*The Last Supper.* 1592–94.
Oil on canvas, 12′ × 18′8″.
San Giorgio Maggiore, Venice.

**right: 487.** El Greco.
*The Vision of St. John.* c. 1610.
Oil on canvas, 7′3½″ × 6′4″.
Metropolitan Museum of Art,
New York (Rogers Fund, 1956).

# Gianlorenzo Bernini

## *1598–1680*

**G**ianlorenzo Bernini falls into a category we find fascinating in all the arts—the youthful prodigy. Born in Naples, he trained with his father, Pietro, a talented sculptor, and by the age of seventeen had received a commission from the Pope. Too late in history to be a man of the Renaissance, Bernini was nonetheless a Renaissance man—sculptor, painter, architect, stage designer, playwright, composer of music, and, by all accounts, a great wit. He lived into his eighties and displayed throughout his life enough energy and enthusiasm and inventiveness for half a dozen ordinary people.

Nearly all of Bernini's life was spent in Rome, and he outdid even his great predecessor Michelangelo in papal patronage, serving seven popes over a period of half a century. Master always of the grand design, he executed many huge projects, including the Cornaro Chapel group with *St. Teresa in Ecstasy* and the piazza and colonnade of the Vatican. Several outdoor fountains in Rome—elaborate figural sculptures—are also of his design. This last is typical of Bernini, for, grand showman that he was, he loved to incorporate such effects as light, smoke, or in this case water in his creations. Often he was called upon to plan important public events, such as state funerals or celebrations in honor of the saints.

As a sculptor, Bernini excelled at the portrait bust—the head and shoulders likeness in marble of an individual. One of the loveliest of these depicts Costanza Bonarelli, the wife of Bernini's assistant who was also Bernini's mistress. Sometime in the mid-1630s the current pope, Urban VIII, urged the artist to terminate this relationship and take a wife. So in 1639 Bernini, then forty-one years old, married a young woman half his age, Caterina Tezio. The story is told that Bernini felt compelled to give away the portrait bust of Costanza Bonarelli, which until then he had kept in his home. The artist's wife eventually bore him eleven children, nine of whom survived to maturity.

Bernini's fame as an architect and sculptor spread throughout Europe. In 1665 Louis XIV, king of France, summoned the artist to Paris to work on a new design for the Louvre palace. The trip was not a success. Bernini's plan for the Louvre was rejected, and the artist alienated his hosts by expressing his preference for Italian art and contempt for most French art. He returned to Rome, where he remained until his death.

One major work did result from Bernini's sojourn in Paris—a splendid portrait bust of Louis carved after Bernini had made numerous sketches of the king going about his daily activities. It was in Paris, too, that the artist reportedly explained the problems of portrait sculpture: "If a man whitened his hair, beard, eyebrows and—were it possible—his eyeballs and lips, and presented himself in this state to those very persons that see him every day, he would hardly be recognized by them. . . . Hence you can understand how difficult it is to make a portrait, which is all of one color, resemble the sitter."[3]

---

Gianlorenzo Bernini. *Self-Portrait.* c. 1625. Oil on canvas. Galleria Borghese, Rome.

Baroque art differs from that of the Renaissance in several important respects. Whereas Renaissance art stressed the calm of reason and enlightenment, Baroque art is full of emotion, energy, and movement. Colors are more vivid in Baroque art than in Renaissance, with greater contrast between colors and between light and dark. In architecture and sculpture, where the Renaissance sought a classic simplicity, the Baroque favored ornamentation, as rich and complex as possible. Baroque art has been called dynamic, sometimes even theatrical. This theatricality is clearly evident in the work of the Baroque's leading interpreter, the artist Gianlorenzo Bernini.

Bernini would have been a fascinating character in any age, but if ever an artist and a style were perfectly suited for one another, this was true of Bernini and the Baroque. With a taste for drama and overstatement, a flair for the grand gesture, Bernini found great success in an era that appreciated such expression (**437**). Bernini's background was in the theater, in stage and scene design; he was also an unsurpassed sculptor and architect. All these talents were brought to bear in his masterpiece, the Cornaro Chapel in the church of Santa Maria della Vittoria in Rome (**488**). The chapel itself, shown here in an 18th-century painting, is a brilliantly integrated scheme of architecture, painting, sculpture, and lighting. On the ceiling is painted a vision of heaven, with angels and billowing clouds. At either side of the chapel sit sculptured figures of the Cornaro family, donors of the chapel, in animated conversation, watching the drama before them as though from opera boxes. The whole arrangement is lighted dramatically by sunlight streaming through a concealed yellow-glass window.

The centerpiece of the chapel is Bernini's sculptured group known as *St. Teresa in Ecstasy* (**489**). Teresa was a Spanish mystic, founder of a strict order of nuns, and an important figure in the Counter Reformation. She claimed to be subject for many years to religious trances, in which she saw visions of Heaven and Hell and was visited by angels. It is in the throes of such a vision that Bernini has portrayed her. Teresa wrote:

**left: 488.** Anonymous artist.
*Cornaro Chapel,*
*Santa Maria della Vittoria, Rome.*
18th century. Oil on canvas.
Staatliches Museum, Schwerin,
East Germany.

**right: 489.** Gianlorenzo Bernini.
*St. Teresa in Ecstasy.* 1645–52.
Marble and gilt bronze, life-size.
Cornaro Chapel,
Sta. Maria della Vittoria, Rome.

Beside me, on the left hand, appeared an angel in bodily form, such as I am not in the habit of seeing except very rarely. . . . He was not tall but short, and very beautiful; and his face was so aflame that he appeared to be one of the highest rank of angels, who seem to be all on fire. . . . In his hands I saw a great golden spear, and at the iron tip there appeared to be a point of fire. This he plunged into my heart several times so that it penetrated to my entrails. When he pulled it out, I felt that he took them with it, and left me utterly consumed by the great love of God. The pain was so severe that it made me utter several moans. The sweetness caused by this intense pain is so extreme that one cannot possibly wish it to cease. . . . This is not a physical, but a spiritual pain, though the body has some share in it—even a considerable share.

Bernini shows the saint in a swoon, ready for another thrust of the angel's spear. She falls backward, yet is lifted up on a cloud, the extreme turbulence of her garments revealing her emotional frenzy. We can almost hear the moans Teresa spoke of in describing her passionate experience. The angel, wielding his spear, has an expression on his face of tenderness and love; in other contexts he might be mistaken for a Cupid. A work like *St. Teresa in Ecstasy* could never have emerged from the Renaissance. Artists of the Renaissance looked backward to the cool, restrained style of Greece in the Classical period. But the Baroque artist was far more interested in the later Hellenistic period of Greek art, typified by the *Laocoön Group* (**453**). Both in composition and in the intensity of emotion portrayed, there is a kinship between the *Laocoön* and *St. Teresa* sculptures.

The Baroque fondness for dramatic composition and lighting revealed in the Cornaro Chapel also is apparent in works by the painter Caravaggio. His magnificent *Deposition* (**490**) depicts the moment when the dead Christ has been removed from the Cross and is being prepared for burial. The body is lowered by two of Christ's followers—his disciple St. John and the Jewish ruler Nicodemus, to whom Christ had counseled that a man must be "born again" to enter Heaven. The group also includes the three Marys—Christ's mother, the Virgin Mary, at left; Mary Magdalene, center; and Mary Cleophas, at right—who look on in despair. Caravaggio's structure is a strong (though complex and twisting) diagonal leading from the upraised hand at top right down through the cluster of figures to Christ's face. The light source seems to be coming from somewhere outside the top left edge of the picture. Light falls on the participants in different ways, but always enhances the sense of drama. Mary Magdalene's face, for example, is almost totally in shadow, but a bright light illuminates her shoulder to create a contrast with the bowed head. Light also catches the pathetic outstretched hand of the Virgin. Christ's body is the only figure lit in its entirety; the others stand in partial darkness.

When one sees this painting, the most immediate impact comes from the stark dead-white of Christ's form, in contrast to the vivid garments and flesh tones of the others. The viewer's experience of this poignant scene is intensified by the fact that we observe it from "a worm's-eye view," from a position below that of the participants in the drama, who stand on a stage-like slab. Certain elements of the composition almost seem to project forward out of the painting—the corner of the slab, Christ's feet, Nicodemus' elbow. Because the deposition group breaks out of the picture plane, we are drawn into the scene, we become a part of it.

We might compare Caravaggio's *Deposition* to a work painted just a few years later, *The Raising of the Cross* (**491**) by the Flemish artist Peter Paul Rubens. Although he spent most of his life in Antwerp (in modern Belgium), Rubens had traveled to Italy and studied the works of Italian masters, including Caravaggio. There are similarities between these two paintings—in the sharply diagonal composition and dramatic lighting—but we also find several differences in the two masters' styles. Caravaggio's figures seem almost frozen in a moment of anguish, but Rubens' painting teems with movement and energy, each of the participants balanced precariously and straining at their

**below: 490.** Caravaggio. *The Deposition.* 1604.
Oil on canvas, 9'9⅛" × 6'7¾".
Pinacoteca, Vatican, Rome.

**right: 491.** Peter Paul Rubens.
*The Raising of the Cross.* 1609–10.
Oil on panel, 15'2" × 11'2". Antwerp Cathedral.

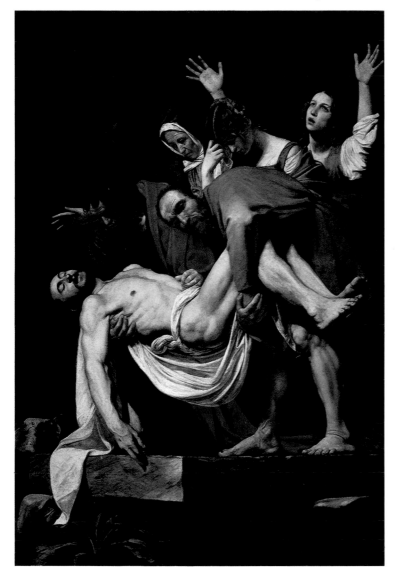

task. While the Caravaggio group projects from the picture plane, its action is contained on four sides within the frame of the canvas. Rubens' figures, in contrast, burst outside the picture in several directions, suggesting that the action continues beyond the painting. In addition, Rubens, like other Northern artists, is far more interested than Caravaggio in textural details—precise rendering of foliage, hair, the curly dog, and so on. Rubens' lifelike treatment of musculature in the bodies recalls Michelangelo's paintings on the Sistine Chapel ceiling (**39,478**), but the writhing S-curve of Christ's body is typically Baroque.

Baroque painting in mid-17th century France seems relatively subdued in contrast to the work of Southern artists of this period and even to that of Rubens. This was due to the French interest in Classical Greek and Roman art, particularly evident in the paintings of Nicolas Poussin. Poussin, born a Frenchman, spent much of his career in Rome, but he struck a different path

# Peter Paul Rubens
## 1577–1640

In all the history of art, one of the most civilized figures was the Flemish painter Peter Paul Rubens. Rubens was born in the German town of Siegen, but he returned with his mother at the age of ten to her native Antwerp (then in the Spanish-controlled Netherlands, now a city of Belgium) after the death of his father. There he was placed as a page in a wealthy home—a post that seems to have taught him the tact and courtly manners that would serve him well in the years to come. Coupled with these was an innate intelligence and pleasant disposition, all of which contributed to an enormously productive, rewarding life.

Rubens began his art studies in Antwerp. At the age of twenty-two, however, he set out for Italy, where he was to remain for eight years. During this time he traveled widely through all the major cities, studied the works of the great Italian masters, and was employed as court painter by the Duke of Mantua.

When the final illness of Rubens' mother called him home in 1608, the artist fully expected to return to Italy. But several inducements persuaded him to remain in Antwerp, which became his base for the rest of his life. For one thing, he was immediately successful as an artist and found many lucrative commissions. For another, the political and intellectual climate satisfied him. Perhaps most important, Rubens met, fell in love with, and married a young woman of Antwerp, Isabella Brant. This union lasted for seventeen years, produced three children, and was an extremely happy one. Rubens painted their wedding portrait, shown here.

In an atmosphere of domestic fulfillment, Rubens settled down to work. He became court painter to the Archduke Albert and his wife (also named Isa-

bella), who were at the time rulers of the Netherlands. Over many years he also served them as political emissary and diplomat to foreign courts, often being entrusted with the most secret of negotiations. Artistic commissions poured in from all parts of Europe. Rubens was able to fulfull them mainly because he had a well-organized studio and many assistants. For certain large works, Rubens would make preliminary drawings, assistants would execute routine parts of the canvas, and then the master would make corrections and provide finishing touches.

Rubens' personal life took a stunning blow in 1626, when his wife died suddenly. Four years later, however, the artist remarried. His second wife was Hélène Fourment, and at the time of their marriage she was sixteen, Rubens fifty-three. This marriage, too, seems to have been a most successful one and produced five children. It was cut short by the artist's death, at sixty-three, from heart failure brought on by gout.

The workshop approach perfected by Rubens occasionally got him into trouble. In 1621 he was forced to write this letter to a dissatisfied client: "I am quite willing that the picture painted for My Lord Ambassador Carleton be returned to me and that I should paint another . . . making rebate as is reasonable for the amount already paid, and the new picture to be entirely by my own hand without admixture of the work of anyone else, which on the word of a gentleman I will carry out."[4]

---

Peter Paul Rubens. *The Honeysuckle Bower (Self-Portrait with Wife)*, detail. c. 1609. Oil on canvas, 5'10½" × 4'5½". Alte Pinakothek, Munich.

from that of the Italian artists. His *Rape of the Sabine Women* (**492**) depicts a famous episode in Roman myth. Romulus, the legendary founder and first king of Rome, was concerned that the men of his city had no wives and so could not establish families. To remedy this problem, he announced a festival and invited the people from the neighboring town of Sabina to attend. Poussin shows us the climax of this event. Romulus, standing at upper left on the steps of the temple, gives a signal—opening his cloak—and each of the Roman men seizes a Sabine woman to carry off, killing the Sabine men as necessary.

Despite the violent and dramatic nature of the occasion, Poussin's treatment seems curiously restrained and reflects his admiration for classical art. Poussin based his background on what he believed to be authentic Roman architecture, and he modeled his figures after ancient Greek and Roman sculptures. The two women at left, with their arms upraised, strike us more as carefully posed statues than as terrified maidens about to be carted away into wedlock by rather brutish strangers. There is little sense of continuous action. We almost have the impression that these are actors, arranged into a living tableau with appropriate facial expressions, who will momentarily break the pose and go about their business. Poussin's art is above all rational and intellectual. He wants us to understand the dramatic import of the scene from his careful composition and ordering of the figures, not from any overt display of passion. The "classicizing" tendencies of Poussin had much influence on French artists for the next century.

To grasp fully the flavor of the Baroque in France, we should look once again at a king who for all time exemplifies the term "absolute monarch"—Louis XIV. In Chapter 3 we discussed how his portrait by Rigaud (**73**) both captured and enhanced the ideal of regal power. But in Louis's reign official portraiture was, so to speak, just the tip of the iceberg. Every aspect of the king's life and environment was calculated to present the image of divine rule. Louis's statement *"L'Etat c'est moi"* ("I am the state") was not just an expression of ego. It was the truth.

Louis ascended the throne of France in 1643, at the age of four. He assumed total control of the government in 1661 and reigned, in all, for seventy-two years. During that time he made France the artistic and literary center of Europe, as well as a political force to be reckoned with. Showing the unerring instincts of a master actor, he created an aura around his own person that bolstered the impression of divinity. Each day, for example, two ceremo-

**492.** Nicolas Poussin.
*Rape of the Sabine Women.* c. 1636–37.
Oil on canvas, 5′1″ × 6′10½″.
Metropolitan Museum of Art, New York
(Harris Brisbane Dick Fund, 1946).

nies took place. In the morning half the court would file into Louis's chambers, in full pageantry, to participate in the king's *lever*—the king's "getting up." At night the same cast of characters arrived to play ritual roles in the king's *coucher*—his "going to bed."

A life in which the simple act of climbing in and out of bed required elaborate ceremony must surely also need an appropriate setting, and Louis did not neglect this matter. He summoned Bernini from Rome to Paris to work on completion of the Louvre palace (although the final design of the building was the work of others, **425**). But Louis's real love was the Palace of Versailles, in a suburb of the capital, and it was from this remarkable structure that the power of kingship flowed forth.

In all, Versailles occupies an area of about 200 acres, including the extensive formal gardens. The palace itself (**493**), substantially rebuilt and enlarged during Louis's reign, is an immense structure, more than a quarter of a mile wide. Of the countless rooms inside, the most famous is the Hall of Mirrors, 240 feet long and lined with large reflective glasses. At the beginning of this discussion we said the Baroque style was characterized by ornamentation, dynamism, theatricality, and overstatement. What could better exemplify this style than the reign of Louis XIV and the Palace of Versailles?

The French court clearly was a model of pomp and pageantry, and the Spanish court to the south was eager to emulate that model. King Philip IV of Spain reigned for a shorter time than his French counterpart and could not begin to match Louis in either power or ability. Philip had one asset, however, that Louis never quite managed to acquire—a court painter of the first rank. That painter was one of three great geniuses of Spanish art—Diego Velázquez.

In his capacity as court painter Velázquez created his masterpiece, *Las Meninas (The Maids of Honor)* (**494**). At left we see the artist, working on a very large canvas, but we can only guess at the subject he is painting. Perhaps it is the young princess, the *infanta,* who stands regally at center surrounded by her attendants ("*las meninas*"), one of whom is a dwarf. Or perhaps Velázquez is actually painting the king and queen, whom we see reflected in a mirror on the far wall. Their participation is clear, but where are they standing? Possibly they are outside the picture, standing next to us, the observers. This ambiguity is part of the picture's fascination, as is the dual nature of the scene. Although it shows a formal occasion, the painting of an official portrait, Velázquez has given the scene a warm, "everyday" quality, almost like that of a genre painting. Some experts believe Velázquez is painting the king and queen, and the little *infanta* has just wandered in to disrupt the proceedings.

Like Caravaggio, Velázquez uses light to create drama and emphasis, but light also serves here to organize and unify a complex space. The major light source comes from outside the top right corner of the painting, falling most brilliantly on the *infanta,* leaving the others in various degrees of shadow. Another light source illuminates the mysterious figure in the open doorway at back. Velázquez may have put him there to direct attention to the reflected images of the king and queen. Light also strikes the artist's face and the mirror

**493.** Versailles Palace and gardens. 1661–88.

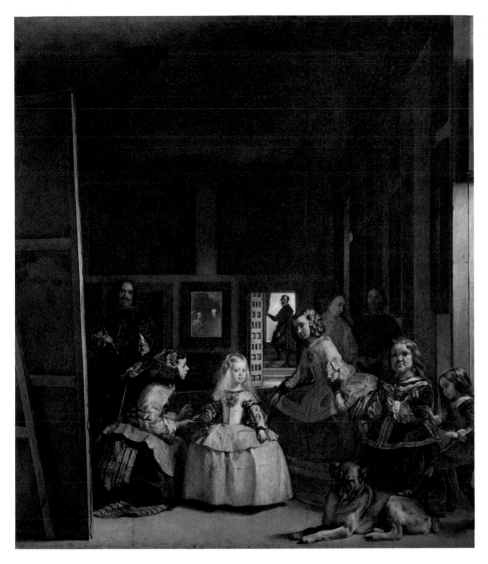

**494.** Diego Velázquez. *Las Meninas (The Maids of Honor)*. 1656. Oil on canvas, $10'5\frac{1}{4}'' \times 9'\frac{3}{4}''$. Prado, Madrid.

reflection. What could have been a very disorderly scene has been pulled together by the device of spotlighting, much as a designer of stage lighting would control what the audience sees. The theatricality of the Baroque is more subtle in Velázquez than in Bernini, but it is no less skillful.

To end this discussion of 17th-century art, we move north, to the Netherlands. The Dutch Baroque, sometimes called the "bourgeois Baroque," is quite different from Baroque movements in France, Spain, and Italy. In the North, Protestantism was the dominant religion, and the outward symbols of faith—imagery, ornate churches, and clerical pageantry—were far less important. Dutch society, and particularly the wealthy merchant class, centered not on the church but instead on the home and family, the land and the community. We see this focus in the work of two great Dutch artists with very different styles—Rembrandt and Jacob van Ruisdael.

In this book we have already considered several works by Rembrandt (**204,234,264**, p. 186). He was master of so many media that we return to him again and again in discussions of art. For most people, though, Rembrandt's special appeal lies in his portraits, and especially his self-portraits. He did more of these than practically any other artist. Through them we trace not only his maturation as a painter but his path through life as a human being—from rather humble beginnings to a period of great prosperity and happiness to the disappointments of his later life (p. 186).

The portrait shown here (**495**) represents a high point in the artist's life and is among the most charming of his self-explorations. Rembrandt portrays himself and his first wife, Saskia van Uijlenburgh, as an elegant and worldly young Amsterdam couple. Both are dressed in fine clothing (Rembrandt in the guise of a cavalier); they are surrounded by splendid material possessions, and the artist lifts his wine glass high as though to say, "This is the good life!" And so it was for an artist of Rembrandt's incomparable talents.

The 17th century was the great age of landscape painting in the Netherlands. Of course, Rembrandt drew and painted many landscapes (**204**), but his style in this area as in every other was a personal one. More typical of the Dutch landscape painting was the work of Jacob van Ruisdael. Van Ruisdael's *Extensive Landscape with a View of the Town of Ootmarsum* (**496**) shows not only

**above: 495.** Rembrandt. *Self-Portrait with Saskia.* c. 1634. Oil on canvas, 5'3½" × 4'3½". Gemäldegalerie, Dresden.

**left: 496.** Jacob van Ruisdael. *Extensive Landscape with a View of the Town of Ootmarsum.* 1660s. Oil on canvas, 23¼ × 28⅞". Alte Pinakothek, Munich.

**opposite: 497.** Antoine Watteau. *Gersaint's Signboard.* 1720–21. Oil on canvas, 5'3⅞" × 10'1". Staatliche Museen, West Berlin.

the famed flatness of the Dutch landscape, but also the artist's reaction to that flatness as an expression of the immense, limitless grandeur of nature. The artist makes a contrast between the land—where human order has been established in the form of buildings and cultivation—and the sky, with its billowing clouds, yielding to the wind, which mere people can never tame. The horizon line is set quite low, and, significantly, only the church steeple rises up in silhouette against the sky, perhaps symbolizing that humankind's one connection with the majesty of nature is through the church.

Despite this emphasis on the church building, Van Ruisdael's art is essentially secular, as is that of Velázquez and Rembrandt. Although religious subjects continued to appear in art—and do so even now—never again would religious art dominate as it did in the Renaissance and Italian Baroque periods. No doubt this is largely because of the change in sponsorship; popes and cardinals became less important as patrons, while kings, wealthy merchants, and the bourgeoisie became more so. We can follow this increasing secularization of art as we move out of the 17th century into the 18th.

# The 18th Century

The first half to three-quarters of the 18th century is often thought of as the age of *Rococo*—a development and extension of the Baroque style. The term "rococo" was a play on the word "baroque," but it also refers to the French words for "rocks" and "shells," forms that appeared as decorative motifs in architecture, furniture, and occasionally in painting. Like the Baroque, Rococo is an extravagant, ornate style, but there are several points of contrast. Baroque, especially in the South, was an art of cathedrals and palaces; Rococo is more intimate, suitable for the aristocratic home and the drawing room (although there are a number of very grand Rococo buildings). Baroque colors are intense; Rococo leans more toward the gentle pastels. Baroque is large in scale, massive, dramatic; Rococo has a smaller scale and a light-hearted, playful quality. And, as suggested earlier, the Baroque—at least in its origins—was a religious art; Rococo is far more secular and, in its extreme forms, charmingly romantic, more than a little erotic.

The art of Antoine Watteau is typical of the carefree, aristocratic impulse of the Rococo. In *Gersaint's Signboard* (**497**) Watteau gives us a picture of fashionable French society out for a day of shopping—shopping for pictures to decorate the opulent home. All is elegance, verging on the pretentious—the men in their powdered wigs, the women in their silks, everyone maintaining a pose of bored nonchalance. At right the gallery owner, Gersaint, displays a painting to prospective customers, while the adjacent group seem more taken with the charms of a lap dog. At left, paintings are being crated, presumably for shipment to purchasers. Watteau celebrates in painting a class of people whose most serious concern was maintaining a chic life style.

Somewhat outside this predominant trend toward aristocratic art was another French artist, younger by about fifteen years than Watteau, the painter Jean Baptiste Siméon Chardin. Chardin specialized in the still life (**156**) and the middle-class genre scene. His works have a quiet, meditative appeal and show ordinary people in ordinary activities. Pictures of children at play, as in *The House of Cards* (**498**), were a favorite theme. Here the boy, dressed in the very proper middle-class attire of the day, is caught up in the concentration of building his card house. There is a tension between his still pose and the precarious balance of the cards. Like the card house, Chardin's picture is perfectly but precariously balanced. The boy leans into his project, and Chardin's masterfully calculated light strikes three areas—the face, the upright cards, and the half-open drawer—to create a tight triangle of interest (**499**). The fact that this triangle is balanced on one of its points adds subtly to the tension of the moment.

Two painters in particular, also French, have become almost synonymous with the Rococo. To admirers their art is sumptuous and delightful; to detractors it is frivolous and decadent. The first is Jean-Honoré Fragonard, whose work we saw in Chapter 4 (**130**). The other is François Boucher. In Boucher's paintings all the people are pretty. The women are frequently nude and, if so, are very pink and voluptuous. (Fragonard's women are more often clothed but equally pink.) If the women are dressed, they are stunningly dressed. Everybody is in love.

Boucher's art suited perfectly the ideals of the French court presided over by Louis XV, great-grandson of the builder of Versailles. Form without substance, beauty without character, extravagance with little regard for paying the bills—such was the reign of Louis XV, and so it was chronicled by Boucher. In 1759 Boucher painted the *Marquise de Pompadour* (**500**), Louis's mistress and influential advisor. How beautiful she looks, how romantic—posed languidly in her lace-frilled dress, resting lightly against a classical statue. Boucher flattered her physically (she was a good deal fatter and less gifted with

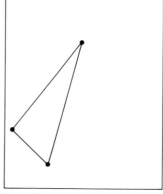

**left: 498.**
Jean Baptiste Siméon Chardin.
*The House of Cards.* c. 1741.
Oil on canvas, 32⅜ × 26″.
National Gallery of Art,
Washington, D.C.
(Andrew W. Mellon Collection, 1937).

**above: 499.** Line analysis
of Chardin's *The House of Cards.*

392

**500.** François Boucher.
*Marquise de Pompadour.* 1759.
Oil on canvas, $35\frac{7}{8} \times 27\frac{1}{4}''$.
Wallace Collection, London.

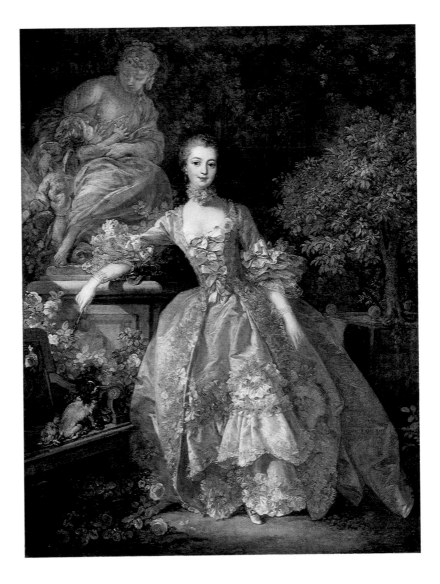

regular features), and he failed to record the steely political brain that lurked behind the soft face. During the reign of Louis XV, the government of France was on the brink of collapse. The king himself is reputed to have said, *"Après moi, le déluge"* ("After me, the flood"). But for a little while—with Louis XV on the throne, the Marquise de Pompadour at his side, and Boucher at his easel—appearances were kept up.

The lower classes did not participate in this world. They could not afford to wear lace-frilled dresses and had no time to be charmingly in love. Many, in fact, were on the brink of starvation. Louis—if he really said it—was right. The flood was coming, and a mere thirty years after Boucher painted his so-lovely portrait of the Marquise de Pompadour, France was engulfed.

## Revolution

Repeatedly in this book we have pointed out that art responds to the culture from which it emerges. To get a sense of how dramatic was the revolution that shook France in 1789 (and had implications for much of western civilization), we might compare Boucher's painting with a work done in France less than three decades later. In 1787, two years before the onset of the French Revolution, Jacques Louis David painted *The Death of Socrates* (**501**). Here there is nothing pretty, charming, or romantic. Instead, the mood is somber and

**501.** Jacques Louis David. *The Death of Socrates.* 1787. Oil on canvas, 4'3" × 6'5". Metropolitan Museum of Art, New York (Wolfe Fund, 1931; Catharine Lorillard Wolfe Collection).

speaks of a world in which the good and noble of character (David meant the French lower classes) were sacrificed to satisfy the vanities of the weak in character (the French upper classes). David has skillfully drawn a parallel between the sacrifice of the downtrodden French and the sacrifice of the ancient Greek philosopher Socrates. In the picture we see Socrates as he prepares to die for his ideals. A teacher as well as a philosopher, Socrates was regarded with suspicion by the Athenian state and eventually was convicted by trial of "corrupting the morals of the young" with radical ideas. His sentence was death by poison, and in David's picture he reaches for the cup of hemlock that will kill him, while his followers look away in grief.

The French Revolution was built on goals like those David attributed to Socrates—liberty, equality, fraternity, and participation by all levels of society in the government and economy of France. In practice, however, the noble ideals of the revolution soon disintegrated into wholesale slaughter of aristocrats (including the king and his family) and, in time, of anyone who disagreed with those momentarily in power. Art such as David's projected the *image* the leaders of the revolution wished to have of themselves, just as Boucher's art had projected the image desired by the French monarchs.

Two other revolutions occurred at more or less the same time as that in France. The first was the American Revolution, preceding the French by thirteen years, in which a small group of colonies in an untamed land broke free of England to create what is now the United States. The other was the Industrial Revolution—not a political uprising but an economic and social upheaval. The Industrial Revolution began slowly in the last half of the 18th century and, many would argue, in still going on.

It is difficult to overestimate the impact—social, economic, and ultimately political—of the change from labor done by hand to labor done by machine. Within the space of a few decades the machine drastically altered a way of life that had prevailed for millennia. People who had formerly worked in their homes or on farms suddenly were herded together in factories, creating a new social class—the industrial worker. Fortunes were made virtually overnight by members of another new class—the manufacturers. Naturally, all this upheaval was reflected in art. At the beginning of the 19th century, then, western civilization faced a totally new world.

# 17

# The Modern World

A chapter covering the art of the 19th and 20th centuries presents certain difficulties, not the least of which is its title. Many writers designate the art of this period as "modern," a term that means "characteristic of the present or the recent past," and so we have chosen to call it. However, this poses a problem: When did "modern" start? There are those who would say that truly modern art did not exist until the Impressionists in the 1860s, or until the period just before World War I, or even until the late 1940s. Moreover, we must remember that people in other periods of history undoubtedly thought of their own art as "modern," and perhaps even called it that.

If modern refers to the present and the recent past, we are faced with another puzzle: When does "modern" stop? In other words, what do we call everything that follows the present? Some writers, obviously at a loss for new labels, have coined the terms "post-modern" and "anti-modern," but these are awkward at best. Very likely the period we call "modern" will be given an entirely different name by future generations.

Whatever we call it, we cannot ignore the fact that the art produced during the 19th and 20th centuries offers a variety of expression unprecedented in the history of art. If you flip through the chapter quickly, you will see an amazing range of styles—works so diverse they seem to have little in common with one another. Our discussion begins with a portrait of a woman, to our eyes not markedly different from paintings of the previous four hundred years. It ends with a work *by* a woman in which there is no tangible substance at all, nothing to hang on the wall or place on a pedestal. No wonder many people find "modern" art bewildering!

Despite the dizzying variety and complexity of modern styles, we have one great advantage in approaching the art of this period. We live now. About three-quarters of the art we shall consider in this chapter was made during the lifetimes of people still alive today. While we can have only limited success in getting "inside" the minds of Michelangelo or Rembrandt—or those of the

**502.** Jean Auguste Dominique Ingres. *La Grande Odalisque.* 1814. Oil on canvas, 2'11¼" × 5'3¾". Louvre, Paris.

audiences for whom they worked—we inhabit the same world as contemporary artists and, as a result, often share their sensibility. It is not inconceivable that you could meet and talk with several of the artists whose work is illustrated here, could question them about their inspirations, their goals, their reasons for working the way they do. Throughout this text it has been stressed that art is a product of the culture that produces it. In this chapter, then, and especially in the latter part of the chapter, we come to *our* art, the art of our own culture. We see works made by artists who have walked the same streets we have, watched the same television programs, felt the same tides of history washing over us. If we take the trouble to look and study, we may find that this is the art with which we feel the closest connection.

To get to the art of the present we begin at the turn of the 19th century, when the seeds of most modern art movements were sown. The center of Western art was France, and so it remained (with a few digressions) until the onset of World War I.

## France, Early 19th Century: Neoclassicism, Romanticism, Realism

As we have seen in earlier chapters, most periods in the history of art had one dominant style—the High Renaissance style or the Baroque style, for instance—that major artists of the time followed. But French art of the early 19th century is not like that. It is customarily divided into three broad categories: classic, romantic, and realist. The fact that artists of the first rank were working in each of these styles gives a hint of the great diversity that was soon to come.

Representing the classic style—or, as it is usually called, *Neoclassical* ("new classical")—was the work of Jean Auguste Dominique Ingres; we saw one of his drawings in Chapter 7 (**198**). Ingres was a pupil of Jacques Louis David (**501**), and he inherited his master's preference for sharp outline, reserved emotions, and studied (often geometric) composition—all characteristics of the Neoclassical style. We see these qualities in *La Grande Odalisque* (**502**). "Odalisque" is a French word derived from the Turkish, meaning a concubine in a harem. It is typical of Ingres that, in portraying the nude figure, he placed it in an exotic situation. (The nude was acceptable to contemporary standards of morality only when separated from everyday life.) This nude, while unquestionably sensual, seems also rather distant and aloof. In Classical Greek art (**452**) and in much art of the High Renaissance (**476**) a cool detachment was deemed ideal. The Neoclassical style followed this trend. Ingres has outlined this figure very clearly, isolating it from its background, and the composition is perfectly balanced—the drape at right offsetting the raised torso on the left. Although a classicist, Ingres was capable of certain romantic touches. Here the figure of the odalisque has been considerably adjusted in its proportions. The long curving spine gives the figure an unearthly elegance, and the graceful arm that connects the two halves of the composition surely outreaches that of any human female.

Ingres's lifelong rival was Eugène Delacroix, champion of the Romantic movement. We can get as clear a picture of the differences between the two men by comparing their drawings (**198,111**) as we can in a comparison of the paintings shown here. The Romantic ideal stressed intense colors, turbulent emotions, and complex composition, all of which are evident in Delacroix's masterpiece, *Liberty Leading the People* (**503**). In 1830 France was rocked by a brief uprising of the people, an aftershock of the French Revolution forty years earlier. Although not personally involved, Delacroix chose to depict an imaginary moment in this uprising as a statement of sympathy with the democratic ideals of the Revolution. Prominent in the composition is the figure of a woman, symbolizing Liberty and France—powerful, striding across the barricades, holding aloft the tricolor flag of France. Participants in the uprising stream behind her, following her lead—the artist does not tell us where, but presumably to the abstract goal of Freedom.

If we compare this passionate scene to the polished perfection of Ingres, the differences are obvious. Ingres's figure is motionless, languid; Delacroix's composition seethes with energy and violence. Ingres's *Odalisque* is beautifully contained within the frame of the picture, whereas Delacroix's figures march-

**503.** Eugène Delacroix.
*Liberty Leading the People, 1830.*
1830. Oil on canvas,
8'6" × 10'10".
Louvre, Paris.

# Edouard Manet
## *1832–1883*

Edouard Manet was a gentleman. That old-fashioned word aptly describes one of the most civilized, elegant figures in the history of art. Unfortunately for Manet, through most of his career he was also a gentleman scorned. Few artists have had to endure as much public derision and abuse as Manet did, and few have been as poorly equipped to tolerate abuse as he. To the end of his life he sought popular success for his art, but always it eluded him.

Manet was born in Paris of well-to-do parents. At first he contemplated a naval career, but after two unsuccessful attempts to gain admittance to the naval academy, he turned to painting. He studied at the Ecole des Beaux-Arts and also in the studio of the painter Thomas Couture, but the major influences on his work were Dutch and Spanish art, particularly the paintings of the great Spanish artist Diego Velázquez. In 1859, when he was just twenty-seven, Manet submitted work to the Salon, the annual government-sponsored art exhibition. This submission was rejected, but two years later Manet placed two paintings in the Salon, one of them a portrait of his parents. Then in 1863 came the great scandal of *Le Déjeuner sur l'herbe*, which was rejected by the Salon, hung in the Salon des Refusés, called "immodest" by the French Emperor, and heaped with abuse by critics and the public alike. Nevertheless, Manet continued to send paintings to the Salon each year, considering it the only true "field of battle" for an artist.

Surprisingly little is known about Manet's private life. He married Suzanne Leenhoff, who had been his piano teacher, in 1863. Though he earned little money from his art, his private means were suf-ficient to enable him to live comfortably. From time to time he traveled in Europe, but he always returned quickly to Paris, his spiritual as well as actual home. Manet was the quintessential Parisian. The well-dressed, well-mannered, well-spoken artist played an important role in intellectual society of the time. His closest friends were the writer/journalist Emile Zola and the poet Charles Baudelaire. Although he never exhibited with the Impressionist painters—most of whom were younger than he—Manet was considered by the Impressionists to be their natural leader.

Sometime in the early 1880s Manet was struck by a serious illness, the exact nature of which is unknown. This illness resulted in the amputation of a gangrenous leg, and ultimately in his death at the age of fifty-one. As has happened with so many artists, recognition came to Manet just a bit too late. Seven years after his death, his painting *Olympia* was accepted by the Louvre.

Manet never got over his surprise at the public's contempt for his art, nor his bitterness about the rejection. In 1878 he wrote to Edgar Degas: "If there were no rewards, I wouldn't invent them: but they exist. And one should have everything that singles one out . . . when possible. It is another weapon. In this beastly life of ours, which is wholly struggle, one is never too well armed. I haven't been decorated? But it is not my fault, and I assure you that I shall be if I can and that I shall do everything necessary to that end."[1]

Henri Fantin-Latour. *Edouard Manet.* 1867. Oil on canvas, $46 \times 35\frac{1}{2}''$. Art Institute of Chicago (Stickney Fund).

ing toward us in a diagonal movement seem about to burst out of the composition, giving the impression of one frame in a continuous drama. Ingres's outlines are clear and refined; Delacroix's free brushstrokes give us a sense of blurred motion, of flickering light and confusion. Yet, in spite of its dynamism, Delacroix's composition is every bit as carefully composed as that of Ingres. The composition is stable, based on a triangle, with the apex in the hand and flag of Liberty, and the two sides moving down through the upraised rifle at left, the boy's arm and pistol at right. In their concern for the structure of painting Ingres and Delacroix were not as far apart as they appeared, but—because of the bitterness of their rivalry—neither would have admitted it.

The Realist movement in French art came somewhat later than Neoclassicism and Romanticism and was, in effect, a reaction against both. Realist artists sought to depict the everyday and the ordinary (**3,268**), rather than the heroic or the exotic. Their concerns were very much rooted in the present. One of the leaders of the Realist movement was Gustave Courbet, who in 1855 exhibited a huge painting, *The Artist's Studio* (**504**), subtitled *A Real Allegory Summing Up Seven Years of My Life as an Artist.* To this day, more than a century later, art historians debate the meaning of the "allegory," or symbolic story.

At the center of the canvas sits Courbet himself, at work on a landscape painting. Although a great many people crowd into the studio, the artist seems aloof from them, as though his aesthetic concerns are all-consuming. A little boy (usually identified as Innocence) gawks up at the work in progress. Behind the artist stands a nude model, whom some consider to be his Muse, or inspiration, others the personification of Truth (that is, the "naked truth"). All the figures to the left of the composition are common people; they are "types," not individuals, derived from Courbet's origins in a rural village. At right are the artist's "intellectual" friends, many of them identifiable figures—his patrons, other artists, writers, and so on. Perhaps Courbet is saying the artist represents a special elite, fed by his origins and by his comrades, but apart from them, alone with Innocence and Truth. We know from Courbet's work as a whole that here the artist was trying to make a particular point—that everyday activities, such as an artist working at his easel or peasants toiling in the fields, were fit subject matter for grand-scale art. In an age when only paintings of religious or historical or mythological scenes were considered "great art," this was indeed a revolutionary idea.

Each of the three paintings we have considered so far in this chapter has included a nude or semi-nude woman. Why are the women unclothed? Their

**504.** Gustave Courbet. *The Artist's Studio: A Real Allegory Summing Up Seven Years of My Life as an Artist.* 1855. Oil on canvas, 11′9¾″ × 19′6⅝″. Louvre, Paris.

nudity has a specific, accepted purpose—the exotic (Ingres's odalisque is a harem woman); the heroic (Delacroix's Liberty is bare-breasted as a mythical Amazon); the allegorical (Courbet's model may be the nude figure of Truth). These conventions satisfied contemporary tastes. But eight years after Courbet exhibited *The Artist's Studio*, a painting was placed on display in Paris that portrayed female nudity without any apparent justification at all. It caused a terrific scandal—the first of many artistic scandals that would shock the art world in the decades to come. The artist responsible for this earthquake was a mild, conventional, well-to-do gentleman: Edouard Manet.

## France, Late 19th Century: Impressionism and Post-Impressionism

In 19th-century France the mark of an artist's success was acceptance at the annual "Salon," a state-sponsored exhibition of paintings. Artists submitted their work for consideration by an official jury, whose members varied from year to year but tended to be conservative, if not downright stodgy. Art critic John Russell has described an ideal Salon painting of the period as containing the following ingredients:

> . . . a knight in armor, a group of cardinals, some tropical vegetation, some counterfeit stained glass, a medieval feast with every dish and goblet shown in meticulous detail, a distant view of Constantinople through a window in the background, and in the foreground, three or four naked women, dancing.[2]

Russell wrote this description with tongue in cheek, but there can be no doubt the Salon pictures followed a predictable formula.

In 1863 the Salon jury rejected four thousand of the submitted paintings, which caused such an uproar among the spurned artists and their supporters that a second official exhibition was mounted—the "Salon des Refusés" (showing of those who had been refused). Among the artists who were refused were Whistler and Cézanne. Among the works in the "refused" show—and soon the most notorious among them—was Edouard Manet's painting, *Le Déjeuner sur l'herbe* (**505**).

*Luncheon on the Grass*, as it is usually translated, shows a kind of outdoor picnic. Two men, dressed in the fashions of the day, relax and chat in a woodland setting. Their companion is a woman who has, for no apparent reason, taken off all her clothes. In the background another woman, wearing only a filmy garment, bathes in a pool. With this one painting Manet had broken several "rules" held dear by French artists and art-lovers alike, and it would be difficult to decide which transgression shocked the viewing public most.

The nude woman is not a goddess, not a harem slave, not an allegorical figure. Then why is she naked, and why sitting nonchalantly with two men who are clothed? Why does she gaze out at the viewer so calmly and matter-of-factly? Nudity in some classical guise was quite acceptable to Manet's audience, but nudity for its own sake was not. With the wisdom of hindsight we can now understand that Manet regarded the nude figure as a study in painted form, an exercise to display his newfound insights into light and shape. His contemporaries had no such understanding. To make matters worse, Manet had "borrowed" certain compositional elements from well-known masterpieces of the past—not at all an unusual practice among artists, but considered presumptuous in the hands of such a "bad" painter as Manet.

Bad, indeed, his technical skills must have seemed to the Salon jurors, for Manet was breaking new ground in the way he interpreted forms on canvas. The artist simplified round, three-dimensional shapes into a series of flat planes. He took a fresh look at the way light strikes a subject, concentrating on brilliant highlights and deep shadow, all but eliminating the middle transitional tones. The whole image seems to have been caught in an instantaneous flash of brilliant light.

**505.** Edouard Manet.
*Le Déjeuner sur l'herbe.* 1863.
Oil on canvas, 7′ × 8′10″.
Louvre, Paris.

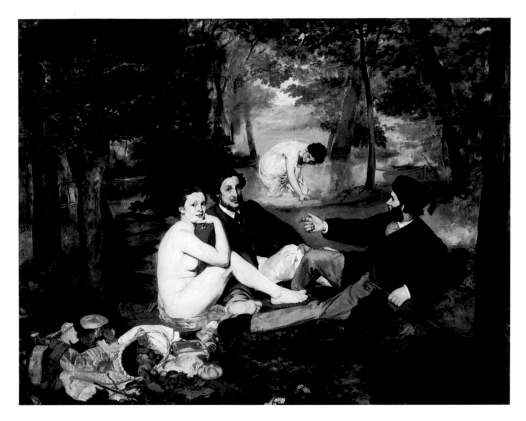

Today's viewer sees *Le Déjeuner sur l'herbe* as one of the first steps toward concerns that would dominate 20th-century art, especially in the use of light and shadow and in the deemphasis of absolute naturalism. Manet's contemporaries, on the whole, thought him just a clumsy painter. Poor Manet was subjected to a storm of outrage and scorn from critics and the art-viewing public alike. We may find it ironic, therefore, that little over a hundred years later, when a major Manet exhibition was organized in Paris and then moved to the United States, *Le Déjeuner sur l'herbe* was not included in the traveling show. It is considered priceless—and far too precious to leave France.

In the years following Manet's sensation in the Salon des Refusés, young French artists increasingly sought alternatives to the Salon. One group in particular looked to Manet as their philosophical leader, although he never consented to exhibit with them. The group was formed in 1874 and staged private showings each year until 1886. Because of the diversity of their techniques, the artists had difficulty finding a name for their association. Then a critic, after seeing a painting by Claude Monet (a member of the group) entitled *Impression: Sunrise,* scornfully dubbed the artists "impressionists." Rather than taking offense, the group happily adopted the name, and their work was known thereafter as *Impressionism.*

As was mentioned in Chapter 7 (pp. 184–185), Impressionism sought to capture the fleeting moment, the transitory effects of light. We see this in the work of Pierre Auguste Renoir, whose lovely painting of Monet in his garden is on the cover of this book. It is also evident in canvases *by* Monet, the artist who perhaps best typifies the Impressionist style. (Despite the similarity of their names, Manet and Monet were not related.) Monet was far less interested in depicting the solidity of natural forms than in showing how forms look to the eye, how light affects our perception of color and shape. He preferred to work outdoors, in daylight, and labored diligently to record on canvas the exact "impression" created by light striking a surface. Best known of Monet's paintings—and those showing the most developed Impressionist style—were the canvases of the water garden he built outside his home, the famous "water lilies" series (**506**). Although we can identify trees, reeds, a bridge, the floating lily pads, our overall impression is of shimmering light and color, the sparkling effect produced by sunlight reflecting off the water. Monet's technique of combining many small, vivid brush strokes of pure color gives the painting a dazzling brilliance.

Another artist associated with the Impressionist group, and one firmly dedicated to its goals, was Berthe Morisot. Morisot had an early success in the Salon and exhibited in this "establishment" forum several years running, but after she took up with the Impressionists she refused ever again to submit

**left: 506.** Claude Monet.
*Pool of Waterlilies.* 1900.
Oil on canvas, $35\frac{3}{8} \times 39\frac{3}{4}''$.
Art Institute of Chicago
(Mr. and Mrs. Lewis Larned Coburn
Memorial Collection).

**below: 507.** Berthe Morisot.
*La Lecture.* 1888.
Oil on canvas, $29\frac{1}{4} \times 36\frac{1}{2}''$.
Museum of Fine Arts,
St. Petersburg, Fla.

**508.** Edgar Degas. *The Tub.* 1886. Pastel, $23\frac{1}{2} \times 32\frac{1}{8}''$. Louvre, Paris.

work to the Salon. Like Monet's, Morisot's paintings are suffused with light; they sparkle with the immediacy of the quick glimpse. Morisot, however, was not so committed as Monet to painting outdoors. Often she posed her figures in a charming room or on a balcony, as in *La Lecture* (**507**). Her brushwork is somewhat freer than Monet's, and is sometimes described as "nervous," with its long flamelike flicks of color. But according to Edgar Degas, an artist whose praise was highly valued by his colleagues and followers, Morisot's airy style "conceals the purest draftsmanship."

Degas was well-equipped to comment on Morisot's draftsmanship, being the finest, most sure-handed draftsman of the Impressionist group. Considering his great interest in line, some critics question whether he can be called an Impressionist at all. Yet Degas's concerns were similar to those of Monet and Renoir and Morisot—to record the fleeting moment, to capture on canvas an instantaneous perception of the eye. As we have noted in other chapters, Degas was absorbed by the unusual angle of sight, the "peephole" view of a scene, and his composition was strongly influenced by the complex spatial relationships in Japanese prints (**137**). *The Tub* (**508**), a work of the mid-1880s, shows the artist in masterful control of these effects. We see a nude at her bath, viewed from above. We glimpse her as though we are quickly looking in a window while passing by. She is crouched rather awkwardly, pushing back her hair, her body almost filling the left side of the canvas. On the right is a table or shelf that increases the picture's spatial ambiguity. We assume that it is above the figure, but the space is so compressed that the left and right sections might be in the same plane. These spatial relations appear to be haphazard, but actually they reflect a meticulously planned composition. To appreciate the originality of Degas's conception, we might speculate how Ingres or Delacroix might have posed a nude bathing, barely half a century earlier.

The Impressionists profoundly influenced the major artists who followed them, especially in the lightness and brightness of colors. However, the work of the members of this next generation is so diverse in so many respects that no one stylistic label seems to fit all of them, and they generally are known as

# Paul Gauguin

*1848–1903*

When Gauguin set sail from France in 1891, headed for the remote island of Tahiti in the South Pacific, he wrote a new chapter in the legend of the romantic, bohemian artist. To this day the legend persists. Many people want an artist to be—and Gauguin himself perhaps wanted to be—a dramatic, tormented soul who turns away from the comforts of modern civilization, who is not subject to society's conventions, who thrives in an exotic climate.

Paul Gauguin's origins gave but little hint of what was to come. Born in Paris, he spent part of his childhood in Peru, then returned with his family to France. After a six-year stint in the merchant marine, he settled down and established himself as a stockbroker in Paris. When his career prospered, he married a young Danish woman, Mette Gad, who eventually bore him five children. Sometime in this period he took up painting as a hobby.

Over the years this hobby gradually came to be an obsession. In 1883, when he was thirty-five, Gauguin suddenly announced to his wife that he intended to quit his job and become a full-time painter. His attempts to support himself in this profession were not rewarding; eventually, Gauguin's wife rejoined her family in Denmark, taking the children, and the couple never lived together again. In 1886 Gauguin made the first of three visits to Brittany, the westernmost province of France. By this time he had already begun to establish his style of painting in broad shapes and flat color areas. A year later the artist journeyed to the island of Martinique, in the Caribbean, where the lush tropical colors heightened his palette even further. Late in 1888 Gauguin paid a brief—and disastrously unpleasant—visit to Van Gogh in the south of France. Finally, disillusioned with Western society and its values, Gauguin departed for Tahiti.

In Tahiti, Gauguin "went native." He lived in a grass hut and took as his *vahine*, or woman, a thirteen-year-old Tahitian girl, who gave birth to his son. At first all seemed idyllic, but even in the tropics one could not live for free, and Gauguin's finances were tight. He returned to Paris in 1893, hoping to sell his paintings and raise money, but the trip was not a success. Two years later Gauguin again set sail for Tahiti—never to return home.

During the second Tahitian period, Gauguin's fortunes went from bad to ghastly. He was wracked by a severe case of syphilis, suffered from a broken ankle that would not heal, and was desperately poor. At lowest ebb he attempted suicide, but the arsenic he swallowed was vomited up, causing him great agony. In 1901 he made his final voyage, to the Marquesas Islands, where—after a series of strokes—he died, penniless and completely alone. Three years after his death a memorial exhibition of Gauguin's work was organized in Paris. The show was a triumph. Gauguin was at last recognized as one of the great artists of his time.

Through all his ordeals, Gauguin seems to have considered the sacrifice worth it—necessary to achieve the vision he sought in art. As he wrote to his wife, "I am a great artist. . . . I am a great artist and know it. It is because of what I am that I have endured so many sufferings so as to pursue my vocation, otherwise I would consider myself a rogue."[3]

Paul Gauguin. *Les Miserables (Self-Portrait)*. 1888. Oil on canvas, 28 × 35".
National Museum Vincent van Gogh, Amsterdam.

the *Post-Impressionists.* They include Vincent van Gogh, Paul Cézanne, Paul Gauguin, and Georges Seurat (**128,129,202**).

We have already seen several paintings by Van Gogh in this book (**21,22,53,190,205,** p. 16). His style is characterized by intense, high-key colors; loose brushwork often with a heavy impasto; a swirling, agitated composition; and a subject matter emphasizing those things closest to him—the landscapes he inhabited, buildings in which he dwelled, his friends, himself. Among his best-known paintings—almost a self-portrait in itself—is *The Artist's Room at Arles* (**509**). The narrow little room, bare except for the bed, two straight chairs, a small table, and (significantly) several paintings on the wall, speaks eloquently of a lonely artist dedicated to his work. The composition is an unusual one. Nearly half the canvas is devoted to bare floor and the blank footboard of the bed. All the main items of interest—Van Gogh's toilet articles on the table, his clothes on a peg, his looking glass, the pillows on his bed, and above all his paintings—are clustered (we might even say crammed) into the top half of the composition. The artist might be showing us that he lived in a tiny, compressed world—the world of his mind, his body, and his extraordinary art.

Paul Cézanne took a different approach in building on the work of the Impressionists. His search was for a solidity and a geometric order in the visual world, and he explored this problem in landscapes (**85**), in figural compositions (**96**), in still lifes, even in portraits (p. 78). A solitary and uncommunicative figure nearly all his life, Cézanne had enormous influence on artists of succeeding generations.

Paul Gauguin worked in the Impressionist style early in his career, but he soon became dissatisfied. Like his contemporaries Van Gogh and Cézanne, he felt the need for more substance, more solidity of form than could be found in optical perceptions of light. Beyond this, Gauguin was interested in expressing a spiritual meaning in his art. All these he sought on the sun-drenched islands of the South Pacific. Gauguin's paintings made in Tahiti have brilliant high-keyed colors, thus revealing his debt to the Impressionists. But to this color effect he has added his own innovations: flattened forms and broad color areas, a strong outline, a taste for the exotic, an aura of mystery, and an interest in the primitive.

**509.** Vincent van Gogh. *The Artist's Room at Arles.* 1888–89. Oil on canvas, 29 × 36". Art Institute of Chicago (Helen Birch Bartlett Memorial Collection).

*Nafea Faaipoipo (When Are You to be Married?)* (**510**) was painted soon after the beginning of Gauguin's first long stay in Tahiti, and it shows all these characteristics. The figures of the two young women are so flat that we feel we could cut around them like paper dolls and simply pull them out of the painting. Strong outlines define them; this is especially apparent in the skirt and face of the woman at left. The landscape is rendered in broad, flat color areas receding backward: green grass of the foreground, a large yellow middle ground, deep blue shadow under the trees, purple mountain in the background. We know that the women of Tahiti, especially the young girls, were slender and lithe. Gauguin has given them a heavy, monumental solidity in keeping with his interest in broad form, and perhaps also because it fulfilled his fantasies about what a "noble savage" ought to look like. Mystery and magic are conveyed by the stylized gesture of the woman at right and the secretive expressions of both women. Perhaps the magic was more in Gauguin's mind than in the subjects he painted. Nevertheless, in the South Pacific he found the ideal environment to foster a unique artistic vision.

When Gauguin moved to this remote island thousands of miles from France, he still kept in touch with his colleagues and dealers in Paris—an indication that we are approaching 20th-century standards of travel and communication. Of course, artists always have traveled. Even the ancient Greek sculptors occasionally set out on the "wine-dark sea" celebrated by the poet Homer. But at the turn of the 20th century, travel across the great oceans had become so convenient and commonplace as to be taken for granted. This ease

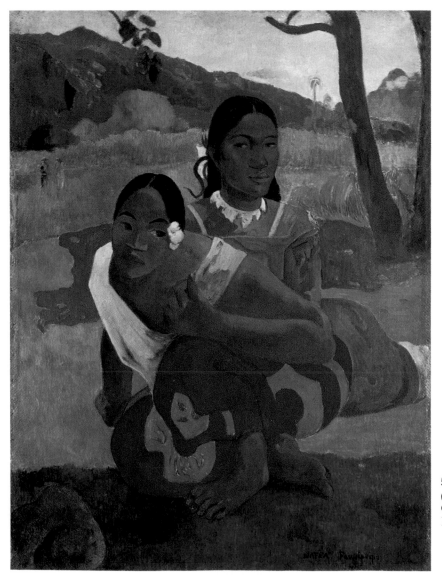

**510.** Paul Gauguin. *Nafea Faaipoipo (When Are You to be Married?).* 1892. Oil on canvas, $41\frac{1}{4} \times 30\frac{1}{2}''$. Rudolf Staechelin Foundation, Basel.

**511.** James Abbott McNeill Whistler. *Arrangement in Gray and Black, No. 1 (The Artist's Mother).* 1871. Oil on canvas, 4'9" × 5'4½". Louvre, Paris.

of movement gave rise to a new phenomenon—trans-Atlantic cultivation of the arts. American artists and writers flocked to London and Paris to learn from the masters there. European artists and writers flocked to the United States, where they found an eager market among certain discerning collectors. Two worlds were rapidly becoming one.

## Bridging the Atlantic: Late 19th Century

Since the early days of the Colonies, American artists had journeyed to Europe, the better to learn their craft. Toward the end of the 19th century, however, the pace of this traveling accelerated. Some artists based in the United States, including Winslow Homer (**258**) and Thomas Eakins (**106,118,119**), made brief visits to Europe and then returned home. Others, born in the United States and considered to be American artists, actually spent much of their working lives in Europe. This latter group includes Mary Cassatt (**267**), Maurice Prendergast (**235**), James Abbott McNeill Whistler, and John Singer Sargent.

Whistler was born in Massachusetts but eventually settled in London. His most famous painting (**511**) has been done a great injustice—and become a cliché—through generations of use on Mother's Day cards, advertisements, and comic posters, thus earning the unfortunate title *Whistler's Mother*. But the artist himself wondered aloud why anyone should care about the identity of the model; his own title, *Arrangement in Gray and Black, No. 1*, speaks far more to Whistler's intent. This image, which has entered the public consciousness as an expression of a son's devotion to his aged mother, actually was meant, and succeeds, as a subtle study of formal composition, light, and color. Whistler's harmony of values—principally soft black and grays—gives the painting a warm, mellow quality. But even more striking is the composition's exquisite visual balance—the elderly woman arranged in profile at right, balanced against the drape at left, the perfect placement of the picture on the wall just off center, even the second picture barely visible at upper right. If any of these elements were changed or removed, Whistler's elegant composition would fall apart. (Indeed, the drape at left is often cropped out in commercial reproductions; you can see how awkward the picture becomes if you cover this portion with your hand.) *Arrangement in Gray and Black* demonstrates a new interest among artists in using the visual elements for their own sake, not to serve the needs of a particular subject matter.

Although John Singer Sargent was an American citizen, he actually spent very little time in the United States. Born in Italy of American parents, Sargent established his primary studio in London, with only occasional trips to New York and Boston. He made his reputation early as a portrait painter, and throughout his career he remained wildly in demand by the rich and fashionable on both sides of the Atlantic. The best of Sargent's portraits succeed because they create an aura of elegance and aristocratic glamor. A typical example is the notorious *Madame X* (**512**), painted in 1884. This portrait of Mme. Gautreau, an American society woman, caused a scandal when it was exhibited in Paris, in equal parts because of the subject's low cut dress—quite daring for a "nice" woman of the time—and her haughty expression. A century later, however, we see both of these factors as contributing to the effectiveness of the picture. Mme. Gautreau's pose, the essence of grace, is enhanced by the elegant full profile of her head. The abundance of creamy white skin contrasts dramatically with the velvety tones of her dress. Shocking as the portrait might have been, we can well imagine that wealthy women of the period would pay handsomely to be made to look like this.

If Paris was startled by *Madame X,* worse upsets were soon to come. Change was everywhere, signaled by the Impressionists and the Post-Impressionists. How far and how fast art was moving will be obvious when we look at the next "portrait" reproduced here, a work painted just twenty-one years after *Madame X.*

## France, Early 20th Century: Fauvism, Cubism, and Other Movements

A public that could be shocked by *Madame X*—to our eyes a lovely but rather conventional painting—was hardly prepared for the explosion that shook the art world soon afterward. In 1903 the Salon d' Automne (autumn salon) was organized in Paris as an alternative to the establishment Salon. Two years later the Salon d'Automne exhibited the work of a new group of artists whose style caused a critic to label them *fauves*—"wild beasts"—and the label stuck. Among the artists who elicited this angry characterization was Henri Matisse.

The Matisse painting illustrated here (**513**) is technically a portrait of the artist's wife, but it is usually known by a more descriptive title, *The Green Stripe.* Mme. Matisse is portrayed recognizably, though the contours of her face are flattened and her features abstracted. Most remarkably, the artist, building on precedents Gauguin had explored a generation earlier (**510**), has painted this image in purely arbitrary colors, that is, colors unrelated to the natural appearance of his wife. While the left side of the face is rendered in close-to-normal flesh tones, the right side is a harsh greenish-yellow, and the hair is dark blue. The background is divided into sections of green, red-orange, and rose-violet; these sections do not define a setting, but are simply color patches. Most startling of all, Matisse has drawn a vivid green stripe down the middle of the subject's face, from her hair to her neckline. Three-quarters of a century later, we are accustomed to the use of color for its own sake and can scarcely comprehend how outrageous this painting must have seemed to Matisse's audience. Its clear message is that color need not be subordinated to nature. With *The Green Stripe* color became a tool, one of many tools in the artist's kit, to be used as the artist sees fit for a given composition.

**left: 512.** John Singer Sargent.
*Madame X (Mme Gautreau).* 1884.
Oil on canvas, 6'10⅛" × 3'11¼".
Metropolitan Museum of Art, New York
(Arthur H. Hearn Fund, 1916).

**above: 513.** Henri Matisse.
*The Green Stripe (Mme Matisse).* 1905.
Oil on canvas, 16 × 12¾".
Statens Museum for Kunst, Copenhagen.

The Fauve movement did not last very long, a mere three years or so.
Matisse went on to explore other aspects of painting, as did his fellow exhibitors at the 1905 Salon d'Automne. Yet the Fauve experiment was crucial for the development of modern art, in that it broke once and for all a longstanding taboo about the boundaries and conventions of art. Never again would artists feel they must confine themselves to replicating the "real" colors of the natural world, although they might do so if they wished. The artistic bag, so to speak, was open.

No sooner had the color rule been broken than artists began to break more daringly than ever before with conventions of shape and space. At the forefront of this experimentation was an artist, just a dozen years younger than Matisse, who broke nearly every rule art had long followed and who emerged as one of the greatest masters of all time: Pablo Picasso. Many consider a painting done relatively early in the artist's career to be pivotal in the

**514.** Pablo Picasso.
*Les Demoiselles d'Avignon.* 1907.
Oil on canvas, 8′ × 7′8″.
Museum of Modern Art, New York
(acquired through
the Lillie P. Bliss Bequest).

development of 20th-century art. That painting is called *Les Demoiselles d'Avignon* (**514**).

Les Demoiselles d'Avignon was not Picasso's title but was given to the painting years later by a friend of his. It translates literally as "the young women of Avignon" and refers to the prostitutes in Avignon Street, a notorious district of Barcelona. In early sketches for the painting Picasso included a sailor entering at left to purchase the prostitutes' services, but in the finished canvas the sailor has been omitted. Picasso had become so involved with the formal components of his painting—the relations of form and space—that he all but forgot its original content.

If these are prostitutes, then how extraordinary they are! They are far from enticing. Picasso has chopped them up into planes—flat, angular segments that still hint at three-dimensionality but have no conventional modeling. Almost as an affront to traditional pictures of curvaceous nude bathers, the artist has defined his nudes in sharp geometric shapes. Figure and ground lose their importance as separate entities; the "background"—that is, whatever is not the five figures—is treated in much the same way as the women's bodies. As a result, the entire picture appears flattened; we have no sense of looking "through" the painting into another world, as we did with Delacroix (**503**) or even Manet (**505**).

To many people who see *Les Demoiselles* for the first time, the faces cause discomfort. The three at left seem like reasonable enough, if abstract, depictions of faces, except for the fact that the figure at far left, whose face is in profile, has an eye staring straight ahead, much as in an Egyptian painting. But the two faces at right are clearly masks—images borrowed from "primitive" art—and they create a disturbing effect when set atop the nude bodies of European females.

In *Les Demoiselles* Picasso was experimenting with several ideas that he would explore in his art for years to come. First, there was the inclusion of Nonwestern elements. Picasso had recently seen sculptures from ancient Iberia (Spain before the Roman Empire), as well as art from Africa. In breaking with Western art traditions that reach back to ancient times, Picasso looked for inspiration from other, equally ancient, traditions. Second, there is the merging of figure and ground, reflecting the assumption that all portions of the work participate in its expression. And third, there is the fragmenting of the figures and other elements into flat planes, especially evident in the breasts of the figure at upper right and the mask just below. This last factor proved especially significant for an artistic journey on which Picasso was soon to embark—the movement known as *Cubism*.

Picasso's partner in this venture was the artist Georges Braque. Braque met Picasso in 1907 and saw *Les Demoiselles* in Picasso's studio. By all reports, Braque was at first dismayed and puzzled by the painting, but later he came to understand Picasso's goals. Both artists had been strongly influenced by the late works of Paul Cézanne (**85**) and by Cézanne's idea that natural forms could be reduced to geometric solids—the cone, the sphere, and the cylinder. Picasso and Braque also were interested in the inherent geometry of forms, but they took as their starting point an angular, rather than a curved, solid—the cube.

In 1909 Braque and Picasso began working closely together, and they continued to do so for several years. By 1910, when Braque's *Violin and Pitcher* (**515**) was painted, their experiments were so closely intertwined that it is difficult to tell their work apart. Cubism is an art of facets, like the facets in a

**515.** Georges Braque. *Violin and Pitcher.* 1910. Oil on canvas, $46\frac{1}{8} \times 28\frac{3}{4}''$. Kunstmuseum, Basel.

411

diamond. Forms are flattened into planes, broken apart, and reassembled to make a striking visual (but nonrepresentational) reality. We see the same form, such as Braque's violin, from several angles simultaneously. Top, bottom, side, and frontal views may be combined into one image. Figure and ground are treated in the same way and have equal weight in the composition; the two blend together into a coherent whole. Both artists deliberately restricted their palettes, concentrating on muted browns and grays so as not to distract attention from their explorations of form.

Cubism was a final, dramatic declaration of independence from Renaissance ideals of natural representation and linear perspective (p. 120). Braque's painting is clearly *not* an attempt to show us exactly what a violin and a pitcher look like. Instead, it is a study of these forms for their aesthetic possibilities, a statement that a work of art has its own reality and need not be a mirror of the natural world. Neither Braque nor Picasso completely abandoned naturalism. Some of Picasso's works after Cubism (**42**) are as faithful representations of the natural world as anyone could ask for. However, with Cubism the principle was firmly established that a painting is *paint on canvas*—an arrangement of shapes and colors and lines chosen to suit the artist's expressive purpose, whatever that might be.

# Early 20th Century: Expressionism

If Picasso and Braque in this period were experimenting with a purely visual reality, some of their contemporaries were more interested in exploring a psychological one. During the first two decades of this century a movement developed in Germany that came to be known as *Expressionism*. Centered around a group of artists based in Dresden who called themselves *Die Brucke* ("The Bridge"), Expressionism had many roots. It was strongly influenced by Van Gogh and Gauguin, took its intense color effects from Fauvism, and admired the stark, emotional works of the Norwegian artist Edvard Munch (**271**). At the time when Expressionism flourished, Sigmund Freud was active in Vienna, publishing his new theories about the role of the unconscious, the meaning of dreams, and the practice of psychoanalysis. The Expressionists were entirely in sympathy with Freud's goal of probing the unconscious and hoped to take the process one step further—to translate their inner explorations into a meaningful art.

Ernst Ludwig Kirchner, a leader of *Die Brucke,* painted himself in 1915 as a soldier with an amputated hand (**516**). This canvas has the quality of a dream, a dream in which the separate elements seem to have a psychological connection that we cannot quite identify. The artist presents himself as a gaunt, shrunken figure, with his cigarette dangling from his mouth and the stump of his hand—his painting hand—offered matter-of-factly for our inspection. In the background, inexplicably, stands a nude woman. In fact, this image *is* a dream—or a waking expression of Kirchner's deepest fears and emotions—for the artist was never actually wounded.

It is difficult to find similarities in the painting styles of the Expressionist artists. Their one thread of connection is the desire or need to probe their deepest emotions and to express those emotions in their work. Other artists generally associated with the Expressionist movement include Käthe Kollwitz (**54,208**, p. 168), Paula Modersohn-Becker (**81**), Gustav Klimt (**133**), Oskar Kokoschka (**229,230**), and Emil Nolde (**254**).

# Synthesis and Awakening: The Armory Show

European art, by the second decade of the 20th century, had run through a series of "isms"—Impressionism, Post-Impressionism, Fauvism, Cubism, Expressionism. The artists connected with these styles certainly were aware of each other's work and were influenced by one another. But each group tended to exhibit with other members of that group—Impressionists with Impressionists, Cubists with Cubists, and so on. Never had the various movements been brought together in one place to make the statement that *here* is modern art—or, rather, here are the many directions of modern art. Moreover, this extraordinary activity in European art had gone largely unnoticed in the United States. Some few American artists and collectors had followed the new styles, but the public at large was unaware of them. All this changed abruptly in 1913. In that year a show of European and American art was organized by a group of progressive American artists. The show opened at the 69th Regiment Armory in New York, and, although there have been many art exhibitions in many armories, this one is still known simply as the Armory Show.

European art of the previous four decades was well represented, and the show caused an immediate sensation. So abusive was the press in its criticism that the general public became intrigued and flocked to the Armory to laugh at the art (and its makers). The critics singled out one work in particular for their greatest scorn, and that work soon became the star attraction. It is a Cubist-derived painting by Marcel Duchamp known as *Nude Descending a Staircase* (**517**).

As in a more "orthodox" Cubist painting, Duchamp has taken an image, here the nude figure, and flattened it into planes, which are then reshuffled and rearranged. However, he has also repeated the image many times over, creating a sharp, choppy rhythm that makes the figure appear to descend the staircase. When we first look at *Nude Descending a Staircase*, we may be tempted to echo the comment of a viewer at the Armory Show, who called the painting "an explosion in a shingle factory." But on closer inspection the forms begin to emerge, although they are abstracted: the rounded shape moving diagonally across the center of the canvas is a hip, the lower section of the painting a series of repeated legs. Duchamp had adopted the rather static forms of Cubism and set them in motion.

Another artist represented in the Armory Show was the Romanian-born sculptor Constantin Brancusi. Brancusi worked briefly in the studio of the great French sculptor Auguste Rodin (**342,357**) but soon departed with the now-famous statement, "No other trees can grow in the shadow of an oak tree." By 1910 Brancusi's work had become very abstract, as evidenced by *The Kiss* (**518**)—one of a long series of sculptures on this theme. *The Kiss* represents two of Brancusi's main preoccupations—fidelity to materials and a search for the essence of form. Here Brancusi's material is stone, and he has carved it in such a way that we are very much aware of its nature as stone, not as an attempt to mimic flesh. So highly simplified is the shape that the kiss itself, the union of two souls and bodies, becomes more important than the individuals who take part in it. Even sex differences between the two are barely suggested (the woman, at right, by longer flowing hair and a rounded breast). Brancusi said: "Simplicity is not an end in art, but one arrives at simplicity in spite of oneself, in approaching the real sense of things."

left: **518.** Constantin Brancusi.
*The Kiss.* 1910.
Stone, height 19¾".
Musée National d'Art Moderne,
Paris.

right: **519.** Auguste Rodin.
*The Kiss.* 1886–98.
Marble, height 5'11¼".
Musée Rodin, Paris.

**520.** Wassily Kandinsky. *Picture with an Archer.* 1909. Oil on canvas, 5'9" × 4'9". Museum of Modern Art, New York (fractional gift of Mrs. Bertram Smith).

We can see how far Brancusi has moved from the style of his teacher—how nearly he had arrived at simplicity—by comparing a work of Rodin's, also called *The Kiss*, carved just about a decade earlier (**519**). Rodin's version of the same subject is far more naturalistic, the figures modeled to a smooth perfection and grace. The embrace of the lovers is both romantic and erotic—qualities missing from Brancusi's interpretation. Yet so idealized are the figures that Rodin's *Kiss*, like Brancusi's, acts as a symbol; it is not any two individuals, but all lovers kissing for all time.

The Armory Show introduced not only French artists to the United States, but Russian as well, most notably Wassily Kandinsky, whose early gouache painting we saw in Chapter 8 (**237**). Born in Moscow, Kandinsky spent long periods of time in both Paris and Munich. He was influenced by the Post-Impressionists and the Fauves, but by about 1905 he had begun to move toward a much greater abstraction than that attempted by either group. *Picture with an Archer* (**520**), painted in 1909, is roughly contemporary with both Matisse's *Green Stripe* and Picasso's *Les Demoiselles d'Avignon*, yet it is remarkably different in approach. Neither Picasso nor Matisse ever completely abandoned figural references in their work, but Kandinsky strove increasingly to eliminate representation. His canvases explode with color and energy derived from his own emotional experience—an expression of "inner necessity"—and he considered subject matter "detrimental" to this expression. For this artist, "The harmony of color and form must be based solely upon the principle of proper contact with the human soul."

While the Armory Show attracted much negative criticism, it was a commercial success; about 350 works were sold. Moreover, the show firmly established the position of modern art and introduced its principles to the United States. As we have seen, Marcel Duchamp was the most controversial figure in the show, exhibiting a work influenced by Cubism. Within a very short time, however, Duchamp had shifted his interest to quite a different mode of expression. He became a leader in the first of two movements that, in their own ways, were fully as revolutionary as Cubism.

## Europe, During and After World War I: Dada and Surrealism

During World War I in Europe there arose an art movement known as *Dada,* which came into being as a reaction against the unprecedented carnage of world war. The artists associated with Dada felt that any civilization that could tolerate such brutality must be swept away, and all of its institutions, including traditional art, along with it. Dada, therefore, was anti-everything, even anti-meaning (the name "dada" is said to have been chosen at random from a French dictionary). Representative of Dada's art is Duchamp's work known as *L.H.O.O.Q.* (**521**). Duchamp selected the one painting that for the western world symbolizes art with a capital *A* and gleefully drew a moustache and goatee on a reproduction of the *Mona Lisa.* As if that irreverence were not enough, he penciled in the letters at the bottom, which, when pronounced in the French way, make a vulgar pun suggestive of nymphomania. *L.H.O.O.Q.* is thus a kind of artistic blasphemy—poking fun at one of the most cherished institutions of art.

*Surrealism,* as we have seen (p. 83), is an art based on the unconscious, often taking its subject matter and its imagery from dreams and fantasies. Conceived as a reaction to the more "intellectual" art movements, such as Cubism, Surrealism, according to its manifesto published in 1924, aimed at "pure psychic automation by which one intends to express verbally, in writing, or by other method, the real functioning of the mind." Artists who worked in the Surrealist mode are generally separated into two categories—those whose imagery is predominantly figural, including Salvador Dali (**89**) and René Magritte (**180**); and those following a more abstract style, such as Joan Miró (**113**).

While both Dada and Surrealism, as movements, were relatively short-lived, they had great influence on artistic developments in the second half of this century. Meanwhile, another aesthetic—one equally dedicated to altering the course of modern art—had taken root in Germany. It centered on what is perhaps the most famous of all art schools: The Bauhaus.

## Between the World Wars: 1918–1938

The Bauhaus was founded as a school of design in 1919 in Weimar, Germany. It moved to Dessau in 1925 and then briefly to Berlin, before being closed by the Nazis in 1933. Throughout its short existence, a mere fourteen years, it had an enormous impact on all the art and design of its time, and the influence of the Bauhaus continues to be felt in many fields. Actually, the Bauhaus was less important as a school than as an *idea.* Although its faculty included some of the most noteworthy names in 20th-century art and architecture, it produced few students of particular talent. But many of the principles that guided its curriculum are alive and well today.

Architect Walter Gropius founded the Bauhaus, and he was also the prime theorist in the development of the school's philosophy. Briefly, the Bauhaus hoped to erase the lines separating painters, sculptors, architects, craftsmen, and industrial designers. All artists and designers, whatever their form of expression, were considered essentially craftsmen, committed to using

L.H.O.O.Q.

materials and forms in the most straightforward manner, without artificially applied decoration. The word "Bauhaus" translates roughly as "building house," and its leaders sought to "build" a new guiding principle of design compatible with 20th-century technology. In its later years the school focused more and more on architecture and industrial design, with a view toward reconciling aesthetic design to the capabilities of machine production. Structures, rooms, furniture, and everyday household objects were stripped of superficial embellishment, pared down to the lines necessary for functional use.

Despite this emphasis on industrial design, the painting faculty retained a strong voice. Wassily Kandinsky taught at the Bauhaus for eleven years, and he is only one of several noted artists whose names are associated with the school. Another was Josef Albers, who later emigrated to the United States. Albers' most representative work was done in the 1950s and 1960s, so he will be considered later in this chapter (**528**).

Also on the painting faculty was the Swiss artist Paul Klee. Klee's work is among the most difficult to categorize in the history of art. Most art historians consider him among the great painters of the century, yet he fits no niche or "ism"; there is really no one like Klee. A common first reaction to a Klee painting is "That looks like a child's drawing!" And, indeed, the artist took much of his inspiration from the art of children, but behind the childlike imagery is a technique and sensibility of great sophistication. The apparent playfulness masks a deeply complex, subtle imagination. *Dance You Monster to My Soft Song!* (**522**), a mixed-media watercolor, was done two years after Klee joined the Bauhaus staff. Here the delicate line drawing is masterfully controlled to express the idea of a quite friendly monster dancing away to the tune played by a little girl at a transparent piano. Klee's genius lies in combining inventive imagery with a superior command of line, color, and composition.

Except for Dada and Surrealism, few major art movements emerged during the period between the world wars, although individual artists pursued their own styles. Piet Mondrian was at work in Holland (**112,189**), Henry Moore in England (**215,216**), and Marc Chagall in France (**90**). In the United States Edward Hopper painted his lonely, penetrating visions of the American scene (**187**), while the Mexican muralists were creating grand-scale images of the social scene both above and below the border (**226,239**). Of course, Picasso and Matisse continued to develop their art throughout the period.

Following World War I Europe remained in a state of social and economic turmoil, joined by the United States in 1929, when the entire Western world plunged into the Great Depression. World War II, beginning in 1939 in Europe, 1941 in the United States, brought organized activity in Western art almost to a standstill. Certainly art was made during the war years, but attention was focused on the conflict, and many of the artists were on the battlefield. When the Western nations emerged from war in 1945, it was discovered that the capital of the Western art world had moved—from Paris to New York.

## Art Since 1945

### New York: 1945–1960

In the aftermath of World War II most of Western Europe was completely devastated. The United States, while exhausted, was not. No bombs had fallen or battles been fought in New York, as they had in London and Paris and Amsterdam and most of the cities in Germany. When the time came to resume the normal activities of life, New York became the center of a vibrant art revival. Many of the most progressive European artists had immigrated to the United States, and they served as teachers and inspiration for a new generation of artists—most of them Americans—who gravitated to New York. In fact, painters associated with the first major post-war art movement are referred to as the New York School.

Not a school in the sense of an institution or of instruction, the New York School was a convenient label under which to lump together a group of painters also known as the *Abstract Expressionists*. Primary among them were Jackson Pollock and Willem de Kooning; the group also included Franz Kline, Robert Motherwell (**102**), and Lee Krasner. Abstract Expressionism had many sources—Surrealism, Cubism, the early work of Kandinsky (**520**), freely

opposite: **523.** Jackson Pollock.
*Blue Poles.* 1952. Oil, enamel,
and aluminum paint, glass on canvas;
6'11½" × 16'½".
Australian National Gallery, Canberra
(purchased 1973).

**right: 524.** Lee Krasner.
*The Bull.* 1958.
Oil on cotton duck, 6'5" × 5'10⅛".
Courtesy Robert Miller Gallery,
New York.

brushed and colorful works by Arshile Gorky (**126**), and in some cases even
Eastern art. The artists involved had less in common than seems apparent at
first. One unifying thread is that their paintings, on the whole, are very large
in scale, tending to overwhelm the viewer in their dynamic—even violent—
presence. Most of the works are entirely nonrepresentational, but de Kooning
for one retained figural elements in many of his paintings and thus fits better
the technical definition of "abstract." Abstract Expressionism was characterized by bold, passionate painting—sometimes achieved with sweeping brush
strokes, at other times produced by hurling paint on the canvas, as Pollock did.
The sheer power and energy of this technique caused it to be known as *action
painting.*

The quintessential Abstract Expressionist was Jackson Pollock, who had
perfected his system of "drip painting" by the late 1940s (pp. 46–47, **55**). *Blue
Poles* (**523**) shows Pollock's characteristically dense interweaving of lines and
colors, here punctuated by the almost vertical "poles," which are themselves
filled with intricate patterns of dripped and spattered paint. Even in reproduction this canvas vibrates with energy, so that one can imagine the impact of the
7-by-16-foot painting on a viewer standing before it.

Lee Krasner, who was married to Pollock, came to Abstract Expressionism at about the same time as her husband. Krasner's work, as exemplified by
*The Bull* (**524**), has bolder areas of color and is often characterized by bulbous
shapes that seem to burst out at the viewer. There is a fierce quality in Krasner's work, deriving from the strong colors and tensely drawn—not spattered—
lines. In *The Bull* the rhythms are predominantly circular, except for the
totem-like image at right.

As mentioned earlier, Willem de Kooning often used figural images in his
paintings, especially in his famous "Woman" series (**56**). However, he, too,
could work in an entirely nonrepresentational mode, as evidenced by *Composi-*

# Lee Krasner

## *1908–1984*

In October of 1983 the first major retrospective exhibition of paintings by Lee Krasner opened at the Museum of Fine Arts in Houston. Later, the same show toured the United States. Krasner did not live to see it arrive in New York—once the hub of the Abstract Expressionist movement—because she died just eight months after the Houston opening. Amazingly, this remarkable woman, whom critics now consider to be "an artist of the first rank," expressed little bitterness about the fact that she worked so long under the shadow of Abstract Expressionism's "golden boy"—Jackson Pollock.

Krasner, born Lenore, was the sixth child of Russian immigrant parents who had settled in Brooklyn. By the age of thirteen she had decided to become an artist. She enrolled first at Cooper Union, later at the Art Students League in New York. She also studied for several years with the painter Hans Hoffman, from whom she learned the principles of Cubism, and under whose tutelage she took her first steps toward Abstract Expressionism. Like many other young artists of the Depression period, Krasner supported herself by working for the government-sponsored Federal Art Project. Her first exhibition—part of a group show—came in 1937, in New York.

In 1942 Krasner, having heard about the work of Jackson Pollock, went to his studio one day and introduced herself. Soon the couple were living together, and in 1945 they married. This union proved to be a successful working partnership. Wherever they lived, in New York or at their house on Long Island, Krasner and Pollock maintained joint studios. While their individual painting styles usually remained separate, the two seemed to sustain and encourage each other's work.

Unfortunately for Krasner, the climate of the times was not receptive to a woman who painted in such an assertive style as Abstract Expressionism. Of the New York School of artists she later said, "There were very few painters in that so-called circle who acknowledged I painted at all." Krasner was relegated to the status of "Pollock's wife." Not long afterward, in 1956, she became "Pollock's widow," when her husband was killed in a car crash.

Gradually, after Pollock's death, the critics began to take a fresh look at the work of Lee Krasner, to evaluate it for its own sake. Through it all she continued to paint and to exhibit. And she remained true to the principles of Abstract Expressionism. Other fashions came and went, but this artist continually sought the development of her personal style. By the late 1970s "Pollock's widow" was again Lee Krasner.

Krasner's ideas about painting were her own, not an echo of Pollock's. She has said: "Painting, for me, when it really 'happens' is as miraculous as any natural phenomenon—as, say, a lettuce leaf. . . . One could go on forever as to whether the paint should be thick or thin, whether to paint the woman or the square, hard-edge or soft, but after a while such questions become a bore. . . . The painting I have in mind . . . transcends technique, transcends subject and moves into the realm of the inevitable—then you have the lettuce leaf."[4]

Lee Krasner. *Self-Portrait.* c. 1930.
Oil on linen, 30⅛ × 25⅛".
Courtesy Robert Miller Gallery, New York.

*tion* (**525**). A saturated blood-red dominates this canvas, seeming to spill out from between the jagged lines and patches of other colors, taking on the intensity of a scream. Abstract Expressionism as interpreted by de Kooning is emotion exploding before your eyes.

Krasner, de Kooning, and Pollock usually worked in color, but two other Abstract Expressionists—Robert Motherwell and Franz Kline—are more closely identified with the bold use of black. Kline's painting *Chief* (**526**), named after a locomotive that passed through the Pennsylvania town where the artist was born, resembles an actual locomotive only in its raw, almost

**right: 525.** Willem de Kooning.
*Composition.* 1955.
Oil, enamel, and charcoal on canvas;
6'7⅝" × 5'9⅛".
Solomon R. Guggenheim Museum,
New York.

**below: 526.** Franz Kline. *Chief.* 1950.
Oil on canvas, 4'10¾" × 6'1½".
Museum of Modern Art, New York
(gift of Mr. and Mrs. David M. Solinger).

menacing power. Above all, Kline's art is based on the gesture—the tense sweep of a broad brush held at arm's length, the dramatic contrast of black against white in large scale.

Another form of abstraction that came into prominence in the post-war period is known as Color Field painting. As the name implies, imagery is reduced to a large "field" or area of color, in some cases one pure color filling the entire canvas. In contrast to the dynamic emotionalism of Abstract Expressionism, Color Field paintings have a meditative tranquility that draws the viewer in and invites contemplation. The work of Mark Rothko in the late forties through the sixties (527) usually features one or more soft-edged color rectangles floating in the larger color rectangle of the canvas. The inner rectangle has sides parallel to the canvas edges, and its boundaries are blurred and gently blended, causing the inner sections to float. Very large scale is also characteristic of Rothko's work, so the viewer is enveloped in an atmosphere of sensuous color.

Superficially the work of Josef Albers (528) seems much like that of Rothko, especially when reproduced in a book. In fact, the two artists' paintings have very little in common. Rothko's canvases are huge, Albers' quite small. Rothko's edges are soft and blurred, Albers' precise. Most important, Rothko's expression is emotional, Albers' more intellectual. In the 1950s Albers began a long series of paintings—finally there were hundreds—all entitled *Homage to the Square.* All are "nests" of three or four squares centered in the canvas. What varies is the color, and this was Albers' chief preoccupation.

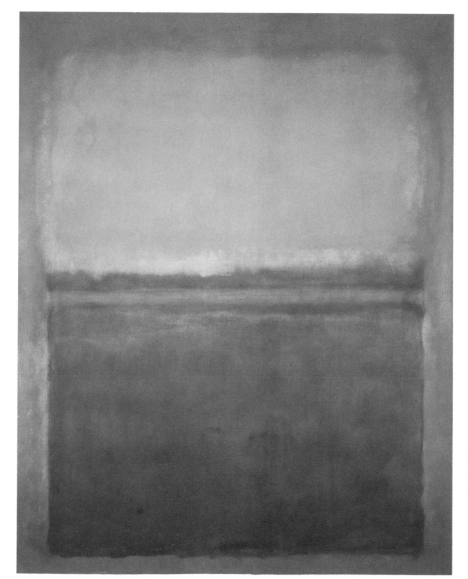

**527.** Mark Rothko. *Orange and Yellow.* 1956. Oil on canvas, 7′7″ × 5′11″. Albright-Knox Art Gallery, Buffalo, N.Y. (gift of Seymour H. Knox, 1956).

above: **528.** Josef Albers.
*Homage to the Square: Ascending.* 1953.
Oil on composition board, 43½″ square.
Whitney Museum of American Art, New York (purchase).

right: **529.** Richard Anuszkiewicz. *Splendor of Red.* 1965.
Liquitex on canvas, 6′ square.
Yale University Art Gallery, New Haven, Conn.
(gift of Seymour H. Knox).

Albers hoped to show the dynamic interaction of colors—how they work together when placed side by side, how some colors advance while others recede, how colors intensify or deintensify each other (pp. 110–112). By restricting himself to the square, he avoided distractions of form, so that the viewer can concentrate on the pure, saturated color. Because it is a series, *Homage to the Square* makes the point that there is no one "best" way a painting can be done, but many different possibilities.

## Art Styles of the Sixties

Albers taught at Yale University, and among his students was Richard Anuszkiewicz, who in the 1960s became associated with the movement known as Op Art, or art based on optical principles. Op Art deals in complex color interactions, to the point where colors and lines actually seem to vibrate before the eyes. We have already seen this effect in the work of Bridget Riley (**150**), who was also part of the Op movement. In Anuszkiewicz' painting *Splendor of Red* (**529**) red and blue lines radiate outward from a central diamond shape of intense red. As a viewer looks at the painting, the lines begin to pulsate, and a halo forms around the red diamond. The Op artists were exploring visual phenomena in a wholly new way, generating a clash between what the eye records and the brain perceives. Some critics dismissed the paintings as "just designs," but in fact Op works suggest a new approach to painting—as a challenging optical experience.

Coexisting with Op Art was the often controversial style known as Pop Art, so called because it took its imagery from the popular culture. Pop Art arose in part as a reaction to Abstract Expressionism. The artists connected

**530.** Roy Lichtenstein.
*Masterpiece.* 1962.
Oil on canvas, 4'6" square.
Private collection, New York.

with the movement wanted to depict, in a naturalistic way, objects from the world, and so, swinging as far from Abstract Expressionism as possible, they chose for their subject matter the most mundane objects of mass-produced culture—billboards, commercial packages, and the like. Andy Warhol's *200 Campbell Soup Cans* (**159**) was but one example of this trend. Another artist, Roy Lichtenstein, based his imagery on the comic book. Many of Lichtenstein's paintings (**530**) are huge, meticulously rendered frames adapted from comic strips, accurate down to the dialogue in "balloons" and the dot pattern of cheap newspaper reproduction. The artist did not hesitate to introduce a

**531.** Tony Smith. *Die.* 1962.
Steel, 6' cube.
Private collection, New York.

touch of irony by poking fun at himself and the art world in proclaiming this work a "masterpiece." Pop Art attempted to show that a detached look at the overfamiliar objects of daily life could give them new meaning as visual emblems. In the process it stretched even more the scope of legitimate subjects for art.

A third movement of the sixties was Minimal Art, which reduced the art elements to a "minimum"—simple (often geometric) shapes and sometimes color. Minimal Art can be seen as a kind of celebration of the artist's basic materials. A painting is paint on canvas, a sculpture is metal or stone or wood or similar material. By stripping art down to these substances, the Minimal artist attempted to reaffirm the worth of art for its own sake, not as a reflection of anything else. In sculpture, an excellent example of the Minimal is Tony Smith's *Die* (**531**), a 6-foot cube of plain black steel that Smith ordered by telephone from the foundry. *Die* cannot be said to have much emotional content. It has no color, no variations of texture, no movement, no rhythm, no focal point. What it does have is *scale*, and that scale gives it a presence, a monumentality. *Die* conveys the idea that form can exist for its own sake in art.

In painting, the Minimal style is often referred to as "hard-edge." Lines are drawn as though with a ruler, colors are pure and unshaded, shapes are precise. Frank Stella's *Sinjerli Variation IV* (**532**) illustrates these characteristics. Its shapes are as regular as those drawn with a compass and a protractor; its rhythms simple and repetitive. Geometric shape in one way or another has been a part of painting for centuries. For example, Raphael based many of his compositions on the triangle (**103**), and Hopper structured a picture around a series of rectangles (**187**). The Minimalists of the 1960s stripped away such figural references and concentrated on geometry alone.

The decade of the sixties was a time of testing, a time of breaking rules, in many spheres—political, social, economic, artistic. Then emerged the sexual revolution, the struggle for racial equality, the peace movement, the feminist movement, the space age, and the computer era. In art a similar kind of testing took place. Merely the fact that there coexisted three art movements—radically different in philosophy and visual effect—demonstrates the vitality of art and the quest for new frontiers. During the following decades, then, artists as well as those in other fields had to confront a basic question: If all the rules have been broken, where does one go next?

**532.** Frank Stella.
*Sinjerli Variation IV*. 1968.
Fluorescent acrylic on canvas,
diameter 10′. Collection
Mr. and Mrs. Burton Tremaine.

**533.** Frank Stella. *Pergusa.* 1981. Mixed media on etched magnesium panel, 5'3" × 7'8" × 1'11". Courtesy M. Knoedler & Co., New York.

## Art of the Seventies and Eighties

A good way to introduce the art of the last two decades is to consider another work by Frank Stella, this one made thirteen years after *Sinjerli Variation IV.* Stella's *Pergusa* (**533**) is obviously by the same artist, yet he has transformed the hard-edge geometry into a complicated interweaving of incredible richness and variety. Creative artists, in general, build on what they have done before. Stella has taken his Minimal expressions of the sixties and translated them into a joyous visual exuberance for the eighties. *Sinjerli*'s movement is slow and measured; our eyes move rhythmically around and through its precise curves. But *Pergusa* is alive with movement, a roller-coaster ride of shapes. There is another big difference between the two works. *Sinjerli* of the sixties is two-dimensional—as flat as a bull's-eye. *Pergusa* of the eighties has moved out into the third dimension. It has elements of relief attached to the background surface and projecting to almost 2 feet.

The variety of options extends also to the styles in which contemporary artists work. Earlier periods in the history of art often pitted fashion against

Like many works of contemporary art, *Pergusa* is difficult to categorize. It looks like a painting when reproduced in this book, and sections of it are painted, but it has more depth than many sculptures. Strictly speaking, it is neither a painting nor a sculpture, but a little of both. Similarly, many of Robert Rauschenberg's works (**77,274**) have areas that are painted, sections that are silkscreened, sometimes applied pieces of fabric, occasionally three-dimensional objects attached to the background. This should not seem surprising in view of the enormous diversity of materials in our lives. A living room, for example, might contain an array of state-of-the-art electronic equipment in a chrome cabinet resting on an antique Oriental rug, and few people would find this combination odd. Just as people select whatever ingredients they wish to support a particular life style, artists choose different ingredients to satisfy their expressive needs.

The variety of options extends also to the styles in which contemporary artists work. Earlier periods in the history of art often pitted fashion against

**534.** Pat Adams. *In the Beginning.* 1982. Isobutyl methacrylate oil on linen, 3′9¼″ × 10′10″. Courtesy Zabriskie Gallery, New York.

anti-fashion. As recently as the 1950s, when Abstract Expressionism held sway, few important museums or galleries would mount shows by contemporary artists working in a naturalistic style, because such work was considered old-fashioned, even trivial. Now the situation has changed dramatically. A tour of the major galleries in New York or San Francisco or Dallas will reveal an astonishing range of styles—all fashionable, all taken seriously by critics and the art-viewing public. The art of the seventies and eighties can be said to offer something for nearly everyone. Abstraction, realism, large, small, painting, sculpture, mixed media, art object, no art object—each has its adherents. Beyond this, the individual art-viewer can enjoy a variety of styles, just as one might enjoy having Mexican food one night, Italian food the next night, and so on. The artistic "menu" is a marvelously varied and exciting one. In the next few pages, then, we will look at some of the styles of today.

A number of prominent artists are working in abstract or nonobjective modes, among them the painter Pat Adams. Adams' *In the Beginning* (**534**) is totally nonobjective; it contains no shapes we can recognize. The title is taken from the first words of the Book of Genesis in the Bible. For those familiar with the quotation, the second verse may give insight into the painting: "And the earth was without form, and void; and darkness was upon the face of the deep." This is not to say that Adams was painting the Book of Genesis or even that she meant to portray that pre-creation void. The main interest of this work lies in the interplay of colors, textures, and shapes in turbulent movement. The title, therefore, suggests an art of swirling formless imagery, just as Genesis recalls a world of swirling formless energy.

Existing side-by-side with nonobjective art is what many would consider its antithesis—art that attempts to duplicate faithfully forms in the natural world. The New Realism, as it is sometimes called, almost certainly derives some of its inspiration from Pop Art of the 1960s, but it is more likely to focus on the human figure, and it lacks the association with commercial, mass-produced culture that was so important to Pop Art. The new realist painters of the 1970s and 1980s include Don Eddy (**157**), Chuck Close (**25**), and Audrey Flack (**60**); Duane Hanson (**362**) is among the best-known of the New Realist sculptors. Both Close and Flack often work from photographs, projecting a photographic image onto a canvas and then painting with an airbrush over the image. The paintings that result have such photographic accuracy that the term *Photorealism* was coined to describe them.

Another prominent artist of the new realist style is Philip Pearlstein, who in the late 1960s began painting the nude figure in a *super*realistic way that

left: **535.** Philip Pearlstein.
*Model Seated on Rocking
Rattan Lounge.* 1984.
Oil on canvas, 6 × 5'.
Courtesy Hirschl & Adler Modern,
New York.

above: **536.** Nam June Paik.
Scene from *Global Groove.* 1982.
Video art. Courtesy the artist.

might more accurately be described as "naked" (**535**). Pearlstein's nudes, both male and female, are captured with meticulous, almost brutal accuracy, with all their bulges, wrinkles, warts, hairs, and general imperfections. The "peep-hole" point of view, in which we see the models at odd angles and oddly cut off by the edges of the canvas, is reminiscent of works by Degas (**508**). In recent years Pearlstein has taken to painting his nudes against elaborate backgrounds, such as intricate, colorful Oriental rugs. The interplay of visual textures becomes extremely important, and one cannot help but marvel at the artist's amazingly naturalistic rendering. Pearlstein's figures are not lovely, but his pictures fascinate in their uncompromising look at the real.

So far, all the art we have considered in this section has roots that we can trace back at least to the first decades of this century, if not for hundreds or thousands of years. We turn now to a type of art that could not have existed at all until about thirty years ago. The new electronic art is an expression of space-age technology. If you pick up any shopping catalogue, you are likely to be overwhelmed by the selection of electronic gadgetry available to the consumer. Three decades ago few homes boasted a television set. Today the average middle-class home is likely to have two or more TV sets, half a dozen radios, complex stereo equipment, and possibly a video cassette recorder and a home computer. Everybody is "tuned in" to electronic sound and pictures—including the artist.

One of the pioneers of electronic imagery is Korean-born, New York-based artist Nam June Paik (**536**), who envisioned a new art of video technology as early as 1960. Paik does not *reproduce* images electronically, as network television might show an image of a great painting by Picasso or Renoir. Rather, the image is *produced* and manipulated by means of the electronic equipment itself. What is especially exciting about this approach is its immediacy, its "aliveness." According to Paik, "Most paintings reflect light. So when it's white paint, for example, you see the white light. Whereas television pictures are glowing light. Light is coming out, sprouting out. So it is much more intense physically. . . ."[5] Paik's installations are expensive and take up space; they are not the sort of art that most collectors could expect to have in their homes. Still, at museum exhibitions they draw large crowds. The fascination of flickering, transitory images is inherent in our world. Click—the art is there; click—it's gone; click—it's back again.

Earlier in this book we encountered the work of an artist, Sandro Chia (**131**), who is often referred to as one of the "new" Expressionists, or *Neo-Expressionists*. Some critics avoid this term and refer to Chia and others of his generation simply as "the new European painters." This latter designation is a key to Neo-Expressionism. Although the art world has been centered in New York since 1945, during the seventies and early eighties artists of Western Europe, especially Germany and Italy, have worked to build an artistic expression of their own. The Neo-Expressionists are Italians and Germans who were young children during or after World War II, and their art reflects the consciousness of nations that fought the great war, lost, and began to pick up the pieces afterward.

Neo-Expressionist art is realistic and often contains figures, but its intensity of color and form and energy makes it quite different from the New Realist paintings just discussed. Neo-Expressionist works are full of passion, symbolism, and even story line (**537**). According to *New York Times* critic John Russell, "For the first time in many years, people want to say, 'And what happened next?' when they look at new pictures."[6] Sometimes there is a jarring, unsettling note, as in the paintings of Georg Baselitz, which always look as though they have been hung upside-down.

We said earlier that video art—art recorded only on film or tape or in the memory—has been a major preoccupation of many late-20th-century artists. The farthest extension (to date) of this elusive expression is *conceptual art*. Conceptual art may or may not have any physical substance. What matters is the concept, the *idea*, the process underlying the art, rather than any tangible product. Among the foremost practitioners of conceptual art is Christo.

In 1970 Christo wrapped and tied a section of the Australian coastline with a million square feet of polyethylene sheeting—and then took it down. In 1972 Christo strung a huge orange curtain between two mountains in Colorado—and then took it down. In 1976 thousands of volunteers, at Christo's direction, installed an 18-foot-high white nylon fence across 24½ miles of the California countryside (**367**). And then they took it down. Nothing remains of any of these projects except Christo's drawings, extensive photographs and films of the work in progress and in place, and the memories of the construction team and onlookers.

**537.** Georg Baselitz.
*Nachtessen in Dresden.* 1983.
Oil on canvas, 9′2″ × 14′9″.
Collection
Doris and Charles Saatchi,
London,
courtesy Xavier Fourcade, Inc.,
New York.

Possibly the most ambitious of all was Christo's 1982 project, called *Surrounded Islands* (**538**). Eleven small islands in Biscayne Bay, next to Miami, Florida, were "skirted" in pink polypropylene cloth—6.4 million square feet of it. For a few days a string of rather untidy, trash-strewn islands were transformed into bright pink flowers shimmering on the blue water. And then—yes, inevitably—Christo's volunteers took it all down again. Why would the artist do this? Why would anyone want to create a large, important work that is doomed to be destroyed?

For Christo, the concept is what matters, and the actual time when the installation remains in place—a few days or weeks—is only part of that concept. It begins with the first glimmer of an idea about the project and extends indefinitely into the future. After the idea—a sort of "What if we could. . . ."—there is a thinking through of the project. Next come the drawings to test possibilities for what the project will look like (**539**). Then bureaucracy gets involved. For the *Surrounded Islands* it became necessary to deal with the Army Corps of Engineers, the City of Miami, and platoons of local residents, just in order to get the necessary permits to install the work. In the end Christo engaged two lawyers, a marine biologist, a marine engineer, several other engineers, two ornithologists (biologists specializing in the study of birds), and an expert in marine mammals. Again, Christo considers this part of the operation intrinsic to the overall concept.

At first the local people were hostile to Christo's project. Soon, however, nearby residents became intrigued with the idea. Not least of the factors responsible for the change of heart was the influx of many, many tourist dollars as the project progressed. By the day of the installation, the Miami *Herald* was cheering, "Go for it, Christo!" As the project took shape, was realized, and was disassembled, practically no one was disappointed.

Yet another part of the concept—and one that no doubt prompted the support of local residents—is the fact that Christo's projects often leave the natural landscape in better condition than it was in before. Christo's volunteers clean up after themselves. More than 4 tons of trash was carted away in preparation for the *Surrounded Islands,* and the materials of the project were removed without a trace. There were even some surprising results that Christo himself could not have predicted. The manatee, a local mammal that is a species of sea-cow, increased its mating behavior. (Could anyone have anticipated a bumper crop of baby manatees?) Local birds seemed happier; the pink plastic kept people and boats away. Tides were unaffected, because the gossamer fabric allowed the water to ripple underneath.

Finally it was all over but the telling and the showing—and that, too, is part of the concept. Christo lectures widely on college campuses and in other forums. Pictures and films of his projects are widely available. And the concept remains—a mental perception of what art can be. As one critic wrote, "Where other artists put nature in a frame, Christo goes boldly to the landscape itself, bringing to it elegant artistic effects that recall our attention to the splendors of natural environment (or what's left of it) in the same romantic spirit as the painters of the 19th-century West." In a sense, Christo's installations *remind* us to look at the landscape we so often take for granted.

Another important result of Christo's projects is that they get so many people involved—from the volunteers who help construct them to the bureaucrats who must approve them to the onlookers and those who hear about the projects afterward. A huge project like the *Surrounded Islands* cannot help but attract attention, both on the spot and through the media. Thus it reaches more people than could ever see a single painting hanging in a museum. If art is about communication, then clearly Christo has found an effective way to communicate, through art, with an enormous audience.

Involving a broader audience in art has been one of the main concerns of the late 20th century. Christo undertakes this on a grand scale; other artists have attempted, in a somewhat more limited way, to involve people who might not otherwise be exposed to art. In 1984 the dancer and choreographer Jacques d'Amboise, noted for his work in teaching dance to children—often underprivileged children—in the New York area, decided to stage the "Event of the Year." This was to involve about a thousand schoolchildren, who would dance a ballet based on the creation of the world and the Garden of Eden. For a backdrop, d'Amboise wanted nothing less than "the largest painting in the world," and so he enlisted the artist Red Grooms (**277,363**) to plan a suitable design.

Grooms drew a sketch of the design on two large pieces of paper. Then artists made enlargements of sections from the design on twenty panels, each measuring 9 by 22 feet. The enlargements were distributed among five public schools in the New York City area. In each school a group of thirty children worked at painting their segments of the design (**540**). Finally, just before the dance performance, the entire composition was assembled into an immense mural, 22 by 180 feet. As a spokesman for the dance institute put it, the children "never dreamed of working on such a scale. . . . House painter-sized

**540.** New York schoolchildren celebrating completion of their segment of a Red Grooms design for Jacques d'Amboise's National Dance Institute, 1984.

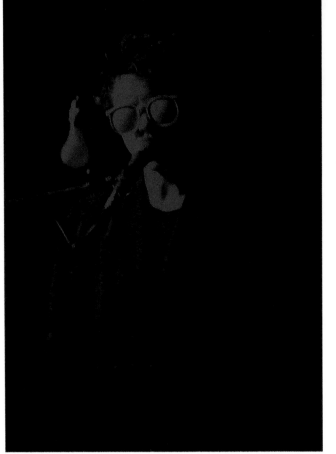

brushes, 50 gallons of ultramarine blue. They had a sense of fulfillment beyond anything they'd ever accomplished." Red Grooms, no stranger to involving the public with art, was equally delighted. According to the artist, "The kids said it presented no problem."

Our next illustration shows a work that originally was conceived on quite a small scale, but grew into an extremely ambitious project involving hundreds of people—Judy Chicago's *The Dinner Party* (**541**). As installed, *The Dinner Party* consists of a triangular table, each side of the table 48 feet long, each side containing thirteen place settings of fabric runner, porcelain plate, knife, fork, spoon, and chalice—for a total of thirty-nine. The place settings are all different, all handmade. Each of them was created to symbolize the life and work of one particular notable woman—the Empress Theodora (**458**), Eleanor of Aquitaine, Queen Elizabeth I, Susan B. Anthony, Emily Dickinson, Georgia O'Keeffe (**86**), and thirty-three others. The table rests on the "Heritage Floor," which lists the names of 999 other notable women in history.

*The Dinner Party* is a remarkable work of art and also a remarkable feminist statement. According to Chicago, "My original idea of representing the history of women in Western civilization took on the additional meaning of a reinterpretation of The Last Supper. I thought 'men had a last supper, but women have had dinner parties.' (Moreover, it was probably women who cooked the food for that famous Last Supper)."[7] To make this point, Chicago developed her project through the traditional areas of "women's work"—embroidery and china painting. The concept, which took form in Chicago's mind in 1974, required five years to realize and eventually involved hundreds of workers, researchers, and studio assistants. Two years were needed just to do the research on the 999 women honored in the "Heritage Floor," thereby underscoring Chicago's point that women have been deprived of their historical heritage, that women throughout time have made great contributions but history has not recorded them in any accessible way. (It would not, after all, take nearly that long to come up with the names and biographies of 999 notable men; one could find them in the encyclopedia.)

Originally there were to be thirteen place settings, the same number as there were men present at the Last Supper. However, as the research progressed, it became clear that there were many more women who should be honored, and so the number was tripled. The triangular table, with three equal sides, symbolizes the goal of feminism—equality. And the tiled floor suggests that the thirty-nine women of the place settings were not isolated in their achievements, but "pulled themselves up" from the efforts of other women who formed a strong support. *The Dinner Party* is so large that it is not often exhibited. In a sense, it is related to conceptual art. The concept is continuous, for it existed well before the physical construction started and persists even when *The Dinner Party* is put away in storage.

Finally, as mentioned at the beginning of this chapter, we come to an artist whose work has no physical substance. During the 1970s the phenomenon known as *performance art* emerged. Performance art undoubtedly took its inspiration from the "Happenings" of the 1950s and 60s, one of which is described on page 220. Happenings are difficult to define; they are visual events in which some activity occurs, often with several people participating, often with audience involvement. They may include music, dance, mime, art, reading, or none of these. Imprecise as it may sound, Happenings are things that happen.

Performance artist Laurie Anderson has developed this idea considerably in the 1980s (**542**). Anderson's performances—no two are alike—contain a bewildering array of elements, pulled together in a way that is meaningful to the artist. She may sing or play the violin or both, and the sounds of voice and instrument may be distorted. Sometimes she will recite a song or story. Complicated electronic imagery flashes—films, slides, lasers. Occasionally a second performer will join her—in one case a black man in women's clothing playing jazz on the bagpipes. There may be sight gags as well; Anderson's lips are made to glow in the dark, or she attaches two extra arms to her body.

Perhaps it is slightly incorrect to say Anderson's art has no physical presence, although it is certainly true that you could not buy it or hang it on the wall. In performance art the art is the artist. What a far cry this is from the art of the Middle Ages, when artists were often anonymous. Their art endures, but the artists' names have been forgotten. In contrast, performance art places the artist at the very center. If you take away the artist, there is no more art. Performance art is the triumph of the artist.

So that is the scope of modern art—from Ingres to Anderson in less than two hundred years. It should be clear now that the question we addressed in Chapter 2 of this book—what is art?—has no convenient answer. It would be almost impossible to construct a meaningful definition of art that would encompass all forty of the works discussed in this chapter. Beyond this, we could be almost certain that a definition formulated now would prove inadequate five or ten years hence. It may seem to us that performance artists like Laurie Anderson have broken all the rules, lowered all the barriers to expression in art. But we must remember that the public so outraged by Manet's *Le Déjeuner sur l'herbe* and Matisse's *Green Stripe* also thought that *those* artists had broken all the rules. The trouble is, no one ever really knows what rules are left.

Artists always seem to be one step ahead of everybody else. If we choose to follow them in their explorations—if we choose to live with art—we may sometimes find the experience unsettling, but we will not find it dull. Living with art is an ongoing adventure.

# 18
# Comparative Styles in World Art

In the previous three chapters we focused on the art of Western civilization—the generally continuous thread of artistic influence stretching from ancient Egypt through Greece and Rome down to Western art styles of today. Here we turn again, as we have often in earlier sections of the book, to a comparison of arts from many different cultures. This final chapter concentrates on the arts in "non-Western" societies—in the Far East, India, Southeast Asia, Africa, Persia, and South America.

One of the most fascinating aspects of art history is its diversity. It can be intriguing to discover what was going on in the world—artistically—at the same time but at different parts of the globe. Often, works of art contemporary with one another but separated geographically are very different; occasionally they are startlingly alike. To get a sense of this cross-cultural diversity, we have selected six periods in the history of art—times when there was significant artistic activity in widely separated areas. For each time period we have illustrated between two and four works of non-Western art and usually compared them with a work of Western art from the same period. And in each case, to make the comparison more interesting, we have chosen works with similar media or themes—sculpture, precious objects, landscape painting, and so forth.

Whether contemporary works of art are similar or dissimilar, we cannot help but wonder how they got that way. In other words, did the art trends of one culture influence those of another, or did certain trends develop independently? A key to the answer is communication. When a culture is isolated from the rest of the world, it will not receive artistic ideas from the outside. Many art historians and others have speculated about possible channels of communication. For example, the explorer Thor Heyerdahl has put forth the theory that sailors of ancient Egypt could have navigated the Atlantic and crossed to South America. But for many of the works illustrated in this chapter, it seems more likely that the creative impulse sprang up without external influence—that artists made wonderful art unaware of the work of their colleagues around the globe.

# 10th to 7th Century B.C.: Sculpture

The two objects illustrated on this page (**543,544**) were made at approximately the same time in history but more than ten thousand miles apart—the first in central China, the second in northern Peru, in South America. The possibility of contact between the cultures that produced them is extremely remote. Yet how remarkably similar in design are these sculptures!

We have already seen the *Tiger* from Zhou Dynasty China in Chapter 12 (**386**). It was made from bronze, cast in a mold that created not only the basic form but also the imprint of the stylized, geometric motifs that cover the animal's body. The feline figure from South America is carved from stone, and its form is chunkier and more compact, probably because of the limitations of stone-carving tools then available. The tail of the cat does not curve outward quite as jauntily as that of the Chinese tiger, and the feet are much closer to the body. But there is great similarity between the designs on the animals' bodies and in their form. Also, both objects had utilitarian functions. The tiger, as noted earlier, probably served as the support for a post, while the Peruvian vessel was meant as a mortar—a receptacle for grinding.

How can it be that two such widely separated peoples developed images that are so much alike? Perhaps like other ideas, the decorated feline figure occurred spontaneously to artists on both sides of the globe.

**right: 543.**
*Tiger*, from China.
Middle Zhou period,
c. 900–600 B.C.
Bronze, length 29⅝".
Freer Gallery of Art,
Smithsonian Institution,
Washington, D.C.

**below: 544.**
Mortar in the form
of a feline, Chavin culture, Peru.
c. 1000–700 B.C.
Stone, length 13".
University Museum, Philadelphia.

**left: 545.**
*Augustus of Prima Porta.*
c. 20 B.C. Marble, height 6'8".
Vatican Museums, Rome.

**right: 546.**
*Cavalryman and Saddle Horse
from Earthenware Army
of First Emperor of Qin.*
c. 210 B.C. Terra cotta,
height of man 5'10½".
Cultural Relics Bureau, Beijing,
and Metropolitan Museum of Art,
New York.

# 3rd Century B.C.
# to A.D. 3rd Century: Sculpture

Made over a period of some three hundred years, the four pieces illustrated in this section (**545,546,547,548**) came from places as far apart as half the circumference of the earth. All four are exquisitely modeled sculptures of figures, two in clay, two in stone. Each represents an important concern for the culture in which it was made, but, because those cultures were very different, the works of art that resulted are unique.

The *Augustus of Prima Porta* (**545**), as we have seen earlier (**71**), was an "official" attempt to glorify the Emperor of Rome and endow him with the stature almost of a god—and thus to solidify his legitimacy as a ruler. In ancient China and India no such needs were apparent. In fact, it is unusual to see a sculpture from Asia depicting a political figure. The first Emperor of China obviously had no doubts about his political clout. Anyone who could commission (or command) an army of ceramic tomb figures—the cavalryman here (**546**) is but one of thousands of similar figures—clearly wielded enormous power.

Throughout most of the history of Eastern art, religious figures have been the most common subjects for sculpture, and a large portion of this sculpture is connected with the Buddhist religion. Typical is a *Seated Buddha* (**547**) from Gandhara, in India (now in Pakistan), the region where Buddhism originated before spreading to China, Japan, and other countries. This image presents an interesting mixture of Eastern and Western art. The yoga-like pose of the Buddha, as well as his meditative expression, are intrinsic to the

Eastern religion; however, the Buddha's draped robe looks very much like a Roman toga (**455**), and his face is reminiscent of naturalistic Greek and Roman statues of gods (**359**). Indeed, it is generally accepted that North Indian art of this period was much influenced by contemporary Roman art.

By contrast, we find little naturalism in a figure from the Zapotec culture in Mexico (**548**). Most pre-Columbian art—or art made in the Americas before the arrival of Columbus in 1492—is stylized and decorative. The Zapotec people, whose settlement was centered around the temple complex of Monte Albán, near modern Oaxaca, were highly civilized. They built sturdy homes of stone and mortar, practiced agriculture, and refined the arts of weaving, metalwork, and ceramics. In the example shown here facial features are exaggerated, the body is compressed into a symmetrical arrangement of arms and hands and feet, and topping the whole is an ornate, perhaps feathered, headdress. Without the climax provided by the majestic headdress, this sculpture would lose most of its power; this is clear if we imagine it with just a simple, round head.

**above: 547.** *Seated Buddha,*
from Gandhara, India (now Pakistan).
Kushan period, A.D. 2nd–3rd century.
Stone, 36 × 22½".
Seattle Art Museum
(Eugene Fuller Memorial Collection).

**left: 548.** Zapotec urn, Mexico,
from Oaxaca. A.D. 100–200.
Clay, height 9".
Dallas Museum of Art.

# 10th to 13th Century: Sculpture

Sculpture of the period that, in European art, we would call the Middle Ages is extremely varied. By this time developed art styles had emerged in many more regions. In this section we show three contemporary pieces—from Europe, Africa, and Asia.

The *Gero Crucifix* (**549**) from Germany has been discussed earlier (**464**). Like so much medieval art, it portrays a religious subject—the crucified Christ—rendered in a naturalistic manner. There is great naturalism, too, in a sculptured head made by the peoples inhabiting Ife, in northern Nigeria (**550**). Artists of this region were not only highly skilled in working with terra cotta, as is obvious here, but were also superb metal-casters. Many heads like this one, all of exceptionally high quality, have been found in the area. It is believed that the heads played a role in ancestor-worship, and that each was an individual, lifelike portrait, perhaps made when the person in question was still alive. After death the sculptured head served as a repository for the soul of that person.

**549.** *The Gero Crucifix.* c. 975–1000.
Wood, height 6'2". Cathedral, Cologne.

**above: 550.** Cast of Ife terra cotta head
called *Lajuwa*, from Nigeria. c. 1200–1300.
American Museum of Natural History, New York.

**right: 551.** *Parvati*, from India.
11th–12th century. Bronze, height 40″.
Freer Gallery of Art.
Smithsonian Institution, Washington, D.C.

A very different approach to depicting the human figure is revealed in
the bronze statue of *Parvati*, from India (**551**). Parvati is a goddess of the
Hindu religion—another major faith of India. She has many names and many
physical guises, but as Parvati she is consort (or wife) of the powerful god Siva.
Parvati is a daughter of the mountain, and mother of the war-god. Here she is
depicted in characteristic Indian style—full-breasted (to show her procreative
powers and strength), narrow-waisted, slender and elegant. The graceful gestures of her hands almost defy the rigid bronze in which this figure was cast.

**far left: 552.** Sesshu.
*Autumn Landscape.*
Late 15th century.
Ink and color on paper,
height 18⅛″.
National Museum, Tokyo.

**left: 553.** Qiu Ying.
*A Lady in a Pavilion
Overlooking a Lake.*
China, Ming Dynasty,
c. 1522–60.
Hanging scroll,
ink and color on paper,
height 35⅛″.
Museum of Fine Arts,
Boston (Chinese and
Japanese Special Fund).

# 15th to 16th Century: Landscape Painting

The painting of the natural world has been an important artistic theme in many cultures, especially in Europe, China, and Japan. Sometimes the goal has been to duplicate the physical landscape as closely as possible, to create a mirror of the natural world. Other artistic styles have attempted to *evoke* the sense of the landscape without actually duplicating it. Let us look at four examples, made in different parts of the world over a period of not more than 150 years.

In 15th-century Japan landscape painting reached a pinnacle of stylistic development, and Sesshu was the great master of this style. His *Autumn Landscape* (**552**) is a wonderfully composed arrangement of diagonals—one from the trees at upper right to the ground at lower left, another cutting from middle left to intersect with the first and focus attention on the pagoda near the center of the painting. Sesshu's brushwork is assured, so sharp and definite that he need give only a few strokes to convey the essence of form. Obviously, this is not a naturalistic depiction of the landscape, such as a European Renaissance artist might hope to achieve; it is instead an evocation of the beauty, majesty, and serenity of nature.

Similar goals motivated the Ming Dynasty Chinese artist Qiu Ying. His *Lady in a Pavilion* (**553**), which we considered in Chapter 7 (**236**), looks like a dream landscape in which no earthly concerns intrude. The pavilion is perched on a hillside, seeming almost to float above the ground to the music of the barely visible harpist. The clump of trees below might be lightly suspending the pavilion on their branches, like a balloon. Qiu Ying's brushwork is fully as delicate and assured as that of his Japanese colleague.

Now we move west and north, to examine a rendering of landscape almost exactly contemporary with the previous two, but made in Europe, in the German city of Nuremberg (**554**). The *Nuremberg Chronicle,* of which this image was a part, was conceived as a "history of the world" up to that time, and therefore depicted, in woodcut, many important people and places. "Portugalia," shown here, seems at first to have several traits in common with the Japanese and Chinese landscapes of the period. It is decorative, rather than naturalistic, in its depiction of physical features, and it focuses attention on the foreground tree and the building at upper left. But the German artist is far more precise and far more interested in filling the space with linear detail. This is partly because of the needs of the woodcut printing process (Chapter 8), but also because the northern European artists of the time emphasized neatness and order. We might also notice that most of the lines in this woodcut are horizontals and verticals—not the sliding diagonals characteristic of the Eastern paintings.

Our fourth example in this section was painted only about ten years after the scene from the *Nuremberg Chronicle.* Yet in a sense the *Nuremberg* woodcut has more in common with its Chinese and Japanese counterparts than it does with a painting made, so to speak, just down the road, in Italy. Giorgione's *The Tempest* (**555**), as discussed earlier (**481**), was a Renaissance attempt to portray the natural landscape as faithfully as possible, and to capture the effects of an approaching storm. But one factor marks this work as drastically different from landscapes of other cultures during this period, and that is the emphasis on people. Giorgione put two important figures in his foreground. We do not know who they are, but clearly they are an essential part of his composition. No figures intrude on the view of "Portugalia"; and the Eastern landscape artists, if they include figures at all, make them tiny and fit them unobtrusively into the majesty of nature. This is an extremely interesting point in comparing works of art from different cultures: Is nature more important, or are people? And how do they fit together?

**below: 554.** Shop of Michael Wolgemut. "Portugalia," from the *Nuremberg Chronicle.* 1493. Woodcut, $9\frac{1}{8} \times 9''$.

**right: 555.** Giorgione. *The Tempest.* c. 1505. Oil on canvas, $32\frac{1}{4} \times 28\frac{3}{4}''$. Academy, Venice.

# 14th to 16th Century: Precious Objects

Not every culture has made paintings or sculptures; but every culture we know has made precious objects—functional articles raised to the level of art because of their ingenious design and fine craftsmanship. In Chapter 16 of this book we focused on the painting and sculpture in the period of Western culture known as the Renaissance. Here we concentrate on decorative objects of the same period, from Europe, Asia, North and South America, and Africa. The dates of some of these pieces are uncertain, but most of them were created between the 14th and 16th centuries.

Benvenuto Cellini was a goldsmith and sculptor of Florence, perhaps one of the greatest masters of fine gold work who ever lived. His best-known piece is the *Saltcellar of Francis I* (**556**), made for the king of France. Cellini's genius was to capture in miniature the physical perfection and grace of figures such as Michelangelo and his colleagues would have carved on a heroic scale—and to surround them with an opulent decoration to satisfy the tastes of monarchs. Ostensibly, this elegant piece was meant to dispense salt and pepper. Neptune, god of the sea, doles out the salt; the goddess Earth is custodian of the pepper. In fact, the *Saltcellar* probably was intended above all to display the virtuosity of Cellini, and at this it succeeds.

Many people automatically associate fine porcelain—vases and decorative objects—with the word "Ming." The Ming Dynasty in China, dating from 1368 to 1644, produced what are unquestionably some of the loveliest specimens of ceramic art ever created. In this example (**557**) the lotus blossoms in the pure white of the base clay gleam through a transparent glaze, surrounded by blue and yellow enamel glazes. The graceful form of the vase is in perfect harmony with the decoration.

Another ceramic vessel (**558**), just as graceful but much simpler in its decoration, was made half a world away, in a portion of the Mississippi Valley now in Louisiana. Very little is known about the culture that made this bottle, which was found in a burial mound. Its swirling, circular decoration, scratched into the clay, is sensitively related to the form. In its simple shape and geometric design, this bottle seems modern enough to have been constructed by a 20th-century craftsman.

Ivory carving has been done in many parts of the world, but we tend to associate it with Africa because the raw material—elephant tusks—has come primarily from that continent. The belt mask illustrated here (**559**) shows the flexibility of the material. In its facial features the mask has a full-fleshed

**left: 556.** Benvenuto Cellini. *The Saltcellar of Francis I.* 1539–43. Gold, 10¼ × 13⅛″. Kunsthistoriches Museum, Vienna.

**right: 557.** *Mei-ping Vase,* from China. Ming Dynasty, late 15th century. Porcelain, height 14¾″. Cleveland Museum of Art (bequest of John L. Severance).

naturalism that recalls the Ife terra cotta heads of a century or two earlier (**550**). But the artist of this mask, working in extremely hard and resistant ivory, has also been able to carve in exquisite detail the many tiny heads that surround the face, representing "hair" and "beard."

As a working material, silver is almost the opposite of ivory. It is very soft, easy to mold, vulnerable to damage—yet far more valuable. The search for silver and gold was a prime motivation for the *conquistadores*, the Spanish conquerors who overtook the ancient cultures of Central and South America in the 16th century. Many of the precious objects found by the Spaniards were shipped back to Europe, there to be melted down for the metal. The *Figure of a Musician* shown here (**560**) survived. Made by the Chimu culture in Peru, this little figure, hammered from sheet silver, demonstrates the cheerful, light-hearted character that has come to be associated with the Chimu. Almost no historical record exists, so what we know of this culture comes from the wonderful metalwork, ceramics, and weaving that have survived.

**above: 558.** Water bottle,
from Ouachita Parish,
Louisiana. 1300–1700.
Ceramic, height 5¾".
Museum of the American Indian,
Heye Foundation, New York
(Clarence B. Moore Collection).

**top: 559.** Belt mask,
from Nigeria. c. 1550.
Ivory, height 9⅜".
Metropolitan Museum of Art, New York
(Michael C. Rockefeller Memorial Collection,
gift of Nelson A. Rockefeller, 1972).

**right: 560.** *Figure of a Musician*, from Peru.
Chimu culture, 14th–15th century.
Silver, height 8¼".
Metropolitan Museum of Art, New York
(Michael C. Rockefeller Memorial Collection,
gift of Nelson A. Rockefeller, 1969).

**561.** Thomas Gainsborough.
*"The Morning Walk,"*
*Mr. and Mrs. Hallett.* 1785.
Oil on canvas, 7'9" × 5'10½".
National Gallery, London.

# 16th to 18th Century: Painting

In this final section we look at the art of painting, which by the 16th century was highly developed in many cultures. To make a clear comparison, we have chosen five works, from widely separated parts of the world, that feature a woman and man together.

Thomas Gainsborough, an English artist, was considered one of the great portraitists of the 18th century. The picture illustrated, usually called *"The Morning Walk,"* (**561**), is not, strictly speaking, a portrait—that is, it is not a portrait of a specific couple so much as a portrait of aristocratic people at leisure. Mr. and Mrs. Hallett are a softly drawn, elegant pair, whose voluptuous forms are just barely defined against the landscape that surrounds them. All parts of the composition are closely integrated: human figures, dog, clouds, background—caught in a swirl of romantic charm.

Gainsborough's work was almost certainly known to, and admired by, a painter of Colonial America—William Williams. (Although the Gainsborough painting illustrated is dated after that of Williams, the English artist's earlier works were familiar in the Colonies.) Williams' painting of *Husband and Wife in a Landscape* (**562**) makes an excellent comparison to Gainsborough's *"The Morning Walk."* In content the two are identical. Each shows a married couple, accompanied by a dog, out for a stroll. But the styles of the two works are not at all alike. Williams has arranged his couple precisely in the center of the canvas, set them apart from the landscape as though they were standing in a stage set, and even placed them in apparent opposition to one another. The husband seems to be pulling one way, the wife the other. All this is in contrast to Gainsborough's painting, which is one smooth flow of movement, from clouds to feet. It would be too easy to say merely that Gainsborough was a

**above: 562.** William Williams, Jr.
*Husband and Wife in a Landscape.* 1775.
Oil on canvas, $33\frac{3}{16} \times 39\frac{1}{8}''$.
Henry Francis du Pont
Winterthur Museum, Winterthur, Del.

**above right: 563.** Okumura Masanobu.
*Lovers.* Japan,
Edo period, 18th century.
Woodcut.
Museum of Fine Arts, Boston
(Ross Collection).

better painter than Williams—although this is undoubtedly true. More important, however, Williams was painting within the fairly austere style of Colonial America, a style that valued a strict presentation of the visual facts. Gainsborough was painting a romantic ideal.

How very different is a work called *Lovers* (**563**) by the Japanese artist Okumura Masanobu, almost exactly contemporary with the previous two. Masanobu includes no landscape. Nothing exists except the two lovers themselves, caught up in their entrancement with each other. The man and woman do not look at each other, but they are drawn together in intimacy and longing. For the viewer this print is delightful in the elaborate decoration of the couple's robes and the sinuous outline of the two figures.

The image of *Krishna and Radha in a Grove* (**564**), contemporary with the previous three but made in India, is much more deliberately sensual. Krishna is an important Hindu god, whom we saw as a child in the guise of "the butter thief" earlier in the book (**360**). As an adult Krishna is often shown in a rendezvous with his beloved, Radha. Indian art contains many examples of meetings, or anticipated meetings, between the couple. There is a passion and intensity in the love between Radha and Krishna—the union of body and soul—that would be unusual in art from other cultures in this period.

Finally, we come to a Persian miniature dated two centuries earlier, *Bahram Gur in the Turquoise Palace on Wednesday* (**565**). Here we see no passion, but only, perhaps, a quiet comradeship. The male and the female figures seem to have been arranged primarily for symmetry, for equal weight in the decorative scheme of the painting, rather than to emphasize any romantic connection between them. Like the background they inhabit, they are flat and ornamental. Persian art strives more for visual appeal than for emotional content.

The temptation to compare the art from here and there, from now and then, is irresistible. We cannot help but be intrigued by the questions: How did it get that way? Why is it so much like other art? Why is it so different? Above all, the study of art from other cultures forces us to set aside preconceived ideas about what art *should* look like. And this openness of mind is valuable for the understanding of all art, from all times and places.

# Chronology

| Style/Period | Political/Social Events and Personalities | Monuments/Major Artists |
|---|---|---|
| **30,000–3,000 B.C.** | | |
| Old Stone Age, 30,000–10,000<br>New Stone Age, 10,000–4,000 | | *Venus of Willendorf*, 30,000–10,000 (**61**)<br>cave paintings, France and Spain, 15,000–10,000 (**4**) |
| **3,000–800 B.C.** | | |
| Sumerian culture, Mesopotamia, c. 2,800–c. 1720<br>Old Kingdom, Egypt, 2686–2181<br>Middle Kingdom, Egypt, 2133–1991<br>Shang Dynasty, China, 1766–1045<br>Assyrian Empire, Mesopotamia, c. 1760–612<br>New Kingdom, Egypt, 1567–1085 | Hammurabi, king of Babylonia, c. 1750–1708<br>Amenhotep IV, pharaoh of Egypt, 1379–1362<br>Tutankhamon, pharaoh of Egypt, 1361–1352<br>Fall of Troy (Trojan Horse), c. 1184 | Square Temple, Tell Asmar, Iraq, c. 2900–2600 (**447**)<br>*Great Sphinx*, Egypt, c. 2530 (**444**)<br>Great Pyramids, Egypt, c. 2500 (**70**)<br>Stonehenge, England, c. 2000–1500 (**62**)<br>Temple of Amen-Mut-Khonsu, Egypt, c. 1390 (**406**) |
| **800 B.C.–A.D. 1** | | |
| Zhou Dynasty, China, 1045–256<br>Etruscan style, Italy, 6th cent.<br>Archaic Period, Greece, c. 560–c. 500<br>Classical Period, Greece, c. 500–c. 400<br>Hellenistic Period, Greece, c. 400–c. 300 | Sargon II, king of Assyria, c. 722–705<br>Nebuchadnezzar II, king of Babylon, 605–562<br>Rome founded, c. 753<br>Buddha, c. 563–483<br>Confucius, c. 551–479<br>Great Wall of China begun, c. 228<br>Augustus, emperor of Rome, 27 B.C.–A.D. 14 | Palace of Sargon II, Iraq, c. 721–705 (**448**)<br>Ishtar Gate, Babylon, c. 575 (**449**)<br>Parthenon, Athens, 447–432 (**65, 407**)<br>Great Stupa, India, 3rd cent. B.C.–A.D. 1st cent. (**66**)<br>*Earthenware Army*, China, c. 210 (**341**)<br>Pont du Gard, France, 1st cent. (**408**)<br>*Laocoön Group*, late 2nd cent. (**453**)<br>*Augustus of Prima Porta*, c. 20 (**71**)<br>Praxiteles (c. 390–c. 330) |
| **A.D. 1–800** | | |
| Roman Empire, 31 B.C.–c. 500<br>Maya culture, Mexico & Central America, c. 300–1500<br>Gupta Period, India, 320–647<br>Byzantine Empire (Europe–Asia), c. 400–1453<br>Tang Dynasty, China, 618–907<br>Islamic Empire, c. 622–900<br>Nara Period, Japan, 645–794 | Jesus Christ (c. 4 B.C.–c. A.D. 29)<br>Pompeii destroyed, 79<br>Constantine, emperor of Rome, 306–337<br>Justinian, emperor of Byzantium, 527–565<br>Mohammed (c. 570–632) | Colosseum, Rome, 72–80 (**457**)<br>Pantheon, Rome, 118–125 (**411**)<br>San Vitale, Ravenna, 527–547 (**460**)<br>Pyramid of the Sun, Mexico, c. 510–660 (**405**)<br>Hagia Sophia, Istanbul, 532–537 (**412**) |
| **A.D. 800–1400** | | |
| Middle Ages, Europe<br>Song Dynasty, China, 960–1279<br>Inca Empire, Peru, c. 1100–1532<br>Kamakura Period, Japan, 1185–1333 | Crusades, Europe, 1096–1270<br>Magna Carta, England, 1215<br>Marco Polo journeys to China, 1271–1295<br>Black Death in Europe, 1348–1357 | Li Cheng (d. 967)<br>*Gero Crucifix*, 975–1000 (**464**)<br>*Bayeux Tapestry*, c. 1073–1088 (**398**)<br>Chartres Cathedral, France, c. 1194–1260 (**67, 410, 432**) |

| Style/Period | Political/Social Events and Personalities | Monuments/Major Artists |
|---|---|---|
| **1400–1600** | | |
| Aztec Empire, Mexico, c. 1350–1521<br>Ming Dynasty, China, 1368–1644<br>Muromachi Period, Japan, 1392–1573<br>Renaissance, Italy, c. 1400–c. 1600<br>Benin "classical" period, Africa, 1550–1680<br>Renaissance, Northern Europe, c. 1500–c. 1600 | Joan of Arc burned at the stake, 1431<br>Lorenzo de' Medici, ruler of Florence, 1469–1492<br>Christopher Columbus landed in the Americas, 1492<br>Henry VIII, king of England, 1509–1547<br>Martin Luther, beginning of Protestant Reformation in Europe, 1517<br>William Shakespeare, 1564–1616 | St. Peter's, Vatican, Rome, c. 1450–1663 (**437, 479**)<br>Aztec Calendar of the Sun, 1479 (**31**)<br>Sistine Chapel frescoes, Rome, 1508–12 (**478**)<br>Jan van Eyck (1370?–1440?)<br>Donatello (1386–1466)<br>Masaccio (1401–1428)<br>Sesshu (1420–1506)<br>Sandro Botticelli (1444?–1510)<br>Hieronymus Bosch (c. 1450–1516)<br>Leonardo da Vinci (1452–1519)<br>Albrecht Dürer (1471–1528)<br>Michelangelo (1475–1564)<br>Raphael (1483–1520)<br>Qiu Ying (d. c. 1560)<br>El Greco (1541?–1614) |
| **1600–1700** | | |
| Baroque Period, Europe<br>Colonial Period, North America<br>Edo Period, Japan, 1615–1868<br>Qing Dynasty, China, 1644–1912 | Catholic Counter Reformation in Europe<br>*Mayflower* landed on coast of North America, 1620<br>Louis XIV, king of France, 1643–1715 | Taj Mahal, India, 1632–53 (**413**)<br>Cornaro Chapel, Rome, 1645–52 (**488, 489**)<br>Versailles Palace, France, 1661–88 (**493**)<br>Peter Paul Rubens (1577–1640)<br>Gianlorenzo Bernini (1598–1680)<br>Diego Velázquez (1599–1660)<br>Rembrandt (1606–1669)<br>Jan Vermeer (1632–1675) |
| **1700–1800** | | |
| Rococo Style, Europe<br>Colonial Period, North America<br>Edo Period, Japan, 1615–1868<br>Qing Dynasty, China, 1644–1912 | Louis XV, king of France, 1715–1774<br>Louis XVI, king of France, 1774–1792<br>American Declaration of Independence, 1776<br>American Revolution, 1775–1783<br>French Revolution, begun 1789 | Antoine Watteau (1684–1721)<br>Jean Baptiste Siméon Chardin (1699–1779)<br>François Boucher (1703–1770)<br>Jean Honoré Fragonard (1732–1806)<br>Francisco de Goya (1746–1828) |
| **1800–1850** | | |
| Neoclassicism, France, early 19th century<br>Romanticism, France, early 19th century<br>Realism, France, mid-19th century<br>Federal style and Greek Revival, United States<br>Edo Period, Japan, 1615–1868<br>Qing Dynasty, China, 1644–1912 | Napoleon I, emperor of France, 1804–1814<br>War of 1812, United States, 1812–1814<br>invention of photography by Daguerre, 1837 | Jacques Louis David (1748–1825)<br>Katsushika Hokusai (1760–1849)<br>Jean Auguste Dominique Ingres (1780–1862)<br>Théodore Géricault (1791–1824)<br>Ando Hiroshige (1797–1858)<br>Eugène Delacroix (1798–1863)<br>Honoré Daumier (1808–1879) |

| Style/Period | Political/Social Events and Personalities | Monuments/Major Artists |
|---|---|---|
| **1850–1900** | | |
| Impressionism, France, c. 1875–1900<br>Post-Impressionism, France, c. 1880–1900 | Victoria, queen of England, 1837–1901<br>Admiral Perry visited Japan, 1853<br>American Civil War, 1861–1865 | Crystal Palace, London, 1851 (**414**)<br>Eiffel Tower, Paris, 1889 (**415**)<br>Statue of Liberty, New York, installed 1886 (**350**)<br>Edouard Manet (1832–1883)<br>James Abbott McNeill Whistler (1834–1903)<br>Edgar Degas (1834–1917)<br>Paul Cézanne (1839–1906)<br>Auguste Rodin (1840–1917)<br>Claude Monet (1840–1926)<br>Berthe Morisot (1841–1895)<br>Pierre Auguste Renoir (1841–1919)<br>Thomas Eakins (1844–1916)<br>Paul Gauguin (1848–1903)<br>Vincent van Gogh (1853–1890)<br>Georges Seurat (1859–1891)<br>Henri de Toulouse-Lautrec (1864–1901) |
| **1900–1945** | | |
| Expressionism, Europe, c. 1900–1920<br>Fauvism, France, begun 1905<br>Cubism, France, c. 1907–1914<br>Dada, Europe, c. 1916–1922<br>Surrealism, Europe, begun 1924 | Wright Brothers' first flight, 1903<br>Armory Show, New York, 1913<br>World War I, 1914–1918<br>Russian Revolution, 1917<br>Bauhaus, Germany, 1919–1933<br>Tutankhamon's tomb found, 1922<br>Great Depression, 1929–1941<br>Spanish Civil War, 1936–1939<br>World War II, 1939–1945 | Edvard Munch (1863–1944)<br>Alfred Stieglitz (1864–1946)<br>Wassily Kandinsky (1866–1944)<br>Käthe Kollwitz (1867–1945)<br>Frank Lloyd Wright (1867–1959)<br>Henri Matisse (1869–1954)<br>Piet Mondrian (1872–1944)<br>Paul Klee (1879–1940)<br>Pablo Picasso (1881–1973)<br>Edward Hopper (1882–1967)<br>Georgia O'Keeffe (b. 1887)<br>Marcel Duchamp (1887–1968)<br>Norman Rockwell (1894–1978)<br>Alexander Calder (1898–1976)<br>Henry Moore (b. 1898)<br>Alice Neel (1900–1984) |
| **1945–present** | | |
| Abstract Expressionism, c. 1945–1960<br>Op Art, 1960s<br>Pop Art, 1960s<br>Minimal Art, 1960s<br>New Realism, 1970s–1980s<br>Neo-Expressionism, 1980s<br>Conceptual Art, 1970s–1980s<br>Computer Art, 1980s<br>Performance Art, 1970s–1980s | atomic bomb dropped on Japan, 1945<br>Korean War, 1950–1953<br>Vietnam War, c. 1961–1973<br>first walk on moon, 1969 | Pablo Picasso (1881–1973)<br>R. Buckminster Fuller (1895–1983)<br>Henry Moore (b. 1898)<br>Louise Nevelson (b. 1899)<br>Willem de Kooning (b. 1904)<br>David Smith (1906–1965)<br>Lee Krasner (1908–1984)<br>Jackson Pollock (1912–1956)<br>Robert Motherwell (b. 1915)<br>Robert Rauschenberg (b. 1925)<br>Andy Warhol (b. 1930)<br>Frank Stella (b. 1936)<br>David Hockney (b. 1937) |

# Bibliography
# and Suggested Readings

## General References

Canaday, John. *What Is Art? An Introduction to Painting, Sculpture, & Architecture.* New York: Knopf, 1980.

Cummings, Paul. *Artists in Their Own Words.* New York: St. Martin's, 1982.

De la Croix, Horst, and Richard G. Tansey. *Art Through the Ages,* 7th ed., 2 vols. New York: Harcourt Brace Jovanovich, 1980.

Feldman, Edmund Burke. *Varieties of Visual Experience,* 2d ed. Englewood Cliffs, N.J.: Prentice-Hall, 1981.

Fine, Elsa H. *Women and Art: A History of Women Painters and Sculptors from the Renaissance to the Twentieth Century.* Montclair, N.J.: Allanheld & Schram, 1978.

Fleming, William. *Arts and Ideas,* 6th ed. New York: Holt, Rinehart and Winston, 1980.

Goldwater, Robert, and Marco Treves, eds. *Artists on Art: From the Fourteenth to the Twentieth Century.* New York: Pantheon, 1974.

Gombrich, E. H. *The Story of Art,* 13th ed. New York: Praeger, 1983.

Harris, Ann Sutherland, and Linda Nochlin. *Women Artists: 1550–1950.* New York: Knopf, 1977.

Hartt, Frederick. *Art: A History of Painting, Sculpture, Architecture,* 2 vols. Englewood Cliffs, N.J.: Prentice-Hall, 1976.

Honour, Hugh, and John Fleming. *The Visual Arts: A History.* Englewood Cliffs, N.J.: Prentice-Hall, 1983.

Janson, H. W. *History of Art,* 2d rev. ed. New York: Abrams, 1977.

Johnson, Ellen H., ed. *American Artists on Art: From 1940 to 1980.* New York: Harper & Row, 1982.

Jones, Lois Swan. *Research Methods and Resources: A Guide to Finding Art Information.* Dubuque, Iowa: Kendall/Hunt, 1983.

Kinneir, Joan, ed. *The Artist by Himself.* New York: St. Martin's, 1979.

Larkin, Oliver. *Art and Life in America.* New York: Holt, Rinehart and Winston, 1960.

Mendelowitz, Daniel M. *A History of American Art.* New York: Holt, Rinehart and Winston, 1970.

Piper, David, ed. *Random House Library of Painting and Sculpture,* 4 vols. New York: Random House, 1981.

## Chapter 1
### Living with Art

Arnheim, Rudolf. *Visual Thinking.* Berkeley: University of California Press, 1980.

Bishop, Robert. *American Folk Sculpture.* New York: Dutton, 1974.

Edwards, Betty. *Drawing on the Right Side of the Brain.* Los Angeles: Tarcher, 1979.

Fein, Sylvia. *Heidi's Horse,* 2d ed. Pleasant Hill, Calif.: Exelrod Press, 1984.

Hemphill, Herbert W., and Julia Weissman. *Twentieth Century American Folk Art and Artists.* New York: Dutton, 1974.

Larkin, David. *Innocent Art.* New York: Ballantine, 1974.

Mendelowitz, Daniel M. *Children Are Artists.* Stanford, Calif.: Stanford University Press, 1963.

Samuels, Mike, and Nancy Samuels. *Seeing with the Mind's Eye: The History, Techniques, and Uses of Visualization.* New York: Random House, 1975.

Segalowitz, Sid J. *Two Sides of the Brain: Brain Lateralization Explored.* Englewood Cliffs, N.J.: Prentice-Hall, 1983.

Smeets, René. *Signs, Symbols and Ornaments.* New York: Van Nostrand Reinhold, 1982.

Springer, Sally P., and Georg Deutsch. *Left Brain, Right Brain.* New York: Freeman, 1981.

Vitale, Barbara Meister. *Unicorns Are Real: A Right-brained Approach to Learning.* Rolling Hills Estates, Calif.: Jalmar Press, 1982.

## Chapter 2
### What Is Art?

Blocker, H. Gene. *Philosophy of Art.* New York: Scribner's, 1979.

Fromme, Babbette Brandt. *Curators' Choice: An Introduction to the Art Museums of the U.S.,* 4 vols. New York: Crown, 1981.

Herbert, Robert L. *Modern Artists on Art: Ten Unabridged Essays.* Englewood Cliffs, N.J.: Prentice-Hall, 1964.

Nelson, George. *How to See: A Guide to Reaching Our Manmade Environments.* Boston: Little, Brown, 1979.

Rader, Melvin, and Bertram Jessup. *Art and Human Values.* Englewood Cliffs, N.J.: Prentice-Hall, 1976.

## Chapter 3
### Themes and Purposes of Art

Clark, Kenneth M. *Civilisation: A Personal View.* New York: Harper & Row, 1969.

Elsen, Albert E. *Purposes of Art,* 4th ed. New York: Holt, Rinehart and Winston, 1981.

Hawkins, Gerald S. *Stonehenge Decoded.* New York: Delta, 1965.

Kris, Ernst, and Otto Kurz. *Legend, Myth, and Magic in the Image of the Artist.* New Haven, Conn.: Yale University Press, 1979.

Norman, Dorothy. *The Hero: Myth/Image/Symbol.* New York and Cleveland: World, 1969.

Pfeiffer, John E. *The Creative Explosion: An Inquiry into the Origins of Art and Religion.* New York: Harper & Row, 1982.

## Chapter 4
### The Visual Elements
and
## Chapter 5
### Principles of Design in Art

Albers, Josef. *Interaction of Color,* rev. ed. New Haven, Conn.: Yale University Press, 1975.

Arnheim, Rudolf. *Art and Visual Perception: A Psychology of the Creative Eye.* Berkeley: University of California Press, 1971.

Bevlin, Marjorie Elliott. *Design Through Discovery,* 4th ed. New York: Holt, Rinehart and Winston, 1984.

Birren, Faber. *Color and Human Response.* New York: Van Nostrand Reinhold, 1978.

Bloomer, Carolyn M. *Principles of Visual Perception.* New York: Van Nostrand Reinhold, 1976.

d'Arbeloff, Natalie. *Designing with Natural Forms.* New York: Watson-Guptill, 1973.

Ehrenzweig, Anton. *The Hidden Order of Art.* Berkeley: University of California Press, 1976.

Ellinger, R. *Color, Structure and Design.* New York: Van Nostrand Reinhold, 1980.

Ernst, Bruno. *The Magic Mirror of M. C. Escher.* New York: Ballantine, 1976.

Gill, Robert W. *Basic Perspective.* London: Thames and Hudson, 1974.

Gregory, R. L. *The Intelligent Eye*. New York: McGraw-Hill, 1970.

Itten, Johannes. *The Art of Color*. New York: Van Nostrand Reinhold, 1974.

———. *Design and Form: The Basic Course at the Bauhaus and Later*. New York: Van Nostrand Reinhold, 1975.

Lauer, David A. *Design Basics*. New York: Holt, Rinehart and Winston, 1979.

Pile, John F. *Design: Purpose, Form and Meaning*. New York: Norton, 1979.

Richardson, John Adkins, Floyd W. Coleman, and Michael J. Smith. *Basic Design: Systems, Elements, Applications*. Englewood Cliffs, N.J.: Prentice-Hall, 1984.

Zelanski, Paul, and Mary Pat Fischer. *Design Principles and Problems*. New York: Holt, Rinehart and Winston, 1984.

### Chapter 6
### Drawing

Ballinger, Louise. *Perspective, Space and Design*. New York: Van Nostrand Reinhold, 1969.

Betti, Claudia, and Teel Sale. *Drawing: A Contemporary Approach*. New York: Holt, Rinehart and Winston, 1980.

Chaet, Bernard. *The Art of Drawing*. New York: Holt, Rinehart and Winston, 1978.

Edwards, Betty. *Drawing on the Right Side of the Brain*. Los Angeles: Tarcher, 1979.

Goldstein, Nathan. *The Art of Responsive Drawing*, 3d ed. Englewood Cliffs, N.J.: Prentice-Hall, 1984.

Mendelowitz, Daniel M. *A Guide to Drawing*, 3d ed. New York: Holt, Rinehart and Winston, 1982.

———. *Drawing*, repr. of 1967 ed. Stanford, Calif.: Stanford University Press, 1980.

Nicolaides, Kimon. *The Natural Way to Draw: A Working Plan for Art Study*. Boston: Houghton Mifflin, 1975.

### Chapter 7
### Painting

Blunden, Maria, and Godfrey Blunden. *Impressionists and Impressionism*. New York: Rizzoli, 1980.

Chaet, Bernard. *An Artist's Notebook: Techniques and Materials*. New York: Holt, Rinehart and Winston, 1979.

Cockcroft, Eva, John Weber, and James Cockcroft. *Toward a People's Art: A Contemporary Mural Movement*. New York: Dutton, 1977.

Goldman, Shifra M. *Contemporary Mexican Painting in a Time of Change*. Austin: University of Texas Press, 1981.

Goldstein, Nathan. *Painting: Visual and Technical Fundamentals*. Englewood Cliffs, N.J.: Prentice-Hall, 1979.

Mayer, Ralph. *The Artist's Handbook of Materials and Techniques*. New York: Viking, 1982.

Sandler, Irving. *The Triumph of American Painting: A History of Abstract Expressionism*. New York: Harper & Row, 1970.

### Chapter 8
### Prints

Gelman, Barbara, ed. *The Wood Engravings of Winslow Homer*. New York: Bounty Books, 1969.

Heller, Jules. *Printmaking Today*, 2d ed. New York: Holt, Rinehart and Winston, 1972.

Hoffman, Detlef. *The Playing Card: An Illustrated History*. Greenwich, Conn.: New York Graphic, 1973.

Lane, Richard. *Masters of the Japanese Print*. Garden City, N.Y.: Doubleday, 1962.

Mayor, A. Hyatt. *Prints and People*. Princeton, N.J.: Princeton University Press, 1980.

Peterdi, Gabor. *Printmaking*. New York: Macmillan, 1971.

Pratt, John Lowell, ed. *Currier and Ives: Chronicles of America*. Maplewood, N.J.: Hammond, 1968.

Saff, Donald, and Deli Sacilotto. *Printmaking: History and Process*. New York: Holt, Rinehart and Winston, 1978.

Salamon, Ferdinando. *The History of Prints and Printmaking from Dürer to Picasso*. New York: American Heritage, 1972.

### Chapter 9
### Photography

Bernard, Bruce, *Photodiscovery: Masterworks of Photography 1840–1940*. New York: Abrams, 1980.

Editors of Time-Life Books. *Great Photographers*. New York: Time-Life, 1971.

Gutman, Judith Mara. *Through Indian Eyes*. New York: Oxford University Press, 1982.

Horan, James D. *Mathew Brady: Historian with a Camera*. New York: Bonanza, 1955.

Newhall, Beaumont. *The History of Photography*. New York: Museum of Modern Art, 1964.

Newhall, Beaumont, and Nancy Newhall, eds. *Masters of Photography*. New York: A & W, 1983.

Sandler, Martin W. *The Story of American Photography*. Boston: Little, Brown, 1979.

Swedlund, Charles. *Photography: A Handbook of History, Materials, and Processes*, 2d ed. New York: Holt, Rinehart and Winston, 1981.

Szarkowski, John. *Looking at Photographs: One Hundred Pictures from the Collection of the Museum of Modern Art*. New York: Museum of Modern Art, 1973.

Thornton, Gene. *Masters of the Camera: Stieglitz, Steichen, and Their Successors*. New York: Holt, Rinehart and Winston, 1976.

Tucker, Anne, ed. *The Woman's Eye*. New York: Knopf, 1973.

Upton, Barbara, and John Upton. *Photography*. Boston: Little, Brown, 1976.

### Chapter 10
### Graphic Design

Buechner, Thomas S. *Norman Rockwell: A Sixty Year Retrospective*. New York: Abrams, 1972.

Deken, Joseph. *Computer Images: State of the Art*. New York: Stewart, Tabori and Chang, 1983.

Glaser, Milton, *Graphic Design*. Woodstock, N.Y.: Overlook, 1983.

Hall, Jim. *Mighty Minutes: An Illustrated History of Television's Best Commercials*. New York: Harmony, 1984.

Johnson, Stewart J. *The Modern American Poster*. New York: Museum of Modern Art, 1983.

Mayor, A. Hyatt. *Popular Prints of the Americas*. New York: Crown, 1973.

Roth, Laszlo. *Package Design*. Englewood Cliffs, N.J.: Prentice-Hall, 1981.

Schlemmer, Richard. *Handbook of Advertising Art Production*. Englewood Cliffs, N.J.: Prentice-Hall, 1974.

### Chapter 11
### Sculpture

Goldwater, Robert. *What Is Modern Sculpture?* New York: Museum of Modern Art, 1969.

Gray, Cleve, ed. *David Smith by David Smith*. New York: Holt, Rinehart and Winston, 1968.

Kaprow, Allan. *Assemblage, Environments and Happenings*. New York: Abrams, 1966.

Mili, Gjon. *Picasso's Third Dimension*. New York: Triton, 1970.

Read, Herbert. *The Art of Sculpture*, 2d ed. Bollingen Series XXXV, 3. Princeton, N.J.: Princeton University Press, 1961.

Selz, Jean. *Modern Sculpture: Origins and Evolution*, trans. Annette Michelson. New York: Braziller, 1963.

Wilkin, Karen. *Smith*. New York: Abbeville, 1984.

### Chapter 12
#### Crafts

Charleston, Robert J., ed. *World Ceramics.* New York: McGraw-Hill, 1968.

Hall, Julie. *Tradition and Change: The New American Craftsman.* New York: Dutton, 1977.

Held, Shirley. *Weaving: A Handbook of the Fiber Arts,* 2d ed. New York: Holt, Rinehart and Winston, 1978.

Morton, Philip. *Contemporary Jewelry,* 2d ed. New York: Holt, Rinehart and Winston, 1976.

Nelson, Glenn C. *Ceramics: A Potter's Handbook,* 5th ed. New York: Holt, Rinehart and Winston, 1984.

Nordness, Lee. *Object U.S.A.* New York: Viking, 1970.

Thomson, F. P. *Tapestry: Mirror of History.* London: David and Charles, 1980.

Waller, Irene. *Textile Sculptures.* London: Studio Vista, 1977.

Westbrook, Adele, and Ann Yarowski, eds. *Design in America: The Cranbrook Vision, 1925–1950.* New York: Abrams, 1983.

### Chapter 13
#### Architecture

Fitch, James Marston. *American Building: The Historical Forces That Shaped It.* Boston: Houghton Mifflin, 1966.

Fuller, R. Buckminster, and Robert W. Marks. *The Dymaxion World of R. Buckminster Fuller.* New York: Reinhold, 1960.

Hitchcock, Henry Russell. *In the Nature of Materials: The Buildings of Frank Lloyd Wright, 1887–1941.* New York: Da Capo, 1975.

Le Corbusier. *Towards a New Architecture.* New York: Praeger, 1959.

Norberg-Schulz, Christian. *Meaning in Western Architecture.* New York: Praeger, 1975.

Risebero, Bill. *Modern Architecture and Design: An Alternative History.* Cambridge: MIT Press, 1983.

Safdie, Moshe. *Form and Purpose: Is the Emperor Naked.* Boston: Houghton Mifflin, 1982.

Scully, Vincent J. *Modern Architecture: The Architecture of Democracy.* New York: Braziller, 1982.

Stern, Robert A. M. *New Directions in American Architecture.* New York: Braziller, 1977.

### Chapter 14
#### Environmental Design

Bacon, Edmund N. *Design of Cities.* New York: Penguin, 1976.

Bennett, Corwin. *Spaces for People: Human Factors in Design.* Englewood Cliffs, N.J.: Prentice-Hall, 1977.

Mehrabian, Albert. *Public Places and Private Spaces: The Psychology of Work, Play and Living Environments.* New York: Basic Books, 1976.

Rudofsky, Bernard. *Streets for People: A Primer for Americans.* New York: Doubleday, 1969.

### Chapter 15
#### The Ancient World to the Middle Ages

Cowen, Painton. *Rose Windows.* San Francisco: Chronicle, 1979.

Edwards, I. E. S. *Tutankhamun: His Tomb and Its Treasures.* New York: Knopf and Metropolitan Museum of Art, 1977.

Hale, William Harlan. *The Horizon Book of Ancient Greece.* New York: American Heritage, 1965.

Mendelssohn, Kurt. *The Riddle of the Pyramids.* New York: Praeger, 1974.

Swann, Wim. *The Gothic Cathedral.* Garden City, N.Y.: Doubleday, 1969.

### Chapter 16
#### Renaissance to Revolution

Chambers, D. S. *Patrons and Artists in the Italian Renaissance.* Columbia: University of South Carolina Press, 1971.

Cuttler, Charles D. *Northern Painting: From Pucelle to Bruegel.* New York: Holt, Rinehart and Winston, 1968.

Hartt, Frederick. *History of Italian Renaissance Art.* Englewood Cliffs, N.J.: Prentice-Hall, 1979.

Leonardo da Vinci. *Notebooks,* ed. E. MacCurdy. New York: Braziller, 1955.

Levey, Michael. *Rococo to Revolution.* New York: Praeger, 1966.

Mitford, Nancy. *The Sun King.* New York: Crescent, 1966.

Panofsky, Erwin. *The Life and Art of Albrecht Dürer.* Princeton, N.J.: Princeton University Press, 1955.

Van der Kemp, Gerald. *Versailles.* New York: Park Lane, 1981.

Varsari, Giorgio. *Lives of the Artists,* trans. George Bull. New York: Penguin, 1966.

### Chapter 17
#### The Modern World

Arnason, H. H. *History of Modern Art: Painting, Sculpture, Architecture,* rev. ed. New York: Abrams, 1977.

Ashton, Dore. *The New York School: A Cultural Reckoning.* New York: Penguin, 1980.

Battcock, Gregory. *Super Realism: A Critical Anthology.* New York: Dutton, 1975.

———. *Minimal Art: A Critical Anthology.* New York: Dutton, 1968.

Chicago, Judy. *The Dinner Party: A Symbol of Our Heritage.* Garden City, N.Y.: Doubleday, 1979.

Diamonstein, Barbaralee. *Inside New York's Art World.* New York: Rizzoli, 1980.

Hughes, Robert. *The Shock of the New.* New York: Knopf, 1981.

Kaprow, Allan. *Assemblage, Environments and Happenings.* New York: Abrams, 1966.

Lancaster, John. *Introducing Op Art.* New York: Watson-Guptill, 1973.

Liane, John R., and Susan Larsen. *Abstract Painting and Sculpture in America, 1927–1944.* New York: Museum of Art, Carnegie Institute, 1983.

Lippard, Lucy R. *Pop Art.* New York: Praeger, 1966.

Rose, Barbara. *American Art Since 1900.* New York: Praeger, 1975.

Rosenblum, Robert. *Cubism and Twentieth-Century Art.* New York: Abrams, 1966.

Roskill, Mark, ed. *The Letters of Vincent Van Gogh.* New York: Atheneum, 1977.

Rubin, William, ed. *Pablo Picasso: A Retrospective.* New York: Museum of Modern Art, 1980.

Rubin, William S. *Dada and Surrealist Art.* New York: Abrams, 1969.

Seitz, William C. *Abstract Expressionist Painting in America.* Cambridge, Mass.: Harvard University Press, 1983. Washington, D.C.: National Gallery of Art, 1983.

Vogt, Paul. *Contemporary Painting.* New York: Abrams, 1981.

### Chapter 18
#### Comparative Styles in World Art

Baker, Joan Stanley. *Japanese Art.* London: Thames and Hudson, 1984.

Dwyer, Jane Powell, and Edward B. Dwyer. *The Traditional Art of Africa, Oceania, and the Americas.* San Francisco: Fine Arts Museum of San Francisco, 1973.

Emmerich, André. *Art Before Columbus.* New York: Simon & Schuster, 1983.

Fagg, William. *Tribes and Forms in African Art.* New York: Tudor, 1965.

Lee, Sherman. *A History of Far Eastern Art,* 4th ed. Englewood Cliffs, N.J.: Prentice-Hall, 1982. New York: Abrams, 1982.

Rawson, Jessica. *Ancient China: Art and Archaeology.* New York: Harper & Row, 1980.

# Notes to the Text

## Chapter 1

1. Quoted in Dora Jane Hamblin, "A Bright and Happy Four-hundredth-Birthday Year for the Remarkable Uffizi," *Smithsonian* (November 1982), p. 71
2. "In the Name of Art," *The Christian Science Monitor* (November 17, 1983).
3. Sylvia Fein, *Heidi's Horse*, 2d ed. (Pleasant Hill, Calif.: Exelrod Press, 1984).
4. Mark Roskill, ed., *The Letters of Vincent van Gogh* (New York: Atheneum, 1977), p. 188.
5. P. Huisman and M. G. Dortu, *Lautrec by Lautrec* (New York: Viking, 1964), p. 164.

## Chapter 2

1. "A Picture over the Sofa," *The New York Times* (December 1, 1981), p. B2.
2. Michael Brenson, "Art People," *The New York Times* (November 12, 1982).
3. Robert Goldwater and Marco Treves, eds., *Artists on Art: From the Fourteenth to the Twentieth Century* (New York: Pantheon, 1972), p. 421.
4. *Ibid.*, p. 417.
5. Quoted in Irving Sandler, *The Triumph of American Painting: A History of Abstract Expressionism* (New York: Harper & Row, 1976).
6. Goldwater and Treves, p. 82.

## Chapter 3

1. Margaret A. Miller, "Alice Aycock at U.S.F.," in *Alice Aycock Projects 1979–1981* (Tampa: University of South Florida), p. 47.
2. Thucydides, *The Peloponnesian War*, trans. Rex Warner (Baltimore: Penguin, 1954), pp. 118, 121.
3. Paul Zanker and John Pollini, quoted in "Scholar-Detectives Learn How Augustus Idealized His Image," *The New York Times* (January 10, 1984), p. C3.
4. Charles Blitzer and the Editors of Time-Life Books, eds., "Age of Kings," *Great Ages of Man: A History of World's Culture* (New York: Time-Life, 1967), p. 62.
5. Quoted in Gerstle Mack, *Paul Cézanne* (New York: Knopf, 1936), p. 199.
6. Kathleen Jessie Paine, *William Blake* (New York: Praeger, 1970), p. 148.

## Chapter 4

1. Goldwater and Treves, *op. cit.*, p. 74.
2. *Ibid.*, pp. 229–230.
3. Quoted in Peter de Polnay, *Enfant Terrible: The Life and Work of Maurice Utrillo* (New York: Morrow: 1969), p. 190.

## Chapter 5

1. Goldwater and Treves, *op. cit.*, pp. 169–170.

## Chapter 6

1. Quoted in Martha Kearns, *Käthe Kollwitz: Woman and Artist* (Old Westbury, N.Y.: Feminist Press, 1976), p. 48.
2. *Ibid.*, p. 164
3. John Russell, "Henry Moore at Eighty—Many Happy Returns," *Smithsonian* (August 1978), p. 75.
4. Carll Tucker, "Henry Moore," *Saturday Review* (March 1981), p. 44.
5. *Ibid.*, p. 46.

## Chapter 7

1. Thomas Hoving, *Two Worlds of Andrew Wyeth* (Boston: Houghton Mifflin, 1978), p. 176.
2. Joan Kinneir, *The Artist by Himself* (New York: St. Martin's, 1980), p. 101.
3. Barbaralee Diamonstein, *Inside New York's Art World* (New York: Rizzoli, 1979), pp. 261–262.

## Chapter 8

1. Elizabeth Ripley, *Hokusai: A Biography* (Philadelphia: Lippincott, 1968), p. 24.
2. *Ibid.*, pp. 62, 68.
3. Kinneir, *op. cit.*, p. 107.
4. Piri Halasz, "An Artist's World of Passion, Pain and Weird Beauty," *Smithsonian* (December 1978), p. 94.
5. Diamonstein, *op. cit.*, pp. 308–309. Information in this biography is adapted from *Robert Rauschenberg* (Washington, D.C.: National Collection of Fine Arts, 1976).

## Chapter 9

1. John Szarkowski, *Looking at Photographs: One Hundred Pictures from the Collections of the Museum of Modern Art* (New York: Museum of Modern Art, 1973), p. 134.
2. Sue Davidson Lowe, *Stieglitz: A Memoire/Biography* (New York: Farrar Straus Giroux, 1983), pp. xxiii, 441.

## Chapter 10

1. Donald Walton, *A Rockwell Portrait* (Kansas City: Sheed Andrews & McMeel, 1978), p. 7.

## Chapter 11

1. Cleve Gray, ed., *David Smith by David Smith* (New York: Holt, Rinehart and Winston, 1972), p. 25.
2. *Ibid.*, p. 123.
3. Vicki Goldberg, "Louise Nevelson," *Saturday Review* (August 1980), p. 36.
4. Diamonstein, *op. cit.*, p. 271.

## Chapter 12

1. Susan Peterson, *The Living Tradition of Maria Martínez* (New York: Kodansha International, 1977), p. 191.

## Chapter 13

1. Quoted in John Lobell, "A Lucid Mystic Helped Transform Our Architecture," *Smithsonian* (July 1979), p. 40.
2. *The New York Times* (July 3, 1983), p. 17.
3. Ellen Posner, "Learning to Love Ma Bell's New Building," *The Wall Street Journal* (October 12, 1983), p. 26.
4. Frank Lloyd Wright, *A Testament* (New York: Horizon Press, 1957), p. 64.

## Chapter 16

1. Quoted in Robert Wallace and the Editors of Time-Life Books, eds., *The World of Leonardo* (New York: Time Incorporated, 1966), p. 17.
2. Goldwater, *op. cit.*, pp. 60–61.
3. *Ibid.*, p. 134.
4. *Ibid.*, pp. 145–146.

## Chapter 17

1. Nicholas Wadley, *Manet* (London: Paul Hamyln, 1967), pp. 25–26.
2. John Russell and the Editors of Time-Life Books, eds., *The World of Matisse* (New York: Time-Life, 1969), p. 17.
3. Daniel Guérin, ed., *The Writings of a Savage: Paul Gauguin* (New York: Viking, 1974), p. 54.
4. Barbara Rose, *Lee Krasner: A Retrospective* (Houston: Museum of Fine Arts; New York: Museum of Modern Art, 1984), p. 134.
5. Kerry Green, "Nam June Paik," *Video Systems* (July 1982), p. 53
6. John Russell, "The New European Painters," *The New York Times Magazine* (April 24, 1983), p. 31
7. "The Dinner Party: Judy Chicago" (San Francisco: San Francisco Museum of Art, 1979), p. 3.

# Glossary

Words in *italics* are also defined in the glossary. Numbers in **boldface** following the definitions refer to the numbers of figures in the text that best illustrate the definitions.

**abstract** Characteristic of art in which natural *forms* are not rendered in a *naturalistic* or *representational* way, but instead are simplified or distorted to some extent, often in an attempt to convey the essence of form. Compare *nonobjective*. (**49**)

**Abstract Expressionism** Painting style of the late 1940s and 1950s in which *abstract* or *nonobjective forms* were used to convey emotional *content*. Abstract Expressionism emphasized spontaneity and often employed bold colors and/or strong *value* contrasts; the paintings were usually quite large in *scale*. Because this art often involved energetic physical movement by the artist, it is also referred to as *action painting*. (**523**)

**acrylic** A plastic substance commonly used as a *binder* for paints and as a *casting* material for sculpture.

**action painting** Any painting style calling for vigorous physical activity; specifically, *Abstract Expressionism*.

**aesthetic** Pertaining to the beautiful, as opposed to the useful, scientific, or emotional. An aesthetic response is an appreciation of such beauty.

**afterimage** An image that persists after the visual stimulus for that image has been removed. In colors, the tendency of the eyes to see a *hue* after having looked for a time at the *complementary* hue. (**127**)

**aquatint** An *intaglio printmaking* method in which areas of tone are created by dusting resin particles on a plate and then allowing acid to bite around the particles. Also, a *print* made by this method. (**259**)

**arch** A curving architectural *form* usually made of bricks or other masonry, often in the shape of a semicircle but sometimes rising to a point at the top. (**408**)

**Archaic style** In Greek art, the style prevalent from the 8th to the 6th century B.C. (**451**)

**armature** A rigid framework, often of wood or steel, used to support a sculpture or other large work while it is being made.

**Armory Show** An art exhibition held in 1913 at the 69th Regiment Armory in New York, at which avant-garde European art was introduced to the United States.

**Art Deco** An art style of the 1920s and 1930s based on modern materials (steel, chrome, glass) and repetitive geometric patterns. (**428**)

**Art Nouveau** An art style of the 1890s featuring curvilinear shapes based on plant forms.

**assemblage** The technique of creating a sculpture by joining together individual pieces or segments, sometimes "found" objects that originally served another purpose. Also, a sculpture made by this method. (**353**)

**asymmetrical** Not *symmetrical*. (**164**)

**atmospheric perspective** A device for suggesting three-dimensional depth on a two-dimensional surface. Forms meant to be perceived as distant from the viewer are blurred, indistinct, and misty.

**axis** A straight line, often an imaginary vertical line.

**Baroque** A style dominant in European art during the 17th century, characterized by strong colors and *value* contrasts, bold *scale*, dramatic use of light, elaborate ornamentation, and great emotionalism, even theatricality. (**488**)

**barrel vault** A *vault*, or masonry roof, based on an extension of the round *arch;* in effect, many round arches placed one behind the other. (**409**)

**bas relief** Also known as low relief, sculpture in which figures project only slightly from a background, as on a coin. (**354**)

**Bauhaus** A school of design in Germany from 1919 to 1933, best known for its attempts to adapt design principles to machine technology.

**binder** A substance in paints that causes particles of *pigment* to adhere to one another and to a *support*.

**calligraphy** The art of "beautiful writing." Specifically, a style of decorative penmanship highly developed in the Orient, featuring a flowing, controlled line, often with gradations from thick to thin.

**cantilever** A horizontal architectural *form* projecting beyond its supports. (**435**)

**cartoon** 1. A simple drawing with humorous or satirical *content*. 2. A preparatory drawing for a *mural, tapestry,* or other large work.

**casting** The process of making a sculpture or other object by pouring liquid material—clay, metal, plastic—into a mold and allowing it to harden.

**ceramic** Made from fired ("baked") clay.

**chiaroscuro** Literally, "light-dark." In two-dimensional art, the use of different *values* to create *modeling* and to simulate the effects of light and shadow in nature. (**121**)

**chroma** See *intensity*.

**cire-perdue** See *lost wax*.

**Classical style** In Greek art, the style of the 5th century B.C. Loosely, the term "classical" is often applied to all the art of ancient Greece and Rome, as well as to any art based on logical, rational principles and deliberate *composition*. (**452**)

**collage** A work of art made by pasting bits of paper, cloth, or other material onto a flat surface.

**Color Field painting** A style of painting prominent from the 1950s through the 1970s, featuring large "fields" or areas of color, meant to evoke an *aesthetic* or emotional response through the color alone.

**color wheel** A circular arrangement of *hues* based on some particular color theory. Often, an arrangement of the hues in a rainbow, plus intermediary colors. (**123**)

**complementary colors** *Hues* directly opposite one another on the *color wheel* and therefore assumed to be as different from one another as possible. When placed side by side, complementary colors are intensified; when mixed together, they produce a *neutral*. (**123**)

**composition** The organization of lines, shapes, colors, and other art elements in a work of art. More often applied to two-dimensional art; the broader term is *design*.

**computer art** Art generated electronically, within the computer. (**209**)

**conceptual art** An art form in which the underlying idea or concept and the process by which it is achieved are more important than any tangible product. (**538**)

**content** The message conveyed by a work of art—its subject matter and whatever the artist hopes to convey by that subject matter.

**continuous narrative** A device by which two or more episodes in an event are portrayed in the same work of art. (**472**)

**contrapposto** Literally, "counterpoise." A method of portraying the human figure, especially in sculpture, so that it is apparently relaxed and mobile. The result is often a graceful S-curve. (**359**)

**cross-hatching** An area of closely spaced lines intersecting one another, used to create a sense of three-dimensionality on a flat surface, especially in drawing and *printmaking*. See also *hatching, stippling*. (**99**)

**Cubism** A style of art pioneered in the early 20th century by Pablo Picasso and Georges Braque. In the most developed form of Cubism, *forms* are fragmented into *planes* or geometric facets, like the facets in a diamond; these planes are rearranged to foster a pictorial, but not *naturalistic*, reality; forms may be viewed simultaneously from several vantage points; figure and background have equal importance; and colors are deliberately restricted to a range of *neutrals*. (**515**)

**Dada** A movement that emerged during World War I in Europe that purported to be anti-everything, even anti-art. Dada poked fun at all the established traditions and tastes in art with works that were deliberately shocking, vulgar, and nonsensical. (**521**)

**daguerreotype** The earliest form of photograph, invented by Louis Jacques Mandé Daguerre, in which the photographic image is made permanent on a copper plate.

**design** The planned organization of lines, shapes and masses, colors, textures, and space in a work of art. In two-dimensional art especially, often called *composition*.

**distemper** A painting *medium* in which the *binder* is water-soluble glue; also known as poster paint.

**dome** An architectural structure generally in the shape of a hemisphere or half globe; theoretically, an arch rotated 360 degrees on its vertical *axis*. (**412**)

**drypoint** An *intaglio printmaking* technique, similar to *engraving*, in which a sharp needle is used to draw on a metal plate, raising a thin ridge of metal that creates a soft line when the plate is printed. Also, the resultant *print*. (**259**)

**earthenware** *Ceramic* ware, usually coarse and reddish in color, fired in the lowest temperature ranges. See also *terra cotta*.

**edition** In *printmaking*, the number of images made from a single plate or printing stone and authorized by the artist.

**encaustic** A painting *medium* in which the *binder* is hot beeswax. (**224**)

**engraving** An *intaglio printmaking* method in which a sharp tool called a burin is used to scratch lines into a metal plate. The lines are then filled with ink and the image transferred to paper. Also, the resultant *print*. (**259**)

**entasis** In *Classical* architecture, the slight swelling or bulge built into the center of a column to make the column seem straight visually.

**environmental art** 1. Art that is large enough for viewers to enter and move about in. 2. Art designed for display in the outdoor environment. 3. Art that actually transforms the natural landscape. (**366**)

**etching** An *intaglio printmaking* method in which lines and image areas are created by first coating a plate with an acid-resistant substance, then scratching through the substance with a sharp needle, and finally immersing the plate in acid, which "bites" depressions into the exposed sections. Also, the resultant *print*. (**259**)

**Expressionism** Any art that stresses the artist's emotional and psychological expression, often with bold colors and distortions of form. Specifically, an art style of the early 20th century followed principally by certain German artists. See also *Abstract Expressionism*. (**254**)

**Fauvism** A short-lived painting style in early-20th-century France, which featured bold, clashing, arbitrary colors—colors unrelated to the appearance of *forms* in the natural world. Henri Matisse was its best-known practitioner. The word *fauve* means "wild beast." (**513**)

**ferroconcrete** Reinforced concrete; a building material that has metal rods or steel mesh embedded in concrete to provide strength. (**420**)

**figure-ground relationship** In two-dimensional art, the relationship between the principal *forms* and the background. Figure-ground ambiguity suggests equal importance for the two. (**114**)

**foreshortening** A method of portraying *forms* on a two-dimensional surface so that they appear to project or recede from the *picture plane*. (**144**)

**forging** Shaping metal with hammers while it is hot; the method for making wrought iron.

**form** 1. The physical appearance of a work of art—its materials, style, and *composition*. 2. Any identifiable shape or mass, as a "geometric form."

**fresco** A painting *medium* in which colors are applied to wet plaster, thus bonding the image with the painting surface; most often used for *murals*. (**225**)

**genre** Art that depicts the casual moments of everyday life and its surroundings. (**78**)

**geodesic dome** An architectural structure invented by R. Buckminster Fuller, based on triangles arranged into tetrahedrons (or four-faceted solids). (**421**)

**glaze** 1. A coating of glassy, often colored material bonded by heat onto a *ceramic* object. 2. Paint applied in a very thin layer.

**Gothic** A style of architecture and art dominant in Europe from the 12th to the 15th century. Gothic architecture features pointed *arches*, ribbed *vaults*, and often large areas of stained glass. (**410**)

**gouache** A painting *medium* similar to *watercolor* but with the addition of an opaque (nontransparent) white. (**237**)

**groin vault** A *vault*, or masonry ceiling, resulting when two *barrel vaults* intersect. Often used in medieval architecture to roof a square area. (**409**)

**ground** 1. A substance applied to a painting or drawing *support* in preparation for the *pigmented* material. 2. The preparatory substance used as a coating for a *printmaking* plate. 3. The background in a work of two-dimensional art. See also *primer, figure-ground relationship*.

**happening** An event performed by artists, usually spontaneous and unrehearsed, that may include music, dance, mime, art, reading, or any combination of these, often with audience participation.

**hard-edge** A style of art, principally painting, of the mid-20th century in which *forms* are depicted with precise, geometric lines and edges. (**241**)

**hatching** An area of closely spaced parallel lines used to create a sense of three-dimensionality on a flat surface, especially in drawing and *printmaking*. See also *cross-hatching, stippling*. (**99**)

**haut-relief** Also known as high relief, sculpture in which figures are attached to a background but project substantially from that background, usually by at least half their normal depth. (**355**)

**Hellenistic style** In Greek art, the style of the 3rd and 2nd centuries B.C., characterized by drama and emotionalism and, in sculpture, a tendency for *forms* to push out boldly into space. (**453**)

**hue** The property of a color that distinguishes it from others in the *color wheel;* the name of a color. (**123**)

**iconography** Loosely, the "story" depicted in a work of art; people, places, events, and other images in a work, as well as the symbolism and conventions attached to those images by a particular religion or culture.

**illumination** Hand-drawn decoration or illustration in a manuscript, especially prevalent in medieval art. (**461**)

**impasto** A thick application of paint to canvas or other *support.* (**230**)

**Impressionism** An art style of the late 19th century, principally in France, in which artists tried to capture in paint the fleeting effects—or impressions—of light, shade, and color on natural *forms.* (**506**)

**inlay** In woodworking, a technique in which small pieces of wood, often with varying grains and colors, are glued together to make a pattern. (**393**)

**intaglio** Any *printmaking* technique in which the lines or image areas to be printed are recessed below the surface of the printing plate. The major intaglio techniques are *aquatint, drypoint, etching, engraving,* and *mezzotint.* (**248**)

**intensity** The degree of purity or brilliance of a color. Also known as *chroma* or *saturation.* (**124**)

**isometric perspective** A system for depicting three-dimensional depth on a two-dimensional surface, especially common in Eastern art. Isometric perspective resembles *linear perspective* in some ways, except that parallel lines do not converge. Instead, they are parallel to one another, but at an angle to the *picture plane.* (**143**)

**kinetic** Of or relating to movement. Kinetic art is art that incorporates movement as part of its expression. (**149**)

**kore** Greek for "maiden"; an ancient Greek sculpture of a young woman, usually clothed.

**kouros** Greek for "youth" or "boy"; an ancient Greek sculpture of a nude young man. (**451**)

**linear perspective** System for depicting three-dimensional depth on a two-dimensional surface. Linear perspective has two main precepts: 1) *forms* that are meant to be perceived as far away from the viewer are made smaller than those meant to be seen as close; 2) parallel lines receding into the distance converge at a point on the horizon line known as the *vanishing point.* (**140**)

**linocut** Also known as linoleum cut, a *relief printmaking* technique in which a block of linoleum is carved so as to leave image areas raised above the surface of the block; in function, similar to a common rubber stamp. Also, the resultant *print.* (**257**)

**lintel** A beam; a horizontal architectural member usually supported by vertical posts. See also *post-and-lintel.* (**406**)

**lithography** A *planographic* (or flat-surface) *printmaking* technique, based on the premise that oil and water do not mix. Image areas are drawn in greasy crayon on a stone or plate, and the greasy ink used in this method adheres to those areas. (**248**)

**load-bearing** In architecture, capable of sustaining the weight of floors or roof above; usually descriptive of walls.

**logo** Distinctive image consisting of letters, words, picture, or some combination of these, representative of an institution, often a business firm. (**311**)

**lost-wax casting** Also known by the French term *cire-perdue,* a method for *casting* metal sculptures and other objects. Positive and negative *molds* are built around a layer of wax that exactly duplicates the shape and size of the desired sculpture. When this arrangement is heated, the wax melts out (is "lost") and then molten metal is poured into the mold to replace it. (**344**)

**Mannerism** A term sometimes applied to art of late-16th and early-17th-century Europe, characterized by a dramatic use of space and light and a tendency toward elongated figures. (**487**)

**mass** Three-dimensional *form,* often implying bulk, density, and weight.

**medium** 1. The material used to create a work of art. 2. The *binder* for a paint, such as oil. 3. An expressive art form, such as painting, drawing, or sculpture.

**metalpoint** A drawing technique, especially popular in the *Renaissance,* in which the drawing material is a thin wire of metal mounted in a holding device. See also *silverpoint.* (**200**)

**mezzotint** An *intaglio printmaking* method in which the printing plate is first roughened all over with a sharp tool called a rocker to create a pattern of burrs. *Values* from light to medium dark are created by smoothing away the burrs in relative degree. Also, the resultant *print.* (**259**)

**Minimal Art** A style of painting and sculpture in the mid-20th century in which the art elements are restricted to an extreme "minimum"—lines, simple (often geometric) shapes, and sometimes color. (**531**)

**mixed media** Descriptive of any work of art employing more than one *medium*—for example, a work that combines painting, *collage,* and *screenprinting.*

**mobile** A sculpture that incorporates movement, usually effected by air currents. (**368**)

**modeling** 1. In sculpture, shaping a *form* in some *plastic* material, such as clay, wax, or plaster. 2. In drawing, painting, or *printmaking,* the illusion of three-dimensionality on a flat surface created by simulating effects of light and shadow. (**121**)

**mold** A hollow or negative *shape* used for *casting* liquid clay, metal, or *plastic.*

**monochromatic** Having only one color. Descriptive of work in which one *hue*—perhaps with variations of *value* and *intensity*—predominates, and also of works in black and white.

**mosaic** An art form in which small pieces of tile, glass, or stone are fitted together and embedded into a background to make a pattern or image. Often used for floor and wall decoration. (**458**)

**mural** Any large-*scale* wall decoration in painting, *fresco, mosaic,* or other *medium.* (**226**)

**naturalistic** Descriptive of a work of art that closely resembles *forms* in the natural world. Synonymous with *representational.*

**nave** The long central section of a church or cathedral where the congregation stands or sits. (**410**)

**Neoclassicism** "New" classicism—a style in 19th-century Western art that referred back to the *Classical* styles of Greece and Rome. Neoclassical painting is marked by sharp outline, reserved emotions, deliberate (often geometric) *composition,* and cool colors. (**502**)

**Neo-Expressionism** "New" expressionism—a term applied to works by some European artists, primarily German and Italian, who came to maturity in the post-World War II era. Neo-Expressionist works often have intense colors, much emotion and symbolism, and sometimes a "story" line. (**131**)

**neutral** Having no *hue*—black, white, or gray; sometimes a tannish color achieved by mixing two *complementary colors.*

**New York School** See *Abstract Expressionism.*

**nonobjective** Descriptive of works of art that have no reference to the natural world of images. Composed of lines, shapes, and sometimes colors, chosen and arranged for their own expressive potential. Synonymous with *non-representational*. Compare *abstract, stylized*. (**534**)

**nonrepresentational** See *nonobjective*.

**Op Art** Short for optical art, a style popular in the 1960s and based on optical principles. Op Art deals in complex color interactions, to the point where colors and lines seem to vibrate before the eyes. (**150**)

**optical color mixture** The tendency of the eyes to blend patches of individual colors placed near one another so as to perceive a different, combined color. Also, any art style that exploits this tendency, especially the *pointillism* of Georges Seurat. (**128**)

**painterly** Descriptive of paintings in which *forms* are defined principally by color areas, rather than by lines or edges.

**palette** 1. A surface used for mixing paints. 2. The range of colors typically used by an artist or group of artists.

**pastel** 1. A soft, chalky crayon used for drawing; also, the resultant drawing. 2. A light-*value* color.

**patina** A surface coating that develops on metals, particularly copper and bronze, through exposure to weather and oxides, or by the deliberate application of chemicals.

**pediment** The triangular area above the porch on a Greek temple, often decorated with sculptures. Any similar architectural structure.

**pendentive** In architecture, a curving, triangular section that serves as a transition between a *dome* and the four walls of a rectangular building. (**412**)

**performance art** Similar to a *happening*, art in which there is no concrete object, but rather a series of events performed by the artist in front of an audience, possibly including music, sight gags, recitation, audio-visual presentations, or other elements. (**542**)

**perspective** Any system for depicting the illusion of three-dimensional space on a two-dimensional surface. See *atmospheric perspective, isometric perspective, linear perspective*. (**140**)

**Photorealism** A painting style of the mid-20th century in which people, objects, and scenes are depicted with such exact naturalism that the paintings resemble photographs. (**25**)

**pictorial space** The illusory space in a painting or other work of two-dimensional art that seems to recede backward into depth from the *picture plane*; the "window" effect in a painting.

**picture plane** An imaginary flat surface that is assumed to be identical to the surface of a painting. *Forms* in a painting meant to be perceived in deep three-dimensional space are said to be "behind" the picture plane. The picture plane is commonly associated with the foreground of a painting.

**pigment** A coloring material made from various organic or chemical substances. When mixed with a *binder*, it creates a drawing or painting *medium*.

**plane** A flat surface. See *picture plane*.

**planography** A *printmaking* technique in which the image areas are level with the surface of the printing plate; *lithography*. (**248**)

**plastic** 1. Capable of being molded or shaped, as clay. 2. Any synthetic polymer substance, such as *acrylic*.

**pointillism** An art style of the late 19th century, particularly associated with Georges Seurat, in which small patches or "points" of color are placed close together to build *form*. See also *optical color mixture*. (**129**)

**polychromatic** Having many colors.

**Pop Art** An art style of the 1960s, deriving its imagery from the popular, mass-produced culture. Deliberately mundane, Pop Art focused on the overfamiliar objects of daily life to give them new meanings as visual emblems. (**159**)

**porcelain** A *ceramic* ware, usually white, firing in the highest temperature ranges and often used for fine dinnerware, vases, and sculpture.

**post-and-lintel** In architecture, a structural system based on two or more uprights (posts) supporting a horizontal crosspiece (lintel or beam). (**406**)

**Post-Impressionism** A term applied to the work of several artists—French or living in France—from about 1885 to 1900. Although all painted in highly personal styles, the Post-Impressionists were united in rejecting the relative absence of *form* characteristic of *Impressionism*. The group included Vincent van Gogh, Paul Cézanne, Paul Gauguin, and Georges Seurat.

**primary color** A *hue* that, in theory, cannot be created by a mixture of other hues. Varying combinations of the primary hues can be used to create all the other hues of the spectrum. In pigment the primaries are red, yellow, and blue. (**123**)

**primer** A preliminary coating applied to a painting *support* to improve adhesion of paints or to create special effects. A traditional primer is gesso, consisting of a chalky substance mixed with glue and water. A primer is also called a *ground*.

**print** An image created from a master wood block, stone, plate, or screen, usually on paper. Prints are referred to as multiples, because as a rule many identical or similar impressions are made from the same printing surface, the number of impressions being called an *edition*. A print is considered an original work of art and, today, is customarily signed and numbered by the artist. See *relief, intaglio, lithography, screenprinting*. (**248**)

**printmaking** The art of making *prints*.

**proportion** Size relationships between parts of a whole, or between two or more objects perceived as a unit. Compare *scale*. (**180**)

**radial** Projecting outward from a central core like the spokes in a wheel. (**173**)

**Realism** Broadly, any art in which the goal is to portray forms in the natural world in a highly *representational* manner. Specifically, an art style of the mid-19th century, identified especially with Gustave Courbet, which fostered the idea that everyday people and events are fit subjects for important art. (**504**)

**refraction** The bending of a ray of light, for example when it passes through a prism. (**122**)

**registration** In *printmaking*, the precise alignment of impressions made by two or more printing blocks or plates on the same sheet of paper, as when printing an image in several colors.

**relief** Anything that projects from a background. 1. Sculpture in which figures or other images are attached to a background but project from it to some degree. See *bas-relief, haut-relief*. 2. A *printmaking* technique in which portions of a block meant to print are raised above the surface of the block. See *woodcut, linocut, wood engraving*. (**248**)

**Renaissance** The period in Europe from the 14th to the 16th century, characterized by a renewed interest in *Classical* art, architecture, literature, and philosophy. The Renaissance began in Italy and gradually spread to the rest of Europe. In art, it is most closely associated with Leonardo da Vinci, Michelangelo, and Raphael. (**478**)

**representational** Descriptive of a work of art that closely resembles *forms* in the natural world. Synonymous with *naturalistic*.

**rhythm** The ordered repetition of accented elements in a *design*; the patterned occurrence of lines, shapes, colors, etc. in a work of art. (**188**)

**Rococo** A style of art popular in Europe in the first three-quarters of the 18th century. Rococo architecture and furnishings emphasized ornate but small-*scale* decoration, curvilinear *forms*, and *pastel* colors. Rococo painting, also tending toward the use of pastels, has a playful, light-hearted, romantic quality and often pictures the aristocracy at leisure. (**500**)

**Romanesque** A style of architecture and art dominant in Europe from the 9th to the 12th century. Romanesque architecture, based on ancient Roman precedents, emphasizes the round *arch* and *barrel vault*. (**409**)

**Romanticism** A movement in Western art of the 19th century, generally assumed to be in opposition to *Neoclassicism*. Romantic works are marked by intense colors, turbulent emotions, complex *composition*, soft outlines, and sometimes heroic subject matter. (**503**)

**salon** 1. A fashionable gathering of artists, writers, and intellectuals held in a private home. 2. In France, a state-sponsored exhibition of art, held in Paris, controlled by the Academy of Fine Arts. Starting in 1863, opposition to the restrictive, overly conservative jurying of the Salon resulted in alternative exhibitions.

**sarcophagus** A stone or *ceramic* coffin, sometimes decorated with sculpture. (**454**)

**saturation** See *intensity*.

**scale** Size in relation to some "normal" or constant size. Compare *proportion*.

**screenprinting** A *printmaking* method in which the image is transferred to paper by forcing ink through a fine mesh in which the areas not meant to print have been blocked; a stencil technique. (**248**)

**secondary color** A *hue* created by combining two *primary colors*, as yellow and blue mixed together yield green. In pigment the secondary colors are orange, green, and violet. (**123**)

**serigraphy** See *screenprinting*.

**sfumato** From the Italian word for "smoke," a technique of painting in thin *glazes* to achieve a hazy, cloudy atmosphere, often to represent objects or landscape meant to be perceived as distant from the *picture plane*. (**476**)

**shape** A two-dimensional area having identifiable boundaries, created by lines, color or *value* changes, or some combination of these. Broadly, *form*.

**silkscreen** See *screenprinting*.

**silverpoint** A variation of *metalpoint* in which the drawing material is a thin silver wire mounted in a holding device.

**simultaneous contrast** The tendency of *complementary colors* to seem brighter and more intense when placed side by side.

**slab construction** In *ceramics*, a construction method in which objects are formed from sheets of clay rolled out as with a rolling pin. (**374**)

**solvent** Also known as a *vehicle*, the liquid used to thin paints and to clean brushes after painting; for example, water or turpentine.

**still life** A painting or other two-dimensional work in which the subject matter is an arrangement of objects—fruit, flowers, tableware, pottery, and so forth—brought together for their pleasing contrasts of shape, color, and texture. Also, the arrangement of objects itself. (**156**)

**stippling** A pattern of closely spaced dots or small marks used to create a sense of three-dimensionality on a flat surface, especially in drawing and *printmaking*. See also *cross-hatching, hatching*. (**99**)

**stoneware** *Ceramic* ware, usually gray or tan in color, fired in the medium temperature ranges.

**stylized** Descriptive of works based on *forms* in the natural world, but simplified or distorted for *design* purposes. See also *abstract*. (**49**)

**support** The surface on which a work of two-dimensional art is made; for example, canvas, paper, or wood.

**Surrealism** A painting style of the early 20th century that emphasized imagery from dreams and fantasies, as well as an intuitive, spontaneous method of recording such imagery. (**89**)

**suspension** A structural system in architecture, most common in bridges, in which the weight of a horizontal member is suspended from steel cables supported by uprights called pylons. (**418**)

**symbol** An image or sign that represents something else, because of convention, association, or resemblance.

**symmetrical** Descriptive of a design in which the two halves on either side of an imaginary central vertical *axis* form mirror images of one another. (**162**)

**tapestry** A type of weaving in which the crosswise yarns are manipulated freely to create patterned or pictorial effects. (**397**)

**tempera** A painting *medium* in which the *binder* is egg yolk. (**227**)

**tensile strength** In architecture, the ability of a material to span horizontal distances with minimum support from underneath.

**terra cotta** Italian for "baked earth." A *ceramic* ware, usually reddish, fired in the low temperature ranges and therefore somewhat porous and fragile; *earthenware*. (**374**)

**throwing** Forming rounded *ceramic* objects on the potter's wheel. (**376**)

**triptych** A three-part work of art; especially a painting, meant for placement on an altar, with three panels that fold together.

**trompe-l'oeil** French for "fool-the-eye." A painting or other work of two-dimensional art rendered in such an extremely *naturalistic* manner that the viewer is "tricked" into thinking it is three-dimensional. (**48**)

**truss** In architecture, a structural system, used principally with wood and metal, based on the triangle. (**419**)

**value** The relative lightness or darkness of a *hue*, or of a *neutral* varying from white to black. (**120**)

**vanishing point** In *linear perspective*, the point on the horizon line where parallel lines appear to converge. (**140**)

**vault** A masonry (brick or concrete) roof or ceiling, especially in medieval architecture. See also *groin vault, barrel vault*. (**409**)

**vehicle** See *solvent*.

**video art** Any art form based on television. (**536**)

**volume** Similar to *mass*, a three-dimensional *form* implying bulk, density, and weight; but also a void or empty, enclosed space.

**wash** Ink or *watercolor* paint thinned so as to flow freely onto a *support*.

**watercolor** A painting *medium* in which the *binder* is gum arabic.

**woodcut** A *relief printmaking* method in which a block of wood is carved so as to leave the image areas raised from the background. Also, the resultant *print*. (**248**)

**wood engraving** Similar to *woodcut*, a *relief printmaking* process in which the image is cut on the end grain of a wood plank, resulting in a "white-line" impression. (**258**)

# Index

# Photographic Sources

All references are to figure numbers. The following abbreviations have been used throughout:
AR: Art Resource, New York
PR: Photo Researchers, New York
RMN: Service de Documentation Photographique de la Réunion des Musées Nationaux, Paris

**Chapter 1:** 1, Scala/AR; 2, Malcolm Varon; 4, Jean Vertut, Issy-les-Moulineaux, France; 11, Life Picture Service, New York; 12, Rod Bauer, courtesy Pratt Institute Gallery, Brooklyn, N.Y.; 13, © 1976 Craig Aurness, West Light, Los Angeles; 18, © 1979 Douglas Keister, Oakland, Calif.; 19, Las Vegas News Bureau; 26, 31, Lee Boltin Picture Library, Croton-on-Hudson, N.Y.; 32, Sygma, New York.

**Chapter 2:** 33, 35, 39, Alinari/AR; 40, Drawing by Saxon © 1971 The New Yorker Magazine, Inc.; 42, 46, RMN; 48, Dan Lecca, New York; 60, Louis K. Meisel Gallery, New York; p. 46, Hans Namuth, New York.

**Chapter 3:** 62, Fritz Menle/PR; 65, George Holton/PR; 66, Paolo Koch/PR; 67, French Government Tourist Office, New York; 68, O. Zimmermann, Colmar; 70, Hirmer Fotoarchiv, Munich; 72, Alinari/AR; 73, Caisse Nationale des Monuments Historiques et des Sites, Paris; 78, Giraudon/AR; 80, RMN; 82, Allan Finkelman, New York.

**Chapter 4:** 92, Museum of Modern Art, New York; 95, Rudolph Burckhardt; 98, American Museum of Natural History, New York; 100, Giraudon/AR; 102, Ken Cohen, NY; 108, 111, Giraudon/AR; 115, George W. Gardner, Hillsdale, N.Y.; 117, Christopher Springman/TIME Magazine; 130, RMN; 135, Françoise Legrand, Buckingham, England; 138, 141, 144, Alinari/AR; 147, Doisneau/PR; 118, French Government Tourist Office, New York; p. 94, Alinari/AR; p. 96, SEF/AR; p. 124, Le Fevre Gallery, London.

**Chapter 5:** 155, George Holton/PR; 160, MIRA, New York; 165, Robert E. Mates, New York; 166, From *Prairie Fires and Paper Moons*, by Hal Morgan and Andreas Brown, pub. David Godine, Boston; 169, Library of Congress, Washington, D.C.; 170, Philip L. Molten, Tiburon, Calif.; 172, Otto E. Nelson, New York; 173, Alinari/AR; 178, courtesy Toni Mendez, Inc., New York; 183, Hirmer Fotoarchiv, Munich; 187, Geoffrey Clements, New York; 191, Johnson/Burgee architects, New York; p. 132, Caisse Nationale des Monuments Historiques et des Sites; p. 136, Magnum Photos Inc., New York.

**Chapter 6:** 204, Courtauld Institute of Art, London; 209, Melvin L. Prueitt, Los Alamos National Laboratory, author of *Art and the Computer* (McGraw-Hill, 1984); 213, Mira Godard Gallery, Toronto; 214, Regional Economic History Research Center, Wilmington, Del.; 220, courtesy McGraw-Hill Book Company, New York; p. 174, Sanford H. Roth, Rapho/PR.

**Chapter 7:** 224, Giraudon/AR; 225, Scala/AR.

**Chapter 8:** 264, Giraudon/AR; p. 220, Hans Namuth, New York.

**Chapter 9:** 286, 287, 295, PR; 299, United Press International, Inc.; p. 234, Philadelphia Museum of Art.

**Chapter 10:** 313, From Henry Dreyfuss, *Symbol Sourcebook* (New York: McGraw-Hill Book Company, 1972), reproduced with permission.

**Chapter 11:** 343, Anne Kohs & Associates, Inc., San Francisco; 345, Alinari/AR; 347, Mary H. Mills, Dallas; 348, Alinari/AR; 350, © 1978 Jan Lukas/PR; 353, Tom Crane, New York; 354, Egyptian Expedition, Metropolitan Museum of Art, New York; 355, Alinari/AR; 359, Hirmer Fotoarchiv, Munich; 362, D. James Dee; 365, Redevelopment Authority of Philadelphia; 366, © Gianfranco Gorgoni 1984, Contact Press, New York; 367, Jeanne-Claude Christo, New York; p. 274, Lynn Gilbert, courtesy Pace Gallery, New York.

**Chapter 12:** 372, Bruce Handelsman, San Francisco; 375, Jacka Photography, Phoenix; 379, Bill Scott; 381, Jonathan Saadak; 384, Sherman Howe; 387, Bruce Miller; 389, Robert Boni; 398, Giraudon/AR; p. 290, Jacka Photography, Phoenix.

**Chapter 13:** 402, Lee Boltin Picture Library, Croton-on-Hudson, N.Y.; 403, Marc Treib, Berkeley, Calif.; 404, Museum of New Mexico, Santa Fe; 405, Carl Frank/PR; 406, Hirmer Fotoarchiv, Munich; 407, Carl Frank/PR; 408, French Government Tourist Office, New York; 409, Omikron/PR; 410, Rapho/PR; 412, Hirmer Fotoarchiv, Munich; 413, George Holton/PR; 415, French Government Tourist Office, New York; 416, Hedrich-Blessing, Chicago; 417, Ezra Stoller: ESTO; 418, Chris Minerva, FPG International; 419, Joe Aker; 420, Dennis Hallinan, FPG International; 421, David MacLean/Shostal Assoc., New York; 422, Library of Congress, Washington, D.C.; 423, Brown Brothers, Sterling, Pa.; 425, RMN; 426, Robert E. Mates; 427, Bob Wharton; 428, Brown Brothers, Sterling, Pa.; 429, © 1958 Ezra Stoller: ESTO; 431, Wayne Andrews, Grosse Point, Mich.; 432, D. Berretty/PR; 433 left, NYT Pictures; 433 right, © 1984 Marvin Rand, Marina del Rey, Calif.; 434, Harold Meeker, San Carlos, Calif.; 435, Bill Hedrich, Hedrich-Blessing; 436, © 1974 Ezra Stoller: ESTO; p. 320, Theo Westenberger, Liaison, New York; p. 330, UPI/Bettmann Archive.

**Chapter 14:** 437, Alinari/AR; 438, Ewing Galloway; 439, Bettmann Archive, New York; 441, Peter Southwick, Stock Boston; 442, Gregory Glass; 443, photo provided by Citicorp.

**Chapter 15:** 444, Hirmer Fotoarchiv, Munich; 448, Oriental Institute, University of Chicago; 450, RMN; 451, Hirmer Fotoarchiv, Munich; 452, 454, Alinari/AR; 456, Scala/AR; 457, Alinari/AR; 458, Scala/AR; 459, Alinari/AR; 462, Georgia Engelhard, FPG International; 464, Bildarchiv Foto Marburg; 466, RMN; 467, Alinari/AR; 468, Scala/AR.

**Chapter 16:** 469, Alinari/AR; 470, Scala/AR; 471, 472, 473, Alinari/AR; 474, Scala/AR; 475, Alinari/AR; 476, Caisse Nationale des Monuments Historiques et des Sites; 477, Alinari/AR; 478, Scala/AR; 480, 481, Alinari/AR; 482, Scala/AR; 484, Giraudon/AR; 486, 488, Alinari/AR; 490, Scala/AR; 491, © Frans Claes, Antwerp, courtesy Belgian National Tourist Office, New York; 493, Le Coguen, Ratho/PR; p. 370, Scala/AR; p. 382, Scala/AR.

**Chapter 17:** 502, 503, 504, 505, RMN; 507, Hirschl & Adler Galleries, Inc., New York; 508, RMN; 510, colorphoto Hans Hinz, Allschwil; 511, RMN; 513, Hans Petersen, Copenhagen; 522, 525, Robert E. Mates, New York; 530, courtesy Leo Castelli Gallery, New York; 531, courtesy Xavier Fourcade, Inc., New York; 532, courtesy Leo Castelli Gallery, New York; 536, Michael Danowski, courtesy Electronic Arts Intermix, New York; 537, Bruce C. Jones, New York; 538, 539, Wolfgang Volz/Photo Eeva-Inkerti, © Christo; 540 © Carolyn George, New York; 541, courtesy Through the Flower Corporation, photo by Michael Alexander, © Judy Chicago; 542, Lynn Goldsmith/LGI © 1982.

**Chapter 18:** 549, Bildarchiv Foto Marburg; 555, Alinari/AR.

Works by Le Corbusier, Dali, Klee, Matisse, Monet, Picasso, Renoir, Rodin, Valadon, Vuillard, Watteau © S.P.A.D.E.M., Paris/VAGA, New York. Works by Escher, Kollwitz, Mondrian © BEELDRECHT, Amsterdam/VAGA, New York, 1985. Works by © Anuszkiewitz, Kristo, Flack, Lichtenstein, Motherwell, Noland, Rauschenberg, Warhol/VAGA, New York, 1985. Work by © Estate of David Smith/VAGA, New York, 1985. Work by © Estate of Grant Wood/VAGA, New York, 1985. Works by Braque, Brancusi, Calder, Chagall, Duchamp, Kandinsky, Klee, Magritte, Miro © ADAGP, Paris/VAGA, New York, 1985.

## About the Authors

William McCarter is Associate Professor of Art at North Texas State University. He holds bachelor's and master's degrees from the University of Georgia, and earned the doctorate at The Pennsylvania State University. Dr. McCarter's chief interest lies in adapting modern technology to the teaching of art—especially the use of videotapes, multiple slide imagery, and television graphics. Married to Mickey Story McCarter, Dr. McCarter has a teen-aged son, Monte. His interest in history and in Baroque music has developed into a special hobby—the painting of Rococo-style images on harpsichords.

Rita Gilbert holds a bachelor's degree in Fine Arts from New York University. For several years she was the editor responsible for a distinguished publishing program in art at a major publishing house, and now she is consultant in art to Alfred A. Knopf/Random House. A writer by profession and singer by avocation, she lives in a small town north of New York City.